Natural Cures

"Saying Goodbye to Your Illness"

Lead Author

Douglas D. Grant

With Foreword by Dr. Chris Lydon M.D.,

Erica Inc.

Natural Cures
"Saying Goodbye to Your Illness"

By: Douglas D. Grant

Foreword: Chris Lydon M.D.

Editor: Cindy Mathieu, Ph.D

Cover: Tri Star Visual Communications

Book layout: Josh Cox

Contributing researchers: Becky Greer, Emily Brown, Dr. Hudson

Printed in the United States of America

Acknowledgments

Many people have helped with this great project. This book has been completed in a short amount of time though it is the culmination of years of research. A special acknowledgment must go out to certain people who have put in long strenuous hours to make this book become a reality.

Tylene Megley. Without her persistence of getting me and Don together this book wouldn't have happened. She has also been a great spokesperson for holistic health over the years and is a great example of living these great principles and sharing them with others.

Don Lapre. He gave me a timeline that challenged the fiber of my being. He also created the ability for the message in this book to reach millions of people around the world. Thanks for the vision.

Becky Greer and Emily Brown have put in countless hours on the research and writing of the conditions and diseases for the nutritional section of this book. They are both a great inspiration and help to me.

My wife Hilary, who is taking the holistic fitness principles to the limit and inspires me and many others daily. My children who put up with me not coming home till wee hours in the morning and leaving early to meet the deadlines needed to get this in the public's hands. They are my support and strength.

The staff members that make up Optimal Health Systems all need to be commended and thanked. Some worked directly on the book while others kept operations going so the book could be completed. These people are my right hand at getting true holisitic health programs to the public. Randy Grant, Eric Jensen, James Megley, Tim Hawkins, Tanya Hudson, Hal Moore, Steven Conners, Christi Allred, Josh and Kathryn Cox, Marisela Pennington, Teresa Bailey, Camille Watson and Kelly Haynes. Working countless hours, this team definitely went the extra mile, at times spending 24 hours straight on this project.

And finally:

MY PARENTS Lyle and Ione Grant

Who at the ages of 90 and 80, still come over twice a week for their workout. They seek out and have used Crisis care medical intervention but they also take responsibility for their own health. They work on their diet, exercise and take specific supplements. They are a great inspiration and example to all of us.

None of the substances, foods, food components or products mentioned in this book in and of themselves cure or heal anything. And there is no statement made herein to say otherwise, and none are implied or intended. Such supplemental foods, supplements, nutriceuticals, botanicals (herbs) and phytonutrients simply function *as foods do*, which is *to nourish* the body — and, therefore, —they simply aid the body to function and operate normally, and facilitate the body's own inherent ability to fix itself.

All products listed in this book are categorized as foods, nutritional supplements, botanicals (herbs), and/or functional foods and nutriceuticals within the guidelines and standards set by the U.S. Food & Drug Administration (FDA), and as also regulated by the U.S. Federal Trade Commission (FTC) with regard to what can be said about them in accordance with current law. All the products listed herein, furthermore, are generally regarded as inherently non-toxic by current government, industry, and/or historical standards.

Foreword

Everyone who ever wondered why I 'wasted' my medical degree just to become a health writer needs to read this book.

The question, which has been thrust at me like an accusation more times than I can count, speaks legions about our nation's health crisis. The fact that I am able to reach more people as a writer than as a practicing physician should be obvious. That I might actually be *helping* more people through my writing— well, for some reason, that doesn't occur to everyone. Sadly, not everyone thinks it's important to learn about being healthy. By and large, most of us take our health for granted. We want to believe that modern medicine can cure all ills, that regardless of the extent to which we abuse and ignore our bodies, there exists some mystical panacea that will make everything better. We are either in denial about the limitations of medical technology, or so completely overwhelmed by the prospect of assuming responsibility for our own physical well-being, that we simply sit back and surrender to the inevitability of disease.

I used to be like that— until I went to medical school.

Medical school taught me a great deal, both about medicine, and about life in general. I floated into the Yale School of Medicine buoyed by lofty ambitions and naive idealism. Most of what I thought I knew about being a physician I'd gleaned from television shows like *M*A*S*H* and *Saint Elsewhere*. According to my ingenuous notions, modern medicine was a dynamic, almost magical domain of endless possibilities, and doctors were heroic miracle workers. I truly believed that the human body, with the proper inducements, possessed infinite healing potential. My Hollywood version of health care was boundlessly romantic and exciting.

Reality soon smashed my fantasy like a rock through the windshield.

Medical principles derive from decidedly un-magical disciplines like chemistry and biology, which are themselves rooted in the immutable laws of nature. And while medicine *is* advancing, and medical breakthroughs *do* happen, the process is slow, methodical, and halting. I soon discovered that the scope of medical technology lagged at least a century behind my imagination. I also came to realize that doctors are not miracle workers. They're just ordinary people who spent many years studying and training to master their trade. At their core, doctors are exactly like everyone else.

And while the human body *does* possess truly astounding healing potential, I quickly learned from firsthand experience that people don't just 'wake up' from comas as if nothing happened. I learned that crippling injuries were just that— crippling, and permanent. I learned that most people with serious medical conditions would never be 'as good as new.' I learned that *treatable* rarely meant *curable*, and that drug side effects could be just as devastating as the illnesses they were intended to alleviate.

I also discovered that the so-called 'art of medicine' died long ago. In the modern world, patient management is largely governed by insurance companies. For a while I thought the insurance companies were the bad guys. I mean, how can you justify placing a price tag on human life? But there were far more powerful and insidious forces at work— sinister forces disguised as saviors...

Enter the pharmaceutical industry.

As impoverished medical students, we all loved it when the various pharmaceutical companies sent their representatives to visit our wards. What was not to love? The drug reps were always young, good-looking, charismatic, and well spoken. And best of all, they come bearing gifts— food, pens, text books, even medical equipment. A pharmaceutical conference (a.k.a. a drug rep lunch) meant a free meal and complimentary doctor paraphernalia. And all the drug reps ever asked in return was a few minutes to deliver their sales pitch while we ate.

It turns out, deli sandwiches and ball point pens are just the tip of the iceberg. For the practicing physician, drug company incentives can be extravagant. When I was a third year student, I became friends with an attending surgeon who confided that each time he prescribed a particular brand of antibiotic, he earned points toward a free trip. He was two infections away from a month-long, all inclusive vacation around the world.

It would be naive to think that this sort of gentle coercion doesn't exist in every industry. However, in the case of health care, the drug companies don't simply influence treatment protocols. To an alarming degree, the pharmaceutical industry dictates the very essence of medical education. By pouring billions of dollars every year into medical research, drug

To find out more or to speak to a nutritional counselor for free, just visit us at:
www.CuresForTheBody.com

companies subsidize the education of every physician who graduates from an American medical school. The upshot of this arrangement is a medical system which places inordinate emphasis on disease *treatment* without the slightest attention to disease *prevention*. And that is why most doctors don't know the first thing about it!

When I passed through the ivy-covered gates for the last time and bid farewell to the Yale School of Medicine, I left my Hollywood version of healthcare behind. As I set off for southern California to commence my surgical internship, my medical bag contained more than a first-rate medical education. Nestled between the stethoscope and the otoscope was a rapidly depleting supply of optimism. And in its place, a growing disillusionment toward my chosen profession.

Residency training is a brutal rite of passage for the future physician. During my brief taste of this age-old tradition, I spent over one hundred hours per week working in the hospital. I averaged three and one half hours of sleep per night— which included my nights off. As someone who has always reveled in the joys of the outdoors and physical activity, as someone who *needs* regular exercise and adequate sleep to feel sane, I have never been more miserable. *And for what?* I found myself wondering. After all, most of my patients would return to a life that had been permanently altered by their illness or injury. Things would never be the same for them. I was beginning to wonder if anything I did really mattered.

To top it all off, I simply couldn't reconcile the fact that my chosen profession, that of a 'healer,' required me to adhere to a schedule which ultimately, compromised my own health and well being. So, after devoting a decade of my existence to becoming a physician, I found myself frustrated, exhausted, up to my eyeballs in debt, and completely disenchanted with the path my life was taking. I remember getting into my Jeep after a particularly grueling 36-hour shift and driving out of the dank, underground parking structure into the dazzling California sunshine. Suddenly, a feeling of euphoria washed over me and I began to laugh out loud until tears were streaming down my face.

Deep down, I knew *I was never coming back!*

Since that fateful day in October of 1994 when I resigned from my surgical residency, it's become my life's work to educate people about healthy living, disease prevention, and natural alternatives to prescription medication. Obviously, I cannot single-handedly revolutionize health care. Shifting the emphasis from disease treatment to disease prevention would involve a large-scale overhaul of the entire medical establishment—something which is not likely to happen any time soon.

Generation after generation of physicians have been lulled into complacence by the monumental influence of the pharmaceutical industry. Most American doctors are openly hostile to any therapeutic practice which does not involve a prescription pad or an operating room. The very notion of disease prevention has been systematically wiped from their collective consciousness. Even the most progressive health care providers are shockingly ignorant when it comes to nutrition, exercise, and natural supplementation. It's not their fault— they've been brainwashed into thinking that they are *health* experts, when in actuality they are *disease* experts.

In the real world, the only completely reliable way to 'cure' disease is to stop it from happening in the first place. But don't expect to unearth a wealth of knowledge about disease prevention at your doctor's office. Although medical school taught me the basics of physiology, anatomy, and biochemistry, virtually everything I now know about nutrition, exercise, and supplementation I learned *after* receiving my degree. Had I completed my residency training and gone on to practice medicine like most of my peers, it's doubtful that I would know the first thing about healthy living. If I was like most practicing physicians, I would eat a diet rich in processed foods, chemical preservatives, saturated fat, and artificial ingredients. I would consume too much coffee and alcohol and not enough fiber. I would suffer from emotional stress, lack of exercise, and lack of sleep. My body would be gearing up for a myriad of pathological processes including cancer, cardiovascular disease, autoimmune disorders, diabetes, and chronic fatigue syndrome. In other words, I would be the typical unhealthy American.

Tallying all the perils of modern living can be overwhelming. *Who will save you?* Who will be there to tell you what to eat? Who will make you exercise? Who will direct you to the crucial vitamins, minerals, and other natural compounds that reduce your risk for chronic disease? Even if your GP happens to be one of the enlightened few with a grasp of what healthy living entails, your doctor can't force you to adopt a healthy lifestyle. The only person who can reliably make healthy life choices is *YOU!*

Being healthy is not overwhelmingly complex. You won't need an an advanced degree to develop an understanding of healthy living or an encyclopedic memory to implement a healthy lifestyle. You *will* need ready access to information that is both comprehensive and comprehendible.

Unfortunately, in the largely unregulated realm of alternative remedies and holistic health care, it can be an arduous undertaking to distill the authentic from the bogus. That's why it's nice to have someone like Douglas Grant on your side! Accredited Nutritionist, certified fitness expert, and author of *Natural Cures "Saying Goodbye to Your Illness,"* Grant is an outspoken proponent of responsible living who has made it his life's work to raise public awareness of legitimate nutritional approaches to disease treatment and prevention. Grant didn't create this work alone. To make his vision a reality, Grant assembled a team of leading experts like myself to contribute their insights to the final product.

Whatever your personal background, Natural Cures "Saying Goodbye to Your Illness," will provide you with the necessary tools for optimizing your health and well-being. Don't be afraid to take responsibility for your health. You will reap the pleasures of your decision in ways that are too many to count, too marvelous to imagine, and too important to miss.

Enjoy!
–Chris Lydon, MD

To find out more or to speak to a nutritional counselor for free, just visit us at:
www.CuresForTheBody.com

Introduction

Henry David Thoreau once said, "Our chief want in life is someone to help us do what we can." I learned many years ago that in order to accomplish big things in life, I must surround myself with experts in the fields in which I want to excel. A life changing event in my early 20s led me to embrace that philosophy. At that time, I was working in a tire warehouse and fell from some scaffolding to the cement floor below; I damaged the L4-L5 vertebrae in my back leaving me paralyzed for a time. I was 23 years old and facing a long and painful recovery. However, the events that unfolded in the ensuing months became more to me than just physical healing. They permanently changed the way I view the health care system. They changed my career path and aspirations. They changed the way I take care of myself physically and mentally. Simply put, those events changed my life. They helped me to understand this important principle of success: that we alone are responsible for our success in the game of life.

After my accident, when it came time for me to ask difficult questions of my doctors, it became extremely obvious that they were only going to give me their opinions from their particular specialty. For example, a surgeon recommended surgery for my injured lower back. A physical therapist recommended exercise therapy, my M.D. recommended drugs and rest, and my chiropractor recommended massage, ultrasound, and manipulation. He also told me to look into nutrition and other areas of health care that might help. When he said this, I realized that although I should continue to get the best tests and opinions I could, ultimately the responsibility for my recovery fell squarely upon my shoulders.

It dawned on me then that I had learned this at a young age; I remembered my father's teachings while growing up, specifically that I must learn all I can and then make my own decisions, before others make them for me. My Father had credibility in teaching this lesson. In WW II, he made the decision to join the Air Force. He became the ball-turret gunner

To find out more or to speak to a nutritional counselor for free, just visit us at:
www.CuresForTheBody.com

in a B-17 bomber plane. On a mission over Munster Germany, his plane was shot down. He was eventually captured by the German Gestapo and spent time in the abhorrent prison camps. After he spent considerable time being carefully observant and gathering information, he made the bold decision to escape. He endured weeks of starvation and freezing rain, and could only travel at night, but he made it back into American lines and to freedom[1]. He definitely knows something about making decisions and being able to follow through with them. Most importantly, he has lived his life courageously, making bold and difficult decisions, knowing that he alone is responsible for his life's path.

My father's example took on new meaning for me as I faced the healing obstacles in my own life. I continued to ask more questions of the medical doctors. What I learned astonished me. I realized that our medical system is not about curing or fixing problems, but is meant to help people in crisis care get relief from pain and then hopefully get back on the right track, on your own. The problem has become that we as a population rely on the "crisis" experts as our sole source of guidance for health. We have unjustly put medical doctors in the powerful position to treat our every concern. However, the only way they know to treat our problems is through drugs: drugs that either mask the true cause of the problem (e.g., cholesterol lowering drugs – lowering the cholesterol artificially, but not finding out why cholesterol is high in the first place) or disguise it in the hope the problem will disappear on its own.

My chiropractor was the only health professional that recommended a holistic approach and was open to communicating and networking with other professionals in order to get me the best care possible. His approach struck me as having the most common sense, and I began following his recommendations.

Shortly thereafter, I ran into an unexpected turn that would change my life even more dramatically. As I started researching health principles, I came across the following quote from the Surgeon General: **"you the individual can do more for your health and well being than any doctor, any hospital, any drug, and any exotic medical device."** I felt compelled to research the sciences of nutrition and exercise even more than I had before, so that I could be armed with the knowledge to make the right choices for my overall health. Unfortunately, I was dismayed once again.

---

[1]Call 1-800-890-4547 to order H. Lyle Grant's book: *Shot Down But Not Defeated*

[2]Clark, A.,. "Healthy by choice,' Veg Times, June 1993, pg 7.

To find out more or to speak to a nutritional counselor for free, just visit us at:
www.CuresForTheBody.com

I saw a lack of truths and differences of opinion from registered dieticians, nutritionists and so-called exercise experts. The dietician industry was being courted by big food companies that wanted their method of thinking taught in schools[2]. I naturally became skeptical and realized I could not believe all of the mainstream dietary guidelines, many of which were not based on fact (e.g., the teachings that Aspartame and other harmful ingredients were safe[3] when it actually is not[4]). So then I looked to nutritionists. One nutritionist would teach one diet as the best and another would teach the opposite and still another would go in an even different direction. There were many nutrition programs available but they differed in context also. Exercise experts would differ between how much exercise a person should do and what type was most effective. So what was I left to do?

I remembered a book I had read growing up entitled *"Think and Grow Rich."* This book had been recommended to me by an extremely successful person, who told me this book had allowed him to accomplish more in life than any other book except the Bible. The author of *"Think and Grow Rich"* writes about researching the most prominent and successful people of his day. Through years of research, he found that the most successful individuals were the ones that had surrounded themselves with experts, gleaned knowledge from those experts, and put together a plan for themselves based on all the truths they learned. I have also set out to do that, which is what this book is all about.

It was at this time that I chose to pursue a nutritional degree program based on the works of generations of leading authorities on nutrition. I also sought out and selected four different exercise certifications so that I could make the right decisions with that part of my personal health package.

---

[3] American Dietetic Association. Straight Answers About Aspartame. Food and Nutrition Information Fact Sheets. 2003. ADA.

[4] US Department of Health and Human Services, "Report on adverse reactions in the adverse monitoring system," Feb. 28, 1994.

Mullarkey, B., "Sweet delusion," *Informed Consent,* Sept./Oct. 1994, p. 35 US Air Force, "Aspartame alert," *Flying Safety,* 48:20, 1992.

Louis R., *Sax's Dangerous Properties of Industrial Materials,* 8th ed., Van Nostrand Reinhold, 1992, p. 2251.

Roberts, H., "Does aspartame cause human brain cancer?," *J Advance Med,* 4:236, 1991. Gross, A., *Congressional Record,* SID 835:131, Aug. 1, 1985. Potenza, D., "Aspartame: clinical update," *Connecticut Medicine,* 53:395, 1989. Neuroscience Research. Dr. John W. Olney. Washington School of Medicine.St. Louis, Missiouri. S.D. Searle on Aspartame.

To find out more or to speak to a nutritional counselor for free, just visit us at:
www.CuresForTheBody.com

Although this was a great start, it was not enough, and I could not even come close to accomplishing my goals alone. I started scouring through research journals looking for the true experts in nutrition and exercise. Once I discovered these individuals, I contacted them personally and met with them – with the request that they honor me by being on my advisory board of health. To my astonishment, every single expert I contacted happily agreed to help me, even though I had nothing to give them in return except my commitment to follow their principles and share them with everyone I could.

Over the next few years, my health improved dramatically. My performance increased to a point that I won a gold medal at the Drug Free World Power lifting championships. I found myself teaching others what I had learned. My approach became to share my research of the many leading experts and put together those results in a simple-to-follow program. I became sought after by others because I was committed to helping them, and resolved not to give them "just another opinion," but rather share what I had learned through intensive research. I started teaching and training people while I was still going through therapy and eventually I started a personal training and nutrition center. Thousands of people came through the center and benefited from our no nonsense, holistic approach to achieving optimal health.

It was this business that led to me meeting Danny Ainge, a professional basketball player, who was seeking nutritional guidance because he felt he was not informed properly about anti-inflammatory side effects during his 13 years in the NBA. His liver enzymes were elevated and he had free radical damage along with high cholesterol problems, even though he consumed no alcohol. After following our program for a few months, consuming the proper nutritional foods and nutrients, all of his test numbers improved. He then referred me to other athletes like Dan Majerle and Charles Barkley, and eventually I became the Team Nutritionist for the Phoenix Suns. I have since been working with many teams, players, celebrities and the general public for well over a decade, traveling and holding seminars, teaching and educating on the true health principles necessary to reach optimal health. The majority of my time is now spent training health professionals on nutritional testing and programs for their patients.

In 2002 I was approached by infomercial business guru Don Lapre. Don became educated through the school of hard knocks – he created a tremendous business in the tough arena of television regardless of his lack of formal education. Don had been concerned about some of the health problems of loved ones, and was searching for ways to help them. He was referred to me and shortly thereafter attended one of my seminars. After hearing the research I presented, he determined the problem was with our medical model of health in America. During a conversation afterwards he said that he intuitively thought that both the medical and nutritional hype model of business was wrong, and getting back to the basics of whole foods and sound exercise was the true answer. The research from the seminar confirmed that for him, and we outlined a strategy he could follow.

He then hired my company's services to produce an all-in-one whole food vitamin product that he has sold through his infomercials. His mom was also benefitting tremendously from the nutritional program we recommended. As time brought him to a greater understanding of health, Don became extremely motivated to take our health education to the masses. He saw that the public was still for the most part not taking responsibility for their own health. He told me about his frustrations, and I admitted that those were the same frustrations I have had for over 15 years. The way I handled it was to share with people the true research through simple programs so they can make educated, informed decisions and take charge of their own health. Although we work with thousands of health professionals and many of the top athletes in the world, our educational programs and products were not hitting the masses because we have followed a no-nonsense simple approach without the fancy gimmicks that usually attract people.

I decided to write this book in hopes of influencing a wider audience. I hope to empower readers with knowledge to make informed decisions about their health, rather than relying on just one person's recommendations. By utilizing an infomercial model we could educate more people in a year than I had in a decade. This would then progress into retail markets and stores to expand the awareness about health. Thus, this book was created. I was only one of an entire team that collaborated on the contents of this work, all of us using the principles I learned many years ago through my research. You will not find many opinions in this book, but instead will find researched facts about our medical and nutritional system and a simple plan to help you decide when to choose and how much to choose of each profession's tools for health.

To find out more or to speak to a nutritional counselor for free, just visit us at:
www.CuresForTheBody.com

What this book **is** and **isn't**:

• This book isn't just someone's opinion. It is based on facts and peer-reviewed research.

• This book isn't a tool to create bad feelings between the medical and nutritional systems. In fact, it is the opposite of that. We want to create a great networking between these two groups so that the public will be served properly.

• The book isn't a manual that just leaves you hanging as to where you should go for your health needs.

• This book is a research based tool for the public to become aware of the need to take responsibility for their health.

• It is a reference for the public to learn about medical approaches to conditions and the risks associated with them.

• It is a reference to look up the nutritional approaches that have been proven to help with specific conditions.

• It is a tool to learn the basic nutrition guidelines to start improving your health today.

• It is a tool to guide the public to responsible nutrition companies that can provide education and products.

"*Natural Cures 'Saying Goodbye to Your Illness'*" is a look into our health care system. It will give you a great start on your education and the motivation needed to take responsibility for your own health care. The book is owned by "Erica Inc." I have been hired by Don Lapre to write this book. As I mentioned, my work alone wouldn't do this project justice. I have utilized the top minds in the industry to make this possible. My company Optimal Health Systems sells and promotes holistic programs and products for professional athletes and doctors worldwide. At the end of the book we give you the option to use our services or some of the others we recommend as reputable companies that provide education with their products. If you stick with companies that provide true education with their programs, then you can choose to use them or someone else to help you with your life-style from a nutritional standpoint. No matter what programs you choose to follow, you will become healthier and better educated.

To find out more or to speak to a nutritional counselor for free, just visit us at:
www.CuresForTheBody.com

All of the contributing writers and researchers who helped with this book, along with Don Lapre, hope and pray this work will enlighten the public's understanding about health care, and will in turn empower the reader to take full responsibility for their well being by giving them the tools to make the best decisions for their health and longevity. Healthy reading.

Yours in health,
Douglas D. Grant

To find out more or to speak to a nutritional counselor for free, just visit us at:
www.CuresForTheBody.com

Table Of Contents

Chapter 1

The Truth About our Medical "Crisis" System

Let's first look at statistics that explain why we need to take a long, hard look at our current medical model. Research shows that patients make more visits to complementary care givers such as chiropractors and naturopaths than to family doctors and internists. If all is satisfactory with our medical model of health, then we wouldn't be migrating by millions to alternative medicine treatments.

The following results study were published in an article entitled WHY PATIENTS USE ALTERNATIVE MEDICINE in the *Journal of the American Medical Association*[1]:

• **Americans made 425 million visits to alternative health care providers in 1990. This figure surpassed the number of visits to allopathic primary care physicians during the same period– by almost 100 million visits!**

• **A 1994 survey of physicians from a wide range of medical specialties (in Washington State, New Mexico, and Israel) discovered that more than 60% had suggested alternative therapies to their patients at least once in the preceding year. Furthermore, 38% had done so in the previous month.**

• **Of these physicians, 47% also reported using alternative therapies themselves, and 23% incorporated them into their medical practices.**

---

[1]Why Patients Use Alternative Medicine. *Journal of the American Medical Association* (JAMA). P. 1548-1553. Stanford. John A. Astin, PhD.

To find out more or to speak to a nutritional counselor for free, just visit us at:
www.CuresForTheBody.com

• **The two most frequently endorsed benefits of alternative care were: "I get relief for my symptoms, the pain or discomfort is less or goes away, I feel better," and "The treatment works better for my particular health problem than standard medicines." According to the author of the study, these responses suggest that the underlying factor in the decision to use alternative health care may be its perceived efficacy.**

• **The third most frequently reported benefit was: "The treatment promotes health rather than just focusing on the illness."**

• **Relief of symptoms was the primary benefit reported (the perceived efficacy of alternative medicine was cited nearly twice as often as other reported benefits).**

• **A critical finding was that users of alternative health care are no more dissatisfied with or distrustful of conventional care than nonusers are.**

While we have the world's most advanced health care, the World Health Organization ranked our system 37th in their Health Report 2001.

The goal of the Western model is often the "quick fix." The goal is to "fight" now; worry about the "debris" later. People readily "feel" the effects of the Western approach when their pain is turned off or symptoms are suppressed. There is often the appearance of health, but that appearance is often transitory. The substance of health is frequently missing.

This model has worked well with crisis care. Western medicine has the best system in the world for dealing with life-threatening infections, sophisticated surgeries, and the like. However, it is a fact that chronic, degenerative diseases (statistically those from which most of us will die) have become the most common problems that medicine currently faces, and those diseases are on the rise. Heart disease is up 400% since 1900; diabetes is up 700% since 1959; and cancer is projected to surpass heart disease as the #1 killer in less than 20 years. The Western medical model is not saving us from chronic, degenerative disease and this is why the public is seeking other practitioners for help.

Obviously, the current medical model is not working for HEALTH CARE and more and more people are seeking alternatives. As stated, this is because the medical model is designed for crisis care and it is the best at crisis care, but one of the worst at health care in the modernized world. Let's look at the ancient history of health care and see how it relates to us today.

In ancient Greece, "doctors" worked under the patronage of Asklepios, the god of medicine, but "healers" served Asklepios's daughter, the radiant Hygeia, goddess of health.

"For the worshipers of Hygeia, health is the natural order of things, a positive attribute to which men are entitled if they govern their lives wisely. According to them, the most important function of medicine is to discover and teach the natural laws which will ensure a man a healthy mind in a healthy body. More skeptical, or wiser in the ways of the world, the followers of Asklepios believed that the chief role of the physician is to treat disease, to restore health by correcting any imperfections caused by accidents of birth or life."

The political debates about how to cover the costs of medical care mostly take place among followers of Asklepios. In the West there is no argument about the nature of medicine or people's expectation of it, only about who is going to pay for its services which have become inordinately expensive.

The major focus of scientific medicine has been the identification of external agents of disease and the development of weapons against them. An outstanding success story of this century was the discovery of antibiotics and the subsequent great victories against infectious diseases caused by bacteria. Such victories were a major factor in winning hearts and minds over to the Asklepian side, convincing most people that medical intervention with modern technology was worth any price. However, weapons are dangerous and can backfire causing injury to the user. Just consider the rise of "Infectious Disease" as reported in our next chapter. Organisms are rapidly developing new resistance mechanisms, sometimes outpacing pharmaceutical research in their quest for new drugs less susceptible to current resistance mechanisms. With tuberculosis, we're even reconsidering techniques used in the Sanatoriums in the 1930s such as the removal of ribs and tearing the chest cavities containing resistant organisms. Some infectious disease specialists are now discussing possibilities of reverting to the strict quarantine rules of the 1920s and 1930s.

The medicine of the East, especially in China, is more aligned with the teachings of Hygeia. It focuses on internal healing, increasing internal resistance, and avoiding harmful external influences. Eastern medicine uses herbs and other natural substances to provide a tonic for the body. Resistance never develops to tonics because they're not directed to external forces such as germs, but act within the body's defenses. Therefore, just as Hygeia's followers emphasized the importance of governing one's life wisely, we

To find out more or to speak to a nutritional counselor for free, just visit us at:
www.CuresForTheBody.com

can also change our life-styles and focus on nutrition and exercise to improve our health from the inside out.

WESTERN MEDICINE

Western medicine views the body as a machine. Machines tend to break down. To fix the machine, you replace the bad part without considering how it was damaged in the first place. To fix the body, then, you take drugs or have surgery without considering the underlying cause of the condition.

If drugs and surgery were the answer, our ancestors could not have delivered us, as they did, into the twentieth century, for they did not have access to these modern practices. If drugs and surgery were the answer, we would be a much healthier population than we are today. We are the most medicated population in the world and yet one out of three of us has a chronic disease. Our health is deteriorating not because we have too many organs in our body or because we are deficient in the chemicals that make up prescription drugs. Rather, we are becoming sicker because our immune systems are constantly being called upon to ward off one onslaught after another.

Do not be mistaken: Western medical practices as disease and crisis oriented are the best in the world. If I had a broken arm or a ruptured appendix, there is no country I'd rather be in than the United States with its brilliant doctors and surgeons providing expert care. The problem lies in our insistence that these same doctors treat *all* of our conditions, including our more common, non-crisis symptoms such as headaches, fatigue, and general aches and pains. The doctors, immersed in the philosophy of Western medicine, treat the symptoms rather than the underlying cause. A simple analogy is found in a car's oil light. When the light comes on, the car needs oil. But what if you were to simply put a piece of tape over the light? It is true that the light would no longer concern you, but eventually, your car would no longer run and permanent damage would be caused. All because you didn't give your car a simple substance it needs to run properly.

So, what happens when we try to have our allopathic medical doctors practice more than crisis care?

A close reading of medical peer-review journals and government health statistics shows that American medicine frequently causes more harm than good. The number of people having in-hospital, adverse drug reactions (ADR) to prescribed medicine is 2.2 million.[2] Dr. Richard Besser, of the Center for Disease Control (CDC). In 1995, Dr. Besser said the number of unnecessary antibiotics prescribed annually for viral infections was 20 million. Eight years later, Dr. Besser referred to tens of millions of unnecessary antibiotics.[3,4] The number of unnecessary medical and surgical procedures performed annually is 7.5 million.[5] According to a congressional oversight subcommittee, the number of people exposed to unnecessary hospitalization annually is 8.9 million.[6]

To make this point even more clear, consider the number of deaths caused per year by the top two fatal diseases in America: heart disease killed 699,697 people in 2001 and cancer killed 553,251. Compare these numbers to the total number of iatrogenic (physician induced) deaths each year: 783,936! It is evident that the American medical system is the leading cause of premature death and injury in the United States.

Though some drugs save lives, unfortunately, most drugs also create unwanted side effects and toxicity.

"Millions of Americans swallow pills that are supposed to make them feel better — physically or mentally — but covertly wreak havoc with their body and brain. Many older folks are dismissed as senile, when in fact their drugs are causing their memory lapses and confusion." –Dr. Julian Whitaker, MD

The number of drug company lobbyists increased from 2001 to 2002, along with the amount spent on lobbying activities. In all, the drug industry spent close to $100 million that year—a record amount.

Is it our Medical doctors' fault? NO and YES.

---

[2]United States, Behavioral Risk Factor Survellance System, 2001, Center for Disease Control, National Center for Chronic Disease Prevention and Health Promotion

[3]Lazarou J, Pomeranz B, Corey P. Incidence of adverse drug reactions in hospitalized patients. JAMA. 1998;279:1200-1205.

[4]Rabin R. Caution About Overuse of Antibiotics. Newsday. Sept. 18, 2003.

[5] http://www.cdc.gov/drugresistance/community/

[6]http://hcup.ahrq.gov/HCUPnet.asp (see Instant Tables: 2001 prerun tables: most common procedures) US Congressional House Subcommittee Oversight Investigation. Cost and Quality of Health Care: Unnecessary Surgery. Washington, DC: Government Printing Office, 1976.

To find out more or to speak to a nutritional counselor for free, just visit us at:
www.CuresForTheBody.com

Medical doctors are taught in medical schools. Medical schools are funded in large part by pharmaceutical companies that want their views taught. MDs are taught this crisis care approach to health very little about nutrition. In fact, in 1992, a question was asked of the AMA: "what do United States medical schools teach medical students about nutrition?" Marian Burros in her column entitled *Eating Well* which appeared in the April 1,1992 *New York Times* gives a stunning answer to this question:

"Only about one third of the 125 or so medical schools require students to take courses in nutrition. And, most of the courses are short. The one at Cornell is eight hours... The University of Alabama at Birmingham is one of the exceptions requiring 52 hours of nutrition education for its medical students... The remaining two thirds of this country's medical schools only offer elective courses."

In her article, Burros acknowledges that nutrition is laced through medical school classes including physiology, gastroenterology, cardiology, biochemistry. But it is rarely, if ever, taught as an application to preventive medicine. Many experts who have begun to question the status quo strongly believe that increasing nutrition awareness and knowledge among MDs would greatly decrease the prevalence of disease. The pharmaceutical companies, however, have a huge investment in maintaining the status quo, and, at present, their agenda is the one being taught to our nation's future physicians.

Burros also reports on a 1986 survey that found 85% of medical students were dissatisfied with the amount of nutrition education they received and 60% were dissatisfied with the quality. This study strongly suggests that MDs believe they are going to be taught more about nutrition and are disappointed that they are not. The pharmaceutical companies only have the schools teach what they can profit from!

Is it any wonder that some doctors are nutritionally unenlightened? Is it any wonder why doctors often hide their lack of nutritional knowledge under the aegis: "food provides all the nutrition a person will ever need?"

Furthermore, *The Journal of the American Medical Association*[7] reported a new study that shows a vast majority of doctors who are involved in establishing national disease treatment guidelines have financial connections or relationships to the pharmaceutical drug industry, potentially

---

[7]*Journal of the American Medical Association* (JAMA). P. 287:612-617. 2002.

To find out more or to speak to a nutritional counselor for free, just visit us at:
www.CuresForTheBody.com

swaying their recommendations and unethically influencing thousands of other physicians. *(Eighty-seven of the 100 doctors who responded to a survey and who had published health guidelines for diseases such as diabetes, high blood pressure, and asthma from 1991 to 1999 have financial ties to drug companies whose products they are assessing.)* Also, numerous studies have linked the medication-prescribing behavior of doctors to incentives and gifts supplied by pharmaceutical drug companies (please read Dr. Lydon's foreword).

So our medical problem, in part, has been created by a government and people that have not demanded better care and who have let big business pharmaceuticals blindly control their health. In this respect medical doctors are not responsible. On the other hand, medical doctors, along with other professionals, should know what is right ethically; that just because we are human and common sense, tells us that our body wants to heal, it isn't Prozac (or any other drug) deficiency, but a life-style and nutrient deficiency. This common sense or "gut feeling" should drive health professionals and you to seek other treatments in your health care program.

Many MDs have realized the need for proper nutrition and healthy life-styles and have become educated in nutritional testing and whole food supplementation. These alternative doctors have taken a lot of criticism from the medical establishment because they are going after the cause of the disease. But they are now starting to reap the benefits of their courage to step off the beaten path. They are gaining enormous respect from the thousands of patients they are helping to become responsible for their general health.

Medical doctors do not have to become health care practitioners of life-style but they should at least send their patients to those who are if they truly want to fix this part of our medical model that has turned into a killing machine. As long as the public seeks their medical doctor for health advice instead of just crisis care, MDs should either become educated in life-style recommendations and natural cures, or network and refer to those who do. Only when this happens will our serious drug induced disease situation be controlled and eventually eliminated.

Chapter 2

The Abuse Of Prescription Drugs And The Rise Of Infectious Diseases... Our Current "Medical Mentality"

"If people let government decide what foods they eat and what medicines they take, their bodies will soon be in as sorry a state as are the souls of those who live under tyranny." *--Hippocrates*

One of the biggest problems we face today is the abuse of prescription drugs by both patients and physicians.

To begin, let us first consider the public's abuse of prescription drugs. Dr. Alan I. Leshner, Ph.D., Director of the National Institute on Drug Abuse, has reported an estimated 9 million people age 12 and older used prescription drugs for non-medical reasons in 1999; more than a quarter of that number reported using prescription drugs non-medically (i.e., misusing the medications) for the first time in the previous year.

Kenneth Schmader, MD, of Duke University, stated that persons age 65 or older consume one-third of all prescription drugs, but represent only 13 percent of the U.S. population. These patients are generally less healthy than younger persons and often suffer from multiple diseases for which they take multiple drugs. Therefore, they are more vulnerable than younger patients to unintentionally misusing drugs and becoming habituated to prescription medications. In one study of more than 1,500 elderly patients, 50 patients (roughly 3 percent) were abusing prescription drugs.

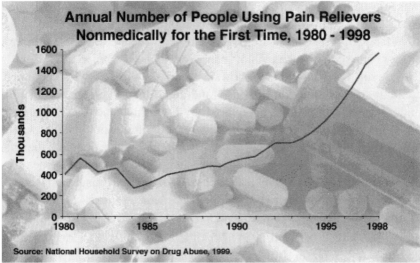

Annual Number of People Using Pain Relievers Nonmedically for the First Time, 1980 - 1998

Source: National Household Survey on Drug Abuse, 1999.

In 1998, roughly 1.6 million people used prescription pain relievers non-medically for the first time; four times as many as in 1980.

In a study of consecutive admissions to a drug treatment program, 80 of 100 elderly patients admitted dependence on sedatives, 49 on opioids, and three on stimulants. Thirty-six were dependent on two drugs and eight were dependent on 3 drugs.

This is just a sample of the documented problems we face as a society in regard to prescription drug abuse. Part of the problem stems from our mentality that drugs are good for us since they supposedly "cure" diseases. As mentioned earlier, drugs are meant for "crisis care." Their primary job is to assist in keeping us alive in critical situations.

However, when the medical crisis has passed, patients should stop using prescription drugs and start focusing on the cause of the disease. Once the cause is pinpointed, all efforts should be made to heal the body through lifestyle changes and nutrition, approaches that do not carry the addictive tendencies and side effects of prescription drugs.

Now let's consider the physician's abuse of prescriptions.

Although ultimately the responsibility of prescribing medication to patients falls to the doctor, many physicians get "pushed" into a corner when it comes to prescribing medication. To make this point, consider what has transpired over the last few decades with the prescription drug industry's use of television advertising.

In order to reach the widest audience possible, drug companies are no longer just targeting medical doctors with their message about medications. By 1995 drug companies had tripled the amount of money allotted to direct advertising of prescription drugs to consumers. The majority of the money is spent on seductive television ads. Consider a commercial selling a cholesterol-lowering pill that shows children playing and says "Grandpa could be alive and playing with his grand-children if only he had taken this pill." Tugs at your heart strings, doesn't it? And how about a commercial for a pill that not only improves sexual performance, but also shows its users as youthful, energetic and happy? What middle-age or elderly person wouldn't want to experience all of these benefits just from taking one little pill? Truly, the emotional appeal of these commercials insures that more and more Americans desire prescriptions to medications.

From 1996 to 2000, spending on advertising rose from $791 million to nearly $2.5 billion.[1] Even though $2.5 billion may seem like a lot of money, it actually only represents 15% of the total pharmaceutical budget. According to medical experts, there is no solid evidence that the efficacy of a drug is improved when a prescription is requested by the consumer. However, the drug companies maintain that direct-to-consumer advertising is educational. Dr. Sidney M. Wolfe of the Public Citizen Health Research Group in Washington, D.C., argues that the public is often misinformed about these ads.[2] People want what they see on television and are told to go to their doctors for a prescription. Doctors in private practice either acquiesce to their patients' demands for these drugs or spend valuable clinic time trying to talk patients out of unnecessary drugs. Dr. Wolfe remarks that one important study found that people mistakenly believe that the "FDA reviews all ads before they are released and allows only the safest and most effective drugs to be promoted directly to the public."[3]

Many of the doctors who have attended our seminars have reported they feel "coerced" into writing a prescription for medication. One doctor commented about a woman and her child who came into his office. The child had a viral infection and the mother expected a prescription for an antibiotic. The doctor informed the mother that antibiotics would not help

---

[1]Rosenthal MB, Berndt ER, Donohue JM, Frank RG, Epstein AM. Promotion of prescription drugs to consumers. New England Journal of Medicine 2002 Feb 14;346(7):498-505.

[2]Wolfe SM. Direct-to-consumer advertising—education or emotion promotion? New England Journal of Medicine 2002 Feb 14;346(7):524-6.

[3]Ibib.

To find out more or to speak to a nutritional counselor for free, just visit us at:
www.CuresForTheBody.com

---

her child, and that the best course of action was for the child to simply rest and drink plenty of fluids. The mother became irate that the doctor wouldn't prescribe any medication. After all, she had waited for hours and her insurance was paying good money. The doctor finally gave in and wrote a prescription.

Not only are there far too many prescriptions being written, but a 2002 study shows that 20% of hospital medications prescribed for patients had dosage mistakes. Of that 20%, nearly 40% were considered potentially harmful to the patient. In a typical 300-patient hospital, the number of errors per day averaged 40. Problems involving patients' medications were even higher in 2003! The error rate intercepted by pharmacists in this study was 24%, making the potential minimum number of patients harmed by prescription drugs 417,908! And this, of course, does not include the inevitable number of prescription errors that are not detected by pharmacists.

Consider the problem of over-prescribed anti-inflammatories. The general public expects these drugs to be harmless, especially when they come with a doctor's prescription. But overuse of these same drugs has caused thousands of patients to experience stomach bleeding, which leads to pain and additional complications in the least, and death at its worst.

And so this much we know: Many prescriptions can cause serious side effects and even death. Drugs can also be addictive and many times they are wrongly prescribed, either through ignorance or coercion. Considering all of these facts, perhaps it's time to take a closer look at our current medical model and re-evaluate our ever-increasing consumption of prescription medication.

How Do We Know Prescription Drugs Are Safe?

Another aspect of scientific medicine that the public takes for granted is the testing reliability of new drugs. In general, drugs are tested on individuals who are fairly healthy and usually not on other medications that can interfere with findings. But when the drugs are declared "safe" and enter the drug prescription books, they are inevitably going to be used by people on a variety of other medications and who have additional health problems. After a drug has been declared "safe", a new phase of drug testing called Post-Approval comes into play. This involves the documentation of side effects after drugs hit the market. In one very telling report, the General Accounting Office (an agency of the U.S. Government) "found that of the 198 drugs approved by the FDA between 1976 and 1985, 102 (or 51.5%) had serious post-approval risks. The serious post-approval risks [included] heart failure, myocardial infarction, anaphylaxis, respiratory depression and arrest, seizures, kidney and liver failure, severe blood disorders, birth defects and fetal toxicity, and blindness."[4]

When the number one killer in a society is the healthcare system, that system must be held responsible and be required to address its own urgent shortcomings. It is a failed system in need of immediate attention.

As disturbing as the abuse, over consumption, and blind faith in prescription medications have become, it was the "unexpected" rise and return of infectious diseases that first opened the eyes of this author.

The Rise, Fall and Rise of Infectious Disease

Most people don't understand that we are in the midst of an unsettling health epidemic... an epidemic that never should have occurred.

In 1968 infectious diseases had been all but eliminated. Infectious diseases did not even make the list of "top ten killers" in the United States. In fact, "The war against infectious diseases has been won," William H. Stewart, U.S. Surgeon General confidently announced in 1969[5], and the world's population breathed a little easier. But the confidence was premature — in fact, the battle was only beginning.

Because, in the past 20 years, the re-emergence of these diseases and the discovery of new strains of "super germs" have created a very disturbing situation for our entire planet.

Towards the end of Louis Pasteur's life, he confessed that germs themselves may not be the cause of disease after all, but may simply be another *symptom* of the disease itself. He had come to realize that germs seem to lead to illness primarily when the person's immune and defense system (what biologists call "host resistance") is not strong enough to combat them. The "cause" of disease is not simply bacteria, but also the factors that compromise host resistance, including the person's hereditary endowment, nutritional state, life stressors and psychological state. In describing one of his experiments with silkworms, Pasteur asserted that the microorganisms present in such large numbers in the intestinal tract of the silk worms he was studying were "more an *effect* than a cause of disease."[6]

---

[4]GAO/PEMD 90-15 FDA DRUG Review: Postapproval Risks 1976-1985, page

[5]US Surgeon General Report 1969

[6]Rene Dubos, <u>Mirage of Health</u>, San Francisco: Harper and Row, 1959, 93-94.

To find out more or to speak to a nutritional counselor for free, just visit us at:
www.CuresForTheBody.com

With these far-reaching insights, Pasteur conceived an ecological understanding of infectious disease. Infectious disease does not simply have a single cause, but is the result of a complex web of interactions inside and outside the diseased individual.

An analogy to help develop an understanding of the ecological perspective of infectious disease can be more easily understood by considering the environmental situation of mosquitoes and swamps. It is commonly known that mosquitoes infest these areas because swamps provide the still waters necessary for the mosquitoes to lay their eggs and for those eggs to be able to hatch without disruption. In essence, swamps provide a perfect environment for the mosquitoes to reproduce.

A farmer might try to rid his land of mosquitoes by spraying insecticide over the swamp. If he's lucky, he will kill all the mosquitoes. However, because the swamp is still a swamp, it remains a perfect environment for new mosquitoes to fly in and to lay their eggs. The farmer then sprays his insecticide again, only to find that more mosquitoes are infesting the swamp. Over time, some mosquitoes do not get sprayed with fatal doses of the insecticide. Instead, they adapt to the insecticide that they have ingested, and with each generation they are able to pass on an increased immunity to the insecticide to their offspring.

Soon, the farmer must use stronger and stronger varieties of insecticide, but due to their "adapted immunity," despite increased exposure to the insecticide, some mosquitoes are able to survive.

Similarly, finding streptococcus in a child's throat does not necessarily mean that streptococcus "caused" the sore throat, any more than one could say that the swamp "caused" the mosquitoes. Streptococcus often inhabits the throat of healthy people without leading to any symptoms of a sore throat. The symptoms of "strep" throat only begin if there are favorable conditions for the strep to reproduce rapidly, and aggressively invade the throat tissue. Strep, like mosquitoes, will only settle and grow in conditions which are conducive for them to multiply.

A child with strep throat generally gets treated with antibiotics. Although the antibiotics may be effective in getting rid of the bacteria temporarily, they do not change the factors that led to the infection in the first place. When the farmer sprays with insecticide, or the physician prescribes antibiotics, but neither changes the conditions that created the problem, both the mosquitoes and the bacteria are able to return to the environments that are favorable for their specific growth.

To find out more or to speak to a nutritional counselor for free, just visit us at:
www.CuresForTheBody.com

The above process, referred to as protective assimilation, is not the only concern created by the use and misuse of modern-day antibiotics. Making matters worse, the antibiotics prescribed also kill the beneficial bacteria along with the harmful bacteria. Since the beneficial bacteria play an important role in digestion, the individual's ability to assimilate necessary nutrients into the body is temporarily limited, ultimately making him more prone to re-infection from the same or another illness during this critical time.

Marc Lappe', PhD, University of Illinois professor and author of *When Antibiotics Fail*, notes that, "When these more benevolent counterparts die off, they leave behind a literal wasteland of vacant tissue and organs. These sites, previously occupied with normal bacteria, are now free to be colonized with new ones. Some of these new ones have caused serious and previously unrecognized diseases."[7]

Some clinicians have found that inappropriate antibiotic usage can transform common vaginal "yeast" infections (*candida albicans*, which are characterized by simple itching) into a system-wide *candida* infection, which can cause a variety of acute and chronic problems.[8] Although the diagnosis of "systemic candidiasis" is controversial, there is general consensus that the frequent use of antibiotics can transform harmless bacteria that normally live in our bodies into irritating and occasionally serious infections that can have dire effects on the elderly, the infirmed, and the immunodepressed.[9]

And, of course, the bacteria learn to adapt to and survive the specific antibiotic. Scientists then must slightly change the antibiotic (there are over 300 varieties of penicillin alone), or make stronger and stronger antibiotics (which generally also have increasingly serious side effects). Despite the best efforts of scientists, Dr. Lappe' asserts that we are creating many more *germs* than we are *medicines*, since each new antibiotic brings to life literally millions of these bacterial "Benedict Arnolds."

Just 20 years ago penicillin was virtually always successful in treating gonorrhea. Today there are gonorrhea bacteria that have learned to resist penicillin, and have now been found in all fifty of the United States and several countries throughout the world. Between the years 1983 to 1984

---

[7]Marc Lappe', *When Antibiotics Fail*, Berkeley: North Atlantic, 1986, xii.

[8]William Crook, *The Yeast Connection*, New York: Vintage, 1986.

[9]Lappe', xiii

To find out more or to speak to a nutritional counselor for free, just visit us at:
www.CuresForTheBody.com

alone, the number of cases in the U.S. with resistant strains of gonorrhea doubled.[10]

Alexander Fleming, the scientist who discovered penicillin, cautioned against the overuse of antibiotics. Unless the scientific community and the general public heed his warning, Harvard professor Walter Gilbert, a Nobel prize winner in chemistry has asserted, "There may be a time down the road when 80% to 90% of infections will be resistant to all known antibiotics."[11]

A majority of the scientific community and the general public have ignored the insights of the late Louis Pasteur and have disregarded the importance of "host resistance" in preventing illness. Most scientists broadly accepted the "germ theory," while only a handful of insightful individuals have acknowledged the importance of the ecological balance of microorganisms in the body. Yet, the wisdom of Pasteur remains relevant, and more and more scientists are beginning to acknowledge the importance of alternatives to antibiotics. Even an editorial in the prestigious *New England Journal of Medicine* affirmed the need for the treatment of infections with "less ecologically disturbing techniques."

So what constitutes "less ecologically disturbing techniques?" First, we need to understand the importance of keeping our friendly bacteria levels "filled up" so that all of the parking places that should be inhabited by these immune boosting microorganisms are occupied. If our friendly bacteria are destroyed by antibiotics or by other factors like stress, alcohol, smoking, etc., pathogenic bacteria can fill these parking places and start a tail gate party that will keep you sick in bed while they're having a great time.

The key answer to this rather silly analogy is that all individuals need to incorporate a **probiotic** supplement into their diet on a daily basis. **Probiotics** are the friendly bacteria that reside in our bodies and help protect us from the invasion of the "unfriendly" bacteria that cause illness. They are our body's "natural antibiotic."[12]

So the question will arise, if *probiotics* are the body's "natural antibiotic," why should an individual need to supplement his or her diet in order to

---

[10]Lappe', xiii

[11]R. Cave, editor. "Those Overworked Miracle Drugs," Newsweek, August 17, 1981, 63.

[12]Reddy, G.V., K.M. Shahani, B.A. Friend and R.C. Chandan, 1983 Natural antibiotic activity of lactobacillus acidophilius and bulgaricaus. Cultured Dairy Prod. J. 18:15-19

To find out more or to speak to a nutritional counselor for free, just visit us at:
www.CuresForTheBody.com

benefit from their presence? Great question! Let's take a look at the history of our nutrition and the cause for decline of our natural probiotics...

In 1970, histamine blockers were created to supposedly help with poor digestion (also known as indigestion). These drugs, which include the likes of Zantac, Pepcid AC, and Tagamet, along with antacids like Tums and Rolaids, have created considerable side effects inside the human body because they are designed to stop or greatly reduce the amount of hydrochloric acid (HCL) used for digestion in our stomachs.

HCL has two main purposes in the body. First, it destroys bacteria that we ingest every time we drink or eat and acts as our first defense against infectious disease by wiping out potentially harmful organisms that would otherwise be traveling, very much alive, into our intestinal tract and blood stream.

Second, HCL lowers the pH level in the stomach and activates enzymes that complete the process of digesting our foods.

The practice of taking products and preparations that stop HCL (and thus leave us defenseless against the bacteria that cause infectious disease) is so prevalent that it has created a huge health problem. Since the introduction of HCL blockers, statistics show that infectious disease is now ranked number *three* as one of the top killers in our society today.

Since indigestion and the need to address indigestion symptoms have been the root of the problem, we should look at what causes the non-digestion of foods.

Enzymes are protein molecules that are present in raw food. These enzymes digest food and deliver the life-giving nutrients to the body on the cellular level. When we heat food to over 118 degrees Fahrenheit, we denature the food and destroy the enzymes, making foods difficult for the body to digest and causing *indigestion* to occur. Then, when these symptoms show up, we take antacids and acid blockers, which only lead to other side effects and increased problems.

The best way to combat the problem of indigestion is to enhance our digestion by eating more raw food. When we eat food that is cooked or processed, enzymes (which we chose to take out of the food when we cooked it) need to be added back into the body in supplemental form.

We have created a major problem in our world today by promoting the use of acid blockers at a time when we are experiencing a significant rise in the spread of infectious diseases, brought on, in part, by the abuse and misuse of antibiotics. As previously mentioned, antibiotic abuse is so

To find out more or to speak to a nutritional counselor for free, just visit us at:
www.CuresForTheBody.com

widespread that it is breeding new strains of germs known as "super germs." Antibiotics are too freely prescribed, and the general public is not aware of the devastating effects that can occur when the prescribed antibiotic does not destroy all the germs it was meant to kill. Many times the antibiotic only destroys the weak germs and the strong ones survive to become even more resistant to future doses of antibiotics. Recommended dosages and potencies are then increased, but ultimately we are still losing the battle.

The Director of the Center for Disease Control and Prevention recently stated, "We are losing the battle with super germs." Antibiotics are not only breeding super germs but they are creating an environment for the pathogenic bacteria to implant and grow. The problem is so severe that the Harvard School of Public Health has predicted that in the near future 40% of all *Streptococcus pneumoniae* strains in the United States will resist both penicillin and erythromycin. This is occurring because the antibiotic (which means literally "against-life") is also destroying our friendly bacteria, which is needed in our intestines. This friendly bacteria, our *probiotics,* is critical to the strength of our immune system.[13] When probiotics are growing and flourishing in the body , the "super germs," or pathogenic bacteria, have no place to implant and grow. If our probiotic levels are up, then the pathogenic bacteria have no choice but to travel straight through our system and are therefore negated from doing us any damage or making us ill.

So we've established that any food that has been heated above 118 degrees Fahrenheit is void of its natural enzymes, thus causing incomplete digestion (or indigestion) when consumed. This not only applies to foods we cook, but also to fruits and vegetables in the supermarket that have been irradiated to help preserve their "shelf life." In order for our digestive system to work the way it was intended, we need the natural food enzymes that are contained within food in its raw state. We have also learned that the use and misuse of antibiotics cause a probiotic *deficit* that can lead to a decrease in our body's immune system to fight these harmful bacteria. This is why the use of *supplemental probiotics* is so important.

The best source of plant enzymes to help aid our bodies in digestion are derived from eating raw foods. Probiotics are best taken in by consuming

---

[13]Perdigon, G., E. Vintini, S. Alvarez. M. Medina, M. Medici, 1999, Study of the possible mechanisms involved in the mucosal immune system activation by lactic acid bacteria, J. Dairy Sci. 82:1108-1114

To find out more or to speak to a nutritional counselor for free, just visit us at:
www.CuresForTheBody.com

fermented foods like Kimchee, sour yogurt, etc. We'll discuss these foods further in Chapter 5.

When choosing a supplemental probiotic, it is extremely important to look for one that contains *stabilized bacteria*.[14] These are bacteria that have been researched and proven to maintain their effectiveness over time.

Here is a quick guide to help with the infectious disease problems we face.

1. **Do not take antacids or acid blockers unless absolutely necessary for crisis care.**
2. **If you are going to take an antibiotic for a bacterial infection, ask your doctor to procure a culture sample to find out what specific bacteria you have, then request the specific antibiotic for that bacteria and finish the prescription completely.**
3. **Replenish your friendly flora with fermented foods or supplemental probiotics, and take plant enzyme supplements when you eat cooked food.**
4. **Try not to consume processed meats that contain antibiotics. If you do eat meat, try to consume organic drug free meats.**

Infectious will be addressed in greater detail in Chapter 4.

Here are a Few Quotes to Motivate You to Take Action Against These Super Germs Today:

"Prayer indeed is good, but while calling on the gods a man should himself lend a hand."
- Hippocrates, *Regimen in Health*

---

[14]Kilara, A., K.M. Shahani and N.K. Das, 1976, Effect of cryoprotective agents on freeze-drying and storage of lactic cultures., Cult. Dairy Prod. J., 11:8-12

"A wise man should consider that health is the greatest of human blessings, and learn how by his own thought to derive benefit from his illnesses."

- Hippocrates, *Regimen in Health*

Additional reasons why our "Medical Mentality" is wrong and we need to create a paradigm shift within ourselves right now…

"Western Medicine has the ability to work with the body in ways that are both life saving and enhancing. It is best for crisis intervention and the last few months of life. It is sickness care more than wellness care.

Traditional Oriental Medicine has a proven track record of dealing with issues of health and aging as well as quality of life. It is wellness care as it focuses on the quality of life and the preservation of the health that we have.

While each is complete in itself, the combination benefits the health of individuals in ways that neither could do alone. Both are necessary in today's modern society."

- Thomas Jefferson *(1743 - 1826)*

"Drugs never cure a disease. They merely hush the voice of nature's protest and pull down the danger signals she erects along the pathway of transgression. Any poison taken into the system has to be reckoned with later even though it palliates present symptoms. Pain may disappear, but the patient is left in a worse condition though unconscious of it at the time."

- Daniel H. Kress, M.D.

To find out more or to speak to a nutritional counselor for free, just visit us at:
www.CuresForTheBody.com

What hope is there for medical science to ever become a true science when the entire structure of medical knowledge is built around the idea that there is an entity called disease which can be expelled when the right drug is found?"

- John H. Tilden, M.D.

"The greater part of all chronic disease is created by the suppression of acute disease by drug poisoning."

- Harry Lindlahr, M.D.

"The body has an innate ability to fight germs and infections and heal itself. Western doctors are frozen in a disease-oriented mode, concentrating on curing disease with drugs and surgery rather than on prevention and stimulating the body's natural healing power. Most drugs just prevent the disease from expressing itself symptomatically. Symptoms disappear but the disease actually gets progressively worse. The true causes of diseases are internal. This point must be stressed: external material objects are never causes of disease, but are merely agents waiting to cause specific symptoms in susceptible hosts. This principle suggests other ways of thinking about prevention and treatment rather than those predominantly in conventional medicine. Rather than warring against disease agents with the hope (in vain, I suspect) of eliminating them, we ought to be strengthening resistance to them and learning to live in balance with them more of the time."

- Andrew Weil, M.D.

"One of the first duties of the physician is to educate the masses not to take medicine."

- Sir William Osler (1849 - 1919)

What have we learned from this chapter? Hopefully you feel more educated and much wiser about the serious effects of taking and abusing prescription drugs. Does this mean you should never take a prescription

To find out more or to speak to a nutritional counselor for free, just visit us at:
www.CuresForTheBody.com

drug? **NOT AT ALL**. What it does mean is that drugs should be used only for "crisis care" and, when used for that purpose, should be taken seriously, following the directions exactly.

Today many people are praying to find a nutritionally oriented health professional because they are "sick and tired" of drugs, hospitals, surgery, and limited myopic thinking. Furthermore, studies reveal that 65% of our health is entirely related to our lifestyle (i.e., diet, mental attitude, relationships, the wearing of seat belts, etc.), 21% is due to environmental factors (pollution, socioeconomic factors, climate) and 14% is based on genetics and health care.

What this tells us is that *You are in control of Your Health*.

The prevailing evidence reveals that "improper lifestyle, faulty dietary habits, environmental pollution, yeast/candida/parasite infestations, misuse/ overuse of medications, vitamin/mineral/nutrient deficiencies, sleep deprivation, lack of exercise, unbalanced mental/emotional states and atherosclerosis can be reversed through diet and lifestyle and stress management practices."[15]

What we have outlined in this book thus far are unsupportable aspects of our contemporary medical system that need to be changed – beginning at its very foundations.

The philosophy many people outside of the medical profession are advocating now is not against the practice of medicine. The philosophy simply insists that Western medicine assume its proper place in the overall scheme of human health. Grassroots health care fully acknowledges the role of medicine in life-threatening crisis situations, for which it is exceedingly well equipped. The fact remains, however, that the modalities used in medicine – drugs and surgery primarily – can be dangerous and are therefore best reserved for those rare situations when all other approaches have failed.

Unfortunately for your health and the health of our future generations this is not what is happening in the world today.

It should be clear to you by now that our medical system is saving and killing us at the same time. There also is no doubt that we as the public are somewhat responsible for this due to our demanding crisis care from our doctors. Much of the problem must be fixed by reform. However, there is an old adage that states "It is tough for a man to change his mind when he

---

[15]Lancet, July 21, 1990.336;129-133

To find out more or to speak to a nutritional counselor for free, just visit us at:
www.CuresForTheBody.com

---

is getting paid not to." Because of this, we know it will take some time for the AMA and pharmaceutical companies to change.

We need to take it upon ourselves to become responsible for our own health care and start to be proactive in our lifestyles and education towards health and disease. Only when we do this will we begin to fix the "Medical Mentality" problem.

To find out more or to speak to a nutritional counselor for free, just visit us at:
www.CuresForTheBody.com

Chapter 3

Why Nutritional Cures and Approaches to Disease are not Promoted More by Companies

For many years there has been a belief among the "nutritionally minded" that big pharmaceutical companies only sell *patented nutrients* because they don't want to advertise for any other company's products. This is not true, at least not for the last decade. Many pharmaceutical companies sell a variety of products that are not patented. In fact, many pharmaceutical giants even own their own nutritional products and nutrition-based companies (take Wyeth for example, which owns "Centrum"). If we examine the research done in this field, we'll get a better understanding of what is going on with "big business" in the medical and health world.

"Business is Business," right? Let's say you were in the business of selling widgets. As part of your marketing plan, you advertised generic widgets on television at the cost of 10 million dollars a month. But, since your widgets are generic, anyone could go out and sell widgets and profit from your hard earned marketing dollars. This does not sound like good business, does it? Of course not. So, you decide to patent a certain widget so that you are the only one that has this particular type, and then you spend 10 million dollars a month to advertise your "patented widget." Now everyone has to come to *you* to buy it! Now that is good business... but only when it comes to selling widgets! When it comes to your health, even though it is still good financial business (pharmaceutical companies are some of the most profitable companies on the planet) is it really ethical?

To find out more or to speak to a nutritional counselor for free, just visit us at:
www.CuresForTheBody.com

Though you can argue both sides of this dilemma, no matter what side you are on, there are some important facts and principles when it comes to your health that must be considered.

Let's say a company sells a patented product (whether widgets or any other consumer product) that they have completely researched and spent time developing - and another company creates a "like" product, also patented, but riding on the coattails of the research completed by the original company. The company who "borrowed" their knowledge may hide some of the detrimental effects of their particular product. The product might not hurt anyone if it is only a widget, so life goes on.

When it comes to pharmaceutical drugs, the situation can become much more serious. Many of us grew up believing that everything our doctor told us about a drug was true. As we grew older we came to understand that the doctors believed what they were teaching us because they themselves were taught these "facts" by the pharmaceutical companies. Since then, new research has proven these beliefs FALSE.

A new study performed at the Institute for Evidence-Based Medicine in Germany found that 94% of the information contained in promotional literature sent to doctors by pharmaceutical companies had absolutely no basis in scientific fact. The study revealed that virtually all of the information in the promotional brochures had been distorted or exaggerated. That means that 19 out of 20 statements made in marketing by pharmaceutical companies are most likely false.

According to this landmark study, medical guidelines from scientific groups are misquoted, the side effects of drugs are minimized, groups of patients are wrongly defined, study results are suppressed, treatment effects are exaggerated and risks are manipulated.

Still, doctors continue to rely on this incorrect information in order to make decisions about what drugs to prescribe to patients. This was understandable in the past, since we had faith in the idea that the pharmaceutical companies were engaged in rigorous scientific studies and clinical trials. As a result, when they received these promotional brochures, they read the material and believe it to be fact, and therefore prescribed these drugs to their patients. And yet, these beliefs are absolutely false.

The following report by the FDA confirms what many other studies have been building up to -- validating the belief that pharmaceutical companies have been suppressing facts for some time.

FDA Public Health Advisory

March 22, 2004

Subject: WORSENING DEPRESSION AND SUICIDALITY IN PATIENTS BEING TREATED WITH ANTIDEPRESSANT MEDICATIONS

Today the Food and Drug Administration (FDA) asked manufacturers of the following antidepressant drugs to include in their labeling a warning statement that recommends close observation of adult and pediatric patients treated with these agents for worsening depression or the emergence of suicidality. The drugs that are the focus of this new Warning are: Prozac (fluoxetine); Zoloft (sertraline); Paxil (paroxetine); Luvox (fluvoxamine); Celexa (citalopram); Lexapro (escitalopram); Wellbutrin (bupropion); Effexor (venlafaxine); Serzone (nefazodone); and Remeron (mirtazapine).

The drugs that are actually supposed to help with depression and anxiety may lead to suicidal depression and violence. This makes one wonder if the anti-pharmaceutical extremists might have known some things we didn't before these subjects became studies and were scrutinized.

Dr. Thomas J. Moore of Georgetown University, Dr. Bruce Psaty of the University of Washington, and Dr. Curt Furberg of Wake Forest University determined that "51% of the approved drugs have serious adverse effects not detected prior to approval.[1]" Think about this: More than half of our drugs, after being deemed "safe" by the FDA and then prescribed to millions of people, are subsequently detected to have previously unrecognized, medically serious side effects. No wonder we have a side effect epidemic. Now take the serious side effect number and look at the statistic that shows Americans purchased 2,587,575,000 prescriptions in 1999 alone. That's nine prescription drugs per person in America.

Because pharmaceutical companies understand business, they manufacture, patent, and advertise drugs so they can make money. But with the above-mentioned findings, they are doing this fraudulently. This is wrong enough, but the important fact is that the public's health should NOT be looked at or treated as NORMAL BUSINESS.

---

[1]Melmon, K.L., Morrelli, H.F., Hoffman, B.B., and Nierenberg, D.W. Melmon and Morrelli's Clinical Pharmacology: Basic Principles in Therapeutics (3rd edition). New York: McGraw-Hill, Inc., 1993

To find out more or to speak to a nutritional counselor for free, just visit us at:
www.CuresForTheBody.com

In the whole food side of the nutrition industry you have a completely different business scenario. The lead author of this book owns a whole food nutritional company and understands this principle well. When you advertise the benefits of whole foods, like Acerola Cherries for Vitamin C or plant enzymes for digestion, you automatically understand that anyone could sell these forms of nutrients and they do. Some of the money you spent on advertising will go to other companies that sell the same nutrients. Your only hope is that you have created a great synergistic blend of the nutrient and give great service so that you will reap enough rewards from the advertising to make a profit. Then you understand the "Law of the Universe" will bring any lost sales back to you through other means because you are helping people. This might sound idealistic and there are definitely a few exceptions to this rule, but the majority of the old school whole food companies have and will always live by this principle because business is NOT business when it comes to people's health. Instead of fraudulently trying to make money by creating patented "only we have it" drugs, whole food nutritional companies are constantly under the gun to always make the purest product with the best service so that the public will choose their products.

Consider the comment at the beginning of this chapter about pharmaceutical companies not selling only patented drugs. During this last decade, more people have visited alternative practitioners for health than medical doctors.[2] Not only that, the nutritional industry has grown and is a prominent voice in the government even though they are much less profitable. Because of this, pharmaceutical companies have brought big business tactics to play again and are buying nutritional companies left and right.[3] By doing this, they will voice their opinions to government even through the nutritional companies. The lead author of this book has repeatedly been offered a buyout of his whole food supplement company by numerous pharmaceutical companies. Watch out -- repercussion of these events will be severe if the public doesn't speak up and take personal responsibility for their own health, and take an active role in defending our health freedoms.

With all this information available to everyone, why hasn't the government bodies that are supposed to teach us about health and nutrition stepped up

---

[2]The results of the study were published in an article entitled WHY PATIENTS USE ALTERNATIVE MEDICINE in the May 20, 1998 edition of Journal of the American Medical Association (JAMA) p. 1548-1553 by Stanford researcher John A. Astin, PhD.

[3]Wyeth, Glaxo, Pfizer etc... Acquisitions 1985-2004

To find out more or to speak to a nutritional counselor for free, just visit us at:
www.CuresForTheBody.com

to the plate with the proper education? This would help us take responsibility for our own health and reduce our risks of disease without relying solely on medical doctors for our health care.

The following is a description of the primary governmental entity that is supposed to disseminate good nutrition information to the public. The U.S. Department of Agriculture (USDA) was created in 1862 by Abraham Lincoln to develop the best seeds. At the time, it had nine employees. Today it has 120,000 employees and in 1992 alone had a budget of $78 billion dollars. One would think with this much money and employee workforce, they would generate great information for the benefit of our health, right? WRONG! The problem is that the USDA has the mandate to have the American public increase their consumption of agricultural products through the national promotional boards. You might be thinking to yourself that this is a good thing because agricultural products are healthy. Consider the boards involved with the USDA:

American Cattlemen's Association

National Dairy Promotion and Research Board

National Pork Board

How healthy are the foods they promote?

American Cattlemen's Association

The American Cattlemen's Association promotes BEEF. Over $11 billion a year is given to this association in the form of subsidies from the USDA. Thus the advertising "Beef, Real Food for Real People." But what does the research say about the beef this association sells?

The China Health Project, the largest study on nutrition to date, was conducted to determine why certain people were healthier than others. Following is one of the observations from this study:

> "People who eat more meat have higher blood cholesterol levels and higher blood albumin levels, which is a function of protein intake. As levels of albumin and cholesterol levels go up, the diseases we tend to get in the west—cancer, heart disease and diabetes—also start going up, its quite remarkable."
>
> - Dr. T Colin Campbell - China Health Project

---

[4] Atkins diet, Protein Power guidelines.

To find out more or to speak to a nutritional counselor for free, just visit us at:
www.CuresForTheBody.com

The average protein intake with the popular protein diets in America is between 60 to 80%.[4] The World Health Organization has reported that a diet with as little as 8% protein has been proven completely healthy and able to reduce your risk of disease dramatically. Even sports nutrition research shows that no more than 20% protein is needed to attain your optimal athletic goals for muscle gain. This includes the top athletes in the world.[5]

Red meat intake from cows has been shown to increase your risk of cancer[6], heart disease[7], diabetes[8], and other diseases.[9]

High protein in general increases your risks of osteoporosis[10], cancer[11], gout[12], kidney stones[13] and rheumatoid arthritis[14].

The problem is that excess protein is broken down into nitrogen waste products (urea, uric acid, creatinine, ammonia) which are excreted in the urine. Over a lifetime, the kidney tissue deteriorates from the increase in

---

[5]Economos, D.D., et al.: Nutritional practices of elite athletes. Practical recommendations. Sports Med., 16:381, 1993.)

[6]Cancer Susceptibility: Role of Genes, Environment, and Diet Highlights From the AACR International Conference on Molecular and Genetic Epidemiology of Cancer; January 18-23, 2003; Waikoloa, Hawaii

[7]Ibid.,

[8]A Prospective Study of Red Meat Consumption and Type 2 Diabetes in Middle-Aged and Elderly Women. The Women's Health StudyPosted 09/21/2004 WebMD Yiqing Song, MD; JoAnn E. Manson, MD, DRPH; Julie E. Buring, SCD; Simin Liu, MD, SCD

[9]Cancer Susceptibility: Role of Genes, Environment, and Diet Highlights From the AACR International Conference on Molecular and Genetic Epidemiology of Cancer; January 18-23, 2003; Waikoloa, Hawaii

[10]Zemel, M., "Calcium utilization: effect of varying level and source of dietary protein,: Am J Clin Nutr, 48:880, 1988 Carroll, K., "Dietary protein and heart disease," Nutrition and the MD, June 1985 Muscari, A., Ann Ital Med Int, 7:7, 1992

[11]Whitney, E., Understanding Normal and Clinical Nutrition, 2nd ed.,West Publishing, 1987, pgs 129-130. Committee on Diet, Nutrition and Cancer of the National Research Council, Diet, Nutrition and Cancer, 1982

[12]Hall, A., "Epidemiology of gout and hyperuricemia: a long-term population study," Am J Med, 42:27, 1967

[13]Vahlensiek, W., "review: the importance of diet in urinary stones," Urological Res, 14:283, 1986 Robertson, P., "The effect of high animal protein intake on the risk of calcium stone-formation in the urinary tract,: Clin Sci, 57:285, 1979

[14]Kjeldsen-Kragh, J., "Controlled trial of fasting and one-year vegetarian diet in rheumatoid arthritis," Lancet, 338:899, 1991

[15] Coats, C., "Negative effects of a high-protein diet," Family Practice Recertification, 12:80, 1990

flow and pressure. By age 80, most Americans have lost 33-50% of their kidney function and excess protein appears to be the primary cause.[15] Is it no wonder why people with kidney disease are placed on low-protein diets.

It is interesting to note that the industry's treatment of meat plays a big role in its disease-causing traits. Red meat from wild animals does not show the same disease-causing effects as lazy cow meat being raised today.[16] Also, the antibiotics, steroids and pesticides that are fed to cows, chicken and other meat producers in the U.S. cause many health problems.[17] So much for the processed meat industry.

National Dairy Promotion and Research Board

Dairy is the leading cause of food allergies.[18] Dairy products are implicated in the cause of insulin-dependent diabetes[19], cataracts[20], multiple

---

[16]NUTRIENT CONTENT OF WILD GAME, Fact sheet from William Henning, Penn State University R. Illingworth and S.L. Connor, Cholesterol content of game meat. JOURNAL OF THE AMERICAN MEDICAL SOCIETY 258, 1532, 1987.
[17]More than 95 percent of all feedlot- raised cattle in the United States are currently receiving growth-promoting hormones and other pharmaceuticals, residues of which may be present in finished cuts of beef. Fred Kuchler et al. "Regulating Food Safety: The Case of Animal Growth Hormones," National Food Review July-December 1989, In order to speed weight gain, feedlot managers administer growth-stimulating hormones and feed additives. Anabolic steroids, in the form of small time-release pellets, are implanted in the animals' ears. The hormones slowly seep into the bloodstream, increasing hormone levels by two to five times. Cattle are given estradiol, testosterone, and progesterone. Jim Mason and Peter Singer, Animal Factories (New York. NY: Harmony· Books, 1990), 51; Jeannine Kenney and Dick Fallert, "Livestock Hormone in the United States," National Food Review, July-September 1989, 22-23.

[18]Bahna, S., Allergies to Milk, Grune and Stratton, 1980

[19]Dosch, H., "Lack of immunity to bovine serum albumin in insulin-dependent diabetes mellitus," New England Journal of Medicine, 330:161, 1994 Verge, C. "Environmental factors in childhood IDDM," Diabetes Care, 17:1381, 1994

[20]Couet, C. "Lactose and cataract in humans: a review," J am Coll Nutr, 10:79, 1991 Simmons, F., "A geographic approach to senile cataracts: possible links with milk consumption, lactose Activity, and galactose metabolism," Digestive Diseases and Sciences, 27:257, 1982

[21]Oski, F., Don't Drink Your Milk, 9th ed., Teach Services, 1992, pg 62

[22]Recker, R., "The effect of milk supplements on calcium metabolism and calcium balance," American Journal of Clinical Nutrition, 41:254, 1985

[23]Cramer, D., "Adult hypolactasia, milk consumption and age-specific fertility," Am J Epidemiol, 139:282, 1994

[24]La Vecchia, C., "Dairy products and the risk of prostatic cancer," Oncology, 48:406, 1991

---

sclerosis[21], osteoporosis[22], female infertility[23], and prostate cancers for men.[24]

It is unlikely you will find unfavorable studies about dairy products before they began to regularly pasteurize and process these foods. The pasteurization of milk uses a very high temperature which changes its molecular structure. It then integrates into the cell membranes of the body.

Research show that undigested proteins found in cow's milk have been found in mother's breast milk. These women had colicky babies and undigested proteins was found to be the cause.[25] Since these proteins can be absorbed into the body and end up in a mother's milk, let's look at the other additives in processed dairy products. An FDA study found 70% of U.S. cheese has pesticides.[26] Another study showed that NO MILK available in the U.S. market is free of pesticide residues.[27] According to the General Accounting Office, up to 82 drugs are used in dairy cows but the FDA only tests for four.[28] The FDA has allowed bovine growth hormone (BGH) to be sold in milk without disclosure since 1985.[29] BGH has been shown to cause allergic and gut tissue reactions in humans.[30]

The American Medical Association and Monsanto jointly produced a 20-minute TV show promoting BGH, which featured the American Dietetic Association (ADA). Then they paid the ADA $100,000.00 to field calls on BGH.[31]

---

[25]Clyne, P., "Human breast milk contains bovine igG. Relationship to infant colic?" Pediatrics, 87:439, 1991

[26]"Effects, Uses, Control and Research of Agricultural Pesticides," A Report by the Surveys and Investigations Staff of USDA, Part 1 pg 174

[27]"Effects, Uses, Control and Research of Agricultural Pesticides," A Report by the Surveys and Investigations Staff of USDA, Part 1 pg 174

[28]US General Accounting Office, "FDA strategy needed to address animal drug residues in milk," 1992

[29]Roberts, J., "US milk cannot be labeled hormone free, says FDS," BJM, 308:495, 1994 Daughaday, W., "Bovine somatotropin supplementation of dairy cows," JAMA, 264:1003, 1990 Townsend Letter for Doctors, Aug./Sept. 1990, pg 7

[30]Mepham, T., "Safety of milk from cows treated with bovine somatotrpin," Lancet, 344:197, 1994

[31]Stauber, J., "Shut up and eat your Frankenfoods," PR Watch, Jan./Mar 1994, pg 8

To find out more or to speak to a nutritional counselor for free, just visit us at:
www.CuresForTheBody.com

Are dairy products beneficial? You be the judge based on the research. Are you starting to see a familiar trend here that shows us that the more processed and mass produced a product is, the more detrimental it is to the health of the human body?

National Pork Board

Promoted as the "Other White Meat," pork has been pushed by the government as a healthy protein choice. In fact, the American Medical Association released a nutritional video clinic to show doctors that they can help lower their patients' cholesterol levels by teaching "Choice, rather than avoidance." The video was provided through a grant by the National Live Stock and Meat Board, the Beef Board and the Pork Board.[32] Pork contains 60% fat on average.[33] Looking at the research, pork is probably the most deceptively harmful promoted meat there is.

If you look at the dilemma, the USDA is in a "No Win" situation. It was developed to teach U.S. citizens about health and nutrition, yet its primary "product" which it must support is the actual cause of much of the disease and degeneration in America today.

With all this information coming from the pharmaceutical companies and from our own government agencies about supposed healthy drugs and foods, are there any simple, honest studies that point in the right direction? YES! There are literally thousands of studies performed by evaluating the cooking and eating habits of the healthiest people in the world. Many other studies have been performed on nutrition and degeneration, and Wales Health Statistics, during World War II, proved that this was no fluke. Again, after the war the death rate rose when we started consuming more meat, dairy, and flour.

The following accounts will give you an example of the type of nutrition program that we will lay out for you throughout the rest of this book.

World War I was a tough time for a lot of people but especially in Denmark. They were blockaded and had a food shortage. To avoid starvation, the Danish Government halted alcohol, meat and white flour

---

[32] AMA VideoClinic ad, "Practical strategies for improving dietary compliance in hypercholesterolemia ," American Medical News, Oct. 26, 1992, pg 25

[33] Nutrition Facts Desk Reference. Dr. Art Ulene, Avery publishing, ISBN 0-89529-623-623

To find out more or to speak to a nutritional counselor for free, just visit us at:
www.CuresForTheBody.com

production. Whole grains were diverted directly to Danish citizens. People consumed more whole grains, fruits and vegetables because nothing else was available. Interestingly, the death rate fell by 34% and Denmark became one of the healthiest nations in Europe. When the war ended and eating habits returned to normal, cancer and heart disease returned to prewar levels.[34] Just to prove that this wasn't a fluke (understanding they did this with the stress of war all around them), similar changes occurred in Norway, Holland, England and Wales during World War II. After the war, the death rate rose as consumption of meat, dairy, and white flour increased.[35]

It is noteworthy that these people reduced their risk of disease and improved their health, vitality and longevity even during an extremely stressful time. This serves as proof that proper nutrition can counter the harmful effects of stress in our lives.

The largest health study ever performed (The China Health Project) showed that only 7% of the Japanese diet consisted of fat and processed foods in the year 1949. As a result, they had a very low rate of disease and premature deaths. In 1991 it was determined that 25% of their diet consisted of fat and processed foods, and that it directly attributed to an enormous increase in disease and degeneration.

In 1850 in America, diets were mainly fruits, vegetables, and meats that were range free. Cancer was almost non-existent.[36]

By 1990 over 100,000 new food chemicals had been introduced along with a dramatic increase in processed foods including white flour, sugar, and soft drinks. The majority of meats were raised (and still are today) with steroids and antibiotics. Today heart disease is the number one killer of the Japanese people and cancer number two.[37]

By now you should be able to see the trend of what the research provides us, and what we need to do to take responsibility for our own health.

---

[34]Hindhede, M., "The effect of food restriction during war on mortality in Coppenhagen," JAMA, 74:381, 1920.

[35]Ingram, D., "Trends in diet and breast cancer mortality in England and Wales, 1928-1977," Nutr and Cancer, 3:75, 1982 Strom, A., "Mortality from circulatory diseases in Norway 1940-1945," Lancet, 1:126, 1951 Malmros, H., "The relation of nutrition to health: a statistical study of the effect of the war-time on Arteriosclerosis, cardiosclerosis, tuberculosis and diabetes," Acta Med Scand Suppl, 246:137, 1950

[36]U.S. Govt. health report and statistics

[37]1990 U.S. Census and health statistics report

To find out more or to speak to a nutritional counselor for free, just visit us at:
www.CuresForTheBody.com

This chapter will be taken by many as a biased stab at pharmaceutical companies and the USDA. The truth of the matter is that these are simply the facts as the research has proven them to us. It isn't the pharmaceutical companies this chapter is exposing, it is our individual choices in our own lives and as a group -- it is the knowledge that we are all responsible for our own health and the health of our families. If we didn't run so willingly into the arms of crisis care every time we have a symptom, we wouldn't spawn these business minded companies to create all of the drugs that just cover up symptoms. Many don't know that drug companies underwrite 70% of all medication research today.[38]

If we would demand more wholesome non-processed foods and purer meats (if we choose to eat them) there wouldn't be such a demand to sell them to us. Wouldn't it be great if our crisis care medical system only had to worry about creating life saving drugs and surgeries? Then we would have a chance to improve our lifestyle and correct the problems that brought us to that desperate position in the first place. We would be much better off if we looked to our own lifestyle choices and nutrition for our health care. We wouldn't be creating the greed that plays on our desire for the instant fix, even if the fix is not a cure.

---

[38]Bodenheimer, T. "Unersy Alliance-Clinical Investigators and the Pharmaceutical Industy." The New England Journal of Medicine, 2000, 342:1539-44.

To find out more or to speak to a nutritional counselor for free, just visit us at:
www.CuresForTheBody.com

Chapter 4

"Conditions and Diseases"

This chapter is designed to prepare you for the rest of the book. Up until now we have considered facts about why we are in this health predicament. No matter what your reason for buying this book, we hope that by now you are even more committed to finding the principles needed to improve your health and well being. In this chapter, you will find a list of many diseases and conditions that are affecting the public today.

This chapter is organized according to the following format: conditions are listed alphabetically. At the beginning of each condition you will learn what the condition is specifically. The explanation about each disease comes from American Medical Association sources along with the national foundations for the condition when available.

Next, you will be guided through the normal medical treatments to this condition based on the guidelines from the American Medical Association, the Physicians Desk Reference and medical doctors' insights from treating patients.

The next section of the disease or condition will focus on the nutritional approach to the treatment including the causes, nutrient recommendations and food choices. The last section of each condition will lay out a suggested nutritional approach to follow that is realistic for most people.

*Important note: The side effects listed for each drug do not include all known side effects. This book would have doubled in size had we included all of the known side effects for each drug. Instead, we chose to list only the major ones. Please check a drug reference for additional side effects before taking any prescription.

To find out more or to speak to a nutritional counselor for free, just visit us at:
www.CuresForTheBody.com

Acid Reflux/Gastroesophageal Reflux (GERD)

Description: Acid reflux occurs when hydrochloric acid (stomach acid) and enzymes, which digest the food in the stomach, back up into the esophagus, causing the sensitive tissues to be irritated and inflamed. The stomach has a protective lining which prevents the acid from irritating the stomach, but the esophagus does not have this lining. Thus, when stomach acid and enzymes flow backward (reflux) into the esophagus, this routinely causes symptoms and in some cases damage.

Acid and enzymes flow into the esophagus when the lower esophageal sphincter, the ring-shaped muscle that normally prevents the contents of the stomach from flowing back into the esophagus, is not functioning properly. Normally, the esophageal sphincter prevents fluid from flowing backward by pinching shut.

Medical Treatment:

Cholinergic drugs

Brand name: Urecholine

Drug Name: Bethanechol

Bethanechol chloride acts principally by producing the effects of stimulation of the parasympathetic nervous system. It increases the tone of the detrusor urinae muscle, usually producing a contraction sufficiently strong to initiate micturition and empty the bladder. It stimulates gastric motility, increases gastric tone and often restores impaired rhythmic peristalsis.

Notable Side Effects:

- *Body as a Whole:* malaise
- *Digestive:* abdominal cramps or discomfort, colicky pain, nausea and belching, diarrhea, borborygmi, salivation
- *Renal:* urinary urgency
- *Nervous System:* headache
- *Cardiovascular:* a fall in blood pressure with reflex tachycardia, vasomotor response
- *Skin:* flushing producing a feeling of warmth, sensation of heat about the face, sweating
- *Respiratory:* bronchial constriction, asthmatic attacks
- *Special Senses:* lacrimation, miosis

Antacids

Brand name: Alka-Seltzer
Drug Name: sodium bicarbonate

Notable Side Effects:

Continual use can result in blood being too alkaline, resulting in nausea, headache, and weakness. (Any acid neutralizer or acid blocker makes it easier for pathogenic bacteria to proliferate the system. This is one of the major causes of the rise of infectious disease today.)

Brand name: Tums, Caltrate, Oscal, Rolaids, Mylanta
Drug Name: calcium carbonate

Calcium carbonate neutralizes stomach acid. Each tablet has an acid-neutralizing capacity of 14.7 mEq and the ability to maintain the pH of stomach contents at 3.5 or greater for a significant period of time.

Notable Side Effects:

Continual use can result in blood being too alkaline, resulting in nausea, headache, and weakness. (Any acid neutralizer or acid blocker makes it easier for pathogenic bacteria to proliferate the system. This is one of the major causes of the rise of infectious disease today.)

To find out more or to speak to a nutritional counselor for free, just visit us at:
www.CuresForTheBody.com

Brand name: Gaviscon, Maalox, Amphogel, Alu-Cap
Drug Name: aluminum hydroxide

Notable Side Effects:

Causes weakness, loss of appetite, constipation

Brand name: Milk of Magnesia, Rolaids, Mylanta, Ex-Lax
Drug Name: magnesium hydroxide

Notable Side Effects:

Can cause diarrhea. (Any acid neutralizer or acid blocker makes it easier for pathogenic bacteria to proliferate the system. This is one of the major causes of the rise of infectious disease today.)

Histamine-2 H2 bockers

(Acid-reducing drugs): promotes ulcer healing by reducing the production of stomach acid. Can cause rash, fever, muscle pains: may cause breast enlargement and erectile dysfunction in men

Brand name: Tagamet
Drug Name: Cimetidine

Cimetidine at prescription doses is known to inhibit various P450 metabolizing isoenzymes, which could.

Notable Side Effects:

Confusion in older people, interference with body's elimination of certain drugs by affecting metabolism and increasing blood concentration. (Any acid neutralizer or acid blocker makes it easier for pathogenic bacteria to proliferate the system. This is one of the major causes of the rise of infectious disease today.)

To find out more or to speak to a nutritional counselor for free, just visit us at:
www.CuresForTheBody.com

Brand name: Pepcid

Drug Name: Famotidine

Famotidine inhibits gastric secretion. Both the acid concentration and volume of gastric secretion are suppressed, while changes in pepsin secretion are proportional to volume output. In normal volunteers and hypersecretors, famotidine inhibited basal and nocturnal gastric secretion, as well as secretion stimulated by food and pentagastrin.

Notable Side Effects:

Headache, dizziness, constipation, and diarrhea. (Any acid neutralizer or acid blocker makes it easier for pathogenic bacteria to proliferate the system. This is one of the major causes of the rise of infectious disease today.)

Brand name: Zantac

Drug Name: Ranitidine

Ranitidine is a reversible inhibitor of the action of histamine at the histamine H_2-receptors, including receptors on the gastric cells. It does not lower serum Ca^{++} in hypercalcemic states, and is not an anticholinergic agent.

Notable Side Effects:

• *Central Nervous System*: Rarely, malaise, dizziness, somnolence, insomnia, and vertigo. Rare cases of reversible mental confusion, agitation, depression, and hallucinations have been reported, predominantly in severely ill elderly patients. Rare cases of reversible blurred vision suggestive of a change in accommodation have been reported. Rare reports of reversible involuntary motor disturbances have been received.

• *Cardiovascular*: As with other H_2-blockers, there have been rare reports of arrhythmias such as tachycardia, bradycardia, atrioventricular block, and premature ventricular beats.

• *Gastrointestinal*: Constipation, diarrhea, nausea/vomiting, abdominal discomfort/pain, and rare reports of pancreatitis.

To find out more or to speak to a nutritional counselor for free, just visit us at:
www.CuresForTheBody.com

• *Hepatic*: There have been occasional reports of hepatocellular, cholestatic, or mixed hepatitis, with or without jaundice. In such circumstances, ranitidine should be immediately discontinued. These events are usually reversible, but in rare circumstances death has occurred. Rare cases of hepatic failure have also been reported. In normal volunteers, SGPT values were increased to at least twice the pretreatment levels in 6 of 12 subjects receiving 100 mg q.i.d. intravenously for 7 days, and in 4 of 24 subjects receiving 50 mg q.i.d. intravenously for 5 days.

•*Musculoskeletal*: Rare reports of arthralgias and myalgias.

• *Hematologic*: Blood count changes (leukopenia, granulocytopenia, and thrombocytopenia) have occurred in a few patients. These were usually reversible. Rare cases of agranulocytosis, pancytopenia, sometimes with marrow hypoplasia, and aplastic anemia and exceedingly rare cases of acquired immune hemolytic anemia have been reported.

• *Endocrine*: Controlled studies in animals and man have shown no stimulation of any pituitary hormone by ZANTAC and no antiandrogenic activity, and cimetidine-induced gynecomastia and impotence in hypersecretory patients have resolved when ZANTAC has been substituted. However, occasional cases of gynecomastia, impotence, and loss of libido have been reported in male patients receiving ZANTAC, but the incidence did not differ from that in the general population.

• *Integumentary*: Rash, including rare cases of erythema multiforme. Rare cases of alopecia and vasculitis. (Any acid neutralizer or acid blocker makes it easier for pathogenic bacteria to proliferate the system. This is one of the major causes of the rise of infectious disease today.)

Proton pump inhibitors:

most potent of acid reducing drugs

Brand name: Prevacid

Drug Name: Lansoprazole

To find out more or to speak to a nutritional counselor for free, just visit us at:
www.CuresForTheBody.com

Lansoprazole inhibits gastric acid secretion.

Notable Side Effects:

Abdominal pain, constipation, diarrhea, nausea, headache

Brand name: Prilosec
Drug Name: Omeprazole

Omeprazole suppresses gastric acid secretion by specific inhibition of the H^+/K^+ ATPase enzyme system at the secretory surface of the gastric parietal cell, but does not exhibit anticholinergic or H_2 histamine antagonistic properties. Because this enzyme system is regarded as the acid (proton) pump within the gastric mucosa, omeprazole has been characterized as a gastric acid-pump inhibitor, in that it blocks the final step of acid production. This effect is dose-related and leads to inhibition of both basal and stimulated acid secretion irrespective of the stimulus.

Notable Side Effects:

Headache, diarrhea, abdominal pain, nausea, URI, dizziness, vomiting, rash, constipation, cough, asthenia, back pain. (Any acid neutralizer or acid blocker makes it easier for pathogenic bacteria to proliferate the system. This is one of the major causes of the rise of infectious disease today.)

Brand name: Protonix
Drug Name: Pantoprazole

Pantoprazole suppresses the final step in gastric acid production by covalently binding to the (H^+,K^+)-ATPase enzyme system at the secretory surface of the gastric parietal cell. This effect leads to inhibition of both basal and stimulated gastric acid secretion irrespective of the stimulus. The binding to the (H^+,K^+)-ATPase results in a duration of antisecretory effect that persists longer than 24 hours for all doses tested.

Notable Side Effects:

Headache, diarrhea, flatulence. (Any acid neutralizer or acid blocker makes it easier for pathogenic bacteria to proliferate the system. This is one of the major causes of the rise of infectious disease today.)

To find out more or to speak to a nutritional counselor for free, just visit us at:
www.CuresForTheBody.com

Brand name: Aciphex

Drug Name: Rabeprazole

Rabeprazole suppresses gastric acid secretion by inhibiting the gastric H $^+$, K $^+$ ATPase at the secretory surface of the gastric parietal cell, but does not exhibit anticholinergic or histamine H $_2$ -receptor antagonist properties. Because this enzyme is regarded as the acid (proton) pump within the parietal cell, rabeprazole has been characterized as a gastric proton-pump inhibitor. Rabeprazole blocks the final step of gastric acid secretion.

Notable Side Effects:

• *Body as a Whole:* asthenia, fever, allergic reaction, chills, malaise, chest pain substernal, neck rigidity, photosensitivity reaction. Rare: abdomen enlarged, face edema, hangover effect.

• *Cardiovascular System:* hypertension, myocardial infarct, electrocardiogram abnormal, migraine, syncope, angina pectoris, bundle branch block, palpitation, sinus bradycardia, tachycardia. Rare: bradycardia, pulmonary embolus, supraventricular tachycardia, thrombophlebitis, vasodilation, QTC prolongation and ventricular tachycardia.

• *Digestive System:* diarrhea, nausea, abdominal pain, vomiting, dyspepsia, flatulence, constipation, dry mouth, eructation, gastroenteritis, rectal hemorrhage, melena, anorexia, cholelithiasis, mouth ulceration, stomatitis, dysphagia, gingivitis, cholecystitis, increased appetite, abnormal stools, colitis, esophagitis, glossitis, pancreatitis, proctitis. Rare: bloody diarrhea, cholangitis, duodenitis, gastrointestinal hemorrhage, hepatic encephalopathy, hepatitis, hepatoma, liver fatty deposit, salivary gland enlargement, thirst.

• *Endocrine System:* hyperthyroidism, hypothyroidism.

• *Hemic & Lymphatic System:* anemia, ecchymosis, lymphadenopathy, hypochromic anemia.

• *Metabolic & Nutritional Disorders:* peripheral edema, edema, weight gain, gout, dehydration, weight loss.

• *Musculo-Skeletal System:* myalgia, arthritis, leg cramps, bone pain, arthrosis, bursitis. Rare: twitching.

To find out more or to speak to a nutritional counselor for free, just visit us at:
www.CuresForTheBody.com

• *Nervous System:* insomnia, anxiety, dizziness, depression, nervousness, somnolence, hypertonia, neuralgia, vertigo, convulsion, abnormal dreams, libido decreased, neuropathy, paresthesia, tremor. Rare: agitation, amnesia, confusion, extrapyramidal syndrome, hyperkinesia.

• *Respiratory System:* dyspnea, asthma, epistaxis, laryngitis, hiccup, hyperventilation. Rare: apnea, hypoventilation.

• *Skin and Appendages:* rash, pruritus, sweating, urticaria, alopecia. (Any acid neutralizer or acid blocker makes it easier for pathogenic bacteria to proliferate the system. This is one of the major causes of the rise of infectious disease today.)

Brand name: Nexium

Drug Name: Esomeprazole

Esomeprazole suppresses gastric acid secretion by specific inhibition of the H^+/K^+-ATPase in the gastric parietal cell. The S- and R-isomers of omeprazole are protonated and converted in the acidic compartment of the parietal cell forming the active inhibitor, the achiral sulphenamide. By acting specifically on the proton pump, esomeprazole blocks the final step in acid production, thus reducing gastric acidity.

Notable Side Effects:

• *Body as a Whole:* abdomen enlarged, allergic reaction, asthenia, back pain, chest pain, chest pain substernal, facial edema, peripheral edema, hot flushes, fatigue, fever, flu-like disorder, generalized edema, leg edema, malaise, pain, rigors.

• *Cardiovascular:* flushing, hypertension, tachycardia.

• *Endocrine:* goiter; *Gastrointestinal:* bowel irregularity, constipation aggravated, dyspepsia, dysphagia, dysplasia GI, epigastric pain, eructation, esophageal disorder, frequent stools, gastroenteritis, GI hemorrhage, GI symptoms not otherwise specified, hiccup, melena, mouth disorder, pharynx disorder, rectal disorder, serum gastrin increased, tongue disorder, tongue edema, ulcerative stomatitis, vomiting.

To find out more or to speak to a nutritional counselor for free, just visit us at:
www.CuresForTheBody.com

• *Hearing:* earache, tinnitus.

• *Hematologic:* anemia, anemia hypochromic, cervical lymphoadenopathy, epistaxis, leukocytosis, leukopenia, thrombocytopenia.

Hepatic: bilirubinemia, hepatic function abnormal, SGOT increased, SGPT increased.

• *Metabolic/Nutritional:* glycosuria, hyperuricemia, hyponatremia, increased alkaline phosphatase, thirst, vitamin B12 deficiency, weight increase, weight decrease.

• *Musculoskeletal:* arthralgia, arthritis aggravated, arthropathy, cramps, fibromyalgia syndrome, hernia, polymyalgia rheumatica.

• *Nervous System/Psychiatric:* anorexia, apathy, appetite increased, confusion, depression aggravated, dizziness, hypertonia, nervousness, hypoesthesia, impotence, insomnia, migraine, migraine aggravated, paresthesia, sleep disorder, somnolence, tremor, vertigo, visual field defect.

• *Reproductive:* dysmenorrhea, menstrual disorder, vaginitis.

• *Respiratory:* asthma aggravated, coughing, dyspnea, larynx edema, pharyngitis, rhinitis, sinusitis.

• *Skin and Appendages:* acne, angioedema, dermatitis, pruritus, pruritus ani, rash, rash erythematous, rash maculo-papular, skin inflammation, sweating increased, urticaria.

• *Special Senses:* otitis media, parosmia, taste loss, taste perversion.

• *Urogenital:* abnormal urine, albuminuria, cystitis, dysuria, fungal infection, hematuria, micturition frequency, moniliasis, genital moniliasis, polyuria.

• *Visual:* conjunctivitis, vision abnormal. (Any acid neutralizer or acid blocker makes it easier for pathogenic bacteria to proliferate the system. This is one of the major causes of the rise of infectious disease today.)

Other common recommendations from medical doctors: Elevate your head off the bed about 6 inches as you sleep. Specific foods (fats & chocoloate) should be avoided, as should smoking and certain drugs, all of which increase the tendency of the lower esophageal sphincter to leak.

To find out more or to speak to a nutritional counselor for free, just visit us at:
www.CuresForTheBody.com

Coffee, alcohol, and other substances that strongly stimulate the stomach to produce acid or that delay stomach emptying should be avoided as well.

Nutritional Approach:

Disease or Condition: Acid Reflux

Causes of Acid Reflux/Heartburn/Indigestion:

Weakness in the muscle that closes the lower esophagus, Overweight, Pregnancy, Diaphragmatic hernia, Over eating and Indigestion. Non-digestion of foods.

Nutritional support

Foods that have been proven to help with Acid Reflux / Heartburn / Indigestion:

Eat small, frequent meals. Eat more raw foods and chew food thoroughly. Avoid: fats, chocolate, peppermint, garlic, onions, orange juice, red-hot sauce, tomatoes, coffee, and alcohol.

Nutrients that have been proven to help with Acid Reflux / Heartburn / Indigestion:

Plant source digestive enzymes[1] have been proven to help dramatically by adding back the enzymes that are missing in the food due to heat and processing. **Probiotics**[2] have been proven to help with the digestion and assimilation of foods partially due to their ability to produce enzymes[3].

Exercises that have been proven to help with Acid Reflux / Heartburn / Indigestion:

Regular exercise helps digestion and can help you lose weight. Being overweight increases your risk of the symptoms of acid reflux disease. Thus, shedding extra pounds can make this risk go down. So it makes sense to include exercise as part of a healthy lifestyle. Exercise does not have to be exhausting to provide benefits. The Center for Disease Control and Prevention recommends that adults engage in moderate-intensity physical activity for at least 30 minutes, five or more days a week.

Basic Acid Reflux / Heartburn / Indigestion Plan:

1. Cut back on fatty foods and eat more complex carbohydrates and protein. Fatty foods are nearly twice as likely to aggravate heartburn in susceptible people as chocolate alone[4].

2. Restrict foods that can **relax the sphincter muscle**, causing it to open and allow stomach acid to backwash into the esophagus: fatty foods, chocolate[5], peppermint, alcohol[6], raw onions[7].

3. Restrict foods that commonly **increase stomach acid secretion**, making them more painful when they wash up into the esophagus: coffee[8] (regular and decaf), colas, all carbonated drinks, beer and whole milk. Drink skim milk if needed.

4. If you suspect your esophagus is sensitive to citrus, tomatoes and spicy foods, avoid them or combine them with plant enzymes. When not properly digested, these foods can **cause irritation and burning to an already damaged esophagus** by direct contact when swallowed. If you have heartburn after eating such irritants, immediately drink water (or other non-acidic liquid) to wash the offending substance out of the esophagus and take a Plant Enzyme, Probiotic formula.

5. **Don't eat too fast or eat too much.** Doing so can overload the stomach, making it overfull, pressuring a weakened sphincter muscle to pop open.

6. **If overweight, lose weight**. Losing 10-15 pounds can cause symptoms to improve. Carrying too much weight around the abdomen can put pressure on the sphincter muscle, weakening it and promoting reflux.

7. **Don't lie down for three hours after eating.** Sleeping with your head elevated also helps avoid heartburn. Lie on your left side rather than your right because the esophagus enters the stomach from the right. Thus, when you lie on your right side, the esophagus is below the stomach opening, making it easier for acid to flow downward and into the esophagus.

8. **Take plant source digestive enzymes** at the beginning of each meal to increase digestion[9].

9. **Take Probiotics** with each meal to increase digestion[10,11,12,13].

Acne

Description: Acne is inflammation of hair follicles that occurs mostly on the face, upper chest, shoulders, and back. It is caused by an interaction between hormones, skin oils, and bacteria.

Acne results when a collection of dried sebum (oily substance), dead skin cells, and bacteria clog the hair follicles, blocking the sebum from leaving through the pores. A blackhead develops with an incomplete blockage, and a whitehead develops with a complete blockage. The blocked sebum-filled hair follicle promotes overgrowth of the bacteria, which are normally present in the hair follicle. The resulting inflammation and infection produce the skin eruptions that are commonly known as acne pimples. If the infection worsens, an abscess may form, which may rupture into the skin, creating even more inflammation.

Acne is considered an inherited disease, and is often considered to be an adolescent problem as the vast majority of teenagers suffers, to some degree, from the condition. Usually, acne has cleared up by a person's mid-twenties. This isn't always the case, however, and adult acne plagues some people throughout their lives unless they seek treatment.

Hormonal changes affect the occurrence of acne. Acne occurs mainly during puberty, when the sebaceous glands are stimulated by increased hormone levels, especially the androgens, resulting in excessive sebum production. Females tend to have flare-ups prior to menstrual periods. This may continue until menopause.

Low grade, persistent acne is often found in professional women, perhaps because chronic stress leads to enhanced secretion of adrenal androgens, resulting in sebaceous hyperplasia and subsequent production of comedones.[14]

The severest forms of acne are most frequently seen in males, but acne is generally more persistent in females.

Medical Treatment:

Over-the-counter Creams:

Dries out the pimples and causes slight sealing

Brand name: Avar

Drug Name: Sulfur

Sulfur: The most widely accepted mechanism of action of sulfonamides is the Woods-Fildes theory which is based on the fact that sulfonamides act as competitive antagonists to para-aminobenzoic acid (PABA), an essential component for bacterial growth. The exact mode of action of sulfur in the treatment of acne is unknown, but it has been reported that it inhibits the growth of Propionibacterium acnes and the formation of free fatty acids.

Notable Side Effects:

Local irritation, dries the skin, may discolor clothing and hair. THE DRYING OF SKIN CAUSES PRE-MATURE AGING.

Topical Antibiotics

Brand name: Duac, Cleocin, Benzaclin

Drug Name: Clindamycin

Clindamycin binds to the 50S ribosomal subunits of susceptible bacteria and prevents elongation of peptide chains by interfering with peptidyl transfer, thereby suppressing protein synthesis. Clindamycin is indicated in the treatment of serious infections caused by susceptible anaerobic bacteria.

Notable Side Effects:

Burning, peeling, dryness, diarrhea

•*Gastrointestinal:* Abdominal pain, pseudomembranous colitis, esophagitis, nausea, vomiting and diarrhea. The onset of pseudomembranous colitis symptoms may occur during or after antibacterial treatment.

• *Hypersensitivity Reactions:* Generalized mild to moderate morbilliform-like (maculopapular) skin rashes are the most frequently reported adverse reactions. Vesiculobullous rashes, as well as urticaria, have been observed during drug therapy. Rare instances of erythema multiforme, some resembling Stevens-Johnson syndrome, and a few cases of anaphylactoid reactions have also been reported.

• *Skin and Mucous Membranes:* Pruritus, vaginitis, and rare instances of exfoliative dermatitis have been reported.

• *Liver:* Jaundice and abnormalities in liver function tests have been observed during clindamycin therapy.

• *Renal:* Although no direct relationship of clindamycin to renal damage has been established, renal dysfunction as evidenced by azotemia, oliguria, and/or proteinuria has been observed in rare instances.

• *Hematopoietic:* Transient neutropenia (leukopenia) and eosinophilia have been reported. Reports of agranulocytosis and thrombocytopenia have been made. No direct etiologic relationship to concurrent clindamycin therapy could be made in any of the foregoing.

• *Musculoskeletal:* Rare instances of polyarthritis have been reported. **As with all anti-biotics, you risk the chance of becoming resistant to the anti-biotic and creating super germs that are even harder to get rid of (see chapter 2 for more details).**

Brand name: EryGel

Drug Name: Erythromycin

Erythromycin acts by inhibition of protein synthesis in susceptible organisms by reversibly binding to 50S ribosomal subunits, thereby inhibiting translocation of aminoacyl transfer-RNA and inhibiting polypeptide synthesis. Antagonism has been demonstrated *in vitro* between erythromycin, lincomycin, chloramphenicol, and clindamycin.

Notable Side Effects:

Peeling, dryness, itching, erythema, and oiliness. Irritation of the eyes and tenderness of the skin have also been reported with the topical use of erythromycin. A generalized urticarial reaction, possibly related to the use of erythromycin, which required systemic steroid therapy has been reported. **As with all anti-biotics, you risk the**

chance of becoming resistant to the anti-biotic and creating super germs that are even harder to get rid of (see chapter 2 for more details).

Brand name: Benzaclin, Brevoxyl

Drug Name: Benzoyl peroxide

Benzoyl peroxide is an antibacterial agent with demonstrated activity against *Propionibacterium acnes.* This action, combined with the mild keratolytic effect of benzoyl peroxide is believed to be responsible for its usefulness in acne. Benzoyl peroxide is a topical agent frequently used in combination with retinoic acid. It is available over-the-counter in the form of soaps, lotions, creams, and gels. The strength ranges from 2.5-10 percent and is applied every other day initially, then twice daily thereafter. If used in combination with retinoic acid, it is generally used once daily approximately 8 to 12 hours after the retinoic acid. Benzoyl peroxide is decomposed on the skin by cysteine, liberating free oxygen radicals that oxidize bacterial proteins.[15] Daily application of 10% benzoyl peroxide for 2 weeks can reduce free fatty acid levels by 50% and *P.acnes* levels by 98%. Benzoyl peroxide increases the sloughing rate of epithelial cells, loosens the follicular plug structure, and thus possesses some degree of comedolytic activity.[16]

Notable Side Effects:

Sensitivity, erythema, peeling, dry skin; may discolor clothing and hair.

Topical: unclogs pores

Brand name: Retin-A

Drug Name: Tretinoin

Tretinoin modifies abnormal follicular keratinization. Comedones form in follicles with an excess of keratinized epithelial cells. Tretinoin promotes detachment of cornified cells and the enhanced shedding of corneocytes from the follicle. By increasing the mitotic activity of follicular epithelia, tretinoin also increases the turnover rate of thin, loosely-adherent corneocytes. Through these actions, the comedo contents are extruded and the formation of the microcomedo, the precursor lesion of acne vulgaris, is reduced. Additionally, tretinoin acts by modulating the proliferation and differentiation of epidermal cells. These effects are mediated by tretinoin's interaction with a family of nuclear retinoic acid receptors. Activation of these nuclear receptors causes changes in gene expression. The exact mechanisms whereby tretinoin-induced changes in gene expression regulate skin function are not understood. The action of topical retinoic acid is to thin the outer horny layer of the epidermis. This reduces hyperkeratosis and loosens existing comedones. It also helps prevent the formation of new lesions.

Notable Side Effects:

Irritates skin; sensitizes skin to sunlight, dryness.

Brand name: Differin

Drug Name: Adapalene

Adapalene acts on retinoid receptors. Biochemical and pharmacological profile studies have demonstrated that adapalene is a modulator of cellular differentiation, keratinization, and inflammatory processes all of which represent important features in the pathology of acne vulgaris. Mechanistically, adapalene binds to specific retinoic acid nuclear receptors but does not bind to the cytosolic receptor protein. Although the exact mode of action of adapalene is unknown, it is suggested that topical adapalene normalizes the differentiation of follicular epithelial cells resulting in decreased microcomedone formation.

Also available as an alternative to retinoic acid, is adapalene a retinoid-mimetic topical gel. Some studies have shown results even slightly better than retinoic acid, when comparing numbers of lesions at week 12. The advantage of adapalene is that it is better tolerated, resulting in less erythema, pruritis, burning, stinging, and peeling.

Notable Side Effects:

Erythema, scaling, dryness, pruritus, some redness, burning, and increases sun sensitivity.

Brand name: Azelez, Finevin

Drug Name: Azelaic acid

Azelaic acid has been shown to possess antimicrobial activity against *Propionibacterium acnes* and *Staphylococcus epidermidis*. The antimicrobial action may be attributable to inhibition of microbial cellular protein synthesis. A normalization of keratinization leading to an anticomedonal effect of azelaic acid may also contribute to its clinical activity. Electron microscopic and immunohistochemical evaluation of skin biopsies from human subjects treated with AZELEX® demonstrated a reduction in the thickness of the stratum corneum, a reduction in number and size of keratohyalin granules, and a reduction in the amount and distribution of filaggrin (a protein component of keratohyalin) in epidermal layers. This is suggestive of the ability to decrease microcomedo formation.

Notable Side Effects:

May lighten skin, pruritus, burning, stinging and tingling. Other adverse reactions such as erythema, dryness, rash, peeling, irritation, dermatitis, and contact dermatitis were reported in less than 1% of subjects. There is the potential for experiencing allergic reactions with use of AZELEX®. In patients using azelaic acid formulations, the following additional adverse experiences have been reported rarely: worsening of asthma, vitiligo depigmentation, small depigmented spots, hypertrichosis, reddening (signs of keratosis pilaris), and exacerbation of recurrent herpes labialis.

Oral Antibiotics

Brand name: Vibramycin

Drug Name: Doxycycline

Doxycycline is primarily bacteriostatic and is thought to exert its antimicrobial effect by the inhibition of protein synthesis. The tetracyclines, including doxycycline, have a similar antimicrobial spectrum of activity against a wide range of gram-positive and gram-negative organisms. Cross-resistance of these organisms to tetracyclines is common. **As with all anti-biotics, you risk the chance of becoming resistant to the anti-biotic and creating super germs that are even harder to get rid of (see chapter 2 for more details).**

Notable Side Effects:

Sensitizes skin to sunlight, yeast infection

• *Gastrointestinal*: anorexia, nausea, vomiting, diarrhea, glossitis, dysphagia, enterocolitis, and inflammatory lesions (with monilial overgrowth) in the anogenital region.

To find out more or to speak to a nutritional counselor for free, just visit us at:
www.CuresForTheBody.com

Hepatotoxicity has been reported rarely. These reactions have been caused by both the oral and parenteral administration of tetracyclines. Rare instances of esophagitis and esophageal ulcerations have been reported in patients receiving capsule and tablet forms of the drugs in the tetracycline class. Most of these patients took medications immediately before going to bed.

• *Skin*: maculopapular and erythematous rashes. Exfoliative dermatitis has been reported but is uncommon. Photosensitivity is discussed above.

• *Renal toxicity*: Rise in BUN has been reported and is apparently dose related.

• *Hypersensitivity reactions*: urticaria, angioneurotic edema, anaphylaxis, anaphylactoid purpura, serum sickness, pericarditis, and exacerbation of systemic lupus erythematosus.

• *Blood*: Hemolytic anemia, thrombocytopenia, neutropenia, and eosinophilia have been reported.

• *Other*: bulging fontanels in infants and intracranial hypertension in adults. **As with all anti-biotics, you risk the chance of becoming resistant to the anti-biotic and creating super germs that are even harder to get rid of (see chapter 2 for more details).**

Brand name: Dynacin

Drug Name: Minocycline

Minocycline is primarily bacteriostatic and is thought to exert its antimicrobial effect by the inhibition of protein synthesis. The tetracyclines, including minocycline, have similar antimicrobial spectra of activity against a wide range of gram-positive and gram-negative organisms. Cross-resistance of these organisms to tetracyclines is common.

Notable Side Effects:

Due to oral minocycline's virtually complete absorption, side effects to the lower bowel, particularly diarrhea, have been infrequent. The following adverse reactions have been observed in patients receiving tetracyclines.

• *Gastrointestinal*: Anorexia, nausea, vomiting, diarrhea, glossitis, dysphagia, enterocolitis, pancreatitis, inflammatory lesions (with monilial overgrowth) in the anogenital region, and increases in liver enzymes have been reported. Rare instances of esophagitis and esophageal ulcerations have been reported in patients taking the tetracycline-class antibiotics in capsule and tablet form. Most of these patients took the medication immediately before going to bed.

• *Skin*: Maculopapular and erythematous rashes. Exfoliative dermatitis has been reported but is uncommon. Fixed drug eruptions have been rarely reported. Lesions occurring on the glans penis have caused balanitis. Erythema multiforme and rarely Stevens-Johnson syndrome have been reported. Photosensitivity is discussed above. Pigmentation of the skin and mucous membranes has been reported.

• *Renal toxicity*: Elevations in BUN have been reported and are apparently dose related. Acute renal failure has been rarely reported and, in most cases is reversible.

• *Hypersensitivity reactions*: Urticaria, angioneurotic edema, polyarthralgia, anaphylaxis, anaphylactoid purpura, pericarditis, exacerbation of systemic lupus erythematosus and rarely pulmonary infiltrates with eosinophilia have been reported. A transient lupus-like syndrome and serum sickness-like reaction have also been reported.

• *Blood*: Hemolytic anemia, thrombocytopenia, neutropenia, and eosinophilia have been reported.

• *Central nervous system*: Bulging fontanels in infants and benign intracranial hypertension (pseudotumor cerebri) in adults have been reported. Headache has also been reported.

• *Other*: When given over prolonged periods, tetracyclines have been reported to produce brown-black microscopic discoloration of the thyroid glands. Very rare cases of abnormal thyroid function have been reported. Tooth discoloration in pediatric patients less than 8 years of age and also, rarely, in adults have been reported. Tinnitus and decreased hearing have been rarely reported in patients on minocycline hydrochloride. **As with all anti-biotics, you risk the chance of becoming resistant to the anti-**

biotic and creating super germs that are even harder to get rid of (see chapter 2 for more details).

Oral: unclogs pores

Brand name: Accutane

Drug Name: Isotretinoin

Isotretinoin inhibits sebaceous gland function and keratinization. The exact mechanism of action of isotretinoin is unknown. Clinical improvement in nodular acne patients occurs in association with a reduction in sebum secretion. The decrease in sebum secretion is temporary and is related to the dose and duration of treatment with Accutane, and reflects a reduction in sebaceous gland size and an inhibition of sebaceous gland differentiation.[1]

Isotretinoin therapy is reserved for patients with severe recalcitrant acne that has not responded to other therapies. Its action is multifaceted in that it decreases sebum production as well as alters the composition of sebum, it inhibits the growth of P.acnes within the follicles, inhibits inflammation, and alters patterns of keratinization. Isotretinoin is a known teratogen, so appropriate precautions are essential when being administered to women of childbearing potential. It is available as a 10, 20, and 40mg capsule and doses are generally in the range of 0.5-1mg/kg/day in two divided doses. Adverse effects are numerous and are often dose-related. Approximately 90% of patients receiving isotretinoin have mucotaneous side effects. Drying of the mucosa of the eye, nose and mouth is the most common problem. Chelitis and skin desquamation occurs in 80% of patients. Other side effects have been reported, and close monitoring is vital. If tolerated, therapy is usually quite successful. Often, one or two 15 to 20 week courses bring severe acne under complete control, with little or no further therapy.

Notable Side Effects:

Can harm a developing fetus; can affect blood cells, liver, and fat levels; dry eyes, chapped lips, drying of the mucous membranes; pain or stiffness of large joints and lower back with high dosages; has been associated with depression, suicidal thoughts, attempted suicide, and completed suicide.

• *Body as a Whole:* allergic reactions, including vasculitis, systemic hypersensitivity, edema, fatigue, lymphadenopathy, weight loss.

To find out more or to speak to a nutritional counselor for free, just visit us at:
www.CuresForTheBody.com

• *Cardiovascular:* palpitation, tachycardia, vascular thrombotic disease, stroke.

• *Endocrine/Metabolic:* hypertriglyceridemia, alterations in blood sugar levels.

• *Gastrointestinal:* inflammatory bowel disease, pancreatitis, bleeding and inflammation of the gums, colitis, esophagitis/esophageal ulceration, ileitis, nausea, other nonspecific gastrointestinal symptoms.

• *Hematologic:* allergic reactions, anemia, thrombocytopenia, neutropenia, rare reports of agranulocytosis.

• *Musculoskeletal:* skeletal hyperostosis, calcification of tendons and ligaments, premature epiphyseal closure, decreases in bone mineral density, musculoskeletal symptoms (sometimes severe) including back pain and arthralgia, transient pain in the chest, arthritis, tendonitis, other types of bone abnormalities, elevations of CPK/rare reports of rhabdomyolysis.

• *Neurological:* pseudotumor cerebri, dizziness, drowsiness, headache, insomnia, lethargy, malaise, nervousness, paresthesias, seizures, stroke, syncope, weakness.

• *Psychiatric:* suicidal ideation, suicide attempts, suicide, depression, psychosis, aggression, violent behaviors, emotional instability. Of the patients reporting depression, some reported that the depression subsided with discontinuation of therapy and recurred with reinstitution of therapy.

• *Reproductive System:* abnormal menses.

• *Respiratory:* bronchospasms (with or without a history of asthma), respiratory infection, voice alteration.

• *Skin and Appendages:* acne fulminans, alopecia (which in some cases persists), bruising, cheilitis (dry lips), dry mouth, dry nose, dry skin, epistaxis, eruptive xanthomas, [7] flushing, fragility of skin, hair abnormalities, hirsutism, hyperpigmentation and hypopigmentation, infections (including disseminated herpes simplex), nail dystrophy, paronychia, peeling of palms and soles, photoallergic/

To find out more or to speak to a nutritional counselor for free, just visit us at:
www.CuresForTheBody.com

photosensitizing reactions, pruritus, pyogenic granuloma, rash (including facial erythema, seborrhea, and eczema), sunburn susceptibility increased, sweating, urticaria, vasculitis (including Wegener's granulomatosis), abnormal wound healing (delayed healing or exuberant granulation tissue with crusting).

• *Hearing:* hearing impairment, tinnitus.

• *Vision:* corneal opacities, decreased night vision which may persist, cataracts, color vision disorder, conjunctivitis, dry eyes, eyelid inflammation, keratitis, optic neuritis, photophobia, visual disturbances.

• *Urinary System:* glomerulonephritis, nonspecific urogenital findings.

• *Laboratory:* Elevation of plasma triglycerides, decrease in serum high-density lipoprotein (HDL) levels, elevations of serum cholesterol during treatment. Increased alkaline phosphatase, SGOT (AST), SGPT (ALT), GGTP or LDH. Elevation of fasting blood sugar, elevations of CPK, hyperuricemia. Decreases in red blood cell parameters, decreases in white blood cell counts, elevated sedimentation rates, elevated platelet counts, thrombocytopenia. White cells in the urine, proteinuria, microscopic or gross hematuria.

Oral Contraceptive

Brand name: Ortho Tri-Cyclen

Drug Name: Norgestimate/ ethinyl estradiol

Ortho Tri-Cyclen may be used in women with moderate acne, since androgen levels correlate with sebum production. The action exhibited is a decrease in unbound, biologically active androgens such as free testosterone. In 1997, the FDA approved its use in anti-acne therapy.

The combination of ethinyl estradiol and norgestimate may increase sex hormone binding globulin (SHBG) and decrease free testosterone resulting in a decrease in the severity of facial acne in otherwise healthy women with this skin condition.

Notable Side Effects:

Thrombophlebitis and venous thrombosis with or without embolism, arterial thromboembolism, pulmonary embolism, myocardial infarction, cerebral hemorrhage, cerebral thrombosis, hypertension, gallbladder disease, hepatic adenomas or benign liver tumors, nausea, vomiting , gastrointestinal symptoms (such as abdominal cramps and bloating), breakthrough bleeding, spotting, change in menstrual flow, amenorrhea, temporary infertility after discontinuation of treatment, edema, melasma which may persist, breast changes (tenderness, enlargement, secretion), change in weight (increase or decrease), change in cervical erosion and secretion, diminution in lactation when given immediately postpartum, cholestatic jaundice, migraine, rash (allergic), mental depression, reduced tolerance to carbohydrates, vaginal candidiasis, change in corneal curvature (steepening), intolerance to contact lenses.

Other common recommendations from medical doctors: gently wash once or twice a day with mild soap. Cosmetics should be water-based. A healthy, balanced diet should be followed. Removal of acnegenic substances should be the first principle of therapy. Some cosmetics, oils, and creams may be capable of producing blockages, and their use should be stopped. Changing from an oral contraceptive containing androgenic progestins to one with more estrogenic ones can help.[17]

Nutritional Approach:

Disease or Condition: Acne

Causes of Acne

The exact cause of acne is unknown, but factors that contribute to the condition include heredity, oily skin, and androgens. Other factors are allergies, stress, the use of certain drugs (especially steroids, lithium, oral contraceptives, and certain antiepileptic drugs), over-consumption of junk food, saturated fats, hydrogenated fats, and animal products; nutritional deficiencies, exposure to industrial pollutants (machine oils, coal tar derivatives, chlorinated hydrocarbons), the use of cosmetics, monthly menstrual cycles, and over-washing or repeated rubbing of the skin.

To find out more or to speak to a nutritional counselor for free, just visit us at:
www.CuresForTheBody.com

Nutritional support
Foods that have been proven to help with Acne:

Avoid: all refined and/or concentrated simple sugars, limiting high-fat foods, milk, milk products, margarine, shortening, and other synthetically hydrogenated vegetable oils, or fried oils.

Eat: corn, chicken, shellfish, whole grains, mushrooms, fresh vegetables, sweet potatoes, carrots, yellow and orange fruits and vegetables (especially green vegetables) fish, eggs, cabbage, dried beans, soy beans, radishes, onions, wheat germ, raw flax seeds and oil, raw hulled hemp seeds and oil, and eat a high fiber diet.

Nutrients that have been proven to help with Acne:

Omega 3 Essential fatty acids[18], Vitamin A[19], Vitamin E[20], Chromium[21], Brewers yeast[22], nutritional yeast[23], Sulfur[24], Zinc[25], Gugglelipid[26], Lipase[27].

Exercises that have been proven to help with Acne:

Exercise can help acne by increasing blood flow and delivering oxygen to the skin cells. Your internal organs will work better to deliver the proper nutrients to your body and rid itself of the toxins that can cause acne. "Exercise rebalances hormones and reduces stress – both are precursors of acne." Some great forms of exercise are jogging, swimming, or even a team sport. Always remember to shower as soon after exercise as possible to remove sweat thereby reducing bacteria growth.

Becoming fit and physically active will also help your mental wellbeing. Acne is renowned for ruining people's self confidence. Exercising releases endorphins which make you feel happier. Exercising regularly will both help reduce your acne and enable you to cope with it better.

Basic Acne Plan:

• Eliminate foods that contain trans-fatty acids, such as milk, milk products, margarine, shortening, and other synthetically hydrogenated vegetable oils and oxidized fatty acids (fried oils)[28]. These fats are toxins. They are thicker and plug up our pores.

• Eat foods that are high in healthy fats; the Omega 3 and 6 essential fatty acid[29]. Raw flax seeds and oil and raw hulled hemp seeds and oil (3 tablespoons seeds or 1 tablespoon oil).

To find out more or to speak to a nutritional counselor for free, just visit us at:
www.CuresForTheBody.com

"EFA rich oils make skin feel and look velvety instead of 'greasy', because their molecules spread out away from each other (disperse) rather than sticking together, and therefore do not produce the 'greaser' forehead streak." *"While the entire nutritional program is important to healthy skin, EFAs hold a main key to skin that is pleasant to look at, beautiful to photograph, and silky to touch."* *–Udo Erasmus*

Caution: never cook with these oils. Their goodness is destroyed by light, oxygen and heat[30]. The seeds can be stored 1 year, but the oil can be stored only 3 months if not kept from light, oxygen and heat.

For your information: Raw hulled hemp seeds became legal in our country in Feb. 2004 when the FDA presented data showing the hulled seeds, oil and protein fibers have no psychoactive ingredients. Fifty years ago it was exiled because of its cousin, marijuana. It was deemed guilty by association, just like raw coconut oil when all saturated fats were lumped in one and deemed bad for you. Both of these great food sources are now making a come back.

• If you won't eat your essential fatty acids, then take a high quality supplement. Pay attention to expiration dates and stability reported by company, as essential fatty acids are very fragile and go rancid quickly when exposed to light, oxygen and heat[31].

• Use raw coconut oil in baking rather than shortening or butter[32]. (great on skin as a topical oil too) . Lauric Acid is antibacterial, decreasing acne flare-ups[33]. Coconut oil also lowers cholesterol according to a report in the Journal of Nutrition 2001.

• Take Lipase enzymes to properly digest fats[34] (use only plant source digestive enzyme).

• Take Gugglelipid.[35]

• Eliminate all refined and/or concentrated simple sugars from the diet. No white flour or processed sugar products. According to reports, there is a strong connection between glucose levels in skin and acne[36].

• Eat foods high in the mineral chromium such as brewers yeast or nutritional yeast, corn, lean chicken, shellfish, whole grains, mushrooms, fresh vegetables[37].

• Take amino acid chelated[38] chromium to help maintain lower insulin levels[39].

• Eat foods high in beta carotene (pro-vitamin A) such as sweet potatoes, carrots, yellow and orange fruits and vegetables and very green vegetables. These foods help protect, heal and regenerate new skin[40].

To find out more or to speak to a nutritional counselor for free, just visit us at:
www.CuresForTheBody.com

• Eating a diet high in fiber helps transport excess fats and toxins out of the body. 25-35 grams/day are recommended[41] (fresh fruits with skins, vegetables, whole grains, and legumes). Get a double bonus with flax seeds. They are high in fiber and omega 3 EFA's.

• Eat foods high in the mineral sulfur such as fish, eggs, cabbage, dried beans, soy beans, radishes, onions, wheat germ. Sulfur, a mineral that is an antioxidant, is also used in the formation of new tissue[42]. It's a beautifying mineral.

• Use a 3-10% topical sulfur preparation. The FDA has approved sulfur as a safe and effective acne treatment.

• Take "Amino Acid" chelated Zinc (highest absorption rate, scientifically proven[43]). Zinc, a mineral, is involved in enzyme function and tissue repair, plus helps to prevent scarring[44].

To find out more or to speak to a nutritional counselor for free, just visit us at:
www.CuresForTheBody.com

Allergies

Description: The immune system includes antibodies, white blood cells, mast cells, complement proteins, and other substances. Normally, it defends the body against foreign substances (antigens), which invade the body, such as bacteria, viruses, and parasites. However, in susceptible people, the immune system can overreact to certain antigens, which are referred to as allergens. Allergens are proteins or low-molecular weight substances that the body identifies as antigenic. An allergic reaction is an inappropriate reaction to a substance that would otherwise be considered harmless. Allergens are harmless in most people. About one third of the people in the United States have an allergy.

You may experience an allergic reaction when an allergen lands on the skin or in the eye, is inhaled, eaten, or injected. An allergic reaction can also occur as part of a seasonal allergy, or be triggered by taking a drug, eating certain foods, or breathing in dust or dander.

In most allergic reactions, the immune system, when first exposed to an allergen, produces a type of antibody called immunoglobulin. Immunoglobulin is responsible for recognizing, destroying, and positioning antigens for removal. The first exposure may make a person sensitive to the allergen but does not cause symptoms. After the first exposure, when the person encounters the same allergen, the cells that have immunoglobulin on their surface release substances that cause swelling or inflammation in the surrounding tissues. These substances include histamine, eosinophil chemotatctic factor of anaphylaxis (ECF-A), leukotrienes, kinins, platelet activating factor (PAF), bradykinin, serotonin, and prostaglandins.[45] Such substances begin a cascade of reactions that irritate and harm tissues.

Allergies appear to be genetic as children of allergic parents are twice as likely to develop allergies.[46] Genetic allergies are referred to as atopic allergies. Allergies can also be stimulated by repeated exposure to specific allergens or pollutants.[47]

To find out more or to speak to a nutritional counselor for free, just visit us at:
www.CuresForTheBody.com

Medical Treatment:

Antihistamines (OTC):

Are used to block histamine activity, interfering with their ability to cause inflammation and increased mucous production in the upper respiratory tract.

Brand name: Dimetapp, Robitussin
Drug Name: Brompheniramine

Brand name: Chlor-Trimeton
Drug Name: Chlorpheniramine

Brand name: Tavist
Drug Name: Clemastine

Brand name: Benadryl
Drug Name: Diphenhydramine

Brand name: Claritin
Drug Name: Loratadine

Brand name: Actifed
Drug Name: Triprolidine

Antihistamines (Rx):

Are used to block histamine activity, interfering with their ability to cause inflammation and increased mucous production in the upper respiratory tract.

Brand name: Zyrtec
Drug Name: Cetirizine

Cetirizine, a metabolite of hydroxyzine, is an antihistamine; its principal effects are mediated via selective inhibition of H_1 receptors.

Notable Side Effects:

Somnolence, fatigue, dry mouth, pharyngitis, dizziness

To find out more or to speak to a nutritional counselor for free, just visit us at:
www.CuresForTheBody.com

Brand name: Periactin

Drug Name: Cyproheptadine

Cyproheptadine is a serotonin and histamine antagonist with anticholinergic and sedative effects.

Notable Side Effects:

• *Central Nervous System:* Sedation and sleepiness (often transient), dizziness, disturbed coordination, confusion, restlessness, excitation, nervousness, tremor, irritability, insomnia, paresthesias, neuritis, convulsions, euphoria, hallucinations, hysteria, faintness.

• *Integumentary:* Allergic manifestation of rash and edema, excessive perspiration, urticaria, photosensitivity.

• *Special Senses:* Acute labyrinthitis, blurred vision, diplopia, vertigo, tinnitus.

• *Cardiovascular:* Hypotension, palpitation, tachycardia, extrasystoles, anaphylactic shock.

• *Hematologic:* Hemolytic anemia, leukopenia, agranulocytosis, thrombocytopenia.

• *Digestive System:* Cholestasis, hepatic failure, hepatitis, hepatic function abnormality, dryness of mouth, epigastric distress, anorexia, nausea, vomiting, diarrhea, constipation, jaundice.

• *Genitourinary:* Urinary frequency, difficult urination, urinary retention, early menses.

• *Respiratory:* Dryness of nose and throat, thickening of bronchial secretions, tightness of chest and wheezing, nasal stuffiness.

• *Miscellaneous:* Fatigue, chills, headache, increased appetite/weight gain.

Brand name: Allegra

Drug Name: Fexofenadine

Fexofenadine hydrochloride is an antihistamine with selective peripheral H_1-receptor antagonist activity. Both enantiomers of fexofenadine hydrochloride displayed approximately equipotent antihistaminic effects.

Fexofenadine inhibited histamine release from peritoneal mast cells in rats. In laboratory animals, no anticholinergic, alpha $_1$ -adrenergic or beta-adrenergic-receptor blocking effects were observed.

Notable Side Effects:

Viral infection, dysmenorrheal, drowsiness, dyspepsia, fatigue, headache, back pain.

Brand name: Atarax

Drug Name: Hydroxyzine

Hydroxyzine action may be due to a suppression of activity in certain key regions of the subcortical area of the central nervous system. Primary skeletal muscle relaxation has been demonstrated experimentally. Bronchodilator activity, and anti-histaminic and analgesic effects have been demonstrated experimentally and confirmed clinically. An antiemetic effect, both by the apomorphine test and the veriloid test, has been demonstrated.

Notable Side Effects:

• *Anticholinergic:* Dry mouth.

• *Central Nervous System:* Drowsiness is usually transitory and may disappear in a few days of continued therapy or upon reduction of the dose. Involuntary motor activity including rare instances of tremor and convulsions have been reported, usually with doses considerably higher than those recommended.

Brand name: Phenergan

Drug Name: Promethazine

Promethazine is an H $_1$ receptor blocking agent. In addition to its antihistaminic action, it provides clinically useful sedative and antiemetic effects.

Notable Side Effects:

• *Central Nervous System:* Drowsiness is the most prominent CNS effect of this drug. Sedation, somnolence, blurred vision, dizziness, confusion, disorientation, and extrapyramidal symptoms such as oculogyric crisis,

To find out more or to speak to a nutritional counselor for free, just visit us at:
www.CuresForTheBody.com

torticollis, and tongue protrusion; lassitude, tinnitus, incoordination, fatigue, euphoria, nervousness, diplopia, insomnia, tremors, convulsive seizures, excitation, catatonic-like states, hysteria. Hallucinations have also been reported.

• *Cardiovascular:* Increased or decreased blood pressure, tachycardia, bradycardia, faintness.

• *Dermatologic:* Dermatitis, photosensitivity, urticaria.

• *Hematologic:* Leukopenia, thrombocytopenia, thrombocytopenic purpura, agranulocytosis.

• *Gastrointestinal:* Dry mouth, nausea, vomiting, jaundice.

• *Respiratory:* Asthma, nasal stuffiness, respiratory depression (potentially fatal) and apnea (potentially fatal).

• *Other:* Angioneurotic edema. Neuroleptic malignant syndrome (potentially fatal) has also been reported.

Corticosteroids:

Anti-inflammatory agents that also reduce mucous production.

Brand name: Decadron

Drug Name: Dexamethasone

Dexamethasone is primarily used for its potent anti-inflammatory effects in disorders of many organ systems.

Notable Side Effects:

• *Fluid and Electrolyte Disturbances:* Sodium retention, fluid retention, congestive heart failure in susceptible patients, potassium loss, hypokalemic alkalosis, hypertension.

• *Musculoskeletal:* Muscle weakness, steroid myopathy, loss of muscle mass, osteoporosis, vertebral compression fractures, aseptic necrosis of femoral and humeral heads, pathologic fracture of long bones, tendon rupture.

• *Gastrointestinal:* Peptic ulcer with possible perforation and hemorrhage, perforation of the small and large bowel, particularly in patients with inflammatory bowel disease, pancreatitis, abdominal distention, ulcerative esophagitis.

To find out more or to speak to a nutritional counselor for free, just visit us at:
www.CuresForTheBody.com

• *Dermatologic:* Impaired wound healing, thin fragile skin, petechiae and ecchymoses, erythema, increased sweating, may suppress reactions to skin tests, other cutaneous reactions, such as allergic dermatitis, urticaria, angioneurotic edema.

• *Neurologic:* Convulsions, increased intracranial pressure with papilledema (pseudotumor cerebri) usually after treatment, vertigo, headache, psychic disturbances.

• *Endocrine:* Menstrual irregularities, development of cushingoid state, suppression of growth in children, secondary adrenocortical and pituitary unresponsiveness, particularly in times of stress, as in trauma, surgery, or illness, decreased carbohydrate tolerance, manifestations of latent diabetes mellitus, hyperglycemia, increased requirements for insulin or oral hypoglycemic agents in diabetics, hirsutism.

• *Ophthalmic:* Posterior subcapsular cataracts, increased intraocular pressure, glaucoma, exophthalmos.

• *Metabolic:* Negative nitrogen balance due to protein catabolism.

• *Cardiovascular:* Myocardial rupture following recent myocardial infarction.

• *Other:* Hypersensitivity, thromboembolism, weight gain, increased appetite, nausea, malaise, hiccups.

Brand name: Azmacort

Drug Name: Triamcinolone

Triamcinolone provides effective local anti-inflammatory activity with reduced systemic corticosteroid effects.

Notable Side Effects:

Sinusitis, pharyngitis, headache, flu syndrome, back pain.

• *Body as a whole:* facial edema, pain, abdominal pain, photosensitivity.

• *Digestive System:* diarrhea, oral monilia, toothache, vomiting.

• *Metabolic:* weight gain.

To find out more or to speak to a nutritional counselor for free, just visit us at:
www.CuresForTheBody.com

• *Musculoskeletal system:* bursitis, myalgia, tenosynovitis.

• *Nervous system:* dry mouth.

• *Respiratory system:* chest congestion, voice alteration.

• *Urogenital system:* cystitis, urinary tract infection, vaginal monilia.

• *Organs of special sense:* rash.

Brand name: Cutivate, Flonase, Flovent

Drug Name: Fluticasone

Fluticasone is a synthetic, trifluorinated corticosteroid with anti-inflammatory activity. The precise mechanism through which fluticasone propionate affects allergic rhinitis symptoms is not known. Corticosteroids have been shown to have a wide range of effects on multiple cell types (e.g., mast cells, eosinophils, neutrophils, macrophages, and lymphocytes) and mediators (e.g., histamine, eicosanoids, leukotrienes, and cytokines) involved in inflammation.

Notable Side Effects:

Headache, pharyngitis, epistaxis, nasal burning/nasal irritation, nausea/vomiting, asthma symptoms, cough, hypersensitivity reactions, including angioedema, skin rash, edema of the face and tongue, pruritus, urticaria, bronchospasm, wheezing, dyspnea, and anaphylaxis/anaphylactoid reactions (which in rare instances were severe) Alteration or loss of sense of taste and/or smell and, rarely, nasal septal perforation, nasal ulcer, sore throat, throat irritation and dryness, cough, hoarseness, and voice changes, Dryness and irritation, conjunctivitis, blurred vision, glaucoma, increased intraocular pressure, and cataracts.

Other

Brand name: Crolom, Intal, Nasalcrom

Drug Name: Cromolyn

Cromolyn sodium inhibits mast cell degranulation and the release of chemical mediators that induce allergic reactions. It can be administered intranasally to protect the mucous membranes of the nasal cavity from allergic rhinitis, or ophthalmically for allergic conjunctivitis. In some cases,

To find out more or to speak to a nutritional counselor for free, just visit us at:
www.CuresForTheBody.com

cromolyn sodium is added to inhalers to augment bronchodilation therapy. Cromolyn sodium is rapidly excreted and has few adverse effects. Cromolyn sodium inhibits the degranulation of sensitized mast cells which occurs after exposure to specific antigens. Cromolyn sodium acts by inhibiting the release of histamine and SRS-A (slow-reacting substance of anaphylaxis) from the mast cell. Another activity demonstrated *in vitro* is the capacity of cromolyn sodium to inhibit the degranulation of nonsensitized rat mast cells by phospholipase A and the subsequent release of chemical mediators. Another study showed that cromolyn sodium did not inhibit the enzymatic activity of released phospholipase A on its specific substrate.

Notable Side Effects:

Transient ocular stinging or burning upon instillation, watery eyes, itchy eyes, dryness around the eye, puffy eyes, eye irritation, and styes, dyspnea, edema, and rash.

Brand name: Epi-Pen

Drug Name: Epinephrine

Epinephrine is a sympathomimetic drug, acting on both alpha and beta receptors. It is the drug of choice for the emergency treatment of severe allergic reactions (Type I) to insect stings or bites, foods, drugs, and other allergens. It can also be used in the treatment of idiopathic or exercise-induced anaphylaxis. Epinephrine when given subcutaneously or intramuscularly has a rapid onset and short duration of action. The strong vasoconstrictor action of epinephrine through its effect on alpha adrenergic receptors acts quickly to counter vasodilation and increased vascular permeability which can lead to loss of intravascular fluid volume and hypotension during anaphylactic reactions. Epinephrine through its action on beta receptors on bronchial smooth muscle causes bronchial smooth muscle relaxation which alleviates wheezing and dyspnea. Epinephrine also alleviates pruritis, urticaria, and angioedema and may be effective in relieving gastrointestinal and genitourinary symptoms associated with anaphylaxis.

Notable Side Effects:

Palpitations, tachycardia, sweating, nausea and vomiting, respiratory difficulty, pallor, dizziness, weakness, tremor, headache, apprehension, nervousness and anxiety. Cardiac arrhythmias may follow administration of epinephrine.

To find out more or to speak to a nutritional counselor for free, just visit us at:
www.CuresForTheBody.com

Other common recommendations from medical doctors: Avoid an allergen by discontinuing drug, keep pets out of the house, install a high quality air filter, avoid eating the particular allergenic food, or move to an area where the allergen is not as prevalent.

Nutritional Approach:

Disease or Condition: Allergies

Causes of Allergies

Allergic reactions appear to be hereditary; however, many factors have to work together to make a person allergic.

Nutritional support:

Foods that have been proven to help with Allergies:

Flax oil (Omega 3 fatty acids). Eat raw foods. They contain enzymes that break up the food during digestion. Also, be sure to chew your food carefully; this allows for the enzymes to be released from the raw foods.

Nutrients that have been proven to help with Allergies:

Vitamin C[48], Quercetin[49,] Omega-3 and certain omega 6 Essential Fatty Acids(GLA)[50], Probiotics[51], Grape Seed Extract[52], Stinging Nettle[53], Coleus[54], Plant source Digestive Enzymes[55].

Exercises that have been proven to help with Allergies:

Vigorous exercise allows you an efficient means of controlling nasal congestion, says Robert S. Zeiger, M.D. People with allergies should avoid excessive heat or cold. This includes over- air-conditioned exercise areas. Make sure to breathe through the nose so allergens will be filtered. It is also a good idea to exercise indoors if you have pollen or smog induced allergies.

Basic Allergy Plan:

    • **Vitamin C** – metabolizes, or detoxifies, histamine.

    – In a chronic allergies study, 10 men and women participated for 6 weeks ingesting a placebo for 4 weeks and 2g/day of vitamin C for 2 weeks. There was a significant rise in plasma ascorbate and a decrease in histamine levels of 38% after vitamin C supplementation indicating that vitamin C's usefulness in allergy treatment may stem from the fact that it metabolizes, or detoxifies, histamine *in vivo*. Use a whole food source Vitamin C (see chapter 5)

– Another study demonstrated that 11 people who had either low vitamin C levels or elevated blood histamine levels, given 1g of vitamin C daily for three days, had their blood histamine levels decline. Use a whole food source Vitamin C (see chapter 5)

– A two week randomized study involving 60 patients suffering from perennial allergic rhinitis were administered a solution of ascorbic acid. The solution caused a decrease in symptoms in 74 percent of patients. Use a whole food source Vitamin C (see chapter 5)

• **Quercetin**

– Reported to reduce allergic reactions by inhibiting the release of histamine from mast cells.

– A bioflavonoid, which is a co-factor of vitamin C.

– In conjunction with vitamin C reportedly helps to reduce the severity of symptoms in individuals with hay fever.

• **Omega-3 and certain omega 6 (GLA) Essential Fatty Acids**

– Some individuals with allergic conditions have been found to have lower delta-6 desaturase enzyme activity, which inhibits the conversion of alpha linolenic acid (omega-3) and linoleic acid (omega-6) to their longer-chain metabolites. This in turn inhibits the production of the important anti-inflammatory prostaglandins.

– Clinical trials indicate that appropriate fatty acid supplementation often alleviates a broad range of allergic-type inflammatory conditions.

– Omega-3 essential fatty acid is the precursor to the series 3 prostaglandins (PGE3), which are anti-inflammatory in nature. The omega-3/omega-6 fatty acid ratios tend to be out of balance in the diets of many people

To find out more or to speak to a nutritional counselor for free, just visit us at:
www.CuresForTheBody.com

in the United States. Proper adjustments of dietary fatty acids can play a key role in the successful management of inflammation associated with atopic diseases. This involves decreasing the intake of oils high in omega-6 (corn, safflower, and sunflower oils) and increasing the intake of omega-3. Flaxseed oil and fish oils are a rich source of omega-3.

– The administration of supplemental GLA has proven to be of therapeutic benefit for patients with conditions such as atopic eczema. Two of the best sources of GLA are borage oil (23%) and evening primrose oil (10%).

– A minimum of an extra 400 IU of natural vitamin E should be taken daily when consuming supplemental omega-3.

• Probiotics

– Probiotics containing lactobacillus acidophilus and bifidobacteria are important supplements for individuals with food allergies or intolerances.

– In one study, every child that was suffering from symptoms related to food allergies was found to have deficiencies of lactobacillus and bifidobacteria, along with an overgrowth of *Enterobacteriaceae*.

• Grape Seed Extracts

– Flavonoid-rich and free radical scavengers.

– It has been reported to enhance the absorption of and work synergistically with vitamin C.

– It has been used for supportive care in allergies and asthma.

– PCO's have been reported to inhibit the release of mediators of inflammation, such as histamine, leukotrienes, and prostaglandins, mechanisms that would be beneficial in multiple inflammatory processes such as allergies and asthma.

• Stinging Nettle

– A randomized, double-blind study of 92 individuals reported that a freeze-dried preparation of stinging nettle leaf was superior to placebo in relieving the symptoms of allergic rhinitis (itching, watery eyes, runny nose).

To find out more or to speak to a nutritional counselor for free, just visit us at:
www.CuresForTheBody.com

• Coleus

– It stimulates thyroid function, increases insulin secretion, inhibits mast cell release of histamine, and increases the burning of fats as fuels.

– Is claimed to inhibit platelet activating factor (PAF) by possibly binding directly to PAF receptor sites. PAF is a key factor in allergic and inflammatory pathways.

Anxiety

Description: Anxiety is a normal reaction as a survival function. It produces the fight-or-flight response that increases blood flow and increases the body's energy and strength to deal with life-threatening situations. However, when anxiety symptoms last longer than normal or are inappropriate for the situation, it is considered a disorder. With the disorder, symptoms happen frequently and intensely and interfere with normal activities. Heredity may be a factor in anxiety, but otherwise the root is generally unknown.

Anxiety has both physical and psychological triggers. Environment stimuli, like a failed relationship or a disaster, cause the person to feel overwhelmed. A drug (cocaine, corticosteroids) or physical disorder (ie, overactive thyroid) can also produce symptoms.

Symptoms of anxiety can come on suddenly or gradually, and can last any amount of time, from a few minutes to several years. These symptoms may include shortness of breath, dizziness, and increased heart rate. For Generalized Anxiety Disorder, a person may feel restlessness, fatigue easily, have difficulty concentrating, be irritable, feel muscle tension, and have disturbed sleep. Anxiety may also lead to depression.

Medical Treatment:

Benzodiazepines:

Most commonly used anti-anxiety drugs. They promote mental and physical relaxation by reducing nerve activity in the brain.

Brand name: Valium

Drug Name: Diazepam

Diazepam appears to act on parts of the limbic system, the thalamus and hypothalamus, and induces calming effects. Valium, unlike

To find out more or to speak to a nutritional counselor for free, just visit us at:
www.CuresForTheBody.com

chlorpromazine and reserpine, has no demonstrable peripheral autonomic blocking action, nor does it produce extrapyramidal side effects; however, animals treated with Valium do have a transient ataxia at higher doses.

Notable Side Effects:

Most commonly reported were drowsiness, fatigue and ataxia. Infrequently encountered were confusion, constipation, depression, diplopia, dysarthria, headache, hypotension, incontinence, jaundice, changes in libido, nausea, changes in salivation, skin rash, slurred speech, tremor, urinary retention, vertigo and blurred vision. Paradoxical reactions such as acute hyperexcited states, anxiety, hallucinations, increased muscle spasticity, insomnia, rage, sleep disturbances and stimulation have been reported; should these occur, use of the drug should be discontinued.

Antidepressants:

Brand Name: Norpramin

Drug Name: Desipramine

Desipramine: While the precise mechanism of action of the tricyclic antidepressants is unknown, a leading theory suggests that they restore normal levels of neurotransmitters by blocking the re-uptake of these substances from the synapse in the central nervous system. Desipramine is not a monoamine oxidase (MAO) inhibitor and does not act primarily as a central nervous system stimulant.

Notable Side Effects:

• *Cardiovascular:* hypotension, hypertension, palpitations, heart block, myocardial infarction, stroke, arrhythmias, premature ventricular contractions, tachycardia, ventricular tachycardia, ventricular fibrillation, sudden death.

• *Psychiatric:* confusional states (especially in the elderly) with hallucinations, disorientation, delusions; anxiety, restlessness, agitation, insomnia and nightmares, hypomania, exacerbation of psychosis.

• *Neurologic:* numbness, tingling, paresthesias of extremities, incoordination, ataxia, tremors, peripheral neuropathy, extrapyramidal symptoms, seizures, alterations in EEG patterns, tinnitus.

• *Anticholinergic:* dry mouth, and rarely associated sublingual adenitis, blurred vision, disturbance of accommodation, mydriasis, increased intraocular pressure, constipation, paralytic ileus, urinary retention, delayed micturition, dilation of urinary tract.

• *Allergic:* skin rash, petechiae, urticaria, itching, photosensitization (sensitivity to sunlight), edema (of face and tongue or general), drug fever, cross-sensitivity with other tricyclic drugs.

• *Hematologic:* bone marrow depressions including agranulocytosis, eosinophilia, purpura, thrombocytopenia.

• *Gastrointestinal:* anorexia, nausea and vomiting, epigastric distress, peculiar taste, abdominal cramps, diarrhea, stomatitis, black tongue, hepatitis, jaundice (simulating obstructive), altered liver function, elevated liver function tests, increased pancreatic enzymes.

• *Endocrine:* gynecomastia in the male, breast enlargement and galactorrhea in the female, increased or decreased libido, impotence, painful ejaculation, testicular swelling, elevation or depression of blood sugar levels, syndrome of inappropriate antidiuretic hormone secretion (SIADH).

• *Other:* weight gain or loss, perspiration, flushing, urinary frequency, nocturia, parotid swelling, drowsiness, dizziness, weakness and fatigue, headache, fever, alopecia, elevated alkaline phosphatase.

• *Withdrawal Symptoms:* Though not indicative of addiction, abrupt cessation of treatment after prolonged therapy may produce nausea, headache, and malaise.

Other common recommendations from medical doctors: Counseling, relaxation, yoga, meditation, exercise, and biofeedback techniques have all proven helpful in reducing the symptoms and severity of symptoms of anxiety.

To find out more or to speak to a nutritional counselor for free, just visit us at:
www.CuresForTheBody.com

Nutritional Approach:

Disease or Condition: Anxiety

Causes of Anxiety

Caused by the perception of real or potential danger that threatens the security of the individual. Everyone experiences a certain amount of nervousness and apprehension when faced with a stressful situation. Usually, the response is reasonable and adaptive, and contains a built-in control mechanism to return to a normal physiologic state.[56] It is during this time that it is best to realize you have a problem and look at your lifestyle and nutrition to stop it from becoming a disease.

Nutritional support:

Foods that have been proven to help with Anxiety:

Anxiety can be enhanced from unstable blood sugar levels and lack of nutrients. Following a diet that consists of Whole grains, Fruits and Vegetables will help balance the body, giving it the best chance at supporting your needs. Anxiety creates an acidic environment, so eating many dark green vegetables will help alkalinize the system. (Refer to the nutritional recommendations in chapter 5 for more specifics.)

Nutrients that have been proven to help with Anxiety:

Probiotics[57], Magnesium[58], Vitamin B[59], 5-Hydorxytryptophan (5-HTP) [60], Tyrosine[61], Vitamin C[62] and Vitamin B3[63], Kava[64], Passionflower[65], Valerian[66], and St. John's Wort[67].

Probiotics–

This benefit may be due not only to the steady biosynthesis of B vitamins, but also to the high production of the amino acid tryptophan during fermentation. Tryptophan is known to relieve anxiety through synthesis of the neurotransmitter serotonin.

Magnesium–

It has been documented that anxiety is one of the symptoms that can occur in individuals with magnesium depletion. In one double-blind trial of women who were being treated with anti-anxiety drugs, the addition of magnesium lactate resulted in a more rapid reduction of psychopathological symptoms, in particular anxiety[68]. Symptoms of magnesium deficiency include anxiety, nervousness, insomnia, muscle fatigue, and tachycardia.

To find out more or to speak to a nutritional counselor for free, just visit us at:
www.CuresForTheBody.com

Vitamin B6–

Vitamin B$_6$ is required for the conversion of tryptophan to serotonin. Therefore, a deficiency of vitamin B$_6$ may result in symptoms of anxiety and depression due to inhibition of serotonin synthesis. In a study of individuals suffering from frequent anxiety attacks, patients were given vitamin B$_6$ (125mg, 3 times daily) and tryptophan (2 grams daily). This regime enabled 70 percent of patients (9 of 13) to become free of anxiety attacks within three weeks[69].

Oral contraceptives are known to deplete vitamin B$_6$, which may cause anxiety in susceptible women. In one particular study, administration of 40mg of vitamin B$_6$ daily restored normal biochemical values and also relieved the clinical symptoms in the vitamin B$_6$ deficient women taking oral contraceptives[70]. Other important categories of drugs that can deplete vitamin B$_6$ include corticosteroids, theophylline-containing medications, hydralazine-containing vasodilators, loop diuretics, and estrogen replacement therapy medications[71].

5-Hydroxytryptophan (5-HTP)–

Tryptophan and 5-hydroxytryptophan (5-HTP) are the precursors for serotonin. Tryptophan is an essential amino acid that the body cannot manufacture. Tryptophan is converted into 5-HTP, which in turn is converted into serotonin. There is ample evidence that tryptophan depletion causes reduced synthesis of serotonin, which can result in anxiety and other mood disorders[72].

In 1989, the FDA removed tryptophan from the market due to some contaminated batches that caused a number of deaths. It is now available by prescription through compounding pharmacies, and it is also used in TPN feeding and infant formulas. However, tryptophan is not available to the general public as a nutritional supplement. The removal of tryptophan is responsible for bringing 5-HTP into the public's awareness as a substitute for tryptophan as a natural therapy for anxiety, depression, and sleep disorders. Either substance can be used to enhance serotonin synthesis in the brain.[73] However, it is now recognized that 5-HTP is more effective at elevating serotonin levels than tryptophan for the following reasons. Intestinal absorption of 5-HTP does not require the presence of a transport molecule, and is not affected by the presence of other amino acids; therefore it may be taken with meals without reducing its effectiveness. Unlike tryptophan, 5-HTP cannot be shunted into niacin or protein production. Also, therapeutic use of 5-HTP bypasses the conversion of tryptophan into 5-HTP by the enzyme tryptophan hydroxylase, which is the rate-limiting step in the synthesis of serotonin. It is reported that 5-HTP is well absorbed from an oral dose, with about 70 percent ending up in the bloodstream. It easily crosses the blood brain barrier and effectively increases central nervous system (CNS) synthesis of serotonin[74].

Studies that induce low levels of tryptophan result in low serotonin levels, which can cause anxiety[75]. This effect may be more pronounced in women than men[76]. In general, the scientific literature indicates that tryptophan and 5-HTP have been used with varying degrees of success in the treatment of various neuropsychiatric disorders[77]. However, the body of scientific literature reporting the use of these supplements for anxiety is not as strong as the literature supporting their use in the treatment of depression.

The average dosage range for 5-HTP is 50-300mg daily. Gas, nausea, and diarrhea are sometimes reported, but are usually minimized or eliminated if 5-HTP is taken with food. Individuals with ulcers or other GI inflammatory conditions such as Crohn's disease or celiac disease should start with low doses, build up gradually, and be sensitive to possible GI irritation.

Patients taking anti-anxiety drugs or other antidepressants should not take tryptophan or 5-HTP without the supervision of a health care professional because it can increase the effects of other antidepressants.

Tyrosine–

Tyrosine is the precursor to the neurotransmitters dopamine, norepinephrine, and epinephrine, which influence and regulate mental and emotional states. In a study with healthy male volunteers, reducing brain tyrosine levels caused a reduction in catecholamine synthesis. This caused decreased calmness, increased tension and anger, and a trend for increased depression. The authors of this study state that brain catecholaminergic dysregulation is involved in pathological anxiety states. In another study, one group of women was placed on a controlled diet that caused the depletion of phenylalanine and tyrosine while a second group was put on a diet that caused the depletion of tryptophan. In both cases, a similar level of anxiety and irritability developed.[78] Oral contraceptives can cause a depletion of tyrosine in women users, which increases the risk of depression.[79] At this time, there are only a few studies that mention the link between tyrosine depletion and anxiety, so this relationship is not strongly supported by scientific documentation.

A plasma amino acid analysis can be useful in identifying individuals with low tyrosine levels, determining appropriate levels of supplementation, and monitoring progress. Without lab assessment guidance, suggested

To find out more or to speak to a nutritional counselor for free, just visit us at:
www.CuresForTheBody.com

dosages start at 500mg three times daily, and can increase to 6 grams per day. People with high blood pressure should only use it under close medical supervision, and it is contraindicated for those with phenylketonuria (PKU) and melanoma.

Vitamin C and Vitamin B3–

Combined supplementation was effective in reducing anxiety in a group of patients following alcohol withdrawal. The patients took 1 gram of vitamin C, 1 gram of niacin, 200mg of vitamin B6, and 200 IU of vitamin E three times daily after meals. After three weeks, patients taking the supplement protocol had significantly decreased levels of anxiety as determined by three different anxiety-testing scales.

Kava–

South Pacific natives have used kava for centuries. The root is used in the preparation of a recreational beverage known by a variety of local names (kava, yaqona, awa) and occupies a prominent position in the social, ceremonial, and daily life of Pacific island peoples as coffee or tea does in the Western cultures. In European phytomedicine, kava has long been used as a safe, effective treatment for mild anxiety states, nervous tension, muscular tension, and mild insomnia[80]. Researchers suggest after a multicenter, randomized, placebo-controlled, double-blind clinical trial that kava may be effective and safe when used for sleep disturbances associated with anxiety disorders[81]. Studies have reported that kava preparations compare favorably to benzodiazepines in controlling symptoms of anxiety and minor depression, while increasing vigilance, sociability, memory, and reaction time[82,83]. Reports are conflicting as to whether kava's anti-anxiety actions are GABA mediated[84,85]. Kavalactones appear to act on the limbic system, in particular the amygdala complex, the primitive part of the brain that is the center of the emotional being and basic survival functions[86]. It is thought that kava may promote relaxation, sleep, and rest by altering the way in which the limbic system modulates emotional processes. Tolerance does not seem to develop with kava use[87,88].

Passionflower–

Passionflower, or maypop, is a common roadside vine in many areas of the United States. Passionflower has been reported to have sedative, hypnotic, antispasmodic, and anodyne properties. It has traditionally been used for neuralgia, generalized seizures, hysteria, nervous tachycardia, spasmodic asthma, and specifically for insomnia. The bioactive constituents maltol and ethylmaltol have been reported to cause CNS sedation, anticonvulsant activity (high doses), and a reduction in spontaneous motor activity (low doses) in laboratory animals.[89] Passionflower extracts have been reported to reduce locomotor activity, prolong sleeping time, raise the nociceptive threshold, and produce an anxiolytic effect in laboratory animals.[90] In humans, passionflower has been reported effective when used in combination with other sedative and anti-anxiety herbs such as valerian, making it beneficial in conditions such as hyperthyroidism where CNS stimulation occurs.[91] These effects may be due to synergism and also due to the potential binding of passionflower constituents to benzodiazepine receptors in vivo.[92,93]

Valerian–

Valerian has long been used as an agent to soothe the nervous system in response to stress. It has been reported that valerian helps improve sleep quality.[94,95] The usefulness of valerian is reported to be due to several principal components, including valepotriates, valeric acid, and pungent oils, which have a sedative effect on the central nervous system, as well as a relaxing effect on the smooth muscles of the GI tract[96,97]. It is felt that both valepotriates and valeric acid bind to receptor sites similar to the benzodiazepines.[98] Valerian's constituents reportedly influence gamma aminobutyric acid (GABA) activity through affinity for receptors in the brain.[99] Valerian does not seem to produce the morning drug hangover effect as seen with some benzodiazepines.[100]

St. John's Wort–

St. John's wort has gained a great deal of attention for its use in minor depression. Its popularity has stemmed from its extensive use by European physicians as an agent of choice in the treatment of mild to moderate depression. There are a variety of studies that are claimed to support the use of St. John's wort in treating depression.[101,102] Studies with St. John's wort have centered around the use of a 0.3 percent hypericin content standardized extract at a dose of 300mg, three times a day. It is viewed as safe and effective in Europe, and its monograph is part of the Commission E Monographs for herbal medicines in Europe. St. John's wort has several possible effects on body chemistry, including: the inhibition of cortisol secretion and the blocking of catabolic hormones, such as interleukin 6 (IL-6);[103] the inhibition of the breakdown of several central nervous system neurotransmitters, including serotonin (it may have mild MAO-inhibiting activity; however, this has not been clearly defined and cannot explain all the activity of St. John's wort, and researchers do not consider this to be its major mechanism of action);[104,105,106] amplification and improvement in the signal produced by serotonin once it binds to its receptor sites in the brain;[107,108] and contains the chemical melatonin (approximately 4.39mcg/ gm), which may also contribute to the antidepressant effects of the plant.[109]

Although the constituent hypericin was originally thought to have the antidepressant effects seen when using St. John's wort, recent research has reported that the constituents pseudo-hypericin and hyperforin may enhance serotonin, catecholamines, and glutamine levels in the brain.[110]

Recent literature has reported cytochrome P-450 enzyme-inducing activity of St. John's wort in human studies. Interactions between St. John's wort and anticoagulants, indinavir, cyclosporin, digoxin, ethinyl estradiol/ desogestrel, and theophylline have been reported.[111] The mechanism of action was believed to be liver enzyme induction and subsequent alterations of drug levels by the herb. Also, several reports have suggested that concurrent use of St. John's wort and SSRIs may result in "serotonin syndrome", including sweating, tremor, confusion, flushing, and agitation.[112,113] St. John's wort should be used with caution if individuals are on these medications.

Exercises that have been proven to help with Anxiety:

Exercise can help to relieve stress, tension, and anxiety. By expelling your excess negative emotions and adrenaline through physical activity, you can enter a more relaxed, calm state of being from which to deal with the issues and conflicts that are causing your anxiety. Exercise is one of the most important coping behaviors to combat anxiety and stress.

Exercise increases blood flow to the brain, releases hormones, stimulates the nervous system, and increases levels of morphine-like substances found in the body (such as beta-endorphin) that can have a positive effect on mood. Exercise may trigger a neurophysiologic high-a shot of adrenaline or endorphins- that produces an antidepressant effect in some, an anti-anxiety effect in others, and a general sense of "feeling better" in most, says Michael H. Sacks, M.D. in *Exercise For Stress Control.*

Arthritis/Osteoarthritis

Description: Osteoarthritis is the most common form of joint disease, and is a chronic disorder of joint cartilage and surrounding tissues. It is a degenerative joint disease and is characterized by pain, stiffness, and loss of function.

Osteoarthritis most often begins with an abnormality of the cells (collagen and proteoglycans) that synthesize the components of cartilage. The slow, progressive changes seen in osteoarthritis consist of an increase in water content, loss of proteoglycans, and reduction of PG aggregates in cartilage. The net result is failure of the cartilage to repair itself.[114] Because of water retention, the cartilage may swell, become soft, and develop cracks on the surface. The bone beneath the cartilage is weakened as tiny cavities form in it. As this process progresses, the joint no longer moves smoothly as the cartilage becomes rough and pitted. Eventually, all of the parts of the joint fail, so the joint is altered.

Osteoarthritis can occur without any known cause (Primary), or it can be based on a known abnormality, overuse, or trauma (Secondary). In secondary Osteoarthritis, people in occupations that require repeated motions of one joint tend to develop Osteoarthritis. Obesity also tends to affect the occurrence of Osteoarthritis, particularly in women.

The chondrocytes control the synthesis and degradation of the ECM by affecting the production of collagen and proteoglycans. The collagens provide tensile strength and maintenance of tissue volume and shape. The proteoglycans (PGs) provide the "stuffing material" for the matrix. The PGs consist of a protein core and at least one or more glycosaminoglycan chains (chondroitin sulfate, keratan sulfate, and dermatan sulfate). These aggregates retain and maintain the water content of the cartilage because of their highly hydrophilic and anionic properties. This is what gives cartilage its resilience and load bearing properties.

To find out more or to speak to a nutritional counselor for free, just visit us at:
www.CuresForTheBody.com

Medical Treatment:

Analgesic: Does not alter the course of osteoarthritis, but reduces symptoms and allows more appropriate exercise

Brand name: Tylenol

Drug Name: Acetaminophen

Acetaminophen inhibits prostaglandin synthetase.

Notable Side Effects:

Light-headedness, dizziness, sedation, nausea and vomiting.

NSAID: Lessen pain and swelling

Brand name: Advil, Motrin

Drug Name: Ibuprofen

Ibuprofen is a nonsteroidal anti-inflammatory drug (NSAID) that possesses anti-inflammatory, analgesic and antipyretic activity. Its mode of action, like that of other NSAIDs, is not completely understood, but may be related to prostaglandin synthetase inhibition. After absorption of the racemic ibuprofen, the [-]R-enantiomer undergoes interconversion to the [+]S-form. The biological activities of ibuprofen are associated with the [+]S-enantiomer.

Notable Side Effects:

• *Cardiovascular system:* Edema, fluid retention (generally responds promptly to drug discontinuation).

• *Digestive system:* Nausea, epigastric pain, heartburn, diarrhea, abdominal distress, nausea and vomiting, indigestion, constipation, abdominal cramps or pain, fullness of Gl tract (bloating and flatulence).

• *Nervous system:* Dizziness, headache, nervousness.

• *Skin and appendages:* Rash (including maculopapular type), pruritus.

• *Special senses:* Tinnitus.

Brand name: Aleve, Anaprox

Drug Name: Naproxen

Naproxen is a nonsteroidal anti-inflammatory drug (NSAID) with analgesic and antipyretic properties. The sodium salt of naproxen has been developed as a more rapidly absorbed formulation of naproxen for use as an analgesic. The naproxen anion inhibits prostaglandin synthesis but beyond this its mode of action is unknown.

Notable Side Effects:

- *Gastrointestinal:* Constipation, heartburn , abdominal pain, nausea, dyspepsia, diarrhea, stomatitis.
- *Central Nervous System:* Headache, dizziness, drowsiness, lightheadedness, vertigo.
- *Dermatologic:* Itching (pruritus), skin eruptions, ecchymoses, sweating, purpura.
- *Special Senses:* Tinnitus , hearing disturbances, visual disturbances.
- *Cardiovascular:* Edema, dyspnea, palpitations.
- *General:* Thirst.

Cyclooxygenase-2 (COX-2) inhibitors: Similar to NSAIDS but have fewer gastrointestinal side effects (454)

Brand name:Celebrex

Drug Name: Celecoxib

Celecoxib is a nonsteroidal anti-inflammatory drug that exhibits anti-inflammatory, analgesic, and antipyretic activities in animal models. The mechanism of action of CELEBREX is believed to be due to inhibition of prostaglandin synthesis, primarily via inhibition of cyclooxygenase-2 (COX-2). At therapeutic concentrations in humans, CELEBREX does not inhibit the cyclooxygenase-1 (COX-1) isoenzyme.

Notable Side Effects:

Abdominal pain, diarrhea, dyspepsia, flatulence, nausea, back pain, peripheral edema, injury-accidental, dizziness, headache, insomnia, pharyngitis, rhinitis, sinusitis, upper respiratory tract infection, rash.

Brand name: Vioxx

Drug Name: Rofecoxib

Rofecoxib is a nonsteroidal anti-inflammatory drug (NSAID) that exhibits anti-inflammatory, analgesic, and antipyretic activities in animal models. The mechanism of action of VIOXX is believed to be due to inhibition of prostaglandin synthesis, via inhibition of cyclooxygenase-2 (COX-2). At therapeutic concentrations in humans, VIOXX does not inhibit the cyclooxygenase-1 (COX-1) isoenzyme.

Notable Side Effects:

Abdominal pain, asthenia/fatigue, dizziness, flu-like disease, lower extremity edema, upper respiratory infection, hypertension, diarrhea, dyspepsia, epigastric discomfort, heartburn, nausea, sinusitis, back pain, headache, bronchitis, urinary tract infection.

SPECIAL NOTE; VIOXX has been taken off the market due to a research study that shows that you can DOUBLE your risk of Heart Attack by taking this drug long term. This is another example of an FDA approved drug that has been prescribed to millions of people. As with most drugs VIOXX never cured any disease and in fact put people at an increased risk of serious complications.

ADDITIONAL CONCERN;

Anti-inflammatory drugs also cause cartilage damage[115]. Thus, you will actually be causing more damage than good.

Other common recommendations from medical doctors: The primary goal in treating Osteoarthritis is to reduce the pain, maintain function, and prevent further destruction. Appropriate exercises are often recommended, including stretching, strengthening, and postural exercises. It is important to rest the painful joint, but not to immobilize joint as this can cause stiffening. Excessively soft chairs, recliners, mattresses, and car seats can also aggravate the joint. Joint replacement may be recommended when function becomes limited, but does not last forever so is often delayed.

A healthy diet and/or dietary counseling may be recommended if you are overweight, as obesity affects the progression of Osteoarthritis, as well as the contraction of the muscles that stabilize the joint.

Nutritional Approach:

Disease or Condition: Arthritis

Causes of arthritis

There are many causes. Age-related changes in collagen-matrix repair mechanisms, altered biochemistry, fractures and mechanical damage, genetic predisposition, hormonal and sex factors, double jointed/ above average flexibility or joint instability, inflammation, inflammatory joint disease, and others.

Nutritional support:

Foods that have been proven to help with arthritis:

Omega 3 and 6 essential fatty acids, avocados and soy beans.

Nutrients that have been proven to help with arthritis:

Supplements containing

–Omega 3 and 6 (EFA's) essential fatty acids (flax seed oil, hemp seed oil, borage oil, DHA)[116]

–Glucosamine[117], Chondroitins[118], Methyl Sulfonyl Methane (MSN)[119], SAMe[120], vitamins C[121], E[122] and B3[123], boron[124], boswellia[125], grape seed extract[126], Cat's claw[127], turmeric[128,] Arzneim and ginger[129].

–Plant source digestive enzymes[130] (i.e. protease, lipase, amylase) especially helpful are the proteolitic enzymes.

Exercises that have been proven to help with arthritis:

The National Institute of Health recognizes three types of exercise are best for people with arthritis: Range-of-motion exercises (e.g., dance) help maintain normal joint movement and relieve stiffness. This type of exercise helps maintain or increase flexibility.

Strengthening exercises (e.g., weight training) help keep or increase muscle strength. Strong muscles help support and protect joints affected by arthritis.

Aerobic or endurance exercises (e.g., bicycle riding) improve cardiovascular fitness, help control weight, and improve overall function. Weight control can be important to people who have arthritis because extra weight puts extra pressure on many joints. Some studies show that aerobic exercise can reduce inflammation in some joints.

To find out more or to speak to a nutritional counselor for free, just visit us at:
www.CuresForTheBody.com

Studies have shown that exercise helps people with arthritis in many ways. Exercise reduces joint pain and stiffness and increases flexibility, muscle strength, cardiac fitness, and endurance. It also helps with weight reduction and contributes to an improved sense of well-being.

Basic Arthritis Plan:

- Eating foods rich in Omega 3 and 6 essential fatty acids or taking supplements containing them (flax seeds/oil, hemp seeds/oil, Borage oil, DHA), are necessary to produce secretions that lubricate our joints[131]. They also help our body produce stage 1 and 3 prostaglandins that inhibit inflammation[132]. They are required to build and deposit bone material and are used to transport minerals. EFA's are also required to build our cells' membranes; those that line our digestive tract help prevent the entrance of undigested foreign material into our bodies. They also strengthen immune cells that inhabit all body surfaces. Further, EFAs and fats and oils of any kind slow down stomach emptying time and thereby allow more time for the complete digestion of foods—especially proteins that could cause allergic reactions[133].

- Eat avocados and soy beans: They are rich in anti-inflammatory chemicals called plant sterols known as unsaponifiables. A team of European researchers found that they cause your body to produce the four types of collagen in the exact same proportions that are found in normal healthy joints! Australian researchers found that after several months cartilage was thicker. The results of two large-scale human studies, with over 200 patients, revealed that those on avocado and soy had greater mobility and less pain, and were able to lower or discontinue their use of aspirin or NSAIDs. Nine different studies have been done on these amazing plant extracts and all have found them effective.

- Consider taking (plant source) digestive enzymes as the help arthritics, at least partly because they promote good digestion. Completely digested proteins turn into amino acids, which cannot cause allergic reactions[134] (i.e. , protease, lipase, amylase).

To find out more or to speak to a nutritional counselor for free, just visit us at:
www.CuresForTheBody.com

• Consider taking higher doses of the proteolitic enzymes to stop inflammation, along with bromelain, boswellia, wheat germ and vitamin C and zinc; all helping decrease inflammation and aiding in tissue repair. Proteolitic enzymes are a natural way to decrease inflammation without the harmful side effects created by NSAIDs[135].

• Consider supplementing Glucosamine[136] and Chondroitins[137] – if you need to rebuild bone cartilage.

• Vitamin C – (whole food is best source) antioxidant – decrease risk of bone cartilage loss and decrease knee pain[138].

• Consider MSM[139] – pain reliever.

• SAMe[140] – anti-inflammatory and pain reliever.

• Cat's claw [141]– plant sterols demonstrate anti-inflammatory activity.

• Turmeric[142] – antioxidant and anti-inflammatory.

• Ginger [143]– an anti-inflammatory.

Arthritis/Rheumatoid

Description: In Rheumatoid Arthritis, joints of the hands and feet are inflamed, resulting in swelling, pain, and often the destruction of joints. Rheumatoid arthritis can occur at any age and occurs when components of the immune system attack the soft tissue that lines the joints and the connective tissue in many other parts of the body (ie, blood vessels and lungs). It is an autoimmune disease that causes chronic inflammation in multiple joints. It attacks the lining of the joints and often produces severe pain and inflammation, joint disfigurement, and loss of joint movement and function.[144] Rheumatoid Arthritis is typically chronic; however, some people will spontaneously enter a remission.[145]

As the immune system attacks the soft tissues of the joints, the cartilage, bone, and ligaments of the joint eventually erode, causing deformity, instability, and scarring within the joint. The joints deteriorate at a highly variable rate.

Many factors, including genetic predisposition[146], poor nutrition[147], and bacterial infection[148] may influence the pattern of the disease. Heavy metals (mercury, cadmium, and lead) are also associated with Rheumatoid Arthritis as they may interfere with collagen synthesis.[149]

A weakening of the immune system from stressful events can exacerbate Rheumatoid Arthritis. For this reason, stress management has been shown to produce clinical benefits for Rheumatoid Arthritis patients.[150]

Medical Treatment:

<u>NSAID:</u> Lessen pain and swelling

Special note: **Harmful Effects Of Pain Medication**

> NEW YORK, July 17 (Reuters) — Too many people are still unaware that chronic use of certain pain-relieving drugs can lead to severe gastrointestinal (GI) complications, such as ulcers, says Dr. Michael Kimmey, a leading

To find out more or to speak to a nutritional counselor for free, just visit us at:
www.CuresForTheBody.com

gastroenterologist, at Thursday's American Medical Association meeting in New York.

Kimmey, director of gastrointestinal endoscopy, professor of medicine, and assistant chief for clinical affairs at the University of Washington Medical Center, in Seattle, estimates that 50 to 80 percent of the people hospitalized for GI bleeding take pain-relieving drugs. "It's a public health problem," he says.

The pain medications most commonly at fault are the non-steroidal anti-inflammatory drugs or NSAIDs, which include: aspirin, ibuprofen (as found in Advil), naproxen (Aleve), and ketoprofen (Orudis). All NSAIDs provide pain relief and alleviate fevers, although at varying degrees of effectiveness.

According to Kimmey, people who take NSAIDs for prolonged periods of time can develop several GI side effects, such as stomach aches, indigestion, or even ulcers. Ulcers can eventually lead to GI bleeding or may even perforate, spilling the contents of the stomach or small intestine into the sterile abdominal cavity. "Every time they come in with bleeding, they have a 10% chance of dying. I don't think people realize that until it may be too late," warns Kimmey.

Ulcers are found in about 15% of the people who use NSAIDs for at least 3 months. Yet, a majority of the individuals with ulcers do not even know they have them because they do not experience any pain. "It's the painless ulcer. That's really part of the problem because those people don't know they have the ulcer until it actually bleeds or perforates," he explains.

The Arthritis, Rheumatism, and Aging Medical Information System reports that approximately 76,000 people are hospitalized each year for GI complications caused by chronic NSAID use. The estimated annual cost for treating these patients is approximately $760 million.

Kimmey believes that pharmaceutical companies and the federal government are not taking adequate measures to warn consumers about the dangers of NSAID use. "There are so many products that contain (NSAIDs) that are available over-the-counter. Unless we teach the public to read the label for what's in there, they will not realize they're taking (NSAIDs)."

Brand name: Advil, Motrin

Drug Name: Ibuprofen

Ibuprofen is a nonsteroidal anti-inflammatory drug (NSAID) that possesses anti-inflammatory, analgesic and antipyretic activity. Its mode of action, like that of other NSAIDs, is not completely understood, but may be related to prostaglandin synthetase inhibition. After absorption of the racemic ibuprofen, the [-]R-enantiomer undergoes interconversion to the [+]S-form. The biological activities of ibuprofen are associated with the [+]S-enantiomer.

Notable Side Effects:

• *Cardiovascular system:* Edema, fluid retention (generally responds promptly to drug discontinuation).

• *Digestive system:* Nausea, epigastric pain, heartburn, diarrhea, abdominal distress, nausea and vomiting, indigestion, constipation, abdominal cramps or pain, fullness of Gl tract (bloating and flatulence).

• *Nervous system:* Dizziness, headache, nervousness.

• *Skin and appendages:* Rash (including maculopapular type), pruritus.

• *Special senses:* Tinnitus.

Brand name: Aleve, Anaprox

Drug Name: Naproxen

Naproxen is a nonsteroidal anti-inflammatory drug (NSAID) with analgesic and antipyretic properties. The sodium salt of naproxen has been developed as a more rapidly absorbed formulation of naproxen for use as an analgesic. The naproxen anion inhibits prostaglandin synthesis but beyond this its mode of action is unknown.

Notable Side Effects:

• *Gastrointestinal:* Constipation, heartburn, abdominal pain, nausea , dyspepsia, diarrhea, stomatitis.

• *Central Nervous System:* Headache, dizziness, drowsiness, lightheadedness, vertigo.

To find out more or to speak to a nutritional counselor for free, just visit us at:
www.CuresForTheBody.com

• *Dermatologic:* Itching (pruritus), skin eruptions, ecchymoses, sweating, purpura.

• *Special Senses:* Tinnitus, hearing disturbances, visual disturbances.

• *Cardiovascular:* Edema, dyspnea, palpitations.

• *General:* Thirst.

Cyclooxygenase-2 (COX-2) inhibitors:

Similar to NSAIDS but have fewer gastrointestinal side effects (454)

Brand name: Celebrex

Drug Name: Celecoxib

Celecoxib is a nonsteroidal anti-inflammatory drug that exhibits anti-inflammatory, analgesic, and antipyretic activities in animal models. The mechanism of action of CELEBREX is believed to be due to inhibition of prostaglandin synthesis, primarily via inhibition of cyclooxygenase-2 (COX-2). At therapeutic concentrations in humans, CELEBREX does not inhibit the cyclooxygenase-1 (COX-1) isoenzyme.

Notable Side Effects:

Abdominal pain, diarrhea, dyspepsia, flatulence, nausea, back pain, peripheral edema, injury-accidental, dizziness, headache, insomnia, pharyngitis, rhinitis, sinusitis, upper respiratory tract infection, rash.

Brand name: Vioxx

Drug Name: Rofecoxib

Rofecoxib is a nonsteroidal anti-inflammatory drug (NSAID) that exhibits anti-inflammatory, analgesic, and antipyretic activities in animal models. The mechanism of action of VIOXX is believed to be due to inhibition of prostaglandin synthesis, via inhibition of cyclooxygenase-2 (COX-2). At therapeutic concentrations in humans, VIOXX does not inhibit the cyclooxygenase-1 (COX-1) isoenzyme.

Notable Side Effects: Abdominal pain, asthenia/fatigue, dizziness, flu-like disease, lower extremity edema, upper respiratory infection, hypertension, diarrhea, dyspepsia, epigastric discomfort, heartburn, nausea, sinusitis, back pain, headache, bronchitis, urinary tract infection.

SPECIAL NOTE: VIOXX has been taken off the market due to a research study that shows that you can DOUBLE your risk of Heart Attack by taking this drug long term. This is another example of an FDA approved drug that has been prescribed to millions of people. As with most drugs VIOXX never cured any disease and in fact put people at an increased risk of serious complications.

Slow-Acting Drugs:

All slow-acting drugs can slow progression of joint damage as well as gradually decrease pain and swelling

Brand Name: Cuprimine

Drug Name: Penicillamine

Penicillamine: The mechanism of action of penicillamine in rheumatoid arthritis is unknown although it appears to suppress disease activity. Unlike cytotoxic immunosuppressants, penicillamine markedly lowers IgM rheumatoid factor but produces no significant depression in absolute levels of serum immunoglobulins. Also unlike cytotoxic immunosuppressants which act on both, penicillamine *in vitro* depresses T-cell activity but not B-cell activity.

Notable Side Effects:

• *Gastrointestinal:* Anorexia, epigastric pain, nausea, vomiting, diarrhea, peptic ulcer, hepatic dysfunction including hepatic failure, pancreatitis, intrahepatic cholestasis and toxic hepatitis, serum alkaline phosphatase, lactic dehydrogenase, and positive cephalin flocculation and thymol turbidity tests; blunting, diminution, or total loss of taste perception; oral ulcerations.

• *Hematological:* Bone marrow depression, leukopenia and thrombocytopenia, thrombotic thrombocytopenic purpura, hemolytic anemia, red cell aplasia, monocytosis, leukocytosis, eosinophilia, and thrombocytosis.

• *Renal:* Proteinuria (6%) and/or hematuria, renal failure.

To find out more or to speak to a nutritional counselor for free, just visit us at:
www.CuresForTheBody.com

• *Central Nervous System:* Tinnitus, optic neuritis and peripheral sensory and motor neuropathies (including polyradiculoneuropathy, i.e., Guillain-Barre syndrome). Muscular weakness. Visual and psychic disturbances; mental disorders; and agitation and anxiety.

– *Neuromuscular:* Myasthenia gravis; dystonia.

• *Other:* Thrombophlebitis; hyperpyrexia; falling hair or alopecia; lichen planus; polymyositis; dermatomyositis; mammary hyperplasia; elastosis perforans serpiginosa; toxic epidermal necrolysis; anetoderma (cutaneous macular atrophy); and Goodpasture's syndrome, a severe and ultimately fatal glomerulonephritis associated with intra-alveolar hemorrhage. Vasculitis, including fatal renal vasculitis, has also been reported. Allergic alveolitis, obliterative bronchiolitis, interstitial pneumonitis and pulmonary fibrosis. Bronchial asthma. Increased skin friability, excessive wrinkling of skin, and development of small white papules; yellow nail syndrome. **As with all anti-biotics, you risk the chance of becoming resistant to the anti-biotic and creating super germs that are even harder to get rid of (see chapter 2 for more details).**

Immunosuppressive Drugs:

Can be used early for severe rheumatoid arthritis; can slow joint damage.

Brand Name:Trexall

Drug Name: Methotrexate sodium

Methotrexate sodium inhibits dihydrofolic acid reductase. Dihydrofolates must be reduced to tetrahydrofolates by this enzyme before they can be utilized as carriers of one-carbon groups in the synthesis of purine nucleotides and thymidylate. Therefore, methotrexate interferes with DNA synthesis, repair, and cellular replication. Actively proliferating tissues such as malignant cells, bone marrow, fetal cells, buccal and intestinal mucosa, and cells of the urinary bladder are in general more sensitive to this effect of methotrexate. When cellular proliferation in malignant tissues is greater than in most normal tissues, methotrexate may impair malignant growth without irreversible damage to normal tissues.

Notable Side Effects:

Liver disease, lung inflammation, an increased susceptibility to infection, suppression of blood cell production in the bone marrow.

• *Alimentary System:* Gingivitis, pharyngitis, stomatitis, anorexia, nausea, vomiting, diarrhea, hematemesis, melena, gastrointestinal ulceration and bleeding, enteritis, pancreatitis.

• *Blood and Lymphatic System Disorders:* Suppressed hematopoiesis causing anemia, aplastic anemia, leukopenia and/or thrombocytopenia. Hypogammaglobulinemia has been reported rarely.

• *Cardiovascular:* Pericarditis, pericardial effusion, hypotension, and thromboembolic events (including arterial thrombosis, cerebral thrombosis, deep vein thrombosis, retinal vein thrombosis, thrombophlebitis, and pulmonary embolus).

• *Central Nervous System:* Headaches, drowsiness, blurred vision, transient blindness, speech impairment including dysarthria and aphasia, hemiparesis, paresis and convulsions have also occurred following administration of methotrexate. Following low doses, there have been occasional reports of transient subtle cognitive dysfunction, mood alteration, unusual cranial sensations, leukoencephalopathy, or encephalopathy.

• *Infection:* There have been case reports of fatal opportunistic infections in patients receiving methotrexate therapy for neoplastic and non-neoplastic diseases. *Pneumocystis carinii* pneumonia was the most common infection. Other reported infections included sepsis, nocardiosis; histoplasmosis, cryptococcosis, *Herpes zoster,* *H. simplex* hepatitis, and disseminated *H. simplex.*

• *Musculoskeletal System:* Stress fracture.

• *Ophthalmic:* Conjunctivitis, serious visual changes of unknown etiology.

• *Pulmonary System:* Respiratory fibrosis, respiratory failure, interstitial pneumonitis deaths have been reported, and chronic interstitial obstructive pulmonary disease has occasionally occurred.

• *Skin:* Erythematous rashes, pruritus, urticaria, photosensitivity, pigmentary changes, alopecia, ecchymosis, telangiectasia, acne, furunculosis, erythema multiforme, toxic epidermal necrolysis, Stevens-Johnson syndrome, skin necrosis, skin ulceration, and exfoliative dermatitis.

• *Urogenital System:*   Severe nephropathy or renal failure, azotemia, cystitis, hematuria; defective oogenesis or spermatogenesis, transient oligospermia, menstrual dysfunction, vaginal discharge, and gynecomastia; infertility, abortion, fetal defects.

Brand Name:Enbrel

Drug Name:Etanercept

Etanercept binds specifically to tumor necrosis factor (TNF) and blocks its interaction with cell surface TNF receptors. TNF is a naturally occurring cytokine that is involved in normal inflammatory and immune responses. It plays an important role in the inflammatory processes of rheumatoid arthritis (RA), polyarticular-course rheumatoid arthritis (JRA), and ankylosing spondylitis and the resulting joint pathology. [1,2] Elevated levels of TNF are found in involved tissues and fluids of patients with ankylosing spondylitis (AS).

Notable Side Effects:

Risk of infection or malignancy, headache, nausea, rhinitis, dizziness, pharyngitis, cough, asthenia, abdominal pain, rash, peripheral edema, respiratory disorder, dyspepsia, sinusitis, vomiting, mouth ulcer, alopecia, pneumonitis.

Other common recommendations from Medical Doctors: Rest, exercise, and physical or occupational therapy are recommended. Therapy is often recommended for keeping your range of motion. Exercise gently and do not freeze joints in one position. Splints can gradually extend tight joints. Orthopedic or athletic shoes can make walking less painful, and devices such as grippers reduce the need to squeeze the hand forcefully. Weight loss is also recommended (if applicable) to help alleviate joint stress.

Surgery is recommended in some patients for tendon repair and joint replacements.

Nutritional Approach:

Disease or Condition: Arthritis

Causes of arthritis

There are many causes. Age-related changes in collagen-matrix repair mechanisms, altered biochemistry, fractures and mechanical damage, genetic predisposition, hormonal and sex factors, double jointed/ above average flexibility or joint instability, inflammation, inflammatory joint disease, and others.

Nutritional support:

Foods that have been proven to help with arthritis:

Omega 3 and 6 essential fatty acids, avocados and soy beans.

Nutrients that have been proven to help with arthritis:

Supplements containing

• Omega 3 and 6 (EFA's) essential fatty acids (flax seed oil, hemp seed oil, borage oil, DHA)[151]

• Glucosamine[152], Chondroitins[153], Methyl Sulfonyl Methane (MSN)[154], SAMe[155], vitamins C[156], E[157] and B3[158], boron[159], boswellia[160], grape seed extract[161], Cat's claw[162], turmeric[163] and ginger[164].

• Plant source digestive enzymes[165] (i.e. protease, lipase, amylase) especially helpful are the proteolitic enzymes[166].

Exercises that have been proven to help with arthritis:

The National Institute of Health recognizes three types of exercise are best for people with arthritis: Range-of-motion exercises (e.g., dance) help maintain normal joint movement and relieve stiffness. This type of exercise helps maintain or increase flexibility.

Strengthening exercises (e.g., weight training) help keep or increase muscle strength. Strong muscles help support and protect joints affected by arthritis.

Aerobic or endurance exercises (e.g., bicycle riding) improve cardiovascular fitness, help control weight, and improve overall function.

To find out more or to speak to a nutritional counselor for free, just visit us at:
www.CuresForTheBody.com

Weight control can be important to people who have arthritis because extra weight puts extra pressure on many joints. Some studies show that aerobic exercise can reduce inflammation in some joints.

Studies have shown that exercise helps people with arthritis in many ways. Exercise reduces joint pain and stiffness and increases flexibility, muscle strength, cardiac fitness, and endurance. It also helps with weight reduction and contributes to an improved sense of well-being.

Basic Arthritis Plan:

• Eating foods rich in Omega 3 and 6 essential fatty acids or taking supplements containing them (flax seeds/oil, hemp seeds/oil, Borage oil, DHA), are necessary to produce secretions that lubricate our joints[167]. They also help our body produce stage 1 and 3 prostaglandins that inhibit inflammation[168]. They are required to build and deposit bone material and are used to transport minerals. EFA's are also required to build our cells' membranes; those that line our digestive tract help prevent the entrance of undigested foreign material into our bodies. They also strengthen immune cells that inhabit all body surfaces. Further, EFAs and fats and oils of any kind slow down stomach emptying time and thereby allow more time for the complete digestion of foods—especially proteins that could cause allergic reactions[169].

• Eat avocados and soy beans. They are rich in anti-inflammatory chemicals called plant sterols known as unsaponifiables. A team of European researchers found that they cause your body to produce the four types of collagen in the exact same proportions that are found in normal healthy joints! Australian researchers found that after several months cartilage was thicker. The results of two large-scale human studies, with over 200 patients revealed that those on avocado and soy had greater mobility and less pain, and were able to lower or discontinue their use of aspirin or NSAIDs. Nine different studies have been done on these amazing plant extracts and all have found them effective.

• Consider taking (plant source) digestive enzymes as they help arthritics, at least partly because they promote good digestion. Completely digested proteins turn into amino acids, which cannot cause allergic reactions[170] (i.e., protease, lipase, amylase).

• Consider taking higher doses of the proteolitic enzymes to stop inflammation, along with bromelain, boswellia, wheat germ and vitamin C and zinc; all help decrease inflammation and aid in tissue repair. Proteolitic enzymes are a natural way to decrease inflammation without the harmful side effects created by NSAIDs[171].

• Consider supplementing Glucosamine[172] and Chondroitins[173]

If you need to rebuild bone cartilage:

• Vitamin C – (whole food is the best source) antioxidant – decrease risk of bone cartilage loss and decrease knee pain[174].

• Consider MSM[175] – pain reliever.

• SAMe[176] – anti-inflammatory and pain reliever.

• Cat's claw [177]– plant sterols demonstrate anti-inflammatory activity.

• Turmeric[178] – antioxidant and anti-inflammatory.

• Ginger [179]– an anti-inflammatory.

Arthritis/Gout

Description: Gout is the most painful of rheumatic diseases. It results from deposits of sodium urate crystals, which accumulate in the joints because of a disorder of uric acid metabolism, leading to attacks of painful joint inflammation. It is caused by either an overproduction or under excretion of uric acid. Normally, uric acid dissolves in the blood and passes through the kidney and into the urine for elimination.

As long as the production of uric acid is balanced with its elimination, it will not accumulate in the body's tissues. When production is greater than elimination, uric acid accumulates.[180] The kidneys typically eliminate about two-thirds of the uric acid through the urine. (The remainder is eliminated through the gastrointestinal tract.) When the kidneys cannot eliminate enough uric acid in the urine, the uric acid level in the blood becomes abnormally high. Too much uric acid in the blood can result in urate crystals being formed and deposited in joints.

Uric acid is a product of purine metabolism, which are found in dietary foods or our bodies. One of the causes of the overproduction of uric acid is that there are several enzymes that regulate the metabolism of purines, and a deficiency of one or more of these enzymes may cause hyperuricemia.

Gout occurrences often increase with age, especially with men.[181] It most commonly affects the joints in the feet, as these joints are cooler than the central part of the body, and urate crystals form readily at cooler temperatures.

Medical Treatment:

<u>NSAID</u>: Lessen pain and swelling

Special note: **Harmful Effects Of Pain Medication**
NEW YORK, July 17 (Reuters) — Too many people
are still unaware that chronic use of certain pain-relieving

To find out more or to speak to a nutritional counselor for free, just visit us at:
www.CuresForTheBody.com

drugs can lead to severe gastrointestinal (GI) complications, such as ulcers, says Dr. Michael Kimmey, a leading gastroenterologist, at Thursday's American Medical Association meeting in New York.

Kimmey, director of gastrointestinal endoscopy, professor of medicine, and assistant chief for clinical affairs at the University of Washington Medical Center, in Seattle, estimates that 50 to 80 percent of the people hospitalized for GI bleeding take pain-relieving drugs. "It's a public health problem," he says.

The pain medications most commonly at fault are the non-steroidal anti-inflammatory drugs or NSAIDs, which include: aspirin, ibuprofen (as found in Advil), naproxen (Aleve), and ketoprofen (Orudis). All NSAIDs provide pain relief and alleviate fevers, although at varying degrees of effectiveness.

According to Kimmey, people who take NSAIDs for prolonged periods of time can develop several GI side effects, such as stomach aches, indigestion, or even ulcers. Ulcers can eventually lead to GI bleeding or may even perforate, spilling the contents of the stomach or small intestine into the sterile abdominal cavity. "Every time they come in with bleeding, they have a 10% chance of dying. I don't think people realize that until it may be too late," warns Kimmey.

Ulcers are found in about 15% of the people who use NSAIDs for at least 3 months. Yet, a majority of the individuals with ulcers do not even know they have them because they do not experience any pain. "It's the painless ulcer. That's really part of the problem because those people don't know they have the ulcer until it actually bleeds or perforates," he explains.

The Arthritis, Rheumatism, and Aging Medical Information System reports that approximately 76,000 people are hospitalized each year for GI complications caused by chronic NSAID use. The estimated annual cost for treating these patients is approximately $760 million.

Kimmey believes that pharmaceutical companies and the federal government are not taking adequate measures to warn consumers about the dangers of NSAID use. "There are so many products that contain (NSAIDs) that are available over-the-counter. Unless we teach the public to read the label for what's in there, they will not realize they're taking (NSAIDs)."

Brand name: Advil, Motrin

Drug Name: Ibuprofen

Ibuprofen is a nonsteroidal anti-inflammatory drug (NSAID) that possesses anti-inflammatory, analgesic and antipyretic activity. Its mode of action, like that of other NSAIDs, is not completely understood, but may be related to prostaglandin synthetase inhibition. After absorption of the racemic ibuprofen, the [-]R-enantiomer undergoes interconversion to the [+]S-form. The biological activities of ibuprofen are associated with the [+]S-enantiomer.

Notable Side Effects:

• *Cardiovascular system:* Edema, fluid retention (generally responds promptly to drug discontinuation).

• *Digestive system:* Nausea, epigastric pain, heartburn, diarrhea, abdominal distress, nausea and vomiting, indigestion, constipation, abdominal cramps or pain, fullness of Gl tract (bloating and flatulence).

• *Nervous system:* Dizziness, headache, nervousness.

• *Skin and appendages:* Rash (including maculopapular type), pruritus.

• *Special senses:* Tinnitus.

Brand name: Aleve, Anaprox

Drug Name: Naproxen

Naproxen is a nonsteroidal anti-inflammatory drug (NSAID) with analgesic and antipyretic properties. The sodium salt of naproxen has been developed as a more rapidly absorbed formulation of naproxen for use as an analgesic. The naproxen anion inhibits prostaglandin synthesis but beyond this its mode of action is unknown.

To find out more or to speak to a nutritional counselor for free, just visit us at:
www.CuresForTheBody.com

Notable Side Effects:

- *Gastrointestinal:* Constipation, heartburn, abdominal pain, nausea , dyspepsia, diarrhea, stomatitis.
- *Central Nervous System:* Headache, dizziness, drowsiness, lightheadedness, vertigo.
- *Dermatologic:* Itching (pruritus), skin eruptions, ecchymoses, sweating, purpura.
- *Special Senses:* Tinnitus, hearing disturbances, visual disturbances.
- *Cardiovascular:* Edema, dyspnea, palpitations.
- *General:* Thirst.

Cyclooxygenase-2 (COX-2) inhibitors:

Similar to NSAIDS but have fewer gastrointestinal side effects (454)

Brand name: Celebrex

Drug Name: Celecoxib

Celecoxib is a nonsteroidal anti-inflammatory drug that exhibits anti-inflammatory, analgesic, and antipyretic activities in animal models. The mechanism of action of CELEBREX is believed to be due to inhibition of prostaglandin synthesis, primarily via inhibition of cyclooxygenase-2 (COX-2). At therapeutic concentrations in humans, CELEBREX does not inhibit the cyclooxygenase-1 (COX-1) isoenzyme.

Notable Side Effects:

Abdominal pain, diarrhea, dyspepsia, flatulence, nausea, back pain, peripheral edema, injury-accidental, dizziness, headache, insomnia, pharyngitis, rhinitis, sinusitis, upper respiratory tract infection, rash.

Brand name: Vioxx

Drug Name: Rofecoxib

Rofecoxib is a nonsteroidal anti-inflammatory drug (NSAID) that exhibits anti-inflammatory, analgesic, and antipyretic activities in animal models. The mechanism of action of VIOXX is believed to be due to inhibition of prostaglandin synthesis, via inhibition of cyclooxygenase-2 (COX-

2). At therapeutic concentrations in humans, VIOXX does not inhibit the cyclooxygenase-1 (COX-1) isoenzyme.

Notable Side Effects: Abdominal pain, asthenia/fatigue, dizziness, flu-like disease, lower extremity edema, upper respiratory infection, hypertension, diarrhea, dyspepsia, epigastric discomfort, heartburn, nausea, sinusitis, back pain, headache, bronchitis, urinary tract infection.

SPECIAL NOTE; VIOXX has been taken off the market due to a research study that shows that you can DOUBLE your risk of Heart Attack by taking this drug long term. This is another example of an FDA approved drug that has been prescribed to millions of people. As with most drugs, VIOXX never cured any disease and in fact it caused disease and risks associated with it.

Slow-Acting Drugs:

All slow-acting drugs can slow progression of joint damage as well as gradually decrease pain and swelling

Brand Name: Cuprimine

Drug Name: Penicillamine

Penicillamine: The mechanism of action of penicillamine in rheumatoid arthritis is unknown although it appears to suppress disease activity. Unlike cytotoxic immunosuppressants, penicillamine markedly lowers IgM rheumatoid factor but produces no significant depression in absolute levels of serum immunoglobulins. Also unlike cytotoxic immunosuppressants which act on both, penicillamine *in vitro* depresses T-cell activity but not B-cell activity.

Notable Side Effects:

• *Gastrointestinal:* Anorexia, epigastric pain, nausea, vomiting, diarrhea, peptic ulcer, hepatic dysfunction including hepatic failure, pancreatitis. Intrahepatic cholestasis and toxic hepatitis, serum alkaline phosphatase, lactic dehydrogenase, and positive cephalin flocculation and thymol turbidity tests; blunting, diminution, or total loss of taste perception; oral ulcerations.

To find out more or to speak to a nutritional counselor for free, just visit us at:
www.CuresForTheBody.com

• *Hematological:* Bone marrow depression. Leukopenia and thrombocytopenia, Thrombotic thrombocytopenic purpura, hemolytic anemia, red cell aplasia, monocytosis, leukocytosis, eosinophilia, and thrombocytosis.

• *Renal:* Proteinuria (6%) and/or hematuria. Renal failure.

• *Central Nervous System:* Tinnitus, optic neuritis and peripheral sensory and motor neuropathies (including polyradiculoneuropathy, i.e., Guillain-Barre syndrome). Muscular weakness. Visual and psychic disturbances; mental disorders; and agitation and anxiety.

– *Neuromuscular:* Myasthenia gravis; dystonia.

• *Other:* Thrombophlebitis; hyperpyrexia; falling hair or alopecia; lichen planus; polymyositis; dermatomyositis; mammary hyperplasia; elastosis perforans serpiginosa; toxic epidermal necrolysis; anetoderma (cutaneous macular atrophy); and Goodpasture's syndrome, a severe and ultimately fatal glomerulonephritis associated with intra-alveolar hemorrhage. Vasculitis, including fatal renal vasculitis, has also been reported. Allergic alveolitis, obliterative bronchiolitis, interstitial pneumonitis and pulmonary fibrosis. Bronchial asthma. Increased skin friability, excessive wrinkling of skin, and development of small white papules; yellow nail syndrome. **As with all anti-biotics, you risk the chance of becoming resistant to the anti-biotic and creating super germs that are even harder to get rid of (see chapter 2 for more details).**

Immunosuppressive Drugs:

Can be used early for severe rheumatoid arthritis; can slow joint damage.

Brand Name:Trexall

Drug Name: Methotrexate sodium

Methotrexate sodium inhibits dihydrofolic acid reductase. Dihydrofolates must be reduced to tetrahydrofolates by this enzyme before they can be utilized as carriers of one-carbon groups in the synthesis of purine nucleotides and thymidylate. Therefore, methotrexate interferes with DNA synthesis, repair, and cellular replication. Actively proliferating tissues such as malignant cells, bone marrow, fetal cells, buccal and intestinal mucosa, and cells of the urinary bladder are in general more sensitive to this effect of methotrexate. When cellular proliferation in malignant tissues is greater than in most normal tissues, methotrexate may impair malignant growth without irreversible damage to normal tissues.

Notable Side Effects:

Liver disease, lung inflammation, an increased susceptibility to infection, suppression of blood cell production in the bone marrow.

• *Alimentary System:* Gingivitis, pharyngitis, stomatitis, anorexia, nausea, vomiting, diarrhea, hematemesis, melena, gastrointestinal ulceration and bleeding, enteritis, pancreatitis.

• *Blood and Lymphatic System Disorders:* Suppressed hematopoiesis causing anemia, aplastic anemia, leukopenia and/or thrombocytopenia. Hypogammaglobulinemia has been reported rarely.

• *Cardiovascular:* Pericarditis, pericardial effusion, hypotension, and thromboembolic events (including arterial thrombosis, cerebral thrombosis, deep vein thrombosis, retinal vein thrombosis, thrombophlebitis, and pulmonary embolus).

• *Central Nervous System:* Headaches, drowsiness, blurred vision, transient blindness, speech impairment including dysarthria and aphasia, hemiparesis, paresis and convulsions have also occurred following administration of methotrexate. Following low doses, there have been occasional reports of transient subtle cognitive dysfunction, mood alteration, unusual cranial sensations, leukoencephalopathy, or encephalopathy.

• *Infection:* There have been case reports of fatal opportunistic infections in patients receiving methotrexate therapy for neoplastic and non-neoplastic diseases. *Pneumocystis carinii* pneumonia was the most common infection. Other reported infections included sepsis, nocardiosis; histoplasmosis, cryptococcosis, *Herpes zoster,* *H. simplex* hepatitis, and disseminated *H. simplex.*

To find out more or to speak to a nutritional counselor for free, just visit us at:
www.CuresForTheBody.com

• *Musculoskeletal System:* Stress fracture.

• *Ophthalmic:* Conjunctivitis, serious visual changes of unknown etiology.

• *Pulmonary System:* Respiratory fibrosis, respiratory failure, interstitial pneumonitis deaths have been reported, and chronic interstitial obstructive pulmonary disease has occasionally occurred.

• *Skin:* Erythematous rashes, pruritus, urticaria, photosensitivity, pigmentary changes, alopecia, ecchymosis, telangiectasia, acne, furunculosis, erythema multiforme, toxic epidermal necrolysis, Stevens-Johnson syndrome, skin necrosis, skin ulceration, and exfoliative dermatitis.

• *Urogenital System:* Severe nephropathy or renal failure, azotemia, cystitis, hematuria; defective oogenesis or spermatogenesis, transient oligospermia, menstrual dysfunction, vaginal discharge, and gynecomastia; infertility, abortion, fetal defects.

Brand Name:Enbrel

Drug Name:Etanercept

Etanercept binds specifically to tumor necrosis factor (TNF) and blocks its interaction with cell surface TNF receptors. TNF is a naturally occurring cytokine that is involved in normal inflammatory and immune responses. It plays an important role in the inflammatory processes of rheumatoid arthritis (RA), polyarticular-course rheumatoid arthritis (PRA), and ankylosing spondylitis and the resulting joint pathology. Elevated levels of TNF are found in involved tissues and fluids of patients with ankylosing spondylitis (AS).

Notable Side Effects:

Risk of infection or malignancy, headache, nausea, rhinitis, dizziness, pharyngitis, cough, asthenia, abdominal pain, rash, peripheral edema, respiratory disorder, dyspepsia, sinusitis, vomiting, mouth ulcer, alopecia, pneumonitis.

Other common recommendations from Medical Doctors: Rest, exercise, and physical or occupational therapy are recommended. Therapy is often recommended for keeping your range of motion. Exercise gently and do not freeze joints in one position. Splints can gradually extend tight joints. Orthopedic or athletic shoes can make walking less painful, and devices such as grippers reduce the need to squeeze the hand forcefully. Weight loss is also recommended (if applicable) to help alleviate joint stress. Surgery is recommended in some patients for tendon repair and joint replacements.

Nutritional Approach:

Disease or Condition: Arthritis
Causes of arthritis

There are many causes. Age-related changes in collagen-matrix repair mechanisms, altered biochemistry, fractures and mechanical damage, genetic predisposition, hormonal and sex factors, double jointed/ above average flexibility or joint instability, inflammation, inflammatory joint disease, and others.

Nutritional support:
Foods that have been proven to help with arthritis:
Omega 3 and 6 essential fatty acids, avocados and soy beans.

Nutrients that have been proven to help with arthritis:
Supplements containing:

- Omega 3 and 6 (EFA's) essential fatty acids (flax seed oil, hemp seed oil, borage oil, DHA)[182]

- Glucosamine[183], Chondroitins[184], Methyl Sulfonyl Methane (MSN)[185], SAMe[186], vitamins C[187], E[188] and B3[189], boron[190], boswellia[191], grape seed extract[192], Cat's claw[193], turmeric[194] and ginger[195].

- Plant source digestive enzymes[196] (i.e. protease, lipase, amylase) especially helpful are the proteolytic enzymes[197].

Exercises that have been proven to help with arthritis:
The National Institute of Health recognizes three types of exercise are best for people with arthritis: Range-of-motion exercises (e.g., dance) help maintain normal joint movement and relieve stiffness. This type of exercise helps maintain or increase flexibility.

To find out more or to speak to a nutritional counselor for free, just visit us at:
www.CuresForTheBody.com

Strengthening exercises (e.g., weight training) help keep or increase muscle strength. Strong muscles help support and protect joints affected by arthritis.

Aerobic or endurance exercises (e.g., bicycle riding) improve cardiovascular fitness, help control weight, and improve overall function. Weight control can be important to people who have arthritis because extra weight puts extra pressure on many joints. Some studies show that aerobic exercise can reduce inflammation in some joints.

Studies have shown that exercise helps people with arthritis in many ways. Exercise reduces joint pain and stiffness and increases flexibility, muscle strength, cardiac fitness, and endurance. It also helps with weight reduction and contributes to an improved sense of well-being.

Basic Arthritis Plan:

• Eating foods rich in Omega 3 and 6 essential fatty acids or taking supplements containing them (flax seeds/oil, hemp seeds/oil, Borage oil, DHA), are necessary to produce secretions that lubricate our joints[198]. They also help our body produce stage 1 and 3 prostaglandins that inhibit inflammation[199]. They are required to build and deposit bone material, and are used to transport minerals. EFAs are also required to build our cells' membranes; those that line our digestive tract help prevent the entrance of undigested foreign material into our bodies. They also strengthen immune cells that inhabit all body surfaces. Further, EFAs and fats and oils of any kind slow down stomach emptying time and thereby allow more time for the digestion of foods—especially proteins that could cause allergic reactions—to be completed[200].

• Eat avocados and soy beans: They are rich in anti-inflammatory chemicals called plant sterols known as unsaponifiables. A team of European researchers found that they cause your body to produce the four types of collagen in the exact same proportions that are found in normal healthy joints! Australian researchers found that after several months cartilage was thicker. The results of two large-scale human studies, with over 200 patients those on avocado and soy had greater mobility and less pain, and were able to lower or discontinue their use of aspirin or

NSAIDs. 9 different studies have been done on these amazing plant extracts and all have found it effective.

• Consider taking (plant source) digestive enzymes as the help arthritics, at least partly because they promote good digestion. Completely digested proteins turn into amino acids, which cannot cause allergic reactions[201]. (i.e. protease, lipase, amylase).

• Consider taking higher doses of the proteolitic enzymes to stop inflammation, along with bromelain, boswellia, wheat germ and vitamin C and zinc; all helping decrease inflammation and aiding in tissue repair. Proteolitic enzymes are a natural way to decrease inflammation without the harmful side effects created by NSAIDs[202].

• Consider supplementing Glucosamine[203] and Chondroitins[204]

SPECIAL NUTRITIONAL INFORMATION ABOUT GOUT

Clinical experience across the nation by many holistic practitioners have found that Proteolytic enzymes (especially Protease and Peptidase) have found to be EXTREMELY effective. The cause of action is the digesting of the proteins that exacerbate and can cause gout. The removal of Red Meats from the diet and taking of proteolytic enzymes is a very effective approach to this condition.

If you need to rebuild bone cartilage:

• Vitamin C – (whole food is best source) antioxidant – decrease risk of bone cartilage loss and decrease knee pain[205].

• Consider MSM[206] – pain reliever.

• SAMe[207] – anti-inflammatory and pain reliever.

• Cat's claw[208] – plant sterols demonstrate anti-inflammatory activity.

• Turmeric[209] – antioxidant and anti-inflammatory.

• Ginger[210]– an anti-inflammatory.

Asthma

Asthma is defined by the American Thoracic Society as a disease characterized by increased responsiveness of the trachea and bronchi to various stimuli and manifested by a widespread narrowing of the airways.[211] Approximately 17 to 18 million people are affected by asthma in the United States. The occurrences of asthma increased dramatically in the last few decades, probably due to either the widespread use of vaccines and antibiotics that shift the activity of certain white blood cells (lymphocytes), or due to the fact that children are spending so much more time indoors and the exposure to potential allergic substances has increased.

Asthma is a disease that affects a person's essential ability to breathe, and is one of the most demanding pathologies on the human being, both physically and mentally. The most important characteristic of asthma is that the airway is obstructed when certain receptors (cholinergic) in the airway cause the muscles to contract. These receptors are hyper-responsive to triggering stimuli, which irritates the airway and causes it to spasm and swell. Mast cells in the bronchi are also triggered by stimuli and release histamines and leukotrienes, which cause the airway to contract, swell, and secrete mucus. The result is wheezing, shortness of breath, and tachycardia.

Asthma can be intrinsic or extrinsic. Intrinsic asthma is triggered by cold air, exercise, or emotional trauma, and usually develops in adulthood. Extrinsic (atopic) asthma is immunologically mediated condition with a rise in serum immonuglobin.

Medical Treatment:

Beta-adrenergic Agonists

Brand Name: Proventil

Drug Name: Albuterol

Albuterol stimulates adenyl cyclase, the enzyme which catalyzes the formation of cyclic-3',5'-adenosine monophosphate (cyclic AMP) from

To find out more or to speak to a nutritional counselor for free, just visit us at:
www.CuresForTheBody.com

adenosine triphosphate (ATP). The cyclic AMP thus formed mediates the cellular responses. In vitro studies and in vivo pharmacologic studies have demonstrated that albuterol has a preferential effect on beta $_2$-adrenergic receptors compared with isoproterenol. While it is recognized that beta $_2$-adrenergic receptors are the predominant receptors in bronchial smooth muscle, recent data indicate that 10% to 50% of the beta-receptors in the human heart may be beta$_2$-receptors. The precise function of these receptors, however, is not yet established. Controlled clinical studies and other clinical experience have shown that inhaled albuterol, like other beta-adrenergic agonist drugs, can produce a significant cardiovascular effect in some patients, as measured by pulse rate, blood pressure, symptoms, and/or electrocardiographic changes.

Notable Side Effects:

Asthma exacerbation, otitis media, allergic reaction, gastroenteritis, cold symptoms, flu syndrome, lymphadenopathy, skin/appendage infection, urticaria, migraine, chest pain, bronchitis, nausea

Brand Name:Advair

Drug Name: Salmeterol

Salmeterol stimulates of intracellular adenyl cyclase, the enzyme that catalyzes the conversion of adenosine triphosphate (ATP) to cyclic-3',5'-adenosine monophosphate (cyclic AMP). Increased cyclic AMP levels cause relaxation of bronchial smooth muscle and inhibition of release of mediators of immediate hypersensitivity from cells, especially from mast cells.

Notable Side Effects:

Upper respiratory tract infection, pharyngitis, upper respiratory inflammation, sinusitis, hoarseness/dysphonia, oral candidiasis, viral respiratory infections, bronchitis, cough, headaches, nausea, vomiting, gastrointestinal discomfort and pain, diarrhea, viral gastrointestinal infections, musculoskeletal pain.

Methylxanthines

Brand Name: Uniphyl

Drug Name: Theophyline

Theophyline has two distinct actions in the airways of patients with reversible obstruction: smooth muscle relaxation (i.e., bronchodilation) and suppression of the response of the airways to stimuli (i.e., non-bronchodilator prophylactic effects).

Notable Side Effects:

Vomiting, abdominal pain, diarrhea, hematemesis, hypokalemia, hyperglycemia, acid/base disturbance, rhabdomyolysis, sinus tachycardia, ventricular premature beats, atrial fibrillation or flutter, multifocal atrial tachycardia, ventricular arrhythmias with hemodynamic instability, hypotension/shock, nervousness, tremors, disorientation, seizures, death.

Anticholinergic Drugs

Brand Name: Atrovent

Drug Name: Ipratropium

Ipratropium is an anticholinergic (parasympatholytic) agent which, based on animal studies, appears to inhibit vagally mediated reflexes by antagonizing the action of acetylcholine, the transmitter agent released from the vagus nerve. Anticholinergics prevent the increases in intracellular concentration of cyclic guanosine monophosphate (cyclic GMP) which are caused by interaction of acetylcholine with the muscarinic receptor on bronchial smooth muscle.

Notable Side Effects:

Palpitations, nervousness, dizziness, headache, rash, nausea, gastrointestinal distress, vomiting, tremor, blurred vision, dry mouth, irritation from aerosol, cough, exacerbation of symptoms.

Mast Cell Stabilizers

Brand Name: Alocril

Drug Name: Nedocromil

Nedocromil is a mast cell stabilizer. Nedocromil sodium inhibits the release of mediators from cells involved in hypersensitivity reactions.

To find out more or to speak to a nutritional counselor for free, just visit us at:
www.CuresForTheBody.com

Decreased chemotaxis and decreased activation of eosinophils have also been demonstrated.

Notable Side Effects:

Ocular burning, irritation and stinging, unpleasant taste, and nasal congestion have been reported to occur in 10-30% of patients. Other events occurring between 1-10% included asthma, conjunctivitis, eye redness, photophobia, and rhinitis.

Leukotriene Modifiers

Brand Name: Singulair

Drug Name: Montelukast

Montelukast is an orally active compound that binds with high affinity and selectivity to the $CysLT_1$ receptor (in preference to other pharmacologically important airway receptors, such as the prostanoid, cholinergic, or (beta)-adrenergic receptor). Montelukast inhibits physiologic actions of LTD_4 at the $CysLT_1$ receptor without any agonist activity.

Notable Side Effects:

Asthenia/fatigue, fever, abdominal pain, trauma, dyspepsia, infectious gastroenteritis, dental pain, dizziness, headache, nasal congestion, cough, flu, rash.

Brand Name: Accolate

Drug Name: Zafirlukast

Zafirlukast is a selective and competitive receptor antagonist of leukotriene D_4 and E_4 (LTD_4 and LTE_4), components of slow-reacting substance of anaphylaxis (SRSA). Cysteinyl leukotriene production and receptor occupation have been correlated with the pathophysiology of asthma, including airway edema, smooth muscle constriction, and altered cellular activity associated with the inflammatory process, which contribute to the signs and symptoms of asthma. Patients with asthma were found in one study to be 25-100 times more sensitive to the bronchoconstricting activity of inhaled LTD_4 than nonasthmatic subjects.

Notable Side Effects:

Headache, infection, nausea, diarrhea, pain, asthenia, abdominal pain, accidental injury, dizziness, myalgia, fever, back pain, vomiting, SGPT elevation, dyspepsia.

Other common recommendations from Medical Doctors: It is important to be educated about what stimulates an asthmatic response and how to treat it, as well as to educate family members and those close to you. It is also useful to write out a treatment plan with your healthcare professional, as this decreases the number of emergency situations.

There are also ways to adjust your lifestyle to reduce the number of attacks, depending on what triggers the asthma. Cigarette smoke should be avoided. Take medication prior to exercise. Air filters, air conditioners, and mattress covers can help control dust and allergens. Allergy shots may also prevent attacks if asthma is induced by allergies.

Nutritional Approach:

Disease or Condition: Asthma

Causes of Asthma

There are both allergic and non-allergic causes of asthma. Some allergic triggers result from interactions with animal dander, grass/tree/plant pollen, dust mites, cat and dog hair and urine. Ingesting foods such as milk, peanuts, corn, citrus, wheat, yeast and foods containing sulfites, MSG, food dyes and other food additives prompt allergic causes. Pharmaceutical drugs such as ASA, beta-blockers, estrogen, NSAIDs, PCN also initiate these causes. Non-allergic causes of asthma include stress, air pollution, nutritional deficiencies (magnesium, omega-3 fatty acids, selenium, vitamin B6 and vitamin C), exercise, gastroesophageal reflux (heart burn), infections (upper respiratory), scents, paint fumes, and tobacco, coal, and wood smoke.

Nutritional support:

Foods that have been proven to help with asthma:

Onions, garlic, vegan diet, spinach, avocadoes, organically grown fruits and vegetables, cold water fish including cod, salmon, mackerel, herring and halibut, extra virgin olive oil, flax seed, rosemary, ginger and turmeric.

Avoid foods containing additives or dyes, refined foods, refined carbohydrates, and beverages containing caffeine and refined sugars, milk and other dairy products, meats, and shellfish.

To find out more or to speak to a nutritional counselor for free, just visit us at:
www.CuresForTheBody.com

Nutrients that have been proven to help with asthma:

Supplements containing

- Vitamins B6 and B12[212], magnesium[213], omega-3 fatty acids[214], selenium[215], and vitamin C[216]
- Digestive enzymes, specifically protease, amylase, and lipase[217]
- Antioxidant nutrients, such as vitamin C, may benefit exercise-induced asthma[218]
- Grape seed extract (contains proanthocyanidins or PCOs) inhibits the release of histamine
- Cordyceps[219], Tylophora[220], Coleus[221,222]

Exercises that have been proven to help with asthma:

If asthma is well controlled with appropriate treatment, exercise does not need to be avoided or limited.

Having asthma does not mean you cannot exercise. Many well-known athletes have managed their asthma to successfully compete in their chosen sports.

Basic Asthma Plan:

• Introduce nutrients into regular diet that will specifically target asthma triggers:

–Eating foods high in or supplementing with Essential Fatty Acids, especially omega 3, EFA's. These fatty acids, fats and oils of any kind slow down stomach emptying time and thereby allow more time for the digestion of foods— especially proteins that could cause allergic reactions[223].

–Supplement with vitamin B6[224]. Individuals taking theophylline drugs, commonly used in asthma treatment, should supplement with vitamin B6. Studies have shown that these drugs create a deficiency in this vitamin[225].

–Eat foods high in or supplement with vitamin B12. This vitamin is effective in reducing the incidence of bronchial asthma attacks in individuals who were sensitive to sulfites[226]. Supplementation of vitamin B12 has also been shown to reduce wheezing, improve breathing upon exertion, assist with better sleep, and improve the general condition of those suffering from these asthma symptoms.[227]

–Eat magnesium rich foods or supplement with magnesium. Magnesium deficiency is associated with many diseases including asthma and allergies. Low magnesium may actually be a causative factor in asthma, increasing both wheezing and hyperactivity of the air passages.[228]

•**Take (plant source) digestive enzymes**.

–Completely digested proteins turn into amino acids, which cannot cause allergic reactions[229]. Ingesting plant source digestive enzymes (i.e., protease, lipase, amylase) aids in the digestion of proteins and inhibits their entry into the blood system.

–If taking NSAIDs, consider proteolitic enzymes instead of these drugs. They are a natural way to decrease inflammation without the harmful side effects created by NSAIDs.[230]

• **Replenish probiotics**.

Some asthma patients may exhibit symptoms of Dysbiosis, dysfunctional intestinal microflora, such as flatulence, bloating, intestinal pain and inflammation, cramping, and constipation and/or diarrhea. Dysbiosis typically results in the overgrowth of Candida albicans. The bacteria imbalance can cause problems associated with fungal overgrowth including allergies, food and chemical sensitivities, malabsorption of nutrients, and asthma. The replenishment of probiotics is especially recommended if undergoing treatments of antibiotics.

Attention Deficit/Hyperactivity Disorder (ADHD)

Description: ADHD is poor attention span and/or hyperactivity in children. It is one of the most frequently diagnosed childhood psychiatric conditions.[231] Although controversial, ADHD can be inherited and affects 5-10% of school-aged children. Signs can be typically seen at age three, but must be seen by age seven to meet the criteria for diagnosis.

ADHD adolescents tend to have poor academic achievement, low self-esteem, anxiety, depression, and difficulty learning proper social behavior. Children with ADHD do not outgrow their inattentiveness, but learn to adapt to their environment as adults. It is easier for them to function effectively in a work environment than a structured school environment. However, if left untreated, the risk for alcohol or substance abuse increases.

Children with fetal alcohol syndrome, lead poisoning, meningitis, or genetic resistance to thyroid hormone have a higher incidence of ADHD.[232, 233] Recent research has indicated that ADHD is caused by abnormalities in neurotransmitters, which affects the nerve impulses in the brain.

ADHD may also be affected by the presence of dysbiotic flora, which destroys probiotics (friendly bacteria) in the intestines. This condition, dysbiosis, is linked to immune function, food sensitivities, and ADHD. This is most likely due to the multiple antibiotic treatments children receive in their first five years without replacing the good intestinal bacteria. A study reported that high levels of antimetabolites were found in the urine of ADHD children, which is consistent with *Candida* related complex.[234]

Some researchers are also linking a deficiency in essential fatty acids (EFAs) to the cause of ADHD. EFAs not only affect the development of brain tissue, but also gut permeability. Essential fatty acids are the substrates for prostaglandin synthesis.[235]

Medical Treatment:

Brand name: Ritalin

Drug Name: Methylphenidate

Methylphenidate is a mild central nervous system stimulant. The mode of action in humans is not completely understood, but Ritalin presumably activates the brain stem arousal system and cortex to produce its stimulant effect. There is neither specific evidence which clearly establishes the mechanism whereby Ritalin produces its mental and behavioral effects in children, nor conclusive evidence regarding how these effects relate to the condition of the central nervous system.

Notable Side Effects:

Nervousness and insomnia are the most common, hypersensitivity (including skin rash, urticaria, fever, arthralgia, exfoliative dermatitis, erythema multiforme with histopathological findings of necrotizing vasculitis, and thrombocytopenic purpura); anorexia; nausea; dizziness; palpitations; headache; dyskinesia; drowsiness; blood pressure and pulse changes; tachycardia; angina; cardiac arrhythmia; abdominal pain; weight loss during prolonged therapy. There have been rare reports of Tourette's syndrome. Toxic psychosis has been reported. Although a definite causal relationship has not been established, the following have been reported in patients taking this drug: instances of abnormal liver function, ranging from transaminase elevation to hepatic coma; isolated cases of cerebral arteritis and/or occlusion; leukopenia and/or anemia; transient depressed mood; a few instances of scalp hair loss. In children, loss of appetite, abdominal pain, weight loss during prolonged therapy, insomnia, and tachycardia may occur more frequently; however, any of the other adverse reactions listed above may also occur.

Brand name: Catapres

Drug Name: Clonidine

Clonidine stimulates alpha-adrenoreceptors in the brain stem. This action results in reduced sympathetic outflow from the central nervous system and in decreases in peripheral resistance, renal vascular resistance, heart rate, and blood pressure. Renal blood flow and glomerular filtration rate remain essentially unchanged. Normal postural reflexes are intact; therefore, orthostatic symptoms are mild and infrequent.

Notable Side Effects: dry mouth and drowsiness, fatigue, headache, lethargy and sedation, insomnia, dizziness, impotence/sexual dysfunction, dry throat and constipation, nausea, change in taste and nervousness.

Other common recommendations from Medical Doctors:

Develop a structure or routine and work with the school to implement a plan. A stable, supportive home environment is also essential. Behavior therapy may be necessary with drug treatment.

Nutritional Approach:

Disease or Condition: Attention Deficit Disorder

Causes of Attention Deficit Disorder (without hyperactivity)

Three factors appear to be particularly relevant to learning disabilities; Otitis media (ear infections), nutrient deficiency, heavy metals.

Nutritional support:

Foods that have been proven to help with Attention Deficit Disorder:

Flax seeds/oils, hemp seeds/oils, fatty fish (salmon), a diet rich in vitamins and minerals (whole grains, fresh fruits and vegetables and good fats), food high in tryptophan (brown rice, cottage cheese, turkey and soy protein). Avoid sources of refined sugars and flour.

Nutrients that have been proven to help with Attention Deficit Disorder:

Omega 3 and 6 essential fatty acids[236] (flax, hemp, DHA, borage, and evening primrose oils), multi-vitamin-and-mineral formula[237] (most deficient in magnesium[238], then chromium and zinc), B vitamin complex[239], GABA[240], Iron[241].

Exercises that have been proven to help with Attention Deficit Disorder:

Regular and vigorous exercise can be very helpful for the Attention Deficit Disorder adult. Attention Deficit Disorder adults tend to have addictive personalities. Exercise is a good addiction. Aside from the obvious health benefits, regular exercise is also a great way to release steam and quiet the mind. Some studies also link regular exercise to decreased depression - a condition common with Attention Deficit Disorder adults.

Basic Attention Deficit Disorder Plan:

• Establish optimal nutrition

Several investigators have demonstrated that correction of even subtle nutritional deficiencies exerts a substantial influence on learning and behavior.

–Highly deficient in EFA's (Omega 3 and 6 essential fatty acids). Children with low levels of total omega 3 fatty acids exhibited significantly more behavioral problems, temper tantrums, and learning, health, and sleep problems than did those with high proportions of omega3 fatty acids.

–Flax seeds or oil, Hemp seeds or oil, DHA[242].

–Supplement organic chelated iron back into your diet (make sure it is A.A. chelated and not ferrous sulfate, which does not absorb well).

–High-absorption multi-vitamin-and-mineral formula.

–Whole food vitamins are optimal.

–B vitamins are needed for correct brain function, enhance digestion and adrenal gland function.

–ADD patients are highly deficient in minerals – most significantly magnesium, then chromium and zinc.

–Take "amino acid chelated" minerals only (highest absorption / least toxicity[243]).

–The chief sources of magnesium in the diet are fruits and vegetables.

–Deficiency symptoms include anxiousness, nervousness, restless limbs, and muscle aches.

–Chromium helps in the proper break down of sugars. ADHD patients have difficulty breaking sugars down properly thus, they become a stimulant to them.

–Zinc is required for the conversion of Essential Fatty Acids to Prostiglandins.

–Iron[244] deficiency is the most common nutrient deficiency in American children. Iron deficiency is associated with markedly decreased attentiveness and narrow attention span.

–GABA is an amino acid that acts as a neurotransmitter in the central nervous system. It is essential for brain metabolism, aiding in proper brain function. Its function is to decrease neuron activity and inhibit nerve cells from over-firing. It is formed in the body by glutamic acid.

–Deficient in amino acid tryptophan – precursor to serotonin. Sleep pattern disturbance with ADD.

–Eat brown rice, cottage cheese, turkey and soy protein.

–Take plant source digestive enzymes to aid in digestion[245]. These help alleviate food allergies that are often associated with ADHD.

• **Elimination of any ear infections[246],** although the frequent use of antibiotics has shown additional contributing factors toward ADD called dybiosis (yeast metabolites); subsequently, altering the absorption of nutrients.

–Take Probiotics to re-implant friendly bacteria, especially if no other choice than to take antibiotics. Anti-biotics kill both good and bad bacteria leaving us open to yeast and fungal infections[247].

• **Detection and elimination of any heavy-metal toxicity.**

–N-Acetyl Cysteine (NAC)[248] a sulfur-containing amino acid that is effective agent for chelation and removal of heavy metal toxins from the body.[249]

Back Pain

Description: Back pain, particularly lower back pain, is one of the only conditions that are considered significant even though it is not life threatening. It is the second most common reason for missing work and affects four out of five people at some time in their lives.

Because the nerves connect along the spine, it is easy to compress the nerve roots when the spine is injured. The lower back, where the chest connects to the pelvis and legs to provide mobility and strength for the body, is involved in most daily activities. So not only is it understandable why so many people injure their back with so much use, but it is also understandable why so many people are affected by this injury because it affects so many common daily activities.

Lifting, exercising, or moving abnormally (or just unexpectedly) is one of the most common causes of an injury to the back. It is easier to experience strains and sprains with poor physical condition and weak back muscles. Other contributors to back injuries include poor posture, improper lifting, being overweight, and fatigue.

Lower back pain is the leading cause of disability for people age 19 to 45, and affects half of those 60 years and older.

Medical Treatment:

NSAIDS

Brand name: Advil, Motrin

Drug Name: Ibuprofen

Ibuprofen is a nonsteroidal anti-inflammatory drug (NSAID) that possesses anti-inflammatory, analgesic and antipyretic activity. Its mode of action, like that of other NSAIDs, is not completely understood, but may be related to prostaglandin synthetase inhibition. After absorption of the racemic ibuprofen, the [-]R-enantiomer undergoes interconversion to the [+]S-form. The biological activities of ibuprofen are associated with the [+]S-enantiomer.

To find out more or to speak to a nutritional counselor for free, just visit us at:
www.CuresForTheBody.com

Notable Side Effects:

Cardiovascular system: Edema, fluid retention (generally responds promptly to drug discontinuation).

Digestive system: Nausea, epigastric pain, heartburn, diarrhea, abdominal distress, nausea and vomiting, indigestion, constipation, abdominal cramps or pain, fullness of Gl tract (bloating and flatulence).

Nervous system: Dizziness, headache, nervousness.

Skin and appendages: Rash (including maculopapular type), pruritus.

Special senses: Tinnitus.

Brand name: Aleve, Anaprox

Drug Name: Naproxen

Naproxen is a nonsteroidal anti-inflammatory drug (NSAID) with analgesic and antipyretic properties. The sodium salt of naproxen has been developed as a more rapidly absorbed formulation of naproxen for use as an analgesic. The naproxen anion inhibits prostaglandin synthesis but beyond this its mode of action is unknown.

Notable Side Effects:

Gastrointestinal: Constipation, heartburn, abdominal pain, nausea, dyspepsia, diarrhea, stomatitis.

Central Nervous System: Headache, dizziness, drowsiness, lightheadedness, vertigo.

Dermatologic: Itching (pruritus), skin eruptions, ecchymoses, sweating, purpura.

Special Senses: Tinnitus, hearing disturbances, visual disturbances.

*Cardiovascular:*Edema, dyspnea, palpitations.

General: Thirst.

Muscle Relaxants

Brand name: Soma

Drug Name: Carisoprodol

To find out more or to speak to a nutritional counselor for free, just visit us at:
www.CuresForTheBody.com

Carisoprodol produces muscle relaxation in animals by blocking interneuronal activity in the descending reticular formation and spinal cord.

Notable Side Effects:

Central Nervous System: Drowsiness and other CNS effects may require dosage reduction. Also observed: dizziness, vertigo, ataxia, tremor, agitation, irritability, headache, depressive reactions, syncope, and insomnia.

Allergic or Idiosyncratic: Allergic or idiosyncratic reactions occasionally develop. They are usually seen within the period of the first to fourth dose in patients having had no previous contact with the drug. Skin rash, erythema multiforme, pruritus, eosinophilia, and fixed drug eruption with cross reaction to meprobamate have been reported with carisoprodol. Severe reactions have been manifested by asthmatic episodes, fever, weakness, dizziness, angioneurotic edema, smarting eyes, hypotension, and anaphylactoid shock.

Cardiovascular: Tachycardia, postural hypotension, and facial flushing.

Gastrointestinal: Nausea, vomiting, hiccup, and epigastric distress.

Hematologic: Leukopenia, in which other drugs or viral infection may have been responsible, and pancytopenia, attributed to phenylbutazone, have been reported. No serious blood dyscrasias have been attributed to carisoprodol.

Brand name: Flexeril

Drug Name: Cyclobenzaprine

Cyclobenzaprine relieves skeletal muscle spasm of local origin without interfering with muscle function. It is ineffective in muscle spasm due to central nervous system disease. Cyclobenzaprine reduced or abolished skeletal muscle hyperactivity in several animal models. Animal studies indicate that cyclobenzaprine does not act at the neuromuscular junction or directly on skeletal muscle. Such studies show that cyclobenzaprine acts primarily within the central nervous system at the brain stem as opposed to spinal cord levels, although its action on the latter may contribute to its overall skeletal muscle relaxant activity. Evidence suggests that the net effect of cyclobenzaprine is a reduction of tonic somatic motor activity, influencing both gamma ((gamma)) and alpha ((alpha)) motor systems.

Notable Side Effects:

Drowsiness, dry mouth, dizziness.

Brand name: Valium

Drug Name: Diazepam

Diazepam appears to act on parts of the limbic system, the thalamus and hypothalamus, and induces calming effects. Valium, unlike chlorpromazine and reserpine, has no demonstrable peripheral autonomic blocking action, nor does it produce extrapyramidal side effects; however, animals treated with Valium do have a transient ataxia at higher doses.

Notable Side Effects:

Most commonly reported were drowsiness, fatigue and ataxia. Infrequently encountered were confusion, constipation, depression, diplopia, dysarthria, headache, hypotension, incontinence, jaundice, changes in libido, nausea, changes in salivation, skin rash, slurred speech, tremor, urinary retention, vertigo and blurred vision. Paradoxical reactions such as acute hyperexcited states, anxiety, hallucinations, increased muscle spasticity, insomnia, rage, sleep disturbances and stimulation have been reported; should these occur, use of the drug should be discontinued.

Other common recommendations from Medical Doctors: To prevent lower back pain, good posture and sitting in chairs with good low back support are important. Learn to lift properly with the knees bent and shoulders back; lift with your legs. Do not sit or stand in one position for long periods of time. Sleep on a firm mattress in a comfortable position, and use pillows for support if necessary. It is important to exercise regularly to reduce the occurrences of low back pain. Exercise improves the body's conditioning and strengthens the low back muscle, which makes it better able to withstand strain. Exercise also stabilizes the spine, improves bone density, and helps you to maintain a desired weight.

To find out more or to speak to a nutritional counselor for free, just visit us at:
www.CuresForTheBody.com

If the back is injured, bed rest, heat or cold, massage, acupuncture, and chiropractic massage can help to ease the pain. Then perform only light activities and/or physical therapy until the back is healed (usually 1-2 weeks).

Nutritional Approach:

Disease or Condition: Back Pain

Causes of Back Pain

Back pain is the one of the most common conditions treated by orthopedic surgeons. Eighty percent of adults experience back pain at some time.[250] Following colds and flu, it is the most common cause of lost work days in adults under the age of 45. Back pain can be caused by a number of factors. The most common causes of back pain include strains, sprains, arthritis, degenerative disc disease, herniated discs, scoliosis and osteoporosis. Less common causes include cancers and tumors of the spine and spinal cord. Factors that contribute to the instability of the back include smoking, increased body weight, and poor nutritional habits.

It is important to review options for conservative, non-surgical treatment since many people with chronic back pain are poor candidates for surgery or fail to benefit from surgery. Many of the surgical procedures are ineffective, with patients reporting no improvement or increased pain after healing from the procedures.[251]

Also see Cancer
Also see Osteoporosis
Also see Osteoarthritis (arthritis)

Nutritional support

Foods that have been proven to help with Back Pain:

Fish containing high amounts of Omega-3 Fatty Acids. Deficiencies in essential fats promote tissue inflammation.[252] Increase consumption of foods that reduce inflammation including fruits, vegetables, fish, ginger, whole grains, focusing on foods rich in antioxidants.

Nutrients that have been proven to help with back pain:

Methyl Sulfonyl Methane (MSM) has many therapeutic benefits in reducing pain is arthritis, muscle soreness, and back pain from herniated disc.[253] Glucosamine[254] and Chondroitin Sulfate[255] help to reduce pain associated with osteoarthritis. Proteolytic enzymes reduce inflammation and show a tremendous benefit over NSAIDS because they don't create more damage[256]. A special form of manganese was used in an animal study with phenomenal results with discs.[257]

There are many nutrients that reduce soft tissue inflammation, such as bromelain.[258]

Pre-surgical administration increases the healing of pain and inflammation.[259,260] Vitamin B1, Vitamin B6, Vitamin B12, Vitamin C, and Caynne pepper reduce pain.[261]

Exercises that have been proven to help with Back Pain:

You can minimize problems with back pain with exercises that make the muscles in your back, stomach, hips and thighs strong and flexible. Some people keep in good physical condition by being active in recreational activities like running, walking, bike riding, and swimming. In addition to these conditioning activities, there are specific exercises that are directed toward strengthening and stretching your back, stomach, hip and thigh muscles.

Focus on stretching hamstrings and tightening abdominals daily.

Basic Back Pain Plan:

• Maintain proper posture. According to the National Institute of Neurological Disorders and Stroke, sit in a chair with a good lumbar support, proper positioning and height. Add a small rolled towel to the small of your back for additional lumbar support. Keep the shoulders back and change positions frequently. When standing, do not slouch.

• Stretch before and after exercising.

• Maintain a healthy body weight. Increased body weight can alter the biomechanics causing stress on the back and predisposing it to injuries. Eat a well balanced diet. According to the American Obesity Association, obesity aggravates simple low back problems and contributes to recurring conditions.

To find out more or to speak to a nutritional counselor for free, just visit us at:
www.CuresForTheBody.com

• Avoid eating red meats, peanuts, foods with caffeine, fried foods, and alcohol.

• Wear low heeled comfortable shoes.

• Chiropractic care; Chiropractic care for patients with low back pain is superior to medical care in terms of scientific evidence of effectiveness, cost, safety, and patient satisfaction.[262] Manipulation is the most effective form of treatment for cervical, thoracic, or lumbar spine dysfunction.[263]

• Avoid smoking. There is a significant association between smoking and lower back pain.[264] Smoking has been associated in causing malnutrition of spinal discs; creating mechanical stress.[265] It also reduces blood flow to the lower spine and causes the discs to degenerate.

Bladder Infections/Urinary Tract Infections (UTI)

Description: In a healthy individual, urine is sterile and contains no bacteria or other infectious organisms. In addition, the channel contains little to no bacteria, as the urine has a low pH and high concentration of urea, which inhibit or kill bacteria. The body usually flushes bacteria out when the bladder is emptied. Bacteria can enter the urinary tract through one of two ways, ascending through the opening of the urethra (blockage from kidney stone, sexual intercourse, leaking valve between the ureter and bladder) or descending through the bloodstream (septicemia, infective endocarditis). Descending UTI's are much less common (about 5%).

UTI's are usually caused by bacteria (85%), but can also be caused by viruses, parasites, and fungi. They are 50 times more common in women than in men between the ages of 20 and 50 years old, probably due to the shorter urethra in their anatomy. Approximately 20% of women suffer from at least one UTI's at some time in their lives.[266]

UTI's can be usually be found in the urethra (urethritis), the bladder (cystitis), the prostate in men (prastatitis), and kidneys (pyelonephritis). Infections in the lower urinary tract, urethritis and cystitis, are the most common. UTI's are usually recognized by painful, burning urination, and a frequent urge to urinate. The urine may be cloudy and contain blood.

Medical Treatment:

Brand name: Bactrim, Septra

Drug Name:Trimethoprim-sulfamethoxazole

Trimethoprim-sulfamethoxazole is a synthetic antibacterial combination product. It is highly effective against most aerobic enteric bacteria except *Pseudomonas aeruginosa*.

Notable Side Effects:

The most common adverse effects are gastrointestinal disturbances (nausea, vomiting, anorexia) and allergic skin reactions (such as rash and urticaria).

Hematologic: Agranulocytosis, aplastic anemia, thrombocytopenia, leukopenia, neutropenia, hemolytic anemia, megaloblastic anemia, hypoprothrombinemia, methemoglobinemia, eosinophilia.

Allergic: Stevens-Johnson syndrome, toxic epidermal necrolysis, anaphylaxis, allergic myocarditis, erythema multiforme, exfoliative dermatitis, angioedema, drug fever, chills, Henoch-Schönlein purpura, serum sickness-like syndrome, generalized allergic reactions, generalized skin eruptions, photosensitivity, conjunctival and scleral injection, pruritus, urticaria, and rash. In addition, periarteritis nodosa and systemic lupus erythematosus have been reported.

Gastrointestinal: Hepatitis, including cholestatic jaundice and hepatic necrosis, elevation of serum transaminase and bilirubin, pseudomembranous enterocolitis, pancreatitis, stomatitis, glossitis, nausea, emesis, abdominal pain, diarrhea, anorexia.

Genitourinary: Renal failure, interstitial nephritis, BUN and serum creatinine elevation, toxic nephrosis with oliguria and anuria, and crystalluria.

Metabolic: Hyperkalemia, hyponatremia.

Neurologic: Aseptic meningitis, convulsions, peripheral neuritis, ataxia, vertigo, tinnitus, headache.

Psychiatric: Hallucinations, depression, apathy, nervousness.

Endocrine: The sulfonamides bear certain chemical similarities to some goitrogens, diuretics (acetazolamide and the thiazides), and oral hypoglycemic agents. Cross-sensitivity may exist with these agents. Diuresis and hypoglycemia have occurred rarely in patients receiving sulfonamides.

Musculoskeletal: Arthralgia and myalgia.

Respiratory System: Cough, shortness of breath, and pulmonary infiltrates.

Miscellaneous: Weakness, fatigue, insomnia.

As with all anti-biotics, you risk the chance of becoming resistant to the anti-biotic and creating super germs that are even harder to get rid of (see chapter 2 for more details).

Brand name: Furadantin, Macrodantin

Drug Name: Nitrofurantoin

Nitrofurantoin is bactericidal in urine at therapeutic doses. The mechanism of the antimicrobial action of nitrofurantoin is unusual among antibacterials. Nitrofurantoin is reduced by bacterial flavoproteins to reactive intermediates which inactivate or alter bacterial ribosomal proteins and other macromolecules. As a result of such inactivations, the vital biochemical processes of protein synthesis, aerobic energy metabolism, DNA synthesis, RNA synthesis, and cell wall synthesis are inhibited. The broad-based nature of this mode of action may explain the lack of acquired bacterial resistance to nitrofurantoin, as the necessary multiple and simultaneous mutations of the target macromolecules would likely be lethal to the bacteria. Development of resistance to nitrofurantoin has not been a significant problem since its introduction in 1953. Cross-resistance with antibiotics and sulfonamides has not been observed, and transferable resistance is, at most, a very rare phenomenon.

Notable Side Effects:

Pulmonary sensitivity reactions. In subacute pulmonary reactions, fever and eosinophilia occur less often than in the acute form. Upon cessation of therapy, recovery may require several months. If the symptoms are not recognized as being drug-related and nitrofurantoin therapy is not stopped, the symptoms may become more severe. Acute pulmonary reactions are commonly manifested by fever, chills, cough, chest pain, dyspnea, pulmonary infiltration with consolidation or pleural effusion on x-ray, and eosinophilia. Cyanosis has been reported rarely.

Hepatic reactions: hepatitis, cholestatic jaundice, chronic active hepatitis, and hepatic necrosis, occur rarely.

Neurologic: Peripheral neuropathy, Fatalities, renal impairment, anemia, diabetes mellitus, electrolyte imbalance, vitamin B deficiency, and debilitating diseases may increase the possibility of peripheral neuropathy, Asthenia, vertigo, nystagmus, dizziness, headache, and drowsiness.

Dermatologic: Transient alopecia also has been reported.

Allergic: A lupus-like syndrome associated with pulmonary reactions to nitrofurantoin. Also, angioedema; maculopapular, erythematous, or eczematous eruptions; pruritus; urticaria; anaphylaxis; arthralgia; myalgia; drug fever; and chills have been reported.

Gastrointestinal: Nausea, emesis, and anorexia occur most often. Abdominal pain and diarrhea are less common gastrointestinal reactions. Sialadenitis and pancreatitis have been reported.

Miscellaneous: Superinfections caused by resistant organisms, e.g., *Pseudomonas* species or *Candida* species, can occur.

Laboratory Adverse Events: Increased AST (SGOT), increased ALT (SGPT), decreased hemoglobin, increased serum phosphorus, eosinophilia, glucose-6-phosphate dehydrogenase deficiency anemia, agranulocytosis, leukopenia, granulocytopenia, hemolytic anemia, thrombocytopenia, megaloblastic anemia. **As with all antibiotics, you risk the chance of becoming resistant to the anti-biotic and creating super germs that are even harder to get rid of (see chapter 2 for more details).**

Brand name: Zithromax

Drug Name: Azithromycin

Azithromycin acts by binding to the 50S ribosomal subunit of susceptible microorganisms and, thus, interfering with microbial protein synthesis. Nucleic acid synthesis is not affected. Azithromycin concentrates in phagocytes and fibroblasts as demonstrated by *in vitro* incubation techniques. Using such methodology, the ratio of intracellular to extracellular concentration was >30 after one hour incubation. *In vivo* studies suggest that concentration in phagocytes may contribute to drug distribution to inflamed tissues.

To find out more or to speak to a nutritional counselor for free, just visit us at:
www.CuresForTheBody.com

Notable Side Effects:

Most common include nausea, vomiting, diarrhea, or abdominal pain. **As with all anti-biotics, you risk the chance of becoming resistant to the anti-biotic and creating super germs that are even harder to get rid of (see chapter 2 for more details).**

Brand name: Monurol

Drug Name: Fosfomycin

Fosfomycin has *in vitro* activity against a broad range of gram-positive and gram-negative aerobic microorganisms which are associated with uncomplicated urinary tract infections. Fosfomycin is bactericidal in urine at therapeutic doses. The bactericidal action of fosfomycin is due to its inactivation of the enzyme enolpyruvyl transferase, thereby irreversibly blocking the condensation of uridine diphosphate-N-acetylglucosamine with p-enolpyruvate, one of the first steps in bacterial cell wall synthesis. It also reduces adherence of bacteria to uroepithelial cells.

Notable Side Effects:

Diarrhea, vaginitis, nausea, headache, dizziness, asthenia, dyspepsia. **As with all anti-biotics, you risk the chance of becoming resistant to the anti-biotic and creating super germs that are even harder to get rid of (see chapter 2 for more details).**

Other common recommendations from Medical Doctors: There are some measures you can take to prevent the occurrence or recurrence of urinary tract infections. Cranberry juice inhibits bacterial growth and also makes the urine more acid, making it less hospitable for bacteria. Drinking more fluids, urinating often, and completely emptying the bladder encourages the flushing of the urinary tract. For women, urinating after sexual intercourse and avoiding spermicides with a diaphragm can also help.

Nutritional Approach:

Disease or Condition: Bladder infection

Causes of bladder infection

To find out more or to speak to a nutritional counselor for free, just visit us at:
www.CuresForTheBody.com

Infection by microbes, mainly bacteria. In men, these symptoms are usually due to an enlarged prostate gland.

Nutritional support

Foods that have been proven to help with bladder infections:
Drink at least 2 quarts of liquids daily.
Cranberry juice has been proven to help with bladder infections[267].
Blueberries, garlic, vegetables.

Nutrients that have been proven to help with bladder infection:
Cranberry in capsules[268] Marshmallow root [269] Probiotics[270,271]

Exercises that have been proven to help with Bladder Infection:

Many studies have shown that an increase in exercise will promote a healthy immune system. With a stronger immune system your body will be able to fight off bacteria and certain viruses better than people who do little or no exercise. Also, studies have shown that exercise can help reduce the chance that a person becomes sick.[272]

Basic Bladder Infection Plan:

• **Drink at least 2 quarts of liquids daily (8 oz./ hour) especially:**

–Pure unsweetened cranberry juice. New findings show that cranberries and blueberries contain unique compounds that block infectious bacteria from clinging to the cells lining the urinary tract and bladder. For years physicians thought they worked by increasing urine acidity. If juice is not available buy cranberry in capsules[273].

• **Increasing the amount of vitamin C in your diet will make your urine more acidic, causing bacteria in it to multiply less rapidly.**

–guava, red and green sweet bell peppers, cantaloupe, papaya, strawberries, Brussels sprouts, and kiwi. Avoid citrus fruit; these produce alkaline urine that encourages bacterial growth.

To find out more or to speak to a nutritional counselor for free, just visit us at:
www.CuresForTheBody.com

• **Probiotics if antibiotic therapy is required. Antibiotics kill good and bad bacteria. To prevent yeast infections and boost your second immune system rapidly, supplement with Probiotics**[274]**.**

•**Avoid: Caffeine. It causes the muscles around the bladder neck to contract, and can cause painful bladder spasms.**[275]

Cancer

Description: Cancer is a group of cells that has uncontrolled growth. It can develop in tissue from any organ and destroys the surrounding tissue. This group of cells becomes a tumor (abnormal growth or mass) and can spread from the initial site throughout the body.

Cancer first begins when the DNA changes in the cell's genetic material. This change can occur spontaneously, or can be caused by a carcinogen (substance that causes cancer). This process is called initiation. Carcinogens include chemicals, tobacco, viruses, radiation, sunlight, etc. Some cells are more susceptible to carcinogens due to genetics or chronic irritation.

Once a cell has changed genetically (during the initiation process), it is then susceptible to the next phase of cancer, promotion. During this process, environmental substances or drugs (promoters) then cause those cells to become cancerous. It is important to note that a cell does not become cancerous from just promoters, but must be acted upon by carcinogens first. However, some carcinogens are powerful enough to cause cancer by themselves, such as ionizing radiation from x-rays, nuclear power plants, and atomic bombs.

There are several risk factors for developing cancer. Genetics affect the risk of cancer because of a gene(s) or an abnormal chromosome. Certain types of cancer are also age related. Young children experience some types of cancer more often (bone, smooth muscle in the intestines). Most cancers are more common as you age, probably due to exposure to carcinogens and a weakened immune system. Environmental factors can also increase the risk of cancer. Pollution, cigarette smoke, chemicals, ultraviolet radiation (sunlight), and ionizing radiation are all contributors to cancer. Certain foods can increase the risk for cancer. Alcohol, tobacco, a high consumption of fats, smoked foods, pickled foods, and barbecued meats are also linked to specific types of cancer.

There is a much better chance of curing cancer if it is treated early. For this reason, it is important to be aware of the warning signs, especially if you experience some of the risk factors. Some of the warning signs include: weight loss, fatigue, night sweats, loss of appetite, new and persistent pain, recurrent nausea or vomiting, blood in urine or stool, enlarged lymph nodes.

Medical Treatment:

Alkylating Agents:

Form chemical bond with DNA, causing breaks in DNA and errors in replication of DNA

Brand name: Leukeran

Drug Name: Chlorambucil

Chlorambucil is a bifunctional alkylating agent of the nitrogen mustard type that has been found active against selected human neoplastic diseases. Chlorambucil is known chemically as 4-[bis(2-chlorethyl)amino] benzenebutanoic acid. Chlorambucil is extensively metabolized in the liver primarily to phenylacetic acid mustard, which has antineoplastic activity. Chlorambucil and its major metabolite spontaneously degrade in vivo forming monohydroxy and dihydroxy derivatives. After a single dose of radiolabeled chlorambucil (^{14}C), approximately 15% to 60% of the radioactivity appears in the urine after 24 hours. Again, less than 1% of the urinary radioactivity is in the form of chlorambucil or phenylacetic acid mustard. In summary, the pharmacokinetic data suggest that oral chlorambucil undergoes rapid gastrointestinal absorption and plasma clearance and that it is almost completely metabolized, having extremely low urinary excretion.

Notable Side Effects:

Hematologic: The most common side effect is bone marrow suppression.

Gastrointestinal: Nausea and vomiting, diarrhea, and oral ulceration occur infrequently.

CNS: Tremors, muscular twitching, myoclonia, confusion, agitation, ataxia, flaccid paresis, and hallucinations have been reported as rare adverse experiences to chlorambucil which resolve upon discontinuation of drug. Rare, focal and/or generalized seizures have been reported to occur in both children and adults at both therapeutic daily doses and pulse-dosing regimens, and in acute overdose.

Dermatologic: Allergic reactions such as urticaria and angioneurotic edema. Skin hypersensitivity (including rare reports of skin rash progressing to erythema multiforme, toxic epidermal necrolysis, and Stevens-Johnson syndrome).

Miscellaneous: Pulmonary fibrosis, hepatotoxicity and jaundice, drug fever, peripheral neuropathy, interstitial pneumonia, sterile cystitis, infertility, leukemia, and secondary malignancies.

Brand name: Alkeran

Drug Name: Melphalan

Melphalan is an alkylating agent of the bischloroethylamine type. As a result, its cytotoxicity appears to be related to the extent of its interstrand cross-linking with DNA, probably by binding at the N^7 position of guanine. Like other bifunctional alkylating agents, it is active against both resting and rapidly dividing tumor cells.

Notable Side Effects:

Hematologic: The most common side effect is bone marrow suppression.

Gastrointestinal: Nausea and vomiting, diarrhea, and oral ulceration occur infrequently. Hepatic disorders ranging from abnormal liver function tests to clinical manifestations such as hepatitis and jaundice.

Miscellaneous: Pulmonary fibrosis and interstitial pneumonitis, skin hypersensitivity, vasculitis, alopecia, and hemolytic anemia. Allergic reactions, including rare anaphylaxis, have occurred after multiple courses of treatment.

Antimetabolites:

Block synthesis of DNA

Brand name: Trexall

Drug Name: Methotrexate

   Methotrexate inhibits dihydrofolic acid reductase. Dihydrofolates must be reduced to tetrahydrofolates by this enzyme before they can be utilized as carriers of one-carbon groups in the synthesis of purine nucleotides and thymidylate. Therefore, methotrexate interferes with DNA synthesis, repair, and cellular replication. Actively proliferating tissues such as malignant cells, bone marrow, fetal cells, buccal and intestinal mucosa, and cells of the urinary bladder are in general more sensitive to this effect of methotrexate. When cellular proliferation in malignant tissues is greater than in most normal tissues, methotrexate may impair malignant growth without irreversible damage to normal tissues.

Notable Side Effects:

The most frequently reported adverse reactions include ulcerative stomatitis, leukopenia, nausea, and abdominal distress. Other frequently reported adverse effects are malaise, undue fatigue, chills and fever, dizziness and decreased resistance to infection. Other adverse reactions that have been reported with methotrexate are listed below by organ system.

Alimentary System: Gingivitis, pharyngitis, stomatitis, anorexia, nausea, vomiting, diarrhea, hematemesis, melena, gastrointestinal ulceration and bleeding, enteritis, pancreatitis.

Blood and Lymphatic System Disorders: Suppressed hematopoiesis causing anemia, aplastic anemia, leukopenia and/or thrombocytopenia. Hypogammaglobulinemia has been reported rarely.

Cardiovascular: Pericarditis, pericardial effusion, hypotension, and thromboembolic events (including arterial thrombosis, cerebral thrombosis, deep vein thrombosis, retinal vein thrombosis, thrombophlebitis, and pulmonary embolus).

Central Nervous System: Headaches, drowsiness, blurred vision, transient blindness, speech impairment including dysarthria and aphasia, hemiparesis, paresis and convulsions have also occurred following administration of methotrexate.

Infection: sometimes fatal opportunistic infections. *Pneumocystis carinii* pneumonia was the most common infection. Other reported infections included sepsis, nocardiosis; histoplasmosis, cryptococcosis, *Herpes zoster,* *H. simplex* hepatitis, and disseminated *H. simplex* .

Musculoskeletal System: Stress fracture.

Ophthalmic: Conjunctivitis, serious visual changes of unknown etiology.

Pulmonary System: Respiratory fibrosis, respiratory failure, interstitial pneumonitis deaths, and chronic interstitial obstructive pulmonary disease have occasionally occurred.

Skin: Erythematous rashes, pruritus, urticaria, photosensitivity, pigmentary changes, alopecia, ecchymosis, telangiectasia, acne, furunculosis, erythema multiforme, toxic epidermal necrolysis, Stevens-Johnson syndrome, skin necrosis, skin ulceration, and exfoliative dermatitis.

Urogenital System: Severe nephropathy or renal failure, azotemia, cystitis, hematuria; defective oogenesis or spermatogenesis, transient oligospermia, menstrual dysfunction, vaginal discharge, and gynecomastia; infertility, abortion, fetal defects.

Antimototics:

Block division of cancer cells.

Brand name: Navelbine

Drug Name: Vinorelbine

Vinorelbine is a vinca alkaloid that interferes with microtubule assembly. The vinca alkaloids are structurally similar compounds comprised of 2 multiringed units, vindoline and catharanthine. Unlike other vinca alkaloids, the catharanthine unit is the site of structural modification for vinorelbine. The antitumor activity of vinorelbine is thought to be due primarily to inhibition of mitosis at metaphase through its interaction with tubulin. Like other vinca alkaloids, vinorelbine may also interfere with: 1) amino acid, cyclic AMP, and glutathione metabolism, 2) calmodulin-dependent Ca^{++}-transport ATPase activity, 3) cellular respiration, and 4) nucleic acid and lipid biosynthesis. In intact tectal plates from mouse embryos, vinorelbine, vincristine, and vinblastine inhibited mitotic microtubule formation at the same concentration (2 µM), inducing a blockade of cells at metaphase. Vincristine produced depolymerization of axonal microtubules at 5 µM, but vinblastine and vinorelbine did not have this effect until concentrations of

30 µM and 40 µM, respectively. These data suggest relative selectivity of vinorelbine for mitotic microtubules.

Notable Side Effects:

Bone marrow: Granulocytopenia, leucopenia, thrombocytopenia, anemia.

General: Asthenia, injection site reactions, injection site pain, phlebitis.

Digestive: Nausea, vomiting, constipation, diarrhea, peripheral neuropathy, dyspnea, alopecia.

Topoisomerase Inhibitors:

Prevent DNA synthesis and repair through blockage of enzymes called topoisomerases.

Brand name: Adriamycin

Drug Name: Doxorubicin

Doxorubicin produces regression in disseminated neoplastic conditions such as acute lymphoblastic leukemia, acute myeloblastic leukemia, Wilms' tumor, neuroblastoma, soft tissue and bone sarcomas, breast carcinoma, ovarian carcinoma, transitional cell bladder carcinoma, thyroid carcinoma, gastric carcinoma, Hodgkin's disease, malignant lymphoma and bronchogenic carcinoma in which the small cell histologic type is the most responsive compared to other cell types.

Notable Side Effects:

Cardiotoxicity.

Cutaneous: Reversible complete alopecia occurs in most cases. Hyperpigmentation of nailbeds and dermal creases, primarily in children, and onycholysis have been reported in a few cases. Recall of skin reaction due to prior radiotherapy has occurred with doxorubicin administration.

Gastrointestinal: Acute nausea and vomiting occurs frequently and may be severe. Mucositis (stomatitis and esophagitis). The effect may leading to ulceration and represents a site of origin for severe infections. Ulceration and necrosis of the colon, especially the cecum, may occur leading to bleeding or severe infections which can be fatal. Anorexia and diarrhea have been occasionally reported.

Vascular: Phlebosclerosis. Facial flushing.

Local: Severe cellulitis, vesication and tissue necrosis will occur if extravasation of doxorubicin occurs during administration. Erythematous streaking along the vein proximal to the site of the injection.

Hematologic: The occurrence of secondary acute myeloid leukemia with or without a preleukemic phase has been reported in patients concurrently treated with doxorubicin in association with DNA-damaging antineoplastic agents. Such cases could have a short (1-3 years) latency period. Pediatric patients are also at risk of developing secondary acute myeloid leukemia.

Hypersensitivity: Fever, chills, and urticaria have been reported occasionally. Anaphylaxis may occur. A case of apparent cross-sensitivity to lincomycin has been reported.

Other: Conjunctivitis and lacrimation occur rarely.

Brand name: Camptosar

Drug Name: Irinotecan

Irinotecan is a derivative of camptothecin. Camptothecins interact specifically with the enzyme topoisomerase I which relieves torsional strain in DNA by inducing reversible single-strand breaks. Irinotecan and its active metabolite SN-38 bind to the topoisomerase I-DNA complex and prevent religation of these single-strand breaks. Current research suggests that the cytotoxicity of irinotecan is due to double-strand DNA damage produced during DNA synthesis when replication enzymes interact with the ternary complex formed by topoisomerase I, DNA, and either irinotecan or SN-38. Mammalian cells cannot efficiently repair these double-strand breaks.

Notable Side Effects:

The most clinically significant adverse events for patients receiving irinotecan-based therapy were diarrhea, nausea, vomiting, neutropenia, and alopecia. The most clinically significant adverse events for patients receiving 5-FU/LV therapy were diarrhea, neutropenia, neutropenic fever, and mucositis. Other significant reactions include the following.

Gastrointestinal: Diarrhea, nausea, abdominal pain, vomiting, anorexia, constipation, mucositis.

Hematologic: Neutropenia, leucopenia, anemia, neutropenic fever, thrombocytopenia, neutropenic infection.

Body as a whole: Asthenia, pain, fever, infection.

Metabolic & nutritional: Up bilirubin.

Dermatologic: Exfoliative dermatitis, rash, alopecia (complete hair loss).

Respiratory: Dyspnea, cough, pneumonia.

Neurologic: Dizziness, somnolence, confusion.

Cardiovascular: Vasodilation, hypotension, thromboembolic events (Includes angina pectoris, arterial thrombosis, cerebral infarct, cerebrovascular accident, deep thrombophlebitis, embolus lower extremity, heart arrest, myocardial infarct, myocardial ischemia, peripheral vascular disorder, pulmonary embolus, sudden death, thrombophlebitis, thrombosis, vascular disorder).

Platinum Derivatives:

Form bonds with DNA causing breaks.

Brand name: Paraplatin

Drug Name: Carboplatin

Carboplatin produces predominantly interstrand DNA cross-links rather than DNA-protein cross-links. This effect is apparently cell-cycle nonspecific. The aquation of carboplatin, which is thought to produce the active species, occurs at a slower rate than in the case of cisplatin. Despite this difference, it appears that both carboplatin and cisplatin induce equal numbers of drug-DNA cross-links, causing equivalent lesions and biological effects. The differences in potencies for carboplatin and cisplatin appear to be directly related to the difference in aquation rates.

Notable Side Effects:

Bone marrow: Thrombocytopenia, neutropenia, leucopenia, anemia, infections, bleeding, transfusions.

Gastrointestinal: Nausea and vomiting, vomiting.

Neurologic: Peripheral neuropathies, ototoxicity, central neurotoxicity.

Renal: Serum creatinine elevations, blood urea elevations.

Hepatic: Bilirubin elevations, SGOT elevations, alkaline phosphatase elevations.

Electrolytes loss: Sodium, potassium, calcium, magnesium.

Other side effects: Pain, asthenia, cardiovascular, respiratory, allergic, genitourinary, alopecia, mucositis.

Other common recommendations from Medical Doctors: To prevent cancer, be aware of your risk factors and screen yourself often if you have a risk for certain types of cancer. Also, be aware of the warning signs of cancer so you can share them with your health practitioner. Overall, you should avoid smoking and tobacco smoke, prolonged exposure to sunlight without protection, and other known carcinogens. You can also limit your intake of high-fat meats and dairy products, increase your intake of fruits and vegetables, exercise, and maintain a healthy weight.

If you have cancer, surgery is usually the most effective method of removal. Most often surgery will be combined with other types of treatment, such as radiation and chemotherapy.

Nutritional Approach:

Disease or Condition: Cancer

Causes of Cancer

1- Lifestyle risk factors: Food, smoking, alcohol, medications.

2- Environmental risk factors: Toxins, pollutions, chemicals

Nutritional support

Foods that have been proven to help with Cancer:

Foods that prevent Cancer: Notably garlic, broccoli, cabbage, soybeans, onions, carrots, tomatoes, all green and yellow vegetables; fruits, especially citrus; fatty fish, flax oils, (omega 3 essential fatty acids), and low-fat or non-fat milk.

Foods that may thwart the spread of cancer: Seafood, garlic, cruciferous vegetables (such as broccoli, cabbage and collard greens).

To find out more or to speak to a nutritional counselor for free, just visit us at:
www.CuresForTheBody.com

<u>Avoid foods that may encourage cancer:</u>   Meat, animal fat and polyunsaturated corn oil, and caffeine[276].

Nutrients that have been proven to help with Cancer:

Garlic[277], Vitamins; C[278], A and E[279]; Omega 3 fatty acids[280]; Probiotics[281]; and Plant source digestive enzymes[282]; Minerals[283]; magnesium, iron, copper, zinc, and selenium.

Exercises that have been proven to help with Cancer:

Evidence seems to support the benefits of exercise as a treatment for cancer. Several studies have examined the relationship between exercise, rehabilitation and quality of life in cancer patients and reported positive findings.

These studies have found that overall; exercise had a positive effect on physical and psychological functioning of cancer patients while in treatment.[284]

Basic Cancer Plan:

What people eat who don't get cancer:

• **They are vegetarians or semi-vegetarian (allowing for some seafood).**

–Favor oily fish like mackerel and salmon (brimming with the omega 3 fatty acids that block cancer) over leaner fish.

–If not much of a fish lover then eat flax seeds and oils (for the essential omega 3 fatty acids).

–Avoid meat and high-saturated–fat animal and dairy foods like cheese and whole milk[285].

–Avoid heavily salted and cured meats.

–If eat meat only turkey breast without the skin – never smoked cured meats like bacon and salami.

–Eat greens and fruits heavily[286], along with cereal brans, notably wheat bran and dried beans, which are high in fiber[287] and nutrients.

The evidence is so overwhelming that Dr. Block, Ph.D., of the University of California at Berkeley, who had done a review of 170 studies from seventeen nations,

To find out more or to speak to a nutritional counselor for free, just visit us at:
www.CuresForTheBody.com

views fruits and vegetables as a powerful preventative drug that could substantially wipe out the scourge of cancer, just as cleaning up the water supply eliminated past epidemics, such as cholera.

- A diet high in fiber (25-35 gm), fruits, and vegetables can detoxify the body in cancer's initial stages. It is thought that certain compounds found in berries, citrus, grapes, walnuts, and caraway also improve prognosis.

–Helps prevent stomach, intestinal and possibly lung cancer: Broccoli[288], soy[289], cabbage, cauliflower, Brussels sprouts, and sauerkraut.

–Fruit in general: lettuce, onions, tomatoes, celery, squash— especially raw vegetables.

–Helps prevent colon cancer: Cruciferous vegetables and carrots.

–Helps prevent lung cancer: Carrots and green leafy vegetables.

–Helps prevent intestinal, uterine, and tongue cancer: Carrots, onions, white cabbage and beets.

–Helps prevent breast cancer: The cabbage family, root vegetables, lettuce, and cucumbers.

–Helps prevent esophageal, oral and pharyngeal cancers: Fruit.

–Helps prevent laryngeal cancer: Fruit and vegetables.

–Helps prevent pancreatic cancer: Fruits and vegetables.

–Helps prevent bladder cancer: Vegetables, specifically carrots, and fruit.

–Helps prevent thyroid cancer: Cruciferous vegetables.

– Helps slow nitrosamine formation: Tomatoes, strawberries, pineapple, and hot peppers.

• **Eat Flax Seeds**

–Lignans in Flax seeds are cyclic molecules with anti-viral, anti-fungal, anti-bacterial, and anti-cancer properties.

–Fresh ground flax seed (the oil has only 2% lignans) 6-8 Tbls. Maximum / day.

–Note: take freshly ground flax seed with five times its volume of fluid, because it absorbs that much liquid.

•Eat healthy fats:

–Olive oil and canola, an omega 9 fatty acid (not essential fatty acids), or fish and flax oils, omega 3 fatty acids (an essential fatty acid), and hemp oil which is perfectly balanced Omega 3 and 6 essential fatty acid, are the right oils and help prevent and fight cancer.

–Use raw coconut oil in baking rather than shortening or butter[290]. Lauric Acid is antibacterial[291]. Coconut oil also lowers cholesterol according to a report in the Journal of Nutrition 2001about the consmption of fat rich in lauric acid vs. fat rich in trans-fatty acids.

–Raw coconut oil was deemed guilty by association when all saturated fats were lumped in one and deemed bad for you. This great food sources is now making a come back.

–Flax oil (the favored of cancer research), is an essential fatty acid means our body needs it but cannot manufacture. Therefore, we can only obtain it from the diet. Omega 3 and 6 fatty acids are essential. However, our diets tend to be too high in omega 6 and not enough omega 3. Too much omega 6 without balancing it with omega 3 is undesirable. Get this balance with fish, flax and hemp. *Caution;* never cook with these oils. Their goodness is destroyed by light, oxygen and heat. The seeds can be stored 1 year but the oil only 3 months if not kept from light, oxygen and heat.

• If you won't eat your essential fatty acids, then take a high quality supplement.

–Pay attention to expiration dates, as essential fatty acids are very fragile and go rancid quickly when exposed to light, oxygen and heat[292].

• Take Lipase enzymes to properly digest fats.[293] (Use only plant source digestive enzyme.)

• Eat heavy, grainy bread without butter or margarine.

• For fats, olive, canola (to cook with) and flax oil (the favored of cancer research).

To find out more or to speak to a nutritional counselor for free, just visit us at:
www.CuresForTheBody.com

• Eat lots of broccoli, carrots, tomatoes, oranges, garlic[294] and onions.

• Eat colorful fruits, like strawberries, raspberries, watermelon, oranges and red grapes.

• Eat yogurt with live cultures (pro-biotics).

–Live cultures in yogurt increase immune functioning by stimulating production of gamma interferon that may slow tumor growth.

• Eat nuts of all kinds for their protective vitamin E and other anticancer agents, but not to excess in gaining weight.

–Brazil nuts for selenium

–Walnuts for ellagic acid

–Almonds for oleic acid

Experts believe that 33-66 percent of all cancers can be traced to poor diet. Excessive consumption of animal fats increases the chance of intestinal cancer and possibly breast cancer as well. Food can be a source of a range of carcinogens, including nitrosamines in cured and smoked meats, fish, and cheeses.

• **Stay away from foods that may encourage cancer:** Meat, animal fat, and polyunsaturated corn oil and caffeine.

–Heavy meat eaters are more vulnerable to cancers of the pancreas, colon, lung and breast.

–Diets high in animal fat encourage cancer growth.

–Trans-fats encourage cancer. (Vegetable oil that has been partially hydrogenated or completely hydrogenated.) These give products a longer shelf life but take life away from you.

–Polyunsaturated corn oil is high in omega 6 and low in omega 3; these need to be in balance.

–Olive oil, an omega 9 fatty acid (not an essential fatty acid), or fish and flax oils, omega 3 fatty acids (an essential fatty acid), and hemp oil which is perfectly balanced Omega 3 and 6 essential fatty acid, are the right oils and help prevent and fight cancer.

–Never cook with flax or hemp oil. It is extremely fragile and needs to be fresh and kept as fresh as possible by refrigerating or freezing to extend its short shelf life. It is sensitive to light, oxygen and heat.

• Avoid caffeinated products – Dr. Kim L. O'Neill, a professor at Brigham Young University, is a microbiologist at BYU's Cancer Research Center. Dr. O'Neill published an article that suggests caffeine may prohibit cancerous cells from dying *(which would mean, caffeine would keep cancer cells alive and thriving). In the study, the cancerous cells that had taken in caffeine didn't die when exposed to a heat shock procedure designed to induce programmed cell suicide.*

• Milk[295] – Low fat or non-fat milk may deter cancer more than drinking whole milk. A study of 1,300 people by researchers at Roswell Memorial Institute in Buffalo found that consumption of low-fat and skim milk showed they had lower odds of cancer (oral, stomach, rectal, lung, and cervical) than drinkers of higher-fat whole milk.

• The immune system is weakened by deficiencies in trace elements such as these minerals:

–magnesium, iron, copper, zinc, and selenium.

Because trace elements are present in unprocessed foods, a healthy, well-balanced diet rich in these foods can ensure sufficient quantities of these substances.

• If supplementing, use only "amino acid" chelated minerals[296]. They have the highest proven absorption with the least toxicity, i.e., magnesium (amino acid chelated).

• Vitamin C (2) inhibits the formation of nitrosamines in the stomach.

–Use only whole food formulas like acreola cherry and or other food types like citrus fruits, not ascorbic acid.

• Vitamin A and E

–Use only whole food formulas[297].

–Vitamin A (pro-vitamin A) – carrots or orange vegetables should be the source.

–Vitamin E – wheat germ oil should be the source.

• Probiotics – Friendly bacteria

–Take only stabilized Probiotics.

• Plant source digestive enzymes

Carpal Tunnel Syndrome

Description: Carpal tunnel syndrome is the compression of the nerve that passes underneath the wrist. This compression comes from swelling or the development of fibrous tissues as a result of repeated forceful movements (i.e., using a screwdriver), improper positioning of a computer keyboard, or prolonged vibrations.

Carpal tunnel syndrome is very common, especially among women. Due to fluid retention and weight gain, pregnant women are at an increased risk. This disorder may also be a secondary syndrome associated with diabetes, an underactive thyroid gland, gout, or rheumatoid arthritis. Symptoms of the disorder include numbness, tingling, pain, and burning.

Medical Treatment:

Corticosteroids

Brand name: Hydrocortone

Drug Name: Hydrocortisone (Cortisol)

Hydrocortisone is an adrenocortical steroids, both naturally occurring and synthetic, which is readily absorbed from the gastrointestinal tract.

Notable Side Effects:

Fluid and Electrolyte Disturbances: Sodium retention, fluid retention, congestive heart failure in susceptible patients, potassium loss, hypokalemic alkalosis, hypertension.

Musculoskeletal: Muscle weakness, steroid myopathy, loss of muscle mass, osteoporosis, vertebral compression fractures, aseptic necrosis of femoral and humeral heads, pathologic fracture of long bones, tendon rupture.

To find out more or to speak to a nutritional counselor for free, just visit us at:
www.CuresForTheBody.com

Gastrointestinal: Peptic ulcer with possible perforation and hemorrhage, perforation of the small and large bowel, particularly in patients with inflammatory bowel disease, pancreatitis, abdominal distention, ulcerative esophagitis.

Dermatologic: Impaired wound healing, thin fragile skin, petechiae and ecchymoses, erythema, increased sweating, may suppress reactions to skin tests, other cutaneous reactions, such as allergic dermatitis, urticaria, angioneurotic edema.

Neurologic: Convulsions, increased intracranial pressure with papilledema (pseudotumor cerebri) usually after treatment, vertigo, headache, psychic disturbances.

Endocrine: Menstrual irregularities, development of cushingoid state, suppression of growth in children, secondary adrenocortical and pituitary unresponsiveness, particularly in times of stress, as in trauma, surgery, or illness, decreased carbohydrate tolerance, manifestations of latent diabetes mellitus, hyperglycemia, increased requirements for insulin or oral hypoglycemic agents in diabetics, hirsutism.

Ophthalmic: Posterior subcapsular cataracts, increased intraocular pressure, glaucoma, exophthalmos.

Metabolic: Negative nitrogen balance due to protein catabolism.

Cardiovascular: Myocardial rupture following recent myocardial infarction.

Other: Hypersensitivity, thromboembolism, weight gain, increased appetite, nausea, malaise.

Other common recommendations from Medical Doctors: Avoid positions that overextend the wrist or that may aggravate the symptoms. If the disorder is a result of an underlying disorder, such as rheumatoid arthritis, it is best to treat the underlying disorder.

To find out more or to speak to a nutritional counselor for free, just visit us at:
www.CuresForTheBody.com

Nutritional Approach:

Disease or Condition: Carpal Tunnel Syndrome
Causes of Carpal Tunnel Syndrome

Compression of the median nerve within the carpal tunnel produces paresthesia in the thumb and the second, third and radial half of the fourth fingers as well as, in some cases, atrophy of thenar musculature.[298]

Nutritional support:

Foods that have been proven to help with Carpal Tunnel Syndrome:

Raw almonds, broccoli, Brewer's yeast, avocado, asparagus, dark leafy greens, mushrooms, wheat bran, wheat germ, and whole grains

Nutritional support that has been proven to help with Carpal Tunnel Syndrome:

Vitamin B6, Vitamin B2, Boswellia, Turmeric, Cayenne

Vitamin B6

Studies conducted and published back in the late-1970s reported that many patients with carpal tunnel syndrome were deficient in vitamin B6, and vitamin B6 supplementation reportedly provided clinical relief and frequently enabled patients to avoid surgical intervention.[299,300] The physician who pioneered this work reported that vitamin B6 (100 to 200 mg daily) for a period of 12 weeks proved helpful for a large percentage of patients and was also useful in diagnosing vitamin B6 deficiency and in making decisions concerning surgery.[301] This research also directs particular attention to prevention of carpal tunnel syndrome during pregnancy.

Other investigators reported that satisfactory improvement was obtained in 68 percent of 494 patients treated with a vitamin B6 at a dosage of 100mg not effective in the treatment of carpal tunnel syndrome.[302]

Vitamin B2

One study reported that a patient with a 3-year history of carpal tunnel syndrome was found to have a vitamin B2 deficiency as determined by the activity of erythrocyte glutathione reductase. Riboflavin for 5 months caused nearly complete disappearance of the carpal tunnel syndrome. Subsequently, combined therapy with vitamin B2 and vitamin B6 normalized B2 and B6-dependent enzyme activities and resulted in a complete disappearance of the patient's carpal tunnel syndrome.[303]

To find out more or to speak to a nutritional counselor for free, just visit us at:
www.CuresForTheBody.com

Boswellia

Animal studies performed in India reported ingesting an extract of boswellia decreased polymorphonuclear leukocyte infiltration and migration, decreased primary antibody synthesis and caused almost total inhibition of the classical complement pathway.[304] An *in vitro* study of the isolated chemical constituent b-boswellic acid on the complement system reported a marked inhibitory effect on both the classical and alternate complement systems.[305]

Boswellia's anti-inflammatory activity seems to be produced by blocking the synthesis of 5-lipoxygenase products, including 5-hydroxyeicosatetraenoic acid (5-HETE) and leukotriene B4 (LTB4).[306,307] Also, it is known that NSAIDs can cause a breakdown of glycosaminoglycan synthesis which can speed up the articular damage in arthritic conditions.[308] Boswellia was reported to significantly reduce the degradation of glycosaminoglycans compared to controls, whereas the NSAID ketoprofen was reported to cause a reduction in total tissue glycosaminoglycan content.[309]

Turmeric

The laboratory and clinical research indicates that turmeric and its phenolics have unique antioxidant and anti-inflammatory properties.[310,311] The anti-inflammatory strength of turmeric is comparable to steroidal drugs such as indomethacin.[312] Turmeric has been reported to be anti-rheumatic, anti-inflammatory and antioxidant.[313] Curcuminoids reportedly inhibit enzymes which participate in the synthesis of inflammatory substances (leukotrienes and prostaglandins) derived from arachidonic acid, and it is claimed they are comparable in activity to the NSAID.[314]

Curcumin reportedly has a similar action to that of aspirin and aspirin-like anti-inflammatory agents.[315] However, an advantage of curcumin over aspirin is claimed, since curcumin, unlike aspirin, is reported to selectively inhibit synthesis of inflammatory prostaglandins but does not affect the synthesis of prostacyclin.[316] Curcumin may be preferable for individuals who are prone to vascular thrombosis and require anti-inflammatory and/or anti-arthritic therapy.

Cayenne

Externally, topical preparations of capsicum oleoresin (0.25-0.75%) is used for pain associated with arthritis, rheumatism, inflammation and cold injuries. Taken orally, capsicum has been reported to increase peripheral circulation and improve digestion.

Capsicum is reported to selectively activate some un-myelinated primary afferent sensory neurons (Type "C"). Many of cayenne's positive effects on the cardiovascular system are thought to be due to excitation of neurons in the vagus nerve.[317] Some of the unmyelinated sensory fibers sensitive to capsaicin contain the neuropeptides Substance P and somatostatin. Capsaicin reportedly stimulates the release of these neuropeptides from both central and peripheral terminals of these primary afferent neurons.[318] The release of the neuropeptide Substance P is associated with desensitization, analgesia and anti-inflammatory activity. Prolonged exposure to capsaicin results in a gradual desensitization to acute effects, potentially due to the depletion of substance P and somatostatin from the primary afferent neurons. Topically, capsaicin has been reported to be useful in alleviating post-herpetic neuralgia, post-mastectomy pain syndrome, arthritis and rheumatoid arthritis, painful diabetic neuropathy, psoriasis, pruritus and other conditions.[319,320]

Exercises that have been proven to help with Carpal Tunnel Syndrome:

> Any exercise that creates movement in the joints will help with healing and improve flexibility. Check with Physical Therapist for specific stretches and exercises for your wrist.

Colds & Flu

Description:

Colds and flu (influenza) are caused by a virus invading the body. These viruses can enter the body through secretions of the eyes or nose, as well as in the air. Psychological stress may also increase the risk and severity of viral infections.[321][322] Viruses invade the cells of the respiratory system and input its DNA into the cell so that it can no longer function. The cell dies, but not before the virus has a chance to replicate itself and send out more viruses into the body. The body fights against the virus with the white blood cells of the immune system (lymphocytes) that attack and destroy the cells the virus has infected. These lymphocytes then remember the virus so that it can respond more quickly when infected by the same virus again. Unfortunately the cold and flu viruses change so much from year to year that it is difficult to treat infections or prevent getting infected with the new viruses.

The common cold virus infects the cells of the nose, sinuses, throat, and large airways. The cold virus is spread when you have contact with an infected person's nasal secretions and then touch your eyes, nose, or mouth. The infection stays in an incubation period from one to five days, and then symptoms can last for up to two weeks. Over $1 billion is spent on over the counter (OTC) treatments of colds. However, these treatments do not treat the disease or underlying condition, but only help the symptoms. Many of these treatments also have side effects such as insomnia, dry mouth, constipation, or drowsiness.

The flu infects the lungs and airways. The flu usually occurs in epidemics, particularly type A and B flu viruses. This virus is spread through an infected person's secretions, or by inhaling droplets that an infected person has breathed, coughed, or sneezed. Symptoms usually occur 24 to 48 hours after infection and are generally more severe than those of the common cold. Those symptoms include a fever, runny nose, sore throat, cough, headache, muscle aches (myalgias), and a general feeling of illness (malaise).

To find out more or to speak to a nutritional counselor for free, just visit us at:
www.CuresForTheBody.com

Medical Treatment:

Antihistamines (OTC): are used to block histamine activity, interfering with their ability to cause inflammation and increased mucous production in the upper respiratory tract.

Brand name: Dimetapp, Robitussin
Drug Name: Brompheniramine

Notable Side Effects:
  drowsiness, dry mouth, blurred vision, difficulty urinating, constipation, light-headedness, and confusion

Brand name: Chlor-Trimeton
Drug Name: Chlorpheniramine

Notable Side Effects: same

Brand name: Tavist
Drug Name: Clemastine

Notable Side Effects: same

Brand name: Benadryl
Drug Name: Diphenhydramine

Notable Side Effects: same

NSAID: relieves fever and aches.
Brand name: Advil, Motrin
Drug Name: Ibuprofen

Ibuprofen is a nonsteroidal anti-inflammatory drug (NSAID) that possesses anti-inflammatory, analgesic and antipyretic activity. Its mode of action, like that of other NSAIDs, is not completely understood, but may be related to prostaglandin synthetase inhibition. After absorption of the racemic ibuprofen, the [-]R-enantiomer undergoes interconversion to the [+]S-form. The biological activities of ibuprofen are associated with the [+]S-enantiomer.

To find out more or to speak to a nutritional counselor for free, just visit us at:
www.CuresForTheBody.com

Notable Side Effects:

Cardiovascular system: Edema, fluid retention (generally responds promptly to drug discontinuation).

Digestive system: Nausea, epigastric pain, heartburn, diarrhea, abdominal distress, nausea and vomiting, indigestion, constipation, abdominal cramps or pain, fullness of Gl tract (bloating and flatulence).

Nervous system: Dizziness, headache, nervousness.

Skin and appendages: Rash (including maculopapular type), pruritus.

Special senses: Tinnitus.

Antiviral Agents: flu only.

Brand Name: Symmetrel

Drug Name: Amantadine

Amantadine interferes with the replication cycle of influenza type A viruses. It appears to mainly prevent the release of infectious viral nucleic acid into the host cell by interfering with the function of the transmembrane domain of the viral M2 protein. In certain cases, amantadine is also known to prevent virus assembly during virus replication. It does not appear to interfere with the immunogenicity of inactivated influenza A virus vaccine.

Notable Side Effects:

nausea, dizziness (lightheadedness), insomnia, depression, anxiety and irritability, hallucinations, confusion, anorexia, dry mouth, constipation, ataxia, livedo reticularis, peripheral edema, orthostatic hypotension, headache, somnolence, nervousness, dream abnormality, agitation, dry nose, diarrhea and fatigue.

Brand Name: Relenza

Drug Name: Zanamivir

Zanamivir inhibits of influenza virus neuraminidase with the possibility of alteration of virus particle aggregation and release. Antiviral agents indicated for the treatment of uncomplicated influenza A and B viruses. These agents are viral neuramidase inhibitors, a critical protein of the surface membrane of the influenza virus, which enables the replicated flu virus to bud from the host cells in the respiratory tract. Inhibition of viral neuramidase prevents newly formed flu virus from escaping the infected cells, interrupting the spread of the infection. To date, reported side effects have been transient, including GI upset, nausea, vomiting, and diarrhea.

Notable Side Effects:
headaches, diarrhea, nausea, vomiting, nasal signs and symptoms, bronchitis, cough, sinusitis, ear-nose-throat infections, dizziness.

Other common recommendations from Medical Doctors: Good hygiene is the best prevention, as the cold virus is generally spread through contact with an infected person. If you have a cold, stay warm, drink fluids, and rest at home, particularly if you have severe symptoms.

To prevent flu infections, vaccinations are considered the best prevention. The young, elderly, those with chronic illnesses, and pregnant women are encouraged to get vaccinations, as they are likely to become very ill. If you become infected, it is important to rest, drink plenty of fluids, and avoid over-exertion.

Nutritional Approach:
Disease or Condition: Colds and Flu
Causes of Colds and Flu
Viruses and low immune system in response to viruses.

Nutritional support:
Foods that have been proven to help with Colds and Flu:
Fruits and vegetables, diluted vegetable juices, non creamy soups.

Nutrients that have been proven to help with Colds and Flu:
Vitamin C[323], E[324], Mineral Zinc[325], Multivitamins[326], Thymus Gland Extract[327], Sterols (Sitosterol) and Sterolins (Sitosterolin)[328], Echinacea[329], Goldenseal[330], Elder[331], Astragalus[332], and Larch Arabinogalactan[333].

Exercises that have been proven to help with Colds & Flu:

To find out more or to speak to a nutritional counselor for free, just visit us at:
www.CuresForTheBody.com

Studies suggest that regular exercise can cut in half the number of days a person suffers from colds and the flu. Exercise stimulates the disease-fighting white blood cells in the body to move from the organs into the bloodstream.

Basic Colds and Flu Plan:

Although the focus in this condition is on the use of natural methods to assist the body in recovery from common colds and flu, prevention is by far the best medicine. Prevention involves strengthening the immune system. The following are recommendations as to what to do if a cold develops.

• **Rest** (bed rest is best)

• **Drink large amounts of fluids** (preferably diluted vegetable juices, soups, and herb teas) for their nutrients.

• **Try to eat more nutrient rich foods**, especially fruits and vegetables.

• **Avoid refined sugar and refined flour** – They slow down white blood cells for several hours after consumption[334].

• **Reduce chronic stress** (it lowers your immunity).

• **Vitamin C** – It may be utilized four to six times the normal rate by white blood cells during active infection. An analysis of sixteen controlled studies evaluating the effects of vitamin C on the common cold provided positive results in decreasing the symptoms and severity of the common cold. There is evidence indicating that vitamin C may play an important role in the efficient functioning of the immune system. Vitamin C demands rise to 5-6 times normal levels within the white blood cells when fighting an infection. Therefore, an increase in Vitamin C during a cold or the flu may be warranted.

–Whole food sources of vitamins are optimal. They are absorbed more significantly and without toxic side effects of synthetics. (i.e., look for acreola cherry, citrus fruits, etc. as the main ingredients, not ascorbic acid).

• **Vitamin E** – Poor immune response has been associated with low levels of vitamin E.

–Whole food sources of vitamins are optimal. They are absorbed more significantly and without toxic side effects of synthetics. (i.e. look for wheat germ oil).

• **Zinc** – Human clinical trials demonstrated that zinc lozenges have a therapeutic effect in treating the common cold. "Amino acid" chelated minerals are proven that they are absorbed the best with the least toxicity.

• **Multivitamins** – Much of our food sources today do not contain the vitamins and minerals that they did in the past due to soil depletion. Multiple vitamin and mineral formulas taken daily is the first choice in prevention.

–Whole food sources of vitamins are optimal. They are absorbed more significantly and without toxic side effects of synthetics.

• **Sterols and Sterolins** – (Phytochemicals; plant "fats") Occur naturally in fruits , vegetables, seeds and nuts, have beneficial effects on humans in many conditions. Seeds are the richest source, but are removed during processing by the food industry. They help in many ways but in regards to colds and flu, they have been reported to increase the function of the immune system, specifically certain T-cells.

• **Echinacea** - Research has reported that echinacea may stimulate white blood cells. Echinacea is also reported to possess antimicrobial activity against bacteria, fungi, and viruses. There have been several randomized, double-blind, placebo controlled clinical studies in Europe conducted on human subjects using echinacea. Benefits reported include improving the symptoms and severity of colds and influenza.

• **Golden Seal** - Due to the antibacterial properties of the alkaloids in golden seal, this herbal medicine may be useful in managing symptoms associated with colds and influenza. Combinations of golden seal and echinacea are one of the leading selling herbal supplements in the U.S. market today.

• **Elder** - An extract of the berries of the black elder (*Sambucus nigra*) has been reported to inhibit the ability of several strains of influenza virus to replicate. It does this by coating the spike-like projections on the virus, preventing it from injecting protein into the host cell

To find out more or to speak to a nutritional counselor for free, just visit us at:
www.CuresForTheBody.com

membrane. In one study using a liquid extract of elder berry, 90 percent of the individuals with symptoms of influenza B were asymptomatic in 2-3 days, while individuals on placebo did not recover for at least 6 days.

• **Astragalus** – enhances the effects of interferon, and may act not only to improve resistance to colds but decrease the duration of a cold. Astragalus improves natural killer and T-cell function, as well as interferon production by the immune system.

• **Larch Arabinogalactan** - Larix is a purified extract of the bark from the Western larch tree. It contains the phytochemical arabinogalactan, an immunomodulating polysaccharide that is also found in *Echinacea spp*. Larix has been reported to increase NK cells, stimulate the reticuloendothelial system, stimulate macrophage activation, and have antiviral effects *in-vitro*. Larix has also been used with positive success in children, specifically in otitis media.

Constipation

Description: Constipation is a condition in which a person has uncomfortable or infrequent bowel movements. The stools are often hard and difficult to pass, and there is a feeling as if the rectum has not been completely emptied. The frequency of bowel movements does not necessary translate to a constipation diagnosis, as not everyone's bowels move the same. However, you may be constipated if you have less than three bowel movements a week and experience a change in the frequency of bowel movements, along with a change in the color or texture of the stools.

Constipation may be accompanied by abdominal pain, nausea, and loss of appetite. In addition, you may develop hemorrhoids (because of increased blood pressure) or increase your risk for diverticular disease because of the increased pressure on the walls of the large intestine. Fecal impaction is also a factor of constipation, which is where the stool in the last part of the large intestine blocks the passage. This condition is accompanied by cramps, rectal pain, and an inability to eliminate the stools. Fecal impaction is more common in the elderly and pregnant women.

Although most people cannot pinpoint an exact cause of constipation, it may be a result of another underlying problem. A lack of fiber and fluids in the diet is probably the most common cause in the United States. Constipation can also be caused from disordered colonic transit or anorectal function as a result of a primary motility disturbance, certain drugs, or in association with a large number of systemic diseases that affect the gastrointestinal tract.[335] Other disorders, such as irritable bowel syndrome, diverticulitis, metabolic disorders (diabetes), or endocrine disorders (hypothyroidism) may also be factors in the cause of constipation.[336]

Medical Treatment:

Bulking Agents:

Prevent or control chronic constipation.

To find out more or to speak to a nutritional counselor for free, just visit us at:
www.CuresForTheBody.com

Brand Name: Citrucel
Drug Name: Methylcellulose

Notable Side Effects:
　Flatulence, bloating

Brand Name: Metamucil
Drug Name: Psyllium

Notable Side Effects:
　Flatulence, bloating

Stool Softeners:

Treat constipation and are often used to help prevent it.
Brand Name: Colace, Dulcolax, Phillips', Senokot
Drug Name: Docusate

Notable Side Effects:
　Stomach pain, nausea, vomiting.

Osmotic Agents:

Treats constipation.
Brand Name: Kristalose
Drug Name: Lactulose

Lactulose is poorly absorbed from the gastrointestinal tract and no enzyme capable of hydrolysis of this disaccharide is present in human gastrointestinal tissue. As a result, oral doses of lactulose reach the colon virtually unchanged. In the colon, lactulose is broken down primarily to lactic acid, and also to small amounts of formic and acetic acids, by the action of colonic bacteria, which results in an increase in osmotic pressure and slight acidification of the colonic contents. This in turn causes an increase in stool water content and softens the stool.

Notable Side Effects:

Initial dosing may produce flatulence and intestinal cramps, which are usually transient. Excessive dosage can lead to diarrhea with potential complications such as loss of fluids, hypokalemia, and hypernatremia. Nausea and vomiting have been reported.

Brand Name: K-Phos

Drug Name: Sodium phosphate

Sodium phosphate: Phosphorus has a number of important functions in the biochemistry of the body. The bulk of the body's phosphorus is located in the bones, where it plays a key role in osteoblastic and osteoclastic activities. Enzymatically catalyzed phosphate-transfer reactions are numerous and vital in the metabolism of carbohydrate, lipid and protein, and a proper concentration of the anion is of primary importance in assuring an orderly biochemical sequence. In addition, phosphorus plays an important role in modifying steady-state tissue concentrations of calcium. Phosphate ions are important buffers of the intracellular fluid, and also play a primary role in the renal excretion of hydrogen ion.

Notable Side Effects:

Gastrointestinal upset (diarrhea, nausea, stomach pain, and vomiting) may occur with phosphate therapy. Also, bone and joint pain (possible phosphate-induced osteomalacia) could occur. The following adverse effects may be observed (primarily from sodium or potassium): headaches; dizziness; mental confusion; seizures; weakness or heaviness of legs; unusual tiredness or weakness; muscle cramps; numbness, tingling, pain, or weakness of hands or feet; numbness or tingling around lips; fast or irregular heartbeat; shortness of breath or troubled breathing; swelling of feet or lower legs; unusual weight gain; low urine output; unusual thirst.

Stimulant Laxatives:

Brand Name: Dulcolax

Drug Name: Bisacodyl

Bisacodyl acts directly on the colonic mucosa-where it stimulates sensory nerve endings to produce parasympathetic reflexes resulting in increased peristaltic contractions of the colon. The contact action of the drug is restricted to the colon, and motility in the small intestine is not appreciably influenced.

Notable Side Effects:

Abdominal pain (cramps); prolonged use can damage the large intestine.

Brand Name: Senekot
Drug Name: Senna

Senna is designed to relieve both aspects of functional constipation—bowel inertia and hard, dry stools. Providing a natural neuroperistaltic stimulant combined with a classic stool softener, standardized senna concentrate gently stimulates the colon while docusate sodium softens the stool for smoother and easier evacuation.

Notable Side Effects:

Abdominal pain (cramps); prolonged use can damage the large intestine.

Other common recommendations from Medical Doctors:

Exercise, fluids, and a high fiber diet are the best preventative measures for constipation. The best sources of fiber are fruits, vegetables, and whole grains or bran. However, fiber works best when consumed with plenty of fluids. If you are prescribed a drug that has a side effect of constipation, increase your fiber and fluid intake and take a laxative along with the prescription.

Nutritional Approach:

Causes of Constipation:

Diet; Highly refined and low-fiber foods (most common cause); Inadequate fluid intake.

Others causes include the following:

To find out more or to speak to a nutritional counselor for free, just visit us at:
www.CuresForTheBody.com

Physical inactivity; Inadequate exercise; Prolonged bed rest.

Pregnancy

Advanced Age

Drugs; Anesthetics; Antacids (aluminum and calcium salts); Anticholinergics (bethanechol, carbachol, pilocarpine, physostigmine, ambenonium); Anticonvulsants; Antidepressants (tricyclics, monoamine oxidase inhibitors); Antihypetensives; Anti-Parkinsonism drugs; Antipsychotics (phenothiazines); Beta-adrenergic blocking agents (proprandolo); Bismuth salts; Diuretics; Iron salts; Laxatives and cathartics (chronic use); Muscle relaxants; Opiates.

Metabolic abnormalities; Low potassium stores; Diabetes; Kidney disease.

Endocrine abnormalities; Low thyroid function; Elevated calcium levels; Pituitary disorders.

Structural abnormalities; Abnormalities in the structure or anatomy of the bowel.

Bowel diseases; Diverticulosis; Irritable bowel syndrome (alternating diarrhea and constipation); Tumor.

Neurogenic abnormalities; Nerve disorders of the bowel (aganglionosis, autonomic neuropathy); Spinal cord disorders (trauma, multiple sclerosis, tabes dorsalis).

Nutritional support:

Foods that have been proven to help with Constipation:

Foods high in fiber (fresh fruits, vegetables and whole grains), increase water intake. Fermented foods like kim chee, miso soup, and fresh sauerkraut.

Nutrients that have been proven to help with Constipation:

Probiotics[337], Flaxseeds, Fiber[338], Aloe Vera[339], Cascara Sagrada[340], Psyllium Seeds[341], and Digestive Enzymes[342].

Exercises that have been proven to help with Constipation:

Moderate exercise helps you to avoid and to relieve constipation. It's generally recommended that you exercise at least three times a week, steadily for 20 to 30 minutes, or enough to raise your heart rate.

Basic Constipation Plan:

• **Drink lots of water (Many times constipation is caused by a lack of fluids).**

• **Find and eliminate known causes of constipation.**

• **Never repress an urge to have a bowel movement.**

• **Take Probiotics. Research has shown that friendly bacteria is one of the best proven remedies for constipation.**

• **Take Digestive enzymes to completely digest your food so that there is no residual left to block up your system.**

• **Eat a high-fiber diet (25-35 grams/day), particularly fruits, vegetables and whole grains.**

–It is well accepted that increasing the level of fiber in the diet is an effective treatment for chronic constipation.

–High levels of dietary fiber increase both the frequency and quantity of bowel movements, decrease the transit time of stools and the absorption of toxins from the stool, and appear to be a preventive factor in many diseases.

• **Psyllium seeds**

–Psyllium is rich in dietary fiber, which is the most satisfactory prophylactic and treatment for functional constipation. Dietary fiber increases the mass of stools, their water content, and the rate of colonic transit. Psyllium has traditionally been used as a bulk-forming laxative; however, recent research points to other uses including hypercholesterolemia, irritable bowel syndrome, and ulcerative colitis. In February 1998, the FDA gave permission to allow food manufactures to make a health claim on the packaging of food products regarding psyllium. The claim reads: "Eating soluble fiber from foods such as psyllium as part of a diet low in saturated fat and cholesterol may reduce the risk of heart disease." These findings make

To find out more or to speak to a nutritional counselor for free, just visit us at:
www.CuresForTheBody.com

psyllium a potential agent for reducing the risks of cardiovascular diseases.

• Flax seeds

–Flaxseed oil acts as a lubricant in the gastrointestinal tract. Although flaxseed oil is not regarded as a primary therapeutic modality for constipation, its lubricating properties may help facilitate bowel movements. Since the diets of most people are deficient in omega-3 fatty acids, taking one tablespoonful of flaxseed oil daily may help to alleviate constipation and also improve overall health.

• Sit on the toilet at the same time every day whether you have the urge or not, but especially after breakfast and exercise.

• Stop using laxatives and enemas.

• Cascara Sagrada

–Anthranoid laxatives, or stimulant laxatives, are widely used in nonprescription products and dietary supplements. They are carried unabsorbed to the large bowel, where metabolism to the active aglycone form takes place. The aglycones exert their laxative effect by damaging epithelial cells, which leads directly and indirectly to changes in absorption, secretion, and motility.

• Aloe Vera

–It has long been recognized that the latex from aloe is an anthranoid stimulant laxative. Studies have reported the effects of aloe as a laxative.

• Use laxatives only to reestablish bowel activity as follows:

–Week one: Every night before bed, take a stimulant laxative containing either cascara sagrada or senna. Take the lowest amount necessary to reliably ensure a bowel movement every morning.

–Weekly: Each week, decrease the laxative dosage by half. If constipation recurs, go to the previous week's dosage. Decrease the dosage if diarrhea occurs.

Chronic Fatigue Syndrome

Description: Chronic fatigue syndrome refers severe and disabling fatigue for at least six months without a proven physical or psychological cause. Although the cause of chronic fatigue is unknown, it has been postulated that psychological factors, viruses or toxic chemical agents, or abnormalities of the immune system may be significant contributors.

Chronic fatigue syndrome usually sets in after a cold or other illness during which the lymph nodes are swollen. Patients experience extreme fatigue that is not relieved by sleep or rest. Most have abdominal pain, headaches, and pain in the muscles and joints. Over time, the symptoms lessen and are less as debilitating.

The greatest frequency of the disease is experienced by people between 20 and 50 years of age, and seems to correlate most with psychological and/or immunological factors. Some believe that chronic fatigue is actually a psychological disorder as depression often accompanies it, and the depressed immune system is caused by the psychological stress. However, there have also been sporadic outbreaks in various locations throughout the years, which suggests that it is more than just a psychological disturbance.

Since the exact cause is unknown, there are no tests or procedures that can be performed to determine if a patient has chronic fatigue syndrome. Health practitioners must rule out other diseases with similar symptoms before they can diagnose their patient with chronic fatigue. In the past, other diagnoses were used to describe what we now group together as chronic fatigue, such as the vapors, neurasthenia, effort syndrome, hyperventilation syndrome, chronic brucellosis, epidemic neuromyasthenia, myalgic encephalomyelitis, hypoglycemia, multiple chemical sensitivity syndrome, chronic candidiasis, chronic mononucleosis, chronic Epstein-Barr virus infection, and post-viral fatigue syndrome.[343]

Medical Treatment:

Antidepressants:

Brand Name: Norpramin

Drug Name: Desipramine

Desipramine: While the precise mechanism of action of the tricyclic antidepressants is unknown, a leading theory suggests that they restore normal levels of neurotransmitters by blocking the re-uptake of these substances from the synapse in the central nervous system. Desipramine is not a monoamine oxidase (MAO) inhibitor and does not act primarily as a central nervous system stimulant.

Notable Side Effects:

Cardiovascular: Hypotension, hypertension, palpitations, heart block, myocardial infarction, stroke, arrhythmias, premature ventricular contractions, tachycardia, ventricular tachycardia, ventricular fibrillation, sudden death

Psychiatric: Confusional states (especially in the elderly) with hallucinations, disorientation, delusions; anxiety, restlessness, agitation; insomnia and nightmares; hypomania; exacerbation of psychosis.

Neurologic: Numbness, tingling, paresthesias of extremities; incoordination, ataxia, tremors; peripheral neuropathy; extrapyramidal symptoms; seizures; alterations in EEG patterns; tinnitus.

Anticholinergic: Dry mouth, and rarely associated sublingual adenitis; blurred vision, disturbance of accommodation, mydriasis, increased intraocular pressure; constipation, paralytic ileus; urinary retention, delayed micturition, dilation of urinary tract.

Allergic: Skin rash, petechiae, urticaria, itching, photosensitization (avoid excessive exposure to sunlight), edema (of face and tongue or general), drug fever, cross-sensitivity with other tricyclic drugs.

Hematologic: Bone marrow depressions including agranulocytosis, eosinophilia, purpura, thrombocytopenia.

Gastrointestinal: anorexia, nausea and vomiting, epigastric distress, peculiar taste, abdominal cramps, diarrhea, stomatitis, black tongue, hepatitis, jaundice (simulating obstructive), altered liver function, elevated liver function tests, increased pancreatic enzymes.

Endocrine: Gynecomastia in the male, breast enlargement and galactorrhea in the female; increased or decreased libido, impotence, painful ejaculation, testicular swelling; elevation or depression of blood sugar levels; syndrome of inappropriate antidiuretic hormone secretion (SIADH).

Other: Weight gain or loss; perspiration, flushing; urinary frequency, nocturia; parotid swelling; drowsiness, dizziness, weakness and fatigue, headache; fever; alopecia; elevated alkaline phosphatase.

Withdrawal Symptoms: Though not indicative of addiction, abrupt cessation of treatment after prolonged therapy may produce nausea, headache, and malaise.

Corticosteroids:

Immunosuppresive drugs

Brand Name: Hydrocortone

Drug Name: Hydrocortisone

Hydrocortisone is an adrenocortical steroids, both naturally occurring and synthetic, which are readily absorbed from the gastrointestinal tract.

Notable Side Effects:

Fluid and Electrolyte Disturbances: Sodium retention, fluid retention, congestive heart failure in susceptible patients, potassium loss, hypokalemic alkalosis, hypertension.

Musculoskeletal: Muscle weakness, steroid myopathy, loss of muscle mass, osteoporosis, vertebral compression fractures, aseptic necrosis of femoral and humeral heads, pathologic fracture of long bones, tendon rupture.

Gastrointestinal: Peptic ulcer with possible perforation and hemorrhage, perforation of the small and large bowel, particularly in patients with inflammatory bowel disease, pancreatitis, abdominal distention, ulcerative esophagitis.

Dermatologic: Impaired wound healing, thin fragile skin, petechiae and ecchymoses, erythema, increased sweating, may suppress reactions to skin tests, other cutaneous reactions, such as allergic dermatitis, urticaria, angioneurotic edema.

Neurologic: Convulsions, increased intracranial pressure with papilledema (pseudotumor cerebri) usually after treatment, vertigo, headache, psychic disturbances.

Endocrine: menstrual irregularities, development of cushingoid state, suppression of growth in children, secondary adrenocortical and pituitary unresponsiveness, particularly in times of stress, as in trauma, surgery, or illness, decreased carbohydrate tolerance, manifestations of latent diabetes mellitus, hyperglycemia, increased requirements for insulin or oral hypoglycemic agents in diabetics, hirsutism.

Ophthalmic: Posterior subcapsular cataracts, increased intraocular pressure, glaucoma, exophthalmos.

Metabolic: Negative nitrogen balance due to protein catabolism.

Cardiovascular: Myocardial rupture following recent myocardial infarction.

Other: Hypersensitivity, thromboembolism, weight gain, increased appetite, nausea, malaise.

Other common recommendations from Medical Doctors: Regular, non-strenuous exercise is important once the initial symptoms have subsided. It is important not to exercise too heavily as it will lead to increased fatigue. A healthy diet is also important, especially in avoiding caffeine and alcohol. Also avoid eating heavy meals in the evening as it can make it harder to sleep.

Nutritional Approach:
Disease or Condition: Chronic Fatigue Syndrome
Causes of Chronic Fatigue Syndrome

To find out more or to speak to a nutritional counselor for free, just visit us at:
www.CuresForTheBody.com

There are no consistent initiators to this condition, but Chronic Fatigue Syndrome is most often preceded by infections of viruses, bacteria, fungi, or yeast; allergies[344]; flu-like conditions; or stressful situations. Some researchers suspect mercury poisoning from amalgam fillings or infection with the Candida albicans fungi. This syndrome typically arises suddenly in normally active individuals.

Nutritional support:

Foods that have been proven to help with Chronic Fatigue Syndrome:

Soluble fiber found in flax, psyllium, and okra. Garlic[345], Reishi mushrooms[346], and shitake mushrooms[347]. Raw foods and raw juices (preferably vegetable juices), raw nuts, deep-water fish and acidophilus found in yogurt and kefir should be added to the diet.[348]

Avoid processed nutrient poor foods, simple/refined sugars, hard and altered fats, stimulants such as coffee, tea, and sodas; fried foods, white flours, and heavy meals.

Nutrients that have been proven to help with Chronic Fatigue Syndrome:

Coenzyme Q10 (CO-Q10)[349], magnesium[350], omega 3 and omega 6 essential fatty acids[351](flax and evening primrose), L- carnitine[352], zinc, copper, potassium, phosphate, calcium, vitamins A, B, C, and D, amino acids and proteins.[353]

Exercises that have been proven to help with Chronic Fatigue Syndrome:

In studies on chronic fatigue therapies, both fatigue and quality of life improved with three months of exercise therapy, writes researcher M. Edmonds with the Cochrane Collaboration research group. Edmonds' report provides a review of data from five studies (involving more than 300 chronic fatigue patients) comparing results of treatments including exercise therapy.

Exercise therapy is typically defined as three to five exercise sessions every week for 12 weeks; each session involves 30 minutes of moderate to intense levels of aerobic exercise.

Basic Chronic Fatigue Syndrome Plan:

• Establish optimal nutrition.

–Most occurrences of chronic fatigue syndrome are preceded by infection. Improving immune system function along with overall nutrition and digestion is necessary. Echinacea pupurea, astragalus, and maitake as well as friendly bacteria (lactobacillus acidophilus) to combat candidiasis are great immune nutrients.

–Introduce foods into the diet that are rich in omega 3 and omega 6 essential fatty acids such as avocados. These enhance immune system functions by improving the immune cells' ability to produce hydrogen peroxide (produced when essential fatty acids are oxidized) which helps eliminate bugs.[354]

• Nutrient regiments consisting of EFAs along with zinc, vitamins A and C as well as antioxidants, assist the body in the elimination and disposal of those bugs that may lead to chronic fatigue.

• Take plant source digestive enzymes to aid in digestion[355]. These help alleviate food allergies that may trigger chronic fatigue.

• Drink plenty of water.

–Drinking plenty of water and vegetable juices aide in the removal of toxins and relief of muscle pain.

• Replenish friendly bacteria.

–Since bacteria infections or viruses are typically precursors to chronic fatigue syndrome, treatments with antibiotics may have occurred. It is very important to replenish the body's supply of friendly bacteria, since antibiotics do not discriminate and kill both good and bad bacteria.

To find out more or to speak to a nutritional counselor for free, just visit us at:
www.CuresForTheBody.com

Depression

Description: The goals of treatment include reducing the symptoms of depression and facilitating the patient's return to functioning at the level prior to the onset of illness. Usually the treatment includes psychotherapy and the use of pharmacologic agents. The most commonly used medications for uncomplicated depression are the **tricyclic antidepressants** (TCAs) and **selective serotonin reuptake inhibitors** (SSRIs). If a patient is refractory to the actions of one agent, therapy is often switched to the other. Of the tricyclic antidepressants, **amitriptyline** and **imipramine** are the most extensively studied and used. All TCAs potentiate the activity of norepinephrine and serotonin by blocking their re-uptake. Because TCAs affect other receptor systems, anticholinergic, neurologic, and cardiovascular adverse events are frequently reported.[356] SSRIs were developed from the perceived need for improved efficacy and adverse effects profile compared with traditional TCAs. Patients who fail to respond to TCAs often respond to an SSRI, and visa versa.

If a patient is unresponsive to either agent, others are considered, including **buproprion,** which blocks reuptake of dopamine, **mirtazapine, a tetracyclic antidepressant** with mixed serotonin/norepinephrine effects, or a **triazolopyridine** (trazodone or nefazodone), which has a dual action as a serotonin antagonist and also a re-uptake inhibitor.

Monoamine oxidase inhibitors (phenelzine, tranylcypromine) are used in cases of atypical depression. Clinical features of atypical depression that predict preferential response to MAOIs include mood reactivity, irritability, hypersomnia, hyperphagia, psychomotor agitation, and hypersensitivity to rejection.[357]

Medical Treatment:

Tricyclics and related drugs:

Brand Name: Norpramin

Drug Name: Desipramine

Desipramine: While the precise mechanism of action of the tricyclic antidepressants is unknown, a leading theory suggests that they restore normal levels of neurotransmitters by blocking the re-uptake of these substances from the synapse in the central nervous system. Desipramine is not a monoamine oxidase (MAO) inhibitor and does not act primarily as a central nervous system stimulant.

Notable Side Effects:

Cardiovascular: Hypotension, hypertension, palpitations, heart block, myocardial infarction, stroke, arrhythmias, premature ventricular contractions, tachycardia, ventricular tachycardia, ventricular fibrillation, sudden death.

Psychiatric: Confusional states (especially in the elderly) with hallucinations, disorientation, delusions; anxiety, restlessness, agitation; insomnia and nightmares; hypomania; exacerbation of psychosis.

Neurologic: Numbness, tingling, paresthesias of extremities; incoordination, ataxia, tremors; peripheral neuropathy; extrapyramidal symptoms; seizures; alterations in EEG patterns; tinnitus.

Anticholinergic: Dry mouth, and rarely associated sublingual adenitis; blurred vision, disturbance of accommodation, mydriasis, increased intraocular pressure; constipation, paralytic ileus; urinary retention, delayed micturition, dilation of urinary tract.

Allergic: Skin rash, petechiae, urticaria, itching, photosensitization (avoid excessive exposure to sunlight), edema (of face and tongue or general), drug fever, cross-sensitivity with other tricyclic drugs.

Hematologic: Bone marrow depressions including agranulocytosis, eosinophilia, purpura, thrombocytopenia.

To find out more or to speak to a nutritional counselor for free, just visit us at:
www.CuresForTheBody.com

Gastrointestinal: Anorexia, nausea and vomiting, epigastric distress, peculiar taste, abdominal cramps, diarrhea, stomatitis, black tongue, hepatitis, jaundice (simulating obstructive), altered liver function, elevated liver function tests, increased pancreatic enzymes.

Endocrine: Gynecomastia in the male, breast enlargement and galactorrhea in the female; increased or decreased libido, impotence, painful ejaculation, testicular swelling; elevation or depression of blood sugar levels; syndrome of inappropriate antidiuretic hormone secretion (SIADH).

Other: Weight gain or loss; perspiration, flushing; urinary frequency, nocturia; parotid swelling; drowsiness, dizziness, weakness and fatigue, headache; fever; alopecia; elevated alkaline phosphatase.

Withdrawal Symptoms: Though not indicative of addiction, abrupt cessation of treatment after prolonged therapy may produce nausea, headache, and malaise.

Selective serotonin reuptake inhibitors:

Brand Name: Sarafem

Drug Name: Fluoxetine

Fluoxetine is presumed to be linked to its inhibition of CNS neuronal uptake of serotonin. Studies at clinically relevant doses in humans have demonstrated that fluoxetine blocks the uptake of serotonin into human platelets. Studies in animals also suggest that fluoxetine is a much more potent uptake inhibitor of serotonin than of norepinephrine. Antagonism of muscarinic, histaminergic, and (alpha) $_1$ -adrenergic receptors has been hypothesized to be associated with various anticholinergic, sedative, and cardiovascular effects of certain psychoactive drugs. Fluoxetine has little affinity for these receptors.

Notable Side Effects:

Body as a whole: Asthenia, flu, headache, fever, infection, accidental injury.

Digestive System: Nausea, diarrhea.

Nervous Systems: Insomnia, nervousness, libido decreased, abnormal dreams, dizziness, tremor, thinking abnormal.

Respiratory system: Pharyngitis, rhinits.

Monoamine oxidase inhibitors:

Brand Name: Nardil

Drug Name: Phenelzine

Phenelzine oxidase is a complex enzyme system, widely distributed throughout the body. Drugs that inhibit monoamine oxidase in the laboratory are associated with a number of clinical effects. Thus, it is unknown whether MAO inhibition per se, other pharmacologic actions, or an interaction of both is responsible for the clinical effects observed. Therefore, the physician should become familiar with all the effects produced by drugs of this class.

Notable Side Effects:

Nervous System: Dizziness, headache, drowsiness, sleep disturbances (including insomnia and hypersomnia), fatigue, weakness, tremors, twitching, myoclonic movements, hyperreflexia.

Gastrointestinal: Constipation, dry mouth, gastrointestinal disturbances, elevated serum transaminases (without accompanying signs and symptoms).

Metabolic: Weight gain.

Cardiovascular: Postural hypotension, edema.

Genitourinary: Sexual disturbances, e.g., anorgasmia and ejaculatory disturbances and impotence.

Less common mild to moderate side effects (some of which have been reported in a single patient or by a single physician) include:

Nervous System: Jitteriness, palilalia, euphoria, nystagmus, paresthesias.

Genitourinary: Urinary retention.

Metabolic: Hypernatremia.

Dermatologic: Pruritus, skin rash, sweating.

Special Senses: Blurred vision, glaucoma.

Although reported less frequently, and sometimes only once, additional severe side effects include:

Nervous System: Ataxia, shock-like coma, toxic delirium, manic reaction, convulsions, acute anxiety reaction, precipitation of schizophrenia, transient respiratory and cardiovascular depression following ECT.

Gastrointestinal: To date, fatal progressive necrotizing hepatocellular damage has been reported in a very few patients. Reversible jaundice.

Hematologic: Leukopenia.

Immunologic: Lupus-like syndrome.

Metabolic: Hypermetabolic syndrome (which may include, but is not limited to, hyperpyrexia, tachycardia, tachypnea, muscular rigidity, elevated CK levels, metabolic acidosis, hypoxia, coma and may resemble an overdose).

Respiratory: Edema of the glottis.

General: Fever associated with increased muscle tone. Withdrawal may be associated with nausea, vomiting, and malaise.

Psychostimulants:

Brand name: Ritalin

Drug Name: Methylphenidate

Methylphenidate is a mild central nervous system stimulant. The mode of action in man is not completely understood, but Ritalin presumably activates the brain stem arousal system and cortex to produce its stimulant effect. There is neither specific evidence which clearly establishes the mechanism whereby Ritalin produces its mental and behavioral effects in children, nor conclusive evidence regarding how these effects relate to the condition of the central nervous system.

Notable Side Effects:

Nervousness and insomnia are the most common, hypersensitivity (including skin rash, urticaria, fever, arthralgia, exfoliative dermatitis, erythema multiforme with histopathological findings of necrotizing vasculitis, and thrombocytopenic purpura); anorexia; nausea; dizziness; palpitations; headache; dyskinesia; drowsiness; blood pressure and pulse changes, both up and down; tachycardia; angina; cardiac arrhythmia; abdominal pain; weight loss during prolonged therapy. There have been rare reports of Tourette's syndrome. Toxic psychosis has been reported. Although a definite causal relationship has not been established, the following have been reported in patients taking this drug: instances of abnormal liver function, ranging from transaminase elevation to hepatic coma; isolated cases of cerebral arteritis and/or occlusion; leukopenia and/or anemia; transient depressed mood; a few instances of scalp hair loss. In children, loss of appetite, abdominal pain, weight loss during prolonged therapy, insomnia, and tachycardia may occur more frequently; however, any of the other adverse reactions listed above may also occur.

Newer drugs:

Brand Name: Wellbutrin

Drug Name: Bupropion

Bupropion hydrochloride: The neurochemical mechanism of the antidepressant effect of bupropion is not known. Bupropion is a relatively weak inhibitor of the neuronal uptake of norepinephrine, serotonin, and dopamine, and does not inhibit monoamine oxidase. Bupropion produces dose-related central nervous system (CNS) stimulant effects in animals, as evidenced by increased locomotor activity, increased rates of responding in various schedule-controlled operant behavior tasks, and, at high doses, induction of mild stereotyped behavior.

Notable Side Effects:

Cardiovascular: Cardiac arrhythmias, dizziness, hypertension, hypotension, palpitations, syncope, tachycardia.

Dermatologic: pruritus, rash.

Gastrointestinal: anorexia, appetite increase, constipation, diarrhea, dyspepsia, nausea/vomiting, weight gain, weight loss.

Genitourinary: impotence, menstrual complaints, urinary frequency, urinary retention.

Musculoskeletal: arthritis.

To find out more or to speak to a nutritional counselor for free, just visit us at:
www.CuresForTheBody.com

Neurological: akathisia, akinesia/bradykinesia, cutaneous temperature disturbance, dry mouth, excessive sweating, headache/migraine, impaired sleep quality, increased salivary flow, insomnia, muscle spasms, pseudoparkinsonism, sedation, sensory disturbance, tremor.

Neuropsychiatric: agitation, anxiety, confusion, decreased libido, delusions, disturbed concentration, euphoria, hostility.

Nonspecific: Fatigue, fever/chills.

Respiratory: upper respiratory complaints.

Special Senses: auditory disturbance, blurred vision, gustatory disturbance.

Other common recommendations from medical doctors:

Depression is typically treated with a combination of drugs and psychotherapy, or in severe cases electroconvulsive therapy and/or hospitalization (those who contemplate suicide or are too frail from weight loss).

Nutritional Approach:

Disease or Condition: Depression

Causes of Depression:

Mood disorders, depression, and anxiety are common illnesses in our society. Lost work time, family conflicts, personal strife, and other consequences of the disease can eventually lead to complete disruption of one's life. Depression and mood disorders have become increasingly recognized as common, yet under-diagnosed and under-treated conditions.[358]

Nutritional support:

Foods that have been proven to help with Depression:

Dairy, turkey, soy, flaxseed, fish, and whole eggs products

Nutrients that have been proven to help with Depression:

S-Adenosylmethionine, 5-Hydrxytryptophan (5-HTP), Phenylalanie, Dehydroepiandrosterone (DHEA), Omega 3 Fatty Acids, Vitamin B6, Vitamin B12, Folic Acid, St. John's Wort, Ginkgo, and Rodiola.

To find out more or to speak to a nutritional counselor for free, just visit us at:
www.CuresForTheBody.com

Exercises that have been proven to help with Depression:

The link between exercise and depression has been the focus of many scientific studies. This research repeatedly shows that exercise really does help depression. Exercise has been shown to be as effective or better in reducing depression symptoms as antidepressants, individual and group psychotherapy and cognitive therapy.

S-Adenosylmethionine (SAMe)

S-adenosyl methionine (SAMe) is one of the most studied non-drug antidepressants available today. SAMe is a naturally occurring substance synthesized in the body from the amino acid methionine. It is critical for the synthesis of neurotransmitters.

When Italian researchers were testing SAMe as a treatment for schizophrenia in the 1970's, they discovered its antidepressant effects, setting in motion clinical studies. A recent meta-analysis concluded, "The efficacy of SAMe in treating depressive syndromes and disorders is superior with that of placebo and comparable to that of standard tricyclic antidepressants. Since SAMe is a naturally occurring compound with relatively few side effects, it is a potentially important treatment for depression."[359] Several studies report that SAMe is more effective than tricyclics.[360,361]

The results of clinical trials highlight another benefit when SAMe is used as an antidepressant agent, which is the fact that it provides a rapid therapeutic response.[362] The excitement surrounding SAMe's effectiveness as a natural antidepressant is balanced by the fact that it is a relatively costly supplement, if the therapeutic dosage is maintained.

5-Hydroxytryptophan (5-HTP)

5-hydroxytryptophan (5-HTP) and tryptophan are the precursors for serotonin. Tryptophan is an essential amino acid that the body cannot manufacturer. Tryptophan is converted into 5-HTP, which in turn is converted into serotonin.[363] There is ample evidence that tryptophan depletion causes reduced synthesis of serotonin, which results in depression and other mood disorders.[364]

In 1989, the FDA removed tryptophan from the market due to some contaminated batches that caused a number of deaths. It is now available by prescription through compounding pharmacies, and it is also used in TPN feeding and in infant formulas. However, tryptophan is still not available to the general public as a nutritional supplement. Without tryptophan on the market, 5-HTP has entered into the public's awareness as an effective and natural therapy for anxiety, depression, and sleep disorders. Either substance can be used to enhance serotonin synthesis in the brain.[365] It is now recognized that 5-HTP is more effective at elevating serotonin levels than tryptophan for the following reasons.

1. Intestinal absorption of 5-HTP does not require the presence of a transport molecule, and is not affected by the presence of other amino acids; therefore it may be taken with meals without reducing its effectiveness. Unlike tryptophan, 5-HTP cannot be shunted into niacin or protein production.

2. Therapeutic use of 5-HTP bypasses the conversion of tryptophan into 5-HTP by the enzyme tryptophan hydroxylase, which is the rate-limiting step in the synthesis of serotonin. The 5-HTP is well absorbed from an oral dose, with about 70 percent ending up in the bloodstream. It easily crosses the blood brain barrier and effectively increases central nervous system (CNS) synthesis of serotonin.[366]

The scientific literature on tryptophan's effectiveness as an antidepressant agent is mixed. However, it appears that there are certain types of depressed patients who respond well to tryptophan therapy. Scientific studies have reported the usefulness of using tryptophan supplementation for the treatment of mild forms of depression.[367,368,369]

5-HTP has been compared to antidepressant drugs in several clinical trials. Several studies have reported 5-HTP's antidepressant activity to be equal to tricyclic antidepressants. A multicenter trial in Switzerland reported that 5-HTP alleviated depression more effectively than Luvox.[370,371] In Europe, 5-HTP is frequently taken along with a drug named carbidopa, which prevents 5-HTP from being converted to serotonin in the body. This allows more 5-HTP to cross the blood brain barrier and be converted to serotonin in the brain. Using carbidopa with 5-HTP is somewhat controversial because studies report that 5-HTP is more effective and has fewer side effects when taken alone.[372]

Phenylalanine

Phenylalanine and tyrosine are the precursors to the neurotransmitters dopamine, norepinephrine, and epinephrine, which all influence and regulate mental and emotional states.

Antidepressant activity has been reported in studies using D-phenylalanine or with a mixture of both isomers called DL-phenylalanine (DLPA). Several studies have reported results equal to or better than tricyclic antidepressants without side effects.[373,374] People usually respond within two to four weeks, and in one study, severely depressed patients responded well.[375]

Tyrosine is synthesized from phenylalanine and thus it is not an essential amino acid. However, like phenylalanine, tyrosine is also intimately involved in the synthesis of dopamine, epinephrine, and norepinephrine. Therefore, the benefits and effects of tyrosine are similar to those reported for phenylalanine. Although several small trials with depressed patients have reported impressive results,[376,377] no large well-controlled studies on tyrosine and depression have been conducted to date.

Suggested dosages for tyrosine start at 500mg, three times daily and can go up to 6 grams per day. As with phenylalanine, people with high blood pressure should only use it under close medical supervision, and it is contraindicated for those with PKU and melanoma.

Dehydroepiandrosterone (DHEA)

Dehydroepiandrosterone (DHEA), when given to a small group of six depressed middle-aged and elderly patients at a dosage of 30-90 mg/day for four weeks, resulted in improvements in both depression and memory performance.[378] In a double-blind trial with 22 patients suffering from major depression, DHEA provided a significant improvement in depressive symptoms.[379] DHEA appears to be safe and without significant side effects; however, long-term human trials have not been conducted. Therapy with DHEA is contraindicated in individuals with a history of prostate or breast cancer. Dosing is best monitored through physiologic measurements of DHEA.

Omega-3 Fatty Acids

Studies report that the a ratio of low omega-3 to high omega-6 fats correlates positively with clinical symptoms of depression.[380,381] The quantity and ratio of omega-3 to omega-6 is critical because they are the precursors to the prostaglandins, which are a group of hormone-like substances that regulate many important aspects of biological function throughout the body. In a book titled *Omega-3 Oils,* Donald O. Rudin, M.D. reports that giving patients omega-3 supplements often improves mood and relieves depression within one to two weeks.[382]

A randomized, double-blind placebo controlled trial evaluated the antidepressant effects of ethyl-eicosapentaenoate in 70 patients using an adequate dose of a standard antidepressant yet continuing to experience depression. Using three different depression rating scales, the group taking 1gram/day (g/d) of ethyl-eicosapentaenoate had significantly better outcomes than placebo on all three rating scales. The 2g/d and 4g/d, at best, displayed nonsignificant trends toward improvement.[383]

Experimental evidence suggests that only a small percentage of omega-3 gets converted into its longer chain metabolites EPA and DHA.[384] Because of this, some people with depression should consider taking fish oil capsules, which contain a mixture of EPA and DHA. Individuals are encouraged to take at least 400 IU of vitamin E daily when consuming fatty acid nutritional supplements.

Vitamin B6

Vitamin B6 is required for the conversion of tryptophan to serotonin. Therefore, a deficiency of vitamin B6 may result in symptoms of anxiety and depression, due to inhibition of serotonin synthesis.[385] Numerous drugs have been known to deplete vitamin B6, which could then lead to depression.

Oral contraceptives are known to deplete vitamin B6, which may cause depression in susceptible women. In one particular study, administration of 40mg of vitamin B6 daily restored normal biochemical values and also relieved the clinical symptoms in the vitamin B6-deficient women taking oral contraceptives.[386] Other important categories of drugs that may deplete vitamin B6 include corticosteroids, theophylline-containing medications, hydralazine-containing vasodilators, loop diuretics, and estrogen replacement therapy medications.[387]

Vitamin B12

Vitamin B12 deficiency can result in depression, and this deficiency is a condition that occurs much more frequently in the elderly.[388,389] A Norwegian mental hospital conducted a test in which every patient over 30 years old that was admitted during a one-year period underwent evaluation for vitamin B12 status. The results indicated that the percentage of mental patients with below normal levels of vitamin B12 was 30 times higher than in the normal population in that area.[390] It is important to realize that a vitamin B12 deficiency may cause depression in the absence of anemia.[391]

Folic Acid

According to doctors from the Department of Psychiatry at Harvard Medical School, depressive symptoms are the most common neuropsychiatric manifestation of folate deficiency. Low serum folate levels have been found in 15-38% of adults diagnosed with depression.[392] In one double-blind placebo-controlled study, 41 patients with major depression who had depressed red cell folate levels were treated with methylfolate (15 mg/day) or a placebo. At both three and six months, patients exhibited substantial improvements in clinical outcome scores compared to the placebo controls allowing the authors to determine that folate supplementation might enhance recovery from psychiatric illness.[393,394]

St. John's Wort

St. John's wort has gained a great deal of attention for its use in minor depression. Its popularity has stemmed from its extensive use by physicians in Europe as an agent of choice in the treatment of mild to moderate depression. There are a variety of studies that are claimed to support the use of St. John's wort in treating depression.[395,396,397] Studies with St. John's wort have centered around the use of a 0.3% hypericin content standardized extract at a dose of 300mg, three times a day. It is viewed as safe and effective in Europe, and its monograph is part of the Commission E Monographs for herbal medicines in Europe.

St. John's wort has several possible effects on body chemistry, including: the inhibition of cortisol secretion and the blocking of catabolic hormones, such as interleukin 6 (IL-6);[398] the inhibition of the breakdown of several central nervous system neurotransmitters, including serotonin (it may have mild MAO-inhibiting activity; this has not been clearly defined and cannot explain all the activity of St. John's wort; researchers do not consider this to be its major mechanism of action);[399,400,401] amplification and improvement in the signal produced by serotonin once it binds to its receptor sites in the brain;[402,403] and contains the chemical melatonin (approximately 4.39 mcg/gm), which may also contribute to the antidepressant effects of the plant.[404]

Although the constituent hypericin was originally thought to have the antidepressant effects seen when using St. John's wort, recent research has reported that the constituents pseudo-hypericin and hyperforin may enhance serotonin, catecholamines, and glutamine levels in the brain.[405]

Literature has reported cytochrome P-450 enzyme-inducing activity of St. John's wort in human studies. Interactions between St. John's wort and anticoagulants, indinavir, cyclosporin, digoxin, ethinyl estradiol/desogestrel, and theophylline have occurred.[406] The mechanism of action was believed to be liver enzyme induction and subsequent alterations of drug levels by the herb. Also, several reports have suggested that concurrent use of St. John's wort and SSRIs may result in "serotonin syndrome", including sweating, tremor, confusion, flushing, and agitation.[407,408] Use St. John's wort with caution if individuals are on these medications.

Ginkgo

Ginkgo is among the oldest living species on earth and has been used extensively as a medicinal agent worldwide for centuries. It is the most frequently prescribed medicinal herb in Europe. The most dramatic benefits are reported in improving circulation in the elderly.[409,410] This can lead to enhanced memory, delaying the onset of Alzheimer's,[411] and reducing senile dementia,[412] tinnitus,[413] and vertigo.[414] Ginkgo's memory-enhancing effects are reported in younger populations as well. The main active components of ginkgo are the flavoglycosides. These compounds act as free radical scavengers or antioxidants.[415] Ginkgo is also reported to inhibit platelet activating factor (PAF), which could reduce the adhesive nature of platelets, possibly through competitive binding. Ginkgo may foster vasodilation by stimulating endothelium releasing factor and prostacyclin.[416] It may also stimulate venous tone and improve the clearance of homotoxins during ischemic episodes.[417] Gingko reportedly acts as a tonic for the circulatory system. It may increase cerebral brain flow, and therefore improve delivery of nutrients to the brain, enhancing elimination of the byproducts of cell metabolism and oxygenating the tissues. Ginkgo may normalize acetylcholine receptors and improve cholinergic function.[418]

Ginkgo has also been used to treat impotence, especially when associated with antidepressant therapy.[419,420] Ginkgo has traditionally been used as an adjunctive agent in resistant depression, often used in combination with St. John's wort.[421]

Rhodiola

Rhodiola has long been used in traditional folk medicine in China, Serbia, and the Carpathian Mountains of the Ukraine. In the former Soviet Union, it has long been used as an adaptogen, decreasing fatigue and increasing the body's natural resistance to various stresses. Rhodiola seems to enhance the body's physical and mental work capacity and productivity, working to strengthen the nervous system, fight depression, enhance immunity, elevate the capacity for exercise, enhance memorization, improve energy levels, and possibly prolong the life span.[422] The effect of alcohol-aqueous extract from rhodiola roots on the processes of learning and memory was studied in rats.[423] For the treatment of depression extracts of rhodiola, namely rosavin and salidroside, in animal studies seem to enhance the transport of serotonin precursors, tryptophan, and 5-hydroxytryptophan into the brain and decrease the action of COMT (catechol-O-methyltransferase), an enzyme that degrades serotonin.[424] Russian scientists have used Rhodiola alone or in combination with antidepressants to enhance mental state and decrease the symptoms of SAD or Seasonal Affective Disorder common to Northern European countries. Additional studies need to be performed to verify its effectiveness for this particular function.

Basic Plan for Depression

• Eliminate sugar, caffeine, and alcohol.

• Identify and eliminate food allergies.

• Exercise.

• Stress reduction can take form in a variety of ways. Some of the more structured forms include counseling, tai chi, yoga, meditation, and deep breathing.

Diabetes Mellitus

Description: When you eat carbohydrates, the body breaks them down into sugars (glucose) in the blood. The sugars are then absorbed into the bloodstream and the pancreas is stimulated to produce insulin. Insulin allows sugar to move out of the bloodstream and into the cells to be used for energy or to be stored for energy in the future. Because of this, blood sugar varies throughout the day, rising for a few hours after you eat and then returning back to normal.

When a person has diabetes mellitus, their bodies do not have enough insulin available for its needs. It is not hyperglycemia. The combination of too much sugar in their blood and not enough sugar in their cells produces the symptoms of diabetes, as well as the complications.

Diabetes increases the risk of other chronic diseases, such as cardiovascular disease, blindness, immune deficiencies, kidney disease, and vascular insufficiency and amputation.

Type 1

Description: In Type 1 diabetes, the insulin producing cells of the pancreas have been destroyed so that the pancreas produces little or no insulin. About 90% of the cells are permanently destroyed so that the person is insulin dependent. Type 1 diabetes usually manifests itself before the age of 30.

The destruction of the insulin producing cells in the pancreas may be due to a virus or poor nutrition, and some people may have a genetic predisposition for those cells to be destroyed. Vaccination and fungal mycotoxins may also be contributors to the disease.

Type 2

Description: In contrast to Type 1 diabetes where the body does not produce enough insulin, the body produces plenty of insulin Type 2 diabetes but is resistant to the insulin init. Type 2 diabetes is much more common; 90% of diabetics are Type 2.

This type of diabetes usually manifests itself after age 30, and the risk increases with age. Obesity is a factor in Type 2 diabetes as the body uses a large amount of insulin. In fact, 80-90% of people with Type 2 diabetes are obese. Obesity or being overweight is the single most important predictor for diabetes.[425]

Type 2 diabetes can also be caused by certain drugs that affect the way the body uses insulin. These include corticosteroids. Pregnancy can also be a factor in altering the way the body uses insulin (gestational diabetes), as well as diseases that damage the pancreas.

Medical Treatment:

Brand Name: Lantus

Drug Name: Insulin

Insulin regulates glucose metabolism. Insulin and its analogs lower blood glucose levels by stimulating peripheral glucose uptake, especially by skeletal muscle and fat, and by inhibiting hepatic glucose production. Insulin inhibits lipolysis in the adipocyte, inhibits proteolysis, and enhances protein synthesis.

Notable Side Effects:

> allergic reactions, injection site reaction, lipodystrophy, pruritus, rash, hypoglycemina

Brand Name: GlucaGen

Drug Name: Glucagon

Glucagon induces liver glycogen breakdown, releasing glucose from the liver. Blood glucose concentration rises within 10 minutes of injection and maximal concentrations are attained at approximately a half hour after injection. Hepatic stores of glycogen are necessary for glucagon to produce an antihypoglycemic effect.

Notable Side Effects: Nausea, vomiting may occur occasionally especially with doses above 1 mg or with rapid injection (less than 1 minute). [1] Glucagon exerts positive inotropic and chronotropic effects (tachycardia). A transient increase in both blood pressure and pulse rate may occur following the administration of glucagon.

Brand name: Avandamet

Drug Name: Metformin

Metformin is an antihyperglycemic agent, which improves glucose tolerance in patients with type 2 diabetes, lowering both basal and postprandial plasma glucose. Its pharmacologic mechanisms of action are different from other classes of oral antihyperglycemic agents. Metformin decreases hepatic glucose production, decreases intestinal absorption of glucose and increases peripheral glucose uptake and utilization. Unlike sulfonylureas, metformin does not produce hypoglycemia in either patients with type 2 diabetes or normal subjects (except in special circumstances) and does not cause hyperinsulinemia. With metformin therapy, insulin secretion remains unchanged while fasting insulin levels and daylong plasma insulin response may actually decrease.

Notable Side Effects:

> Upper respiratory tract infection, injury, headache, back pain, hyperglycemia, fatigue, sinusitis, diarrhea, viral infection, arthralgia, anemia.

Brand name: Diabinese

Drug Name: Chlorprapamide

Chlorprapamide appears to lower the blood glucose acutely by stimulating the release of insulin from the pancreas, an effect dependent upon functioning beta cells in the pancreatic islets. The mechanism by which Diabinese lowers blood glucose during long-term administration has not been clearly established. Extra-pancreatic effects may play a part in the mechanism of action of oral sulfonylurea hypoglycemic drugs. While chlorpropamide is a sulfonamide derivative, it is devoid of antibacterial activity.

Notable Side Effects:

Hypoglycemia.

Gastrointestinal: Cholestatic jaundice may occur rarely, nausea, diarrhea, vomiting, anorexia, and hunger.

Dermatologic: Pruritus. Porphyria cutanea tarda and photosensitivity reactions have been reported with sulfonylureas. Skin eruptions rarely progressing to erythema multiforme and exfoliative dermatitis have also been reported.

Hematologic: Leukopenia, agranulocytosis, thrombocytopenia, hemolytic anemia, aplastic anemia, pancytopenia, and eosinophilia have been reported with sulfonylureas.

Metabolic: Hepatic porphyria and disulfiram-like reactions have been reported with Diabinase.

Endocrine: On rare occasions, chlorpropamide has caused a reaction identical to the syndrome of inappropriate antidiuretic hormone (ADH) secretion. The features of this syndrome result from excessive water retention and include hyponatremia, low serum osmolality, and high urine osmolality. This reaction has also been reported for other sulfonylureas.

Brand name: Prandin

Drug Name: Repaglinide

Repaglinide lowers blood glucose levels by stimulating the release of insulin from the pancreas. This action is dependent upon functioning beta cells in the pancreatic islets. Insulin release is glucose-dependent and diminishes at low glucose concentrations. Repaglinide closes ATP-dependent potassium channels in the beta-cell membrane by binding at characterizable sites. This potassium channel blockade depolarizes the beta-cell, which leads to an opening of calcium channels. The resulting increased calcium influx induces insulin secretion. The ion channel mechanism is highly tissue selective with low affinity for heart and skeletal muscle.

Notable Side Effects:

Metabolic: Hypoglycemia.

Respiratory: URI, sinusitis, rhinitis, bronchitis.

Gastrointestinal: Nausea, diarrhea, constipation, vomiting, dyspepsia.

Musculoskeletal: Arthralgia, back pain.

Other: Headache, paresthesia, chest pain, urinary tract infection, tooth disorder, allergy.

Brand name: Actos

Drug Name: Pioglitazone

Pioglitazone is a thiazolidinedione antidiabetic agent that depends on the presence of insulin for its mechanism of action. ACTOS decreases insulin resistance in the periphery and liver resulting in increased insulin-dependent glucose disposal and decreased hepatic glucose output. Unlike sulfonylureas, pioglitazone is not an insulin secretagogue. Pioglitazone is a potent and highly selective agonist for peroxisome proliferator-activated receptor-gamma (PPAR(gamma)). PPAR receptors are found in tissues important for insulin action such as adipose tissue, skeletal muscle, and liver. Activation of PPAR(gamma) nuclear receptors modulates the transcription of a number of insulin responsive genes involved in the control of glucose and lipid metabolism.

Notable Side Effects: Upper respiratory tract infection, headache, sinusitis, myalgia, tooth disorder, aggravated diabetes mellitus, pharyngitis.

Brand name: Precose

Drug Name: Acarbose

Acarbose does not enhance insulin secretion. The antihyperglycemic action of acarbose results from a competitive, reversible inhibition of pancreatic alpha-amylase and membrane-bound intestinal alpha-glucoside hydrolase enzymes. Pancreatic alpha-amylase hydrolyzes complex starches to oligosaccharides in the lumen of the small intestine, while the membrane-bound intestinal alpha-glucosidases hydrolyze oligosaccharides, trisaccharides, and disaccharides to glucose and other monosaccharides in the brush border of the small intestine. In diabetic patients, this enzyme inhibition results in a delayed glucose absorption and a lowering of postprandial hyperglycemia.

Notable Side Effects:

Abdominal pain, diarrhea, and flatulence, elevated serum transaminase levels, small reductions in hematocrit, low serum calcium and low plasma vitamin B_6 levels, rash, edema.

Other common recommendations from Medical Doctors: Diet, exercise, and education are the most important factors in living with diabetes and keeping your blood sugar in the normal range. Drugs are also important for some people. Complications are much less likely to develop when you keep your blood sugar levels under control. Treating high blood pressure and high cholesterol also reduce the risk for complications.

Healthy diet and weight are important and can reduce the need for drugs, especially with Type 2 diabetes. And even with insulin dependent Type 1 diabetes patients, diet, weight, and exercise help your body maintain normal blood sugar levels.

Nutritional Approach:

Diabetes Mellitus Type 2 (non-insulin-dependent, or adult on-set diabetes)

About 90 percent of all diabetes are Type 2 and not dependent upon insulin.

Causes of Type 2 Diabetes:

Although genetic factors appear important in susceptibility to diabetes, lifestyle factors are required to trigger diabetes. Obesity is significantly affected by lifestyle factors, as ninety percent of diabetics are obese.

Nutritional support:

Foods that have been proven to help with Type 2 Diabetes:

High fiber foods (whole grains, fresh fruit and vegetables, and legumes), omega 3 and 6 essential fatty acids (raw flax seeds or oil, raw hulled hemp seeds or oil), fenugreek seeds, fish, high-chromium foods (i.e., broccoli and barley), and onions.

Nutrients that have been proven to help with Type 2 Diabetes:

Omega 3 and 6 essential fatty acids (flax oil, hemp oil, DHA, Evening Primrose oil[426]) Chromium[427], Vitamin E[428], vitamin C[429], vitamin B6, Biotin[430], Magnesium[431], Vanadium[432], Zinc [433]Cyclo (His-Pro)[434], Gymnema[435], Bitter Melon[436], Lipase enzymes.[437]

Exercises that have been proven to help with Type 2 Diabetes:

Exercise, in combination with a healthy diet, is one of the best things you can do to take care of yourself if you have diabetes. Exercise burns calories, which will help you lose weight or maintain a healthy weight.

Regular exercise can help your body respond to insulin and is known to be effective in managing blood glucose. Exercise can lower blood glucose and possibly reduce the amount of medication you need to treat diabetes, or even eliminate the need for medication. Exercise can also improve your circulation, especially in your arms and legs, where people with diabetes can have problems.

Basic Type 2 Diabetes Plan:

To reduce the risk of developing the complications of diabetes, it is important to control against elevations in blood sugar by careful monitoring. Much research on diet is directed toward preventing the long march from insulin resistance, or glucose intolerance, to full-blown diabetes. Eating certain foods can help keep diabetes away. Dietary modification and treatment is fundamental to the successful treatment of Diabetes.

- **Follow Dietary plan in chapter 5.**
- **Gradually increase fiber to a high fiber diet (25-35 grams/day).**

–Fiber slows down the digestion of sugars. Whole grains are better than refined for that very reason, not to mention the increase in nutrients.

- **Eat Omega 3 and 6 fatty acids (predominately Omega 3).**

–Researchers at the University of Sydney Australia took cells from the muscles of older non-diabetic men and women undergoing surgery. They measured the saturated fatty acids in the cell membranes and tested the patients for insulin resistance. They found that the more saturated fatty acids in cells, the greater the insulin resistance. On the other hand, higher tissue levels of polyunsaturated fat, particularly fish oil (omega 3 fatty acid), indicated better insulin activity and less resistance. In fact, the researchers also reported that feeding animals omega 3 fish oils effectively overcame their insulin resistance.

–Cut down on saturated dairy and animal fats and eat more fish and raw flax and raw hemp oils.

• Onions and garlic have demonstrated blood-sugar-lowering action in several studies and help reduce the risk of cardiovascular disease; the more onions eaten the lower the blood sugar.

• Eat high chromium foods – Broccoli, nuts, oysters, mushrooms, whole grains, barley, wheat cereal, rhubarb, brewer's yeast, nutritional yeast (read about chromium below).

• Chromium plays a major role in the sensitivity of cells to insulin.

–Supplementing - "Amino acid chelated" minerals have the highest proven absorption with the least toxicity.

• Eat foods rich in magnesium.

– Soybeans, fresh green vegetables, raw wheat germ, apples, almonds, raw nuts, honey, peaches, brown rice, figs, lemons, grapefruit, bran, yellow corn, seeds.

–It is well documented that low magnesium may aggravate diabetic conditions. It's involved in glucose metabolism and insulin secretion.

–Supplementing - "Amino acid chelated" minerals have the highest proven absorption with the least toxicity.

• Eat foods rich in vitamins B, C and E (fruits, vegetables, whole grains).

The treatment of diabetes requires nutritional supplementation, as diabetics have a greatly increased need for many nutrients.

• Vitamin C – Since the transport of vitamin C into cells is facilitated by insulin, many diabetics do not have enough intracellular vitamin C.

To find out more or to speak to a nutritional counselor for free, just visit us at:
www.CuresForTheBody.com

–Whole food vitamins are perfectly balanced without side effects. Use acreola cherry and fruit formulas known to have high quantities of vitamin C.

• **Vitamin B6** – Appears to offer significant protection against development of diabetic nerve disease.

–Whole food vitamins are perfectly balanced without side effects. Use Nutritional Yeast.

• **Vitamin E** – Diabetics appear to have an increased requirement.

–Whole food vitamins are perfectly balanced without side effects. Use wheat germ oil.

• **Biotin** – Improves glucose tolerance and insulin resistance.

• **Vanadium** – Studies show that it reduces fasting blood sugar.

–"Amino acid chelated" minerals have the highest proven absorption with the least toxicity.

• **Zinc** – Necessary for proper wound healing.

–"Amino acid chelated" minerals have the highest proven absorption with the least toxicity.

• **Gymnema sylvestre** – Recent scientific investigation has upheld its effectiveness.

• **Bitter melon –** Oral administrations of preparations has shown good results in clinical trials.

• **Cyclo (His-Pro)** – A thyrotropin releasing hormone metabolite, thought to be a useful agent in improving blood sugar regulation. Main function is improving zinc utilization which is important because it plays a role in over 300 different enzymatic functions. This extract not only contains high levels of zinc, but also several cofactors reported to stimulate intestinal zinc absorption. Zinc is important for diabetics; it is involved in wound healing, immune function, and skin integrity.

• **Lipase Enzymes** – breaks down fat for better utilization for energy production rather than storage.

–Plant source are the best form. Don't use pancreatic enzymes.

To find out more or to speak to a nutritional counselor for free, just visit us at:
www.CuresForTheBody.com

• **Digestive Enzymes**[438] - help to break food down completely, so that all the nutrients possible can be absorbed and utilized within the body, thus increasing nutrient absorption.

–Plant sources are the best. Don't use pancreatic enzymes.

• **Probiotics**[439] – re-implant the good friendly bacteria in the bowels. When sugars aren't broken down and used they remain in the blood and system for bacteria, yeast and fungal forms to feast on. Taking friendly flora helps to strengthen your immune system.

–Take only stabilized Probiotics that don't need to be refrigerated.

Diarrhea

Description: Diarrhea is not only the increase in frequency of bowel movements, but also an increase in the wateriness of the stools. It is often accompanied by gas, cramping, abdominal pain, nausea, vomiting, and an urgency to move the bowels.

Diarrhea occurs when not enough water is removed from the stool as it moves through the digestive tract. Stools normally contain 60-90% water, and diarrhea occurs when the stools are over 90% water. There are many reasons why this may happen, including if food travels too quickly through the digestive tract, certain medications, virus/bacterial/parasitic infections, chemicals, stress, and other disorders (i.e., irritable bowel syndrome).

Medical Treatment:

Absorbents:
Brand Name: Kaopectate, Pepto-Bismol
Drug Name: Bismuth subsalicylate

Intestinal Muscle Relaxants: Relaxes the muscles of the intestines.
Brand Name: Imodium
Drug Name: Loperamide
Loperamide acts by slowing intestinal motility and by affecting water and electrolyte movement through the bowel.

Other common recommendations from Medical Doctors: Diarrhea is a symptom of an underlying cause, and so the cause must be addressed in order for the diarrhea to be remedied. For example, if the diarrhea is a symptom of a viral infection, it will probably go away in 24 to

48 hours as your body fights the virus. While the diarrhea persists, it is important to drink plenty of fluids with a balance of water, sugar and salts to avoid dehydration.

Nutritional Approach:

Causes of Diarrhea

Stress, antibiotics, diseases and infections, and junk foods (fatty and sugary).

Functional disorders

Irritable bowel syndrome

• Symptoms: Recurring diarrhea with a feeling of fullness, gas or bloating, nausea.

• Self help: Don't hold gas in. Don't repress bowel movements[440].

• Nutrition: Eat smaller more frequent meals, eating slowly and chewing food thoroughly, eat fiber rich, varied foods and keep a regular meal time. Don't drink alcohol or carbonated beverages. Drink minimum of 6-8 glasses of water per day.

• Supplement: Plant source digestive enzymes and Probiotics.

• Regular exercise (walking, gymnastics, swimming, hiking, cycling) keeps the bowels in motion.

Nutritional support:

Foods that have been proven to help with Diarrhea:

Cereals, bananas, rice, tapioca, root vegetables such as carrots and potatoes, and all fermented foods.

Foods to avoid: Gaseous foods, such as beans, cabbage and onions, which cause discomfort, cramps and bloating. High-fiber bulky foods, such as course fruits and vegetables, fruit and vegetable peels. Milk, notably if you have any intolerance to milk-sugar (lactose). High-sugar liquids, including soft drinks and juices.

Coffee and other caffeine-containing beverages. Caffeine robs the body of needed fluids. Very diluted soups. Although often recommended as fluids, they are not nutritionally sufficient and are usually too high in sodium.

Nutrients that have been proven to help with Diarrhea:

Probiotics[441], potassium[442], magnesium[443], folic acid[444], zinc[445]

Exercises that have been proven to help with Diarrhea:

Exercise on a regular basis can improve your immune system along with supporting a healthy gastrointestinal system.[446] Yoga has its own exercises to support regular digestion and reduce nervousness. Relaxation techniques can support behavioral changes when symptoms appear as a result of conflicts or excitement.

Diet Prescription to Curb Diarrhea

If diarrhea is chronic, the cause, whether in infants, children or adults, could be a reaction to something in the diet.

To find a cause of chronic diarrhea:

- First, give up milk and dairy products to see if the diarrhea ceases.
- Rid the diet of sorbitol.
- If that doesn't work, give up coffee, both caffeinated and decaf (good to give up anyway).
- Avoid gaseous foods.
- In toddlers, cut back on fruit juices, especially apple juice.

To treat diarrhea:

- Reestablish Probiotics (friendly bacteria)

   –Probiotics have been used by Underdahl[447], in the treatment of diarrheal diseases in man. Lewenstein et al[448] carried a clinical observation with 14 patients, suffering from different diarrheal disorders. Patients were given three or four capsules of probiotics a day during a six- to 10-day period. They observed that the diarrheal and abdominal pain, which were very strong during the start of the treatment, disappeared in all cases between day 1 and day 3. The starting pH values of the feces ranged from 7.5 to 8.5 and fell to 7.0 in two to three days. The ratio of gram-negative to gram-positive flora reached normalcy in two to four days. The enteropathogenic E. Coli was never detected in the cultures of the feces after only two days of treatment. No abnormality was detected in blood chemistry examination.

During diarrhea symptoms, the intestinal microecology gets out of balance. In such a diseased state antibiotics are administered. Antibiotics then destroy the gut microbiota, resulting in proliferation and inhabitation of drug-resistant microbes. Thus it is essential to treat these symptoms with care without changing the microbial environment of the gastrointestinal tract.

Following the consumption of cultured dairy products, lactobacillus, or other lactic acid producing bacteria, there occurs an alteration in the intestinal microflora, particularly an increase in the lactobacillus population, as observed in the feces.[449]

The control of infant and adult diarrhea by lactobacilli has been attempted in recent years with much success, prompting researchers to conclude that even simple dietary improvements involving probiotic supplementation, without antibiotic therapy, can be effective.[450]

For infant diarrhea, the standard remedy includes oral administration of B. bifidum in human milk, cream of rice cereal, some electrolytes, and a high fluid diet. For adult diarrhea, the recommendation is for 3-4 capsules daily of a supplement containing B. bifidum taken for 6-10 days, and sufficient liquids to rehydrate.[451]

In the early mid 1980's, it was observed that in Bangladesh that diarrhea was so rampant that a child died every 6 seconds. Research work for the World Health Organization (WHO) of the United Nations and the International Center for Diarrheal Disease Research, Bangladesh (ICDDRB) showed that diarrhea could be effectively controlled by administering Flora coupled with rice oral rehydration solution containing electrolytes.

• Keep hydrated with lots of low-sugar, low-sodium fluids.

• Try cereal soup or drink made from any starchy food, such as rice, corn, wheat or potatoes. Favorites around the world are lentil soup, rice porridge, carrot soup, tapioca pudding, coconut juice and chicken noodle soup. Starchy liquids, unlike sugary ones, tend to diminish vomiting, reduce the amount of fluid lost and speed recovery time.

• Continue to eat regular foods, such as soft starchy foods like cooked carrots, potatoes and tapioca.

• Avoid irritating high fiber grains, gaseous foods and certainly milk if lactose intolerant.

• Shun high sugar fluids like fruit drinks and sugar-sweetened carbonated sodas and diet sodas.

• Avoid dairy products.

 –With the exception of live-cultured yogurt.

• Use carob or pectin (alone or in combination with kaolin).

• Brewed teas of roasted carob powder (rich in dietary fiber and polyphenols)[452].

• Pectin (a fruit fiber found in citrus fruits, apples, and many other fruits and vegetables), alone or in combination with kaolin (clay) as a bulking agent to improve the consistency of the stool.

• Reestablish Probiotics (friendly bacteria).

 –Nutritional: Yogurt with live-cultures.

• Supplemental: Take stabilized Probiotics and plant source digestive enzymes[453].

Foods That Can Trigger Diarrhea:
• Milk, fruit juices, sorbitol and coffee

Foods That Relieve or Prevent Diarrhea:
• Starchy soups and cereals, and yogurt

Foods That Can Delay Recovery:
• Caffeine, high-sugar juices and soft drinks, "Rest the Bowel" diets.

To find out more or to speak to a nutritional counselor for free, just visit us at:
www.CuresForTheBody.com

Diagnostic Criteria for Common Causes of Diarrhea[454]:
Intestinal viral infections

Enterovirus, rotavirus

Intestinal bacterial infections

Campylobacter jejuni, Shigella, Salmonella, Yersinai enterocolitica

Intestinal bacterial toxins

Clostridium difficele, pathogenic Escherichia coli, Staphylococcus, Vibrio parahaemolytica, Vibrio cholerae

Parasitic infections

Giardia lamblia, Entamoeba histolytica, Cryotisoirium, Isospora

• Symptoms for the 4 above causes: Diarrhea with stomach pain, fever, headache, muscle pain, vomiting.

• Self help: Nutritional: Drink plenty of liquids, eat yogurt with live-cultures.[455]

• Supplement: Take stabilized probiotics.

• Call your doctor if infection persists after 3 days.

Inflammatory bowel disease

Crohn's disease, ulcerative colitis, diverticulitis

• Symptoms: Diarrhea with blood and mucus in the stool. Fever may be present.

• Self help for Crohn's disease: A fiber rich diet, plenty of rest, and a stress-free lifestyle. [456]

• Self help for ulcerative colitis: A varied diet containing plenty of fiber.[457]

• Supplement: Take plant source digestive enzymes and stabilized Probiotics for all of these[458].

Side effects of many medicines, especially:

Antibiotics, cough and asthma medicines, medicines containing iron, medicines for heart and circulatory disorders, medicines for stomach and intestinal disorders, rheumatism and gout medicines.[459]

To find out more or to speak to a nutritional counselor for free, just visit us at:
www.CuresForTheBody.com

• Symptoms: Diarrhea after taking certain medicines.

–Self help: If your medication is over the counter and does not list diarrhea as a side effect, stop taking it[460].

• If your medicine is by prescription and you were not alerted to possible side effects, call your doctor[461].

• Taking antibiotics[462]:

–Nutritional self help: Eat yogurt with live-cultures.

–Supplement: Stabilized Probiotics.

Inadequate bile secretion

Hepatitis, bile duct obstruction.

• Self help: Supplement: Take plant source digestive enzymes for fat digestion (Lipase).

Malabsorption states

Celiac sprue (severe wheat allergy), short small bowel, lactose Intolerance.

• **Self help for Celiac sprue:**

• Nutrition: Switch to a diet completely free of gluten. Use cornmeal, buckwheat, rice, millet, potato, quinoa, legumes, tapioca. Fruits, vegetables, dairy products, eggs, poultry, fish, etc. may be eaten. Eat small frequent meals.

• Avoid: thickening agents, stabilizers, emulsifiers, MSG, starch, gluten, hydrogenated vegetable protein.

• Supplemental: Take plant source digestive enzymes with meals. Whole food vitamins, amino acid chelated minerals, especially calcium.[463]

• **Self help for lactose intolerance:**

• Nutritional and Supplement: Avoid dairy milk or take plant source digestive enzymes that include lactase. Yogurt is usually fine because it has already gone through the first stage of digestion and contains live-cultures.

Pancreatic disease:

• Pancreatic insufficiency, pancreatic tumor

Self help:

–Nutritional: Eat as many raw fruits, vegetables, raw nuts, and sprouted seeds (lessening the burden of the pancreas to provide enzymes for cooked foods).

–Supplemental: Plant source digestive enzymes.

Reflex from other areas
Pelvic inflammatory disease

Neurological disease
Syphilis, diabetic neuropathy

Metabolic disease
Hyperthyroidism

Bowel Cancer
• Symptoms: Diarrhea alternating with constipation over a long period of time, bloody stool, passing stool whilempassing gas, weight loss.

• Self help: Take plant source digestive enzymes and stabilized Probiotics.

Eye Problems/Macular Degeneration

Description: Macular degeneration is an age-related condition in which there is a gradual vision loss due to the progressive damage to the macula. One study showed that macular degeneration affects about 2% of Americans between 52-64 years of age, 11% between 65-74 years of age, and 28% that are 75 years and older.[464] Macular degeneration occurs equally between men and women, but is more common among fair-skinned individuals and those who smoke. Macular degeneration rarely leads to complete blindness, although it can severely damage vision.

There are two types of macular degeneration. Dry (atrophic) macular degeneration results as the macula tissues thin and disappear. There is no scarring, bleeding, or other fluid in the eye. The first symptoms of dry macular degeneration are fuzzy central vision and a loss of fine detail.

In wet macular degeneration, abnormal blood vessels under the macula leak fluid and blood, resulting in scar tissue under the retina. The first symptoms of wet macular degeneration can be a distortion of vision. Loss of vision tends to progress quickly.

Some researchers show that arteriosclerosis, oxidative damage, photic damage, inflammation, diet, vitamin and rare element deficiencies, and genetics are contributors to macular degeneration. One study also showed that depression may exacerbate the progression of macular degeneration and that by treating the depression, you can improve the outcomes of the macular degeneration.[465]

Medical Treatment:

No drugs are currently available to slow or stop the progression of macular degeneration of either type.

To find out more or to speak to a nutritional counselor for free, just visit us at:
www.CuresForTheBody.com

Other common recommendations from Medical Doctors: In dry macular degeneration, there are currently no drug treatments that have been shown to be effective in slowing or stopping the progression of the disease. However, high doses of antioxidants (Vitamins A,C,E, and Selenium), copper, and zinc have shown to be beneficial.

In wet macular degeneration, various laser or photodynamic therapies can be used to destroy the abnormal blood vessels.

Low vision specialists can provide counseling to those with macular degeneration to help them adjust to their limited vision. Reading glasses and other types of magnifiers for the TV, computer, etc., can be an aid.

Nutritional Approach:

Disease or Condition: Macular Degeneration/ Eye Problems
Causes of Macular Degeneration:

Macular degeneration is a major cause of gradual, painless, central vision loss in the elderly[466]. It occurs as a result of geographic atrophy, serous detachment of the retinal pigment epithelium, and / or choroidal neovascularization. Although it is widely accepted that the primary loci of the disease are the choriocapillaris, Bruch's membrane, and the retinal pigment epithelium, the visual loss in age-rated macular degeneration results for dysfunction and death of the overlying photoreceptors.[467]

Nutritional support:
Foods that have been proven to help with macular degeneration:

Foods with high lutein and zeaxanthin content include green leafy vegetables, egg yolk, corn, orange peppers, kiwi fruit, grapes, spinach, orange juice, zucchini, and different kinds of squash.[468]

Nutrients that have been proven to help with Macular Degeneration:

Vitamin A,[469] Zinc,[470] Lutein and Zeaxanthin[471],Lycopene,[472] Vitamin E[473],Vitamin C,[474] Bilberry,[475] Grape Seed Extract,[476] Green Tea.[477]

Zinc

Studies have reported lower serum zinc levels in individuals with macular degeneration.[478,479,480]

To find out more or to speak to a nutritional counselor for free, just visit us at:
www.CuresForTheBody.com

Lutein and Zeaxanthin

Lutein and zeaxanthin are the primary carotenoids comprising the macular pigment of the eyes. In addition to acting as optical filters, evidence suggests that they also function as antioxidants in the human retina by inhibiting the peroxidation of long-chain polyunsaturated fatty acids.[481]

Foods with high lutein and zeaxanthin content include green leafy vegetables, egg yolk, corn, orange peppers, kiwi fruit, grapes, spinach, orange juice, zucchini, and different kinds of squash.[482]

Lycopene

Lycopene is the most abundant carotenoid in the serum. One study reported that individuals with levels of lycopene in the lowest quintile were twice as likely to have age-related macular degeneration. Surprisingly, this study also reported finding that serum levels of the carotenoids that predominate in the macular pigment (lutein and zeaxanthin) were unrelated to ARMD.[483]

Vitamin E

Much of the research on the etiology of age-related macular degeneration and other eye diseases has focused on the role of nutritional antioxidants. Evidence from epidemiological studies suggests that nutritional antioxidants, such as vitamin E, may play a role in delaying the onset of these age-related vision disorders.[484] It is now known that vitamin E is distributed within retinal tissues.[485] Some research results indicate that patients with age-related macular degeneration have significantly lower serum vitamin E levels compared to age-matched controls.[486]

Vitamin C

Evidence from epidemiological studies indicates that vitamin C is one of the antioxidant nutrients that may play a role in delaying the onset of age-related macular degeneration and other visual disorders.[487] However, other studies report finding that vitamin C levels are not associated with a reduced risk to macular degeneration.[488,489] The multicenter Eye Disease Case-Control Study involved 356 case subjects and 520 control subjects. The results from this study found no statistically significant protective effects for vitamin C or E or selenium individually, but an antioxidant index that combined the micronutrients revealed statistically significant risk reductions with increasing levels of the index.[490]

Basic Macular Degeneration Plan
• Avoid smoking.

To find out more or to speak to a nutritional counselor for free, just visit us at:
www.CuresForTheBody.com

• Avoid excess UV sunlight.

• Supplement with above mentioned vitamins and minerals.

• Consume adequate amounts of antioxidant fruits and vegetables(these foods are bright in color like broccoli and dark fruits).

To find out more or to speak to a nutritional counselor for free, just visit us at:
www.CuresForTheBody.com

Fibromyalgia

Description: Fibromyalgia is the aching, pain, and stiffness of the soft tissues of the body (muscles, ligaments, and tendons).It is not a life-threatening condition, but can be very disruptive to daily activities and lifestyle. The symptoms of fibromyalgia may be worsened by physical or mental stress, poor sleep, injury, or exposure to the cold.

There are three variations of fibromyalgia: primary, secondary, and localized.

Primary fibromyalgia is the most common type of fibromyalgia and is much more common in women than men (7 times). The aching, pain, and stiffness usually develop gradually and are widespread throughout the body. It is not associated with any other disease or underlying condition. Primary fibromyalgia symptoms are typically accompanied by other symptoms, including poor sleep, anxiety, depression, fatigue, and irritable bowel syndrome.

Secondary fibromyalgia occurs in patients in which the symptoms of fibromyalgia are a result of an underlying condition, such as hypothyroidism. Secondary fibromyalgia is also widespread in the body.

Localized fibromyalgia is more common in men and the symptoms come on more rapidly than in primary or secondary fibromyalgia. The symptoms are usually a result of an occupation or sports, and are generally localized in a particular area of the body.

Medical Treatment:

Brand name: Tylenol

Drug Name: Acetaminophen

Acetaminophen inhibits prostaglandin synthetase.

To find out more or to speak to a nutritional counselor for free, just visit us at:
www.CuresForTheBody.com

Notable Side Effects:

Light-headedness, dizziness, sedation, nausea and vomiting.

<u>NSAIDS</u>: Lessen pain and swelling. NSAIDS do not heal or cure this condition. **Anti-inflammatory drugs also cause cartilage damage[491]. With this understanding, you will actually be causing more damage than good in the long run so use as sparingly as possible.**

Brand name: Advil, Motrin

Drug Name: Ibuprofen

Ibuprofen is a nonsteroidal anti-inflammatory drug (NSAID) that possesses anti-inflammatory, analgesic and antipyretic activity. Its mode of action, like that of other NSAIDs, is not completely understood, but may be related to prostaglandin synthetase inhibition. After absorption of the racemic ibuprofen, the [-]R-enantiomer undergoes interconversion to the [+]S-form. The biological activities of ibuprofen are associated with the [+]S-enantiomer.

Notable Side Effects:

Cardiovascular system: Edema, fluid retention (generally responds promptly to drug discontinuation).

Digestive system: Nausea, epigastric pain, heartburn, diarrhea, abdominal distress, nausea and vomiting, indigestion, constipation, abdominal cramps or pain, fullness of Gl tract (bloating and flatulence).

Nervous system: Dizziness, headache, nervousness.

Skin and appendages: Rash (including maculopapular type), pruritus.

Special senses: Tinnitus.

Brand name: Aleve, Anaprox

Drug Name: Naproxen

Naproxen is a nonsteroidal anti-inflammatory drug (NSAID) with analgesic and antipyretic properties. The sodium salt of naproxen has been developed as a more rapidly absorbed formulation of naproxen for use as an analgesic. The naproxen anion inhibits prostaglandin synthesis but beyond this its mode of action is unknown.

To find out more or to speak to a nutritional counselor for free, just visit us at:
www.CuresForTheBody.com

Notable Side Effects:

Gastrointestinal: Constipation, heartburn, abdominal pain, nausea, dyspepsia, diarrhea, stomatitis.

Central Nervous System: Headache, dizziness, drowsiness, lightheadedness, vertigo.

Dermatologic: Itching (pruritus), skin eruptions, ecchymoses, sweating, purpura.

Special Senses: Tinnitus, hearing disturbances, visual disturbances.

Cardiovascular: Edema, dyspnea, palpitations.

General: Thirst.

Other common recommendations from Medical Doctors:

Avoid the activities that exacerbate the symptoms of fibromyalgia. Physical therapy, relaxation, and psychological counseling have proven helpful in some cases.

Nutritional Approach:

Disease or Condition: Fibromyalgia

Causes of Fibromyalgia:

The exact causes of fibromyalgia are not known, but there are several triggers that precede the onset of this condition. Triggers include viral and bacterial infections, the candida albicans fungus, physical traumas, development of other health problems such as rheumatoid arthritis, lupus "leaky gut" syndrome, or hypothyroidism, psychological stress, immune or endocrine abnormalities, mitochondrial uncoupling of energy production, or biochemical abnormalities in the central nervous system.

Nutritional support:

Foods that have been proven to help with Fibromyalgia:

Soybeans, whole wheat and buckwheat flours, raw almonds and cashews, brown rice, and many legumes.

Avoid meat, dairy and other foods high in saturated fats, fried and processed foods, white flour products, shellfish, caffeine, alcohol or sugar (including fructose and honey).

To find out more or to speak to a nutritional counselor for free, just visit us at:
www.CuresForTheBody.com

Nutrients that have been proven to help with Fibromyalgia:

S-adenosylmethionine[492], magnesium and malic acid, essential amino acid tryptophan and 5-hydroxytryptophan (5-HTP)[493], melatonin[494], L-glutamine (lactobacillus acidophilus), vitamin B1[495], lecithin, manganese[496], proteolytic enzymes[497], grapeseed extract, vitamins A and C.

Exercises that have been proven to help with Fibromyalgia:

Current research indicates that patients with fibromyalgia who participate in a specially designed, carefully controlled exercise program can improve physical function and mood and even decrease pain, in many cases; overall quality of life is greatly enhanced.[498]

Slow, strength training exercises along with stretching have been proven to be the most beneficial.

Basic Fibromyalgia Plan:

• **Establish optimal nutrition.**

–Studies show that 60% of individuals with gastrointestinal disorders have fibromyalgia, 70% of individuals with fibromyalgia experience symptoms of irritable bowel syndrome, and 50% complain of symptoms of functional dyspepsia. These individuals typically have abnormal levels of microbial in the gastrointestinal tract. These digestive problems can cause "leaky gut" syndrome which is a possible trigger of fibromyalgia.[499] These gastrointestinal problems may be combated with digestive enzymes.

–Malabsorption is common in individuals with fibromyalgia; therefore, ensuring the highest absorption of nutrients is vital. Minerals should be amino acid chelated minerals, as they are the readily absorbed into the body in this from.[500]

–Eating foods with high levels of vitamins A, B6, B12, C, and E are essential in the support of the immune system.[501]

• **Drink plenty of liquids.**

–Vegetable juices and water should be consumed to flush out toxins in the body.

• **Replenish friendly bacteria.**

–Supplementation with probiotics can combat candida albicans and promote a balance of good and bad bacteria.[502]

Heart Disease

Description: Angina is chest pain or a sensation of pressure that occurs while the heart muscle is not receiving enough oxygen. This can be due to narrowing of the arteries because of fatty deposits, or due to another abnormality that interferes with the body's ability to give the heart blood and oxygen. This is a very common condition in the United States and affects nearly 6.5 million people.

Angina is typically triggered by physical exertion, weather, and sometimes emotional stress. In these instances, the heart has to work hard and its need for oxygen is increased. Although unusual, if the arteries are narrowed more than 70%, symptoms of angina can be felt while at rest. Most people feel an ache or pressure under the breastbone, and can also feel pain in the shoulder, arm, back, throat, or jaw.

Angina is related to coronary artery disease, and some people experience angina because of it. Coronary artery disease is the buildup of fatty materials in the arteries due to atherosclerosis. As the fatty materials build up in the arteries, the blood flow to the heart is limited.

Medical Treatment:

Anticoagulants:

Prevent blood from clotting. Used to treat people who have unstable angina or who have had a heart attack

Brand name: Coumadin

Drug Name: Warfarin

Warfarin is an anticoagulant which acts by inhibiting vitamin K-dependent coagulation factors. Vitamin K is an essential cofactor for the post ribosomal synthesis of the vitamin K dependent clotting factors. The vitamin promotes the biosynthesis of (gamma)-carboxyglutamic acid residues

To find out more or to speak to a nutritional counselor for free, just visit us at:
www.CuresForTheBody.com

in the proteins which are essential for biological activity. Warfarin is thought to interfere with clotting factor synthesis by inhibition of the regeneration of vitamin K_1 epoxide.

Notable Side Effects:

Fatal or nonfatal hemorrhage from any tissue or organ. This is a consequence of the anticoagulant effect. The signs, symptoms, and severity will vary according to the location and degree or extent of the bleeding. Hemorrhagic complications may present as paralysis; paresthesia; headache, chest, abdomen, joint, muscle or other pain; dizziness; shortness of breath, difficult breathing or swallowing; unexplained swelling; weakness; hypotension; or unexplained shock. Therefore, the possibility of hemorrhage should be considered in evaluating the condition of any anticoagulated patient with complaints which do not indicate an obvious diagnosis. Bleeding during anticoagulant therapy does not always correlate with PT/INR. Bleeding which occurs when the PT/INR is within the therapeutic range warrants diagnostic investigation since it may unmask a previously unsuspected lesion, e.g., tumor, ulcer, etc. Necrosis of skin and other tissues.

Antiplatelet drugs:

Prevent platelets from clumping and blood clots from forming. They also reduce the risk of a heart attack. They are used to treat people who have stable or unstable angina or who have had a heart attack. Aspirin is taken as soon as a heart attack is suspected. People with an allergy to aspirin may take clopidogrel or ticlopidine as an alternative.

Brand name: Bayer, Ecotrin

Drug Name: Aspirin

Aspirin is a more inhibitor of both prostaglandin synthesis and platelet aggregation.

Notable Side Effects:

Body as a Whole: Fever, hypothermia, thirst.

To find out more or to speak to a nutritional counselor for free, just visit us at:
www.CuresForTheBody.com

Cardiovascular: Dysrhythmias, hypotension, tachycardia.

Central Nervous System: Agitation, cerebral edema, coma, confusion, dizziness, headache, subdural or intracranial hemorrhage, lethargy, seizures.

Fluid and Electrolyte: Dehydration, hyperkalemia, metabolic acidosis, respiratory alkalosis.

Gastrointestinal: Dyspepsia, GI bleeding, ulceration and perforation, nausea, vomiting, transient elevations of hepatic enzymes, hepatitis, Reye's Syndrome, pancreatitis.

Hematologic: Prolongation of the prothrombin time, disseminated intravascular coagulation, coagulopathy, thrombocytopenia.

Hypersensitivity: Acute anaphylaxis, angioedema, asthma, bronchospasm, laryngeal edema, urticaria.

Musculoskeletal: Rhabdomyolysis.

Metabolism: Hypoglycemia (in children), hyperglycemia.

Reproductive: Prolonged pregnancy and labor, stillbirths, lower birth weight infants, antepartum and postpartum bleeding.

Respiratory: Hyperpnea, pulmonary edema, tachypnea.

Special Senses: Hearing loss, tinnitus. Patients with high frequency hearing loss may have difficulty perceiving tinnitus. In these patients, tinnitus cannot be used as a clinical indicator of salicylism.

Urogenital: Interstitial nephritis, papillary necrosis, proteinuria, renal insufficiency and failure.

Brand name: Plavix

Drug Name: Clopidogrel

Clopidogrel is an inhibitor of ADP-induced platelet aggregation acting by direct inhibition of adenosine diphosphate (ADP) binding to its receptor and of the subsequent ADP-mediated activation of the glycoprotein GPIIb/IIIa complex.

Notable Side Effects:

Severe bleeding, chest pain, accidental/inflicted injury, flu-like symptoms, pain, fatigue, edema, hypertension, headache, dizziness, abdominal pain, dyspepsia, diarrhea, nausea, hypercholesterolemia, arthralgia, back pain, purpura/bbruising, epistaxis, depression, upper respitory tract infection, dyspnea, rhinitis, bronchitis, coughing, rash, pruritus, urinary tract infection.

Brand Name: Ticlid

Drug Name: Ticlopidine

Ticlopidine causes a time- and dose-dependent inhibition of both platelet aggregation and release of platelet granule constituents, as well as a prolongation of bleeding time. Ticlopidine hydrochloride, after oral ingestion, interferes with platelet membrane function by inhibiting ADP-induced platelet-fibrinogen binding and subsequent platelet-platelet interactions. The effect on platelet function is irreversible for the life of the platelet, as shown both by persistent inhibition of fibrinogen binding after washing platelets ex vivo and by inhibition of platelet aggregation after resuspension of platelets in buffered medium.

Notable Side Effects:

Diarrhea, nausea, dyspepsia, rash, GI pain, neutropenia, purpura, vomiting, flatulence, pruritus, dizziness, anorexia, abnormal liver function.

Glycoprotein inhibitors:

These drugs prevent platelets from clumping and blood clots from forming. They are used to treat people who have unstable angina or who are undergoing percutaneous transluminal coronary angioplasty after a heart attack.

Brand name: ReoPro

Drug Name: Abciximab

Abciximab is the Fab fragment of the chimeric human-murine monoclonal antibody 7E3. Abciximab binds to the glycoprotein (GP) IIb/IIIa receptor of human platelets and inhibits platelet aggregation. Abciximab also binds to the vitronectin ((alpha) $_v$ (beta) $_3$) receptor found on platelets and vessel wall endothelial and smooth muscle cells. The chimeric 7E3 antibody is produced by continuous perfusion in mammalian cell culture. The 47,615 dalton Fab fragment is purified from cell culture supernatant by a series of steps involving specific viral inactivation and removal procedures, digestion with papain and column chromatography.

Notable Side Effects:

Bleeding, intracranial hemorrhage and stroke, thrombocytopenia, hypotension, bradycardia, nausea, vomiting, abdominal pain, back pain, chest pain, headache, puncture site pain, peripheral edema.

Brand name: Integrilin
Drug Name: Eptifibatide

Eptifibatide reversibly inhibits platelet aggregation by preventing the binding of fibrinogen, von Willebrand factor, and other adhesive ligands to GP IIb/IIIa. When administered intravenously, eptifibatide inhibits *ex vivo* platelet aggregation in a dose- and concentration-dependent manner. Platelet aggregation inhibition is reversible following cessation of the eptifibatide infusion; this is thought to result from dissociation of eptifibatide from the platelet.

Notable Side Effects:

Bleeding, intracranial hemorrhage and stroke, thrombocytopenia, allergic reactions.

Brand name: Aggrastat
Drug Name: Tirofiban

Tirofiban, a non-peptide antagonist of the platelet glycoprotein (GP) llb/llla receptor, inhibits platelet aggregation.

Notable Side Effects:

Bleeding, edema/swelling, pelvic pain, vasovagal reaction, bradycardia, coronary artery dissection, leg pain, dizziness, sweating.

Beta-blockers:

Reduce the workload of the heart and the risk of a heart attack and sudden death. They are used to treat people who have stable or unstable angina or syndrome X or who have had a heart attack.

Brand name: Tenormin

Drug Name: Atenolol

Atenolol is a beta$_1$-selective (cardioselective) beta-adrenergic receptor blocking agent without membrane stabilizing or intrinsic sympathomimetic (partial agonist) activities. This preferential effect is not absolute, however, and at higher doses, atenolol inhibits beta$_2$-adrenoreceptors, chiefly located in the bronchial and vascular musculature.

Notable Side Effects:

Bradycardia, cold extremities, postural hypotension, leg pain, dizziness, vertigo, light-headedness, tiredness, fatigue, lethargy, drowsiness, depression, dreaming, diarrhea, nausea, wheeziness, dyspenea.

Brand name: Betoptic

Drug Name: Betaxolol

Betaxolol, a cardioselective (beta-1-adrenergic) receptor blocking agent, does not have significant membrane-stabilizing (local anesthetic) activity and is devoid of intrinsic sympathomimetic action. Orally administered beta-adrenergic blocking agents reduce cardiac output in healthy subjects and patients with heart disease. In patients with severe impairment of myocardial function, beta-adrenergic receptor antagonists may inhibit the sympathetic stimulatory effect necessary to maintain adequate cardiac function.

Notable Side Effects:

Ocular: blurred vision, corneal punctate keratitis, foreign body sensation, photophobia, tearing, itching, dryness of eyes, erythema, inflammation, discharge, ocular pain, decreased visual acuity and crusty lashes.

Systemic reactions following administration of BETOPTIC S Ophthalmic Suspension 0.25% or

To find out more or to speak to a nutritional counselor for free, just visit us at:
www.CuresForTheBody.com

BETOPTIC Ophthalmic Solution 0.5% have been rarely reported. These include:

Cardiovascular: Bradycardia, heart block and congestive failure.

Pulmonary: Pulmonary distress characterized by dyspnea, bronchospasm, thickened bronchial secretions, asthma and respiratory failure.

Central Nervous System: Insomnia, dizziness, vertigo, headaches, depression, lethargy, and increase in signs and symptoms of myasthenia gravis.

Other: Hives, toxic epidermal necrolysis, hair loss, and glossitis. Perversions of taste and smell have been reported.

Brand name: Zebeta

Drug Name: Bisoprolol

Bisoprolol is a synthetic, beta$_1$-selective (cardioselective) adrenoceptor blocking agent. Bisoprolol fumarate also inhibits beta$_2$-adrenoceptors, chiefly located in the bronchial and vascular musculature.

Notable Side Effects:

Central Nervous System: Dizziness, unsteadiness, vertigo, syncope, headache, paresthesia, hypoesthesia, hyperesthesia, somnolence, sleep disturbances, anxiety/restlessness, decreased concentration/memory, reversible mental depression progressing to catatonia, hallucinations, an acute reversible syndrome characterized by disorientation to time and place, emotional lability, slightly clouded sensorium.

Autonomic Nervous System: Dry mouth.

Cardiovascular: Bradycardia, palpitations and other rhythm disturbances, cold extremities, claudication, hypotension, orthostatic hypotension, chest pain, congestive heart failure, dyspnea on exertion.

Psychiatric: Vivid dreams, insomnia, depression.

Gastrointestinal: Gastric/epigastric/abdominal pain, gastritis, dyspepsia, nausea, vomiting, diarrhea, constipation, peptic ulcer, mesenteric arterial thrombosis, ischemic colitis.

To find out more or to speak to a nutritional counselor for free, just visit us at:
www.CuresForTheBody.com

Musculoskeletal: Muscle/joint pain, arthralgia, back/neck pain, muscle cramps, twitching/tremor.

Skin: Rash, acne, eczema, psoriasis, skin irritation, pruritus, flushing, sweating, alopecia, dermatitis, angioedema, exfoliative dermatitis, cutaneous vasculitis.

Special Senses: Visual disturbances, ocular pain/pressure, abnormal lacrimation, tinnitus, decreased hearing, earache, taste abnormalities.

Metabolic: Gout.

Respiratory: Asthma/bronchospasm, bronchitis, coughing, dyspnea, pharyngitis, rhinitis, sinusitis, URI.

Genitourinary: Decreased libido/impotence, Peyronie's disease, cystitis, renal colic, polyuria.

Hematologic: Agranulocytosis, thrombocytopenia, thrombocytopenic purpura.

General: Fatigue, asthenia, chest pain, malaise, edema, weight gain, angioedema.

Allergic: Fever, combined with aching and sore throat, laryngospasm, respiratory distress.

Brand name: Toprol-XL

Drug Name: Metoprolol

Metoprolol is a $beta_1$-selective (cardioselective) adrenergic receptor blocking agent. This preferential effect is not absolute, however, and at higher plasma concentrations, metoprolol also inhibits $beta_2$-adrenoreceptors, chiefly located in the bronchial and vascular musculature. Metoprolol has no intrinsic sympathomimetic activity, and membrane-stabilizing activity is detectable only at plasma concentrations much greater than required for beta-blockade. Animal and human experiments indicate that metoprolol slows the sinus rate and decreases AV nodal conduction. Clinical pharmacology studies have confirmed the beta-blocking activity of metoprolol in man, as shown by (1) reduction in heart rate and cardiac output at rest and upon exercise, (2) reduction of systolic blood pressure upon exercise, (3) inhibition of isoproterenol-induced tachycardia, and (4) reduction of reflex orthostatic tachycardia.

Notable Side Effects:

Central Nervous System: Tiredness and dizziness have occurred in about 10 of 100 patients. Depression has been reported in about 5 of 100 patients. Mental confusion and short-term memory loss have been reported. Headache, somnolence, nightmares, and insomnia have also been reported.

Cardiovascular: Shortness of breath and bradycardia have occurred in approximately 3 of 100 patients. Cold extremities; arterial insufficiency, usually of the Raynaud type; palpitations; congestive heart failure; peripheral edema; syncope; chest pain; and hypotension have been reported in about 1 of 100 patients.

Respiratory: Wheezing (bronchospasm) and dyspnea have been reported in about 1 of 100 patients.

Gastrointestinal: Diarrhea has occurred in about 5 of 100 patients. Nausea, dry mouth, gastric pain, constipation, flatulence, digestive tract disorders, and heartburn have been reported in about 1 of 100 patients.

Hypersensitive Reactions: Pruritus or rash have occurred in about 5 of 100 patients. Worsening of psoriasis has also been reported.

Miscellaneous: Peyronie's disease has been reported in fewer than 1 of 100,000 patients. Musculoskeletal pain, blurred vision, decreased libido, and tinnitus have also been reported.

Brand name: Nadolol Tablets, Corzide

Drug Name: Nadolol

Nadolol is a nonselective beta-adrenergic receptor blocking agent. Clinical pharmacology studies have demonstrated beta-blocking activity by showing (1) reduction in heart rate and cardiac output at rest and on exercise, (2) reduction of systolic and diastolic blood pressure at rest and on exercise, (3) inhibition of isoproterenol-induced tachycardia, and (4) reduction of reflex orthostatic tachycardia. Nadolol specifically competes with beta-adrenergic receptor agonists for available beta receptor sites; it inhibits both the $beta_1$ receptors located chiefly in cardiac muscle and the $beta_2$ receptors located chiefly in the bronchial and vascular musculature, inhibiting the chronotropic, inotropic, and vasodilator responses to beta-adrenergic stimulation proportionately.

Notable Side Effects:

Cardiovascular: Bradycardia with heart rates of less than 60 beats per minute, and heart rates below 40 beats per minute and/or symptomatic bradycardia were seen in about 2 of 100 patients. Symptoms of peripheral vascular insufficiency. Cardiac failure, hypotension, and rhythm/conduction disturbances. First degree and third degree heart block have been reported; intensification of AV block is a known effect of beta-blockers.

Central Nervous System: Dizziness or fatigue paresthesias, sedation, and change in behavior.

Respiratory: Bronchospasm.

Gastrointestinal: Nausea, diarrhea, abdominal discomfort, constipation, vomiting, indigestion, anorexia, bloating, and flatulence.

Miscellaneous: Rash; pruritus; headache; dry mouth, eyes, or skin; impotence or decreased libido; facial swelling; weight gain; slurred speech; cough; nasal stuffiness; sweating; tinnitus; blurred vision. Reversible alopecia.

Central Nervous System: Reversible mental depression progressing to catatonia; visual disturbances; hallucinations; an acute reversible syndrome characterized by disorientation for time and place, short-term memory loss, emotional lability with slightly clouded sensorium, and decreased performance on neuropsychometrics.

Gastrointestinal: Mesenteric arterial thrombosis; ischemic colitis; elevated liver enzymes.

Hematologic: Agranulocytosis; thrombocytopenic or nonthrombocytopenic purpura.

Allergic: Fever combined with aching and sore throat; laryngospasm; respiratory distress.

Miscellaneous: Pemphigoid rash; hypertensive reaction in patients with pheochromocytoma; sleep disturbances; Peyronie's disease.

Calcium channel blockers:

Prevent blood vessels from narrowing and can counter artery spasm. Diltiazem and verapamil reduce the heart rate. Calcium channel blockers are used to treat people who have stable angina.

Brand name: Norvasc

Drug Name: Amlodipine

Amlodipine reduces the total peripheral resistance (afterload) against which the heart works and reduces the rate pressure product, and thus myocardial oxygen demand, at any given level of exercise in exertional Angina. In Vasospastic Angina, Amlopidine has been demonstrated to block constriction and restore blood flow in coronary arteries and arterioles in response to calcium, potassium epinephrine, serotonin, and thromboxane A $_2$ analog in experimental animal models and in human coronary vessels *in vitro* . This inhibition of coronary spasm is responsible for the effectiveness of NORVASC in vasospastic (Prinzmetal's or variant) angina.

Notable Side Effects:

Edema, dizziness, flushing, palpitation, headache, fatigue, nausea, abdominal pain, somnolence.

Nitrates:

These drugs relieve angina, prevent episodes of angina, and reduce the risk of a heart attack and sudden death. 8-12 hour periods without taking the drug are needed daily to maintain the long-term effectiveness.

Brand name: Nitrostat

Drug Name: Nitroglycerin

Nitroglycerin relaxes the vascular smooth muscle. Although venous effects predominate, nitroglycerin produces, in a dose-related manner, dilation of both arterial and venous beds. Dilation of postcapillary vessels, including large veins, promotes peripheral pooling of blood, decreases venous return to the heart, and reduces left ventricular end-diastolic pressure (preload). Nitroglycerin also produces arteriolar relaxation, thereby reducing peripheral vascular resistance and arterial pressure (afterload), and dilates large epicardial coronary arteries; however, the extent to which this latter effect contributes to the relief of exertional angina is unclear.

Notable Side Effects:

Headache which may be severe and persistent may occur immediately after use. Vertigo, dizziness, weakness, palpitation, and other manifestations of postural hypotension may develop occasionally, particularly in erect, immobile patients. Marked sensitivity to the hypotensive effects of nitrates (manifested by nausea, vomiting, weakness, diaphoresis, pallor, and collapse) may occur at therapeutic doses. Syncope due to nitrate vasodilatation has been reported. Flushing, drug rash, and exfoliative dermatitis have been reported in patients receiving nitrate therapy.

Opioids:

Relieve anxiety and pain if the pain persists despite use of other drugs

Brand name:

Drug Name: Morphine

Morphine produces a wide spectrum of pharmacologic effects including analgesia, dysphoria, euphoria, somnolence, respiratory depression, diminished gastrointestinal motility and physical dependence. Opiate analgesia involves at least three anatomical areas of the central nervous system: the periaqueductal-periventricular gray matter, the ventromedial medulla and the spinal cord. A systemically administered opiate may produce analgesia by acting at any, all or some combination of these distinct regions. Morphine interacts predominantly with the [micro]-receptor. The [micro]-binding sites of opioids are very discretely distributed in the human brain, with high densities of sites found in the posterior amygdala, hypothalamus, thalamus, nucleus caudatus, putamen and certain cortical areas. They are also found on the terminal axons of primary afferents within laminae I and II (substantia gelatinosa) of the spinal cord and in the spinal nucleus of the trigeminal nerve.

Notable Side Effects:

Respiratory depression, respiratory arrest, tolerance and myoclonus, pruritus, urinary retention, constipation, headache, dizziness, euphoria, anxiety, depression of cough reflex, interference with thermal regulation and oliguria, evidence of histamine release, wheals and/or local tissue irritation, nausea, and vomiting.

To find out more or to speak to a nutritional counselor for free, just visit us at:
www.CuresForTheBody.com

Thrombolytic drugs:

Dissolve blood clots. They are used to treat people who have had a heart attack.

Brand name: Activase

Drug Name: Alteplase (Recombinant tissue plasminogen activator)

Alteplase is an enzyme (serine protease) which has the property of fibrin-enhanced conversion of plasminogen to plasmin. It produces limited conversion of plasminogen in the absence of fibrin. When introduced into the systemic circulation at pharmacologic concentration, Activase binds to fibrin in a thrombus and converts the entrapped plasminogen to plasmin. This initiates local fibrinolysis with limited systemic proteolysis.

Notable Side Effects:

Internal bleeding, intracranial hemorrhage, arrhythmias, AV block, cardiogenic shock, heart failure, cardiac arrest, recurrent ischemia, myocardial reinfarction, myocardial rupture, electromechanical dissociation, pericardial effusion, pericarditis, mitral regurgitation, cardiac tamponade, thromboembolism, pulmonary edema. These events may be life threatening and may lead to death. Nausea and/or vomiting, hypotension and fever have also been reported.

Other common recommendations from Medical Doctors: It is important to be aware of your risk factors for heart disease and to adjust your lifestyle to limit the effects of these risk factors on your health. Quitting smoking, a low-fat and varied diet, exercise, and weight loss (if needed) are some of the most important ways that you can reduce your risk factors.

Nutritional Approach:

Disease or Condition: Heart Disease

Causes of Heart Disease

Genes, gender and lifestyle factors (including smoking, lack of exercise and stress).

To find out more or to speak to a nutritional counselor for free, just visit us at:
www.CuresForTheBody.com

Even when scientists eliminate all those things, diet still pops out as vital to whether your arteries clog or your heart gives out.

Nutritional support:

Foods that have been proven to help with Heart Disease:

Fatty fish and or flax oil (loaded with omega 3 fatty acids), fruits, vegetables, nuts, whole grains, legumes, onions, garlic, olive oil, foods high in C and E and Beta Carotene. Fermented foods.

Avoid: Meat and dairy foods high in saturated fat and excessive alcohol.

Nutrients that have been proven to help with Heart Disease:

Probiotics[503], Plant Enzymes (lipase)[504], Vitamin E[505], vitamin C[506], L-Carnitine[507], Coenzyme Q10 (CO-Q10)[508], Magnesium[509], Omega 3 Fatty Acids[510], Potassium[511], Selenium[512], B Complex vitamins[513], Soy Isoflavones[514], Beta-$_{1,3}$, Glucan[515], Lycopene[516], Coleus[517], Hawthorn[518], Garlic[519], Cordyceps[520], Kava[521], Psyllium seed[522], Proteolytic enzymes[523], Probiotics.[524]

Exercises that have been proven to help with Heart Disease:

When you exercise regularly, your entire cardiovascular system benefits. This is because exercise prevents the onset of high blood pressure if you're at increased risk of developing it, lowers your blood pressure if you already have high blood pressure, increases the concentration of high-density lipoprotein (HDL) cholesterol (the "good" cholesterol) and decreases the concentration of low-density lipoprotein (LDL) cholesterol (the "bad" cholesterol) in your blood. It also strengthens your heart so it can pump your blood more efficiently to bring much-needed oxygen and nutrients to the rest of your body.[525]

Basic Heart Disease Plan:

• The number-one advice to keep heart disease away has to be: eat more fatty fish or flax oil (high in omega-3 fatty acids) daily or at minimum 2 times per week.

• Go heavy on garlic, onions and all kinds of other vegetables and fruits.

• Shun fatty animal foods, such as high-fat meat and dairy products.

To find out more or to speak to a nutritional counselor for free, just visit us at:
www.CuresForTheBody.com

• Use cold processed olive oil and canola oil to cook with.

• Use flax oil in salad dressings, smoothies etc. (never cook with it).

• Omega 3 Fatty Acids

–These fatty acids, when incorporated into the diet at levels of about 1 g/d, seem to stabilize myocardial membranes electrically, resulting in reduced susceptibility to ventricular dysrhythmias, thereby reducing the risk of sudden death.

–The recent GISSI study of 11,324 patients showed a 45% decrease in risk of sudden cardiac death and a 20% reduction in all-cause mortality in the group taking 850 mg/d of omega-3 fatty acids.

–These fatty acids have potent anti-inflammatory effects and may also be antiatherogenic.

–Higher doses of omega-3 fatty acids can lower elevated serum triglyceride levels; 3 to 5 g/ d can reduce triglyceride levels by 30% to 50%, minimizing the risk of both coronary heart disease and acute pancreatitis."

• Garlic

–has been reported to lower total cholesterol, LDL cholesterol and triglycerides, and increase HDL cholesterol.

–The antioxidant effect in aged garlic has been reported to be beneficial in preventing stroke and arteriosclerosis.

–A recent study reported no effect of garlic oil on serum lipids. However, the product used was garlic oil, which is processed and heated garlic. The impact of processing is an important fact to keep in mind when recommending garlic supplements. Changes can occur in the active constituents when exposed cooking or other processing which can render the garlic product virtually ineffective. Cooking is known to denature proteins and therefore may inactivate the enzyme (allinase) that is necessary in converting Allinase into allicin, the major bio-active constituent in garlic. Also, research has reported that allinase may be irreversibly inhibited by stomach acid and may fail to form adequate amounts of allicin or other thiosulfinates below pH 3.6. Recommending a quality garlic supplement is essential, and enteric coating may be advantageous.

* Of further note, as reported in a few laboratory studies, is the potential for large amounts of allicin to damage liver tissue if absorbed due to its oxidation potential. However, there are positive studies while using high quality garlic preparations standardized to allicin potential without adverse effects.

• Psyllium Seed

–One of psyllium's findings is in its potential for management of cholesterol levels. 1.78 g/serving given four servings a day as a dietary fiber, has been approved by The US Food and Drug Administration (FDA) to reduce cardiovascular disease risk.

–There have been several clinical trials reporting the effectiveness of psyllium in hypercholesterolemia.

–Fiber in the diet, especially soluble fiber, can reportedly reduce absorption of blood cholesterol and fecal bile acids that can lower cholesterol levels, decreasing the risk for heart disease and stroke.

• Beta-1,3 Glucan – appear to be the major cholesterol lowering agents in oat bran fiber.

–This dietary fiber, 0.75 g/serving and four servings a day, has been approved by The US Food and Drug Administration (FDA) to reduce cardiovascular disease risk.

• Vitamin E

–a well researched substance with evidence suggesting it prevents the oxidative damage that leads to atherosclerosis.

–In the Cambridge Heart Antioxidant Study (CHAOS), over 2000 patients with angiographically proven coronary atherosclerosis were followed for periods ranging from 3 to 910 days (median 510 days). In this double-blind, placebo-controlled trial, three groups of patients were randomly assigned to receive daily doses of 400 IU vitamin E, 800 IU of vitamin E, or a placebo. The patients taking the doses of vitamin E had a 47% reduction in subsequent heart attacks (both fatal and non-fatal) compared to the placebo controls. The overall reduction in non-fatal secondary heart attacks was 77%.

–In another study, 156 men aged 40-59 years with previous coronary artery bypass graft surgery reported that individuals taking 100 IU of vitamin E or more daily had a substantial reduction in the progression of atherosclerosis.

–Even better, take whole food vitamin E – Wheat germ oil.

• Vitamin C

–In a study that was conducted at UCLA, it was reported that men who took 800 mg. of vitamin C daily had a 42% reduction in mortality from cardiovascular disease, compared to men who only consumed the FDA's Recommended Dietary Allowance (RDA) of 60 mg of vitamin C daily. This study also reported that men consuming the larger amounts of vitamin C lived an average of 6 years longer than the men who only consumed the RDA of 60 mg of vitamin C daily.

–In another study, 316 women and 511 men (aged 19-95 years) were administered vitamin C well above RDA. The results were improved lipid profiles corresponding to possible reduced risk of cardiovascular disease.

–Even better, take whole food vitamin C – Acreola cherry and citrus fruit formulas.

• B Complex Vitamin

–Several studies have documented the fact that supplementation with folic acid, vitamin B6, and vitamin B12 can effectively lower homocysteine levels.

–There are wide variations in the dosages of these B-vitamins used in different studies.

–A deficiency of any one of these three B-vitamins can lead to elevated homocysteine.

–It is now recognized that even moderate elevations of homocysteine represent a strong independent risk to cardiovascular disease.

–There are numerous examples of people who had been taking vitamins B6, B12, and folic acid at substantially greater than RDA levels, who when tested, still had

To find out more or to speak to a nutritional counselor for free, just visit us at:
www.CuresForTheBody.com

elevated homocysteine. The only way to ensure appropriate doses of these B-vitamins to maintain low homocysteine levels is by lab assessment.

• **Magnesium** – It performs functions similar to numerous cardiovascular drugs.

–It inhibits platelet aggregation (like aspirin), thins the blood (like warfarin), blocks calcium uptake (like nifedipine), and relaxes blood vessels (like ACE inhibitors such as enaparil).

–Magnesium also increases oxygenation of the heart muscle by improving cardiac contractibility.

–Adequate magnesium is associated with reduced incidence of angina, cardiac spasms, and arrhythmias, as well as having relaxing and antispasmodic effects of the blood vessels. On the other hand, magnesium deficiency is associated with increased incidence of atherosclerosis, hypertension, strokes, and heart attacks.

–It is now recognized that many heart attacks happen to individuals with relatively healthy hearts. It is a magnesium deficiency that causes a cardiac spasm, which results in death.

• **Potassium** – Epidemiological evidence reveals that increasing potassium intake can lower blood pressure in individuals who have essential hypertension and:

–can result in a reduction of antihypertensive medications.

–Diets high in potassium have also been reported to protect against death from strokes.

• **Selenium**

–Low plasma selenium (less than 45 micrograms/L) has been considered a significant risk factor for cardiovascular disease.

–Selenium's protective mechanisms include selenium's role in the enzyme glutathione peroxidase, which helps remove hydrogen peroxide and lipid peroxides. Lipid peroxidation may damage cell membranes and it may also activate the liberation of arachidonic acid from phospholipids, which may ultimately increase the risk to thrombogenesis, platelet aggregation and vasoconstriction.

To find out more or to speak to a nutritional counselor for free, just visit us at:
www.CuresForTheBody.com

–Selenium is antagonistic to cadmium, mercury, and lead which have been related to hypertension and it is also antagonistic to other cardiotoxic elements. Selenium has a cardioprotective effect against drugs and other xenobiotics that are cardiotoxic (e.g., Adriamycin). Selenium has a known antiviral capability, which may protect the heart from agents such as the coxsackie B4 viruses.

• **Soy Isoflavones**

–Studies have found that supplementation with soy isoflavones exerted favorable effects on blood pressure symptoms and a reduction in LDL and an increase in HDL levels.

–Specifically, genistein reportedly inhibits platelet aggregation and smooth muscle cell proliferation. Smooth muscle cells are one of the primary cell types comprising plaques.

• **Lycopene**

–One study matched a control group of 483 healthy middle-aged to elderly women to an equivalent group that had CVD. Blood levels of lycopene, other carotenoids, and retinol were measured in both groups. The results of this study were adjusted for smoking, cholesterol, and age. The results found that those who had the highest blood levels of lycopene had a 50% reduced risk of CVD when compared to those who had the lowest levels. These results were not seen in the other carotenoids measured. The authors concluded that the results of this study warrant further investigations into the mechanisms of lycopene.

• **L-Carnitine**

–Studies report that carnitine can be therapeutically useful in the treatment of various forms of cardiovascular disease such as angina, acute myocardial infarction, congestive heart failure, peripheral vascular disease, arrhythmias and abnormal blood lipids.

• **Coenzyme Q10 (CO-Q10)**

–In one double-blind study, patients with severe congestive heart failure who were given 150 mg/day of CoQ10 had a 38% decrease in hospitalizations due to worsening of heart failure compared to the control group. At the same time, episodes of pulmonary edema decreased by 60% and angina episodes decreased by 53%. In another study it was shown that the symptoms of cardiovascular disease got progressively worse as CoQ10 levels declined. Treatment with 100 mg of coenzyme Q10 daily resulted in both subjective and objective improvement in 69% of patients with cardiomyopathy and 43% of patients with ischemic heart disease.

–The authors of one study noted that coenzyme Q10 is transported throughout the body packaged into the LDL and VLDL fractions of cholesterol. They emphasized that the transport of CoQ10 by LDL-cholesterol means that CoQ10 is acting as an antioxidant to prevent the oxidation of LDL-cholesterol and the subsequent development of atherosclerosis.

–Numerous categories of prescription drugs can inhibit the body's ability to synthesize coenzyme Q10. Drugs that can deplete coenzyme Q10 include sulfonylureas, biguanides, beta-blockers, hydralazine-containing vasodilators, thiazide diuretics, centrally-acting antihypertensives (clonidine and methyldopa), the "statin" cholesterol-lowering drugs, tricyclic antidepressants, and phenothiazines.

• **Coleus**

–stimulates thyroid function

–increases insulin secretion

–inhibits mast cell release of histamine and

–increases the burning of fats as fuels.

–claimed to inhibit platelet activating factor (PAF) by possibly directly binding to PAF receptor sites.

• **Hawthorne**

–Studies have reported a reduction in blood pressure due to arteriosclerosis and chronic nephritis with the use of hawthorn.

–It has a slight diuretic effect which may help lower high blood pressure.

–Its bioflavonoids reportedly dilate both peripheral and coronary blood vessels. This leads to its use in decreasing angina attacks.

–Laboratory studies have reported that proanthocyanidins;,which are a component of hawthorne, may actually aid in reversing atherosclerotic plaque.

–In Europe, physicians have found that it helps maintain digoxin levels while decreasing the need for the pharmaceutical medication.

• **Proteolytic enzymes** – Lipase enzymes have been shown to lower blood lipid levels dramatically. In clinical applications in hundreds of doctors' offices around the country, Lipase supplementation has consistently lowered blood cholesterol levels. This is the favored nutritional approach of the lead author.

• **Probiotics** - A study of hypercholesterolemic individuals showed that probiotics created a distinct increase in the HDL/LDL ratio. Another study showed a cholesterol lowering capability of L.Acidophilus in infants and in adults.

• **Kava** – Decreasing and managing stress may also play a key role in improving cardiovascular health.

–Studies have reported that kava preparations compare favorably to benzodiazepines in controlling symptoms of anxiety and minor depression, while increasing vigilance, sociability, memory, and reaction time.

–Tolerance does not seem to develop with kava use.

High Blood Pressure/ Hypertension

Description: Hypertension is a condition of high blood pressure regardless of the cause. It is more common in blacks, and the risk increases with age. One-fourth of people in the United States between the ages of 20-74 have hypertension, and three-fourths of women and two-thirds of men over 75 have hypertension.

Blood pressure is described by two values: the highest pressure in the arteries when the heart contracts (systolic pressure), and the lowest pressure just before the heart contracts (diastolic pressure). Blood pressure is considered high when the systolic pressure is above 140 and the diastolic pressure is above 90 for mild hypertension.

When a change in blood pressure occurs, the body has compensatory means of returning it back to normal. These include changing the amount of blood that the heart pumps, controlling the diameter of the arteries, and changing the volume of blood in the bloodstream. The kidneys can also help control blood pressure by excreting salt and water in the blood so that the blood volume decreases, which returns the pressure to normal.

For those that have primary hypertension, the cause is unknown. However, the increase in pressure may be due to a change in the heart and blood vessels or an increase in the blood volume. Other factors contributing to hypertension include an inherited abnormality, obesity, sedentary lifestyle, stress, smoking, excessive alcohol, and salt.

Most people with hypertension experience no symptoms from hypertension itself, so it often goes a long time without being treated. However, once damage has occurred to other organs as a result of hypertension (brain, eyes, heart, kidneys), symptoms of those conditions may manifest themselves as headaches, fatigue, nausea, vomiting, shortness of breath, restlessness, and blurred vision.

To find out more or to speak to a nutritional counselor for free, just visit us at:
www.CuresForTheBody.com

Hypertension increases for other conditions. The higher the pressure, the more likely you are to experience a stroke, mycardial infarction, angina, heart failure, renal failure, or early death from a cardiovascular cause.[526]

Medical Treatment:

Diuretics

Brand Name: Dyazide

Drug Name: Hydrochlorothiazide

Hydrochlorothiazide component blocks the reabsorption of sodium and chloride ions, and thereby increases the quantity of sodium traversing the distal tubule and the volume of water excreted. A portion of the additional sodium presented to the distal tubule is exchanged there for potassium and hydrogen ions. With continued use of hydrochlorothiazide and depletion of sodium, compensatory mechanisms tend to increase this exchange and may produce excessive loss of potassium, hydrogen and chloride ions. Hydrochlorothiazide also decreases the excretion of calcium and uric acid, may increase the excretion of iodide and may reduce glomerular filtration rate. The exact mechanism of the antihypertensive effect of hydrochlorothiazide is not known.

Notable Side Effects:

Hypersensitivity: Anaphylaxis, rash, urticaria, photosensitivity. *Cardiovascular:* Arrhythmia, postural hypotension. *Metabolic:* Diabetes mellitus, hyperkalemia, hyperglycemia, glycosuria, hyperuricemia, hypokalemia, hyponatremia, acidosis, hypochloremia. *Gastrointestinal:* Jaundice and/or liver enzyme abnormalities, pancreatitis, nausea and vomiting, diarrhea, constipation, abdominal pain. *Renal:* Acute renal failure (one case of irreversible renal failure has been reported), interstitial nephritis, renal stones composed primarily of triamterene, elevated BUN and serum creatinine, abnormal urinary sediment. *Hematologic:* Leukopenia, thrombocytopenia and purpura, megaloblastic anemia. *Musculoskeletal:* Muscle cramps.

Central Nervous System: Weakness, fatigue, dizziness, headache, dry mouth. *Miscellaneous:* Impotence, sialadenitis.

To find out more or to speak to a nutritional counselor for free, just visit us at:
www.CuresForTheBody.com

Thiazides alone have been shown to cause the following additional adverse reactions:

Central Nervous System: Paresthesias, vertigo. *Ophthalmic:* Xanthopsia, transient blurred vision. *Respiratory:* Allergic pneumonitis, pulmonary edema, respiratory distress. *Other:* Necrotizing vasculitis, exacerbation of lupus. *Hematologic:* Aplastic anemia, agranulocytosis, hemolytic anemia. *Neonate and infancy:* Thrombocytopenia and pancreatitis—rarely, in newborns whose mothers have received thiazides during pregnancy.

Adrenergic blockers

Brand name: Nadolol Tablets

Drug Name: Nadolol

Nadolol is a nonselective beta-adrenergic receptor blocking agent. Clinical pharmacology studies have demonstrated beta-blocking activity by showing (1) reduction in heart rate and cardiac output at rest and on exercise, (2) reduction of systolic and diastolic blood pressure at rest and on exercise, (3) inhibition of isoproterenol-induced tachycardia, and (4) reduction of reflex orthostatic tachycardia. Nadolol specifically competes with beta-adrenergic receptor agonists for available beta receptor sites; it inhibits both the beta $_1$ receptors located chiefly in cardiac muscle and the beta $_2$ receptors located chiefly in the bronchial and vascular musculature, inhibiting the chronotropic, inotropic, and vasodilator responses to beta-adrenergic stimulation proportionately.

Notable Side Effects: *Cardiovascular:* Bradycardia with heart rates of less than 60 beats per minute, and heart rates below 40 beats per minute and/or symptomatic bradycardia were seen in about 2 of 100 patients. Symptoms of peripheral vascular insufficiency. Cardiac failure, hypotension, and rhythm/conduction disturbances. First degree and third degree heart block have been reported; intensification of AV block is a known effect of beta-blockers. *Central Nervous System:* Dizziness or fatigue paresthesias, sedation, and change in behavior. *Respiratory:* Bronchospasm. *Gastrointestinal:* Nausea, diarrhea, abdominal discomfort, constipation, vomiting, indigestion, anorexia, bloating, and flatulence. *Miscellaneous:* Rash; pruritus; headache; dry mouth, eyes, or skin; impotence or decreased libido; facial swelling; weight gain; slurred speech; cough; nasal stuffiness; sweating; tinnitus; blurred vision. Reversible alopecia. *Central Nervous System:* Reversible mental depression progressing to catatonia; visual disturbances; hallucinations; an acute reversible syndrome characterized by disorientation for time and place, short-term memory loss, emotional lability with slightly clouded sensorium, and decreased performance on neuropsychometrics. *Gastrointestinal:* Mesenteric arterial thrombosis; ischemic colitis; elevated liver enzymes. *Hematologic:* Agranulocytosis; thrombocytopenic or nonthrombocytopenic purpura. *Allergic:* Fever combined with aching and sore throat; laryngospasm; respiratory distress. *Miscellaneous:* Pemphigoid rash; hypertensive reaction in patients with pheochromocytoma; sleep disturbances; Peyronie's disease.

Centrally acting alpha-agonists

Brand Name: Aldoril

Drug Name: Methyldopa

Methyldopa is an aromatic-amino-acid decarboxylase inhibitor in animals and in man. Although the mechanism of action has yet to be conclusively demonstrated, the antihypertensive effect of methyldopa probably is due to its metabolism to alpha-methylnorepinephrine, which then lowers arterial pressure by stimulation of central inhibitory alpha-adrenergic receptors, false neurotransmission, and/or reduction of plasma renin activity.

Notable Side Effects: Sedation, Headache, asthenia, or weakness. *Cardiovascular:* Aggravation of angina pectoris, congestive heart failure, prolonged carotid sinus hypersensitivity, orthostatic hypotension (decrease daily dosage), edema or weight gain, bradycardia. *Digestive:* Pancreatitis, colitis, vomiting, diarrhea, sialadenitis, sore or "black" tongue, nausea, constipation, distention, flatus, dryness of mouth. *Endocrine:* Hyperprolactinemia. *Hematologic:* Bone marrow depression, leukopenia, granulocytopenia, thrombocytopenia, hemolytic anemia; positive tests for antinuclear antibody, LE cells, and rheumatoid factor, positive Coombs test. *Hepatic:* Liver disorders including hepatitis, jaundice, abnormal liver function tests. *Hypersensitivity:* Myocarditis, pericarditis, vasculitis, lupus-like syndrome, drug-related fever, eosinophilia. *Nervous System/Psychiatric:* Parkinsonism, Bell's palsy, decreased mental acuity, involuntary choreoathetotic movements, symptoms of cerebrovascular insufficiency, psychic disturbances including nightmares and reversible mild psychoses or depression, headache, sedation, asthenia or weakness, dizziness, lightheadedness, paresthesias. *Metabolic:* Rise in BUN. *Musculoskeletal:* Arthralgia, with or without joint swelling; myalgia. *Respiratory:* Nasal stuffiness. *Skin:* Toxic epidermal necrolysis, rash. *Urogenital:* Amenorrhea, breast enlargement, gynecomastia, lactation, impotence, decreased libido. *Hydrochlorothiazide Body as a Whole:* Weakness. *Cardiovascular:* Hypotension including orthostatic hypotension (may be aggravated by alcohol, barbiturates, narcotics or antihypertensive drugs). *Digestive:* Pancreatitis, jaundice (intrahepatic cholestatic jaundice), diarrhea, vomiting, sialadenitis, cramping, constipation, gastric irritation, nausea, anorexia. *Hematologic:* Aplastic anemia, agranulocytosis, leukopenia, hemolytic anemia, thrombocytopenia. *Hypersensitivity:* Anaphylactic reactions, necrotizing angiitis (vasculitis and cutaneous vasculitis), respiratory distress including pneumonitis and pulmonary edema, photosensitivity, fever, urticaria, rash, purpura. *Metabolic:* Electrolyte imbalance, hyperglycemia, glycosuria, hyperuricemia. *Musculoskeletal:* Muscle spasm. *Nervous System/Psychiatric:* Vertigo, paresthesias, dizziness, headache, restlessness. *Renal:* Renal failure, renal dysfunction, interstitial nephritis. *Skin:* Erythema multiforme including Stevens-Johnson syndrome, exfoliative dermatitis including toxic epidermal necrolysis, alopecia. *Special Senses:* Transient blurred vision, xanthopsia. *Urogenital:* Impotence.

Angiotensin-converting enzyme (ACE) inhibitors

Brand Name:

Drug Name: Captopril

Captopril is a specific competitive inhibitor of angiotensin I-converting enzyme (ACE), the enzyme responsible for the conversion of angiotensin I to angiotensin II. The mechanism of action of captopril has not yet been fully elucidated. Its beneficial effects in hypertension and heart failure appear to result primarily from suppression of the renin-angiotensin-aldosterone system. However, there is no consistent correlation between renin levels and response to the drug. Renin, an enzyme synthesized by the kidneys, is released into the circulation where it acts on a plasma globulin substrate to produce angiotensin I, a relatively inactive decapeptide. Angiotensin I is then converted by angiotensin converting enzyme (ACE) to angiotensin II, a potent endogenous vasoconstrictor substance. Angiotensin II also stimulates aldosterone secretion from the adrenal cortex, thereby contributing to sodium and fluid retention.

Notable Side Effects:*Renal:* Proteinuria, renal insufficiency, renal failure, nephrotic syndrome, polyuria, oliguria, and urinary frequency. *Hematologic:* Neutropenia/ agranulocytosis has occurred. Cases of anemia, thrombocytopenia, and pancytopenia have been reported. *Dermatologic:* Rash, often with pruritus, and sometimes with fever, arthralgia, and eosinophilia, a reversible associated pemphigoid-like lesion, and photosensitivity have also been reported. Flushing or pallor. *Cardiovascular:* Hypotension may occur. Tachycardia, chest pain, and palpitations have each been observed in approximately 1 of 100 patients. Angina pectoris, myocardial infarction, Raynaud's syndrome, and congestive heart failure. *Dysgeusia:* Approximately 2 to 4 (depending on renal status and dose) of 100 patients developed a diminution or loss of taste perception. Taste impairment is reversible and usually self-limited (2 to 3 months) even with continued drug administration. Weight loss may be associated with the loss of taste. *Angioedema:* Angioedema involving the extremities, face, lips, mucous membranes, tongue, glottis or larynx. Angioedema involving the upper airways has caused fatal airway obstruction. *Gastrointestinal:* Cough, gastric irritation, abdominal pain, nausea, vomiting, diarrhea, anorexia, constipation, aphthous ulcers, peptic ulcer, dizziness, headache, malaise, fatigue, insomnia, dry mouth, dyspnea, alopecia, paresthesias.

Other clinical adverse effects reported since the drug was marketed are listed below by body system. In this setting, an incidence or causal relationship cannot be accurately determined.

Body as a Whole: Anaphylactoid reactions. *General:* Asthenia, gynecomastia. *Cardiovascular:* Cardiac arrest, cerebrovascular accident/insufficiency, rhythm disturbances, orthostatic hypotension, syncope. *Dermatologic:* Bullous pemphigus, erythema multiforme (including Stevens-Johnson syndrome), exfoliative dermatitis. *Gastrointestinal:* Pancreatitis, glossitis, dyspepsia. *Hematologic:* Anemia, including aplastic and hemolytic. *Hepatobiliary:* Jaundice, hepatitis, including rare cases of necrosis, cholestasis. *Metabolic:* Symptomatic hyponatremia. *Musculoskeletal:* Myalgia, myasthenia. *Nervous/Psychiatric:* Ataxia, confusion, depression, nervousness, somnolence. *Respiratory:* Bronchospasm, eosinophilic pneumonitis, rhinitis. *Special Senses:* Blurred vision. *Urogenital:* Impotence

Angiotensin II blockers

Brand Name: Avapro

Drug Name: Irbesartan

Irbesartan: Angiotensin II is a potent vasoconstrictor formed from angiotensin I in a reaction catalyzed by angiotensin-converting enzyme (ACE, kininase II). Angiotensin II is the principal pressor agent of the renin-angiotensin system (RAS) and also stimulates aldosterone synthesis and secretion by adrenal cortex, cardiac contraction, renal resorption of sodium, activity of the sympathetic nervous system, and smooth muscle cell growth. Irbesartan blocks the vasoconstrictor and aldosterone-secreting effects of angiotensin II by selectively binding to the AT_1 angiotensin II receptor. There is also an AT_2 receptor in many tissues, but it is not involved in cardiovascular homeostasis. Blockade of the AT_1 receptor removes the negative feedback of angiotensin II on renin secretion, but the resulting increased plasma renin activity and circulating angiotensin II do not overcome the effects of irbesartan on blood pressure.

Notable Side Effects: abdominal pain, anxiety/ nervousness, chest pain, dizziness, edema, headache, influenza, musculoskeletal pain, pharyngitis, nausea/ vomiting, rash, rhinitis, sinus abnormality, tachycardia and urinary tract infection.

Calcium Channel Blockers

Brand Name: Procardia XL

Drug Name: Nifedipine (extended release)

Nifedipine works in two ways: relaxation and prevention of coronary artery spasm, and reduction of oxygen utilization.

1. *Relaxation and Prevention of Coronary Artery Spasm:*

Nifedipine dilates the main coronary arteries and coronary arterioles, both in normal and ischemic regions, and is a potent inhibitor of coronary artery spasm, whether spontaneous or ergonovine-induced. This property increases myocardial oxygen delivery in patients with coronary artery spasm, and is responsible for the effectiveness of nifedipine in vasospastic (Prinzmetal's or variant) angina. Whether this effect plays any role in classical angina is not clear, but studies of exercise tolerance have not shown an increase in the maximum exercise rate-pressure product, a widely accepted measure of oxygen utilization. This suggests that, in general, relief of spasm or dilation of coronary arteries is not an important factor in classical angina.

2. *Reduction of Oxygen Utilization*: Nifedipine regularly reduces arterial pressure at rest and at a given level of exercise by dilating peripheral arterioles and reducing the total peripheral vascular resistance (afterload) against which the heart works. This unloading of the heart reduces myocardial energy consumption and oxygen requirements, and probably accounts for the effectiveness of nifedipine in chronic stable angina.

Notable Side Effects: (*most common*) Headache, fatigue, dizziness, constipation, nausea. *Body as a Whole/ Systemic:* Asthenia, flushing, pain. *Cardiovascular:* palpitations. *Central Nervous System:* insomnia, nervousness, paresthesia, somnolence. *Dermatologic:* pruritus, rash. *Gastrointestinal:* abdominal pain, diarrhea, dry mouth, dyspepsia, flatulence. *Musculoskeletal:*

arthralgia, leg cramps.*Respiratory:*   chest pain (nonspecific), dyspnea. *Urogenital:*   impotence, polyuria.

Other common recommendations from Medical Doctors: There are several ways to naturally reduce blood pressure if you fit into one or more risk categories. These include obtaining and maintaining a desirable weight, eating a healthy diet, reducing alcohol and sodium intake, and stopping smoking. Regular moderate exercise can also help to regulate blood pressure. It is also recommended to monitor your blood pressure at home as it makes it easier to implement the lifestyle changes necessary to lower your blood pressure and to follow your doctor's recommendations.

Nutritional Approach:

Disease or Condition: High Blood Pressure

Causes of High Blood Pressure

According to the American Heart Association, the cause of 90-95% of High Blood Pressure cases is unknown. These cases are referred to as primary hypertension. The other 5-10% of the cases are caused by kidney abnormalities, structural abnormality of the aorta, or narrowing of arteries; known as secondary hypertension. The National Heart, Lung, Blood Institute (National Institute of Health) states that high blood pressure can be prevented and controlled. High blood pressure increases the risk for stroke, myocardio infaction, heart failure, renal failure, and early death from cardiovascular problems.[527]

Nutrional Support:

Foods that have been proven to help with High Blood Pressure

Complex carbohydrates, garlic, onions, shallots, chives, leeks, oats, wheat germ, olives, nuts, organ meats, eggs, raspberries, cranberries, grapes, red wine, black currant red cabbage, green tea.

Nutrients that have been proven to help with High Blood Pressure

Plant enzymes[528], Potassium[529], Calcium[530], Magnesium[531,532], Omega 3 Fatty Acids[533], Vitamin E[534,535]; and Garlic[536].

Exercise that have been proven to help with High Blood Pressure

A new study published in Archives of Internal Medicine provides further proof that exercise, especially in combination with weight loss, can help keep high blood pressure under control. Exercise will decrease the amount of fat present in the body which puts extra stress on the cardiovascular system.[537]

Potassium, Calcium, and Magnesium

Help with blood flow by providing electrolytes. These minerals have been proven to help with blood pressure by providing mineral support to the blood.

Omega 3 Fatty Acids, Vitamin E, and Garlic

Provide essential oils that support the lipid lining of the red blood cells and improve blood pressure. These nutrients have been proven to help with Platelet function, Thromboxane formation, and blood pressure control durning supplementation.[538]

Herbs

Astragalus, Ginkgo Biloba, Maitake Mushrooms – Improves circulation.

Basic High Blood Pressure Plan

Enzymes such as bromelain, proteases, amylase, and lipase improve circulation, blood vessel integrity, and strengthen capillary walls. They also breakdown circulating proteins, fats, and carbohydrates.

1. Reduce stress.
2. Maintain an optimal weight.
3. Select foods high in antioxidants.
4. Select low sodium foods.
5. Select foods rich in enzymes – raw foods.
6. Exercise regularly.
7. Avoid foods high in saturated fats
8. Avoid coffees, teas, and sodas – increases blood pressure temporarily

High Cholesterol

Description: Lipid disorders are when you have excess fatty substances in your blood. These substances include cholesterol, triglycerides, and lipoproteins. Lipid disorders are an important risk factor in developing atherosclerosis and heart disease.

Alternative Names: Lipid disorders; hyperlipoproteinemia; Hyperlipidemia

Causes, incidence, and risk factors: Certain types of lipid disorders may be caused by genetic factors (hereditary diseases) or by secondary factors, such as fatty diets and diabetes.

Forms of lipids in the blood are cholesterol, triglycerides, and lipoproteins, which are molecules of fat and cholesterol linked to protein. Types of lipoproteins include very low-density lipoproteins (VLDL), low-density lipoproteins (LDL), and intermediate-density lipoproteins (IDL).

Chylomicrons are also classified as lipoproteins, and are composed of triglycerides, cholesterol and protein. High-density lipoproteins (HDL), or "good cholesterol," actually reduce the risk of heart disease risk, and are therefore protective factors.

There are 6 types of hyperlipidemia, which are differentiated by the types of lipids that are elevated in the blood. Some types may be caused by a primary disorder such as a familial hyperlipidemia, and some are due to secondary causes. Secondary causes of hyperlipidemia are related to disease risk factors, dietary risk factors, and drugs associated with hyperlipidemia.

Disease risk factors include type 1 diabetes, type 2 diabetes, hypothyroidism, Cushing's syndrome, and certain types of kidney failure. Drug risk factors include birth control pills; hormones such as estrogen and corticosteroids; certain diuretics; and beta-blockers.

Dietary risk factors include: dietary fat intake greater than 40% of total calories; saturated fat intake greater than 10% of total calories; cholesterol intake greater than 300 milligrams per day; habitual excessive alcohol use; and obesity. Cigarette smoking with hyperlipidemia increases the risk for heart disease.

Hyperlipidemia is more common in men than women.

Signs and tests: Laboratory tests may be performed to identify secondary causes of hyperlipidemia or hereditary disorders, if a lipoprotein test is elevated.

Fasting lipid (or lipoprotein test) analysis breaks down cholesterol into four groups:

• Total cholesterol

• Low density lipoproteins (LDL), "bad" cholesterol

• High density lipoproteins (HDL), "good" cholesterol

• Triglycerides

A defined "high" cholesterol (lipid) level depends on other risk factors including smoking, high blood pressure, low HDL, family history of heart disease, male over 45 or woman over 55. Total cholesterol values over 200 may indicate an increased risk for heart disease.

However, LDL levels better predict risk factor for heart disease. Those with known heart disease (previous heart attack or peripheral vascular disease) or diabetes should have levels under 100.

LDL over 130, with two or more of the above risk factors, is abnormal. An LDL over 160, with one or fewer of the risk factors, is also abnormal. HDL cholesterol more than or equal to 60 takes away one risk factor and decreases your risk for heart disease. Levels under 40 add a risk factor.

Normal triglyceride levels are under 150. However, as with other components of the lipid test, fasting less than 9-12 hours may alter triglyceride results.

Other tests to help determine risk for heart disease are:

• Lipoprotein(a) analysis

• C-reactive protein analysis

• Merck Manual

Medical Treatment:

The most common prescription for high cholesterol is statin drugs

Statin medications

Statins are a class of drugs used to lower blood cholesterol. They work in your liver to block a substance needed to make cholesterol. They may also help your body reabsorb cholesterol that has accumulated in plaques on your artery walls. This helps prevent further blockage in your blood vessels. Long-term use of statins may even reduce existing blockage in narrowed blood vessels.

Statins have few important side effects. The most common side effects are headache, nausea, vomiting, constipation, diarrhea, headache, rash, weakness, and muscle pain. The most serious side effects are liver failure and rhabdomyolysis. Rhabdomyolysis is a serious side effect in which there is damage to muscles. Rhabdomyolysis often begins as muscle pain and can progress to loss of muscle cells, kidney failure, and death. It occurs more often when statins are used in combination with other drugs that themselves cause rhabdomyolysis or with drugs that prevent the elimination of statins and raise the levels of statins in the blood. Since rhabdomyolysis may be fatal, unexplained joint or muscle pain that occurs while taking statins should be brought to the attention of a healthcare provider for evaluation.

In addition, another potentially serious side effect is: Elevated liver enzymes. Occasionally, statin use causes an increase in liver enzymes. If the increase is only mild, you can continue to take the drug. If the increase is severe, you may need to stop taking it, which usually reverses the problem. Certain other cholesterol-lowering drugs, such as gemfibrozil (Lopid) and niacin, increase the risk of liver problems in people who take statins. Because liver problems may develop without symptoms, people who take statins should have their liver function tested periodically.

Avoid taking statins with grapefruit juice, which alters your body's metabolism of these drugs.

Information from Mayo Clinic and Physicians desk reference.:

With which drugs do statins interact?

Statins have some important drug interactions. The first type of interaction involves the elimination of statins by the liver. Liver enzymes (specifically the cytochrome P-450 liver enzymes) are responsible for

To find out more or to speak to a nutritional counselor for free, just visit us at:
www.CuresForTheBody.com

eliminating all statins from the body with the exception of pravastatin. Therefore, drugs that block the action of these liver enzymes increase the levels of simvastatin, lovastatin, fluvastatin, and atorvastatin (but not pravastatin) in the blood and can lead to the development of rhabdomyolysis.

Drugs or agents that block these enzymes include protease inhibitors (used in treating AIDS), erythromycin, itraconazole, clarithromycin, diltiazem, verapamil, and grapefruit juice. Another important drug interaction occurs between statins and niacin or fibric acids, e.g., gemfibrozil (Lopid), clofibrate (Atromid-S), and fenofibrate (Tricor). Fibric acids and niacin can cause rhabdomyolysis or liver failure when used alone and combining them with statins increases the likelihood of rhabdomyolysis or liver failure. Nevertheless, fibric acids and niacin are often used with caution in combination with most statins. Cholestyramine (Questran) as well as colestipol (Colestid) bind statins in the intestine and reduce their absorption into the body. To prevent this binding within the intestine, statins should be taken one hour before or four hours after cholestyramine or colestipol.

Brand name: Lipitor

Drug name: Atorvastatin

Atorvastatin is an oral drug that lowers the level of cholesterol in the blood. It belongs to a class of drugs referred to as statins which includes lovastatin (Mevacor), simvastatin, (Zocor), fluvastatin (Lescol0, and pravastatin (Pravachol). All statins, including atorvastatin, prevent the production of cholesterol by the liver by blocking the enzyme that makes cholesterol, HMGCoA reductase. They lower total blood cholesterol as well as LDL cholesterol levels. (LDL cholesterol is believed to be the "bad" cholesterol that is primarily responsible for the development of coronary artery disease.) Lowering LDL cholesterol levels retards progression and may even reverse coronary artery disease. Unlike the other drugs in this class, atorvastatin also can reduce the concentration of triglycerides in the blood. High blood concentrations of triglycerides also have been associated with coronary artery disease. Atorvastatin was approved by the FDA in December of 1996.

Notable Side Effects:

Atorvastatin is generally well-tolerated, and side effects are rare. Minor side effects include constipation, diarrhea, fatigue, gas, heartburn and headache. Atorvastatin should be used with caution in patients with alcohol or other liver

To find out more or to speak to a nutritional counselor for free, just visit us at:
www.CuresForTheBody.com

diseases. Persistently abnormal liver tests during treatment are rare but may require discontinuation of the medication. Rare cases of muscle inflammation (myositis) and breakdown have been reported with other drugs in this class (HMGCoA reductase antagonists), and it is assumed that this side effect also may occur with atorvastatin. Muscle breakdown causes the release of muscle protein (myoglobin) into the blood and accumulation of the protein in the kidney tubules, resulting in kidney failure.

Brand name: Zocor

Drug Name: Simvastatin

Simvastatin is a cholesterol-lowering medicine. It inhibits the production of cholesterol by the liver. It lowers overall blood cholesterol as well as blood LDL cholesterol levels. LDL cholesterol is believed to be the "bad" cholesterol that is primarily responsible for the development of coronary artery disease. Lowering LDL cholesterol levels retards progression and may even reverse coronary artery disease.

> **Notable Side Effects:** Simvastatin is generally well-tolerated and side effects are rare. Minor side effects include constipation, diarrhea, fatigue, gas, heartburn, and headache. Major side effects include abdominal pain or cramps, blurred vision, dizziness, easy bruising or bleeding, itching, muscle pain or cramps, rash, and yellowing of the skin or eyes.

Brand Name: Mevacor, Altocor

Drug Name: Lovastatin

Lovastatin is a cholesterol-lowering medicine. It inhibits the production of cholesterol by the liver. It lowers overall blood cholesterol as well as blood LDL cholesterol levels. LDL cholesterol is believed to be the "bad" cholesterol that is primarily responsible for the development of coronary artery disease. Lowering LDL cholesterol levels retards progression and may even reverse coronary artery disease.

> **Notable Side Effects:** Side effects are rare. Minor side effects include constipation, diarrhea, gas, heartburn,

headache, insomnia. Major side effects include abdominal pain or cramps, blurred vision, dizziness, itching, muscle pain or cramps, rash, yellowing of the skin or eyes.

Brand Name: Lopid
Drug Name: Gemfibrozil

Gemfibrozil is a lipid and cholesterol-modifying medicine. It reduces triglycerides and increases cholesterol carried in high density lipoprotein (HDL) in the blood. HDL cholesterol is sometimes called "good" cholesterol because higher concentrations of HDL cholesterol in the blood are associated with a reduced risk of heart disease. The decrease in triglycerides is thought to be in part due to reduced release of triglycerides from fat tissue in the body. In one large study, gemfibrozil decreased the risk of heart attacks but did not affect the overall survival of persons with high cholesterols.

> **Notable Side Effects:** The most common side effects of gemfibrozil are upset stomach (1 in 5 patients), diarrhea (1 in 14 patients), tiredness (1 in 30 patients) and nausea or vomiting (1 in 40 patients). Others may experience dizziness, tiredness, tingling in the extremities, headache, decreased sexual drive, impotence, depression, or blurred vision. Less common are muscle aches, pains, weakness or tenderness. Rarely, these muscle-related symptoms are associated with damage to the muscles which releases chemicals into the blood that then damage the kidney. Muscle damage is of concern primarily when gemfibrozil is being taken along with one of the "statin" medications.

Important information about Statin drugs and memory loss

Duane Graveline, MD, MPH, a retired family doctor and former NASA scientist/astronaut, recounted his own hair-raising experience taking the popular statin drug Lipitor for only six weeks. Soon after he went for a walk, Dr. Graveline was found wandering, confused, and reluctant to enter his own home because he didn't recognize it or remember his wife's name. Six hours later–after being examined by a neurologist and undergoing an MRI–he came to his senses. Transient global amnesia (TGA) was diagnosed. Neither he nor his physician suspected Lipitor, so Dr. Graveline was restarted on one-half the previous dose. Again, at six weeks, the TGA returned. This time, he regressed to his teen-age years with no memory for his time in college, medical school, or the recent past. "Many decades of my life were obliterated," he said. "The diagnosis was TGA: cause unknown."

To verify his growing suspicion that Lipitor might be the cause, Dr. Graveline wrote to Joe and Teresa Graedon, the husband and wife team that writes the syndicated column called The People's Pharmacy, which specializes in warning the public about drug side effects. The Graedons asked for permission to print his letter in their column, and once it appeared, hundreds of people wrote in to say they, too, had experienced severe memory loss while on Lipitor. "Patients are reluctant to report amnesia, or they attribute the symptoms to old age or early Alzheimer's," explained Dr. Graveline. "And doctors are reluctant to see that the drug they prescribed was the cause." Still, the official word on Lipitor is that memory loss is not a statin side effect. "Thousands of cases of memory dysfunction have been reported to the FDA's Medwatch program," he said, "but after two years, the agency still hasn't acted. And most practicing physicians are unaware of the problem." Lipitor is not the only statin linked to this side effect, observed Dr. Graveline.

A reporter pointed out also that FDA-required trials do not report memory loss in people taking statins. An explanation was offered by Joel M. Kauffman, PhD, research professor of chemistry and biochemistry at the University of the Sciences in Philadelphia. "In drug trials, the pharmaceutical companies often divide similar adverse effects into six or seven different categories to keep the scarier side effects under 1%." To illustrate his point, Dr. Kauffman said that amnesia could be divided into confusion, memory loss, senility, and cognitive impairment. There is general acknowledgment, however, that muscle pain, weakness, fatigue, peripheral neuropathy, and rhabdomyolysis, a potentially fatal muscle disease, are statin side effects, though they are thought to be rare.

Nutritional Approach:

Disease or Condition: Hypercholesterolemia

Causes of High Cholesterol

Genes, gender and lifestyle factors all contribute to high cholesterol. But even when scientist eliminate all those things, diet still pops out as vital to whether your arteries clog or your heart gives out.

Nutrional Support:

Foods that have been proven to lower bad LDL Cholesterol:

Almonds, apple, avocado, barley, dried beans, carrot, garlic, grapefruit pulp, oats, olive oil, rice bran, shiitake mushrooms, soybeans, walnuts. Essential fatty acid Omega 3, rich fish and/or flax oil, Hemp oil (rich in Omega 3 and 6 essential fatty acids), fruits and vegetables focusing on the high ORAC values; especially blueberries, nuts, whole grains, legumes, onions, garlic, foods high in C and E.

Foods that may keep LDL Cholesterol from becoming oxidized and toxic to arteries:

Foods high in vitamin C like dark colored fruits and vegetables, foods high in beta carotene, foods high in vitamin E, foods high in co-enzyme Q-10, foods high in monounsaturated fat (olive oil, avocado, almonds).

Nutrients that have been proven to help lower cholesterol:

Chromium[539,540], Vitamin C[541,542], Vitamin B5[543], Omega 3 Fatty Acids[544,545], Omega 6 and GLA[546], Sterols and Sterolins[547,548], Vitamin E[549], Coenzyme Q10 (CO-Q10)[550], Soy Isoflavones[551], Beta-1,3 Glucan[552], Policosanol[553], Guggul[554], Garlic[555], Red Yeast Rice[556], Psyllium seed[557], Coleus[558], Lipase enzymes[559,560,561,562], Probiotics[563].

Exercise that have been proven to help with High Cholesterol:

Exercise burns excess fat and sugar to be utilized as energy rather than stored. Also, it increases metabolism.

Basic High Cholesterol Plan:

• Go heavy on garlic, onions and a variety of vegetables and fruits.

• Shun fatty animal foods, such as high-fat meat and dairy products.

• Use olive oil and canola oil to cook with.

• Use flax oil in salad dressings, smoothies etc. (never cook with it).

Chromium

    • Chromium produces a beneficial effect on blood cholesterol levels.

    • In a double-blind crossover study, 28 individuals were administered either 200mcg of chromium or a placebo daily for 42 days. The ones taking the chromium experienced a significant decrease in total cholesterol and LDL-cholesterol levels, and a slight elevation of HDL-cholesterol.

• Chromium has also been reported to improve blood sugar and Hmg A1C levels in diabetics. This will have a positive impact on the process of glycosylation and thus reduce cardiovascular risk.

• In general, American diets are chromium-poor and therefore, place the population at added risk.

• Those with diets high in refined sugar, athletes, pregnant women, and the elderly are all at additional risk for chromium deficiency.

• Chromium is biologically active only in the trivalent state in which it forms complexes with organic compounds. The most important of these complexes is glucose tolerance factor (GTF) which is comprised of trivalent chromium, niacin, glycine, glutamic acid, and cysteine.

Blueberries

Dr. Agnes Rimando and her team studied the effect of the chemical pterostilbene and three other blueberry compounds on rat liver cells.

Pterostilbene showed the most potent effect in stimulating a receptor protein in the cells which plays an important role in lowering cholesterol and other blood fats.

This is similar to the way the commercial cholesterol-lowering drug ciprofibrate works.

Ciprofibrate is effective but can cause muscle pain and nausea in some people, but because the blueberry compound targets the liver cell receptor more accurately, Dr Rimando believes it is likely to have fewer side effects.

There were no signs of side effects in the study.

Similar antioxidants have already been identified in grapes and red wine. Other research suggests pterostilbene may help fight cancer and ward off diabetes.

Dr Rimando said: "We are excited to learn that blueberries, which are already known to be rich in healthy compounds, may also be a potent weapon in the battle against obesity and heart disease."

To find out more or to speak to a nutritional counselor for free, just visit us at:
www.CuresForTheBody.com

But she said until studies were conducted in humans, it would be impossible to know how many blueberries a person would need to eat to lower their cholesterol.

Belinda Linden from the British Heart Foundation said: "Research has suggested that natural chemicals found in fruit, including blueberries, have potent antioxidant properties which may reduce the harmful type of cholesterol, low density lipoprotein (LDL).

"This study claims that blueberries are particularly efficient at reducing cholesterol in a laboratory; we will be interested to see if similar results emerge from long-term studies involving people."

Eating other dark colored fruits and vegetables will also lower your risk for heart disease.

Vitamin C –

Vitamin C is another nutrient that reportedly produces favorable changes in blood cholesterol levels.

- Vitamin C was given to 10 women in a double-blind study at a dose of 1,000mg daily for four weeks. A 16 percent reduction in LDL-cholesterol along with a slight improvement in HDL-cholesterol levels resulted.

- Similar results were obtained in a much larger study with 256 men and 221 women. In men and women, those taking large doses of vitamin C, greater than 1000mg per day, experienced larger reductions in total cholesterol, LDL-cholesterol and triglycerides, elevations of HDL-cholesterol, and an improvement in the total cholesterol to HDL ratio.

- Because vitamin C is an antioxidant, it may also help to prevent the oxidation of LDL, which could possibly lower the risks for developing atherosclerosis.

- In another study, 316 women and 511 men (aged 19-95 years) were administered vitamin C well above RDA. The results were improved lipid profiles corresponding to possible reduced risk of cardiovascular disease.

For optimal results, take whole food vitamin C – Acreola cherry and citrus fruit formulas.

Vitamin B5

• Pantethine is the active form of vitamin B5, which is also known as pantothenic acid.

• Pantethine has been reported to lower elevated triglycerides and LDL cholesterol while raising levels of the beneficial HDL cholesterol.

• Pantethine apparently helps lower the amount of cholesterol that is made in the liver. In one study, 24 women with cholesterol levels above 240ng/dl were given 900mg of pantethine daily.

• After 16 weeks, eighty percent of the women experienced significant lowering of total cholesterol and LDL-cholesterol levels without side effects.

Omega 3 Fatty Acids

• Higher doses of omega-3 fatty acids can lower elevated serum triglyceride levels; 3 to 5 g/ d can reduce triglyceride levels by 30% to 50%, minimizing the risk of both coronary heart disease and acute pancreatitis.

Omega 6 Fatty Acids and Gamma Lineolic Acid (GLA)

• Omega-6 fatty acid, also known as linoleic acid, is a dietary fat that helps lower LDL-cholesterol levels. Under normal conditions, the body converts omega-6 into a longer chain fatty acid known as gamma-linolenic acid (GLA).

• It has been determined that GLA plays a role in the metabolism of LDL-cholesterol, converting it to bile acids, which can be eliminated via the colon.

• Researchers have reported that GLA is 170 times more effective at lowering LDL-cholesterol levels than omega-6. It is important to note that trans fats from partial hydrogenation can decrease this benefit by inhibiting the conversion of omega-6 to GLA.

• It is important to carefully read labels and avoid consuming processed foods where partially hydrogenated fats and oils are contained in the list of ingredients.

To find out more or to speak to a nutritional counselor for free, just visit us at:
www.CuresForTheBody.com

• Borage oil, black currant oil, and evening primrose oil all contain relatively high amounts of GLA, 26%, 18% and 9% respectively. Therefore, consuming supplemental amounts of one of these oils on a daily basis is one of the most effective ways to lower LDL-cholesterol levels. These oils must be kept refrigerated.

Sterols (Sitosterol) and Sterolins (Sitosterolin)

• There are many chemical constituents (termed phytochemicals) found in plant medicines that have beneficial pharmacological effects in humans. Some bioactive phytochemicals include tannins, resins, polysaccharides, saponins, glycosides and volatile oils among others. Recent literature has reported that two of these phytochemicals, sterols and sterolins (plant "fats"), occur naturally in fruits, vegetables, seeds and nuts, and have beneficial effects in human subjects in many conditions.

• Sterol is found in all plant-based foods, and sterolin is a glucoside moiety joined to the sterol chemical structure. Both sterols and sterolins were identified as early as 1922. In the natural state, these plant "fats" are bound to the fibers of the plant, making the sterols and sterolins difficult to be absorbed during the normal transit of digested food through our gut. Seeds are the richest source of the sterols and sterolins, but are usually removed during processing by the food industry.

• Plant sterols and sterolins have been reported to be effective adjunctive agents in the management and treatment of disease states such as high cholesterol levels, benign prostatic hyperplasia, pulmonary tuberculosis, stress-induced immune suppression, and HIV, among others. Some of the most promising uses of these plant "fats" is in the management of autoimmune disorders such as lupus, multiple sclerosis, rheumatoid arthritis and myasthenia gravis. Of note is that the sterols should be combined with sterolin in order to be an effective agent for the immune system.

To find out more or to speak to a nutritional counselor for free, just visit us at:
www.CuresForTheBody.com

• Sterols and sterolins have been reported to modulate the function of T-cells, significantly enhancing the proliferation of the CD-4 TH-1 cells and increasing the production of the interleukin 2 (IL2) and gamma-interferon (FN-g and IFN-y). These results indicate that sterols and sterolins are adaptogenic in that they modulate the immune and stress response.

• Care should be taken if an individual is taking immunosuppressive agents. Based on pharmacology, if an individual is taking hypocholesterolemic agents concurrently with plant sterols and sterolins, a dosage adjustment in the pharmaceutical medication may be necessary.

Vitamin E

• Studies suggest that vitamin E is one of the most effective nutrients in preventing the oxidation of LDL-cholesterol. It reduces platelet adhesion and, more importantly, reduces lipid peroxidation of LDL cholesterol.

• Vitamin E is a well researched substance with evidence suggesting it prevents the oxidative damage that leads to atherosclerosis.

In the Cambridge Heart Antioxidant Study (CHAOS), over 2000 patients with angiographically proven coronary atherosclerosis were followed for periods ranging from 3 to 910 days (median 510 days). In this double-blind, placebo-controlled trial, three groups of patients were randomly assigned to receive daily doses of 400 IU vitamin E, 800 IU of vitamin E, or a placebo. The patients taking the doses of vitamin E had a 47% reduction in subsequent heart attacks (both fatal and non-fatal) compared to the placebo controls. The overall reduction in non-fatal secondary heart attacks was 77%.

• Some experts feel that using a combination of antioxidants including carotenoids, Vitamin C, and selenium along with Vitamin E is the best way to supplement.

• Vitamin E includes eight compounds, which include four tocopherols: alpha, beta, gamma, and delta. The natural form of Vitamin E, d-alpha tocopherol, has been reported to have greater bioavailability than synthetic iso-forms of the vitamin.

In another study, 156 men aged 40-59 years with previous coronary artery bypass graft surgery reported that individuals taking 100 IU of vitamin E or more daily had a substantial reduction in the progression of atherosclerosis. **<u>For optimal results, take whole food vitamin E – Wheat germ oil.</u>**

Coenzyme Q10 (CoQ10)

• The authors of one study noted that coenzyme Q10 is transported throughout the body packaged into the LDL and VLDL fractions of cholesterol. They emphasized that the transport of CoQ10 by LDL-cholesterol means that CoQ10 is acting as an antioxidant to prevent the oxidation of LDL-cholesterol and the subsequent development of atherosclerosis.

• Numerous categories of prescription drugs can inhibit the body's ability to synthesize coenzyme Q10. Drugs that can deplete coenzyme Q10 include sulfonylureas, biguanides, beta-blockers, hydralazine-containing vasodilators, thiazide diuretics, centrally-acting antihypertensives (clonidine and methyldopa), the "statin" cholesterol-lowering drugs, tricyclic antidepressants, and phenothiazines.

• CoQ10 is an antioxidant that can reportedly help to prevent the oxidation of LDL cholesterol as well as reduce risks associated with several other aspects of cardiovascular disease. CoQ10 is carried throughout the body on LDL-cholesterol molecules. Adequate coenzyme Q10 is an important nutrient to protect LDL-cholesterol from damage, which substantially reduces an individual's risk for developing atherosclerosis.

• Many individuals with high cholesterol will be using a cholesterol-lowering drug, likely a member of the class of drugs known as the "statins." These effective agents inhibit the body's ability to manufacture coenzyme Q10. The drug known as gemfibrozil may also deplete coenzyme Q10. As was mentioned above, coenzyme Q10 helps protect LDL-cholesterol from being damaged. CoQ10 also plays a role in the generation of energy at the cellular level. The heart is the most energy-demanding muscle in the body; a deficiency of coenzyme Q10 could affect the heart.

Soy Isoflavones

• Studies have found that supplementation with soy isoflavones exerted favorable effects on blood pressure symptoms and a reduction in LDL and an increase in HDL levels.

• Soy protein has been reported to be hypocholesterolemic in individuals with elevated cholesterol. This possibility that soy protein diets, rather than animal protein diets, can lower serum cholesterol levels tends to be well documented among animal studies, but has historically been inconclusive in humans.

One meta-analysis of 38 controlled human clinical trials evaluated the relationship between serum cholesterol and soy protein intake. This evaluation concluded that an average soy protein intake of 47g per day led to significant decreases in lipid levels. The soy based diets led to a 9.3% decrease in total cholesterol, a 12.9% decrease in low-density lipoprotein (LDL) cholesterol, a 10.5% decrease in triglycerides and a nonsignificant 2.4% increase in high-density lipoprotein (HDL) cholesterol.

• Specifically, genistein reportedly inhibits platelet aggregation and smooth muscle cell proliferation. Smooth muscle cells are one of the primary cell types comprising plaques.

Beta 1,3 Glucan

• Appear to be the major cholesterol lowering agents in oat bran fiber.

• This dietary fiber, 0.75 g/serving and four servings a day, has been approved by The US Food and Drug

Administration (FDA) to reduce cardiovascular disease risk.

• Studies reveal that soluble beta-1,3 glucans in oat bran can lower total cholesterol and LDL cholesterol levels in patients with hyperlipidemia.

• Similar cholesterol lowering effects are reported in studies where barley is used as the source of beta-1,3 glucans.

• A randomized crossover study fed a high-fiber (beta-glucan or psyllium) and a control low-fat, low-cholesterol diet for 1 month each to 68 hyperlipidemic adults. Reductions in numerous cholesterol measures and ratios were observed.

Policosanol

• Policosanol is a natural mixture of higher aliphatic primary alcohols isolated from sugar cane wax. It has demonstrated cholesterol-lowering effects in experimental models and in patients with type II hyperlipoproteinemia. A new proprietary product has been developed that is made from beeswax, and is reported to be a more stable form than other products.

• There have been several reports of policosanol lowering cholesterol levels in human subjects.

• One study has compared policosanol to HMG-CoA reductase inhibitors in patients with Type II hypercholestrolemia. Patients with a LDL cholesterol over 160 mg/dl were included in the study. A 24% LDL cholesterol reduction was obtained with policosanol, compared with a 22% reduction with lovastatin and a 15% reduction with simvastatin. HDL cholesterol significantly increased in patients on policosanol and did not change in the other treatment groups. Adverse effects of policosanol were mild and unspecific, with no changes in hepatic enzymes were observed. The authors concluded that policosanol is a safe and effective cholesterol-lowering agent.

• A large double-blind, randomized, placebo controlled study of 437 patients was conducted to study the effects of policosanol in reducing serum cholesterol levels. Policosanol (5 and 10 mg/day) significantly reduced serum low-density lipoprotein cholesterol (18.2% and 25.6%, respectively), and cholesterol (13.0% and 17.4%), and it significantly raised HDL cholesterol (15.5% and 28.4%). Triglycerides remained unchanged after the first 12 weeks and lowered significantly at study completion. Policosanol was reported safe and well tolerated, and no drug-related interactions and adverse effects were observed.

• Policosanol has been reported to lower elevated levels of cholesterol and LDL cholesterol in non-insulin-dependent diabetes mellitus (NIDDM) patients, potentially decreasing the development of coronary artery disease through the direct action of hyperglycemia on the arteries as well as the dyslipidemia induced by NIDDM. Policosanol (10 mg/day) significantly reduced total cholesterol by 17.5% and LDL cholesterol by 21.8% compared with baseline and placebo.

• In a laboratory animal study, oral administration of policosanol in rats provided a partial inhibition of lipid peroxidation, protecting against membrane lipid peroxidation and to some extent against free radical-associated diseases. Policosanol has also been reported to protect against the development of atherosclerotic lesions in laboratory animal studies.

Guggul

• Guggul oleoresin has been used in the Indian (Ayurvedic) medical system for centuries as an anti-arthritic, carminative, antispasmodic, diaphoretic, and aphrodisiac. In the early 1960's, researchers began to explore the ancient Sanskrit description of guggul being used by Ayurvedic physicians in the management of lipid disorders. After years of research and scientific studies, guggul was approved for marketing in India in 1986 as a lipid-lowering drug. Guggul has also been reported to inhibit platelet aggregation and have fibrinolytic activity, as well as being an antioxidant, preventing the heart from being damaged by free radicals.

• The lipid lowering effects of guggul may be explained by four proposed mechanisms of action. First, guggul reportedly inhibits the biosynthesis of cholesterol in the liver, interfering with the formation of lipoproteins (LDL, VLDL). Secondly, it may increase the fecal excretion of bile acids and cholesterol, resulting in a low rate of absorption of fat and cholesterol in the intestines. Thirdly, it is claimed to stimulate the LDL receptor binding activity in the liver cellular membranes, reducing serum LDL levels. Lastly, guggul reportedly stimulates thyroid function, which may lead to blood lipid lowering and weight loss. In addition to its lipid lowering effects, guggul has been reported to prevent the formation of atherosclerosis and aid in the regression of pre-existing atherosclerotic plaques in animals.

Garlic

• Has been reported to lower total cholesterol, LDL cholesterol and triglycerides, and increase HDL cholesterol.

• The antioxidant effect in aged garlic has been reported to be beneficial in preventing stroke and arteriosclerosis.

• A recent study reported no effect of garlic oil on serum lipids. However, the product used was garlic oil, which is processed and heated garlic. The impact of processing is an important fact to keep in mind when recommending garlic supplements. Changes can occur in the active constituents when exposed cooking or other processing which can render the garlic product virtually ineffective. Cooking is known to denature proteins and therefore may inactivate the enzyme (allinase) that is necessary in converting Allinase into allicin, the major bio-active constituent in garlic. Also, research has reported that allinase may be irreversibly inhibited by stomach acid and may fail to form adequate amounts of allicin or other thiosulfinates below pH 3.6.

• Recommending a quality garlic supplement is essential, and enteric coating may be advantageous.

To find out more or to speak to a nutritional counselor for free, just visit us at:
www.CuresForTheBody.com

• Of further note, as reported in a few laboratory studies, is the potential for large amounts of allicin to damage liver tissue if absorbed due to its oxidation potential. However, there are positive studies which utilized high quality garlic preparations standardized to allicin potential without adverse effect.

Red Yeast Rice

• In 1976, Japanese researchers reported the discovery of mevastatin, a fungal metabolite isolated from the cultures of *Penicillium citrinum* and *P. brevicompactin*. Mevastatin was found to be a potent inhibitor of the enzyme 3-hydroxy-3-methylglutaryl coenzyme A reductase (HMG-CoA reductase), the enzyme that is the rate-limiting step in the synthesis of cholesterol. These agents play a prominent role in the management of hypercholesterolemia, a significant risk factor for coronary artery disease.

• In recent years, at least 34 separate clinical studies (17 controlled and 17 open-label) in China and the United States have assessed the efficacy of *M. purpureus* red yeast rice as a cholesterol-lowering agent. One major randomized, single-blind, multicenter clinical trial involved 446 hyperlipidemic subjects. After eight weeks, blood levels of total cholesterol, low-density lipoprotein cholesterol, and triglycerides in the red yeast rice treatment group were reduced by 22.7, 30.9, and 34.1 percent, respectively. In addition, HDL-c levels increased by 19.9 percent in the red yeast rice treatment group. This increase was significantly greater than the 8.4 percent increase observed in the control group.

• In a major prospective double-blind, randomized clinical trial involving 152 subjects, total cholesterol was reduced by 19 percent compared to 1.5 percent in the placebo group. Triglycerides were reduced by 36 percent compared to 10 percent in the placebo group.

• In another double-blind, placebo-controlled randomized clinical study, researchers evaluated the efficacy and safety of a proprietary red yeast rice product. After eight weeks, total cholesterol levels of the treatment group decreased by 18 percent while those in the placebo group remained unchanged. No serious adverse effects were observed in the study group.

• Released findings of a U.S. multi-center, open-label trial confirmed the consistent cholesterol-lowering effects of red yeast rice. In a two-month study involving 187 subjects, a twice-daily regimen of a proprietary red yeast rice product was found to reduce total cholesterol and LDL-c levels by 16 and 22 percent, respectively. Moreover, when the treatment was discontinued, these levels returned to pretreatment values within two weeks.

• Red yeast rice was compared with pravastatin in a randomized, single-blind, controlled study. Forty-four subjects diagnosed with essential hyperlipidemia were randomly divided into two equal groups. After four weeks, both treatments caused significant and comparable reductions in total serum cholesterol and LDL-c. The clinical evidence strongly suggests that red yeast rice is an effective, natural dietary supplement for controlling serum cholesterol, and that the product is well tolerated in humans.

Psyllium Seed

• One of psyllium's findings is in its potential for management of cholesterol levels. 1.78 g/serving given four servings a day as a dietary fiber, has been approved by The US Food and Drug Administration (FDA) to reduce cardiovascular disease risk.

• There have been several clinical trials reporting the effectiveness of psyllium in hypercholesterolemia.

• Fiber in the diet, especially soluble fiber, can reportedly reduce absorption of blood cholesterol and fecal bile acids that can lower cholesterol levels, decreasing the risk for heart disease and stroke.

Coleus

• stimulates thyroid function

To find out more or to speak to a nutritional counselor for free, just visit us at:
www.CuresForTheBody.com

• increases insulin secretion

• inhibits mast cell release of histamine and

• increases the burning of fats as fuels.

• claimed to inhibit platelet activating factor (PAF) by possibly directly binding to PAF receptor sites.

Lipase enzymes

• Lipase enzymes have been shown to lower blood lipid levels dramatically.

• In clinical applications in hundreds of doctor's offices around in the U.S., lipase supplementation has consistently lowered blood cholesterol levels. This is the favored nutritional approach of the lead author.

Probiotics

• A study of hypercholesterolemic individuals showed that probiotics created a distinct increase in the HDL/LDL ratio. Another study showed a cholesterol lowering capability of L.Acidophilus in infants and in adults.

Infections/Bacterial

Description: Bacteria naturally exists all around us in the environment, on the skin, in our airways, in our mouths, in our digestive tract, and in our genitourinary tract. Only a few types of these bacteria cause disease, however.

Bacteria is classified by different factors. These factors include their shape (i.e., spherical, rod-like, etc.), the color they turn after being stained (blue=gram-positive, pink=gram-negative), and their tolerance of oxygen (aerobic, anaerobic).

Gram-positive and gram-negative bacteria have different characteristics, produce different types of infections, and are likely to be killed by different antibiotics. Gram-positive bacteria create illness by producing a toxin that is released into the body. However, they are not very difficult to kill with antibiotics. On the other hand, gram-negative bacteria have a unique outer membrane that is much more difficult for antibiotics to penetrate and so are more resistant to antibiotics. In addition, they can mutate to become resistant to antibiotics and share their DNA with other bacteria so that the other strains become resistant as well. Gram-negative bacteria can be life-threatening as molecules on their outer membrane (lipopolysccharides) trigger high fevers and a drop in blood pressure.

The bacteria's tolerance to oxygen can also determine how it affects your body. Anaerobic bacteria can tolerate little to no oxygen. This type of bacteria typically lives harmless on and in the body. Your immune system and your body's supply of good bacteria (probiotics) keep these bacteria in check. However, anaerobic bacteria take advantage of situations in which they can thrive in cells with little oxygen, such as tissue damaged from an injury, decaying tissue, and wounds. A weakened immune system also allows these bacteria to cause infection in the body.

Medical Treatment:

To find out more or to speak to a nutritional counselor for free, just visit us at:
www.CuresForTheBody.com

Brand name: Vibramycin

Drug Name: Doxycycline

Doxycycline is primarily bacteriostatic and is thought to exert its antimicrobial effect by the inhibition of protein synthesis. The tetracyclines have a similar antimicrobial spectrum of activity against a wide range of gram-positive and gram-negative organisms. Cross-resistance of these organisms to tetracyclines is common.

> **Notable Side Effects:** Sensitizes skin to sunlight, yeast infection *Gastrointestinal*: anorexia, nausea, vomiting, diarrhea, glossitis, dysphagia, enterocolitis, and inflammatory lesions (with monilial overgrowth) in the anogenital region. Hepatotoxicity has been reported rarely. These reactions have been caused by both the oral and parenteral administration of tetracyclines. Rare instances of esophagitis and esophageal ulcerations have been reported in patients receiving capsule and tablet forms of the drugs in the tetracycline class. Most of these patients took medications immediately before going to bed. *Skin*: maculopapular and erythematous rashes. Exfoliative dermatitis has been reported but is uncommon. Photosensitivity is discussed above. *Renal toxicity*: Rise in BUN has been reported and is apparently dose related. *Hypersensitivity reactions*: urticaria, angioneurotic edema, anaphylaxis, anaphylactoid purpura, serum sickness, pericarditis, and exacerbation of systemic lupus erythematosus. *Blood*: Hemolytic anemia, thrombocytopenia, neutropenia, and eosinophilia have been reported. *Other*: bulging fontanels in infants and intracranial hypertension in adults.

Brand name: Zithromax

Drug Name: Azithromycin

Azithromycin acts by binding to the 50S ribosomal subunit of susceptible microorganisms and, thus, interfering with microbial protein synthesis. Nucleic acid synthesis is not affected. Azithromycin concentrates in phagocytes and fibroblasts as demonstrated by *in vitro* incubation techniques. Using such methodology, the ratio of intracellular to extracellular concentration was >30 after one hour incubation. *In vivo* studies suggest that concentration in phagocytes may contribute to drug distribution to inflamed tissues.

Notable Side Effects: *(most common)* nausea, vomiting, diarrhea, or abdominal pain.

Brand Name: Bicillin

Drug Name: Penicillin

Penicillin exerts a bactericidal action against penicillin-susceptible microorganisms during the stage of active multiplication. It acts through the inhibition of biosynthesis of cell-wall mucopeptide. It is not active against the penicillinase-producing bacteria, which include many strains of staphylococci.

Notable Side Effects: *General:* Hypersensitivity reactions including the following: skin eruptions (maculopapular to exfoliative dermatitis), urticaria, laryngeal edema, fever, eosinophilia; other serum sickness-like reactions (including chills, fever, edema, arthralgia, and prostration); and anaphylaxis including shock and death. Note: Urticaria, other skin rashes, and serum sickness-like reactions may be controlled with antihistamines and, if necessary, systemic corticosteroids. *Gastrointestinal:* Pseudomembranous colitis. Onset of pseudomembranous colitis symptoms may occur during or after antibacterial treatment. *Hematologic:* Hemolytic anemia, leukopenia, thrombocytopenia. *Neurologic:* Neuropathy. *Urogenital:* Nephropathy. The following adverse events have been temporarily associated with parenteral administration of penicillin G benzathine. *Body as a Whole:* Hypersensitivity reactions including allergic vasculitis, pruritus, fatigue, asthenia, and pain; aggravation of existing disorder; headache. *Cardiovascular:* Cardiac arrest; hypotension; tachycardia; palpitations; pulmonary hypertension; pulmonary embolism; vasodilation; vasovagal reaction; cerebrovascular accident; syncope. *Gastrointestinal:* Nausea, vomiting; blood in stool;

intestinal necrosis. *Hemic and Lymphatic:* Lymphadenopathy. *Injection Site:* Injection site reactions including pain, inflammation, lump, abscess, necrosis, edema, hemorrhage, cellulitis, hypersensitivity, atrophy, ecchymosis, and skin ulcer. Neurovascular reactions including warmth, vasospasm, pallor, mottling, gangrene, numbness of the extremities, and neurovascular damage. *Metabolic:* Elevated BUN, creatinine, and SGOT. *Musculoskeletal:* Joint disorder; periostitis; exacerbation of arthritis; myoglobinura; rhabdomyolysis. *Nervous System:* Nervousness; tremors; dizziness; somnolence; confusion; anxiety; euphoria; transverse myelitis; seizures; coma. A syndrome manifested by a variety of CNS symptoms such as severe agitation with confusion, visual and auditory hallucinations, and a fear of impending death (Hoigne's syndrome), has been reported after administration of penicillin G procaine and, less commonly, after injection of the combination of penicillin G benzathine and penicillin G procaine. Other symptoms associated with this syndrome, such as psychosis, seizures, dizziness, tinnitus, cyanosis, palpitations, tachycardia, and/or abnormal perception in taste, also may occur. *Respiratory:* Hypoxia; apnea; dyspnea. *Skin:* Diaphoresis. *Special Senses:* Blurred vision; blindness. *Urogenital:* Neurogenic bladder; hematuria; proteinuria; renal failure; impotence; priapism.

Brand name: EryGel

Drug Name: Erythromycin

Erythromycin acts by inhibition of protein synthesis in susceptible organisms by reversibly binding to 50S ribosomal subunits, thereby inhibiting translocation of aminoacyl transfer-RNA and inhibiting polypeptide synthesis. Antagonism has been demonstrated *in vitro* between erythromycin, lincomycin, chloramphenicol, and clindamycin.

Notable Side Effects: peeling, dryness, itching, erythema, and oiliness. Irritation of the eyes and tenderness of the skin have also been reported with the topical use of erythromycin. A generalized urticarial reaction, possibly related to the use of erythromycin, which required systemic steroid therapy has been reported.

NOTE: Please read chapter 2 to understand the long term consequences of taking anti-biotics. The misuse and overuse of anti-biotics has caused a tremendous problem with infectious diseases that are resilient to anti-biotics.

Other common recommendations from Medical Doctors: Most important is to keep the immune system strong with a healthy diet, exercise, and maintaining a healthy weight. By strengthening the immune system, you use your body's best defense against the invasion of bacteria. If necessary, take antibiotics that are specific to the strain of bacteria causing the infection so that the bacteria does not become resistant and the good bacteria (probiotics) in the body are not needlessly killed.

Nutritional Approach:

Disease or Condition: Bacterial Infections
Causes of Infections/Bacterial:

Low functioning immune system

Allowing the internal environment to be succeptible to pathogenic bacteria.

Anti-biotic abuse can lead to more harmful infections if not taken properly.

Nutritional support:
Foods that have been proven to help with Bacterial Infections:

Antioxidant containing foods like: dark colored fruits and vegetables. Yogurt with Probiotics, Garlic and Flax seeds

Avoiding refined flour and refined sugars.

Nutrients that have been proven to help with Bacterial Infections

Vitamin C[564], E[565], Mineral Zinc[566], Sterols (Sitosterol) and Sterolins (Sitosterolin)[567], Echinacea[568], Goldenseal[569], Astragalus[570], Larch

Arabinogalactan[571], Probiotics[572], Cat's Claw[573], Olive Leaf[574], Garlic[575], Tea Tree Oil[576], Grapefruit Seed[577], Multivitamins and minerals[578], and Flax seeds[579].

Exercises that have been proven to help with Bacterial Infections

Exercising regularly will promote a strong immune system which will make you less susceptible to bacterial infections. Also some studies have shown that exercising will cut the time that it takes to get over an illness in half.[580]

Basic Bacterial Infection Plan:

Although the focus in this section is on the use of natural methods to assist the body in recovery from bacterial infections, prevention is by far the best medicine. Prevention involves strengthening the immune system.

• **Drink plenty of water.**

• **Try to eat more nutrient rich foods**, especially fruits and vegetables.

• **Avoid refined sugar and refined flour**.

– They slow down white blood cells for several hours after consumption.[581]

• **Reduce chronic stress** (it lowers your immunity).

• **Eat Foods with Antibacterial Activity:** Apple, banana, basil, beet, blueberry, cabbage, carrot, cashew, celery, chili pepper, chives, coconut, cranberry, cumin, dill, garlic, ginger, honey, horseradish, licorice, lime, black mustard seed, nori (seaweed) , nutmeg, olive, papaya, plum, purslane, onion, sage, yogurt.

–Food compounds destroy bacteria's synthesis of protein, folic acid and transpeptidase so they cannot multiply. Blueberries and cranberries not only can inhibit bacteria, but also block their attachment to human cells.

• **Garlic**

– It has antibacterial, antifungal, antiviral, and antiparasitic activities. There are several important actions that are attributed to the sulfur-containing compounds in garlic. These compounds (allicin and alliin) are reported to have anti-infective effects against bacteria and fungi.

–The impact of processing is an important fact to keep in mind when recommending garlic supplements. Changes can occur in the active constituents when exposed cooking or other processing which can render the garlic product virtually ineffective. Cooking is known to denature proteins and therefore may inactivate the enzyme (allinase) that is necessary in converting alliin into allicin, the major bio-active constituent in garlic.

–Tests show that garlic kills or cripples at least seventy-two infectious bacteria that spread diarrhea, dysentery, botulism, tuberculosis and encephalitis, among other diseases.

• Probiotics

–Most clinicians now agree on the importance of maintaining homeostatis of the microflora in health and disease.

• Eat yogurt with live cultures.

• When supplementing, use stabilized Probiotics for best results[582].

* Important to take Probiotics if you have to take antibiotics. This replenishes your supply of good friendly "microflora" that antibiotics kill in the process of killing the bad bacteria.

• Vitamin C

–It may be utilized four to six times the normal rate by white blood cells during active infection. There is evidence indicating that vitamin C may play an important role in the efficient functioning of the immune system. Vitamin C demands rise to 5-6 times normal levels within the white blood cells when fighting an infection. Therefore, an increase in Vitamin C during a bacterial infection may be warranted.

–Whole food sources of vitamins are optimal. They are absorbed more significantly and without toxic side effects of synthetics. (i.e., look for acreola cherry, citrus fruits etc. as the main ingredients not ascorbic acid).

• **Vitamin E** – Poor immune response has been associated with low levels of vitamin E.

–Whole food sources of vitamins are optimal. They are absorbed more significantly and without toxic side effects of synthetics. (i.e., look for wheat germ oil).

• Sterols and Sterolins – (Phytochemicals; plant "fats")

– Occur naturally in fruits, vegetables, seeds and nuts, have beneficial effects on humans in many conditions. Seeds are the richest source, but are removed during processing by the food industry.

–They help in many ways but for our purposes here they have been reported to increase the function of the immune system; specifically certain T-cells.

• **Flax Seed Lignans** - Lignans are cyclic molecules with anti-viral, anti-fungal, anti-bacterial, and anti-cancer properties.

• Fresh ground flax seed (the oil has only 2% lignans) 6-8 Tbls. maximum / day.

• Note: take freshly ground flax seed with five times its volume of fluid, because it absorbs that much liquid.

• **Zinc** – is necessary for proper immune system function and healing.

• **Echinacea**

– Research has reported that echinacea may stimulate white blood cells and to fight against infection.

– Echinacea is also reported to possess antimicrobial activity against bacteria, fungi, and viruses.

– There have been several randomized, double-blind, placebo controlled clinical studies in Europe conducted on human subjects using echinacea.

• **Golden Seal**

– Due to the antibacterial properties of the alkaloids in golden seal, this herbal medicine may be useful.

– Combinations of golden seal and echinacea are one of the leading selling herbal supplements in the U.S. market today.

• **Astragalus**

– Enhances the effects of interferon, and may act not only to improve resistance to infections but decrease the duration of an infection.

– Astragalus improves natural killer and T-cell function, as well as interferon production by the immune system.

• **Larch Arabinogalactan (LA)** - purified extract of the bark from the Western larch tree.

– Because of the immune-enhancing properties, LA is receiving increased attention as a clinically useful immunomodulating agent, and is effective against many bacteria, viruses, and fungi (including candida).

– Reported to enhance immunity by various methods.

– May be a good therapeutic choice for individuals with recurrent immune system problems.

– Has been used with positive success in children, specifically in ear infection.

– Contains the phytochemical arabinogalactan, an immunomodulating polysaccharide that is also found in *Echinacea spp.*

–Has been reported to increase NK cells, stimulate the reticuloendothelial system, stimulate macrophage activation, and have antiviral effects *in-vitro*.

– Studies report that LA stimulates natural killer cell cytotoxicity, enhances other functional aspects of the immune system, and inhibits the metastasis of tumor cells to the liver.

• Cat's claw

– The glycosides are also reported to enhance and stimulate phagocytosis, which if true would be a key part of cat's claw's immune function activity.

– Isopteridine, an alkaloid which has been isolated, is claimed to have immuno-stimulatory properties.

– Triterpenoid alkaloids and quinovic acid glycosides have been isolated and studied for antiviral activity, possibly inhibiting replications of some DNA viruses.

– Colon toxicity has been somewhat ignored in Western medicine. It is now becoming apparent that bowel hygiene and proper flora are essential to good health. If the colon flora is out of balance (dysbiosis) or if food is not being properly digested and assimilated, toxic metabolites and mutagens may be produced. Cat's claw is reported to have the ability to soothe irritated and inflamed tissues and help eliminate pathogens from the GI tract.

• Olive Leaf

– Olive leaf extract has been reported to be an effective antimicrobial agent against a wide variety of pathogens (including some penicillin-resistant strains), causal agents of intestinal or respiratory tract infections in man.

– Oleuropein also has been reported to directly stimulate macrophage (white blood cell) activation in laboratory studies.

• Tea Tree Oil

– As early as 1930, the antiseptic properties of the plant were recognized by the Australian dental profession.

– Of recent interest is a study that determined the susceptibility of methicillin-resistant *Staphylococcus aureus* (MRSA) to tea tree oil in vitro. MRSA is a common pathogen recognized in hard to treat hospital acquired infections. In the study all 60 MRSA tested against tea tree oil by the disc diffusion method and modified broth microdilution were susceptible, with MICs and MBCs of 0.25% and 0.5% respectively. Also tested were mupirocin-susceptible and mupirocin-resistant MRSA, and there was no difference in tea tree oil susceptibility between the two.

– The universal susceptibility to tea tree oil of all MRSA isolated tested, including those who were mupirocin-resistant, represents a significant result which may find application in the control of MRSA.

– A recent report also supports the use of tea tree oil in the hospital and community setting to help prevent spread of multi-resistant bacteria such as MRSA, glycopeptide-resistant enterococci, aminoglycoside-resistant klebsiellae, *Pseudomonas aeruginosa,* and *Stenotrophomonas maltophilia.*

• Grapefruit Seed

– Grapefruit seed extract has been reported to be a broad-spectrum antimicrobial.

– Studies indicate that the antimicrobial activity of grapefruit seed extract exists in the cytoplasmic membrane of the invading bacteria, where the uptake of amino acids is prevented, there is disorganization of the cytoplasmic membrane and leakage of low molecular weight cellular contents ultimately resulting in inhibition of cellular respiration and death.

– Grapefruit seed extract also inhibits the growth of H. pylori and C. jejuni, both causative agents in gastrointestinal ulcers. Grapefruit seed extract is a useful agent in maintaining bowel integrity.

– In human study, an improvement in constipation, flatulence, abdominal distress, and night rest were noticed after 4 weeks of therapy.

• Multi-vitamins and minerals – First choice in prevention!

Much of our food sources today do not contain the vitamins and minerals that they did in the past due to soil depletion. Multiple vitamin and mineral formulas taken daily is the first choice in prevention.

– Whole food sources of vitamins are optimal. They are absorbed more significantly and without toxic side effects of synthetics.

– "Amino acid" chelated minerals are proven to have the highest absorption with the least toxicity.

• Take action to build the immune system!

Irritable Bowel Syndrome (IBS)

Description: Irritable Bowel Syndrome is the most commonly treated gastrointestinal disorders by health practitioners today. It is a disorder of the motility of the entire digestive tract, where patients will experience abdominal pain and cramping, constipation, and sudden/urgent diarrhea. This symptoms are generally not classified as IBS however unless they have persisted for at least three months.

It is unknown what causes IBS, but the extra-sensitive digestive tract is triggered by stimuli that are normally not irritating. A flare-up of IBS results in stronger and more frequent contractions of the digestive tract, which causes food to pass more quickly and cause diarrhea. These stimuli may include a high-calorie diet, a high-fat diet, wheat, dairy, coffee, tea, citrus, etc. Strong emotions, such as stress, anxiety, and fear, can also lead to flare-ups of irritable bowel syndrome, as well as other irritants, such as certain drugs or hormones.

Along with the alternating diarrhea and constipation typical of IBS, other symptoms are also characteristic of IBS. These include abdominal distention, abdominal pain relief following a bowel movement, increased frequency of stools, changes in the consistency of the stools, passage of mucus, and the sensation of incomplete evacuation.[583] Other symptoms may also accompany IBS, such as bloating gas, nausea, headaches, fatigue, depression, anxiety, and difficultly concentrating.

Medical Treatment:

<u>Bulking Agents</u>: prevent or control chronic constipation.
Brand Name: Citrucel
Drug Name: Methylcellulose

Notable Side Effects: flatulence, bloating

Brand Name: Metamucil
Drug Name: Psyllium

Notable Side Effects: flatulence, bloating

<u>Anti-Spasmodic</u>
Brand Name: Nulev
Drug Name: Hyoscyamine Sulfate

Hyoxcyamine sulfate inhibits specifically the actions of acetylcholine on structures innervated by postganglionic cholinergic nerves and on smooth muscles that respond to acetylcholine but lack cholinergic innervation. These peripheral cholinergic receptors are present in the autonomic effector cells of the smooth muscle, cardiac muscle, the sinoatrial node, the atrioventricular node, and the exocrine glands. At therapeutic doses, it is completely devoid of any action on autonomic ganglia. Hyoscyamine sulfate inhibits gastrointestinal propulsive motility and decreases gastric acid secretion. Hyoscyamine sulfate also controls excessive pharyngeal, tracheal and bronchial secretions.

> **Notable Side Effects:** dryness of the mouth; urinary hesitancy and retention; blurred vision; tachycardia; palpitations; mydriasis; cycloplegia; increased ocular tension; loss of taste; headache; nervousness; drowsiness; weakness; dizziness; insomnia; nausea; vomiting; impotence; suppression of lactation; constipation; bloated feeling; allergic reactions or drug idiosyncrasies; urticaria and other dermal manifestations; ataxia; speech disturbance; some degree of mental confusion and/or excitement (especially in elderly persons); and deceased sweating.

Brand Name: Zelnorm

To find out more or to speak to a nutritional counselor for free, just visit us at:
www.CuresForTheBody.com

Drug Name: Tegaserod

Tegaserod is a 5-HT $_4$ receptor partial agonist that binds with high affinity at human 5-HT $_4$ receptors, whereas it has no appreciable affinity for 5-HT $_3$ or dopamine receptors. It has moderate affinity for 5-HT $_1$ receptors. Tegaserod, by acting as an agonist at neuronal 5-HT $_4$ receptors, triggers the release of further neurotransmitters such as calcitonin gene-related peptide from sensory neurons. The activation of 5-HT $_4$ receptors in the gastrointestinal tract stimulates the peristaltic reflex and intestinal secretion, as well as inhibits visceral sensitivity. *In vivo* studies showed that tegaserod enhanced basal motor activity and normalized impaired motility throughout the gastrointestinal tract. In addition, studies demonstrated that tegaserod moderated visceral sensitivity during colorectal distension in animals.

> **Notable Side Effects:** *Gastrintestinal System Disorders:* abdominal pain, diarrhea, nausea, flatulence. *Central and Peripheral Nervous System:* headache, dizziness, migraine. *Body as a whole:* accidental trauma, leg pain. *Musculoskeletal System Disorders:* back pain, arthropathy.

Brand Name: Lotronex
Drug Name: Alosetron Hydrochloride

Alosetron is a potent and selective 5-HT3 receptor antagonist. 5-HT3 receptors are nonselective cation channels that are extensively distributed on enteric neurons in the human gastrointestinal tract, as well as other peripheral and central locations. Activation of these channels and the resulting neuronal depolarization affect the regulation of visceral pain, colonic transit and gastrointestinal secretions, processes that relate to the pathophysiology of irritable bowel syndrome (IBS). 5-HT3 receptor antagonists such as alosetron inhibit activation of non-selective cation channels which results in the modulation of the enteric nervous system.

> **Notable Side Effects:** *Gastrointestinal:* constipation, abdominal discomfort and pain, nausea, gastrointestinal discomfort and pain, abdominal distention, regurgitation and reflux, hemorrhoids.

To find out more or to speak to a nutritional counselor for free, just visit us at:
www.CuresForTheBody.com

Other common recommendations from Medical Doctors: Understanding your symptoms and triggers of IBS flare-ups can be your best treatment for IBS. Avoid the foods that trigger your symptoms, which may include dairy, high-fat/calorie meals, fructose (sugar in fruits and berries), sorbitol (artificial sweetener), and difficult to digest foods (beans, cabbage). If your symptoms are triggered by a psychological factor, find out if you can treat an emotional disorder. Many patients find that when they address psychosocial factors, they experience a clinical improvement in their condition.[584]

There are also pro-active preventative measures you can take. Exercise helps to improve the motility of the digestive system. Frequent, small meals and fiber also help food to pass through more easily without triggering a flare-up.

Nutritional Approach:

Disease or Condition: Irritable Bowel Syndrome (IBS)

Causes of Irritable Bowel Syndrome (IBS)

Usually caused by; food allergies, stress, or a lack of fiber in the diet.

Nutritional support:

Foods that have been proven to help with IBS

Increasing the intake of plant foods in the diet is effective in most cases.

Eat foods high in omega 3 and 6 essential fatty acids (i.e. flax, hemp and fish).

Eat a low refined flour and sugar diet, eliminate allergenic foods.

Nutrients that have been proven to help with IBS

Fiber[585] (psyllium[586]), glutamine[587], zinc[588], omega 3 and 6 essential fatty acids (i.e. flax oil, hemp oil, DHA, EPO)[589], Broad spectrum plant source digestive enzymes[590], Probiotics[591] (friendly flora), enteric coated peppermint oil[592], cat's claw[593], olive leaf extract[594], grapefruit seed extract[595], and artichoke leaf extract.[596]

Exercises that have been proven to help with IBS

To find out more or to speak to a nutritional counselor for free, just visit us at:
www.CuresForTheBody.com

People with irritable bowel syndrome should engage in regular physical exercise. This helps relieve the symptoms of anxiety and also promotes good bowel function. Efforts should be made to deal with any stresses that may be contributing to the problem.[597]

Basic IBS Plan:
•Increase intake of fiber-rich foods

– In general, researchers suggest that it is best to recommend that patients with IBS judge for themselves whether increased fiber helps or worsens their symptoms[598]. One group of physicians studying the relationship of fiber to various diseases suggested that the most suitable fiber for patients with irritable bowel syndrome is methylcellulose or polycarbophil.

– Psyllium Seed - has been reported effective in supporting the management of irritable bowel syndrome (IBS) and ulcerative colitis. Psyllium is rich in dietary fiber. In IBS, psyllium has been reported to increase bowel movements, appearing to be a major reason for the therapeutic success.

• Eliminate allergenic foods

– Numerous studies report that dietary food allergies are frequently responsible for many of the symptoms experienced by patients with irritable bowel syndrome. Careful avoidance of the offending foods resulted in the following symptomatic improvements: distention was relieved in 88%, colic in 90%, diarrhea in 85% and constipation in 65%. Seventy-nine percent of the patients also reported improvements other conditions such as hay fever, sinusitis, asthma, eczema and hives. Food triggers were twice as frequent as inhalants, which included danders, grasses and perfumes[599].

• **Avoid milk and dairy**. Lactose intolerance may be a contributing factor. Avoiding lactose can decrease symptoms and reduce medication use[600].

• Taking a **broad spectrum Digestive Enzyme product** when you eat helps significantly with food allergies. If foods are not broken down completely, then food can become a toxin to us and our body reacts in many ways; allergies are just one evidence of food not being broken down completely.

– Take plant source enzymes only. Do not use pancreatic enzymes.

• Take **Probiotics** – Not only does friendly flora aid in digestion[601], but it has been thought that some of the symptoms in patients with IBS are due to imbalances in the intestinal microflora. A 12 month study reported that at the 12-month follow-up, it became apparent that the patients that had consumed the Lactobacillus-containing product had maintained a better overall level of gastrointestinal function than the patients given placebos[602]. Our body produces thousands of friendly flora. It is beneficial to supplement more than just one strain to re-supply the intestinal microflora. Most clinicians now agree on the importance of maintaining healthy function of the microflora in health and disease.

– Use only stabilized Probiotics that don't need to be refrigerated.

• Take **Zinc**

– Low zinc levels have been reported in patients with irritable bowel disease. Zinc helps in the healing process and immummity.

– "Amino Acid Chelated" minerals have the highest proven absorption with the least toxicity.

• **Omega 3 and 6 fatty acids** - Supplementation with essential fatty acids has been shown to prevent zinc deficiency, thereby potentially improving immunity. Fatty acids are an important part of normal function of the body. The human body can produce all but two fatty acids - omega-3 and omega-6 fatty acids. Both must be obtained through the diet or by the use of supplements. Obtaining a balance of these two fatty acids is essential. Essential fatty acids are needed for building cell membranes and are precursors for production of hormones and prostaglandins.

• Eat flax seeds or oil, hemp seeds or oil, and deep sea cold water fish.

– Supplement with flax oil, hemp oil, fish oil, DHA, EPO.

• **Grapefruit Seed Extract** - a broad-spectrum antimicrobial. It also inhibits the growth of H. pylori and C. jejuni, both causative agents in gastrointestinal ulcers. In a human study, an improvement in constipation, flatulence, abdominal distress and night rest were noticed after 4 weeks of therapy.

• **Avoid refined sugar, highly processed foods** – these raise blood sugar level too fast and too much; then the sugars become food for the bad bacteria to feast on.

• **Avoid caffeine**[603]- can be bowel irritating for those with IBS.

• **Glutamine** - Research indicates that glutamine is therapeutically useful for maintaining the integrity of intestinal mucous membranes and their permeability to luminal toxins in animal models for inflammatory bowel disease.

• **Enteric coated peppermint oil** - Eight randomized, controlled trials have reported positive benefits in IBS when using enteric coated peppermint oil, confirming the antispasmodic, pain-relieving action of peppermint oil when administered as enteric coated tablets.

• **Cat's Claw (root)** - has the ability to soothe irritated and inflamed tissues and help eliminate pathogens from the GI tract.

• **Olive Leaf Extract** - an effective antimicrobial agent against a wide variety of pathogens, including some penicillin-resistant strains.

• **Artichoke Leaf Extract -** As many as 96% of those tested, claimed that the artichoke leaf extract was well tolerated and that it worked at least as well as other therapies used for their symptoms of IBS.

Kidney Stones

Description: Most people describe hard masses that form in the urinary tract as kidney stones. However, these stones can be formed anywhere in the urinary tract: the bladder, ureter, or the kidney. Stones are more common in older adults, particularly men. Those at higher risk include people with certain diseases, such as hypertension, and those who eat a high-protein diet or don't drink enough water.

Stones may be various sizes, from microscopic to 1 inch in diameter. They may be caused for various reasons. The urine may become saturated with salts, or may lack the inhibitors that prevent stones form forming. Most (80%) of stones are made of calcium, and the rest are made of uric acid, cystine, and struvite.

Symptoms of stones include pain in the lower abdomen that can be excruciating and intermittent. Other symptoms include nausea and vomiting, abdominal distention, chills, fever, and blood in the urine.

Stones may result in a urinary tract infection if they stones block the urinary tract and cause the urine to back up and pool. This can eventually put pressure on and distend the kidneys, leading to eventual damage.

Medical Treatment:

NSAID: Lessen pain

Brand name: Advil, Motrin

Drug Name: IbuprofenIbuprofen

IbuprofenIbuprofen is a nonsteroidal anti-inflammatory drug (NSAID) that possesses anti-inflammatory, analgesic and antipyretic activity. Its mode of action, like that of other NSAIDs, is not completely understood, but may be related to prostaglandin synthetase inhibition. After absorption of the racemic ibuprofen, the [-]R-enantiomer undergoes interconversion to the

[+]S-form. The biological activities of ibuprofen are associated with the [+]S-enantiomer.

> **Notable Side Effects:** *Cardiovascular system:* Edema, fluid retention (generally responds promptly to drug discontinuation). *Digestive system:* Nausea, epigastric pain, heartburn, diarrhea, abdominal distress, nausea and vomiting, indigestion, constipation, abdominal cramps or pain, fullness of Gl tract (bloating and flatulence). *Nervous system:* Dizziness, headache, nervousness. *Skin and appendages:* Rash (including maculopapular type), pruritus. *Special senses:* Tinnitus.

Brand name: Aleve, Anaprox

Drug Name: Naproxen

Naproxen is a nonsteroidal anti-inflammatory drug (NSAID) with analgesic and antipyretic properties. The sodium salt of naproxen has been developed as a more rapidly absorbed formulation of naproxen for use as an analgesic. The naproxen anion inhibits prostaglandin synthesis but beyond this its mode of action is unknown.

> **Notable Side Effects:** *Gastrointestinal:* constipation, heartburn, abdominal pain, nausea, dyspepsia, diarrhea, stomatitis. *Central Nervous System:* headache, dizziness, drowsiness, lightheadedness, vertigo. *Dermatologic:* itching (pruritus), skin eruptions, ecchymoses, sweating, purpura. *Special Senses:* tinnitus, hearing disturbances, visual disturbances. *Cardiovascular:* edema, dyspnea, palpitations. *General:* thirst.

Opioids: Relieve anxiety and pain if the pain persists despite use of other drugs

Brand name:

Drug Name: Morphine

Morphine produces a wide spectrum of pharmacologic effects including analgesia, dysphoria, euphoria, somnolence, respiratory depression, diminished gastrointestinal motility and physical dependence. Opiate analgesia involves at least three anatomical areas of the central nervous system: the periaqueductal-periventricular gray matter, the ventromedial medulla and the spinal cord. A systemically administered opiate may produce analgesia by acting at any, all or some combination of these distinct regions. Morphine interacts predominantly with the [micro]-receptor. The [micro]-binding sites of opioids are very discretely distributed in the human brain, with high densities of sites found in the posterior amygdala, hypothalamus, thalamus, nucleus caudatus, putamen and certain cortical areas. They are also found on the terminal axons of primary afferents within laminae I and II (substantia gelatinosa) of the spinal cord and in the spinal nucleus of the trigeminal nerve.

> **Notable Side Effects:** Respiratory depression, respiratory arrest, tolerance and myoclonus, pruritus, urinary retention, constipation, headache, dizziness, euphoria, anxiety, depression of cough reflex, interference with thermal regulation and oliguria, evidence of histamine release, wheals and/or local tissue irritation, nausea, and vomiting.

Other common recommendations from Medical Doctors: Drinking plenty of fluids is important. A low calcium diet may help for those who excrete a lot of calcium in the urine. Decreasing foods containing oxalate (contributes to calcium formation) rhubarb, spinach, cocoa, nuts, pepper, and tea. For people who get stones of uric acid should eat a diet low in meat, fish, and poultry.

Nutritional Approach:

Disease or Condition: Kidney Stones

Cause of Kidney Stones:

There are generally three types of kidney stones and all three of them have to do with the indigestion of certain foods in our diet. Specifically Uric Acid stones from Proteins (hard to digest proteins consist of animal meats, especially red meat). Calcium Phosphate stones from undigested fats (fried and hydrogenated fats). And Calcium Oxalate from junk foods (heavily processed foods like white flour and table sugar).

A person with a family history of Kidney Stones may be more likely to develop them.

To find out more or to speak to a nutritional counselor for free, just visit us at:
www.CuresForTheBody.com

Nutritional Support:

Foods that have been proven to help with Kidney Stones:

Acerola cherries, Strawberries, Mustard Greens, Orange, Kiwi

Proven Nutrients to help dissolve kidney stones:

Vitamin C[604], Digestive Plant Enzymes[605], Probiotics[606].

Basic Nutrition Plan for Specific Types of Kidney Stones:

• Uric Acid stones are formed from poor protein digestion. Protease enzymes have been proven to be absorbed into the body[607]. Protease enzymes digest proteins and can help digest the Uric Acid stones[608].

• Calcium phosphate (fat) stones are common and easily dissolve in urine acidified by Vitamin C. Acidic urine or slightly acidic urine reduces the union of calcium and oxalate, reducing the possibility of stones. "Vitamin C in the urine tends to bind calcium and decrease its free form. This means less chance of calcium's separating out as calcium oxalate (stones)." Also, the diuretic effect of vitamin C reduces the static conditions necessary for stone formation in general. Fast moving rivers deposit little silt[609].

• Since Calcium Phosphate stones contain undigested fats, the plant enzyme Lipase will help since it digests dietary fats in the bloodstream[610].

• Magnesium ammonium phosphate (struvite stones) are much less common, often appearing after an infection. They dissolve in vitamin C acidified urine[611].

• Calcium oxalate (junk food) stones are also common but they do not dissolve in acid urine[612]. A balanced Digestive Enzyme needs to be taken to ensure all of the different types of undigested foods will be broken down[613].

• Increase intake of fluids and drink cranberry juice.

• Increase B6 (salmon, banana, tomatoes, watermelon).

• Omit foods containing purines (i.e., shellfish, organ meats, red meat, anchovies, mackerel, yeast).

• Limit oxalate-containing foods (coffee, black tea, chocolate, spinach, eggplant).

• Uric acid stones result from a problem metabolizing purines (the chemical base of adenine, xanthine, theobromine [in chocolate] and uric acid). They may form in a condition such as gout[614]. Specific Enymes that easily digest Protein completely down to there most usable form.

–Protease, Peptidase, Bromelains

To find out more or to speak to a nutritional counselor for free, just visit us at:
www.CuresForTheBody.com

• Cystine stones result from a hereditary inability to reabsorb cystine (proteins). Most children's stones are this type, and these are rare[615].

To find out more or to speak to a nutritional counselor for free, just visit us at:
www.CuresForTheBody.com

Lupus

Description: Lupus is a chronic disorder where the connective tissue is inflamed, and subsequently affects the joints, kidneys, mucous membranes, and blood vessel walls. The immune system functions abnormally and forms antibodies that attack the connective tissues of the body. Lupus generally affects young women, from their late teens to their 30's. In fact, 90% of lupus patients fit in this category.

The cause of lupus is generally unknown. However, certain drugs can sometimes cause lupus, the symptoms disappear after their use is discontinued. Some researchers also suggest that lupus can be triggered after susceptible people are exposed to a triggering agent, possibly in the environment.[616] People with lupus have an extremely large amount of antibodies in their bodies, which are the underlying problem. These antibodies determine which symptoms the person will develop and can affect any organ system.

The onset of lupus is usually noticed with initial symptoms if a migraine headache, epilepsy, or severe mental disorders. The progression of lupus can then either be sudden or gradual. And most will experience occasional flare-ups. Lupus is also usually chronic and relapsing with symptom free periods.

Other symptoms of lupus can include rash, sensitivity to light, fluid around lungs, kidney dysfunction, loss of hair, chest pain. Ninety percent of lupus patients experience joint inflammation, and long standing joint inflammation can lead to deformity of the joints.

Medical Treatment:

NSAIDS

Brand name: Bayer, Ecotrin

Drug Name: Aspirin

To find out more or to speak to a nutritional counselor for free, just visit us at:
www.CuresForTheBody.com

Aspirin is a more inhibitor of both prostaglandin synthesis and platelet aggregation.

Notable Side Effects:

Body as a Whole: Fever, hypothermia, thirst. *Cardiovascular:* Dysrhythmias, hypotension, tachycardia. *Central Nervous System:* Agitation, cerebral edema, coma, confusion, dizziness, headache, subdural or intracranial hemorrhage, lethargy, seizures. *Fluid and Electrolyte:* Dehydration, hyperkalemia, metabolic acidosis, respiratory alkalosis. *Gastrointestinal:* Dyspepsia, GI bleeding, ulceration and perforation, nausea, vomiting, transient elevations of hepatic enzymes, hepatitis, Reye's Syndrome, pancreatitis. *Hematologic:* Prolongation of the prothrombin time, disseminated intravascular coagulation, coagulopathy, thrombocytopenia. *Hypersensitivity:* Acute anaphylaxis, angioedema, asthma, bronchospasm, laryngeal edema, urticaria. *Musculoskeletal:* Rhabdomyolysis. *Metabolism:* Hypoglycemia (in children), hyperglycemia. *Reproductive:* Prolonged pregnancy and labor, stillbirths, lower birth weight infants, antepartum and postpartum bleeding. *Respiratory:* Hyperpnea, pulmonary edema, tachypnea. *Special Senses:* Hearing loss, tinnitus. Patients with high frequency hearing loss may have difficulty perceiving tinnitus. In these patients, tinnitus cannot be used as a clinical indicator of salicylism. *Urogenital:* Interstitial nephritis, papillary necrosis, proteinuria, renal insufficiency and failure.

Brand Name: Plaquenil

Drug Name: Hydroxychloroquine

Hydroxychloroquine exerts a beneficial effect in lupus erythematosus (chronic discoid or systemic) and acute or chronic rheumatoid arthritis. The precise mechanism of action is not known.

Notable Side Effects: mild and transient headache, dizziness, and gastrointestinal complaints (diarrhea, anorexia, nausea, abdominal cramps and, on rare occasions, vomiting) may occur. Cardiomyopathy has been rarely reported with high daily dosages of hydroxychloroquine.

Brand Name: Aralen

Drug Name: Chloroquine

Chloroquine inhibits certain enzymes, its effect is believed to result, at least in part, from its interaction with DNA. However, the mechanism of plasmodicidal action of chloroquine is not completely certain.

Notable side Effects: *Ocular:* Irreversible retinal damage in patients receiving long-term or high-dosage 4-aminoquinoline therapy; visual disturbances (blurring of vision and difficulty of focusing or accommodation); nyctalopia; scotomatous vision with field defects of paracentral, pericentral ring types, and typically temporal scotomas, e.g., difficulty in reading with words tending to disappear, seeing half an object, misty vision, and fog before the eyes. *Auditory:* Nerve type deafness; tinnitus, reduced hearing in patients with pre-existing auditory damage. *Musculoskeletal system:* Skeletal muscle myopathy or neuromyopathy leading to progressive weakness and atrophy of proximal muscle groups, which may be associated with mild sensory changes, depression of tendon reflexes and abnormal nerve conduction, have been noted. *Gastrointestinal system:* Anorexia, nausea, vomiting, diarrhea, abdominal cramps. *Skin and appendages:* Pleomorphic skin eruptions, skin and mucosal pigmentary changes; lichen planus-like eruptions, pruritus, photosensitivity and hair loss and bleaching of hair pigment. *Hematologic system:* Rarely, aplastic anemia, reversible agranulocytosis, thrombocytopenia and neutropenia. *Central Nervous system:* Convulsive seizures. Mild and transient headache. Neuropsychiatric changes including psychosis, delirium, personality changes and depression. *Cardiovascular system:* Rarely, hypotension, electrocardiographic change (particularly, inversion or depression of the T-wave with widening of the QRS complex), and cardiomyopathy.

Corticosteroid
Prednisone

Immunosuppressive Drugs
Brand Name: Azasan

Drug Name: Azathioprine

Azathioprine: The mechanisms whereby azathioprine affects autoimmune diseases are not known. Azathioprine is immunosuppressive, delayed hypersensitivity and cellular cytotoxicity tests being suppressed to a greater degree than are antibody responses. In the rat model of adjuvant arthritis, azathioprine has been shown to inhibit the lymph node hyperplasia which precedes the onset of the signs of the disease. Both the immunosuppressive and therapeutic effects in animal models are dose-related.

> **Notable Side Effects:** *Hematologic:* Leukopenia and/or thrombocytopenia are dose dependent. Infection may occur as a secondary manifestation of bone marrow suppression or leucopenia. Macrocytic anemia and/or bleeding have been reported. *Gastrointestinal:* Nausea and vomiting, and may be accompanied by symptoms such as diarrhea, fever, malaise, and myalgias. Vomiting with abdominal pain may occur rarely with a hypersensitivity pancreatitis. Hepatotoxicity manifest by elevation of serum alkaline phosphatase, bilirubin, and/or serum transaminases is known to occur. *Others:* Additional side effects of low frequency have been reported. These include skin rashes, alopecia, fever, arthralgias, diarrhea, steatorrhea and negative nitrogen balance.

Other common recommendations from Medical Doctors: Patients should be educated about the disease and give their bodies plenty of rest, eat a good diet, and avoid smoking. Limiting the exposure to sunlight and wearing sunscreen is also helpful.

Nutritional Approach:

To find out more or to speak to a nutritional counselor for free, just visit us at:
www.CuresForTheBody.com

Disease or Condition: Lupus

Causes of Lupus:

An autoimmune disease that many experts believe is caused by an unidentified virus. Additional factors may play a role in the body succumbing to this condition including genetic, environmental, and hormonal factors. Some theorize that the condition lay dormant until it is triggered by an event. Women using or who have used previously postmenopausal horomones were found to have an increased risk for developing lupus.[617]

Nutritional support:

Foods that have been proven to help with Lupus

Fruits, nuts, seeds, vegetables containing sterolins (plant "fats"), fatty acid containing foods like: avocados, raw nuts, and flax seed.

Nutrients that have been proven to help with Lupus

DHEA (Dehydroepiandrosterone)[618], Omega 3 and 6 (EFA's) essential fatty acids (flax seed oil, hemp seed oil, borage oil, DHA)[619], Vitamin B12[620], Vitamin E[621], Astragalus[622], Oregano[623], Grapefruit seed extract[624], Plant source digestive enzymes (i.e. protease, lipase, amylase) especially helpful are the proteolitic enzymes[625], Sterols and Sterolins[626], Probiotics.[627]

Exercises that have been proven to help with Lupus

Because lupus causes joint pain and inflammation, muscle pain, and fatigue, the very thought of exercising can be a challenge. In addition, because lupus is a disease that requires a large amount of rest, you might wonder why exercise is so important. Although rest is important in managing fatigue, too much rest can be harmful to muscles, bones, joints, and overall fitness. Keeping fit through an exercise program planned just for you can help you feel better, both mentally and physically. There are many types of exercises that are appropriate for lupus patients, such as swimming and walking. Regular exercise will increase your muscle strength, help prevent your joints from getting stiff, help prevent osteoporosis, help keep your weight under control, improve your cardiovascular health, and help reduce stress.[628]

Basic Lupus Plan

To find out more or to speak to a nutritional counselor for free, just visit us at:
www.CuresForTheBody.com

• Consider supplementing with Vitamin B12 using a whole food source such as, nutritional yeast, since studies have shown deficiencies in lupus patients.[629]

• Eating foods rich in Omega 3 and 6 essential fatty acids or taking supplements containing them (flax seeds/oil, hemp seeds/oil, Borage oil, DHA),. They also help our body produce stage 1 and 3 prostaglandins that inhibit inflammation. They also strengthen immune cells that inhabit all body surfaces.

• Consider taking higher doses of the proteolitic enzymes (protease and peptidase) to stop inflammation, along with bromelain, boswellia, wheat germ and vitamin C and zinc; all helping decrease inflammation and aiding in tissue repair. Proteolitic enzymes are a natural way to decrease inflammation without the harmful side effects created by NSAIDs.

• Probiotics balance the pH levels and ecology of the intestines. They help with the reconstruction of the immune system.

Migraine Headaches

Description: A migraine headache is usually a band-like pain that affects the whole head. Throbbing pain on one side of the head is typically experienced, which can sometimes be severe and incapacitating. Nausea and vomiting may also accompany the headache.

Migraine headaches are three times more common in women than men, and can also run in families. Migraines typically begin between the ages of 10 and 40, and typically resolve or become less severe after age 60.

A typical theory of what causes a migraine suggests that the pain is caused by the arteries in the brain narrowing and widening. However, this theory is too simple and does not explain the changes in blood flow that occur.

There are some known factors that can trigger a migraine. Estrogen can trigger a migraine, which partly explains why it is more common in women than in men. Many women will typically experience their migraines during puberty, menstrual periods, and when taking oral contraceptive. Insomnia, changes in barometric pressure, and hunger can also trigger a migraine headache. Once a migraine is triggered, physical activities, light, sounds, and smells can make it worse.

Most people will experience a prodrome, aura, and postdrome along with the pain of the headache. The prodrome can occur up to 24 hours before the pain of the headache and involves a change in mood or behavior. The aura can occur up to an hour before the headache and involves disturbances in vision, sensation, balance, movements, or speech. The aura usually subsides at the onset of pain of the migraine. In the postdrome, there is another change in mood or behavior after the migraine has subsided.

Medical Treatment:

Abortive:

Brand Name: Axert

Drug Name: Almotriptan

Almotriptan: Current theories on the etiology of migraine headache suggest that symptoms are due to local cranial vasodilatation and/or to the release of vasoactive and pro-inflammatory peptides from sensory nerve endings in an activated trigeminal system. The therapeutic activity of almotriptan in migraine can most likely be attributed to agonist effects at 5-$HT_{1B/1D}$ receptors on the extracerebral, intracranial blood vessels that become dilated during a migraine attack, and on nerve terminals in the trigeminal system. Activation of these receptors results in cranial vessel constriction, inhibition of neuropeptide release, and reduced transmission in trigeminal pain pathways.

Notable Side Effects:

(Most common) nausea, dry mouth, paresthesia (nervous system).

Body: Frequent was headache. Infrequent were abdominal cramp or pain, asthenia, chills, back pain, chest pain, neck pain, fatigue, and rigid neck. Rare were fever and photosensitivity reaction.

Cardiovascular: Infrequent were vasodilation, palpitations, and tachycardia. Rare were hypertension and syncope.

Digestive: Infrequent were diarrhea, vomiting, and dyspepsia. Rare were colitis, gastritis, gastroenteritis, esophageal reflux, increased thirst, and increased salivation.

Metabolic: Infrequent were hyperglycemia and increased serum creatine phosphokinase. Rare were increased gamma glutamyl transpeptidase and hypercholesteremia.

Musculoskeletal: Infrequent were myalgia and muscular weakness. Rare were arthralgia, arthritis, and myopathy.

Nervous: Frequent were dizziness and somnolence. Infrequent were tremor, vertigo, anxiety, hypesthesia, restlessness, CNS stimulation, insomnia, and shakiness. Rare were change in dreams, impaired concentration, abnormal coordination, depressive symptoms, euphoria, hyperreflexia, hypertonia, nervousness, neuropathy, nightmares, and nystagmus.

To find out more or to speak to a nutritional counselor for free, just visit us at:
www.CuresForTheBody.com

Respiratory: Infrequent were pharyngitis, rhinitis, dyspnea, laryngismus, sinusitis, bronchitis, and epistaxis. Rare were hyperventilation, laryngitis, and sneezing.

Skin: Infrequent were diaphoresis, dermatitis, erythema, pruritus, and rash.

Special Senses: Infrequent were ear pain, conjunctivitis, eye irritation, hyperacusis, and taste alteration. Rare were diplopia, dry eyes, eye pain, otitis media, parosmia, scotoma, and tinnitus.

Urogenital: Infrequent was dysmenorrhea.

Analgesic:

Brand name: Tylenol

Drug Name: Acetaminophen

Acetaminophen inhibits prostaglandin synthetase.

Notable Side Affects:

Light-headedness, dizziness, sedation, nausea and vomiting.

Brand name: Bayer, Ecotrin

Drug Name: Aspirin

Aspirin is a more inhibitor of both prostaglandin synthesis and platelet aggregation.

Notable Side Effects:

Body as a Whole: Fever, hypothermia, thirst.

Cardiovascular: Dysrhythmias, hypotension, tachycardia.

Central Nervous System: Agitation, cerebral edema, coma, confusion, dizziness, headache, subdural or intracranial hemorrhage, lethargy, seizures.

Fluid and Electrolyte: Dehydration, hyperkalemia, metabolic acidosis, respiratory alkalosis.

Gastrointestinal: Dyspepsia, GI bleeding, ulceration and perforation, nausea, vomiting, transient elevations of hepatic enzymes, hepatitis, Reye's Syndrome, pancreatitis.

Hematologic: Prolongation of the prothrombin time, disseminated intravascular coagulation, coagulopathy, thrombocytopenia.

Hypersensitivity: Acute anaphylaxis, angioedema, asthma, bronchospasm, laryngeal edema, urticaria.

Musculoskeletal: Rhabdomyolysis.

Metabolism: Hypoglycemia (in children), hyperglycemia.

Reproductive: Prolonged pregnancy and labor, stillbirths, lower birth weight infants, antepartum and postpartum bleeding.

Respiratory: Hyperpnea, pulmonary edema, tachypnea.

Special Senses: Hearing loss, tinnitus. Patients with high frequency hearing loss may have difficulty perceiving tinnitus. In these patients, tinnitus cannot be used as a clinical indicator of salicylism.

Urogenital: Interstitial nephritis, papillary necrosis, proteinuria, renal insufficiency and failure.

Brand name: Aleve, Anaprox

Drug Name: Naproxen

Naproxen is a nonsteroidal anti-inflammatory drug (NSAID) with analgesic and antipyretic properties. The sodium salt of naproxen has been developed as a more rapidly absorbed formulation of naproxen for use as an analgesic. The naproxen anion inhibits prostaglandin synthesis but beyond this its mode of action is unknown.

Notable Side Effects:

Gastrointestinal: constipation, heartburn, abdominal pain, nausea, dyspepsia, diarrhea, stomatitis.

Central Nervous System: headache, dizziness, drowsiness, lightheadedness, vertigo.

Dermatologic: itching (pruritus), skin eruptions, ecchymoses, sweating, purpura.

Special Senses: tinnitus, hearing disturbances, visual disturbances.

Cardiovascular: edema, dyspnea, palpitations.

General: thirst.

To find out more or to speak to a nutritional counselor for free, just visit us at:
www.CuresForTheBody.com

Other common recommendations from Medical Doctors: overuse of caffeine or analgesics can make migraine worse. Avoid environmental triggers (cigarette smoke, loud noise, and bright, flickering lights), psychological triggers (stress, anxiety, or depression), dietary triggers (alcohol, chocolate, caffeine, or tyramine containing foods, food additives, or citrus fruit), or lifestyle triggers (inadequate or excessive sleep, fasting or dieting, fatigue, skipping meals, or strenuous exercise).

Nutritional Approach:

Disease or Condition: Migraine

Causes of Migraine

Migraines are considered vascular headaches and although the exact cause of this condition is unknown, many triggers exist including food allergies, blood sugar disturbances, stress, injury, and hormonal fluctuations.

Many clinical experiences have found iron deficiency to be common in migraine headaches, especially in women.

Nutritonal Support:

Foods that have been proven to help with Migraines:

Peppers. Increasing fluid intake and incorporating foods rich in omega-3 fatty acids, like flaxseed, walnuts (which contain alpha-linolenic acid [ALA], an important omega-3 fatty acid), and fish, into your diet may help stave off migraines.

Avoid: caffeine, chocolate, alcohol, foods containing additives or citrus fruit, dairy products, tuna, mackerel, processed meats (bacon, hot dogs, salami, cured meats), nuts, peanut butter, fermented or pickled foods, and onions.

Nutrients that have been proven to help with Migraine:

Magnesium[630], Vitamin B2[631], Vitamin D and Calcium[632], Iron[633], Probiotics[634], Bitter melon[635], Chasteberry[636], Black cohosh[637], Kava[638], Evening primrose oil.[639]

Exercises that have been proven to help with Migraine:

A moderate aerobics program can lessen the frequency and intensity of the migraine when it occurs. However, continuous and strenuous exercise may in fact precipitate migraine headache. So you have to be very careful as to the type of exercises you choose.

Basic Migraine Plan:

• Establish Optimal Nutrition

–Since migraines may be brought about by food allergies eat as many raw fruits and vegetables as possible and avoid processed sugars, white flour, and fried foods. If processed foods are being consumed, taking (plant source) digestive enzymes help allergies in part, because they promote good digestion (i.e. protease, lipase, amylase). Completely digested proteins turn into amino acids, which cannot cause allergic reactions.[640]

–Reduce and eliminate the consumption of NSAIDS and other anti-inflammatories. Proteolytic enzymes, minerals, herbs, and antioxidants that reduces inflammation.

–Women suffering from (hormonal triggered) migraines would benefit from the consumption of black cohosh or supplementation of a whole food vitamin containing the herb[641]. This herb is found to have a balancing effect in the female reproductive system.[642]

–Tumeric – has anit-inflammatory strengths[643]

–Feverfew – anti-inflammatory[644]

–Eat foods or supplement with gamma-linolenic acid as in evening primrose[645](an omega-6 fatty acid). Omega-6 fatty acids decrease inflammatory response.

–Take amino acid chelated magnesium (has the highest absorption rate)[646] Magnesium's role in the pathogenesis of migraine headaches has been clearly established in numerous clinical and experimental studies. Magnesium was also found to be effective in the prophylaxis of menstrual migraines. In a double-blind trial, women taking 360 mg/day of magnesium for two months reported a reduction in the number of days with headaches in addition to overall improvement in premenstrual complaints.[647]

–Take amino acid chelated calcium (has the highest absorption rate).[648]

Amino acid's role in the body is to make 5-HTP from tryptophan (an amino acid that is obtained from the diet) and convert it to an important brain chemical known as serotonin. 5-HTP dietary supplements help raise serotonin levels in the brain, which may have a positive effect on sleep, mood, anxiety, aggression, appetite, temperature, sexual behavior, and pain sensation.

–The chasteberry tree finds its origins in the Mediterranean. Its fruit is harvested and dried for medicinal purposes. It has a long folk history of use in women's health and in hormonal regulation. Chasteberry has been recommended for use in mild to moderate female complaints, especially in endometriosis, menopause, and PMS symptoms.

Multiple Sclerosis

Description: Multiple Sclerosis (MS) is a disorder in which the myelin and the nerve fibers are damaged and destroyed. According to one theory, MS is the result of an autoimmune response against the myelin surrounding the nerve fibers by the action of macophages, T-killer cells, lymphokines, antibodies, or a combination of these elements.[649] The process of demyelination causes disruptions in the transmission of nerve impulses, which therefore, results in symptoms specific to the nerve fibers damaged.

The cause of MS is unknown; however, it may be due to a virus or other unknown antigen. This disorder is typically found in temperate climates, and is rarely if ever found in tropical climates. MS typically occurs between the ages of 20 and 40 years. Heredity may also play a factor in the occurrence of MS as approximately 10 percent of those with MS have siblings that also have the disease.[650]

Some of the most common early symptoms of MS include numbness, tingling, pain, burning, itching, mood swings, and giddiness. Some cognitive symptoms may also include memory disturbances, decreased judgement, and inattention. However, the symptoms experienced depend on which nerve fibers have been affected. In addition, symptoms may come and go as the myelin is damaged, repaired, and then more myelin is damaged.

Most people with MS have a normal lifespan. Generally 20% have no functional limitation, 70% will be limited or unable to perform major daily activities, and 75% will be unemployed.

Medical Treatment:

Corticosteroids:

Recommended for people with inflammation of the optic nerve and no other symptoms.

Brand Name: Solu-Medrol

Drug Name: Methyl-prednisolone

Methyl-prednisolone is a naturally occurring glucocorticoids (hydrocortisone and cortisone), which also have salt-retaining properties, are used as replacement therapy in adrenocortical deficiency states. Their synthetic analogs are primarily used for their potent anti-inflammatory effects in disorders of many organ systems. Glucocorticoids cause profound and varied metabolic effects. In addition, they modify the body's immune responses to diverse stimuli. Methylprednisolone is a potent anti-inflammatory steroid with greater anti-inflammatory potency than prednisolone and even less tendency than prednisolone to induce sodium and water retention.

Notable Side Effects:

Fluid and Electrolyte Disturbances: Sodium retention, Fluid retention, Congestive heart failure in susceptible patients, Potassium loss, Hypokalemic alkalosis, Hypertension.

Musculoskeletal: Muscle weakness, Steroid myopathy, Loss of muscle mass, Severe arthralgia, Vertebral compression fractures, Aseptic necrosis of femoral and humeral heads, Pathologic fracture of long bones, Osteoporosis, Tendon rupture, particularly of of the Achilles tendon.

Gastrointestinal: Peptic ulcer with possible perforation and hemorrhage, Pancreatitis, Abdominal distention, Ulcerative esophagitis,Increases in alanine transaminase (ALT, SGPT), aspartate transaminase (AST, SGOT), and alkaline phosphatase have been observed following corticosteroid treatment.

Dermatologic: Impaired wound healing, Thin fragile skin, Petechiae and ecchymoseds, Facial erythema, Increased sweating, May suppress reactions to skin tests.

Neurological: Increased intracranial pressure with papilledema (pseudo-tumor cerebri) usually after treatment, Convulsions, Vertigo, Headache.

Endocrine: Development of Cushingoid state, Suppression of growth in children, Secondary adrenocortical and pituitary unresponsiveness, particularly in times of stress, as in trauma, surgery or illness, Menstrual irregularities,

Decreased carbohydrate tolerance, Manifestations of latent diabetes mellitus, Increased requirements for insulin or oral hypoglycemic agents in diabetics.

Ophthalmic: Posterior subcapsular cataracts, Increased intraocular pressure, Glaucoma, Exophthalmos.

Metabolic: Negative nitrogen balance due to protein catabolism.

Interferon-beta injections:

Reduce the frequency of relapses and may help prevent later disability.

Brand Name: Copaxone

Drug Name: Glatiramer acetate

Glatiramer acetate is thought to act by modifying immune processes that are currently believed to be responsible for the pathogenesis of MS. This hypothesis is supported by findings of studies that have been carried out to explore the pathogenesis of experimental allergic encephalomyelitis (EAE), a condition induced in several animal species through immunization against central nervous system derived material containing myelin and often used as an experimental animal model of MS. Studies in animals and *in vitro* systems suggest that upon its administration, glatiramer acetate-specific suppressor T-cells are induced and activated in the periphery. Because glatiramer acetate can modify immune functions, concerns exist about its potential to alter naturally occurring immune responses. Results of a limited battery of tests designed to evaluate this risk produced no finding of concern; nevertheless, there is no logical way to absolutely exclude this possibility.

Notable Side Effects:

Body as a Whole: asthenia, back pain, bacterial infection, chest pain, chills, cyst, face edema, fever, flu syndrome, infection, injection site erythema, injection site hemorrhage, injection site induration, injection site inflammation, injection site mass, injection site pain, injection site pruritus, injection site urticaria, injection site welt, neck pain, pain.

Cardiovascular System: migraine, palpitations, syncope, tachycardia, vasodilatation.

Digestion system: anorexia, diarrhea, gastroenteritis, gastrointestinal disorder, nausea, vomiting.

Hemic and lymphatic System: ecchymosis, lymphadenopathy.

Metabolic and Nutritional: edema, peripheral edema, weight gain.

Musculoskeletal system: arthralgia.

Nervous System: agitation, anxiety, confusion, foot drop, hypertonia, nervousness, nystagmus, speech disorder, tremor, vertigo.

Respiratory System: bronchitis, dyspnea, laryngismus, rhinitis.

Skin and Appendages: erythema, herpes simplex, pruritus, rash, skin nodule, sweating, urticaria.

Special Senses: ear pain, eye disorder.

Urogenital system: dysmenorrheal, urinary urgency, vaginal moniliasis.

Beta-Blocker:

Reduces severity of tremors

Brand Name: Inderal LA

Drug Name: Propranolol

Propranolol is a nonselective, beta-adrenergic receptor-blocking agent possessing no other autonomic nervous system activity. It specifically competes with beta-adrenergic receptor-stimulating agents for available receptor sites. When access to beta-receptor sites is blocked by Inderal, the chronotropic, inotropic, and vasodilator responses to beta-adrenergic stimulation are decreased proportionately. The mechanism of the antihypertensive effect of Inderal has not been established. Among the factors that may be involved in contributing to the antihypertensive action are: (1) decreased cardiac output, (2) inhibition of renin release by the kidneys, and (3) diminution of tonic sympathetic nerve outflow from vasomotor centers in the brain. Although total peripheral resistance may increase initially, it readjusts to or below the pretreatment level with chronic use. Effects on plasma volume appear to be minor and somewhat variable. Inderal has been shown to cause a small increase in serum potassium concentration when used in the treatment of hypertensive patients.

Notable Side Effects:

Cardiovascular: Bradycardia; congestive heart failure; intensification of AV block; hypotension; paresthesia of hands; thrombocytopenic purpura; arterial insufficiency, usually of the Raynaud type.

Central Nervous System: Light-headedness, mental depression manifested by insomnia, lassitude, weakness, fatigue; reversible mental depression progressing to catatonia; visual disturbances; hallucinations; vivid dreams; an acute reversible syndrome characterized by disorientation for time and place, short-term memory loss, emotional lability, slightly clouded sensorium, and decreased performance on neuropsychometrics. For immediate formulations, fatigue, lethargy, and vivid dreams appear dose related.

Gastrointestinal: Nausea, vomiting, epigastric distress, abdominal cramping, diarrhea, constipation, mesenteric arterial thrombosis, and ischemic colitis.

Allergic: Pharyngitis and agranulocytosis, erythematous rash, fever combined with aching and sore throat, laryngospasm, and respiratory distress.

Respiratory: Bronchospasm.

Hematologic: Agranulocytosis, nonthrombocytopenic purpura, and thrombocytopenic purpura.

Autoimmune: In extremely rare instances, systemic lupus erythematosus has been reported.

Miscellaneous: Alopecia, LE-like reactions, psoriasiform rashes, dry eyes, male impotence, and Peyronie's disease have been reported rarely. Oculomucocutaneous reactions involving the skin, serous membranes, and conjunctivae reported for a beta blocker (practolol) have not been associated with propranolol.

Muscle Relaxant:

Relieves muscle spasms

Brand name: Valium

Drug Name: Diazepam

Diazepam appears to act on parts of the limbic system, the thalamus and hypothalamus, and induces calming effects. Valium, unlike chlorpromazine and reserpine, has no demonstrable peripheral autonomic blocking action, nor does it produce extrapyramidal side effects; however, animals treated with Valium do have a transient ataxia at higher doses.

Notable Side Effects:

Most commonly reported were drowsiness, fatigue and ataxia. Infrequently encountered were confusion, constipation, depression, diplopia, dysarthria, headache, hypotension, incontinence, jaundice, changes in libido, nausea, changes in salivation, skin rash, slurred speech, tremor, urinary retention, vertigo and blurred vision. Paradoxical reactions such as acute hyperexcited states, anxiety, hallucinations, increased muscle spasticity, insomnia, rage, sleep disturbances and stimulation have been reported; should these occur, use of the drug should be discontinued.

Cholinergic Drug:

Brand name: Urecholine

Drug Name: Bethanechol

Bethanechol chloride acts principally by producing the effects of stimulation of the parasympathetic nervous system. It increases the tone of the detrusor urinae muscle, usually producing a contraction sufficiently strong to initiate micturition and empty the bladder. It stimulates gastric motility, increases gastric tone and often restores impaired rhythmic peristalsis.

Notable Side Effects:

Body as a Whole: malaise

Digestive: abdominal cramps or discomfort, colicky pain , nausea and belching , diarrhea , borborygmi, salivation

Renal: urinary urgency

Nervous System: headache

Cardiovascular: a fall in blood pressure with reflex tachycardia, vasomotor response

Skin : flushing producing a feeling of warmth, sensation of heat about the face , sweating

Respiratory: bronchial constriction, asthmatic attacks

Special Senses: lacrimation, miosis

Antiviral Agents: may help relieve fatigue

Brand Name: Symmetrel

Drug Name: Amantadine

Amantadine appears to mainly prevent the release of infectious viral nucleic acid into the host cell by interfering with the function of the transmembrane domain of the viral M2 protein. In certain cases, amantadine is also known to prevent virus assembly during virus replication. It does not appear to interfere with the immunogenicity of inactivated influenza A virus vaccine.

Notable Side Effects:

Nausea, dizziness (lightheadedness), and insomnia, depression, anxiety and irritability, hallucinations, confusion, anorexia, dry mouth, constipation, ataxia, livedo reticularis, peripheral edema, orthostatic hypotension, headache, somnolence, nervousness, dream abnormality, agitation, dry nose, diarrhea and fatigue.

Other common recommendations from Medical Doctors: Regular exercise helps maintain cardiovascular, physical, and psychological health. Physical therapy helps maintain balance, walking ability, and range of motion. Exercise reduces spasticity and weakness. Avoid high temperatures and other possible triggers of flare-ups.

Nutritional Approach:

Disease or Condition: Multiple Sclerosis (MS)

Causes of Multiple Sclerosis

The exact cause(s) are unknown. An autoimmune theory does exist. The non-digestion of foods and processed chemicals from our diet had also been theorized as possible contributers. Nutritional foods

Nutritional support:

Foods that have been proven to help with Multiple Sclerosis:

To find out more or to speak to a nutritional counselor for free, just visit us at:
www.CuresForTheBody.com

Fresh vegetables, whole grains, fatty acid rich foods (avocado, raw nuts, salmon).

Nutrients that have been proven to help with Multiple Sclerosis:

Calcium[651], Magnesium[652], Vitamin B12[653], Zinc[654], Reishi Mushroom[655], Essential Fatty Acids[656], Selenium[657], Plant Digestive Enzymes[658], Probiotics.[659]

Exercises that have been proven to help with Multiple Sclerosis:

In addition to improving overall health, cardiovascular fitness, range of motion, and flexibility exercises can help increase energy, improve balance, decrease muscle atrophy, and better perform activities of daily living.[660]

Basic Multiple Sclerosis Plan:
• Establish optimal nutrition

–A significant number of those with MS may have some degree of Malabsorbtion.[661] Digestive enzymes and probiotic have been proven to help digestion and absorption of foods. Take a plant enzyme probiotic supplement with each meal.

–Consuming foods and or supplementing with Omega-3 and Omega-6 Fatty Acids such as those found in evening primrose, flax oil have been shown to have significant results in the occurrence of MS relapse and deterioration, especially when treatment with these essential fatty acids is implemented at early stages. Evening primrose has also been shown to prevent zinc deficiency[662]

–Vitamin B deficiencies are significant in MS patients. Eating foods high in vitamin B12 or supplementing with a whole food vitamin is important, as a deficiency in this vitamin may irritate MS and stifle recovery. There are remarkable similarities in the epidemiology of MS and pernicious anemia. It has been suggested that vitamin B12 deficiency should always be looked for in MS, and it is important to remember that a vitamin B12 deficiency may aggravate MS and/or impair recovery.[663]

–Magnesium deficiencies have been noted to create an environment in the cells that produces peroxinitrite, an extremely powerful free radical that can cause damage especially in MS patients. Eating foods with high magnesium content or supplementing with magnesium would be beneficial.[664]

To find out more or to speak to a nutritional counselor for free, just visit us at:
www.CuresForTheBody.com

–Zinc levels in MS patients especially during exacerbations of MS are decreased. This leads to increased levels of superoxides that induce free radical damage.[665]

–Omega-3 and Omega-6 Fatty Acids used for dietary therapy in MS patients, which emphasized high levels of essential fatty acids, while limiting the intake of other fats. High sensitivity to fats suggests that saturated animal fats are directly involved in the genesis of multiple sclerosis.[666]

–Phytochemicals, sterols and sterolins (plant "fats"), occur naturally in fruits, vegetables, seeds, and nuts are, have clinically beneficial effects in human subjects in many conditions.[667]

–Reishi mushroom is called the "mushroom of immortality" in China and has been used as a tonic and strengthening medicine for thousands of years. Uses in traditional healing include increasing intellectual capacity and memory, promoting agility and lengthening the life span. Reishi is reported to have some of the most active polysaccharides in the plant kingdom. Polysaccharides are claimed to have immunomodulating activity. Reishi is also reported beneficial as an antioxidant, antihypertensive, hypoglycemic, antiviral and hepatoprotective agent.[668]

–Omega-6 fatty acids reportedly reduce the arachidonic acid cascade and decrease inflammation through inhibiting the formation of inflammatory mediators in this process. Supplementation with essential fatty acids such as EPO has been shown to prevent zinc deficiency, thereby potentially enhancing immunity.[669] Essential Fatty Acid oils may also be effective in reducing the disabling effects, number of relapses, severity and duration of relapses in patients with multiple sclerosis.[670]

–Schisandra has been used as an adaptogen, increasing the body's natural ability to fight off disease and stresses from chemical, physical, mental and environmental sources.[671] Schisandra has been reported to increase human endurance and mental and physical performance.[672]

Obesity

Description: Obesity is the accumulation of excess body fat. Obesity can occur as a result of several factors. Your metabolic rate (how fast you burn calories), exercise, diet, alcohol, or metabolic disorders (diabetes) can have a significant effect on your weight. Obesity may also be genetic. Some theories suggest that two obese parents have a higher risk of having children with weight problems in their adulthood.[673] Obesity is also more common among women, and varies by race and age.

Obesity changes the overall appearance of an individual, but also can cause structural changes as you have to adjust to your size. For example, you may walk abnormally and widen your stance, which contributes significantly to osteoarthritis, low back pain, and swollen feet and ankles. They also typically have difficulty breathing or become short of breath easily when the lungs are compressed by excess fat.

Obesity also dramatically increases the risk of developing heart disease, high blood pressure, stroke, varicose veins, psychological stress, osteoarthritis, hyperlipidemia, and diabetes.[674,675] In addition, the risk of premature death may be doubled or even tripled.

Obesity can be determined by your body mass index (BMI) and body composition. BMI is your weight (in kilograms) divided by their height (in meters squared). BMI standards state that you are overweight when your BMI is between 25 and 29.9, and obese when your BMI is 30 or greater. Body composition is the percentage of fat and muscle in the body.

Medical Treatment:

Brand Name: Xenical

Drug Name: Orlistat

Orlistat is a reversible inhibitor of lipases. It exerts its therapeutic activity in the lumen of the stomach and small intestine by forming a covalent

To find out more or to speak to a nutritional counselor for free, just visit us at:
www.CuresForTheBody.com

bond with the active serine residue site of gastric and pancreatic lipases. The inactivated enzymes are thus unavailable to hydrolyze dietary fat in the form of triglycerides into absorbable free fatty acids and monoglycerides. As undigested triglycerides are not absorbed, the resulting caloric deficit may have a positive effect on weight control. Systemic absorption of the drug is therefore not needed for activity. At the recommended therapeutic dose of 120 mg three times a day, orlistat inhibits dietary fat absorption by approximately 30%.

Notable Side Effects:

Gastrointestinal System: abdominal pain/discomfort, nausea, infectious diarrhea, rectal pain/discomfort, tooth disorder, gingival disorder, vomiting.

Respiratory System: Influenza, upper respiratory infection, lower respiratory infection, ear-nose-throat symptoms.

Musculoskeletal System: back pain, lower extremity pain, arthritis, myalgia, joint disorder, tendonitis.

Central Nervous System: headache dizziness.

Body as a Whole: fatigue, sleep disorder.

Skin & Appendages: rash, dry skin.

Female Reproductive: menstrual irregularity, vaginitis.

Urinary System: urinary tract infection.

Psychiatric Disorder: psychiatric anxiety, depression.

Hearing & Vestibular Disorders: otitis.

Cardiovascular Disorders: pedal edema.

Brand Name: Meridia

Drug Name: Sibutramine

Sibutramine produces its therapeutic effects by norepinephrine, serotonin and dopamine reuptake inhibition. Sibutramine and its major pharmacologically active metabolites (M_1 and M_2) do not act via release of monoamines. Sibutramine exerts its pharmacological actions predominantly via its secondary (M_1) and primary (M_2) amine metabolites. The parent compound, sibutramine, is a potent inhibitor of serotonin (5-hydroxytryptamine, 5-HT) and norepinephrine reuptake *in vivo*, but not *in vitro* . However, metabolites M_1 and M_2 inhibit the reuptake of these neurotransmitters both *in vitro* and *in vivo.*

To find out more or to speak to a nutritional counselor for free, just visit us at:
www.CuresForTheBody.com

Notable Side Effects:

Body as a Whole: headache, back pain, flu syndrome, injury accident, asthenia, abdominal pain, chest pain, neck pain, allergic reaction.

Cardiovascular System: tachycardia, vasodilation, migraine, hypertension, palpitation.

Digestive System: anorexia, constipation, increased appetite, nausea, dyspepsia, gastritis, vomiting, rectal disorder.

Metabolic & Nutritional: thirst, generalized edema.

Musculoskeletal System: arthralgia, myalgia, tenosynovitis, joint disorder.

Nervous System: dry mouth insomnia, dizziness, nervousness, anxiety, depression, paresthesia, somnolence, CNS stimulation, emotional lability.

Respiratory system: rhinitis, pharyngitis, sinusitis, cough increase, laryngitis.

Skin & Appendages: rash, sweating, herpes simplex, acne.

Special Senses: taste perversion, ear disorder, ear pain.

Urogenital System: dysmenorrheal, urinary tract infection, vaginal monilia, metrorrhagia.

Brand Name: Ionamin

Drug Name: Phentermine

Phentermine is a sympathomimetic amine with pharmacologic activity similar to the prototype drug of this class used in obesity, amphetamine (d- and d|Sj-amphetamine). Actions include central nervous system stimulation and elevation of blood pressure. Tachyphylaxis and tolerance have been demonstrated with all drugs of this class in which these phenomena have been looked for. Drugs of this class used in obesity are commonly known as "anorectics" or "anorexigenics." It has not been established, however, that the action of such drugs in treating obesity is primarily one of appetite suppression. Other central nervous system actions, or metabolic effects may be involved.

Notable Side Effects:

Cardiovascular: Primary pulmonary hypertension, palpitation, tachycardia, elevation of blood pressure.

Central Nervous System: Overstimulation, restlessness, dizziness, insomnia, euphoria, dysphoria, tremor, headache; rarely psychotic episodes at recommended doses with some drugs in this class.

Gastrointestinal: Dryness of the mouth, unpleasant taste, diarrhea, constipation, other gastrointestinal disturbances.

Allergic: Urticaria.

Endocrine: Impotence, changes in libido.

Other common recommendations from Medical Doctors: If untreated, obesity tends to worsen. Typical recommendations for lowering your body fat is: to reduce your intake of calories and exercise more. Exercise produces lean muscle, which burns fat at a much higher rate. Some people benefit from joining a group or organized program to provide support, as well as nutritional counseling.

Nutritional Approach:

Disease or Condition: Obesity

Causes of Obesity

Obesity occurs from numerous conditions. The most major cause of Obesity is the over consumption of processed foods, consumption of high fat, high-sugar foods and lack of exercise. Other contributors on a lower percentage include: Imbalance of the basal metabolic rate; metabolic disorders, disorders such as hypothyroidism, hypopituitarism, Cushing's syndrome, insulin resistance, impaired glucose tolerance, and hyperinsulinemia. Genetics also plays a role.

Nutritional support:

Foods that have been proven to help with Obesity:

Raw fruits and vegetables, whole grains and easily digested proteins.

Avoid: refined sugars, refined flours, fried foods.

Nutrients that have been proven to help with Obesity:

To find out more or to speak to a nutritional counselor for free, just visit us at:
www.CuresForTheBody.com

Plant Enzymes (Lipase)[676], Essential Fatty Acids[677], Chromium[678], garcinia,[679] Probiotics,[680] Citrus Aurantium.[681]

Linoleic Acid (CLA)

Conjugated linoleic acid (CLA) is a type of fat that helps to reduce body fat, which has prompted researchers to suggest that it is an obesity-preventing agent.[682] CLA is necessary for the transport of dietary fats into cells where it can be utilized to build muscle or to produce energy. Animal and human studies indicate that the reduction in body fat could be significant.[683,684] These results from these studies indicate that CLA reduces body fat by several mechanisms, including a reduced energy intake, increased metabolic rate, and increased utilization of fats for energy.

Formerly, beef and dairy products contained approximately 3 percent CLA. However, there has been nearly a 70 percent reduction in the amount of CLA in the food supply in the last 40 years, due to changes in how cattle are fed, and people switching from whole milk to low fat or skim milk. Some researchers suggest that the disappearance of CLA in the food chain is one of the reasons why Americans have continued to become fatter.

Chromium

Chromium is a mineral that plays a role in the metabolism of carbohydrates and fats as well as in the production of insulin. Chromium enhances insulin's ability to transport glucose into energy producing cells, which reduces the amount of glucose that gets converted into body fat.[685] In addition to its effects on glucose, insulin, and lipid metabolism, chromium has been reported to increase lean body mass and decrease the percentage of body fat, which may lead to weight loss in humans. Claims that chromium improves lean body mass in humans remains controversial, but this effect has been reported in animal studies.[686] Note that if no chromium deficiency is present, chromium will not have any additional benefit for weight loss.

Garcinia

The use of garcinia cambogia has been growing rapidly in the United States due to the increased desire of people to lose weight. Unlike appetite suppressant drugs, garcinia has no reported CNS stimulant activity. Research indicates that it may modulate blood fat levels and have a positive effect on energy and metabolism.[687,688]

The appetite-suppressant mechanism of garcinia is thought to be due in part to the production of glycogen in the liver and small intestine.[689] The conversion of carbohydrates to fat requires the enzyme, adenosine triphosphate citrate lyase. Garcinia temporarily inhibits this enzyme.[690] At the same time, the liver produces more glycogen and this sends a satiety signal to the brain. Obese individuals have less glycogen storage and more triglyceride storage than thin individuals. The storage mechanism for glycogen in the peripheral muscle tissue is thought to be defective in the obese and in patients with type 2 diabetes. Studies have reported that individuals using garcinia, combined with niacin-bound chromium and a reduction in dietary fats, had three times the weight loss of those on diet alone.[691] Obesity is often seen in individuals with diets high in refined foods and saturated fat. A recent study reported no benefits in the management of obesity in human subjects when given 1,500mg of garcinia per day.[692] A higher dosage may be required. To date, evidence is not convincing for the use of garcinia alone.

Exercises that have been proven to help with Obesity

The key to long term fat loss is to create a better Fat to Muscle ration since muscle burns many more calories than fat. Strength training the whole body 2-3 times a week for 30-40 minutes will create the most strength the fastest. Also do an aerobic program consisting of 30-45 minutes a day of increased heart rate activity 6 days a week.[693]

Basic Obesity Plan:
• Establish optimal nutrition

–Avoid refined foods: Consuming refined foods that are nutrient deficient cause people to overeat. They also use less energy to digest leaving more calories to produce fat[694]. Refined sugars are absorbed into the blood rapidly and our body rapidly turns them into fat to prevent toxic reactions of the sugars in our blood. Also, different foods are absorbed at different rates into the body. Because refined sugars are absorbed so quickly into the body, they do not leave hunger cravings satisfied as long as other foods such as fats, proteins and complex carbohydrates.[695] Follow diet recommendations in Chapter 5.

–Chromium metabolizes carbohydrates and fats. It also enhances the body's ability to turn glucose into energy which leaves less glucose to turn to fat. It increases lean body mass while decreasing body fat. Eat a diet containing or supplementing with chromium (amino acid chelated has highest absorption).

–Consume foods rich in Essential Fatty Acids especially Omega-3 fatty acids. Omega-3 Fatty Acids assist in weight loss from numerous angles. They assist in the production of prostaglandins which help the kidneys get rid of excess water retention (edema). Omega-3s also increase metabolic and oxidation rates and energy production. This increase energy is a residual effect that also helps in weight loss.[696]

–Lipase - vital to break down fat to make it usable as energy by the body.[697]

–Bladderwrack – a marine plant that is iodine rich is used to manage weight loss and hypothyroidism. This plant is also high in minerals such as potassium, magnesium, calcium, iron, zinc, and others.[698]

–Guggul – has been reported to stimulate thyroid function which may lead to weight loss.[699]

–Probiotics combined with Enzymes taken at each meal will help stop foods from not being digested. Undigested foods can be stored as fat.[700]

Osteoporosis

Description: Osteoporosis is a progressive loss of bone density and is often called the "silent killer" because it can go undetected until it is severe and fractures begin to occur. Approximately 8 million women and 2 million men in the United States have osteoporosis.

Bone is continuously being broken down and reformed to adjust to your changing body. Throughout your lifetime, old bone is removed (resorption) and new bone is added to the skeleton (formation). During childhood and teenage years, new bone is added faster than old bone is removed. As a result, bones become larger, heavier, and denser. Bone formation continues at a pace faster than resorption until peak bone mass (maximum bone density and strength) is reached around age 30. After age 30, bone resorption slowly begins to exceed bone formation. Osteoporosis develops when bone resorption occurs too quickly or if replacement occurs too slowly.

To maintain bone density, it is important to have an adequate supply of calcium, other minerals, and proper amounts of several hormones. When the body doesn't get the proper amount of calcium from our diet into the bloodstream, the bones surrender calcium to maintain the amounts needed in the blood for other bodily functions. Increased amounts of phosphorus from sources such as carbonated beverages, fast foods, and preservatives can contribute to calcium deficiency by lowering available blood calcium. Surveys show few people consume the necessary amounts of bone building nutrients in their diet.

At first, there are very little, if any, symptoms of osteoporosis. As the bones continue to weaken by the decreasing bone density, the bones may collapse or fracture. This can produce sudden pain or a gradual aching and development of deformities. Some people also experience vertebral crush fractures that may crush spontaneously or after a slight injury.

Those at highest risk for osteoporosis are women who are white, fair-skinned, thin, and light framed. Risk is also influenced by age, genetics, pre/post-menopausal, poor nutrition, lack of exercise, and certain drugs.

To find out more or to speak to a nutritional counselor for free, just visit us at:
www.CuresForTheBody.com

Medical Treatment:

Brand Name: Fosomax

Drug Name: Alendronate

Alendronate shows preferential localization to sites of bone resorption, specifically under osteoclasts. The osteoclasts adhere normally to the bone surface but lack the ruffled border that is indicative of active resorption. Alendronate does not interfere with osteoclast recruitment or attachment, but it does inhibit osteoclast activity. Studies in mice on the localization of radioactive [^{3}H]alendronate in bone showed about 10-fold higher uptake on osteoclast surfaces than on osteoblast surfaces. Bones examined 6 and 49 days after [^{3}H]alendronate administration in rats and mice, respectively, showed that normal bone was formed on top of the alendronate, which was incorporated inside the matrix. While incorporated in bone matrix, alendronate is not pharmacologically active. Thus, alendronate must be continuously administered to suppress osteoclasts on newly formed resorption surfaces. Histomorphometry in baboons and rats showed that alendronate treatment reduces bone turnover (i.e., the number of sites at which bone is remodeled). In addition, bone formation exceeds bone resorption at these remodeling sites, leading to progressive gains in bone mass.

Notable Side Effects:

Gastrointestinal: abdominal pain, nausea, dyspepsia, constipation, diarrhea, flatulence, acid regurgitation, esophageal ulcer, vomiting, dysphagia, abdominal distention, gastritis.

Musculosckeletal: bone-muscle-joint pain, muscle cramp.

Nervous System/Psychiatric: headache, dizziness.

Special Senses: taste perversion.

Brand Name: Actonel

Drug Name: Risedronate

Risedronate has an affinity for hydroxyapatite crystals in bone and acts as an antiresorptive agent. At the cellular level, ACTONEL inhibits osteoclasts. The osteoclasts adhere normally to the bone surface, but show evidence of reduced active resorption (e.g., lack of ruffled border). Histomorphometry in rats, dogs, and minipigs showed that ACTONEL treatment reduces bone turnover (activation frequency, i.e., the rate at which

To find out more or to speak to a nutritional counselor for free, just visit us at:
www.CuresForTheBody.com

bone remodeling sites are activated) and bone resorption at remodeling sites.

Notable Side Effects:

Body as a Whole: infection, back pain, pain, abdominal pain, neck pain, asthenia, chest pain, neoplasm, hernia.

Cardiovascular: hypertension, cardiovascular disorder, angina pectoris.

Digestive: nausea, diarrhea, flatulence, gastritis.

Gastrointestinal Disorder: rectal disorder, tooth disorder.

Hemic and Lymphatic: ecchymosis, anemia.

Musculoskeletal: arthralgia, joint disorder, myalgia, bone pain, bone disorder, leg cramps, bursitis, tendon disorder.

Nervous: depression, dizziness, insomnia, anxiety, neuralgia, vertigo, hypertonia, paresthesia.

Respiratory: pharyngitis, rhinitis, dyspnea, pneumonia.

Skin and Appendages: rash, pruritus, skin carcinoma.

Special Senses: cataract, conjunctivitis, otitis media.

Urogenital: urinary tract infection, cystitis.

Brand Name: Miacalcin

Drug Name: Calcitonin

Calcitonin causes a marked transient inhibition of the ongoing bone resorptive process. With prolonged use, there is a persistent, smaller decrease in the rate of bone resorption. Histologically, this is associated with a decreased number of osteoclasts and an apparent decrease in their resorptive activity. Decreased osteocytic resorption may also be involved. There is some evidence that initially bone formation may be augmented by calcitonin through increased osteoblastic activity. However, calcitonin will probably not induce a long-term increase in bone formation.

Notable Side Effects:

Gastrointestinal System: Nausea with or without vomiting has been noted in about 10% of patients treated with calcitonin. It is most evident when treatment is first initiated and tends to decrease or disappear with continued administration.

Dermatologic/Hypersensitivity: Local inflammatory reactions at the site of subcutaneous or intramuscular injection have been reported in about 10% of patients. Flushing of face or hands occurred in about 2-5% of patients. Skin rashes, nocturia, pruritus of the ear lobes, feverish sensation, pain in the eyes, poor appetite, abdominal pain, edema of feet, and salty taste have been reported in patients treated with calcitonin-salmon. Administration of calcitonin-salmon has been reported in a few cases to cause serious allergic-type reactions (e.g. bronchospasm, swelling of the tongue or throat, and anaphylactic shock), and in one case, death attributed to anaphylaxis

Other common recommendations from Medical Doctors: Eat a balanced, healthy diet to make sure you receive enough calcium and Vitamin D. Weight bearing exercise will also increase bone density and can help to prevent a fracture.

Nutritional Approach:

Disease or Condition: Osteoporosis

Causes of Osteoporosis

Carbonated drinks[701], inactivity, poor nutrition, cigarette smoking, and caffeine[702]. Estrogen loss in women, androgen loss in men[703], aging[704], decreased absorption rates of calcium[705,706], genetics, use of anticonvulsant and glucocorticoids increase risk.

Nutritional support:

Foods that have been proven to help with Osteoporosis:

Dark green leafy vegetables, broccoli, raw nuts, whole grains, legumes.

Avoid foods containing phosphorus, phosphate, phoshoirc acid and oxalic acid such as animal protein, soft drinks, and tea. Sugars.

To find out more or to speak to a nutritional counselor for free, just visit us at:
www.CuresForTheBody.com

Nutrients that have been proven to help with Osteoporosis:

Calcium[707,708], Ipriflavone[709], Magnesium[710], Vitamin K[711], Maganese[712], Boron[713], Soy Isoflavones[714], Horsetail[715] and Red Clover.[716]

Exercises that have been proven to help with Osteoporosis:

For patients who have osteoporosis, strength training exercises are an essential part of treatment. Just as regular workouts build muscle, they also maintain and may even increase bone strength. By strengthening your muscles and bones and improving your balance, exercise can reduce the risk of falls and resulting fractures.[717]

Basic Osteoporosis Plan:
• Establish optimal nutrition

–Eat foods high in calcium or take a high quality supplement containing calcium (amino acid chelated have the highest absorption rates

–Stop calcium loss by avoiding caffeine, alcohol, salt which excrete calcium in urine[718,719]. Avoid foods containing phosphorus such as soda beverages and animal proteins that strip calcium from the body.[720]

–Eat soy beans because of their isoflavone content. Isoflavones have been shown to support mineralization of bones. Also, supplemention with Ipriflavone, a isoflavone, has been documented in the maintenance of bone density.[721,722,723,724]

–Eat foods high in magnesium or take high quality supplements containing magnesium (amino acid chelated). Magnesium works to metabolize calcium, synthesis of Vitamin D, and the development of bone. Consuming magnesium from raw food sources is important since the mineral is very sensitive to food processings unless it is in the AA chelated form.

Pain and Inflammation

Description: Pain is the number one reason why people seek medical advice.[725] Many people experience pain and inflammation as a result of an injury due to sports, occupation, or daily activities. Injuries usually result as muscles, tendons, and ligaments are subjected to forces greater than their inherent strength.

These injuries can occur due to overuse or repeated motions, misuse (ie: turning the wrong way or lifting improperly), structural abnormalities (stress part of the body unevenly), pronation of the feet (affecting posture), and everyday wear and tear.

When an injury occurs, you will typically experience pain along with inflammation.

Inflammation causes swelling, warmth, tenderness, and impairs the function of the area. Pain can be acute or chronic, and can present itself as somatic, visceral, or neuropathic. Acute pain comes on suddenly and signals your body that there has been an injury. Acute pain is also typically accompanied with increased heart rate and blood pressure.

Chronic pain includes low back pain, headaches, neuralgia, and cancer pain. Chronic pain is typically associated with a chronic disease or injury, and the pain lasts longer than the expected healing time.

Medical Treatment:

Acute/Chronic Pain

Brand name: Tylenol

Drug Name: Acetaminophen

Acetaminophen inhibits prostaglandin synthetase.

Notable Side Affects:

Light-headedness, dizziness, sedation, nausea and vomiting.

To find out more or to speak to a nutritional counselor for free, just visit us at:
www.CuresForTheBody.com

NSAIDS

Brand name: Advil, Motrin

Drug Name: Ibuprofen

Ibuprofen is a nonsteroidal anti-inflammatory drug (NSAID) that possesses anti-inflammatory, analgesic and antipyretic activity. Its mode of action, like that of other NSAIDs, is not completely understood, but may be related to prostaglandin synthetase inhibition. After absorption of the racemic ibuprofen, the [-]R-enantiomer undergoes interconversion to the [+]S-form. The biological activities of ibuprofen are associated with the [+]S-enantiomer.

Notable Side Effects:

Cardiovascular system: Edema, fluid retention (generally responds promptly to drug discontinuation).

Digestive system: Nausea, epigastric pain, heartburn, diarrhea, abdominal distress, nausea and vomiting, indigestion, constipation, abdominal cramps or pain, fullness of Gl tract (bloating and flatulence).

Nervous system: Dizziness, headache, nervousness.

Skin and appendages: Rash (including maculopapular type), pruritus.

Special senses: Tinnitus.

Brand name:Aleve, Anaprox

Drug Name: Naproxen

Naproxen is a nonsteroidal anti-inflammatory drug (NSAID) with analgesic and antipyretic properties. The sodium salt of naproxen has been developed as a more rapidly absorbed formulation of naproxen for use as an analgesic. The naproxen anion inhibits prostaglandin synthesis but beyond this its mode of action is unknown.

Notable Side Effects:

Gastrointestinal: constipation, heartburn, abdominal pain, nausea, dyspepsia, diarrhea, stomatitis.

Central Nervous System: headache, dizziness, drowsiness, lightheadedness, vertigo.

Dermatologic: itching (pruritus), skin eruptions, ecchymoses, sweating, purpura.

To find out more or to speak to a nutritional counselor for free, just visit us at:
www.CuresForTheBody.com

Special Senses: tinnitus, hearing disturbances, visual disturbances.

Cardiovascular: edema, dyspnca, palpitations.

General: thirst.

Opioids:

Relieve anxiety and pain if the pain persists despite use of other drugs

Brand name: Kadian

Drug Name: Morphine

Morphine produces a wide spectrum of pharmacologic effects including analgesia, dysphoria, euphoria, somnolence, respiratory depression, diminished gastrointestinal motility and physical dependence. Opiate analgesia involves at least three anatomical areas of the central nervous system: the periaqueductal-periventricular gray matter, the ventromedial medulla and the spinal cord. A systemically administered opiate may produce analgesia by acting at any, all or some combination of these distinct regions. Morphine interacts predominantly with the [micro]-receptor. The [micro]-binding sites of opioids are very discretely distributed in the human brain, with high densities of sites found in the posterior amygdala, hypothalamus, thalamus, nucleus caudatus, putamen and certain cortical areas. They are also found on the terminal axons of primary afferents within laminae I and II (substantia gelatinosa) of the spinal cord and in the spinal nucleus of the trigeminal nerve.

Notable Side Effects:

Respiratory depression, respiratory arrest, tolerance and myoclonus, pruritus, urinary retention, constipation, headache, dizziness, euphoria, anxiety, depression of cough reflex, interference with thermal regulation and oliguria, evidence of histamine release, wheals and/or local tissue irritation, nausea, and vomiting.

Muscle Relaxants

Brand name: Soma

Drug Name: Carisoprodol

Carisoprodol produces muscle relaxation in animals by blocking interneuronal activity in the descending reticular formation and spinal cord.

To find out more or to speak to a nutritional counselor for free, just visit us at:
www.CuresForTheBody.com

Notable Side Effects:

Central Nervous System: Drowsiness and other CNS effects may require dosage reduction. Also observed: dizziness, vertigo, ataxia, tremor, agitation, irritability, headache, depressive reactions, syncope, and insomnia.

Allergic or Idiosyncratic: Allergic or idiosyncratic reactions occasionally develop. They are usually seen within the period of the first to fourth dose in patients having had no previous contact with the drug. Skin rash, erythema multiforme, pruritus, eosinophilia, and fixed drug eruption with cross reaction to meprobamate have been reported with carisoprodol. Severe reactions have been manifested by asthmatic episodes, fever, weakness, dizziness, angioneurotic edema, smarting eyes, hypotension, and anaphylactoid shock.

Cardiovascular: Tachycardia, postural hypotension, and facial flushing.

Gastrointestinal: Nausea, vomiting, hiccup, and epigastric distress.

Hematologic: Leukopenia, in which other drugs or viral infection may have been responsible, and pancytopenia, attributed to phenylbutazone, have been reported. No serious blood dyscrasias have been attributed to carisoprodol.

Brand name: Flexeril

Drug Name: Cyclobenzaprine

Cyclobenzaprine relieves skeletal muscle spasm of local origin without interfering with muscle function. It is ineffective in muscle spasm due to central nervous system disease. Cyclobenzaprine reduced or abolished skeletal muscle hyperactivity in several animal models. Animal studies indicate that cyclobenzaprine does not act at the neuromuscular junction or directly on skeletal muscle. Such studies show that cyclobenzaprine acts primarily within the central nervous system at brain stem as opposed to spinal cord levels, although its action on the latter may contribute to its overall skeletal muscle relaxant activity. Evidence suggests that the net

To find out more or to speak to a nutritional counselor for free, just visit us at:
www.CuresForTheBody.com

effect of cyclobenzaprine is a reduction of tonic somatic motor activity, influencing both gamma and alpha motor systems.

Notable Side Effects:

Drowsiness, dry mouth, dizziness.

Brand name: Valium

Drug Name: Diazepam

Diazepam appears to act on parts of the limbic system, the thalamus and hypothalamus, and induces calming effects. Valium, unlike chlorpromazine and reserpine, has no demonstrable peripheral autonomic blocking action, nor does it produce extrapyramidal side effects; however, animals treated with Valium do have a transient ataxia at higher doses.

Notable Side Effects:

Most commonly reported were drowsiness, fatigue and ataxia. Infrequently encountered were confusion, constipation, depression, diplopia, dysarthria, headache, hypotension, incontinence, jaundice, changes in libido, nausea, changes in salivation, skin rash, slurred speech, tremor, urinary retention, vertigo and blurred vision. Paradoxical reactions such as acute hyperexcited states, anxiety, hallucinations, increased muscle spasticity, insomnia, rage, sleep disturbances and stimulation have been reported; should these occur, use of the drug should be discontinued.

Other common recommendations from Medical Doctors: When an injury first occurs, the best recommendation is RICE (rest, ice, compression, and elevation). You can also prevent or correct dysfunction that is causing the pain or injury. Strengthening exercises help to strengthen the muscles and stabilize the spine. Also, good posture, shoe inserts to correct pronation, and proper lifting techniques can also reduce stress on the body.

Nutritional Approach:

Disease or Condition: Pain and Pain Management

Causes of Pain: Types of pain include acute and chronic. Acute pain can result from injury from trauma, surgery, and damage from disease.

To find out more or to speak to a nutritional counselor for free, just visit us at:
www.CuresForTheBody.com

Chronic pain does not have specific etiologies, but typically results from chronic diseases.

Nutritional support:

Foods that have been proven to help with Pain:

Raw fruits and vegetables containing Methyl Sulfonyl Methane (MSM) as even slight food processing destroys this nutrient.

Nutrients that have been proven to help with Pain:

Proteolytic enzymes[726], Methyl Sulfonyl Methane (MSM)[727], Chondroitin Sulfate [728,729], and Glucosamine[730,731], Valerian Root[732]

Exercises that have been proven to help with Pain

A regular exercise regiment will help to reduce the amount of pain associated with joints and many other parts of the body. While excess exercise can induce inflammation moderate; exercise will help move toxins and redistribute inflammation throughout you body so that it can heal the cause of the inflammation.[733] Consult a exercise specislist or Physical Therapist for specific exercises for your condition.

Basic Pain and Pain Management Plan:

• Establish optimal nutrition

–Proteolytic enzymes have been proven to reduce inflammation and pain for many years. It is the main natural nutrient used for pain and inflammation reduction in professional sports.

–Glucosamine does not occur in foods, and therefore taking a high quality supplement is containing glucosamine sulfate or glucosamine hydrochloride (HCL) is essential.

–Chondroitin sulfate has been shown as an anti-inflammatory by inhibiting enzymes that damage the joint.[734] Chondroitin sulfate is naturally produced in the body. It does not occur in foods, and therefore taking a high quality supplement is essential for use of its anti-inflammatory.

–Methyl sulfonyl methane (MSM) relieves pain by inhibiting pain impulses, reducing inflammation and muscle spasms, and promotes blood flow to speed up healing. It is an organic sulfur that occurs in meats and plants and is also present in the body.

–The following herbs aide in pain relief. Tumeric – has anti-inflammatory along with beneficial antioxidant properties[735]. Ginger [736,737,738], Feverfew[739], and Willow[740] all have anti-inflammatory resultants.

▪ Switching Hot and Cold packs on painful site has been proven beneficial. 20 minutes each is the norm with this procedure.

Pre-Menstrual Syndrome (PMS)

Description: Premenstrual syndrome are the physical and emotional symptoms a woman experiences associated with her menstrual cycle. They can occur up to 14 days before her period begins, and usually end at the start of the period. Most women experience PMS at some point during their lives, but the symptoms vary greatly. PMS affects 20-50% of women, and severe PMS (dysphoric disorder) affects 5% of women. In dysphoric disorder, the symptoms are so severe, that work, social activities, and relationships are affected.

Symptoms for PMS vary greatly between women, but may include a bad mood, irritability, bloating, and breast tenderness. In addition, other disorders may worsen or flare-up, such as seizures, lupus, rheumatoid arthritis, allergies, and congestion. These symptoms are generally followed by a very painful period.

PMS may occur because of the changing levels progesterone and estrogen hormones in the body. These levels fluctuate during the menstrual cycle, and may also be broken down differently in the body during the cycle. Another theory is that PMS may be due to an aberration in blood viscosity and red blood cell hydration during the menstrual cycle.[741]

Medical Treatment:

Diuretic:
Reduce edema by increasing the excretion of sodium ions by the kidneys.

Brand Name: Dyazide

Drug Name: Hydrochlorothiazide

Hydrochlorothiazide component blocks the reabsorption of sodium and chloride ions, and thereby increases the quantity of sodium traversing the distal tubule and the volume of water excreted. A portion of the additional sodium presented to the distal tubule is exchanged there for potassium and hydrogen ions. With continued use of hydrochlorothiazide and depletion of sodium, compensatory mechanisms tend to increase this exchange and may produce excessive loss of potassium, hydrogen and chloride ions. Hydrochlorothiazide also decreases the excretion of calcium and uric acid, may increase the excretion of iodide and may reduce glomerular filtration rate. The exact mechanism of the antihypertensive effect of hydrochlorothiazide is not known.

Notable Side Effects:

Hypersensitivity: anaphylaxis, rash, urticaria, photosensitivity.

Cardiovascular: arrhythmia, postural hypotension.

Metabolic: diabetes mellitus, hyperkalemia, hyperglycemia, glycosuria, hyperuricemia, hypokalemia, hyponatremia, acidosis, hypochloremia.

Gastrointestinal: jaundice and/or liver enzyme abnormalities, pancreatitis, nausea and vomiting, diarrhea, constipation, abdominal pain.

Renal: acute renal failure (one case of irreversible renal failure has been reported), interstitial nephritis, renal stones composed primarily of triamterene, elevated BUN and serum creatinine, abnormal urinary sediment.

Hematologic: leukopenia, thrombocytopenia and purpura, megaloblastic anemia.

Musculoskeletal: muscle cramps.

Central Nervous System: weakness, fatigue, dizziness, headache, dry mouth.

Miscellaneous: impotence, sialadenitis.

Thiazides alone have been shown to cause the following additional adverse reactions:

Central Nervous System: paresthesias, vertigo.

Ophthalmic: xanthopsia, transient blurred vision.

Respiratory: allergic pneumonitis, pulmonary edema, respiratory distress.

Other: necrotizing vasculitis, exacerbation of lupus.

Hematologic: aplastic anemia, agranulocytosis, hemolytic anemia.

Neonate and infancy: thrombocytopenia and pancreatitis—rarely, in newborns whose mothers have received thiazides during pregnancy.

NSAID: Lessen pain and swelling by inhibiting prostaglandin formation by interfering with the enzyme cyclooxygenase. They have demonstrated some benefit in symptomatic management of PMS and dysmenorrheal.[742] Because the inhibition of prostaglandins is non-selective, beneficial prostaglandins are also inhibited. Therefore, it is recommended that NSAIDs be used only for short-term treatment of PMS symptoms.

Brand name: Advil, Motrin

Drug Name: Ibuprofen

Ibuprofen is a nonsteroidal anti-inflammatory drug (NSAID) that possesses anti-inflammatory, analgesic and antipyretic activity. Its mode of action, like that of other NSAIDs, is not completely understood, but may be related to prostaglandin synthetase inhibition. After absorption of the racemic ibuprofen, the [-]R-enantiomer undergoes interconversion to the [+]S-form. The biological activities of ibuprofen are associated with the [+]S-enantiomer.

Notable Side Effects:

Cardiovascular system: Edema, fluid retention (generally responds promptly to drug discontinuation).

Digestive system: Nausea, epigastric pain, heartburn, diarrhea, abdominal distress, nausea and vomiting, indigestion, constipation, abdominal cramps or pain, fullness of Gl tract (bloating and flatulence).

Nervous system: Dizziness, headache, nervousness.

Skin and appendages: Rash (including maculopapular type), pruritus.

Special senses: Tinnitus.

Brand name: Aleve, Anaprox

Drug Name: Naproxen

Naproxen is a nonsteroidal anti-inflammatory drug (NSAID) with analgesic and antipyretic properties. The sodium salt of naproxen has been developed as a more rapidly absorbed formulation of naproxen for use as an analgesic. The naproxen anion inhibits prostaglandin synthesis but beyond this its mode of action is unknown.

Notable Side Effects:

Gastrointestinal: constipation, heartburn, abdominal pain, nausea, dyspepsia, diarrhea, stomatitis.

Central Nervous System: headache, dizziness, drowsiness, lightheadedness, vertigo.

Dermatologic: itching (pruritus), skin eruptions, ecchymoses, sweating, purpura.

Special Senses: tinnitus, hearing disturbances, visual disturbances.

Cardiovascular: edema, dyspnea, palpitations.

General: thirst.

AntiDepressant:

The selective serotonin re-uptake inhibitors (SSRIs) have demonstrated effectiveness in relieving premenstrual dysphoria. SSRIs can be taken for relief of irritability, anger, sadness, cravings, and tension.[743]

Brand Name:Sarafem

Drug Name: Fluoxetine

Fluoxetine is presumed to be linked to its inhibition of CNS neuronal uptake of serotonin. Studies at clinically relevant doses in humans have demonstrated that fluoxetine blocks the uptake of serotonin into human platelets. Studies in animals also suggest that fluoxetine is a much more potent uptake inhibitor of serotonin than of norepinephrine. Antagonism of muscarinic, histaminergic, and (alpha) $_1$-adrenergic receptors has been hypothesized to be associated with various anticholinergic, sedative, and cardiovascular effects of certain psychoactive drugs. Fluoxetine has little affinity for these receptors.

Notable Side Effects:

Body as a whole: asthenia, flu, headache, fever, infection, accidental injury.

Digestive System: nausea, diarrhea.

Nervous Systems: insomnia, nervousness, libido decreased, abnormal dreams, dizziness, tremor, thinking abnormal.

Respiratory system: pharyngitis, rhinits.

Other common recommendations from Medical Doctors: Exercise and stress reduction can help ease the symptoms. Reducing salt from the diet can help to reduce fluid retention and bloating. Reducing caffeine may also help. Calcium and other nutrients, such as magnesium and B vitamins can also lessen symptoms.

Nutritional Approach:

Disease or Condition: Premenstrual Syndrome (PMS)

Causes of Premenstrual Syndrome

The most common causative factors are: Excess estrogen levels, progesterone deficiency, Others include; elevated prolactin levels, Hypothyroidism, Stress, endogenous opioid deficiency, and adrenal dysfunction, depression, nutritional factors (macronutrients disturbances/ excesses and micronutrient deficiency).

Moderate to severe PMS can be divided into four subtypes.[744]

PMS-A (Anxiety) is the most common type of PMS.

Symptoms include anxiety, irritability, and nervous tension.

Elevated serum estrogen and low progesterone are associated with this type.

PMS-C (Cravings) is characterized by an increase in appetite, craving for simple carbohydrates, and fluctuations in blood sugar. Indulgence in simple sugars results in fatigue, headaches, palpitations, dizziness, or fainting. This type of PMS is attributed to a deficiency in prostaglandin synthesis, excessive insulin response, and impaired glucose tolerance.

Low cellular magnesium levels have been reported among this subgroup.

PMS-D (Depression) is the least common but most serious manifestation of PMS.

To find out more or to speak to a nutritional counselor for free, just visit us at:
www.CuresForTheBody.com

Symptoms include depression, tearfulness, confusion, insomnia, and withdrawal.

Low levels of estrogen, high progesterone, and elevated adrenal androgens are implicated in this subtype. Abnormal sertonenergic responses have been found among women with PMS-D, suggesting a neurochemical cause.

PMS-H (Hyperhydration) is associated with symptoms of...

water retention, abdominal bloating, breast tenderness, and weight gain. Elevated serum aldosterone may be a causative factor, which is thought to increase in the presence of stress, excess estrogen, magnesium deficiency, and dopamine deficiency.

Nutritional support:

Foods that have been proven to help with PMS:

Plant foods (vegetables, fruits, legumes, whole grains, nuts, and seeds particulary flax and hemp), soy protein.

Avoid: commercial animal protein and commercial dairy, refined carbohydrates and caffeine.

Nutrients that have been proven to help with PMS:

Magnesium[745], Omega 3 and 6 Essential Fatty Acids, Soy Isoflavones[746], Probiotics[747], vitamin B6[748], Vitamin E[749], Black Cohosh[750], Chasteberry[751], Dong Quai[752], Dandelion Leaf[753], Kava[754], St. John's Wort[755], and Natural Progesterone cream.[756]

Exercises that have been proven to help with PMS:

Exercise can have many positive psychological and physical benefits for PMS sufferers, so try to include some form of exercise in your daily routine. Exercise can help to deal with stress many other factors contributing to PMS.[757]

Basic PMS Plan:

Our American diet causes us so many problems; too many refined foods and not enough nutrient dense foods. With countless over-the-counter medications claiming to help with certain symptoms and the prevalence of hormone replacement therapy, it's easy to confuse the issue. The problem isn't solved by taking one drug or another. Instead, addressing the root cause of the problem comes down to examining what nutrients are missing from the body and how to replace those to create optimal hormone balance.

• All subtypes need to eat more plant foods (vegetables, fruits, legumes, whole grains, nuts, and seeds particularly flax and hemp), and soy protein.

Avoid: commercial animal protein and commercial dairy because of hormones injected in cows to increase their growth and production.

• Consider taking Magnesium – Sub-optimal levels of magnesium have been noted in women suffering from PMS. Use AA chelated magnesium because of its higher absorbtion rate.

• Eat or take as a supplement Essential fatty acids like raw flax seeds or oil and raw hulled hemp seeds or oil, borage oil, evening primrose oil. They help reduce inflammatory prostaglandins and increase prostaglandins that relieve menstrual cramping, breast pain, water gain, and increased clotting; which can relieve PMS complaints.

• Consider using Soy Isoflavones - reported to reduce PMS symptoms, support bone mineralization, and decrease the risk of some cancers.

• Probiotics - Many women with chronic yeast infections, a history of antibiotic use, a high intake of refined foods, high stress, chronic corticosteroid use, or birth control pill use may have a bowel flora imbalance (dysbiosis). A program to enhance bowel flora can be of benefit in these conditions.

• Vitamin B6, has reported benefits for reducing PMS symptoms.

–Use whole food vitamins like nutritional yeast, balancing all B vitamins.[758]

• Vitamin E – reportedly, produced significant improvement in certain affective and physical symptoms in some women with PMS.

• Black Cohosh, - Clinical studies have reported positive effects on <u>menopausal and postmenopausal</u> complaints when using standardized extracts of black cohosh. Also, the constituent black cohosh is reported to affect the hypothalamus-pituitary system, producing a hormonal balancing effect in the female reproductive system. The hypothalamus and pituitary glands control many aspects of human biochemistry, including hormonal release and regulation.

• Chasteberry - has been recommended for use in mild to moderate complaints, especially in endometriosis, menopause, and PMS symptoms. Several clinical studies have reported beneficial results using chasteberry in treating women with infertility associated with corpus luteum deficiency.

• Dong Quai – Is a Phytoestrogen. Phytoestrogens have a weaker effect on binding sites than do their drug counterparts. During PMS when estrogen levels are elevated, phytoestrogens bind to estrogen-binding sites, leaving the endogenous estrogen to be metabolized by the liver and thus reducing overall excess estrogenic effects. When estrogen levels are low, as in the case of menopause, phytoestrogens bind to estrogen-binding sites, activating the receptor site in a milder fashion than drug counterparts.

• Dandelion Leaf – A natural diuretic. A study demonstrated that the usual potassium loss seen with many conventional diuretics was not seen in dandelion's use, due to the high potassium content in the leaves.

• Kava - Studies have reported that kava preparations compare favorably to benzodiazepines in controlling symptoms of anxiety and minor depression, while increasing vigilance, sociability, memory, and reaction time.

• St. John's wort – Many effects on the body.

–Inhibits cortisol secretion and blocks catabolic hormones.

–Inhibits breakdown of several central nervous system neurotransmitters, including serotonin.

–Contains melatonin – may contribute to the antidepressant effect of the plant.

To find out more or to speak to a nutritional counselor for free, just visit us at:
www.CuresForTheBody.com

Warning - Interactions between St. John's wort and anticoagulants, indinavir, cyclosporin, digoxin, ethinyl estradiol/desogestrel, and theophylline have occurred. The mechanism of action was believed to be liver enzyme induction and subsequent alterations of drug levels by the herb. Also, several reports have suggested that concurrent use of St. John's wort and SSRIs may result in "serotonin syndrome", including sweating, tremor, confusion, flushing, and agitation. Use St. John's wort with caution if individuals are on these medications. 400 mg. / oz.

Prostratitis

Description: Prostatis is a condition that causes pain and swelling of the prostate gland. Prostatitis is a common affliction of men over the age of 50.[759] The cause of prostatitis is typically unknown, but may be the result of a bacterial infection, and more rarely a fungal, viral, or protozoal infection.

Symptoms of prostatitis are the result of muscle spasms of the bladder and pelvis. Some of the symptoms caused by these spasms include pain in the perineum, pain in the lower back, pain in the in the penis and testes, the need to urinate frequently and urgently, and urinating may be painful and burning. The pain may also make erection and ejaculation difficult. Some also experience constipation with prostatitis.

Acute bacterial prostatits is caused by a bacterial infection. This may include the symptoms listed previously, as well as a fever, difficulty urinating, and blood in the urine. Chronic prostatitis causes many urinary tract infections in men and can be a cause of infertility.

Medical Treatment:

Analgesics & NSAIDS:

Relieve pain & swelling.

Brand name: Tylenol

Drug Name: Acetaminophen

Acetaminophen inhibits prostaglandin synthetase.

Notable Side Affects:

Light-headedness, dizziness, sedation, nausea and vomiting.

Brand name: Advil, Motrin

Drug Name: Ibuprofen

Ibuprofen is a nonsteroidal anti-inflammatory drug (NSAID) that possesses anti-inflammatory, analgesic and antipyretic activity. Its mode of action, like that of other NSAIDs, is not completely understood, but may be related to prostaglandin synthetase inhibition. After absorption of the racemic ibuprofen, the [-]R-enantiomer undergoes interconversion to the [+]S-form. The biological activities of ibuprofen are associated with the [+]S-enantiomer.

Notable Side Effects:

Cardiovascular system: Edema, fluid retention (generally responds promptly to drug discontinuation).

Digestive system: Nausea, epigastric pain, heartburn, diarrhea, abdominal distress, nausea and vomiting, indigestion, constipation, abdominal cramps or pain, fullness of Gl tract (bloating and flatulence).

Nervous system: Dizziness, headache, nervousness.

Skin and appendages: Rash (including maculopapular type), pruritus.

Special senses: Tinnitus.

Brand name: Aleve, Anaprox

Drug Name: Naproxen

Naproxen is a nonsteroidal anti-inflammatory drug (NSAID) with analgesic and antipyretic properties. The sodium salt of naproxen has been developed as a more rapidly absorbed formulation of naproxen for use as an analgesic. The naproxen anion inhibits prostaglandin synthesis but beyond this its mode of action is unknown.

Notable Side Effects:

Gastrointestinal: constipation, heartburn, abdominal pain, nausea, dyspepsia, diarrhea, stomatitis.

Central Nervous System: headache, dizziness, drowsiness, lightheadedness, vertigo.

Dermatologic: itching (pruritus), skin eruptions, ecchymoses, sweating, purpura.

To find out more or to speak to a nutritional counselor for free, just visit us at:
www.CuresForTheBody.com

Special Senses: tinnitus, hearing disturbances, visual disturbances.

Cardiovascular: edema, dyspnea, palpitations.

General: thirst.

Alpha-adrenergic blockers:

Treat prostate enlargement

Brand Name: Cardura

Drug Name: Doxazosin

Doxazosin antagonizes phenylephrine (alpha $_1$ agonist)-induced contractions, *in vitro*, and binds with high affinity to the alpha $_{1c}$ adrenoceptor. The receptor subtype is thought to be the predominant functional type in the prostate. Doxazosin acts within 1-2 weeks to decrease the severity of BPH symptoms and improve urinary flow rate. Since alpha $_1$ adrenoceptors are of low density in the urinary bladder (apart from the bladder neck), Doxazosin should maintain bladder contractility.

Notable Side Effects:

Body as a Whole: back pain, chest pain, fatigue, headache, flu-like symptoms, pain.

Cardiovascular System: hypotension, palpitation.

Digestive System: abdominal pain, diarrhea, dyspepsia, nausea.

Metabolic & Nutritional: edema.

Nervous System: dizziness, dry mouth, somnolence.

Respiratory System: dyspnea, respiratory disorder.

Special Senses: abnormal vision.

Urogenital System: impotence, urinary tract infection.

Skin & Appendages: increased sweating.

Psychiatric Disorders: anxiety, insomnia.

Brand Name: Hytrin

Drug Name: Terazosin

Terazosin, an alpha-1-selective adrenoceptor blocking agent. The symptoms associated with BPH are related to bladder outlet obstruction, which is comprised of two underlying components: a static component and a dynamic component. The static component is a consequence of an increase in prostate size. Over time, the prostate will continue to enlarge. However, clinical studies have demonstrated that the size of the prostate does not correlate with the severity of BPH symptoms or the degree of urinary obstruction. The dynamic component is a function of an increase in smooth muscle tone in the prostate and bladder neck, leading to constriction of the bladder outlet. Smooth muscle tone is mediated by sympathetic nervous stimulation of alpha-1 adrenoceptors, which are abundant in the prostate, prostatic capsule and bladder neck. The reduction in symptoms and improvement in urine flow rates following administration of terazosin is related to relaxation of smooth muscle produced by blockade of alpha-1 adrenoceptors in the bladder neck and prostate. Because there are relatively few alpha-1 adrenoceptors in the bladder body, terazosin is able to reduce the bladder outlet obstruction without affecting bladder contractility.

Notable Side Effects:

Body as a Whole: asthenia, flu syndrome, headache.
Cardiovascular System: hypotension, palpitations, postural hypotension, syncope.
Digestive System: nausea.
Metabolic & Nutritional: peripheral edema, weight gain.
Nervous System: dizziness, somnolence, vertigo.
Respiratory System: dyspnea, nasal congestion/rhinitis.
Special Senses: blurred vision/amblyopia.
Urogenital System: impotence, urinary tract infection.

Antibiotics:

Oral antibiotics that can penetrate the prostate tissue.
Brand Name: Floxin
Drug Name: Ofloxacin

Ofloxacin is a quinolone antimicrobial agent. The mechanism of action of ofloxacin and other fluoroquinolone antimicrobials involves inhibition of bacterial topoisomerase IV and DNA gyrase (both of which are type II topoisomerases), enzymes required for DNA replication, transcription, repair and recombination. Ofloxacin has *in vitro* activity against a wide range of gram-negative and gram-positive microorganisms. Ofloxacin is often bactericidal at concentrations equal to or slightly greater than inhibitory concentrations.

Notable Side Effects:

Nausea, insomnia, headache, dizziness, diarrhea, vomiting, rash, pruritus, external genital pruritus in women, vaginitis, dysgeusia, abdominal pain and cramps, chest pain, decreased appetitie, dry mouth, dysgeusia, fatigue, flatulence, gastrointestinal distress, nervousness, pharyngitis, pruritus, fever, rash, sleep disorders, somnolence, trunk pain, vaginal discharge, visual disturbances, and constipation.

Brand name: Septra
Drug Name:Trimethoprim-sulfamethoxazole

Trimethoprim-sulfamethoxazole is a synthetic antibacterial combination product. It is highly effective against most aerobic enteric bacteria except *Pseudomonas aeruginosa*.

Notable Side Effects:

The most common adverse effects are gastrointestinal disturbances (nausea, vomiting, anorexia) and allergic skin reactions (such as rash and urticaria).

Hematologic: Agranulocytosis, aplastic anemia, thrombocytopenia, leukopenia, neutropenia, hemolytic anemia, megaloblastic anemia, hypoprothrombinemia, methemoglobinemia, eosinophilia.

Allergic: Stevens-Johnson syndrome, toxic epidermal necrolysis, anaphylaxis, allergic myocarditis, erythema multiforme, exfoliative dermatitis, angioedema, drug fever, chills, Henoch-Schönlein purpura, serum sickness-like syndrome, generalized allergic reactions, generalized skin eruptions, photosensitivity, conjunctival and scleral injection, pruritus, urticaria, and rash. In addition, periarteritis nodosa and systemic lupus erythematosus have been reported.

Gastrointestinal: Hepatitis, including cholestatic jaundice and hepatic necrosis, elevation of serum transaminase and bilirubin, pseudomembranous enterocolitis, pancreatitis, stomatitis, glossitis, nausea, emesis, abdominal pain, diarrhea, anorexia.

Genitourinary: Renal failure, interstitial nephritis, BUN and serum creatinine elevation, toxic nephrosis with oliguria and anuria, and crystalluria.

Metabolic: Hyperkalemia, hyponatremia.

Neurologic: Aseptic meningitis, convulsions, peripheral neuritis, ataxia, vertigo, tinnitus, headache.

Psychiatric: Hallucinations, depression, apathy, nervousness.

Endocrine: The sulfonamides bear certain chemical similarities to some goitrogens, diuretics (acetazolamide and the thiazides), and oral hypoglycemic agents. Cross-sensitivity may exist with these agents. Diuresis and hypoglycemia have occurred rarely in patients receiving sulfonamides.

Musculoskeletal: Arthralgia and myalgia.

Respiratory System: Cough, shortness of breath, and pulmonary infiltrates.

Miscellaneous: Weakness, fatigue, insomnia.

Other common recommendations from Medical Doctors: A healthy diet and exercise can keep the immune system strong. In addition, the symptoms may be relieved by periodic prostate massage (by a doctor), frequent ejaculation, sitting in a warm bath, and relaxation techniques.

Nutritional Approach:

Disease or Condition: Prostate Health

Causes of Prostatitis/BPH/Prostate Cancer

Several main prostate conditions may occur: Prostatitis is caused by bacterial infection of the prostate and can be acute or chronic. A diet consisting of high fats and red meats increases your risk of prostate diseases and cancer[760]. Benign prostate hyperplasia (BPH) is the enlargement of the prostate caused by the non-canerous production of prostate cells. Prostate cancer is the most common cancer in men, but little is known

To find out more or to speak to a nutritional counselor for free, just visit us at:
www.CuresForTheBody.com

about the on set of it except that risk factors include family history and is higher for black men.

Nutritional support:

Foods that have been proven to aide in Prostate Health:

Tomatoes, garlic, onions, oregano, basil, and anise

Avoid saturated fats and hydrogenated and partially hydrogenated oils

Nutrients that have been proven to aide in Prostate Health:

Saw Palmetto[761], Zinc[762], Lycopene[763], Selenium[764], Vitamin E[765], Pygeum[766], and Stinging Nettle[767], Omega-3 fatty acids[768], proteolytic enzymes.[769]

Exercises that have been proven to help with Prostate Health:

In may cases exercising on a regular basis has reduced the risk of prostratitis and prostrate cancer. Exercising helps you body's immune system stay strong along with strengthening the muscles that can cause prostratitis. Kaegle exercises can be helpful because of the strengthening of the muscles in the pelvic region.

Basic Prostate Health Plan:

• **Establish optimal nutrition**

–Avoid Hydrogenated and partially hydrogenated oils. During the hydrogenation process remnants of the often used catalyst containing nickel and aluminum are left behind and later consumed. Aluminum is associated with several health conditions including cancer[770]. These trans-fats can be combated with highly unsaturated fats (flax, hemp, and cold water fish oils)[771].

–Eat foods containing Essential Fatty Acids (both Omega-3 and Omega-6). EFAs help bring oxygen into the body to fight against degenerative diseases. They are high in antioxidants as well.

–Nutritional deficiencies play a large role in the degenerative diseases, such as cancer. Specific to this disease, vitamin B3, potassium, iodine, hydrochloric acid, digestive enzymes, EFAs, vitamins C and E, carotene, sulphur, and selenium should all be considered in the diet.

–Eat a diet high in raw fruit, vegetables, and nuts. These foods have their own digestive enzymes and do not rob the body of its enzyme reserve. When digestive enzymes are needed from the body during the digestion process, it must sacrifice metabolic enzymes which are vital to the development of blood, nerves, tissues, and organs and therefore the protection from disease[772]. If processed foods are consumed, supplement the digestion process by adding (plant) enzymes.

–Proteolytic enzymes have been proven to reduce inflammation. They also help with circulation that is a problem with prostate conditions.

–Zinc – helps prevent enlargement of the prostate gland. It also helps shrink an already swollen prostate.[773]

–Lycopene – especially beneficial in protecting against prostate cancer. Consuming foods high in lycopene (tomatoes) have shown lower incidence of prostate cancerr.[774] Lycopene is also effective against free radicals.[775]

–Selenium – especially beneficial in protecting against prostate cancer along with colorectal and lung cancers.[776]

–Vitamin E - shown to reduce incidence of prostate cancer.[777]

–Saw Palmetto – should be supplemented to prevent and treat men suffering from benign prostatic hyperplasia (BPH).[778,779,780] Saw Palmetto also contains zinc and fatty acids.[781]

–Stinging Nettle root – great for the treatment of BPH.[782,783]

Sexual Dysfunction/Impotence

Description: Impotence is an erectile dysfunction, or the inability to achieve or maintain an erection. The occasional inability to achieve an erection is normal. The condition is considered a dysfunction when a man is continuously and frequently unable to achieve an erection. Mild erectile dysfunction is characterized occasionally being able to achieve a full erection, although more often his erections are inadequate for penetration. Severe erectile dysfunction occurs when a man is rarely able to achieve an erection.

Impotence is more common as men age; however, it is not a natural aging process. Half of men over 65 years old, and three-fourths of men over 80 experience erectile dysfunction. This condition may be caused by several factors that affect the blood flow into and out of the penis. Certain disorders (atherosclerosis, diabetes, blood clot) can narrow the arteries to the penis and restrict the blood flow. Impotence may also be the result of psychologic issues (depression, anxiety, fear) or drugs that interfere with the ability to cause an erection (antihypertensive, antidepressants, etc).

Men with erectile dysfunction will often experience decreased sex drive (libido) and have a difficult time engaging in intercourse. They may also stop having erections during sleep or upon awakening.

Medical Treatment:

Brand Name: Viagra

Drug Name: Sildenafil

Sildenafil has no direct relaxant effect on isolated human corpus cavernosum, but enhances the effect of nitric oxide (NO) by inhibiting phosphodiesterase type 5 (PDE5), which is responsible for degradation of cGMP in the corpus cavernosum. The physiologic mechanism of erection of the penis involves release of nitric oxide (NO) in the corpus cavernosum during sexual stimulation. NO then activates the enzyme guanylate cyclase,

To find out more or to speak to a nutritional counselor for free, just visit us at:
www.CuresForTheBody.com

which results in increased levels of cyclic guanosine monophosphate (cGMP), producing smooth muscle relaxation in the corpus cavernosum and allowing inflow of blood. When sexual stimulation causes local release of NO, inhibition of PDE5 by sildenafil causes increased levels of cGMP in the corpus cavernosum, resulting in smooth muscle relaxation and inflow of blood to the corpus cavernosum. Sildenafil at recommended doses has no effect in the absence of sexual stimulation.

Notable Side Effects:

Headache, flushing, dyspepsia, nasal congestion, urinary tract infection, abnormal vision, diarrhea, dizziness, rash.

Brand Name: Androderm

Drug Name: Testosterone

Testosterone delivers physiologic amounts of testosterone producing circulating testosterone concentrations that approximate the normal circadian rhythm of healthy young men. Androderm (testosterone transdermal system) delivers testosterone, the primary androgenic hormone.Testosterone is responsible for the normal growth and development of the male sex organs and for maintenance of secondary sex characteristics. These effects include the growth and maturation of the prostate, seminal vesicles, penis, and scrotum; development of male hair distribution, such as facial, pubic, chest, and axillary hair; laryngeal enlargement; vocal cord thickening; and alterations in body musculature and fat distribution.

Notable Side Effects:

Pruritus at application site, burn-like blister reaction under system, erythema at application site, vesicles at application site, prostate abnormalities, headache, allergic contact dermatitis to the system, burning at application site, induration at application site, depression, rash, gastrointestinal bleeding.

Brand Name: Caverject

Drug Name: Alprostadil

Alprostadil has a wide variety of pharmacological actions; vasodilation and inhibition of platelet aggregation are among the most notable of these effects. In most animal species tested, alprostadil relaxed retractor penis and corpus cavernosum urethrae *in vitro* . Alprostadil also relaxed isolated preparations of human corpus cavernosum and spongiosum, as well as cavernous arterial segments contracted by either noradrenaline or PGF $_{2a}$ *in vitro* . In pigtail monkeys (*Macaca nemestrina*), alprostadil increased cavernous arterial blood flow *in vivo* . The degree and duration of cavernous smooth muscle relaxation in this animal model was dose-dependent. Alprostadil induces erection by relaxation of trabecular smooth muscle and by dilation of cavernosal arteries. This leads to expansion of lacunar spaces and entrapment of blood by compressing the venules against the tunica albuginea, a process referred to as the corporal veno-occlusive mechanism.

Notable Side Effects:

Penile pain, prolonged erection, penile fibrosis, injection site hematoma, penis disorder (including numbness, yeast infection, sensitivity, phimosis, pruritus, erythema, venous leak, penile skin tear, strange feeling of penis, discoloration of penile head, itch at tip of penis), injection site ecchymosis, penile rash, penile edema.

Other common recommendations from Medical Doctors:

If a drug is causing the erectile dysfunction, you may consider discontinuing its use. Psychological therapy can be used to improve mental and emotional factors if they contribute to the dysfunction. Constriction or vacuum devices can also be used to aid in obtaining and sustaining an erection.

Nutritional Approach:

Disease or Condition: Impotence
Causes of Impotence

May stem from or be a side effect of endocrine, vascular, neurologic, or psychiatric diseases. Medications may also initiate impotence.

Nutritional support:
Foods that have been proven to help with Impotence:

Arginine found in meats, nuts, eggs, milk and cheese. Cordyceps.

Nutrients that have been proven to help with Impotence:

Ashwagandha[784], Astragalus[785], Rhodiola[786], Vitamin B6[787], Vitamin B12[788], Folic Acid[789], Niacin[790], Chromium[791], and Pantethine.[792]

Exercises that have been proven to help with Impotence:

Exercise of the muscles that surround the sexual organs and glands can help to overcome many forms of sexual dysfunction. While exercised vary between men and women it is possible of exercising to help overcome sexual dysfunction. Increased oxygen is proven to help with Sexual Disfunction. Aerobics for 30 4-5 times a week improves oxygen absorbtion in blood.

Basic Impotence Plan:
• Establish optimal nutrition

–Follow a diet that is highly digestible, low in red meat and balanced like the one described in chapter 5.

–Arginine – an amino acid that is a precursor of nitric oxide which permits penile erection.[793] It is produced in the body, but can also be found in meats, nuts, eggs, milk and cheese.

–Ashwagandha – aka winter cherry or Indian ginseng- used in the treatment of impotence. Ashwagandha also contains amino acid arginine[794] and increased sexual performance in 71% of men in a recent study.[795]

–Cordyceps – reported to decrease impotence in men, and enhance sexual vitality in both genders.[796] Also thought to reverse impotence caused by pharmaceuticals.[797]

–Rhodiola – has been used for treatment of sexual disorders in both genders.

• Atherosclerosis: In an animal model that produced experimental atherosclerosis, 93% of the animals with 50% or greater occlusion to arteries in the region of the groin exhibited erectile dysfunction. Atherosclerosis is also reported to be one of the most common causes of erectile dysfunction in humans. Thus, substances that slow down

or reduce the risks of developing atherosclerosis might be helpful in the prevention and/or treatment of male impotence. These substances include **vitamin B6, vitamin B12** and **folic acid**, which help to lower homocysteine levels, since homocysteine is a known atherogenic risk factor.

• Elevated cholesterol is also a risk to atherosclerosis. **Niacin** and **chromium** have both been found to aid in lowering elevated cholesterol levels and so has **pantethine**, which is the active form of vitamin B5. Gamma Linolenic acid (GLA) is reportedly very effective at lowering elevated cholesterol levels by increasing the metabolism and excretion of cholesterol from the body.

• Antioxidants such as vitamin C,[798] vitamin E,[799] and coenzyme Q10[800] can help to prevent the oxidation of LDL-cholesterol. Thus, they too may be helpful in preventing and/or slowing down the progression of both atherosclerosis and impotence.

Skin Disorders/Eczema and Psoriasis

Description: Many skin problems are limited to the skin, but may also reveal a disorder of other parts of the body. Two common skin disorders are dermatitis (eczema) and psoriasis.

Eczema appears as a red, itchy rash, and is a condition of itching, blisters, swelling, oozing, scabbing, and/or scaling as a result of inflammation of the upper layers of skin. These symptoms may be triggered due to irritation or an allergic reaction. It may result as a reaction to something that comes into contact with the skin or a substance that is swallowed. Because the hands and feet are more vulnerable to trigger substances, the rash usually appears on these areas of the body.

Psoriasis is a chronic disease that occurs because of the rapid growth of skin cells. It results in raised, red patches that have a distinct border. These patches may cover large areas of the body in some, but usually starts as small patches on the scalp, elbows, knees, back, or buttocks. Flare-ups may be triggered by irritation to the skin (sunburn), minor injuries, infections, and in stressful situations. The patches are often obvious, although they are not necessarily uncomfortable.

All age groups are susceptible to psoriasis, although it is more common in people between the ages of 10 and 40. The symptoms usually come and go throughout life, and usually are lessened when exposed to more sunlight.

Medical Treatment:

Antihistamines:

Brand name: Atarax

Drug Name: Hydroxyzine

To find out more or to speak to a nutritional counselor for free, just visit us at:
www.CuresForTheBody.com

Hydroxyzine action may be due to a suppression of activity in certain key regions of the subcortical area of the central nervous system. Primary skeletal muscle relaxation has been demonstrated experimentally. Bronchodilator activity, and anti- histaminic and analgesic effects have been demonstrated experimentally and confirmed clinically. An antiemetic effect, both by the apomorphine test and the veriloid test, has been demonstrated.

Notable Side Effects:

Anticholinergic: Dry mouth.

Central Nervous System: Drowsiness is usually transitory and may disappear in a few days of continued therapy or upon reduction of the dose. Involuntary motor activity including rare instances of tremor and convulsions have been reported, usually with doses considerably higher than those recommended.

Brand name: Zyrtec

Drug Name: Cetirizine

Cetirizine, a metabolite of hydroxyzine, is an antihistamine; its principal effects are mediated via selective inhibition of H_1 receptors.

Notable Side Effects:

Somnolence, fatigue, dry mouth, pharyngitis, dizziness

Corticosteroid creams

Brand Name: Cortizone

Drug Name: Hydrocortisone

Psoriasis

Brand Name: Psoriatec

Drug Name: Anthralin

Anthralin is a synthetic compound whose precise mechanism of anti-psoriatic action is not yet fully understood. Numerous studies, however, have demonstrated anti-proliferative and anti-inflammatory effects of anthralin on psoriatic and normal skin. The anti-proliferative effects of anthralin appear to result from both an inhibition of DNA synthesis as well as from its strong reducing properties. Recently, anthralin's effectiveness as an anti-psoriatic agent has also been in part attributed to its abilities to inactivate epidermal 12-lipoxygenase and reduce levels of endothelial adhesion molecules which are markedly elevated in psoriatic patients. Inactivation of 12-lipoxygenase by anthralin substantially reduces levels of 12-hydroperoxyeicosatetraenoic acid and its inflammatory metabolites, which are present in high concentrations in psoriatic plaques. Anthralin does not appear to affect liver microsomal enzyme activity. Systemic absorption of anthralin after topical application of Psoriatec has not been determined in humans.

Notable Side Effects:

Very few instances of contact allergic reactions to anthralin have been reported. However, transient primary irritation of the normal skin or uninvolved skin surrounding the treated lesions is more frequently seen. If the initial treatment produces excessive soreness or if the lesions spread, reduce frequency of application and, in extreme cases, discontinue use and consult a physician. Psoriatec cream may stain skin, hair or fabrics. Some temporary discoloration of hair and fingernails may arise during the period of treatment but should be minimized by careful application. Staining of fabrics may be permanent, so contact should be avoided.

Brand Name:Trexall

Drug Name: Methotrexate sodium

Methotrexate sodium inhibits dihydrofolic acid reductase. Dihydrofolates must be reduced to tetrahydrofolates by this enzyme before they can be utilized as carriers of one-carbon groups in the synthesis of purine nucleotides and thymidylate. Therefore, methotrexate interferes with DNA synthesis, repair, and cellular replication. Actively proliferating tissues such as malignant cells, bone marrow, fetal cells, buccal and intestinal mucosa, and cells of the urinary bladder are in general more sensitive to this effect of methotrexate. When cellular proliferation in malignant tissues is greater than in most normal tissues, methotrexate may impair malignant growth without irreversible damage to normal tissues.

Notable Side Effects:

Liver disease, lung inflammation, an increased susceptibility to infection, suppression of blood cell production in the bone marrow.

Alimentary System: Gingivitis, pharyngitis, stomatitis, anorexia, nausea, vomiting, diarrhea, hematemesis, melena, gastrointestinal ulceration and bleeding, enteritis, pancreatitis.

Blood and Lymphatic System Disorders: Suppressed hematopoiesis causing anemia, aplastic anemia, leukopenia and/or thrombocytopenia. Hypogammaglobulinemia has been reported rarely.

Cardiovascular: Pericarditis, pericardial effusion, hypotension, and thromboembolic events (including arterial thrombosis, cerebral thrombosis, deep vein thrombosis, retinal vein thrombosis, thrombophlebitis, and pulmonary embolus).

Central Nervous System: Headaches, drowsiness, blurred vision, transient blindness, speech impairment including dysarthria and aphasia, hemiparesis, paresis and convulsions have also occurred following administration of methotrexate. Following low doses, there have been occasional reports of transient subtle cognitive dysfunction, mood alteration, unusual cranial sensations, leukoencephalopathy, or encephalopathy.

Infection: There have been case reports of sometimes fatal opportunistic infections in patients receiving methotrexate therapy for neoplastic and non-neoplastic diseases. *Pneumocystis carinii* pneumonia was the most common infection. Other reported infections included sepsis, nocardiosis; histoplasmosis, cryptococcosis, *Herpes zoster, H. simplex* hepatitis, and disseminated *H. simplex*.

Musculoskeletal System: Stress fracture.

Ophthalmic: Conjunctivitis, serious visual changes of unknown etiology.

Pulmonary System: Respiratory fibrosis, respiratory failure, interstitial pneumonitis deaths have been reported, and chronic interstitial obstructive pulmonary disease has occasionally occurred.

Skin: Erythematous rashes, pruritus, urticaria, photosensitivity, pigmentary changes, alopecia, ecchymosis, telangiectasia, acne, furunculosis, erythema multiforme, toxic epidermal necrolysis, Stevens-Johnson syndrome, skin necrosis, skin ulceration, and exfoliative dermatitis.

Urogenital System: Severe nephropathy or renal failure, azotemia, cystitis, hematuria; defective oogenesis or spermatogenesis, transient oligospermia, menstrual dysfunction, vaginal discharge, and gynecomastia; infertility, abortion, fetal defects.

Other common recommendations from Medical Doctors: avoid contact with trigger substances. Barrier creams and clothing may also help to avoid contact with substances that irritate the skin externally. Keeping the skin moisturized is also recommended. Sunlight may also help to lessen symptoms and flare-ups.

Nutritional Approach

Disease or Condition: Skin Condition Eczema

Eczema is caused by a cascade of immune mechanisms. The itching of eczema is a result of allergens interacting with IgG on the surface of mast cells and macrophages under the skin. This leads to the flooding of histamines, prostaglandins, and other inflammatory components, along with T lymphocytes (type 2 T-helper cells) and macrophages to the skin

Nutritional support:

Foods that have been proven to help with Eczema:

Any foods high in raw fatty acids, like: avacadoes and raw nuts. Use raw oils, like: Extra Virgin Olive Oil and Flaxseed Oil.

Nutrients that have been proven to help with Eczema:

Olive leaf[801], Proboitics[802], Digestive enzymes, Milk Thistle[803], GLA[804], DGLA[805], AA Zinc[806], Silymarin[807], Grapefruitseed Extract[808], Artichoke.[809]

To find out more or to speak to a nutritional counselor for free, just visit us at:
www.CuresForTheBody.com

Exercises that have been proven to help with Skin Disorders:

Many studies have shown that exercised can help to prevent or even overcome many skin disorders. This is because of the cleansing effect that sweating has on the body. It is important to remember the sweating releases toxins from the body and they need to be removed from the skin so that it does not worsen the disorder. It is recommended to shower immediately after exercising.

Basic Eczema Plan:
- Avoid food allergens, alcohol, caffeine, and smoking.
- Rule out hypochlorhydria/achlorhydria.
- Identify and eliminate food allergies.

–Food allergies frequently cause dermatological problems such as eczema. In fact, it is estimated that approximately one third of young children with atopic eczema suffer from clinically significant food allergies.[810] This study is an evaluation of 10 breastfed infants with atopic eczema who were allergic to cow's milk. Lactobacillus GG was given to the nursing mothers at a dose of 2×10^{10} colony- forming units twice daily for one month. Over a one-month period, this therapeutic intervention with Lactbacillus GG resulted in significant symptomatic improvements. There was a substantial reduction in alpha1-antitrypsin in the treated infants, but not in the group receiving the whey formula without Lactobacillus GG.

- Therapy with **probiotic** bacteria may reduce GI inflammation, promote intestinal health and cause improvements in eczema in patients with food allergies.

- **Olive leaf** extract has been reported to be an effective antimicrobial agent against a wide variety of pathogens, including *Salmonella typhi*, *Vibrio parahaemolyticus* and *Staphylococcus aureus* (including penicillin-resistant strains); and *Klebsiella pneumonia* and *Escherichia coli*, causal agents of intestinal or respiratory tract infections in man. The component usually associated with olive leaf's antimicrobial properties is oleuropein.[811], Oleuropein has also been reported to directly stimulate macrophage activation in laboratory studies.[812] If intestinal flora disturbances are suspected as a cause of eczema, olive leaf may inhibit the offending pathogen.

• **Milk Thistle** Historically, milk thistle was used as a digestive tonic; a general tonic for the spleen, stomach, and liver; for the gallbladder; to promote bile flow; and as a stimulant for milk flow in nursing mothers.

• One aspect of atopic eczema seems to be a block or inhibition of delta-6 desaturase enzyme activity, which is necessary for the conversion of linoleic acid to gamma-linolenic acid (GLA), dihomogamma-linolenic acid (DGLA), and arachidonic acid (AA). Frequently all three of these linoleic acid metabolites are all reduced in patients with eczema. In most but not all studies, treatment with GLA produces substantial improvement in skin roughness and a normalization of the elevated blood catecholamine levels in patients with atopic eczema. It is suggested that atopic eczema may be a minor genetic abnormality of essential fatty acid metabolism.

• **Zinc**- The results of some studies report that patients with eczema have low zinc levels whereas others do not. For example, the results from one clinical trial revealed that the mean serum zinc level in 65 children with ectopic eczema was slightly but significantly lower than normal controls. Six out of eleven children with serum zinc below 10 mumol/l had recurrent skin infections, which was a significantly greater proportion than occurred in patients whose serum zinc was 10 mumol/l or above. Even though this study reports an association between low zinc and eczema, an 8 week double-blind placebo-controlled trial reported that zinc was not effective in the treatment of children with atopic eczema.[813] Even though low zinc levels may be a secondary rather than a primary aspect of eczema, it still may be helpful to evaluate patients' zinc levels and treat any deficiencies that are found.

• **Silymarin**- reportedly acts by inhibiting the passage of toxins into the liver cells, by altering the membranes of the hepatic cells, and by stimulating regeneration of new liver cells through increased protein synthesis. Silymarin has been demonstrated to increase glutathione content in the liver by more than 35 percent, increasing its antioxidant capacity.[814]

• **Grapefruit seed extract** inhibits causative agents of bowel dysbiosis (the imbalance of normal bacterial flora in the GI tract) including *Candida sp. In vivo*, grapefruit seed extract is a useful agent in maintaining bowel integrity. In this human study, an improvement in constipation, flatulence, abdominal distress and night rest were noticed after four weeks of therapy. Most clinicians now agree on the importance of maintaining homeostasis of the microflora in health and disease.[815] Grapefruit seed extract may provide value in the event that eczema symptoms are initiated by GI tract dysbiosis.

• **Artichoke**The flower head of the globe artichoke has been used as a food and medicinal agent for centuries. In medicine, the globe artichoke has historically been used for poor digestion, along with "sluggish" liver, skin problems such as eczema, atherosclerosis, elevated cholesterol levels, and as a mild diuretic. Artichoke leaf is claimed to be a potent antioxidant. Dyspeptic complaints take artichoke as a supplement, symptoms rapidly disappear, reducing pain, nausea, retching, and the sensation of fullness. The constituent cynarin has been stated to be most active in this capacity.

Sleeping Disorders/Insomnia

Description: Insomnia is habitual sleeplessness, characterized by the inability to fall asleep or stay asleep. Sleep is also often inadequate and unrefreshing. Insomnia itself is not a disorder however. Insomnia is a symptom of other issues. It is most often caused by emotional issues and stress.

Other issues of insomnia may include an irregular schedule, physical disorders, drug use, alcohol use, emotional problems and stress. An irregular schedule can also cause a sleep-wake schedule disorder where the sleeping patterns are disrupted by jet lag, work schedules, those who have been hospitalized and awakened frequently in the night, or excessive use of alcohol. Many people with insomnia experience symptoms such as irritability, fatigue during the day, problems concentrating, and difficulty performing under stress.

About 10% of adults have chronic insomnia and 50% of adults have occasional insomnia. However, many older people mistake their changing sleep patterns for insomnia as the need for sleep decreases with age. Older people may awaken more at night also.

Medical Treatment:

Antihistamines:
Brand Name: Benadryl
Drug Name: Diphenhydramine

Notable Side Effects:
Drowsiness, dry mouth, blurred vision, difficulty urinating, constipation, light-headedness, and confusion

To find out more or to speak to a nutritional counselor for free, just visit us at:
www.CuresForTheBody.com

Brand Name: Unisom

Drug Name: Doxylamine

Hypnotics:

Brand Name: Ambien

Drug Name: Zolpidem

Zolpidem is a hypnotic agent with a chemical structure unrelated to benzodiazepines, barbiturates, or other drugs with known hypnotic properties, however, it interacts with a GABA-BZ receptor complex and shares some of the pharmacological properties of the benzodiazepines. In contrast to the benzodiazepines, which nonselectively bind to and activate all omega receptor subtypes, zolpidem in vitro binds the ((omega) $_1$) receptor preferentially with a high affinity ratio of the alpha $_1$/alpha $_5$ subunits. The ((omega) $_1$) receptor is found primarily on the Lamina IV of the sensorimotor cortical regions, substantia nigra (parsreticulata), cerebellum molecular layer, olfactory bulb, ventral thalamic complex, pons, inferior colliculus, and globus pallidus. This selective binding of zolpidem on the ((omega) $_1$) receptor is not absolute, but it may explain the relative absence of myorelaxant and anticonvulsant effects in animal studies as well as the preservation of deep sleep (stages 3 and 4) in human studies of zolpidem at hypnotic doses.

Notable Side Effects:

Most commonly observed adverse events in controlled trials: During short-term treatment (up to 10 nights) with Ambien at doses up to 10 mg, the most commonly observed adverse events associated with the use of zolpidem and seen at statistically significant differences from placebo-treated patients were drowsiness (reported by 2% of zolpidem patients), dizziness (1%), and diarrhea (1%). During longer-term treatment (28 to 35 nights) with zolpidem at doses up to 10 mg, the most commonly observed adverse events associated with the use of zolpidem and seen at statistically significant differences from placebo-treated patients were dizziness (5%) and drugged feelings (3%).

Benzodiazepines:

Manage anxiety

Brand Name: ProSom

To find out more or to speak to a nutritional counselor for free, just visit us at:
www.CuresForTheBody.com

Drug Name: Estazolam

Notable Side Effects:

> *Body as a Whole:* headache, asthenia, malaise, lower extremity pain, pack pain, body pain, abdominal pain, chest pain.
>
> *Digestive System:* nausea, dyspepsia.
>
> *Musculoskeletal System:* stiffness.
>
> *Nervous System:* somnolence, hypokinesia, nervousness, dizziness, coordination abnormal, hangover, confusion, depression, dream abnormal, thinking abnormal.
>
> *Respiratory System:* cold symptoms, pharyngitis.
>
> *Skin Appendages:* pruritus.

Other common recommendations from Medical Doctors: If the insomnia is a symptom of another disorder, it is always best to treat that disorder. In addition it is helpful to follow a regular sleep schedule. Light therapy to reset the biological clock may be helpful to some who experience sleep-wake reversal.

Nutritional Approach:

Disease or Condition: Insomnia/ Sleep Disorder

Causes of Insomnia:

Physical and emotional disorders such as chronic illnesses, pregnancy, alcohol intake, stress and depression may trigger the onset of insomnia. Nutrient deficientcies of vitamins and minerals have been proven to cause insomnia.

Nutritional support:

Foods that have been proven to help with Insomnia:

Ginger, tangerines, spearmint, basil, tomatoes, red pepper, thyme, cinnamon, pennyroyal.

Nutrients that have been proven to help with insomnia:

To find out more or to speak to a nutritional counselor for free, just visit us at:
www.CuresForTheBody.com

Melatonin[816], and 5-hydroxytryptophan (5-HTP)[817], Kava,[818] Passionflower[819], Valerian[820], Chamomile[821], Hops[822], Magnesium[823], Iron.[824]

- Deficiencies or imbalances in amino acids can indicate fundamental reasons for numerous disorders. Amino acid malabsorption syndrome or imbalanced amino patterns reflect abnormal organ and glandular processes that have critical bearing on optimal function. Several amino acids have impact on healthy sleep patterns.[825]

- Stress activates the HPA axis and has impact on the immune system, particularly through the adrenal hormones. In assessing the HPA axis, adrenal functional abnormalities are relatively simple to identify and address (e.g., when compared to hypothalamic dysregulation or pituitary imbalance).

- Melatonin an antioxidant, is considered important in the healthy sleep cycle.[826]

- Insulin and Cortisol: The interactions of these hormones in the sleep-wake cycle have been found to be significant.[827]

- Kava has long been used as a safe, effective treatment for mild anxiety states, nervous tension, muscular tension, and mild insomnia.[828]

- Passionflower has been reported to have sedative, hypnotic, antispasmodic, and anodyne properties. It has traditionally been used for neuralgia, generalized seizures, hysteria, nervous tachycardia, spasmodic asthma, and specifically for insomnia.[829]

- Valerian has long been used as an agent to soothe the nervous system in response to stress. It has been reported that valerian helps improve sleep quality.[830] Because of fewerside effects, valerian could prove to be a less troublesome alternative to drugs in the treatment of insomnia.[831]

- Chamomile has been used as a medicinal herb for centuries. It is most frequently used as a mild sedative for individuals with minor anxiety or nervousness.[832]

Exercises that have been proven to help with insomnia:

People who regularly engage in exercise have fewer episodes of sleeplessness. Exercise promotes improved sleep quality by allowing smoother and more regular transition between the cycles and phases of sleep. Moderate exercises lasting 20 to 30 minutes three or four times a week will help you sleep better and give you more energy.

Basic insomnia plan:

• Avoid caffeine and alcohol in the afternoon and evening. Some people report that small amounts of caffeine can keep them awake, even 8-10 hours after consumption.

• Maintain a consistent bedtime routine. Go to bed and wake up at the same time every day, even on weekends.

• Exercise during the day can improve sleep at night.

• Increase your body temperature slightly before bed in a warm bath or shower. The subsequent decline can help induce and maintain sleep.

• Try to stop work or doing tasks that keep the mind active earlier in the evening.

• Avoid television before bed. The lights and sounds can over-stimulate the nervous system.

• If the insomnia is stress induced, try and learn stress reduction techniques. This is different for many, but exercise, yoga, tai chi, or any activity that will bring joy and calmness is a big step in the right direction.

• Some people who wake up during the middle of the night do so because of hypoglycemia. Consuming a small snack just before bedtime helps to stabilize blood sugar levels throughout the night. Ideally, snacks should consist of complex carbohydrates, along with a little fat and protein. This allows for more of a timed-release breakdown and release of energy into the body.

To find out more or to speak to a nutritional counselor for free, just visit us at:
www.CuresForTheBody.com

Thyroid/Hypothyroidism

Description: The thyroid gland is responsible for secreting the hormone that controls the body's metabolic rate (chemical functions). It stimulates the tissues in every part of the body and especially influence the body's vital functions, such as the heart rate, the respiratory rate, the rate calories are burned, growth, heat production, fertility, and digestion.

Hypothyroidism is the underactivity of the thyroid, which therefore results in the slowing of vital body functions. It is more common in older people, particularly in women.

There are many causes to hypothyroidism, the most common being Hashimoto's thyroiditis. This condition causes the thyroid to become inflamed and damaged. Subacute thyroiditis can also cause hypothyroidism, although the thyroid is not destroyed. Radioactive iodine or the surgical remove can also be a cause, as well as rare causes, such as inherited enzyme abnormalities. A chronic lack of iodine can also cause hypothyroidism, but this condition is rare in the United States as table salt and dairy products (due to the sterilization process in retrieving milk) contain iodine.

There are many symptoms associated with hypothyroidism as the body's functions begin to slow. Most symptoms are subtle and develop gradual, and may at first resemble depression. Some symptoms include: slow speech, droopy eyelids, puffy eyes and face, weight gain, inability to tolerate cold, sparse/coarse/dry hair, dry and scaly skin, slower pulse, and other symptoms resembling Alzheimer's disease (confused, forgetful, demented). Severe hypothyroidism can lead to anemia, a low body temperature, heart failure and coma if left untreated.

Medical Treatment:

To find out more or to speak to a nutritional counselor for free, just visit us at:
www.CuresForTheBody.com

Brand Name: Cytomel

Drug Name: Liothyronine sodium

Liothyronine: The mechanisms by which thyroid hormones exert their physiologic action are not well understood. These hormones enhance oxygen consumption by most tissues of the body, increase the basal metabolic rate and the metabolism of carbohydrates, lipids and proteins. Thus, they exert a profound influence on every organ system in the body and are of particular importance in the development of the central nervous system.

Notable Side Effects:

Allergic skin reactions. (Side effects are rare.)

Brand Name: Levothroid

Drug Name: Levothyroxine

Levothyroxine: The principal effect of exogenous thyroid hormone is to increase the metabolic rate of body tissues. The thyroid hormones are also concerned with growth and differentiation of tissues. In deficiency states in the young there is retardation of growth and failure of maturation of the skeletal and other body systems, especially in failure of ossification in the epiphyses and in the growth and development of the brain. The precise mechanism of action by which thyroid hormones affect thermogenesis and cellular growth and differentiation is not known. It is recognized that these physiologic effects are mediated at the cellular level primarily by T_3, a large part of which is derived from T_4 by deiodination in the peripheral tissues. Thyroxine (T_4) is the major component of normal secretions of the thyroid gland and is thus the primary determinant of normal thyroid function.

Notable Side Effects:

hyperthyroidism (Side effects are rare.)

Nutritional Approach:

Disease or Condition: Hypothyroid

Causes of Hypothyroid:

95% of all cases are due to the thyroid gland and not the pituitary gland. Most patients with hypothyroidism are not born with it; they develop it as adults.

Iodine deficiency leads to hypothyroidism and/or the development of an enlarged thyroid gland.

Currently, the most common cause is due to an autoimmune disease known as Hashimoto's disease. In this disease, antibodies are formed that bind to the thyroid and prevent the manufacture of sufficient levels of thyroid hormone. In addition to binding to thyroid tissue, antibodies may also bind to the adrenal glands, pancreas, and acid-producing cells of the stomach.

A lack of thyroid hormones leads to...

A general decrease in the rate of utilization of fat, protein, and carbohydrate.

Moderate weight gain combined with sensitivity to cold weather (demonstrated by cold hands or feet) is a common finding.

Cholesterol and triglyceride levels are increased in even the mildest forms of hypothyroidism. This elevation greatly increases the risk of serious cardiovascular disease. Studies have shown an increased rate of heart disease due to atherosclerosis in individuals with hypothyroidism[833].

Dry, rough skin covered with fine, superficial scales is seen in most hypothyroid individuals, while their hair is course, dry and brittle. Hair loss can be quite sever. The nails become thin and brittle and typically show transverse grooves.

Depression, weakness, and fatigue are usually the first symptoms of hypothyroidism. Later, the hypothyroid individual will have difficulty concentrating and become extremely forgetful.

Nutritional support:

Foods that have been proven to help with Hypothyroid:

Iodine and Selenium rich foods; whole grains are the best dietary source of selenium followed by seafood, garlic, liver, eggs, and some vegetables including cabbage, celery, cucumbers, and radishes.

Avoid naturally goitrogen-containing foods (anti-thyroid or more specifically, foods that impair the use of iodine): Brussels sprouts, kale, cauliflower, asparagus, broccoli, raw soybeans, lettuce, peas, turnips greens and watercress.

To find out more or to speak to a nutritional counselor for free, just visit us at:
www.CuresForTheBody.com

Nutrients that have been proven to help with Hypothyroid:

Iodine[834], Selenium[835], Bladderwrack.[836]

Exercises that have been proven to help with Hypothyroid:

A daily exercise regiment can help to keep weight in balance. Having a balanced weight will help with your overall health as well as promoting the healing of the thyroid. Strength training twice a week and 30-40 minutes of aerobics 5 times a week is a good routine.

Basic Hypothyroid Plan:

Eat foods high in:

    Iodine

    –Generally, hypothyroidism is treated by giving the patient supplemental thyroid hormone. However, occasionally iodine supplementation is used to increase the production of thyroid hormone.

    Selenium

    –Iodothyronine 5'-deiodinase, which is primarily responsible for the conversion of thyroxine (T4) to triiodothyronine (T3), has recently been demonstrated to be a selenium-containing enzyme. This raises the possibility that low dietary selenium intake could create a hypothyroid-like condition due to a lack of T4 to T3 conversion.

    –Selenium deficiency may cause an inhibition of deiodinase enzyme activity, which could result in elevated levels of circulating T4, and a corresponding decrease in the concentration of T3 in peripheral tissues.

    –Low levels of selenium may also accelerate the depletion of iodine from the thyroid gland and increase some of the problems associated with iodine deficiency.

    –Selenium deficiency may also be involved in the occurrence and development of iodine deficiency disorders. In China, Keshan disease, which is primarily due to selenium deficiency, was also observed to alter thyroid hormone metabolism.

    –It has also been noted that selenium deficiency may cause a lowering of glutathione peroxidase activity in the thyroid gland. This in turn could allow hydrogen peroxide produced during thyroid hormone synthesis to be more cytotoxic.

–In individuals who are deficient in both selenium and iodine, selenium supplementation may aggravate hypothyroidism by stimulating thyroxin metabolism via the selenoenzyme type I iodothyronine 5'-deiodinase. In cases of combined selenium and iodine deficiencies, selenium supplementation is not used without iodine and thyroid hormone supplementation.

Bladderwrack

–Is a rich source of iodine, and is traditionally used in weight loss and for hypothyroidism.

–Also contains potassium, magnesium, calcium, iron, zinc, and other minerals.

–Historically, it has been used in the dairy and baking industries, due to the gelling properties of the constituent algin.

–Is thought to stimulate the thyroid gland, thus increasing basal metabolism.

–It is recommended that products be used in which the iodine content is assayed to avoid potential iodine toxicity problems.

–Low levels of vitamin B12 have been occasionally reported in patients with hyperthyroidism. One study identified malabsorption as the probable cause in two patients.[837] Other studies evaluating hyperthyroid patients have reported finding normal vitamin B12 levels. Vitamin B12 depletion appears to be only an occasional occurrence in hyperthyroidism, but practitioners should be aware of the possibility.

–Oxidative processes have been implicated as playing roles in the genesis of hyperthyroidism-induced damage. In a study with animals, researchers investigated the effects of vitamins C and E on plasma lipid peroxidation and the susceptibility of apolipoprotein B (apo B)-containing lipoproteins to oxidation Malondialdehyde levels were measured as an indicator of plasma lipid peroxidation. The results indicated an increased susceptibility of apo B-containing lipoproteins to oxidation, and that supplementation with vitamins C and E could provide protection from copper-induced oxidation.[838] In another study of 24 human subjects, vitamin C was found to increase glutathione concentration and glutathione peroxidase activity indicating the potentiation of antioxidant status and a reduction in oxidative stress.[839]

–Experimental studies have revealed elevated oxidative stress in humans during hyperthyroidism, which can be reduced by treatment. In one study, 22 patients with hyperthyroidism exhibited increased plasma levels of thiobarbituric acid reactive substances (TBARS) with a reduction in coenzyme Q10 and vitamin E, confirming the presence of oxidative stress in hyperthyroidism[840].

−Studies have been published that indicate L-carnitine antagonizes thyroid hormone in some tissues. A study by Benvenga, et al evaluated the clinical impact of these findings on hyperthyroid patients. This double-blind, placebo-controlled trial evaluated 50 hyperthyroid women for six months. The women were randomized to one of 5 groups ranging from strictly placebo to either 2 or 4 grams of carnitine per day for a period alternating with placebo use for a period. The trial concluded that the use of L-carnitine is effective in preventing and reducing the nine hyperthyroid related symptoms evaluated and has a beneficial effect on bone mineralization based on biochemical parameters evaluated.[841]

Ulcer/Ulcerative Colitis

Description: Ulcerative colitis is a condition where the large intestine is inflamed and ulcerated (perforated). This condition is usually manifest by bout of bloody diarrhea, abdominal cramps, and a fever.

Most people with ulcerative colitis begin seeing symptoms between the ages of 15 and 30. Although less common, people may also experience this disorder between 50 and 70 years of age.

This condition usually begins in the rectum and may eventually spread up into the lower part of the large intestine. It is rarely found in the small intestine. The cause of this condition is unknown. However, heredity and an over-reactive immune system may be contributors.

Symptoms experienced during a flare-up of ulcerative colitis include violent diarrhea, high fever, abdominal pain, inflammation of the abdominal cavity lining., mild cramps, visible blood and mucus in stool. If the condition has moved further up the intestine, symptoms may also include a fever, poor appetite, and a loss of weight.

Medical Treatment:

Antidiarrheal Drugs:

Brand Name: Imodium

Drug Name: Loperamide

Loperamide acts by slowing intestinal motility and by affecting water and electrolyte movement through the bowel.

Anti-Inflammatory Drugs:

Brand Name: Azulfidine

Drug Name: Sulfasalazine

Sulfasalazine's action is still under investigation, but may be related to the anti-inflammatory and/or immunomodulatory properties that have been observed in animal and in vitro models, to its affinity for connective tissue, and/or to the relatively high concentration it reaches in serous fluids, the liver and intestinal walls, as demonstrated in autoradiographic studies in animals. In ulcerative colitis, clinical studies utilizing rectal administration of SSZ, SP and 5-ASA have indicated that the major therapeutic action may reside in the 5-ASA moiety. The relative contribution of the parent drug and the major metabolites in rheumatoid arthritis is unknown.

NotableSide Effects:

The most common adverse reactions associated with sulfasalazine in ulcerative colitis are anorexia, headache, nausea, vomiting, gastric distress, and apparently reversible oligospermia. These occur in about one-third of the patients. Less frequent adverse reactions are pruritus, urticaria, rash, fever, Heinz body anemia, hemolytic anemia and cyanosis, which may occur at a frequency of 1 in 30 patients or less. Experience suggests that with a daily dose of 4 g or more, or total serum sulfapyridine levels above 50 μg/mL, the incidence of adverse reactions tends to increase.

Brand Name: Dipentum

Drug Name: Olsalazine

Olsalazine's mechanism of action is unknown, but appears to be topical rather than systemic. Mucosal production of arachidonic acid (AA) metabolites, both through the cyclooxygenase pathways, i.e., prostanoids, and through the lipoxygenase pathways, i.e., leukotrienes (LTs) and hydroxyeicosatetraenoic acids (HETEs) is increased in patients with chronic inflammatory bowel disease, and it is possible that mesalamine diminishes inflammation by blocking cyclooxygenase and inhibiting prostaglandin (PG) production in the colon.

Notable Side Effects:

Diarrhea/loose stools, nausea, abdominal pain, rash/itching, headache, heartburn, rectal bleeding, insomnia, dizziness, anorexia, light headedness, depression.

Immunomodulating Drugs:

Brand Name: Azasan

Drug Name: Azathioprine

Azathioprine suppresses disease manifestations as well as underlying pathology in animal models of autoimmune disease. For example, the severity of adjuvant arthritis is reduced by azathioprine. The mechanisms whereby azathioprine affects autoimmune diseases are not known. Azathioprine is immunosuppressive, delayed hypersensitivity and cellular cytotoxicity tests being suppressed to a greater degree than are antibody responses. In the rat model of adjuvant arthritis, azathioprine has been shown to inhibit the lymph node hyperplasia which precedes the onset of the signs of the disease. Both the immunosuppressive and therapeutic effects in animal models are dose-related. Azathioprine is considered a slow-acting drug and effects may persist after the drug has been discontinued.

Notable Side Effects:

Hematologic: Leukopenia and/or thrombocytopenia. Infection may occur as a secondary manifestation of bone marrow suppression or leukopenia, but the incidence of infection in renal homotransplantation is 30 to 60 times that in rheumatoid arthritis. Macrocytic anemia and/or bleeding have been reported in two patients on azathioprine.

Gastrointestinal: Nausea and vomiting may occur within the first few months of AZASAN™ therapy, and occurred in approximately 12% of 676 rheumatoid arthritis patients. The frequency of gastric disturbance often can be reduced by administration of the drug in divided doses and/or after meals. However, in some patients, nausea and vomiting may be severe and may be accompanied by symptoms such as diarrhea, fever, malaise, and myalgias. Vomiting with abdominal pain may occur rarely with a hypersensitivity pancreatitis. Hepatotoxicity manifest by elevation of serum alkaline phosphatase, bilirubin, and/or serum transaminases is known to occur following azathioprine use, primarily in allograft recipients. Hepatotoxicity has been uncommon (less than 1%) in rheumatoid arthritis patients. Hepatotoxicity following transplantation most often occurs within 6 months of transplantation and is generally reversible after interruption of AZASAN™. A rare, but life-threatening hepatic veno-occlusive disease associated with chronic administration of azathioprine has been described in transplant patients and in one patient receiving AZASAN™ for panuveitis. Periodic measurement of serum transaminases, alkaline phosphatase, and bilirubin is indicated for early detection of hepatotoxicity. If hepatic veno-occlusive disease is clinically suspected, AZASAN™ should be permanently withdrawn.

Others: Additional side effects of low frequency have been reported. These include skin rashes (approximately 2%), alopecia, fever, arthralgias, diarrhea, steatorrhea and negative nitrogen balance (all less than 1%).

Other common recommendations from Medical Doctors: Ulcerative colitis is typically a chronic condition, so the goal of sufferers is to prevent flare-ups. Dietary changes may reduce the irritation of the intestine and reduce the risk of flare-ups. Raw fruits and vegetables may injure the lining of an inflamed intestinal lining. Reducing dairy intake may also reduce the irritation of the lining. Iron supplements may provide useful in offsetting the blood lost in the stool.

Nutritional Approach:

Disease or Condition: Peptic Ulcer

Causes of Peptic Ulcer: h-pylori bacteria, stress, chemicals, Anti-inflammatory drugs (NSAIDS)

Nutritional support:

Foods that have been proven to help with Peptic Ulcer:

Raw cabbage juice, bananas and plantains, broccoli, cauliflower, Brussels sprouts, kale and turnips, fenugreek seeds, fig, ginger, and licorice.

Nutrients that have been proven to help with Peptic Ulcer:

Vitamin C[842], A[843], and E[844], Zinc[845], L-Glutamine[846], Licorice[847], Olive Leaf[848], Mastic[849], Aloe Vera[850], Probiotics[851], Plant Source Digestive Enzymes.[852]

To find out more or to speak to a nutritional counselor for free, just visit us at:
www.CuresForTheBody.com

Exercises that have been proven to help with Peptic Ulcer:

Exercising daily has been proven in many studies to relieve stress and promote a strong immune system. Since ulcers can be linked to the h. pylori bacteria and healthy immune system is important in preventing this bacteria from causing ulcers.[853]

Basic Peptic Ulcer Plan:

  • Foods with Anti-Ulcer Activity:

–Bananas and plantains – studies showed 20% thickening of stomach wall.

–Raw cabbage juice – has been remarkably successful in treating ulcers. One quart of the fresh juice is prepared daily and taken in divided doses throughout the day. The juice can be prepared by using a standard juicing machine or putting the cabbage along with some water in a high speed blender. In one study, this therapy produced complete healing of ulcers in approximately ten days.

*An interesting note is that cabbage juice is very rich in L-glutamine.

*Indian researchers photographed the rejuvenation of ulcerated cells in guinea pigs. The healing was due to increased mucins, substances that shield the stomach lining from damage, produced by drinking cabbage juice.

• Other cruciferous vegetables (broccoli, cauliflower, Brussels sprouts, kale and turnips).

• Fenugreek seeds, fig, ginger, and licorice.

• Eating antibacterial foods such as…

–yogurt, cabbage and licorice may be more appropriate medicine against ulcers and gastritis, an inflammation of the stomach lining, than previously imagined.

–Physicians have discovered that a microbe known as H. pylori appears to be a cause of the two maladies in many cases. Ulcer treatment now often includes antibiotics. Antibacterial foods might also help cure the ulcer.

–Use raw coconut oil in baking rather than shortening or butter.[854]

Raw coconut oil was deemed guilty by association when all saturated fats were lumped in one and deemed bad for you. This great food source is now making a come back.

–It is rich in Lauric Acid which is antibacterial.[855] It also lowers cholesterol according to a report in the Journal of Nutrition 2001 "Consumption of a Solid Fat Rich in Lauric Acid Results in a More Favorable Serum Lipid Profile in Healthy Men and Women than Consumption of a solid fat rich in trans-fatty acids."

• **Take Plant Source Digestive Enzymes**

–People on anti-ulcer drugs such as Tagament and Zantac actually develop candida over- growth.in the stomach.[856] Lactobacillus Acidophilus(the good friendly bacteria) thrives on stomach acids and when it is neutralized by the antacid medication, it dies and bad bacteria flourish. This is why doctors prescribe antibiotics with stomach ulcers. A better solution for heartburn and acid reflux is plant source digestive enzymes. They help you digest the cooked food so that you don't experience indigestion and then you don't develope stomach ulcers and require antacids to heal it and in turn set the stage for candida overgrowth.

–Never use animal pancreatic enzymes.

• **Take Probiotics and Eat Yogurt**

–Eat yogurt – with live Probiotic cultures.

–Numerous studies report that Lactobacillus acidophilus bacteria inhibit the growth of Candida albicans and some studies report that ingestion of products containing lactobacillus acidophilus can be helpful in the prevention and treatment of intestinal and vaginal candidiasis.

–Most clinicians now agree on the importance of maintaining homeostatis of the microflora in health and disease.

*If supplementing Probiotics, it's best to take stabilized Probiotics.[857]

• If you won't eat your essential fatty acids, then take a high quality supplement.

–Pay attention to expiration dates, as essential fatty acids are very fragile and go rancid quickly when exposed to light, oxygen and heat.

• Take Lipase enzymes to properly digest fats.[858] (use only plant source digestive enzyme).

• Avoid alcohol, coffee and other caffeine-containing products, decaffeinated coffee, milk, sugar, and smoking.

• **Vitamin C**

Numerous studies report that individuals with ulcers have low levels of plasma vitamin C.

–Scientists have learned that most ulcers are caused by bacteria known as *Helicobacter pylori*, or *H. pylori*. In a study involving patients who had symptoms of painful digestion, proven chronic gastritis, and who were verified to be harboring *H. pylori* bacteria. In this 4-week study, one group of patients took 5 grams of vitamin C daily. By the end of the 4 weeks, 30% (8 of 27) of these patients had complete eradication of their H. pylori infections.

• **Vitamin A**

–Vitamin A has also proven to be an effective therapy in patients with chronic gastric ulcers. Patients in a clinical trial consumed 150,000 IU of vitamin A daily for four weeks. Endoscopic examination at the end of the 2nd and 4th weeks verified that there was significant reduction in the size of the ulcers and a progressive healing of the ulcers.

• **Vitamin E**

–In one study, researchers found that patients with gastric ulcers had very low levels of gastric antioxidants. They also reported that vitamin E levels were depleted in patients with gastritis and with gastric ulcers.

–Two studies published in the late 1950's reported that individuals on vitamin E deficient diets have a greater risk of developing gastric ulcers.

–Results from a study using the Shay's pylorus ligation model found that vitamin E helped provide protection against experimentally induced ulcers in animals. In addition to protecting the gastric mucosa against ulcers produced by either stress or chemicals, vitamin E also lowered the secretion of gastric acid. It was notable that the inhibition of acid secretion and the protection against the development of ulcers was much greater when vitamin E and selenium were administered together.

–A couple of small clinical trials with humans have reported that supplementation with vitamin E may be therapeutically useful in the healing of peptic ulcers.

• Zinc

–The results of an animal study indicate that zinc deficiency delays the rate of healing in gastric ulcers.

–Numerous studies report that zinc compounds are therapeutically useful in the treatment of ulcers. A compound named zinc acexamate reportedly reduces acid production and increases mucus secretion.

–In an animal study, it was reported that administration of zinc sulfate caused an increase production of mucus in the gastric wall in both stressed and non-stressed animals. The authors suggest that a similar mechanism may explain zinc's ulcer-reducing effects in man.

–A major side effect of diclofenac and most other NSAID medications is gastric irritation with frequent ulceration. When zinc was administered in conjunction with the diclofenac, it significantly reduced the ulcerogenic activity that normally occurs with the use of that anti-inflammatory drug.

–Ingestion of supplemental zinc for prolonged periods of time can result in a copper deficiency. Many physicians recommend 1 to 3 mg of copper daily when patients are taking 25 mg of zinc or more daily.

• L-Glutamine

–Glutamine is necessary for the growth of new tissue and the repair of injured tissue. It is especially useful in healing tissues in the gastrointestinal tract in conditions such as peptic ulcers and ulcerative colitis. Several decades ago studies began to publicize glutamine's healing effects on the gastric mucosa and its therapeutic usefulness in the treatment of peptic ulcers.

To find out more or to speak to a nutritional counselor for free, just visit us at:
www.CuresForTheBody.com

In one trial, glutamine provided a substantial level of protection against aspirin-induced gastric ulcers in both active and healed stages.

–In a double-blind, placebo-controlled human clinical trial, 57 patients received either glutamine (400 mg 4 times daily) or lactose along with the standard medical treatments. At the end of the 4-week trial, x-ray examinations revealed that 22 of 24 patients taking glutamine experienced a complete healing of their ulcers.

• **Licorice**

–Deglycyrrhizinated (DGL) licorice has the ability to protect irritated mucous membranes. In cases where the intestinal lining is inflamed, DGL licorice reportedly stimulates the production of mucus, and is used to reduce symptoms.

–When compared with cimetidine in several clinical studies, a proprietary DGL licorice product performed as effectively as the pharmaceutical counterpart.

• **Olive Leaf**

–Olive leaf extract has been reported to be an effective antimicrobial agent against a wide variety of pathogens.(including some penicillin-resistant strains), causal agents of intestinal or respiratory tract infections in man.

–Oleuropein also has been reported to directly stimulate macrophage (white blood cell) activation in laboratory studies.

• **Mastic**

–Mastic gum has been reported to inhibit *H. pylori in vitro.*

–Mastic gum also has been reported to have *in vitro* antifungal activity.

Mastic gum also has reported antibacterial activity, being active *in vitro* against *E. coli* and *Staph. Aureus.*

• **Aloe Vera**

Aloe vera leaf gel has also been reported useful in peptic ulcer disease.

–The constituent aloe-emodin also was reported to inhibit the growth of H. pylori *in vitro.*

To find out more or to speak to a nutritional counselor for free, just visit us at:
www.CuresForTheBody.com

Yeast Infections/Candidiasis

Description: Yeast infections are fungal infections caused by the candida species. There are more than 150 species of known Candida, but only eight are considered to be pathogenic to humans.[859] Candida normally lives on the skin, in the gastrointestinal tract, and in the female genital tract without causing an infection.

An infection usually only develops when the immune system is weakened and the body's normal checks do not keep it under control. The use of antibiotics can also increase the risk of Candidiasis as it destroys the good bacteria in the body that helps to keep the yeast in check. Immunosuppressive drugs increase the risk as they suppress the immune system.

Vaginal Candidiasis is more common in pregnant women, obese women, and women with diabetes. In addition, women who take hormone replacement therapy after menopause increase their risk of yeast infections.

Symptoms of a yeast infection generally include irritation and vaginal discharge. Redness and swelling may also be present. Occasionally, severe itching and burning may accompany an infection.

Medical Treatment:

Brand Name: Gynazole-1

Drug Name: Butoconazole Nitrate

Butoconazole Nitrate is presumed to function as other imidazole derivatives via inhibition of steroid synthesis. Imidazoles generally inhibit the conversion of lanosterol to ergosterol, resulting in a change in fungal cell membrane lipid composition. This structural change alters cell permeability and, ultimately, results in the osmotic disruption or growth inhibition of the fungal cell. Butoconazole nitrate is an imidazole derivative that has fungicidal activity *in vitro* and is clinically effective against vaginal infections due to *Candida albicans* .

Notable Side Effects:

Of the 314 patients treated with GYNAZOLE•1® for 1 day in controlled clinical trials, 18 patients (5.7%) reported complaints such as vulvar/vaginal burning, itching, soreness and swelling; pelvic or abdominal pain or cramping; or a combination of two or more of these symptoms. In 3 patients (1%) these complaints were considered treatment-related. Five of the 18 patients reporting adverse events discontinued the study because of them.

Brand Name: Diflucan

Drug Name: Fluconazole

Fluconazole is a highly selective inhibitor of fungal cytochrome P-450 sterol C-14 alpha-demethylation. Mammalian cell demethylation is much less sensitive to fluconazole inhibition. The subsequent loss of normal sterols correlates with the accumulation of 14 alpha-methyl sterols in fungi and may be responsible for the fungistatic activity of fluconazole.

Notable Side Effects:

(For a single dose) headache, nausea, and abdominal pain. Other side effects reported with an incidence equal to or greater than 1% included diarrhea, dyspepsia, dizziness, and taste perversion.

Other common recommendations from Medical Doctors: Good hygiene is the best preventative measure against a yeast infection. It is important to keep the genital area clean and wash with a mild soap daily. You should always wipe front to back after urinating and defecating. Also, wearing loose and absorbent clothing helps to keep the area dry.

Nutritional Approach:

Disease or Condition: Yeast (candidiasis) / Fungal Infections

To find out more or to speak to a nutritional counselor for free, just visit us at:
www.CuresForTheBody.com

Causes of Yeast (candidiasis) / Fungal Infections

Predisposing factors to Candida overgrowth: Altered bowel flora, Decreased digestive secretions, Dictary factors (high sugar diet), Drugs (particularly antibiotics), Impaired immunity, Impaired liver function, Nutrient deficiency, Prolonged antibiotic use, Underlying disease states.

Prolonged antibiotic use is believed to be the most important factor in the development of chronic candidiasis. Antibiotics suppress the immune system and the normal intestinal bacteria that prevent yeast over-growth, strongly promoting the proliferation of candida.

There is little argument that, when used appropriately, antibiotics save lives. However, there is also little argument that antibiotics are seriously overused. The widespread use and abuse of antibiotics is becoming increasingly alarming, not only because of the chronic candidiasis epidemic, but also due to the development of "superbugs" that are resistant to currently available antibiotics. According to the World Health Organization, we are coming dangerously close to arriving at a "postantibiotic era," in which many infectious diseases will once again become almost impossible to treat.[860]

Nutritional support:

Foods that have been proven to help with Yeast (candidiasis) / Fungal Infections:

Yogurt with probiotic cultures, Garlic and Flax seeds.[861]

Avoid refined flour and refined sugars and large amounts of honey, maple syrup, and fruit juice.

Avoid milk and other dairy products.

Avoid alcoholic beverages, cheeses, dried fruits, and peanuts.

Nutrients that have been proven to help with Yeast (candidiasis) / Fungal Infections:

Probiotics,[862] Plant Source Digestive Enzymes,[863] Cat's Claw,[864] Olive Leaf,[865] Garlic,[866] Tea Tree Oil,[867] Grapefruit Seed,[868] Larch Arabinogalactan.[869]

Exercises that have been proven to help with Yeast (candidiasis) / Fungal Infections:

To find out more or to speak to a nutritional counselor for free, just visit us at:
www.CuresForTheBody.com

In many cases yeast infections are caused by a weak immune system. A daily exercise routine will help promote a strong immune system which will help you to prevent and over come infections such as a yeast infection.[870]

Basic Yeast (candidiasis) / Fungal Infections Plan:
• **Sugar is the chief nutrient for Candida albicans**.

–Most people do well by simply avoiding refined flour, sugar and large amounts of honey, maple syrup and fruit juice.

–Milk's high lactose content (milk sugar) promotes the overgrowth of candida.

–Milk is one of the most common food allergens.

–Milk may contain trace levels of antibiotics, which can further disrupt the gastrointestinal bacterial flora and promote candida overgrowth.

• **Avoid** food with a high content of yeast or mold, including …

–alcoholic beverages, cheeses, dried fruits, and peanuts. (these may not cause you a problem, but it is best to avoid them until the condition is under control).

• Take Plant Source Digestive Enzymes

–Food Allergies are another common finding. Food allergies can be greatly eleviated by using Plant Source Digestive Enzymes. When we can't break down our food effectively we build up toxins and our body reacts to them.

–People on anti-ulcer drugs such as Tagament and Zantac actually develop candida over-growth in the stomach.[871] Lactobacillus Acidophilus(the good friendly bacteria) thrives on stomach acids and when it is neutralized by the antacid medication, it dies and bad bacteria flourish. This is why doctors prescribe antibiotics with stomach ulcers. A better solution for heartburn and acid reflux is plant source digestive enzymes. They help you digest the cooked food so that you don't experience indigestion and then you don't develope stomach ulcers and require antacids to heal it and in turn set the stage for candida overgrowth.

–Never use animal pancreatic enzymes.

• Take Probiotics

–Numerous studies report that Lactobacillus acidophilus bacteria inhibit the growth of Candida albicans and some studies report that ingestion of products containing lactobacillus acidophilus can be helpful in the prevention and treatment of intestinal and vaginal candidiasis.

To find out more or to speak to a nutritional counselor for free, just visit us at:
www.CuresForTheBody.com

–Most clinicians now agree on the importance of maintaining homeostatis of the microflora in health and disease.

–Even better, take stabilized Probiotics.[872]

• **Eat yogurt** – with live Probiotic cultures.

• **Eat and supplement garlic**

–It has antibacterial, antifungal, antiviral, and antiparasitic activities. There are several important actions that are attributed to the sulfur-containing compounds in garlic. These compounds (allicin and alliin) are reported to have anti-infective effects against bacteria and fungi.

–The impact of processing is an important fact to keep in mind when recommending garlic supplements. Changes can occur in the active constituents when exposed cooking or other processing which can render the garlic product virtually ineffective. Cooking is known to denature proteins and therefore may inactivate the enzyme (allinase) that is necessary in converting alliin into allicin, the major bio-active constituent in garlic.

• **Eat Flax Seeds**

–**The Lignans** in flax seeds are cyclic molecules with anti-viral, anti-fungal, anti-bacterial, and anti-cancer properties.

–Fresh ground flax seed (the oil has only 2% lignans) 6-8 Tbls. Maximum / day.

*Note: take freshly ground flax seed with five times its volume of fluid, because it absorbs that much liquid.

• **Cat's claw**

–The glycosides are also reported to enhance and stimulate phagocytosis, which if true would be a key part of cat's claw's immune function activity.

–Isopteridine, an alkaloid which has been isolated, is claimed to have immuno-stimulatory properties.

–Triterpenoid alkaloids and quinovic acid glycosides have been isolated and studied for antiviral activity, possibly inhibiting replications of some DNA viruses.

–Colon toxicity has been somewhat ignored in Western medicine. It is now becoming apparent that bowel hygiene and proper flora are essential to good health. If the colon flora is out of balance (dysbiosis) or if food is not being properly digested and assimilated, toxic metabolites and mutagens may be produced. Cat's claw is reported to have the ability to soothe irritated and inflamed tissues and help eliminate pathogens from the GI tract.

• **Olive Leaf**

To find out more or to speak to a nutritional counselor for free, just visit us at:
www.CuresForTheBody.com

–Olive leaf extract has been reported to be an effective antimicrobial agent against a wide variety of pathogens.(including some penicillin-resistant strains), causal agents of intestinal or respiratory tract infections in man.

–Oleuropein also has been reported to directly stimulate macrophage (white blood cell) activation in laboratory studies.

• Tea Tree Oil

–The therapeutic use of tea tree oil is largely based on its antiseptic and antifungal properties. This claim is supported by its effectiveness against a wide range of organisms including *Candida albicans, Propionibacterium acnes, Pseudomonas aeruginosa, Staphylococcus aureus, Staphylococcus epidermis, Streptococcus pyrogenes, Trichomonas vaginalis,* and *Trichomonas mentagrophytes.*

–Tea tree oil has historically been used in many conditions including the treatment of acne, aphthous stomatitis, tinea pedis, boils, burns, carbuncles, corns, gingivitis, herpes, empyema, impetigo, infections of the nail bed, insect bites, lice, mouth ulcers, pharyngitis, psoriasis, root canal treatment, ringworm, sinus infections, skin and vaginal infections, thrush, and tonsillitis - a literal panacea for topical infectious conditions.

–In vaginal candidiasis, tea tree oil suppositories or douche may be compounded by the pharmacist.

–Data indicates that some essential oils are active against *Candida* spp., suggesting that they may be useful in the topical treatment of superficial candida infections. Recent tests on three intra-vaginal tea tree oil products showed these products to have MICs and minimum fungicidal concentrations comparable to those of non-formulated tea tree oil, indicating that the tea tree oil contained in these products has retained its anti-candidal activity.

• Grapefruit Seed

–Grapefruit seed extract has been reported to be a broad-spectrum antimicrobial.

–Studies indicate that the antimicrobial activity of grapefruit seed extract exists in the cytoplasmic membrane of the invading bacteria, where the uptake of amino acids is prevented, there is disorganization of the cytoplasmic membrane and leakage of low molecular weight cellular contents ultimately resulting in inhibition of cellular respiration and death.

–Grapefruit seed extract also inhibits the growth of H. pylori and C. jejuni, both causative agents in gastrointestinal ulcers. Grapefruit seed extract is a useful agent in maintaining bowel integrity.

–In human study, an improvement in constipation, flatulence, abdominal distress, and night rest were noticed after 4 weeks of therapy.

• **Larch Arabinogalactin**

–Because of the immune-enhancing properties, LA is receiving increased attention as a clinically useful immunomodulating agent, and is effective against many bacteria, viruses, and fungi (including candida).

• **Take action to boost the immune system!**

Chapter 4 Footnotes

[1] "Enzyme Therapy of Digestive Disorders" by David Y. Graham in Enzymes as Drugs edited by John S. Holcenberg and Joseph Roberts. (New York: John Wiley & Sons, 1981).

[2] Shahani, K.M. and A.D. Ayebo, 1980, Role of dietary lactobacilli in gastrointestinal microecology, Proc. VI International Symposium on Intestinal Microecology, American Journal of Clinical Nutrition, 33 (11), 2448-2457.

[3] Fernandes, C.F., and K.M. Shahani, 1989, Lactose intolerance and its modulation with lactobacilli and other microbial supplements, Journal of Applied Nutrition, 41:50-64

[4] Becker, D. J.: A comparison of high and low fat meals on postprandial esophageal acid exposure. American Journal of Gastroenterology 1989; 84 (7):782-85

[5] Murphy, D. W.: Chocolate and heartburn: evidence of increased esophageal acid exposure after chocolate ingestion. American Journal of Gastroenterology 1988;83 (6):633-36.

[6] Vitale, G. C.: The effect of alcohol on nocturnal gastroesophageal reflux. Journal of American Medical Association 1987; 258:2077-79.

[7] Allen, M. L.: The effect of raw onions on acid reflux and reflux symptoms. American Journal of Gastroenterology 1990; 85 (4): 377-80.

[8] Price, S. F.: Food sensitivity in reflux esophagitis, Gastroenterology 1978; 75:240-43.

[9] "Enzyme Therapy of Digestive Disorders" by David Y. Graham in Enzymes as Drugs edited by John S. Holcenberg and Joseph Roberts. (New York: Joshn Wiley & Sons, 1981)

[10] K.M. Shahani and K.C. Chandan, 1979, Nutritional and Healthful Aspects of Cultured and Culture Continaing Dairy foods, Journal of Dairy Science 62:1685-94

[11] Ayebo A.D., I.A. Angelo and K.M. Shahani, 1981, Effect of ingesting Lactobacillus acidophilus milk upon fecal flor and enzyme activity in humans. Milchwissenschaft, 35: 730-733

[12] Shahani, K.M. and B.A. Friend, 1983, Properties of and prospects for cultured dairy products. In Food Microbiology)Skinner, F.A. and T.A. Roberts, eds), Academic Press, inc., London, pp. 257-269

[13] Fernandes, C.F., and K.M. Shahani, 1989 lactose intolerance and its modulation with lactobacilli and other microbial supplements, Journal of Applied Nutrition, 41:50-64

[14] Kligman AM. Postadolescent acne in women. Cutis. 1991;48:75-77

[15] Arndt KA, ed. Acne. In: Manual of Dermatologic Therapeutics, 5th ed. Boston: Little & Brown; 1995. 3-15.

[16] Melski JW, et al. Topical therapy for acne. N Engl J Med. 1980;302:503-506.

[17] Reisner RM. Management of acne. In: Goroll AH, May LA, Mulley AG, eds. Prinary Care Medicine, Office Evaluation and Management of the Adult Patient 3rd Ed. Philadelphia: Lippincott-Raven; 1995:911-914.

[18] Horrobin, D.F. *Essential Fatty Acids: A Review.*In: Horrobin, D.F. (ed) Clinical Uses of Essential Fatty Acids. London, England. Eden Press. 1982.

[19] Peck , S., Glick, A., Sobotka, H., and Chargin, L., 'Vitamin A studies in cases of keratosis folliculitis (Darier's disease)', Arch., Dermatol. Syph., 1943, 48, pp. 17-31 A. Kugman, O. Mills, J. Leyden, et al., :Oral Vitamin A in Acne Vulgaris," Int J Dermatol 20 (1981): 278-85

[20] Ayres S Jr, et al. Synergism of vitamins A and E with dermatologic applications. Cutis. May1979;23(5):600-3, 689-90.

[21]McCarthy, M., 'High Chromium Yeast for Acne?' Med. Hypoth., 1984, 14, pp. 307-10. Offenbach, E. and Pistunyer, F., 'Beneficial effect of chromium-rich yeast on glucose tolerance and blood lipids in elderly patients', Diabetes, 1980, 29, pp. 919-25.

Abdel, K.M., El Mofty, A., Ismail, A. and Bassili, F. , 'Glucose tolerance in blood and skin of patients with acne vulgaris', Ind. J. Derm., 1977, 22, pp 139-49.

[22]McCarthy, M., 'High Chromium Yeast for Acne?' Med. Hypoth., 1984, 14, pp. 307-10. Offenbach, E. and Pistunyer, F., 'Beneficial effect of chromium-rich yeast on glucose tolerance and blood lipids in elderly patients', Diabetes, 1980, 29, pp. 919-25.

[23]McCarthy, M., 'High Chromium Yeast for Acne?' Med. Hypoth., 1984, 14, pp. 307-10.

Offenbach, E. and Pistunyer, F., 'Beneficial effect of chromium-rich yeast on glucose tolerance and blood lipids in elderly patients', Diabetes, 1980, 29, pp. 919-25.

[24] FDA has approved sulfur as a safe and effective acne treatment.

[25] Verma KC. Oral zinc sulphate therapy in acne vulgaris: a double-blind trial. Acta Derm Venereol. Jan1980;60(4):337-40.

[26] Thappa DM, et al. Nodulocystic acne: oral gugulipid versus tetracycline. J Dermatol. Oct1994;21(10):729-31.

[27] Effect of lipase ingestion on blood lipid levels" James C. McPherson, et al. *Proceedings of the Society of Experimental Biology and Medicine* 115: 514-17 (1964).

[28] Enig, M.G. *Trans-Fatty Acids in the Food Supply: a comprehensive report covering 60 years of research.*Silver Springs, MD, Enig Associates. 1993.

[29] Lees, R. & Karel, M. *Omega 3 Fatty Acids in Health and Disease.* Basel, Switxerland. Dekker. 1990.

[30] Jung MO et al. *Effects of temperature and agitation rate on the formation of conjugated linoleic acids in soybean oil during hydrogenation process.* J Agric Food Chem 2001 Jun; 49(6): 3010-6.

[31] Minor, L. *Standards for Fats and Oils.* Westport, CT. Avi Publishing. 1985.

[32] De Roos, Nicole M, et al. "Consumption of a Solid Fat Rich in Lauric Acid Results in a More Favorable Serum Lipid Profile in Healthy Men and Women than Consumption of a Solid Fat Rich in trans-fatty Acids," Journal of Nutrition (2001): 131:242-245.

Prior, I. A., et al. "Cholesterol, coconuts, and diet on Polynesian atolls: a natural experiment: the Pukapuka and Tokelau Island studies," American Journal of Clinical Nutrition (1981): 34: 1552-1561.

St-Onge, Marie-Pierre, P.J.H. Jones, "Physiological Effects of Medium-Chain Triglycerides: Potential Agents in the Prevention of Obesity," Journal of Nutrition (2002): 132:329-332.

[33] Petschow, Byron W., et al. "Susceptiblity of Helicobacter pylori to Bactericidal Properties of Medium-Chain Monoglycerides and Free Fatty Acids ," Antimicrobial Agents and Chemotherapy (February 1996): 302-306.

[34] Effect of lipase ingestion on blood lipid levels" James C. McPherson, et al. *Proceedings of the Society of Experimental Biology and Medicine* 115: 514-17 (1964).

[35] Thappa DM, et al. Nodulocystic acne: oral gugulipid versus tetracycline. J Dermatol. Oct1994;21(10):729-31.

[36] Abdel, K.M., El Mofty, A., Ismail, A. and Bassili, F. , 'Glucose tolerance in blood and skin of patients with acne vulgaris', Ind. J. Derm., 1977, 22, pp 139-49.

H. Semon and F. Herrmann, "Some Observatins on the Sugar Metabolism in Acne Vulgaris, and it's Treatment by Insulin," Br J Derm 52 (1940)

[37] McCarthy, M., 'High Chromium Yeast for Acne?' Med. Hypoth., 1984, 14, pp. 307-10.

Offenbach, E. and Pistunyer, F., 'Beneficial effect of chromium-rich yeast on glucose tolerance and blood lipids in elderly patients', Diabetes, 1980, 29, pp. 919-25.

[38] Mowat. D.N. Chang x and Yang. W.Z. Can J An Science. 1993 Vol 73:49-55

[39] Abdel, K.M., El Mofty, A., Ismail, A. and Bassili, F. , 'Glucose tolerance in blood and skin of patients with acne vulgaris', Ind. J. Derm., 1977, 22, pp 139-49.

[40] Peck , S., Glick, A., Sobotka, H., and Chargin, L., 'Vitamin A studies in cases of keratosis folliculitis (Darier's disease)', Arch., Dermatol. Syph., 1943, 48, pp. 17-31 A. Kugman, O. Mills, J. Leyden, et al., :Oral Vitamin A in Acne Vulgaris," Int J Dermatol 20 (1981): 278-85

[41] FDA Consumer, July - August 1997, Revised September 1998: Healthy Pregnancy, Healthy Baby.

[42] FDA has approved sulfur as a safe and effective acne treatment.

[43] Ashmead, H.D., A Peptide Dependent Intestinal Pathway for the Absorption of Essential Minersals, Bioavailability Conference 88, Norwich, England.

[44] Zorrilla P, Salido JA, Lopez-Alonso A, Silva A. Serum zinc as a prognostic tool for wound healing in hip hemiarthroplasty. Clin Orthop. Mar2004;(420):304-8.

[45] Smeltzer SC, Bare BG. Medical-Surgical Nursing. Philadelphia: JB Lippincott Co; 1992.

[46] Hara H, et al. Short chain fatty acids suppress cholesterol synthesis in rat liver and intestine. J Nutr. May1999;129(5):942-8.

[47] Marz RB. Medical Nutrition from Marz. Portland, OR: Omni-Press; 1997.

[48] Ruskin SL. High dose vitamin C in allergy. Am J Dig Dis. 1945;12:281.

Johnston CS, et al. Antihistamine effect of supplemental ascorbic acid and neutrophil chemotaxis. J Am Coll Nutr. Apr1992;11(2):172-6.

To find out more or to speak to a nutritional counselor for free, just visit us at:
www.CuresForTheBody.com

[49] Bronner C, Landry Y. Kinetics of the inhibitory effect of flavonoids on histamine secretion from mast cells. Agents Actions. 1985;16(3-4):147-151.

Clemetson CA. Histamine and ascorbic acid in human blood. J Nutr. Apr1980;110(4):662-8.

Podoshin L, et al. Treatment of perennial allergic rhinitis with ascorbic acid solution. Ear Nose Throat J. Jan1991;70(1):54-5.

Pauling L. How to Live Longer and Feel Better. New York: W.H. Freeman and Company; 1986:201.

Middleton E, Drzewicki G. Effect of ascorbic acid and flavonoids on human basophil release. J Allerg Clin Immunol. Jan1992:278.

[50] Galland L. Increased requirements for essential fatty acids in atopic individuals: a review with clinical descriptions. J Am Coll Nutr. 1986;5(2):213-28.

Kankaanpaa P, et al. Dietary fatty acids and allergy. Ann Med. Aug1999;31(4):282-7.

Horrobin DF. Essential fatty acid metabolism and its modification in atopic eczema. Am J Clin Nutr. Jan2000;71(1 Suppl):367S-72S.

[51] Kuvaeva IB, et al. Microecology of the gastrointestinal tract and the immunological status under food allergy. Nahrung. 1984;28(6-7):689-93.

[52] Maffei Facino R, et al. Regeneration of Endogenous Antioxidants, Ascorbic Acid, Alpha Tocopherol, by the Oligomeric Procyanide Fraction of Vitus vinifera L:ESR Study. Boll Chim Farm. 1997;136(4):340-44.

Maffei Facino R, et al. Procyanidines from Vitis vinifera Seeds Protect Rabbit Heart from Ischemia/Reperfusion Injury: Antioxidant Intervention and/or Iron and Copper Sequestering Ability. Planta Med. 1996;62(6):495-502.

Maffei Facino R, et al. Free Radicals Scavenging Action and Anti-enzyme Activities of Procyanidines from Vitis vinifera. A Mechanism for Their Capillary Protective Action. Arzneim-Forsch/Drug Res. 1994;44(5):592-601.

Bernstein CK, Deng C, Shuklah R, et al. Abstract 1018 Double Blind Placebo Controlled (DBPC) Study of Grapeseed Extract in the Treatment of Seasonal Allergic Rhinitis (SAR). American Academy of Allergy, Asthma and Immunology (AAAAI) 57th Annual Meeting. Mar2001.

Lagrue G, et al. A Study of the Effects of Procyanidol Oligomers on Capillary Resistance in Hypertension and in Certain Nephropathies. Sem Hop. 1981;57(33-36):1399-1401.

Fitzpatrick DF, et al. Endothelium-dependent Vasorelaxing Activity of Wine and Other Grape Products. Am J Physiol. 1993;265(2 Pt 2):H774-H778.

Uchida S, et al. Active Oxygen Free Radicals Are Scavenged by Condensed Tannins. Prog Clin Biol Res. 1988;280:135-38.

Hatano T, et al. Effects of Interaction of Tannins with Co-existing Substances. VII. Inhibitory Effects of Tannins and Related Polyphenols on Xanthine Oxidase. Chem Pharm Bull (Tokyo). 1990;38(5):1224-29.

Mittman P. Randomized, Double-blind Study of Freeze-dried Urtica dioica in the Treatment of Allergic Rhinitis. Planta Med. Feb1990;56(1):44-47.

[53] Mittman P, et al. Randomized, Double-blind Study of Freeze-dried Urtica dioica in the Treatment of Allergic Rhinitis. Planta Medica. Feb1990;56(1):44.

[54] Bhat SV, et al. The Antihypertensive and Positive Inotropic Diterpene Forskolin: Effects of Structural Modifications on Its Activity. J Med Chem. 1983;26:486-92.

To find out more or to speak to a nutritional counselor for free, just visit us at:
www.CuresForTheBody.com

Baumann G, et al. Cardiovascular Effects of Forskolin (HL 362) in Patients with Idiopathic Congestive Cardiomyopathy — A Comparative Study with Dobutamine and Sodium Nitroprusside. Cardiovasc Pharmacol. 1990;16(1):93-100.

Seamon KB, et al. Forskolin: Its Biological and Chemical Properties," Advances in Cyclic Nucleotide and Protein Phosphorylation Research, vol 20. New York: Raven Press; 1986:1-150.

Doi K, et al. The Effect of Adenylate Cyclase Stimulation on Endocochlear Potential in the Guinea Pig. Eur

[55] Kreutner RW. Bronchodilator and Antiallergy Activity of Forskolin.European Journal of Pharmacology.

1985;111:1-8.

[56] Kirkwood CK, in DiPiro JT, et al. Pharmacotherapy, A Pathophysiologic Approach, 4th ed. Stamford,Conn: Appleton & Lange; 1999:1182-1196.

[57] Wingrove, J., A.J. Bond, A.J. Cleare and R. Sherwood, 1999, Plasma tryptophan and trait aggression, J. Psychopharmacology. 13: 235-237.

[58] Seelig MS, et al. Latent tetany and anxiety, marginal magnesium deficit, and normocalcemia. Dis Nerv Syst. Aug1975;36(8):461-5.

[59] Bockova E, et al. Potentiation of the effects of anxiolytics with magnesium salts. Cesk Psychiatr. Aug1992;88(3-4):141-4.

[60] Birdsall TC. 5-Hydroxytryptophan: a clinically-effective serotonin precursor. Altern Med Rev. Aug1998;3(4):271-80.

[61] McCann UD, et al. The effects of L-dihydroxyphenylalanine on alertness and mood in alpha-methyl-para-tyrosine-treated healthy humans. Further evidence for the role of catecholamines in arousal and anxiety. Neuropsychopharmacology. Aug1995;13(1):41-52.

[62] Replogle WH, Eicke FJ. Megavitamin therapy in the reduction of anxiety and depression among alcoholics. J Orthomol Med. 1989;4(4):221-224.

[63] Replogle WH, Eicke FJ. Megavitamin therapy in the reduction of anxiety and depression among alcoholics. J Orthomol Med. 1989;4(4):221-224.

[64] Singh YN. Kava: An Overview. J Ethnopharmacol. Aug1992;37(1):13-45.

[65] Newall CA, et al. Herbal Medicines: A Guide for Health Care Professionals. London: The Pharmaceutical Press; 1996:206-207.

[66] Lindahl O, Lindwall L. Double Blind Study of Valerian Preparations. Pharmacol Biochem Behav. 1989;32(4):1065-66.

[67] Volz HP. Controlled Clinical Trials of Hypericum Extracts in Depressed Patients - An Overview. Pharmacopsychiatry. 1997;30(Suppl 2):72-76.

[68] Bockova E, et al. Potentiation of the effects of anxiolytics with magnesium salts. Cesk Psychiatr. Aug1992;88(3-4):141-4.

[69] Hartvig P, et al. Pyridoxine effect on synthesis rate of serotonin in the monkey brain measured with positron emission tomography. J Neural Transm Gen Sect. 1995;102(2):91-7.

[70] Bermond P. Therapy of side effects of oral contraceptive agents with vitamin B6. Acta Vitaminol Enzymol. 1982;4(1-2):45-54.

[71] Pelton R. The Drug-Induced Nutrient Depletion HandbookThe Drug-Induced Nutrient Depletion Handbook. Hudson, OH: Lexi-Comp, Inc; 1999.

[72] Klaassen T, et al. Effects on mood of acute phenylalanine/tyrosine depletion in healthy women. Neuropsychopharmacology. Jan2000;22(1):52-63.

[73] Myers S. Use of neurotransmitter precursors for treatment of depression. Altern Med Rev. Feb2000;5(1):64-71.

[74] Birdsall TC. 5-Hydroxytryptophan: a clinically-effective serotonin precursor. Altern Med Rev. Aug1998;3(4):271-80.

[75] Miller HE, et al. Effect of acute tryptophan depletion on CO2-induced anxiety in patients with panic disorder and normal volunteers. Br J Psychiatry. Feb2000;176:182-8.

[76] Monteiro-Dos-Santos PC, et al. Effects of tryptophan depletion on anxiety induced by simulated public speaking. Braz J Med Biol Res. May2000;33(5):581-7.

[77] Sandyk R. L-tryptophan in neuropsychiatric disorders: a review. Int J Neurosci. Nov1992;67(1-4):127-44.

[78] Leyton M, et al. Effects on mood of acute phenylalanine/tyrosine depletion in healthy women. Neuropsychopharmacology. Jan 2000; 22(1):52-63.

[79] Moller SE. Effect of oral contraceptives on tryptophan and tyrosine availability: evidence for a possible contribution to mental depression. Neuropsychobiology. 1981;7(4):192-200.

[80] Volz HP, et al. Kava-kava Extract WS 1490 Versus Placebo in Anxiety Disorders - A Randomized Placebo-controlled 25-week Outpatient Trial. Pharmacopsychiatry. Jan1997;30(1):1-5.

[81] Lehrl S. Clinical efficacy of kava extract WS 1490 in sleep disturbances associated with anxiety disorders. Results of a multicenter, randomized, placebo-controlled, double-blind clinical trial. J Affect Disord. Feb2004;78(2):101-10.

[82] Munte TF, et al. Effects of Oxazepam and an Extract of Kava Roots (Piper methysticum) on Event-related Potentials in a Word Recognition Task. Neuropsychobiology. 1993;27(1):46-53.

[83] Drug Therapy of Panic Disorders. Kava-specific Extract WS 1490 Compared to Benzodiazepines. Nervenarzt. Jan1994;65(1Supp):14.

[84] Jussofie A, et al. Kavapyrone Enriched Extract from Piper methysticum as Modulator of the GABA Binding Site in Different Regions of Rat Brain. Psychopharmacology (Berl). Dec1994;116(4):469-74.

[85] Davies LP, et al. Kava Pyrones and Resin: Studies on GABAA, GABAB and Benzodiazepine Binding Sites in Rodent Brain. Pharmacol Toxicol. Aug1992;71(2):120-26.

[86] Holm E, et al. The Action Profile of D,L-kavain. Cerebral Cites and Sleep-wakefulness-Rhythm in Animals. Arzneimittelforschung. Jul1991;41(7):673-83.

[87] Duffield PH, et al. Development of Tolerance to Kava in Mice. Clinical and Experimental Pharmacology & Physiology. 1991;18(8):571-78.

[88] Singh YN. Kava: An Overview. J Ethnopharmacol. 1992;37(1): 13-45.

[89] Kimura R, et al. Central Depressant Effects of Maltol Analogs in Mice. Chem Pharm Bull (Tokyo). Sep1980;28(9): 2570-2579.

[90] Soulimani R, et al. Behavioural Effects of Passiflora incarnata L. and Its Indole Alkaloid and Flavonoid Derivatives and Maltol in the Mouse. J Ethnopharmacol. Jun1997;57(1):11-20.

[91] Bourin M, et al. A Combination of Plant Extracts in the Treatment of Outpatients with Adjustment Disorder with Anxious Mood: Controlled Study Versus Placebo. Fundam Clin Pharmacol. 1997;11(2):127-132.

[92] Wolfman C, et al. Possible Anxiolytic Effects of Chrysin, A Central Benzodiazepine Receptor Ligand Isolated from Passiflora coerulea. Pharmacol Biochem Behav. Jan1994;47(1):1-4.

[93] Spreoni E, et al. Neuropharmacological Activity of Extracts from Passiflora incarnata. Planta Med. Dec1988;54(6):488-91.

[94] Leathwood PD, et al. Aqueous Extract of Valerian Root (Valeriana officinalis L.) Improves Sleep Quality in Man. Pharmacol Biochem Behav. 1982;17:65-71.

[95] Balderer G, et al. Effect of Valerian on Human Sleep. Psvchopharmacology. 1985;87:406-09.

[96] Houghton PJ. The scientific basis for the reputed activity of Valerian. J Pharm Pharmacol. May 1999;51(5):505-12.

[97] Hendriks H, et al. Pharmacological Screening of Valerenal and Some Other Components of Essential Oil of Valeriana officinalis. Planta Medica. 1985;51:28-31.

[98] Houghton PJ. The Biological Activity of Valerian and Related Plants. J Ethnopharmacol. 1988;22(2):121-42.

[99] Santos MS, et al. Synaptosomal GABA Release as Influenced by Valerian Root Extract—Involvement of the GABA Carrier. Arch Int Pharmacodyn Ther. 1994;327(2):220-31.

[100] Leathwood PD, et al. Aqueous Extract of Valerian Root (Valeriana officinalis L.) Improves Sleep Quality in Man. Pharmacol Biochem Behav. 1982;17:65-71.

[101] Muller WE, et al. Effects of Hypericum Extract (LI 160) in Biochemical Models of Antidepressant Activity. Pharmacopsychiatry. 1997;30(Supp 2):102-07.

[102] Linde K, et al. St. John's Wort for Depression—An Overview and Meta-analysis of Randomised Clinical Trials. BMJ 313m. 1996:253-58.

[103] Nordfors M, Hatvig P. Hypericum Perforatum in the Treatment of Mild Depression. Lakrtidningen. 1997;94:2365-67.

[104] Bloomfield H, et al. Can Depression Be Successfully Treated with a Safe, Inexpensive, Medically Proven Herb Available Without a Prescription? Hypericum and Depression. California: Prelude Press; 1996:110-12.

[105] Suzuki O, et al. Inhibition of Monoamine Oxidase by Hypericin. Planta Medica. 1984;50:272-74.

[106] Bladt S, et al. Inhibition of MAO by Fractions and Constituents of Hypericum Extract. J Geriatric Psychiatry and Neurology. 1994;7:S57 S59.

[107] Murray M. Natural Alternatives to Prozac. New York: William Morrow and Company, Inc; 1996:137.

[108] Muller WEG, et al. Effects of Hypericum Extract on the Expression of Serotonin Receptors. J Geriatric Psychiatry and Neurology. 1994;7:S63-S64.

[109] Murch SJ, et al. Melatonin in Feverfew and Other Medicinal Plants. Lancet. Nov1997;350(9091):1598-9.

[110] Kaehler ST, et al. Hyperforin Enhances the Extracellular Concentrations of Catecholamines, Serotonin and Glutamate in the Rat Locus Coeruleus. Neurosci Lett. Mar1999;262(3):199-202.

To find out more or to speak to a nutritional counselor for free, just visit us at:
www.CuresForTheBody.com

[111] Ernst E. Second Thoughts About Safety of St John's wort. Lancet. Dec1999;354(9195):2014-6.

[112] Gordon JB. SSRIs and St.John's Wort: Possible Toxicity? Am Fam Physician. Mar1998;57(5):950,953.

[113] Lantz MS, et al. St. John's wort and Antidepressant Drug Ineractions in the Elderly. J Geriatr Psychiatr Neurol. 1999;12:7-10.

[114] Slater RR, et al. Monoclonal antibodies that detect biochemical markers of arthritis in humans. Arthritis Rheum. May1995;38(5):655-9.

[115] Effects of nonsteroidal anti-inflammatory drugs on chondrocyte metabolism in vitro and in vivo. Brandt KD. Department of Medicine, Indiana University School of Medicine, Indianapolis 46223.

[116] Udo Erasmus, Fats That Heal Fats That Kill, pg. 272,289

[117] McCarty MF. Enhanced synovial production of hyaluronic acid may explain rapid response to high-dose glucosaminein oseteoarthritis. Med Hypotheses. June 1998; (6): 507 10.

Delafuente JC. Glucosamin in the treatment of osteoarthritis. Rheum Dis. Clinica Feb2000:26(1):1-11.

Pavelka K, Gatterova J, Olejararova M, Machacek S, Giacovili G, Rovati LC. Glucosamine Sulfate Use and Delay of Progression of Knee Osteoarthritis: A 3-Year, Randomised Placebo-controlled, Double-blind Study. Arch Intern Med. Oct2002:162(18):211

[118] Bucsi L, Poor G. Efficacy and tolerability of oral chondroitin sulfate as a symptomatic slow-acting drug for osteoarthritis (SYSADOA) in the treatment of knee osteoarthritis Osteoarthritis Cartilage. May1998:6 Suppl A:31-6.

[119] Jacob SW, et al. The Miracle of MSM: The Natural Solution for Pain. New York Putnam's Sons; 199957-58.

[120] Konig B. A long-term (two years) clinical trial with S-adenosylmethionine for the treatment of osteoarthritis. Am J Med. Nov1987:83(5A):89-94.

[121] McAlindon TE, Jacques P, Ahang Y, Hannan MT, Aliabadi P, Weissman B, et al ., antioxidant micronutrients protect against the development and progression of osteoarthritis? Arthritis Rheum. Apr1996:39(4):648-56.

[122] Scherak O, et al. High dosage vitamin E therapy in patients with activated arthritis Rheomatol. Nov1990:49(6(:369-73.

[123] Hoffer A. Treatment of arthritis by nicotinic acid and nicotinamide. Can Med Arthritis Jonas WB, et al. The effect of niacinamide on osteoarthritis: a pilot study. Inflammation Jul1996;45(7):330-4.

[124] Newnham RE. Essentiality of boron for healthy bones and joints. Environ Health Perspect. Nov1994: 102 Suppl 7:83-5

[125] Majeed M, et al. Boswellin: The Anti-Inflammatory Phytonutrient. Piscataway, Nutriscience Publishing; 1996:2

Kimmatkar N, Thawani V, Hingorani L, Khiyani R. Efficacy and tolerability of Boswellia serrata exract in treatment of osteoarthritis of knee—a randomized double blind controlled trial. Phytomedicine. Jan2003;10(1):3-7.

[126] LiWG, Ahang XY, Wu Yj, Tian X. Anti-inflammatory effect and mechanism of proanthocyanidines from grape seeds. Acta Pharmacol Sin. Dec2001:22(12):111;

[127] Sandoval-Chacon M, Thompson JH, Zhang XJ, Liu X, Mannick EE, Sandowska-H, et al. Antiinflammatory actions of cat's claw: the role of NF-KappaB. Aliment Ther. Dec. 1998:12(12):1279-89. Forsch/Drug Res. 1986;36:715-17.

[128] Ammon HP, et al. Mechanismof Anti-inflammatory Actions of Curcumin. J Ethnopharmacol. 1993;38:113. Srivastava V, et al. Effect of Curcumin on Platelet Aggregation and Vascular Prostacyclin Synthesis.

[129] Altman RD, Marcussen KC. Effects of a ginger (Zingiber officinale) in Rheumatism and Musculoskeletal Disorders. Nov2001 ;44(!!) :2531-8.

[130]Donelly, P.K. et al. "The role of protease in immunoregulation." *British Journal of Surgery* 70: 614-22, (1983).

Effects of an oral enzyme preparation upon serum proteins associated with injury in man." *Journal of Medicine* (1974).

[131] Willis, A Handbook of Eicosnoid prostaglandisn and related lipids (Vol-1 Chemical and Biochemical aspects.) Boca Raton, FL CRC Press 1987

[132] Ibid

[133] BeareRogers J. (ed) Dietary Fat Requirements in Health and Development. Champaign, IL. AOCS. 1998

[134] Udo Erasmus, Fats that Heal Fats that Kill, Arthritis, pg. 354

[135] Tarayre, J.P.; Lauressergues, H. "Advantages of a combination of proteolytic enzymes, flavonoids and ascorbic acid in comparison with non-steroid anti-inflammatory agents." *Arzneimittel-Forschung (Drug Research)* 27 (I): 1144-9 (1977).

[136] Pavelka K, Gatterova J, Olejararova M, Machacek S, Giacovili G, Rovati LC. Glucosamine Sulfate Use and Delay of Progression of Knee Osteoarthritis: A 3-Year, Randomised Placebo-controlled, Double-blind Study. Arch Intern Med. Oct2002:162(18):211

[137] Bucsi L, Poor G. Efficacy and tolerability of oral chondroitin sulfate as a symptomatic slow-acting drug for osteoarthritis (SYSADOA) in the treatment of knee osteoarthritis Osteoarthritis Cartilage. May1998:6 Suppl A:31-6.

[138] McAlindon TE, Jacques P, Ahang Y, Hannan MT, Aliabadi P, Weissman B, et al ., antioxidant micronutrients protect against the development and progression of osteoarthritis? Arthritis Rheum. Apr1996:39(4):648-56.

[139] Jacob SW, et al. The Miracle of MSM: The Natural Solution for Pain. New York Putnam's Sons; 199957-58.

[140] Konig B. A long-term (two years) clinical trial with S-adenosylmethionine for the treatment of osteoarthritis. Am J Med. Nov1987:83(5A):89-94.

[141] Sandoval-Chacon M, Thompson JH, Zhang XJ, Liu X, Mannick EE, Sandowska-H, et al. Antiinflammatory actions of cat's claw: the role of NF-KappaB. Aliment Ther. Dec. 1998:12(12):1279-89.

[142] Ammon HP, et al. Mechanismof Anti-inflammatory Actions of Curcumin. J Ethnopharmacol. 1993;38:113.

Srivastava V, et al. Effect of Curcumin on Platelet Aggregation and Vascular Prostacyclin Synthesis. Arzneim Forsch/Drug Res. 1986;36:715-17.

[143] Altman RD, Marcussen KC. Effects of a ginger (Zingiber officinale) in Rheumatism and Musculoskeletal Disorders. Nov2001;44(!!):2531-8.

To find out more or to speak to a nutritional counselor for free, just visit us at:
www.CuresForTheBody.com

[144] Grassi W, De Angelis R, Lamanna G, Cervini C. The clinical features of rheumatoid arthritis. Eur J Radiol. May1998;27(Suppl1):S18-24.

[145] DiPiro JT, et al. Pharmacotherapy, A Pathophysiologic Approach, fourth edition. Stamford, Conn. Appleton and Lange; 1999:1427 1440

[146] Reveille JD. The Genetic Contribution to the Pathogenesis of Rheumatic Arthritis. Curr Opin Rheumatol. May1998; 10(3):187-200

[147] Gio-Fitman J. The Role of Psychological Stress in rheumatoid Arthritis. Medsurg Nurs. Dec1996;5(6):422-26

[148] Henrickson AE, et al. Small Intestinal Bacterial overgrowth in Patients with Rheumatoid Arthritis. Ann Rheum Dis. Jul1993;52(7):503 10

[149] Goldberg RL, et al. Effect of Heavy Metals on Human Rheumatoid Synovial Cell Proliferation and Collagen Synthesis. Biochem Pharmacol. Sep1983;32(18):2763-66

[150] Reveille JD. The Genetic Contribution to the Pathogenesis of Rheumatic Arthritis. Curr Opin Rheumatol. May1998; 10(3):187-200

[151] Udo Erasmus, Fats That Heal Fats That Kill, pg. 272,289 Delafuente JC. Glucosamin in the treatment of osteoarthritis. Rheum Dis. Clinica Feb2000:26(1):1-11.

Pavelka K, Gatterova J, Olejararova M, Machacek S, Giacovili G, Rovati LC. Glucosamine Sulfate Use and Delay of Progression of Knee Osteoarthritis: A 3-Year, Randomised Placebo-controlled, Double-blind Study. Arch Intern Med. Oct2002:162(18):211

[152] McCarty MF. Enhanced synovial production of hyaluronic acid may explain rapid response to high-dose glucosaminein oseteoarthritis. Med Hypotheses. June 1998; (6): 507-10.

[153] Bucsi L, Poor G. Efficacy and tolerability of oral chondroitin sulfate as a symptomatic slow-acting drug for osteoarthritis (SYSADOA) in the treatment of knee osteoarthritis Osteoarthritis Cartilage. May1998:6 Suppl A:31-6.

[154] Jacob SW, et al. The Miracle of MSM: The Natural Solution for Pain. New York Putnam's Sons; 199957-58.

[155] Konig B. A long-term (two years) clinical trial with S-adenosylmethionine for the treatment of osteoarthritis. Am J Med. Nov1987:83(5A):89-94.

[156] McAlindon TE, Jacques P, Ahang Y, Hannan MT, Aliabadi P, Weissman B, et al ., antioxidant micronutrients protect against the development and progression of osteoarthritis? Arthritis Rheum. Apr1996:39(4):648-56.

[157] Scherak O, et al. High dosage vitamin E therapy in patients with activated arthritis Rheomatol. Nov1990:49(6(:369-73.

[158] Hoffer A. Treatment of arthritis by nicotinic acid and nicotinamide. Can Med Arthritis Jonas WB, et al. The effect of niacinamide on osteoarthritis: a pilot study. Inflammation Jul1996;45(7):330-4.

[159] Newnham RE. Essentiality of boron for healthy bones and joints. Environ Health Perspect. Nov1994: 102 Suppl 7:83-5

[160] Majeed M, et al. Boswellin: The Anti-Inflammatory Phytonutrient. Piscataway, Nutriscience Publishing; 1996:2

Kimmatkar N, Thawani V, Hingorani L, Khiyani R. Efficacy and tolerability of Boswellia serrata exract in treatment of osteoarthritis of knee—a randomized double blind controlled trial. Phytomedicine. Jan2003;10(1):3-7.

[161] LiWG, Ahang XY, Wu Yj, Tian X. Anti-inflammatory effect and mechanism of proanthocyanidines from grape seeds. Acta Pharmacol Sin. Dec2001:22(12):111;

[162] Sandoval-Chacon M, Thompson JH, Zhang XJ, Liu X, Mannick EE, Sandowska-H, et al. Antiinflammatory actions of cat's claw: the role of NF-KappaB. Aliment Ther. Dec. 1998:12(12):1279-89.

[163] Ammon HP, et al. Mechanismof Anti-inflammatory Actions of Curcumin. J Ethnopharmacol. 1993;38:113.

Srivastava V, et al. Effect of Curcumin on Platelet Aggregation and Vascular Prostacyclin Synthesis. Arzneim Forsch/Drug Res. 1986;36:715-17.

[164] Altman RD, Marcussen KC. Effects of a ginger (Zingiber officinale) in Rheumatism and Musculoskeletal Disorders. Nov2001;44(!!):2531 8.

[165] Donelly, P.K et al. "The role of protease in immunoregulation." British Journal of Surgery 70: 14-22 (1983). Effects of an oral enzyme preparation upon serum proteins associated with injury in man." Journal of Medicine (1974).

[166] Rathgeber, W.F., "The use of proteolytic enzymes in sporting injuries." South African Medical Journal 45: 181-3 (1971)

[167]Willis, A Handbook of Eicosnoid prostaglandisn and related lipids (Vol-1 Chemical and Biochemical aspects.) Boca Raton, FL CRC Press 1987

[168]Ibid

[169] BeareRogers J. (ed) Dietary Fat Requirements in Health and Development. Champaign, IL. AOCS. 1998

[170] Udo Erasmus, Fats that Heal Fats that Kill, Arthritis, pg. 354

[171] See special note at beginning of chapter

[172] McCarty MF. Enhanced synovial production of hyaluronic acid may explain rapid response to high-dose glucosamine oseteoarthritis. Med Hypotheses. June 1998; (6): 507-10.

Delafuente JC. Glucosamin in the treatment of osteoarthritis. Rheum Dis. Clinica Feb2000:26(1):1-11.

Pavelka K, Gatterova J, Olejararova M, Machacek S, Giacovili G, Rovati LC. Glucosamine Sulfate Use and Delay of Progression of Knee Osteoarthritis: A 3-Year, Randomised Placebo-controlled, Double-blind Study. Arch Intern Med. Oct2002:162(18):211osteoarthritis (SYSADOA) in the treatment of knee osteoarthritis Osteoarthritis Cartilage. May1998:6 Suppl A:31-6.

[173]Bucsi L, Poor G. Efficacy and tolerability of oral chondroitin sulfate as a symptomatic slow-acting drug for osteoarthritis (SYSADOA) in the treatment of knee osteoarthritis. Osteoarthritis Cartilage, Double blind study. Arch Intern Me. Oct 2002: 162(18):211

[174] McAlindon TE, Jacques P, Ahang Y, Hannan MT, Aliabadi P, Weissman B, et al ., antioxidant micronutrients protect against the development and progression of osteoarthritis? Arthritis Rheum. Apr1996:39(4):648-56.

[175] Jacob SW, et al. The Miracle of MSM: The Natural Solution for Pain. New York Putnam's Sons; 199957-58.

[176] Konig B. A long-term (two years) clinical trial with S-adenosylmethionine for the treatment of osteoarthritis. Am J Med. Nov1987:83(5A):89-94.

To find out more or to speak to a nutritional counselor for free, just visit us at:
www.CuresForTheBody.com

[177] Sandoval-Chacon M, Thompson JH, Zhang XJ, Liu X, Mannick EE, Sandowska-H, et al. Antiinflammatory actions of cat's claw: the role of NF-KappaB. Aliment Ther. Dec. 1998:12(12):1279-89.

[178] Ammon HP, et al. Mechanismof Anti-inflammatory Actions of Curcumin. J Ethnopharmacol. 1993;38:113.

Srivastava V, et al. Effect of Curcumin on Platelet Aggregation and Vascular Prostacyclin Synthesis. Arzneim Forsch/Drug Res. 1986;36:715-17.

[179] Altman RD, Marcussen KC. Effects of a ginger (Zingiber officinale) in Rheumatism and Musculoskeletal Disorders. Nov2001;44(!!):2531-8.

[180] Hawkins DW, Rahn DW. Gout and Hyperuricemia. In: DiPiro JT, et al, eds. Pharmacotherapy, A Pathophysiologic Approach, 4th ed. Stamford, CT: Appleton & Lange; 1999

[181] Kelley WN, Worthman RL. Gout and hyperuricemia. In: Kelley WN, Harris EP, Ruddy S, Sledge CB, eds. Textbook of Rheumatology. Philadelphia: Saunders; 1997:1313-1351

[182] Udo Erasmus, Fats That Heal Fats That Kill, pg. 272,289

[183] McCarty MF. Enhanced synovial production of hyaluronic acid may explain rapid response to high-doseglucosaminein oseteoarthritis. Med Hypotheses. June 1998; (6): 507-10.

Delafuente JC. Glucosamin in the treatment of osteoarthritis. Rheum Dis. Clinica Feb2000:26(1):1-11.

Pavelka K, Gatterova J, Olejararova M, Machacek S, Giacovili G, Rovati LC. Glucosamine Sulfate Use and Delay of Progression of Knee Osteoarthritis: A 3-Year, Randomised Placebo-controlled, Double-blind Study. Arch Intern Med. Oct2002:162(18):211

[184]Bucsi L, Poor G. Efficacy and tolerability of oral chondroitin sulfate as a symptomatic slow-acting drug for osteoarthritis (SYSADOA) in the treatment of knee osteoarthritis Osteoarthritis Cartilage. May1998:6 Suppl A:31-6.

[185] Jacob SW, et al. The Miracle of MSM: The Natural Solution for Pain. New York Putnam's Sons; 199957-58.

[186] Konig B. A long-term (two years) clinical trial with S-adenosylmethionine for the treatment of osteoarthritis. Am J

Med. Nov1987:83(5A):89-94.

[187] McAlindon TE, Jacques P, Ahang Y, Hannan MT, Aliabadi P, Weissman B, et al ., antioxidant micronutrients protect against the development and progression of osteoarthritis? Arthritis Rheum. Apr1996:39(4):648-56.

[188] Scherak O, et al. High dosage vitamin E therapy in patients with activated arthritis Rheomatol. Nov1990:49(6(:369-73.

[189]Hoffer A. Treatment of arthritis by nicotinic acid and nicotinamide. Can Med Arthritis Jonas WB, et al. The effect of niacinamide on osteoarthritis: a pilot study. Inflammation Jul1996;45(7):330-4.

[190] Newnham RE. Essentiality of boron for healthy bones and joints. Environ Health Perspect. Nov1994: 102 Suppl 7:83-5

[191] Majeed M, et al. Boswellin: The Anti-Inflammatory Phytonutrient. Piscataway, Nutriscience Publishing; 1996:2

To find out more or to speak to a nutritional counselor for free, just visit us at:
www.CuresForTheBody.com

Kimmatkar N, Thawani V, Hingorani L, Khiyani R. Efficacy and tolerability of Boswellia serrata exract in treatment of osteoarthritis of knee—a randomized double blind controlled trial. Phytomedicine. Jan2003;10(1):3-7.

[192] LiWG, Ahang XY, Wu Yj, Tian X. Anti-inflammatory effect and mechanism of proanthocyanidines from grape seeds. Acta Pharmacol Sin. Dec2001:22(12):111;

[193] Sandoval-Chacon M, Thompson JH, Zhang XJ, Liu X, Mannick EE, SandowskaH, et al. Antiinflammatory actions of cat's claw: the role of NF-KappaB. Aliment Ther. Dec. 1998:12(12):1279-89.

[194] Srivastava V, et al. Effect of Curcumin on Platelet Aggregation and Vascular Prostacyclin Synthesis. Arzneim Forsch/Drug Res. 1986;36:715-17.

[195] Altman RD, Marcussen KC. Effects of a ginger (Zingiber officinale) in Rheumatism and Musculoskeletal Disorders. Nov2001;44(!!):2531-8.

[196] Donelly, P.K et al. "The role of protease in immunoregulation." British Journal of Surgery 70: 14-22 (1983). Effects of an oral enzyme preparation upon serum proteins associated with injury in man." Journal of Medicine (1974).

[197] Rathgeber, W.F., "The use of proteolytic enzymes in sporting injuries." South African Medical Journal 45: 181-3 (1971)

[198] Willis, A Handbook of Eicosnoid prostaglandisn and related lipids (Vol-1 Chemical and Biochemical aspects.) Boca Raton, FL CRC Press 1987

[199] Ibid

[200] 136 BeareRogers J. (ed) Dietary Fat Requirements in Health and Development. Champaign, IL. AOCS. 1998

[201] Udo Erasmus, Fats that Heal Fats that Kill, Arthritis, pg. 354

[202] Sherry, Sol and Fletcher, Anthony P. "Proteolytic enzymes: a therapeutic evaluation." *Clinical Pharmacology and Therapeutics.* 1: 202-6 (1961).

[203] McCarty MF. Enhanced synovial production of hyaluronic acid may explain rapid response to high-dose glucosamine oseteoarthritis. Med Hypotheses. June 1998; (6): 507-10.

Delafuente JC. Glucosamin in the treatment of osteoarthritis. Rheum Dis. Clinica Feb2000:26(1):1-11.

Pavelka K, Gatterova J, Olejararova M, Machacek S, Giacovili G, Rovati LC. Glucosamine Sulfate Use and Delay of Progression of Knee Osteoarthritis: A 3-Year, Randomised Placebo-controlled, Double-blind Study. Arch Intern Med. Oct2002:162(18):211

[204] Bucsi L, Poor G. Efficacy and tolerability of oral chondroitin sulfate as a symptomatic slow-acting drug for osteoarthritis (SYSADOA) in the treatment of knee osteoarthritis Osteoarthritis Cartilage. May1998:6 Suppl A:31-6.

[205] McAlindon TE, Jacques P, Ahang Y, Hannan MT, Aliabadi P, Weissman B, et al ., antioxidant micronutrients protect against the development and progression of osteoarthritis? Arthritis Rheum. Apr1996:39(4):648-56.

[206] Jacob SW, et al. The Miracle of MSM: The Natural Solution for Pain. New York Putnam's Sons; 199957-58.

[207] Konig B. A long-term (two years) clinical trial with S-adenosylmethionine for the treatment of osteoarthritis. Am J Med. Nov1987:83(5A):89-94.

[208] Sandoval-Chacon M, Thompson JH, Zhang XJ, Liu X, Mannick EE, Sandowska-H, et al. Antiinflammatory actions of cat's claw: the role of NF-KappaB. Aliment Ther. Dec. 1998:12(12):1279-89.

[209] Ammon HP, et al. Mechanismof Anti-inflammatory Actions of Curcumin. J Ethnopharmacol. 1993;38:113.

Srivastava V, et al. Effect of Curcumin on Platelet Aggregation and Vascular Prostacyclin Synthesis. Arzneim Forsch/Drug Res. 1986;36:715-17.

[210] Altman RD, Marcussen KC. Effects of a ginger (Zingiber officinale) in Rheumatism and Musculoskeletal Disorders. Nov2001;44(!!):2531-8.

[211] American Thoracic Society. Committee on diagnostic standards for non-tuberculosis respiratory disease: Definition and classification of chronic bronchitis, asthma, and pulmonary edema. Am Rev Resp Dis. 1962;85:762

[212] Hamilton K, Roberson K. Asthma. Sacramento, CA. IT Services; 1997.

[213] Davis WH, Leary WP, Reyes AJ, and Olhaberry JV: Monotherapy with magnesium increases abnormally low high density lipoprotein cholesterol: A clinical assay. Curr Ther Res 36: 341-5, 1984.

[214] Sanders TAB and Roshanai F: The influence of different types of omega-3 polyunsaturated fatty acids on blood lipids and platelet function in healthy volunteers.

[215] Salonen JT: Association between cardiovascular death and myocardial infarction and serum selenium in a matched-pair longitudinal study. Lancet 2: 175-9, 1982.

[216] Turley S. West C. and Horton B: Role of ascorbic acid in the regulation of cholesterol metabolism and the pathogenesis of atherosclerosis. Atherosclerosis 24: 1-18, 1976.

[217] Dr. Edward Howell, Enzyme Nutrition, Enzymes to the Rescue, pg. 143.

[218] Cohen HA, et al. Blocking effect of vitamin C in exercise-induced asthma. Arch Pediatr Adolesc Med. Apr1997;151(4):367-70.

[219] Lei J, et al. Pharmacological Study on Cordyceps sinensis (Berk.) Sacc. and ze-e Cordyceps. Chung Kuo Chung Yao Tsa Chih. Jun1992;17(6):364-66.

[220] Gupta S, et al. Tylophora Indica in Bronchial Asthma—A Double Blind Study. Indian J Med Res. 1979;69:981-89.

[221] Bhat SV, et al. The Antihypertensive and Positive Inotropic Diterpene Forskolin: Effects of Structural Modifications on Its Activity. J Med Chem. 1983;26:486-92

[222] Baumann G, et al. Cardiovascular Effects of Forskolin (HL 362) in Patients with Idiopathic Congestive Cardiomyopathy — A Comparative Study with Dobutamine and Sodium Nitroprusside. Cardiovasc Pharmacol. 1990;16(1):93-100.

[223] Udo Erasmus, Fats that Heal Fats that Kill, Arthritis, pg. 354

[224] Delport R, et al. Theophylline increases pyridoxal kinase activity independently from vitamin B6 nutritional status.

Res Commun Chem Pathol Pharmacol. Mar1993;79(3):325-33.

[225] Delport R, et al.Theophylline increases pyridoxal kinase activity independently from vitamin B6 nutritional status.

Res Commun Chem Pathol Pharmacol. Mar1993;79(3):325-33

[226] Anibarro B, et al.Asthma with sulfite intolerance in children: a blocking study with cyanocobalamin. J Allergy Clin Immunol. Jul1992;90(1):103-9.

[227]Simon SW. Vitamin B12 therapy in allergy and chronic dermatoses. J Allergy. 1951;22:183-185.

[228] Britton J, et al. Dietary Magnesium, Lung Function, Wheezing and Airway Hyperreactivity in a Random Adult Population Sample. Lancet. Aug1994;344:357-62.

[229] Physiology and clinical effects of buccally given proteases. Irving Innerfield, JAMA 170: 9259. 1959.

[230] Deitrick, R.E., MD. "Oral Proteolytic enzymes in the treatment of athletic injuries: a double-blind study." *The Pennsylvania Medical Journal* 68(10): 35-7 (1965).

[231] McGough JJ, McCracken JT. Assessment of attention deficit hyperactivity disorder: a review of recent literature. Curr Opin Pediatr. Aug2000;12(4):319-24.

[232] Cantwell CB. Attention Deficit Disorder: A review of the last 10 years. J Am Acad Child Adolesc Psychiatry. 1996;35:978-987.

[233] Zametkin AJ. Attention Deficit Disorder: Born to be hyperactive? Grand rounds at the Clinical Center of the National Institutes of Health. JAMA. 1995;16:174-184.

[234] Hanna GL, Ornitz EM, Hariharan M. Urinary catecholamine excretion and behavioral differences in ADHD and normal boys. J Child Adolesc Psychopharmacol. 1996;6(1):63-73.

[235] Burgess JR, Stevens L, Zhang W, Peck L. Long-chain polyunsaturated fatty acids in children with attention-deficit hyperactivity disorder. Am J Clin Nutr. Jan2000;71(1 Suppl):327S-30S.

[236] Burgess JR, etal. Long-chain polyunsaturated fatty acids in children with attention deficit hyperactivity disorder (ADHD). Magnes Res. Jun1997:10(2):143.

[237] M. Colgan and L. Colgain, "Do Nutrient Supplements and Dietary Changes Affect learning and emotional Reactions of Childrn with Learning and Emotional Reactions of Children with Learning Disabilities? A controlled Series of 16 Cases," Nutr Health 3 (1984):69-77.

J. Kerschner and W. Hawke, "Magavitmains and Learning Disorders: A Controlled Double-Blind Wxperiment." J Nutr 109 (1979):819-826.

[238] Starobrat-Hermelin B. Assessment of magnesium levels in children with attention deficit hyperactivity disorder (ADHD). Positive response to magnesium oral loading test. Magnes Res. Jun199 (2):149-56.

[239] James F. Balch, M.D. and Phyllis A. Balch, C.N.C., Prescription for Nutritional Healing, Attention Deficit Hyperactivity Discorder, pg.330.

[240] James F. Balch, M.D. and Phyllis A. Balch, C.N.C., Prescription for Nutritional Healing, Attention Deficit Hyperactivity Discorder, pg.330, Gamma-Aminobutyric Acid pg. 38..

[241] Tseng R, Mellon J and Bammer K:

The Relationship Between Nutrition and Student Achievement, Behavior, and Health – A Review of the Literature.

California State Department of Education, Sacramento, Ca. 1980.

[242] Mitchell EA, et al. Clinical characteristics and serum essential fatty acid levels of hyperactive children. Clin. Pediatr (Phila). Aug1987;26(8):406-11.

[243] Albion Mineral Amino Acid Chelates and *Absorbing Story.*Clearfield, UT.

[244] Murray, Michael, N.D., and Pizzorno, Josesph, N.D. Encyclopedia of Natural Healing, Attention Deficit Disorder, Nutrient Deficiency, pg. 279

[245] "Gastrointestinal absorption of intact proteins." Michael LG Gardner. *Annual Review of Nutrition* 8:329-50 (1988)

[246] Hagerman RJ, Falkenstein AR. An association between recurrent otisis media and later hyperactivity. Clin Rediatr (Phila). May1987;26(5):253-7.

[247] Vanderhoof, JA DB Whitney DL Antonson, TL Hanner JV lupon and RJ Young, 1999, Lactobacillus GG in the prevention of Antiboitic-associated diarrhea in children; J Pediatr 135:564-568

[248] Ottenwalder H, Simon P. Differential effect of N-acetylcysteine on excretion of toxic metals hg, cd, Pb and Au. Arch Toxicol. Jul1987;60(5):401-2.

[249] Ottenwalder H, Simon P. Defferential effect of –acetylcysteinne on excretion of toxic metals Hg, Cd, Pb and Au. Arch Toxicol. Jul1987:60(5):401-2.

[250] Rehab Breif: Chronic Back Pain. Vol XV, No. 7 (1993). ISSN: 0732-2623. National Institute of Disability and Rehabilitation Research Office of Special Education and Rehabilitative Services Department of Education, Washington, D.C. 20202

[251] Waddell, Kummel, Lotto, Graha, Hall, & McCulloch, 1979. Failed lumber disc surgery and repeat surgery following industrial injuries. *The Journal of Bone and Joint Surgery*, 61, 201-207.

[252] Erasmus, Udo. Fats that Heal Fats that Kill, Thriteenth Printing. Pg 44

[253] Jacob SW, et al. The Miracle of MSM: The Natural Solution for Pain. New York: GP Putnam's Sons; 1999:57-58.

[254] McAlindon TE, et al. Glucosamine and chondroitin for treatment of osteoarthritis: a systematic quality assessment and meta-analysis. JAMA. Mar2000;283(11):1469.

[255] Leeb BF, et al. A metaanalysis of chondroitin sulfate in the treatment of osteoarthritis. J Rheumatol. Jan2000;27(1):205-11.

[256] Rathgeber, W.F., "The use of proteolytic enzymes in sporting injuries."*South African Medical Journal* 45: 181-3 (1971).

[257] Albion Mineral Amino Acid Chelates an *Absorbing Story.*Clearfield, UT.

[258]Monograph:Bromelain. Altern Med Rev. Aug1998;3(4):302-5.

[259] Tassman GC, Zafran JN, Zayon GM. A double-blind crossover study of a plant proteolytic enzyme in oral surgery. J Dent Med. 1965;20:51-54.

[260] Tassman GC, Zafran JN, Zayon GM. Evaluation of a plant proteolytic enzyme for the control of inflammation and pain. J Dent Med. 1964;19:73-77.

[261] Fusco BM, Giacovazzo M. Peppers and pain. The promise of capsaicin. Drugs 1997;53-909-14.

[262] Manga, P. et al. The effectiveness and cost-effectiveness of chiropractic management of low-back pain. University of Ottawa, Canada: Pran Manga and Associates, 1993.

[263] Meade, TW, Dyer, S. et al. Low back pain of mechanical origin: Randomized comparison of chiropractic and hospital outpatient treatment. British Medical Journal. June 1990, 300, pp. 431-437.

[264] Leboeuf-Yde C, Kyvik KO, Bruun NH. Low back pain and lifestyle. Part 1: Smoking. Information from a population base sample of 29,424 twins. *Spine* 1998;23:2207-13.

[265] Ernst E. Smoking is a risk factor for spinal diseases. Hypothesis of the patomechanism. *Wien Klin Wocenschr* 1992;104:626-30.

To find out more or to speak to a nutritional counselor for free, just visit us at:
www.CuresForTheBody.com

[266] Plumridge RJ, Golledge CL. Treatment of urinary tract infection: Clinical and economic considerations. Pharmacoeconomics. 1996;9:295-306.

[267] Cranberry May Offer Protection Against Antibiotic-Resistant Bacteria That Cause Urinary Tract Infections. June 19, 2002 issue of The Journal of the American Medical Association (JAMA).

[268] Cranberry May Offer Protection Against Antibiotic-Resistant Bacteria That Cause Urinary Tract Infections. June 19, 2002 issue of The Journal of the American Medical Association (JAMA).

[269] Bradley, P.R. (ed.). 1992. British Herbal Compendium, Vol. 1. Bournemouth: British Herbal Medicine Association

[270] Guillot, N., 1958 Elaboration par Lactobacillus aciddophillus d'un produit actif contre Candida albicans, Ann. Inst. Pasteur 95, 194-207

[271] Wood, J.R., Sweet, R.L., Catena. A., Hadley. W.K. and Robbie, M. (1985) In vitro adherence of Lactobacillus species to vaginal epithelial cells. Am. J. Obstet. Gynecol. 153. 740-743.

[272] Source: Lee, I-Min. Harvard Medical School, "Physical Activity and Cancer," PCPFS Research Digest 2:2.

[273] Balch, James and Phyllis Balch Perscriptions for Natural Healing.

[274] Collins, E.B. and P. Hardt, 1980, Inhibition of Candida albicans by Lactobacillus acidophilus J. Dairy Sci. 63, 830-832.

[275] Balch, James and Phyllis Balch Perscriptions for Natural Healing. 158.

[276] Kim L. ONeill, Ph.D., and Bryan S. Poe "Cancer Letters," Irish Journal, Elsevier Science, Dec. 1997 vol. 121 pg..1-6. Author of "Power Foods".

[277] Lau, Benjamin H. S.: Garlic compounds modulate macrophage and T-lymphocyte functions. Molecular Biotherapy 1991; 3:1037.

[278] Henson, D. E.: Ascorbic acid: biologic functions and relation to cancer. Journal of the National Cancer Institute 1991;83(8):547-50.

[279] Schwartz, J. L.: Beta carotene and/or vitamin E as modulators of alkylating agents in SCC-25 human squamous carcinoma cells. Cancer Chemotherapy and Pharmacology 1992; 29(3):207-13.

[280] Karmali, R. A.: Omega-3 fatty acids and cancer. Journal of Internal Medicine 1989;225 (suppl. 1):197-200.

[281] Reddy, G.V. K.M. Shahani and M.R. Ganaerjee, 1973, Effect of yogurt on Ehrlich ascites tumor-cell proliferation", Journal Nat

'l Cancer Institute: 50: 815-817

[282] "Application of Enzyme Supplements" by A.V. Modyanoc and V.R. Zel'ner in Handbook of Nutritional Supplements: Volume II, Agricultural Use edited by Miloslav Rechcigl, Jr. Boca Raton, F1: CRC Press, 1983.

[283] Ann N Y Acad Sci. 1990;587:110-2.

[284] Source: Lee, I-Min. Harvard Medical School, "Physical Activity and Cancer," PCPFS Research Digest 2:2.

[285] Willett, W. C.: Relation of meat, fat, and fiber intake to the risk of colon cancer in a prospective study among women. New England Journal of Medicine 1990; 323:1664-72.

To find out more or to speak to a nutritional counselor for free, just visit us at:
www.CuresForTheBody.com

[286] Ziegler, R. G.: Does beta-carotene explain why reduced cancer risk is associated with vegetable and fruit intake? Cancer Research 1992;52(suppl.7):2060s-66s.

Caragay, A. B.: Cancer-preventative foods and ingredients. Food Technology 1992; 46:65-68.

Steinmetz, K. A.: Vegetables fruit, and cancer. I. Epidemiology. Cancer Causes Control 1991;2(5):325-57.

Steinmetz, K. A.: Vegetables fruit, and cancer. II. Epidemiology. Cancer Causes Control 1991;2(6):427-42.

[287] Howe, G R.: Dietary intake of fiber and decreased risk of cancers of the colon and rectum: evidence from the combined analysis of 13 case-control studies. Journal of the National Cancer Institute 1992; 84(24):1887-96.

[288] Zhang, Yuesheng: A major inducer of anticarcinogenic protective enzymes from broccoli: isolation and elucidation of structure. Proceedings of the National Academy of Sciences 1992:89:2399-2403.

[289] Messina, M.: The role of soy products in reducing risk of cancer. Journal of the National Cancer Institute 1991;83(8):541-46.

[290] De Roos, Nicole M, et al. "Consumption of a Solid Fat Rich in Lauric Acid Results in a More Favorable Serum Lipid Profile in Healthy Men and Women than Consumption of a Solid Fat Rich in trans-fatty Acids," Journal of Nutrition (2001): 131:242-245.

Prior, I. A., et al. "Cholesterol, coconuts, and diet on Polynesian atolls: a natural experiment: the Pukapuka and Tokelau Island studies," American Journal of Clinical Nutrition (1981): 34: 1552-1561.

St-Onge, Marie-Pierre, P.J.H. Jones, "Physiological Effects of Medium-Chain Triglycerides: Potential Agents in the Prevention of Obesity," Journal of Nutrition (2002): 132:329-332.

[291] Petschow, Byron W., et al. "Susceptiblity of Helicobacter pylori to Bactericidal Properties of Medium-Chain Monoglycerides and Free Fatty Acids ," Antimicrobial Agents and Chemotherapy (February 1996): 302-306.

[292] Fats that heal, Udo Errasmus

[293] Effect of lipase ingestion on blood lipid levels, James C. MecPHerson, et al. Proceedings of the Society of Experimental Biology and Medicine 115: 514-17 (1964)

[294] Lau, Benjamin H. S.: Garlic compounds modulate macrophage and T-lymphocyte functions. Molecular Biotherapy 1991; 3:1037.

[295] Mettlin C. J.: Patterns of milk consumption and risk of cancer. Nutrition and Cancer 1990;13(1-2):207-13.

[296] Albion Mineral Amino Acid Chelates and *Absorbing Story.*Clearfield, UT.

[297] "Composition of Foods." Agriculture Handbook, Nov. 8, U.S. Dept. of Agriculture

[298] Cush JJ, Lipsky PE. Approach to Articular and Musculoskeletal disorders. In: Fauci AS, Braunwald E, Isselbacher KJ, et al. eds. Harrison's Principles of Internal Medicine 14th ed. New York: McGraw-Hill; 1998:1933.

[299] Ellis JM, et al. Vitamin B6 deficiency in patients with a clinical syndrome including the carpal tunnel defect. Biochemical and clinical response to therapy with pyridoxine. Res Commun Chem Pathol Pharmacol. Apr1976;13(4):743-57.

[300] Ellis JM, et al. Survey and new data on treatment with pyridoxine of patients having a clinical syndrome including the carpal tunnel and other defects. Res Commun Chem Pathol Pharmacol. May1977;17(1):165-77.

To find out more or to speak to a nutritional counselor for free, just visit us at:
www.CuresForTheBody.com

[301] Ellis JM. Treatment of carpal tunnel syndrome with vitamin B6. South Med J. Jul1987;80(7):882-4.

[302] Franzblau A, et al. The relationship of vitamin B6 status to median nerve function and carpal tunnel syndrome among active industrial workers. J Occup Environ Med. May1996;38(5):485-91.

[303] Folkers K, et al. Enzymology of the response of the carpal tunnel syndrome to riboflavin and to combined riboflavin and pyridoxine. Proc Natl Acad Sci U S A. Nov1984;81(22):7076-8.

[304] Wagner H. Search for New Plant Constituents with Potential Antiphlogistic and Antiallergic Activity. Planta Med. Jun1989;55(3):235-241.

[305] Boswellia serrata. Altern Med Rev. Aug1998;3(4):306-307.

[306] Ammon HP. Salai Guggal - Boswellia serrata: From an Herbal Medicine to a Non-redox Inhibitor of Leukotriene Biosynthesis. Eur J Med Res. May1996;1(8):369-370.

[307] Ammon HP, et al. Inhibition of Leukotriene B4 Formation in Rat Peritoneal Neutrophils by an Ethanolic Extract of the Gum Resin Exudate of Boswellia serrata. Planta Med. Jun1991;57(3):203-207.

[308] Redini F, et al. Modulation of Extracellular Matrix Metabolism in Rabbit Articular Chondrocytes and Human Rheumatoid Synovial Cells by the Non-steroidal Anti-inflammatory Drug Etodolac. II: Glycosaminoglycan Synthesis. Agents Actions. Nov1990;31(3-4):358-367.

[309] Boswellia serrata. Altern Med Rev. Aug1998;3(4):306-307.

[310] Rao CV. Chemoprevention of colon carcinogenesis by dietary curcumin, a naturally occurring plant phenolic compound. Cancer Res. Jan1995;55(2):259-66.

[311] Srivastava KC, et al. Curcumin, A Major Component of Food Spice Turmeric (Curcuma longa) Inhibits Aggregation and Alters Eicosanoid Metabolism In Human Blood Platelets. Prostaglandins Leukot Essent Fatty Acids. Apr1995;52(4): 223-27.

[312] Deodhar SD, et al. Preliminary Studies on Anti-Rheumatic Activity of Curcumin. Ind J Med Res. 1980;71:632.

[313] Ammon HP, et al. Pharmacology of Curcuma longa. Planta Med. Feb1991;57(1):1-7.

[314] Ammon HP, et al. Mechanism of Anti-inflammatory Actions of Curcumin and Boswellic Acids. J Ethnopharmacol. 1993;38:113.

[315] Srivastava V, et al. Effect of Curcumin on Platelet Aggregation and Vascular Prostacyclin Synthesis. Arzneim Forsch/Drug Res. 1986;36;715-17.

[316] Srivastava V, et al. Effect of Curcumin on Platelet Aggregation and Vascular Prostacyclin Synthesis. Arzneim Forsch/Drug Res. 1986;36;715-17.

[317] Nagy JI, et al. Fluoride-resistant Acid Phosphatase-containing Neurones in Dorsal Root Ganglia are Separate from Those Containing Substance P or Somatostatin. Neuroscience. Jan1982;7(1):89-97.

[318] Purkiss JR, et al. Capsaicin Stimulates Release of Substance P from Dorsal Root Danglion Neurons Via Two Distinct Mechanisms. Biochem Soc Trans. Aug1997;25(3):542S.

[319] Magnusson BM. Effects of Topical Application of Capsaicin to Human Skin: A Comparison of Effects Evaluated by Visual Assessment, Sensation Registration, Skin Blood Flow and Cutaneous Impedance Measurements. Acta Derm Venereol. Mar1996;76(2):129-32.

To find out more or to speak to a nutritional counselor for free, just visit us at:
www.CuresForTheBody.com

[320] Rains C, et al. Topical Capsaicin. A Review of Its Pharmacological Properties and Therapeutic Potential in Post-herpetic Neuralgia, Diabetic Neuropathy and Osteoarthritis. Drugs Aging. Oct1995;7(4):317-28.

[321] Padgett DA, et al. Stress exacerbates age-related decrements in the immune response to an experimental influenza viral infection. J Gerontol A Biol Sci Med Sci. 1998;53(5):B347-53.

[322] 5 Gruzelier J, et al. Mind-body influences on immunity: lateralized control, stress, individual differences predictors, and prophylaxis. Ann N Y Acad Sci. 1998;851:487-94.

Van Straten M, Josling P. Preventing the common cold with a vitamin C supplement: a double-blind, placebo-controlled survey. Adv Ther. May2002;19(3):151-9.

Prinz W, et al. The effect of ascorbic acid supplementation of some parameters of the human immunological defense system. Int J Vit Nutr Res. 1977;47:248-256.

Yonemoto RH, et al. Enhanced lymphocyte blastogenesis by oral ascorbic acid. Proceedings of the American Association for Cancer Research. 1976;17:288.

Dahl H, et al. The effect of ascorbic acid on production of human interferon and the antiviral activity in vitro. Acta Pathol Microbiol Scan [B]. 1976;84B:280-84.

[323] Pauling L. How to Live Longer and Feel Better. New York: WH Freeman and Company; 1987:118-21.

Hemila H. Does vitamin C alleviate the symptoms of the common cold? – A review of current evidence. Scan J Infec Dis. 1994;26(1):1-6.

[324] Meydani SN, et al. Antioxidant modulation of cytokines and their biologic function in the aged. Z Ernahrungswiss. 1998;37(1):35-42.

[325] Garland ML, et al. The role of zinc lozenges in the treatment of the common cold. Ann Pharmacother. 1998;32:63-69.

Marshall S. Zinc gluconate and the common cold. Review of randomized controlled trials. Can Fam Physician. 1998;44:1037-42.

Novick SG, et al. Zinc-induced suppression of inflammation in the respiratory tract, caused by infection with HRV and other irritants. Med Hypotheses. 1997;49(4):347-57.

[326] Girodon F, Galan P, Monget AL. Impact of Trace Elements and Vitamin Supplementation on Immunity and Infections in Institutionalized Elderly Patients. Arch Intern Med. 1999;159:748-754.

[327] Kosmala M, et al. Pharmacological Properties of the Extract of Thymus Gland (Thymomodulin-TFX) and Its Effects on Reproduction. Acta Pol Pharm. 1993;50(6):447-52.

[328] Bouic PJD. Immunomodulation in HIV/AIDS: The Tygerberg/Stellenbosch university experience. AIDS Bulletin. Sept1997;6(3):18-20.

Clerici M, Bevilacqua M, Vago T, et al. An Immunoendocrinological Hypothesis of HIV Infection. Lancet. Jun1994;343:1552-1553.

Donald PR, Lamprecht JH, Freestone M, et al. A Randomized Placebo-controlled Trial of the Efficacy of Beta-sitosterol and Its Glucoside as Adjuvants in the Treatment of Pulmonary Tuberculosis. International Journal of Tuberculosis and Lung Disease. Jul1997;1(5):518-522.

Berges RR, Windele J, Trampisch HJ, et al. Randomized, Placebo-controlled, Double-blind Clinical Trial of B-sitosterol in Patients with Benign Prostatic Hyperplasia. Lancet. Jun1995;345(8964):1529-32.

To find out more or to speak to a nutritional counselor for free, just visit us at:
www.CuresForTheBody.com

Plat J, Kerckhoffs DA, Mensink RP. Therapeutic Potential of Plant Sterols and Stanols. Curr Opin Lipidol. Dec2000;11(6):571-6.

Grimm W, et al. A Randomized Controlled Trial of the Effect of Fluid Extract of Echinacea purpurea on the Incidence and Severity of the Colds and Respiratory Infections. Am J of Medicine. 1999;109:139-143.

Turner RB, et al. Ineffectiveness of echinacea for prevention of experimental rhinovirus colds. Antimicrob Agents Chemother. Jun2000;44(6):1708-9.

[329] Snow JM. Echinacea (Moench) spp. Asteraceae. Protocol Journal of Botanical Medicine. 1996;2(2):18-23.

Vomel VT. The effect of a nonspecific immunostimulant on the phagocytosis of erythrocytes and ink by the reticulohistiocyte system in the isolated, perfused liver of rats of various ages. Arzneim Forsch/Drug Res. 1984;34:691-95.

See DM, et al. In vitro effects of echinacea and ginseng on natural killer and antibody-dependent cell cytotoxicity in healthy subjects and chronic fatigue syndrome or acquired immunodeficiency syndrome patients. Immunopharmacology. 1997;35(3):229-35.

Wichtl M, in N. A. Bisset, ed. Herbal Drugs and Phytopharmaceuticals. Stuttgart: Scientific Press; 1994:182-84.

Schoneberger D. The influence of immune-stimulating effects of pressed juice from Echinacea purpurea on the course and severity of colds. Forum Immunologie. 1992;8:2-12.

Braunig B, et al. Echinacea purpurea root for strengthening the immune response in flu-like infections. Zeitschrift Phytother. 1992;13:7-13.

Braunig B, et al. Therapeutical experiences with Echinacea pallida for influenza-like infections. Naturheilpraxis. 1993;1:72-75.

Grimm W, et al. A Randomized Controlled Trial of the Effect of Fluid Extract of Echinacea purpurea on the Incidence and Severity of Colds and Respiratory Infections. Am J Med. Feb1999;106(2):138-43.

Brinkeborn RM, et al. Echinaforce and Other Echinacea Fresh Plant Preparations in the Treatment of the Common Cold. A Randomized, Placebo Controlled, Double-blind Clinical Trial. Phytomedicine. Mar1999;6(1):1-6.

Bauer R, et al. Analysis of alkamides and caffeic acid derivatives from Echinacea simulata and E. paradoxa roots. Planta Medica. 1991;57:447-449.

Wagner H, et al. Immunstimulerend wirkende polysaccharide (heteroglykane) aus hoheren Pflanzen. Arneim-Forsch. 1985;35:1069-1075.

[330] Sabir M, et al. Study of some pharmacological actions of berberine. Indian J Physiol Pharmacol. 1971;15(3):111-32.

Newall CA, et al. Herbal Medicines: A Guide for Health Care Professionals. London, England: The Pharmaceutical Press; 1996:151-52.

Berberine. Altern Med Rev. Apr 2000;5(2):175-7.Zhang MF, et al. Antidiarrheal and anti-inflammatory effects of berberine. Chung Kuo Yao Li Hsueh Pao. 1989;10(2):174-76.

Sun D, et al. Berberine sulfate blocks adherence of Streptococcus pyogenes to epithelial cells, fibronectin, and hexadecane. Antimicrobial Agent and Chemotherapy. 1988;32(9):1370-1374.

Sabir M, et al. Study of Some Pharmacological Actions of Berberine. Indian J Physiol Pharmacol. 1971;15(3):111-32.

[331] Newall CA, et al. Herbal Medicines: A Guide for Health Care Professionals. London, England: The Pharmaceutical Press; 1996:151-52.

Zakay-Rones Z, et al. Inhibition of several strains of influenza virus in-vitro and reduction of symptoms by an elderberry extract (Sambucus nigra L.) during an outbreak of influenza B in Panama. J Altern Complement Med. 1995;1(4):361-369.

Chu DT, et al. Immune restoration of local xenogeneic graft-versus-host reaction in cancer patients in in-vitro and reversal of cyclophosphamide-induced immune suppression in the rat in vivo by fractionated Astragalus membranaceus. Chung Hsi I Chieh Ho Tsa Chih. Jun1989;9:351-54.

Chu DT, et al. Immune Restoration of Local Xenogeneic Graft-versus-host Reaction in Cancer Patients in In-Vitro and Reversal of Cyclophosphamide-induced Immune Suppression in the Rat in vivo by Fractionated Astragalus membranaceus. Chung Hsi I Chieh Ho Tsa Chih. Jun1989;9:351-54.

Geng CS, et al. Advances in immuno-pharmacological studies on Astragalus membranaceus. Chung Hsi I Chieh Ho Tsa Chih. 1986;6(1):62-64.

[332] Chang CY, et al. Effects of Astragalus membranaceus on enhancement of mouse natural killer cell activity. Chung Kuo I Hsueh Ko Hsueh Yuan Hsueh Pao. 1983;5(4):231-34.

Zhao KS, et al. Positive modulating action of shengmaisan with Astragalus membranaceus on anti-tumor activity of LAK cells. Immunopharmacology. 1990;20(3):471.

Chang H, et al. Pharmacology and Application of Chinese Materia Medica. Singapore; Chinese University of Hong Kong. World Scientific. 1987:4.

[333] Hauer J, et al. Mechanism of Stimulation of Human Natural Killer Cytotoxicity by Arabinogalactan from Larix occidentalis. Cancer Immunol Immunother. 1993;36(4):237-44.

Kelly GS. Larch Arabinogalactan: Clinical Relevance of a Novel Immune-enhancing Polysaccharide. Altern Med Rev. Apr1999;4(2):96-103.

[334] A. Sanchez et al. "Role of Sugars in Human Neutrophilic Phagocytosis," Am J Clin Nutr 26 (1973):1180-4.

W. Ringsdorf, E. Cherakin, and R. Ramsay, "Sucrose, Neutrophil Phagocytosis, and Resistance to Disease' Dent Surv 52 (1976):46-8.

J. Bernstein et al., "Depression of Lymphocyte Transformation Following Oral Glucose Ingestion," Am J Clin Nutr 30 (1977):613.

[335] Friedman LS, Isselbacher KJ. Diarrhea and Constipation. In: Fauci AS, Braunwald E, Isselbacher KJ, et al, eds. Harrison's Principles of Internal Medicine, 14th ed. New York: McGraw-Hill; 1998:242-244.

[336] Longe RL, DiPiro JT. Diarrhea and Constipation. In: DiPiro JT, et al, eds. Pharmacotherapy, A Pathophysiologic Approach, 4th ed. Stamford, CT: Appleton & Lange; 1999:606-612.

[337] Dunne C. Adaptation of bacteria to the intestinal niche: probiotics and gut disorder. Inflamm Bowel Dis. May2001;7(2):136-45.

[338] Rodrigues-Fisher L, et al. Dietary fiber nursing intervention: prevention of constipation in older adults. Clin Nurs Res. Nov 1993;2(4):464-77.

[339] Salcido R. Complementary and alternative medicine in wound healing. Adv Wound Care. Nov1999;12(9):438.

[340] Leung A, et al. Encyclopedia of Common Natural Ingredients Used in Foods, Drugs, and Cosmetics. New York: Wiley-Interscience Publication; 1996:128-130.

To find out more or to speak to a nutritional counselor for free, just visit us at:
www.CuresForTheBody.com

[341] Freeman GL. Psyllium hypersensitivity. Ann Allergy. Dec1994;73(6):490-2.

[342] "Gastrointestinal Absorption of intact proteins." Michael LG Gardner. Annual Review of Nutrition 8: 329-50 (1988)

[343] Straus SE. Chronic Fatigue Syndrome. In: Fauci AS, Braunwald E, Isselbacher KJ, et al, eds. Harrison's Principles of Internal Medicine 14th ed. New York: McGraw-Hill; 1998:2483-2485.

[344] Udo Erasmus, Fats that Heal Fats that Kill, pg 361

'Bugs' Candida Yeast, Fungi, Bacteria, and Chronic Fatigue.

[345] Udo Erasmus, Fats that Heal Fats that Kill, pg 361

'Bugs' Candida Yeast, Fungi, Bacteria, and Chronic Fatigue

[346] Jong SC, et al. Medicinal Benefits of the Mushroom Ganoderma. Adv Appl Microbiol. 1992;37:101-34.

[347] Balch, James and Phyllis, Prescription for Nutritional Healing, pgs 200-201

[348] Balch, James and Phyllis, Prescription for Nutritional Healing, pgs 202

[349] Langsjoen PH, et al. Isolated diastolic dysfunction of the myocardium and its response to CoQ10 treatment. Clin Investig. 1993;71(8 Suppl):S140-4.

[350] Cox IM, et al. Red Blood Cell Magnesium and Chronic Fatigue Syndrome. Lancet. Mar1991;337:757-760.

[351] Behan PO. Effect of high doses of essential fatty acids on the postviral fatigue syndrome. Acta Neurol Scand. Sep1990;82(3):209-16.

[352] Plioplys AV, Plioplys S. Serum levels of carnitine in chronic fatigue syndrome: clinical correlates. Neuropsychobiology. 1995;32(3):132-8.

[353] Udo Erasmus, Fats that Heal Fats that Kill, pg 361

'Bugs' Candida Yeast, Fungi, Bacteria, and Chronic Fatigue

[354] Udo Erasmus, Fats that Heal Fats that Kill, pg 360

'Bugs' Candida Yeast, Fungi, Bacteria, and Chronic Fatigue

[355] "Systemic biochemical changes following the oral administration of a proteolytic enzyme, bromelain." R. D. Smyth, et at. *Archives of International Pharmacodynamics* 136: 230-6 (1962).

[356] Bryant SG, Brown CS. Current concepts in clinical therapeutics:Major affective disorders, part 1. Clin Pharm. 1986;5:304-318.

[357] Liebowitz M, Quitkin F, Stewart J, et al. Antidepressant specificity in atypical depression. J Clin Psychiatry. 1988;45:19-21.

[358] Harman JS, Mulsant BH, Kelleher KJ, Schulberg HC, Kupfer DJ, Reynolds CF 3rd. Narrowing the gap in treatment of depression. Int J Psychiatry Med. 2001;31(3):239-53.

[359] Bressa GM. S-adenosyl-l-methionine (SAMe) as antidepressant: meta-analysis of clinical studies. Acta Neurol Scand Suppl. 1994;154:7-14.

[360] Bell KM. et al. S-adenosylmethionine blood levels in major depression : changes with drug treatment. Acta Neurol Scand Suppl. 1994;1540:15-8.

[361] Bell KM, Plon L, Bunney WE Jr, Potkin SG. S-adenosylmethionine treatment of depression: a controlled clinical trial. Am J Psychiatry. Sep1988;145(9):1110-4.

[362] Fava M, et al. Rapidity of onset of the antidepressant effect of parenteral S-adenosyl-L-methionine. Psychiatry Res. Apr1995;56(3):295-7.

[363] Birdsall TC. 5-Hydroxytryptophan: a clinically-effective serotonin precursor. Altern Med Rev. Aug1998;3(4):271-80.

[364] Leyton M, et al. Effects on mood of acute phenylalanine/tyrosine depletion in healthy women. Neuropsychopharmacology. Jan2000;22(1):52-63.

[365] Meyers S. Use of neurotransmitter precursors for treatment of depression. Altern Med Rev. Feb2000;5(1):64-71.

[366] Birdsall TC. 5-Hydroxytryptophan: a clinically-effective serotonin precursor. Altern Med Rev. Aug1998;3(4):271-80.

[367] Riemann D, Vorderholzer V. Treatment of depression and sleep disorders. Significance of serotonin and L-tryptophan in pathophysiology and therapy. Fortschr Med. Nov1998;116(32):40-2.

[368] Boman B. L-tryptophan: a rational anti-depressant and a natural hypnotic? Aust N Z J Psychiatry. Mar1988;22(1):83-97.

[369] Byerly WF, et al. 5-Hydroxytryptophan: a review of its antidepressant efficacy and adverse effects. J Clin Psychopharmacol. Jun1987;7(3):127-37.

[370] Angst J, et al. The treatment of depression with L-5-hydroxytryptophan versus imipramine: Results of two open and one double-blind study. Arch Psychiatr Nervenkr. 1977;224:175-186.

[371] Poldinger W, et al. A functional-dimensional approach to depression: serotonin deficiency as a target syndrome in a comparison of 5-hydroxytryptophan and fluvoxamine. Psychopathology. 1991;24:53-81.

[372] Zmilacher K, et al. L-5-hydroxytryptophan alone and in combination with a peripheral decarboxylase inhibitor in the treatment of depression. Neuropsychobiology. 1988;20:28-33.

[373] Beckman H, et al. DL-phenylalanine versus imipramine: a double-blind controlled study. Arch Psychiatr Nervenkr. Jul1979;227(1):49-58.

[374] Fischer E, et al. Therapy of depression by phenylalanine. Preliminary note. Arzneimittelforschung. Jan1975;(1):132.

[375] Yaryura, et al. Phenylalanine in affective disorders. Adv Biol Psychiatry. 1983;10:137-147.

[376] Goldberg IK, et al. L-tyrosine in depression. Lancet. 1980;2:364.[377]

[377] Gelenberg AJ, et al. Tyrosine for the treatment of depression. Am J Psychiatry. 1980;137:622-623.

[378] Wolkowitz OM, et al. Dehydroepiandrosterone (DHEA) treatment of depression. Biol Psychiatry. Feb1997;41(3):311-8.

[379] Wolkowitz OM, et al. Double-blind treatment of major depression with dehydroepiandrosterone. Am J Psychiatry. Apr1999;156(4):646-9.

[380] Adams PB, et al. Arachidonic acid to eicosapentaenoic acid ratio in blood correlates positively with clinical symptoms of depression. Lipids. Mar1996;31 Suppl:S157-61.

[381] Maes M, et al. Fatty acid composition in major depression: decreased omega 3 fractions in cholesteryl esters and increased C20: 4 omega 6/C20:5 omega 3 ratio in cholesteryl esters and phospholipids. J Affect Disord. Apr1996;38(1):35-46.

[382] Rudin DO, Felix C. Omega-3 Oils. Honesdale, PA: Paragon Press; 1996:216.

To find out more or to speak to a nutritional counselor for free, just visit us at:
www.CuresForTheBody.com

[383] Peet M, Horrobin DF. A dose-ranging study of the effects of ethyl-eicosapentaenoate in patients with ongoing depression despite apparently adequate treatment with standard drugs. Arch Gen Psychiatry. Oct2002;59(10):913-9.

[384] Gerster H. Can adults adequately convert alpha-linolenic acid (18:3n-3) to eicosapentaenoic acid (20:5n-3) and docosahexaenoic acid (22:6n-3)? Int J Vitam Nutr Res. 1998;68(3):159-73.

[385] Hartvig P, et al. Pyridoxine effect on synthesis rate of serotonin in the monkey brain measured with positron emission tomography. J Neural Transm Gen Sect. 1995;102(2):91-7.

[386] Bermond P. Therapy of side effects of oral contraceptive agents with vitamin B6. Acta Vitaminol Enzymol. 1982;4(1-2):45-54.

[387] Pelton R. The Drug-Induced Nutrient Depletion Handbook. Hudson, OH: Lexi-Comp, Inc; 1999:292.

[388] Bell IR, et al. Relationship of normal serum vitamin B12 and folate levels to cognitive test performance in subtypes of geriatric major depression. J Geriatr Psychiatry Neurol. Apr1990;3(2):98-105.

[389] Joosten E, et al. Metabolic evidence that deficiencies of vitamin B-12 (cobalamin), folate, and vitamin B-6 occur commonly in elderly people. Am J Clin Nutr. Oct1993;58(4):468-76.

[390] Edwin E, et al. Vitamin B12 hypovitaminosis in mental diseases. Acta Med Scand. 1965;177:689-699.

[391] Zucker DK, et al. B12 deficiency and psychiatric disorders: Case report and literature review. Biol Psychiatry. 1981;16:197-205.

[392] Alpert JE, Fava M. Nutrition and depression: the role of folate. Nutr Rev. May1997;55(5):145-9.

[393] Procter A. Enhancement of recovery from psychiatric illness by methylfolate. Br J Psychiatry. Aug1991;159:271-2.

[394] Godfrey PS, et al. Enhancement of recovery from psychiatric illness by methylfolate. Lancet. Aug1990;336(8712):392-5.

[395] Volz HP. Controlled Clinical Trials of Hypericum Extracts in Depressed Patients—An Overview. Pharmacopsychiatry. 1997;30(Suppl 2):72-76.

[396] Muller WE, et al. Effects of Hypericum Extract (LI 160) in Biochemical Models of Antidepressant Activity. Pharmacopsychiatry. 1997;30(Supp 2):102-07.

[397] Linde K, et al. St. John's Wort for Depression—An Overview and Meta-analysis of Randomised Clinical Trials. BMJ. 1996;313m:253-58.

[398] Nordfors M, Hatvig P. St John's wort against depression in favour again. Lakrtidningen. 1997;94:2365-67.

[399] Bloomfield H, et al. Can Depression Be Successfully Treated with a Safe, Inexpensive, Medically Proven Herb Available Without a Prescription? Hypericum and Depression. California: Prelude Press; 1996:110-12.

[400] Suzuki O, et al. Inhibition of Monoamine Oxidase by Hypericin. Planta Medica. 1984;50:272-74.

[401] Bladt S, et al. Inhibition of MAO by Fractions and Constituents of Hypericum Extract. J Geriatric Psychiatry and Neurology. 1994;7:S57-S59.

[402] Murray M. Natural Alternatives to Prozac. New York: William Morrow and Company, Inc; 1996:137.

[403] Muller WEG, et al. Effects of Hypericum Extract on the Expression of Serotonin Receptors. J Geriatric Psychiatry and Neurology. 1994;7:S63-S64.

[404] Murch SJ, et al. Melatonin in Feverfew and Other Medicinal Plants. Lancet. Nov1997;350(9091):1598-9.

[405] Kaehler ST, et al. Hyperforin Enhances the Extracellular Concentrations of Catecholamines, Serotonin and Glutamate in the Rat Locus Coeruleus. Neurosci Lett. Mar1999;262(3): 199-202.

[406] Ernst E. Second Thoughts About Safety of St John's wort. Lancet. Dec1999;354(9195):2014-6.

[407] Gordon JB. SSRIs and St.John's Wort: Possible Toxicity?. Am Fam Physician. Mar1998;57(5):950,953.

[408] Lantz MS, et al. St. John's wort and Antidepressant Drug Ineractions in the Elderly. J Geriatr Psychiatr Neurol. 1999;12:7-10.

[409] Kleijnen J, et al. Ginkgo biloba for Cerebral Insufficiency.
Br J Clin Pharm. 1992;34:352-58.

[410] Kleijnen J, et al. Ginkgo biloba. Lancet. 1992;340(8828): 1136-39.

[411] Maurer K, et al. Clinical Efficacy of Ginkgo biloba Special Extract EGb 761 in Dementia of the Alzheimer Type. J Psychiatr Res. 1997;31(6):645-55.

[412] Kanowski S, et al. Proof of Efficacy of the Ginkgo biloba Special Extract EGb 761 in Outpatients Suffering from Mild to Moderate Primary Degenerative Dementia of the Alzheimer Type or Multi-infarct Dementia. Pharmacopsychiatry. 1996;29:47-56.

[413] Meyer B. Multicenter Randomized Double-blind Drug versus Placebo Study of Ginkgo biloba Extract in the Treatment of Tinnitus. Presse Med. 1986;15:1562-64.

[414] Odawara M, et al. Ginkgo biloba. Neurology. 1997;48(3):789-90.

[415] Kose L, et al. Lipoperoxidation Induced by Hydrogen Peroxide in Human Erythrocyte Membranes. 2. Comparison of the Antioxidant Effect of Ginkgo biloba Extract (EGb 761) with Those of Water-soluble and Lipid-soluble Antioxidants. J Intern Med Res. 1995;23:9-18.

[416] Auguet M, et al. Effects of Ginkgo biloba on Arterial Smooth Muscle Responses to Vasoactive Stimuli. Gen Pharmacol. 1982;13(2):169-71.

[417] Bauer U. 6-Month Double-blind Randomised Clinical Trial of Ginkgo biloba Extract Versus Placebo in Two Parallel Groups in Patients Suffering from Peripheral Arterial Insufficiency. Arzneim-Forsch/Drug Res. 1984;34(6):716-20.

[418] Ramassamy C, et al. The Ginkgo biloba Extract, EGb761, Increases Synaptosomal Uptake of 5-hydroxytryptamine: In-vitro and Ex-vivo Studies. J Pharm Pharmacology. 1992;44(11):943-45.

[419] Cohen AJ, et al. Ginkgo biloba for Antidepressant-induced Sexual Dysfunction. J Sex Marital Ther. 1998;24(2):139-43.

[420] Sikora R, et al. Ginkgo biloba Extract in the Therapy of Erectile Dysfunction. J Urol. 1989;141:188A.

[421] LaValle JB, et al. Natural Therapeutics Pocket Guide. Hudson OH: LexiComp, Inc; 2000:441-442.

[422] Rege NN, et al. Adaptogenic Properties of Six Rasayana Herbs Used in Ayurvedic Medicine. Phytother Res. Jun1999;13(4):275-91.

[423] Petkov VD, et al. Effects of Alcohol Aqueous Extract From Rhodiola rosea L. Roots On Learning and Memory. Acta Physiol Pharmacol Bulg. 1986;12(1):3-16.

[424] Saratikov AS, et al. Rhodiola rosea Is a Valuable Medicinal Plant. Tomsk State Medicinal University, Russian Academy of Medicinal Sciences, Russia; 1987.

[425] Hu FB, Manson JE, et al. Diet, lifestyle, and the risk of type 2 diabetes mellitus in women. N Engl J Med. Sep2001;345(11):790-7.

[426] Takahashi R, et al. Evening Primrose Oil and Fish in Non-Insulin-Dependent Diabetes. Prostigladins Leukot Essential Fatty Acids. 1993;492):569-71.

Stevens EJ, et al. Essential Fatty Acid Treatment Prevents Nerve Ischaemia and Associated Conduction Anomalies in Rates with Experimental Diabetes mellitus. Diabetologia. 1993;36(5):397-401.

Cameron NE, et al. Metabolic and Vascular Factors in the Pathogenesis of Diabetic Neuropathy. Diabetes. 1997;46 (Supp 2):S31-S37.

Ghosh D, Bhattacharya B, Mukherjee B, et al. Role of Chromium supplementation in Indians. Int J Biosocial Med Research. 1989;11(2):163-80.

[427] Vincent JB. Mechanisms of chromium action: low-molecule-weight chromium-binding substance. J Am Coll Nutr. 1999;18(1):6-12.

Anderson RA. Chromium as an essential nutrient for humans. Reg Tox Pharmacology 1997;26:S35-S46.

[428] Paolisso G, D'Amore A, Giugliao D, Et al. Pharmacologic doses of vitamin E improve insulin action in healthy subjects and non-insulin-dependent diabetic patients. Am J Nutr. May1993;57(5):650-6.

Tamai H. Diabetes and vitamin levels. Nippon Rinsho. Oct1999;57(10);2362-5.

Tutuncu NB, Bayraktar M, Varli K. Reversal of defective nerve conduction with supplementation in type 2 diabetes: a preliminary study. Diabetes Care Nov1998;21(11):1915-8.

[429] Pecoraro RE, Chen MS. Ascorbic acid metabolism in diabetes mellitus. Ann N Y Acad Sci 1987;498:248-58.

[430] Reddi A, DeAngelis B, Frank O, et al. Biotin supplementation improves glucose and insulin tolerances in genetically diabetic KK mice. Life Sci. 1988;42(13):1323-30.

[431] Elamin A, et al. Magnesium and insulin-dependent diabetes mellitus. Diabetes Res. Clin Pract. 1990;10(3):203-9.

LalJ, Vasudev K, Kela AK, Jain SK. Effect of oral magnesium supplementation on the lipid profile and blood glucose of patients with type 2 diabetes mellitus. J Assoc Physicians India. Jan2003;51:37-42

Tosiello L. Hypomagnesemia and diabetes mellitus: a review of clinical implications. Arch Int Med. 1996;156(11):1143-8.

[432] Brichard SM, et al. The role of vanadium in the management of diabetes. Trends Pharmacol Sci. 1995;16(8):265-70

Poucheret P, et al. Vanadium and diabetes. Mol Cell Biochem. 1998;188(1,2):73-80.

Boden F, et al. Effects of vanadyl sulfate on carbohydrate and lipid metabolism in patients with non-insulin dependent diabetes mellitus. Metabolism. 1996;45(9):1130-5.

[433] Tobia MH. The role of dietary zinc in modifying the onset and severity of spontaneous diabetes in the BB Wistar rat. Mol Genet Metab. Mar1998:63(3):205-13.

[434] Song Mk, et al. Animal Prostate Ameliorates Diabetic Symptoms by Stimulating Intestinal Zinc Absortion in Rats. Diabetes Research. 1996;31:157-70.

Song MK, et al. Effects of bovine prostate powder on zinc, glucose, and insulin metabolism in old patients with non-insulin dependent diabetes mellitus. Metabolism. 1998:47(1):39-43.

[435] Baskaran K, et al. Antidiabetic Effect of a Leaf Extract from Gymnema Sylvestre in Non-insulin-dependent Diabetes Mellitus Patients. J Ethnopharmacol. Oct1990;30(3):295-300.

[436] Rao BK, et al. Antidiabetic and Hypolipidemic Effects fo Momordiac cymbalaria Hook. Fruit Powder in Alloxan-diabetic Rats. J Ethnopharmacol. Oct1999;67(1):103-9.

[437] Abstracts of efficacy studies using acid stable lipase (Aspergillus niger). *British Society of Gastroenterology.*

[438] Effect of lipase ingestion on blood lipid levels. James C. McPherson, et al. Proceedings of the Society of Experimental Biology and Medicine. 115: 514-17. 1964.

[439] Gilliand, S.E. 1990. Health and Nutritional benefits fro lactic acid bacteria. FEMS Microbiol. Rev. 87:175-188

[440] Everything You Need to Know Before You Call the Doctor pg. 403

[441] Lewenstein, A., G: Frigerio and M. Moroni. 1979 Biological properties of streptococcus faecium, a new approach for the treatment of diarrhea.. Curr There. Res., 26:967-981

[442] Kuriyama H, Ito Y et al: Factors modifying contraction-relaxation cycle in vascular smooth muscles. Am J Physiol. 243: H641. 1982.

[443] Wacker WEC and Parisi AF: Magnesium metabolism. N Eng J Med. 278: 658-63, 712-7, 772-86. 1968.

[444] Bailey LB, Wagner PA, Davis CG and Dinning JS: Food frequency related to folacin status in adolescents. J Am Diet Assoc 84: 801-4. 1984.

[445] Shambaugh GE Jr: Zinc: the neglected nutrient. Am J Otol. 10: 156-60. 1989.

[446] Benefits and Recommendations for Physical Activity Programs for All Americans. Circulation. 1996;94:857-862.

[447] Lewenstein, A. G Frigerio and M. Moroni, 1979, Biological properties of Streptococcus faecium, a new approach for the treamen of diarrheal diseases, Curr. Ther. Res., 26:967-981.

[448] Lewenstein, A. G Frigerio and M. Moroni, 1979, Biological properties of Streptococcus faecium, a new approach for the treamen of diarrheal diseases, Curr. Ther. Res., 26:967-981.

[449] Chandan, RC 1999, Enhancing market value of milk by adding cultures, J. Dairy Sci, 82:2245-2256.

[450] Chandan, RC 1999, Enhancing market value of milk by adding cultures, J. Dairy Sci, 82:2245-2256.

[451] Saavedra, HM 1999 Probiotics plus antibiotics: regulation our bacterial environment J> Pediatr., 135:535-537

[452] H. loeb et al., "Tannin-Rich Carob Pod for the Treatment of Acute Onset Diarrhea," J Ped Gastroenterol Nutr 8 (1989): 480-5

To find out more or to speak to a nutritional counselor for free, just visit us at:
www.CuresForTheBody.com

[453] lewenstein, A., G: Frigerio and M. Moroni. 1979 Biological properties of streptococcus faecium, a new approach for the treatment of diarrhea.. Curr There. Res., 26:967-981

[454] Encyclopia of Natural Medicine pg. 434

[455] Everything You Need to Know Before You Call the Doctor pg. 403

[456] Everything You Need to Know Before You Call the Doctor By an international team of doctors from all fields fo medicine. Black Dog & Leventhal Publishers pg. 412

[457] Everything You Need to Know Before You Call the Doctor By an international team of doctors from all fields fo medicine. Black Dog & Leventhal Publishers pg. 413

[458] Encyclopia of Natural Medinine, revised second edition, by Michail Murray, MD and Joseph Pizzono ND Published by Prima Health.

[459]Everything You Need to Know Before You Call the Doctor By an international team of doctors from all fields fo medicine. Black Dog & Leventhal Publishers

[460]Ibid.

[461]Ibid.

[462]Ibid.

[463] Abrams SA. Calcium turnover and nutrition through the life cycle. Proc Nutr Soc. May2001;60(2):283-9.

[464] Leibowitz HM, Krueger DE, Maunder LR, et al. The Framingham Eye Study Monograph: an ophthalmological and epidemiological study of cataract, glaucoma, diabetic retinopathy, macular degeneration, and visual acuity in a general population of 2631 adults, 1973-1975. Surv Ophthalmol. 1980;24(Suppl):335-610.

[465] Rovner BW, Casten RJ, Tasman WS. Effect of Depression on Vision Function in Age-Related Macular Degeneration. Arch Ophthalmol. 2002;120:1041-1044.

[466] Horton JC, Disorders of the eye. In: Fauci AS, Braunwald E, Isselbacher KJ, et al, eds Harrison's Principles of Internal Medicine, 14th ed. New York: McGraw-Hill;1998:168

[467] Young RW, pathophysiology of age-rated macular degeneration. Surv Ophthalmol, 1987;31:291-306

[468] Sommerburg O, et al. Fruits and vegetables that are sources for lutein and zeaxanthin the mucular pigment in human eyes. Br J Ophthalmol. Aug 1998;82 (8):907-10.

[469] Wilhelm Stahl, Ulrike Heinrich, Holger Jungmann, Helmut Sies, and Hagen Tronnier Carotenoids and carotenoids plus vitamin E protect against ultraviolet light–induced erythema in humans

[470] Wu L, et al. Study of pathogenesis of age-related macular degeneration. Yen Ko Hsueh Pao. June 1996; 12(2):58-63   Wu L, et al. Metabolic disturbance in age-related macular degeneration. MPS. 1994;17(1-4):38-40.

[471] Rapp LM, et al. Lutein and zeaxanthin concentrations in rod outer segment membranes from perifoveal and peripheral human retina. Invest Ophthalmol Vis Sci. Apr2000;41(5):1200-9.

[472] Mares-Perlman JA, et al. Serum antioxidants and age-related macular degeneration in a population based case-control study. Arch Ophthalmol. Dec1995;113(12):1518-23.

[473] Jacques PF. The potential preventive effects of vitamins for cataract and age-related macular degeneration. Int J Vitam Nutr Res. May1999;69(3):198-205.

Snodderly DM. Evidence for protection against age-related macular degeneration by carotenoids and antioxidant vitamins. Am J Clin Nutr. Dec1995;62(6 Suppl):1448S-1461S.

To find out more or to speak to a nutritional counselor for free, just visit us at:
www.CuresForTheBody.com

[474] West S, et al. Are antioxidants or supplements protective for age-related macular degeneration? Arch Ophthalmol. Feb1994;112(2):222-7.

[475] Morazonni P, et al. Vaccinium myrtillus. Fitoterapia vol. LXVII, no 1. 1996:3-29.

Jonadet M, et al. Anthocyanosides Extracted from Vitis vinifera, Vaccinium myrtillus and Pinus maritimus, I. Elastase-inhibiting Activities in Vitro, II. Compared Angioprotective Activities in Vivo. J Pharm Belg. 1983;38(1):41-46.

[476] Maffei Facino R, et al. Regeneration of Endogenous Antioxidants, Ascorbic Acid, Alpha Tocopherol, by the Oligomeric Procyanide Fraction of Vitus vinifera L:ESR Study. Boll Chim Farm. 1997;136(4):340-44.

[477] Hirayama O, et al. Evaluation of Antioxidant Activity by Chemiluminescence. Anal Biochem. May1997;247(2):237-41.

[478] Statement on Exercise: Benefits and Recommendations for Physical Activity Programs for All Americans. Circulation. 1996;94:857-862.

[479] Wu L, et al. Study of pathogenesis of age-related macular degeneration. Yen Ko Hsueh Pao. Jun1996;12(2):58-63.

[480] Wu L, et al. Metabolic disturbance in age-related macular degeneration. MPS. 1994;17(1-4):38-40.

[481] Rapp LM, et al. Lutein and zeaxanthin concentrations in rod outer segment membranes from perifoveal and peripheral human retina. Invest Ophthalmol Vis Sci. Apr2000;41(5):1200-9.

[482] Sommerburg O, et al. Fruits and vegetables that are sources for lutein and zeaxanthin: the macular pigment in human eyes. Br J Ophthalmol. Aug1998;82(8):907-10.

[483] Mares-Perlman JA, et al. Serum antioxidants and age-related macular degeneration in a population-based case-control study. Arch Ophthalmol. Dec1995;113(12):1518-23.

[484] Jacques PF. The potential preventive effects of vitamins for cataract and age-related macular degeneration. Int J Vitam Nutr Res. May1999;69(3):198-205.

[485] Snodderly DM. Evidence for protection against age-related macular degeneration by carotenoids and antioxidant vitamins. Am J Clin Nutr. Dec1995;62(6 Suppl):1448S-1461S.

[486] Belda JI, et al. Serum vitamin E levels negatively correlate with severity of age-related macular degeneration. Mech Ageing Dev. Mar1999;107(2):159-64.

[487] Jacques PF. The potential preventive effects of vitamins for cataract and age-related macular degeneration. Int J Vitam Nutr Res. May1999;69(3):198-205.

[488] Seddon JM, et al. Dietary carotenoids, vitamins A, C, and E, and advanced age-related macular degeneration. Eye Disease Case-Control Study Group. JAMA. Nov1994;272(18):1413-20.

[489] Smith W, et al. Dietary antioxidants and age-related maculopathy: the Blue Mountains Eye Study. Ophthalmology. Apr1999;106(4):761-7.

[490] Antioxidant status and neovascular age-related macular degeneration. Eye Disease Case-Control Study Group. Arch Ophthalmol. Jan1993; 111(1):104-9.

[491] Effects of nonsteroidal anti-inflammatory drugs on chondrocyte metabolism in vitro and in vivo. Brandt KD. Department of Medicine, Indiana University School of Medicine, Indianapolis 46223.

[492] Tavoni A, et al. Evaluation of S-adenosylmethionine in primary fibromyalgia. A double-blind crossover study. Am J Med. Nov1987;83(5A):107-10.

[493] Juhl JH, et al. Fibromyalgia and the serotonin pathway. Altern Med Rev. Oct1998;3(5):367-75.

[494] Citera G, et al. The effect of melatonin in patients with fibromyalgia: a pilot study. Clin Rheumatol. 2000;19(1):9-13.

[495] Lonsdale DA: Nutritionist's Guide to the Clinical Use of Vitamin B1. Life Sciences Press, Tacoma, WA. 1987. pp1-209.

[496] Beisel WR: Single nutrients and immunity. Am J Clin Nutr 35 (Suppl): 456. 1982

[497] Influence of any enzyme from Apergillus oryzae, Protease I, on some components of the fibrinolytic system. Hans Kiessling and Roland Svensson. *Acta Chemie Scandinavia.* 24: 569-79. 1970.

[498] Rooks. D.S., Silverman. C.B., Kantrowite, F.G. The effects of progressive strength training and acrobic exercise on muscle strength and cardiovascular fitness in women with fibromyalgia. Arthritis Care and Research 47:22-28, 2002.

[499] Chang L. The association of functional gastrointestinal disorders and fibromyalgia. Eur J Surg Suppl. 1998;(583):32-

[500] Biochemistry and physiology of metal amino acid chelates oas proofs of chelation, Robert B. Jeppsen, Ph.D. Clearfield Utah, Albion Labs,18 Ref.

[501] Balch, James and Phyllis, Prescription for Nutritional Healing, pg 275.

[502] Guillot, N., 1958, Elaboration par Lactobacillus cidophilus d'un produit actif contre Candida Albicans, Ann. Inst. Pasteur 95, 194-207

[503] K.M. Shahani and K.C. Chandan, 1979, Nutritioinal and Healthful aspects of cultured and culture containing dairy foods, Journal of dairy science 62:1685-94

[504] Effect of lipase ingestion on blood lipid levels" James C. McPherson, et al. Proceedings of the Society of Experimental Biology and Medicine 115: 514-17 (1964)

Enzyme therapy in experimentally produced atherosclerosis." L.E. Mawdesley-Thopmas. Enzymologia 31: 65-82 (1966)

[505] Reaven PD, et al. Effect of dietary antioxidant combinations in humans. Protection of LDL by vitamin E but not by beta-carotene. Arterioscler Thromb. Apr1993;13(4):590-600.

Stephens NG, Parsons A, Schofield PM, Kelly F, Cheeseman K, Mitchinson MJ. Randomized controlled trial of vitamin E in patients with coronary disease: Cambridge Heart Antioxidant Study (CHAOS). Lancet. Mar1996;347(9004):781-6.

Gey KF, et al. Inverse Correlation Between Plasma Vitamin E and Mortality from Ischemic Heart Disease in Cross-Cultural Epidemiology. Am J Clin Nutr. 1991;53:326S-334S.

Hodis HN, et al. Serial coronary angiographic evidence that antioxidant vitamin intake reduces progression of coronary artery atherosclerosis. JAMA. Jun1995;273(23):1849-54.

[506] Enstrom JE, et al. Vitamin C intake and mortality among a sample of the United States population. Epidemiology. May1992;3(3):194-202.

Hallfrisch J, et al. High plasma vitamin C associated with high plasma HDL and HDL2 cholesterol. Am J Clin Nutr. 1994;60:100-105.

Kobayashi A, Masumura Y, Yamazaki N. L-carnitine treatment for congestive heart failure— experimental and clinical study. Jpn Circ J. Jan1992;56(1):86-94.

Hiatt WR, Nawaz D, Brass EP. Carnitine metabolism during exercise in patients with peripheral vascular disease.

To find out more or to speak to a nutritional counselor for free, just visit us at:
www.CuresForTheBody.com

J Appl Physiol. Jun1987;62(6):2383-7.

Rizzon P, Biasco G, Di Biase M, et al. High doses of L-carnitine in acute myocardial infarction: metabolic and antiarrhythmic effects. Eur Heart J. Jun1989;10(6):502-8.

Arsenian MA. Carnitine and its derivatives in cardiovascular disease. Prog Cardiovasc Dis. Nov1997;40(3):265-86.

Kishi H, et al. Bioenergetics in clinical medicine. III. Inhibition of coenzyme Q10-enzymes by clinically used anti-hypertensive drugs.
Res Commun Chem Pathol Pharmacol. Nov1975;12(3):533-40.

Ghirlanda G, et al. Evidence of Plasma CoQ10-lowering Effect by HMG-CoA Reductase Inhibitors: A Double-blind, Placebo-controlled Study. J Clin Pharmacol. Mar1993;33(3):226-29.

Kishi T, et al. Inhibition of Myocardial Respiration by Psychotherapeutic Drugs and Prevention by Coenzyme Q10. In: Yamamura Y, Folkers K, Ito Y, eds. Biomedical and Clinical Aspects of Coenzyme Q10. Vol. 2. Amsterdam: Elsevier/North-Holland Biomedical Press;1980:139-54.

Chiba M. A protective action of coenzyme Q10 on chlorpromazine-induced cell damage in the cultured rat myocardial cells. Jpn Heart J. Jan1984;25(1):127-37.

[507] Cacciatore L, Cerio R, Ciarimboli M, et al. The therapeutic effect of L-carnitine in patients with exercise-induced stable angina: a controlled study. Drugs Exp Clin Res. 1991;17(4):225-35.

Cherchi A, Lai C, Angelino F, et al. Effects of L-carnitine on exercise tolerance in chronic stable angina: a multicenter, double-blind, randomized, placebo controlled crossover study. Int J Clin Pharmacol Ther Toxicol. Oct1985;23(10):569-72.

Singh RB, Niaz MA, Agarwal P, et al. A randomised, double-blind, placebo-controlled trial of L-carnitine in suspected acute myocardial infarction. Postgrad Med J. Jan1996;72(843):45-50.

[508] Morisco C, et al. Effect of coenzyme Q10 in patients with congestive heart failure: a long-term multicenter randomized trial. Clin Invest. 1993;71:S134-S136.

Mortensen SA, et al. Coenzyme Q10: clinical benefits with biochemical correlates suggesting a scientific breakthrough in the management of chronic heart failure. Int J Tissue React. 1990;12(3):155-62.

Langsjoen P, et al. Treatment of essential hypertension with coenzyme Q10. Mil Aspects Med. 1994;15 Suppl:S265-72.

Langsjoen H, et al. Usefulness of coenzyme Q10 in clinical cardiology: a long-term study. Mol Aspects Med. 1994;15 Suppl: 165-75.

Mortensen SA, et al. Dose-related decrease of serum coenzyme Q10 during treatment with HMG-CoA reductase inhibitors. Mol Aspects Med. 1977;18 Suppl:S137-44.

Kishi T, et al. Bioenergetics in Clinical Medicine XI. Studies on Coenzyme Q and Diabetes Mellitus. J Med. 1976;7(3-4):307-21.

Kishi T. Bioenergetics in clinical medicine XV. Inhibition of coenzyme Q10-enzymes by clinically used adrenergic blockers of beta-receptors. Res Commun Chem Pathol Pharmacol. May1977;17(1):157-64.

[509] VII International Symposium On Magnesium. Presented by John Hopkins Department of Cardiology and IntraCellular Diagnostics, Inc. Athens, Greece. 1997.

Haigney, Mark CP, MD, Silver, Burton, PhD, et al. Tissue Magnesium Levels and the Arrhythmic Substrate in Humans. Journal of Cardiovascular Electrophysiology, Volume 8 No 9. Armonk, NY: Futura Publishing Company, Inc; Sep1997.

Gaby AR. Magnesium: an inexpensive, safe, and effective treatment for cardiovascular disease. J Advancement Med. 1988;1:179-181.

Al-Delaimy WK, Rimm EB, Willett WC, Stampfer MJ, Hu FB. Magnesium intake and risk of coronary heart disease among men. J Am Coll Nutr. Feb2004;23(1):63-70.

Eisenberg MJ. Magnesium deficiency and sudden death. Am Heart Journal. 1992;124:545-549.

510 O'Keefe JH, Harris WS. From Inuit to implementation: omega-3 fatty acids come of age. Mayo Clin Proc. Jun2000;75(6):607-14.

511 Langford HG. Dietary potassium and hypertension: Epidemiologic data. Am Intern Med. 1983;98(2):770-772.

Krishna G. Potassium and blood pressure regulation. Drug Therapy. 1993;88-92.

Khaw KT, Berrett-Connor E. Dietary potassium and stroke-associated mortality: A 12-year prospective population study. N Eng J Med. 1987;316:235-240.

Oster O, Prellwitz W. Selenium and Cardiovascular Disease. Biological Trace Elements. 1990;24:91-103.

512 Neve J. Physiologic and Nutritional Importance of Selenium. Experientia. 1991;47:187-193.

513 Wilcken DE, et al. B vitamins and homocysteine in cardiovascular disease and aging. Ann N Y Acad Sci. Nov1998; 854:361-70.

Woo KS, Chook P, Lolin YI, Sanderson JE, Metreweli C, Celermajer DS. Folic acid improves arterial endothelial function in adults with hyperhomocystinemia. J Am Coll Cardiol. Dec1999;34(7):2002-6.

Brouwer IA, van Dusseldorp M, Thomas CM, Duran M, Hautvast JG, Eskes TK, et al. Low-dose folic acid supplementation decreases plasma homocysteine concentrations: a randomized trial. Am J Clin Nutr.Jan1999;69(1):99-104.

Landgren F, Israelsson B, Lindgren A, Hultberg B, Andersson A, Brattstrom L. Plasma homocysteine in acute myocardial infarction: homocysteine-lowering effect of folic acid. J Intern Med. Apr1995;237(4):381-8.

Woodside JV, Yarnell JW, McMaster D, Young IS, Harmon DL, McCrum EE, et al. Effect of B-group vitamins and antioxidant vitamins on hyperhomocysteinemia: a double-blind, randomized, factorial-design, controlled trial. Am J Clin Nutr. May1998;67(5):858-66.

Tice JA, Ross E, Coxson PG, Rosenberg I, Weinstein MC, Hunink MG, et al. Cost-effectiveness of vitamin therapy to lower plasma homocysteine levels for the prevention of coronary heart disease: effect of grain fortification and beyond. JAMA. Aug2001;286(8):936-43.

Schnyder G, Roffi M, Pin R, Flammer Y, Lange H, Eberli FR, et al. Decreased rate of coronary restenosis after lowering of plasma homocysteine levels. N Engl J Med. Nov2001:345(22):1593-600.

Schnyder G, Roffi M, Flammer Y, Pin R, Hess OM. Effect of homocysteine-lowering therapy with folic Acid, vitamin B12, and vitamin b6 on clinical outcome after percutaneous coronary intervention: the swiss heart study: a randomized controlled trial. JAMA. Aug2002;288(8):973-9.

Lichtenstein AH. Soy Protein, Isoflavones and Cardiovascular Disease Risk. J Nutr. Oct1998;128(10): 1589-92.

Sagara M, Kanda T, NJelekera M, et al. Effect of Dietary Intake of Soy Protein and Isoflavones on Cardiovascular

[514] Messina MJ, Persky V, Setchell KDR. Soy Intake and Cancer Risk: A Review of the in Vitro and in Vivo Data. Nutr Cancer. 1994;21:113.

Kellie S, Murphy CT, Westwick J. Tyrosine-kinase Activity in Rabbit Platelets Stimulated with Platelet-activating Factor. The Effect of Inhibiting Tyrosine Kinase with Genistein on Platelet-signal-molecule Elevation and Functional Responses. Euro J Biochem. 1993;216:639.

Anthony MS, Clarkson TB, Williams JK. Effects of Soy Isoflavones on Atherosclerosis: Potential Mechanisms. Am J Clin Nutr. Dec1998;68(Suppl6):1390S-93S.

[515] Jenkins DJ, Kendall CW, Vuksan V, Vidgen E, Parker T, Faulkner D, et al. Soluble fiber intake at a dose approved by the US Food and Drug Administration for a claim of health benefits: serum lipid risk factors for cardiovascular disease assessed in a randomized controlled crossover trial. Am J Clin Nutr. May2002;75(5):834-839.

[516] Sesso HD, et al. Plasma lycopene, other carotenoids, and retinol and the risk of cardiovascular disease in women. Am J Clin Nutr. Jan 2004;79(1):47-53.

[517] Seamon KB, et al. Forskolin: Its Biological and Chemical Properties. Advances in Cyclic Nucleotide and Protein Phosphorylation Research. Vol 20. New York: Raven Press; 1986:1-150.

Doi K, et al. The Effect of Adenylate Cyclase Stimulation on Endocochlear Potential in the Guinea Pig. Eur Arch Otorhinolaryngol. 1990;247(1):16-19.

Kreutner RW. Bronchodilator and Antiallergy Activity of Forskolin. European Journal of Pharmacology. 1985;111:1-8.

Christenson JT, et al. The Effect of Forskolin on Blood Flow, Platelet Metabolism, Aggregation and ATP Release. Vasa. 1995;24(1):56-61.

Agarwal KC, et al. Significance of Plasma Adenosine in the Antiplatelet Activity of Forskolin: Potentiation by Dipyridamole and Dilazep. Thromb Haemost. 1989;61(1):106-10.

Marone G, et al. Inhibition of IgE-mediated Release of Histamine and Peptide Leukotriene from Human Basophils and Mast Cells by Forskolin. Biochem Pharmacol. 1987;36(1):13-20.

Taskov M. On the Coronary and Cardiotonic Action of Crataemon. Acta Physiol Pharmacol Bulg. 1977;3(4):53-57.

Petkov E, et al. Inhibitory Effect of Some Flavonoids and Flavonoid Mixtures on Cyclic AMP Phosphodiesterase Activity of Rat Heart. Planta Medica. 1981;43:183-86.

Uchida S, et al. Inhibitory Effects of Condensed Tannins on Angiotensin Converting Enzyme. Jap J Pharmacol. 1987;43(2):242-46.

Wergowski J, et al. The Effect of Procyanidolic Oligomers on the Composition of Normal and Hypercholesterolemic Rabbit Aortas. Biochem Pharm. 1984;33:3491-97.

Bordia A, et al. Protective Effect of Garlic Oil on the Changes Produced by 3 Weeks of Fatty Diet on Serum Cholesterol, Serum Triglycerides, Fibrinolytic Activity and Platelet Adhesiveness in Man. Indian Heart J. 1982;34(2):86-88.

Kendler BS. Garlic (Allium sativum) and Onion (Allium cepa): A Review of Their Relationship to Cardiovascular Disease. Prev Med. 1987;16(5):670-85.

Arora RC, et al. The Long-term Use of Garlic in Ischemic Heart Disease—An Appraisal. Atherosclerosis. 1981;40(2):175-79.

Koscielny J, et al. The Antiatherosclerotic Effect of Allium sativum. Atherosclerosis. May1999;144(1):237-49.

Ide N, et al. Aged Garlic Extract Attenuates Intracellular Oxidative Stress. Phytomedicine. May1999;6(2):125-31.

Garlic Oil: No Impact on Lipids. Harv Heart Lett. Sep1998;9(1):6.

Weber ND, et al. In Vitro Virucidal Effects of Allium sativum (garlic) Extract and Compounds. Planta Med. Oct1992;58(5):417-23.

Freeman F, et al. Garlic Chemistry: Stability of s-2-propenyl)-2-propene-1-sulfinothioate (allicin) in Blood, Solvents, and Simulated Physiological Fluids. J Agric Food Chem. 1995;43:2332-2338.

Egen-Schwind C, et al. Metabolism of Garlic Constituents in the Isolated Perfused Rat Liver. Planta Med. Aug1992;58(4):301-5.

Egen-Schwind C, et al. Pharmacokinetics of Vinyldithiins, Transformation Products of Allicin. Planta Med. Feb1992;58(1):8-13.

Zhou DH, et al. Effect of Jinshuibao Capsule on the Immunological Function of 36 Patients with Advanced Cancer. Chung Kuo Chung Hsi I Chieh Ho Tsa Chih. Aug1995;15(8):476-78.

Chen YJ, et al. Effect of Cordyceps sinensis on the Proliferation and Differentiation of Human Leukemic U937 Cells. Life Sci. 1997;60(25):2349-59.

Yoshida J, et al. Antitumor Activity of an Extract of Cordyceps sinensis (Berk.) Sacc. against Murine Tumor Cell Lines. Jpn J Exp Med. Aug1989;59(4):157-61.

Bao ZD, et al. Amelioration of Aminoglycoside Nephrotoxicity by Cordyceps sinensis in Old Patients. Chung Kuo Chung Hsi I Chieh Ho Tsa Chih. May1994;14(5):271-73.

Zhao X, et al. Cordyceps sinensis in Protection of the Kidney from Cyclosporine A Nephrotoxicity. Chung Hua I Hsueh Tsa Chih. Jul1993;73(7):410-12.

Guan YJ, et al. Effect of Cordyceps sinesis on T-lymphocyte Subsets in Chronic Renal Failure. Chung Kuo Chung Hsi I Chieh Ho Tsa Chih. Jun1992;12(6):338-39.

Zhen F, et al. Mechanisms and Therapeutic Effect of Cordyceps sinensis (CS) on Aminoglycoside Induced Acute Renal Failure (ARF) in Rats. Chung Kuo Chung Hsi I Chieh Ho Tsa Chih. May1992;12(5):288-91.

Zhu J, et al. CordyMax Cs-4: A Scientific Product Review. Pharmanex Phytoscience Review Series. 1997.

Deng X, et al. Clinical study of fermentation product of cordyceps sinensis on treatment of hyposexuality. J Administration Traditional Chinese Med. 1995;5(supp):23-24.

Munte TF, et al. Effects of Oxazepam and an Extract of Kava Roots (Piper methysticum) on Event-related Potentials in a Word Recognition Task. Neuropsychobiology. 1993;27(1):46-53.

Drug Therapy of Panic Disorders. Kava-specific Extract WS 1490 Compared to Benzodiazepines. Nervenarzt. Jan1994;65(1Supp):1-4.

Jussofie A, et al. Kavapyrone Enriched Extract from Piper methysticum as Modulator of the GABA Binding Site in Different Regions of Rat Brain. Psychopharmacology. Berl. Dec1994;116(4):469-74.

To find out more or to speak to a nutritional counselor for free, just visit us at:
www.CuresForTheBody.com

Davies LP, et al. Kava Pyrones and Resin: Studies on GABAA, GABAB and Benzodiazepine Binding Sites in Rodent Brain. Pharmacol Toxicol. Aug1992;71(2):120-26.

Holm E, et al. The Action Profile of D,L-kavain. Cerebral Cites and Sleep-wakefulness-Rhythm in Animals. Arzneimittelforschung. Jul1991;41(7):673-83.

Duffield PH, et al. Development of Tolerance to Kava in Mice. Clinical and Experimental Pharmacology & Physiology. 1991;18(8):571-78.

Haskell WL, et al. Role of water-soluble dietary fiber in the management of elevated plasma cholesterol in healthy subjects. Am J Cardiol. Feb1992;69(5):433-9.

Trautwein EA, et al. Psyllium, not pectin or guar gum, alters lipoprotein and biliary bile acid composition and fecal sterol excretion in the hamster. Lipids. Jun1998;33(6):573-82.

[518] Morelli V. Alternative therapies: Part II. Congestive heart failure and hypercholesterolemia. Am Fam Physician. Sep2000;62(6): 325-30.

Racz-Kotilla E, et al. Salidiuretic and Hypotensive Action of Ribes-Leaves. Planta Medica. 1980;29:110-14.

Wagner H, et al. Cardioactive Drugs IV. Cardiotonic Amines from Crataegus oxyacantha. Planta Medica.

1982;45:99-101.

Rewerski W, et al. Some Pharmacological Properties of Flavan Polymers Isolated from Hawthorn. Arzneim-Forsch/Drug Res. 1967;17:490-91.

[519] Ernst E. Cardioprotection and Garlic. Lancet. 1997; 349(9045):131.

Steiner M, et al. A Double-blind Crossover Study in Moderately Hypercholesterolemic Men that Compared the Effect of Aged Garlic Extract and Placebo Administration on Blood Lipids. Am J Clin Nutr. 1996;64(6):866-70.

Agarwal KC. Therapeutic Actions of Garlic Constituents. Med Res Rev. 1996;16(1):111-24.

Fogarty M. Garlic's Potential Role in Reducing Heart Disease. Br J Clin Pract. 1993;47(2):64-65.

Orekhov AN, et al. Direct Anti-atherosclerosis-related Effects of Garlic. Ann Med. 1995;27(1):63-65.

Kiesewetter H, et al. Effect of Garlic on Platelet Aggregation in Patients with Increased Risk of Juvenile Ischaemic Attack. Eur J Clin Pharmacol. 1993;45(4):333-36.

Bordia A. Effect of Garlic on Blood Lipids in Patients with Coronary Heart Disease. Am J Clin Nutr.

1981; 34(10):2100-03.

[520] Lei J, et al. Pharmacological Study on Cordyceps sinensis (Berk.) Sacc. and ze-e Cordyceps. Chung Kuo Chung Yao Tsa Chih. Jun1992;17(6):364-66.

[521] Volz HP, et al. Kava-kava Extract WS 1490 Versus Placebo in Anxiety Disorders - A Randomized Placebo-controlled 25-week Outpatient Trial. Pharmacopsychiatry. Jan1997;30(1):1-5.

Singh YN. Kava: An Overview. J Ethnopharmacol. Aug1992;37(1):13-45.

[522] Terpstra AH, Lapre JA, de Vries HT, et al. Hypocholesterolemic Effect of Dietary Psyllium in Female Rats. Ann Nutr Metab. Dec2000;44(5-6):223-228.

Davidson MH, et al. Long-term effects of consuming foods containing psyllium seed husk on serum lipids in subjects with hypercholesterolemia. Am J Clin Nutr. Mar1998;67(3):367-76.

Jenkins DJ, Kendall CW, Vuksan V, Vidgen E, Parker T, Faulkner D, et al. Soluble fiber intake at a dose approved by the US Food and Drug Administration for a claim of health benefits: serum lipid risk factors for cardiovascular disease assessed in a randomized controlled crossover trial. Am J Clin Nutr. May2002;75(5):834-839.

Brown L, et al. Cholesterol-lowering effects of dietary fiber: a meta-analysis. Am J Clin Nutr. Jan1999;69(1):30-42.

Anderson JW, et al. Long-term cholesterol-lowering effects of psyllium as an adjunct to diet therapy in the treatment of hypercholesterolemia. Am J Clin Nutr. Jun2000;71(6):1433-1438.

[523] Systemic biochemical changes following the oral administration of a proteolytic enzyme, bromelain. R.D. Smyth, et al. *Archives of International Pharmacodynamics.* 136: 230-6. 1962.

[524] Miller, N.E., D.S. Theille, O.H. Forde, and O.D. Mjies, 1977, High density lipoprotein and coronary heart disease: a prospective case-controlled study. Lancet i: 965-968

[525] Benefits and Recommendations for Physical Activity Programs for All Americans. Circulation. 1996;94:857-862.

[526] Hawkins DW, Bussey HI, Prisant LM. Hypertension In: DiPiro, et al, eds. Pharmacotherapy, A Pathophysiologic Approach, 4th ed. Stamford, CT: Appleton & Lange; 1999:131-151.

[527] Hawkins DW, Bussey HI, Prisant LM. Hypertension In: DiPiro, et al, eds. Pharmacotherapy, A Pathophysiologic Approach, 4th ed. Stamford, CT: Appleton & Lange; 1999:131-151.

[528] Studies on the thrombolytic activity of a protease from Aspergillus oryzae." Rolf Bergkvist and Per Olov Svard. Acta Physiologie Scandanavia 60: 363-71 (1964)

[529] Langford HG. Dietary potassium and hypertension: Epidemiologic data. Am Intern Med. 1983;98(2):770-772.

[530] Olivan Martinez J, et al. Effect of an oral calcium supplement in the treatment of slight-to- moderate essential arterial hypertension. An Med Interna. Apr1989;6(4):192-6.

[531] Widman L, et al. The dose-dependent reduction in blood pressure through administration of magnesium. A double blind placebo controlled cross-over study. Am J Hypertens. Jan1993;6(1):41-5.

[532] Geleijnse JM, et al. Reduction of blood pressure with oral magnesium supplementation in women with mild to moderate hypertension. Am J Clin Nutr. Jul1994;60(1):129-35.

[533] Prisco D, et al. Effect of medium-term supplementation with a moderate dose of n-3 polyunsaturated fatty acids on blood pressure in mild hypertensive patients. Thromb Res. Aug1998;91(3):105-12.

[534] Ide N, et al. Aged Garlic Extract Attenuates Intracellular Oxidative Stress. Phytomedicine. May1999;6(2):125-31.

[535] Agarwal KC. Therapeutic Actions of Garlic Constituents. Med Res Rev. 1996;16(1):111-24.

[536] Kiesewetter H, et al. Effect of Garlic on Platelet Aggregation in Patients with Increased Risk of Juvenile Ischaemic Attack. Eur J Clin Pharmacol. 1993;45(4):333-36.

To find out more or to speak to a nutritional counselor for free, just visit us at:
www.CuresForTheBody.com

[537] *Exercise and weight loss reduce blood pressure in men and women with mild hypertension: effects on cardiovascular, metabolic, and hemodynamic functioning.* J. Blumenthal, et al., Archives of Internal Medicine, 2000, vol. 160, pp. 1947—1957

[538] Circulation. 67: 504-11, 1983   Prinz W, et al. The effect of ascorbic acid supplementation of some parameters of the human immunological defense system. Int J Vit Nutr Res. 1977;47:248-256.

Yonemoto RH, et al. Enhanced lymphocyte blastogenesis by oral ascorbic acid. Proceedings of the American Association for Cancer Research. 1976;17:288.

Dahl H, et al. The effect of ascorbic acid on production of human interferon and the antiviral activity in vitro. Acta Pathol Microbiol Scan [B]. 1976;84B:280-84.

[539] Press RI, et al. The effect of chromium picolinate on serum cholesterol and apolipoprotein fractions in human subjects. West J Med. 1990;152(1):41-45.

[540] Fox GN, et al. Chromium picolinate supplementation for diabetes mellitus. J Fam Prac. 1998;46(1):83-6.

[541] Jacques PF, et al. Ascorbic acid and plasma lipids. Epidemiology. 1994;5(1):19-26. Lynch SM, et al. Ascorbic acid and atherosclerotic cardiovascular disease. Subcell Biochem. 1996;25:331-67. Hallfrisch J, et al. High plasma vitamin C associated with high plasma HDL and HDL2 cholesterol. Am J Clin Nutr. 1994;60:100-105.

[542] Simon JA, et al. Relation of Serum Ascorbic Acid to Serum Lipids and Lipoproteins in US Adults. J Am Coll Nutr. 1998;17(3):250-5.

[543] Bertolini S, et al. Lipoprotein changes induced by pantethine in hyperlipoproteinemic patients: adults and children. Int J Clin Pharmacol Ther Toxicol. 1986;24(11):630-7. Binaghi P, et al. Evaluation of the cholesterol-lowering effectiveness of pantethine in women in perimenopausal age. Minerva Med. Jun1990;81(6):475-479.

[544] O'Keefe JH, Harris WS. From Inuit to implementation: omega-3 fatty acids come of age. Mayo Clin Proc. Jun2000;75(6):607-14.

[545] January 2001 issue Journal of the American Medical Association, fatty acid consumption reduces heart disease risk

[546] Horrobin D. How do polyunsaturated fatty acids lower plasma cholesterol levels? Lipids. Aug1983;18(8):558-562.

[547] Donald PR, Lamprecht JH, Freestone M, et al. A Randomized Placebo-controlled Trial of the Efficacy of Beta-sitosterol and Its Glucoside as Adjuvants in the Treatment of Pulmonary Tuberculosis. International Journal of Tuberculosis and Lung Disease. Jul1997;1(5):518-522. Plat J, Kerckhoffs DA, Mensink RP. Therapeutic Potential of Plant Sterols and Stanols. Curr Opin Lipidol. Dec2000;11(6):571-6.

[548] Berges RR, Windele J, Trampisch HJ, et al. Randomized, Placebo-controlled, Double-blind Clinical Trial of B-sitosterol in Patients with Benign Prostatic Hyperplasia. Lancet. Jun1995;345(8964):1529-32.

[549] Chan AC. Vitamin E and atherosclerosis. J Nutr. 1998;128(10):1593-6. Stephens NG, et al. Randomized controlled trial of vitamin E in patients with coronary disease: Cambridge Heart Antioxidant Study (CHAOS). Lancet. 1996;347:781-6.

[550] Langsjoen PH, et al. Overview of the use of CoQ10 in cardiovascular disease. Biofactors. 1999;9(2-4):273-84.

[551] Sirtori CR, et al. Role of Isoflavones in the Cholesterol Reduction by Soy Proteins in the Clinic. Am J Clin Nutr. Jan1997;65(1):166-67.

To find out more or to speak to a nutritional counselor for free, just visit us at:
www.CuresForTheBody.com

Anderson JW, Cook-Newell ME, Johnstone BM. Meta-Analysis of the Effects of Soy Protein Intake on Serum Lipids. NEJM. Aug1995;333:5.

Anthony MS, Clarkson TB, Williams JK. Effects of Soy Isoflavones on Atherosclerosis: Potential Mechanisms. Am J Clin Nutr. Dec1998;68(Suppl6):1390S-93S.

Lichtenstein AH. Soy Protein, Isoflavones and Cardiovascular Disease Risk. J Nutr. Oct1998;128(10): 1589-92.

[552] Davidson MH, Dugan LD, Burns JH, et al. The hypocholesterolemic effects of beta-glucan in oatmeal and oat bran. A dose-controlled study. JAMA. Apr1991;265(14): 1833-9.

Braaten JT, Wood PJ, Scott FW, et al. Oat beta-glucan reduces blood cholesterol concentration in hypercholesterolemic subjects. Eur J Clin Nutr. Jul1994;48(7):465-74.

McIntosh GH, Whyte J, McArthur R, et al. Barley and wheat foods: influence on plasma cholesterol concentrations in hypercholesterolemic men. Am J Clin Nutr. May1991;53(5):1205-9.

Jenkins DJ, Kendall CW, Vuksan V, Vidgen E, Parker T, Faulkner D, et al. Soluble fiber intake at a dose approved by the US Food and Drug Administration for a claim of health benefits: serum lipid risk factors for cardiovascular disease assessed in a randomized controlled crossover trial. Am J Clin Nutr. May2002;75(5):834-839.

[553] Menendez R, et al. Oral administration of policosanol inhibits in vitro copper ion-induced rat lipoprotein peroxidation. Physiol Behav. Aug1999;67(1):1-7.

Alcocer L, et al. A comparative study of policosanol Versus acipimox in patients with type II hypercholesterolemia. Int J Tissue React. 1999;21(3):85-92.

Batista J, et al. Effect of policosanol on hyperlipidemia and coronary heart disease in middle-aged patients. A 14-month pilot study. Int J Clin Pharmacol Ther. Mar1996;34(3):134-7.

Canetti M, et al. A two-year study on the efficacy and tolerability of policosanol in patients with type II hyperlipoproteinaemia. Int J Clin Pharmacol Res. 1995;15(4):159-65.

Prat H, et al. Comparative effects of policosanol and two HMG-CoA reductase inhibitors on type II hypercholesterolemia. Rev Med Chil. Mar1999;127(3):286-94.

Mas R, et al. Effects of policosanol in patients with type II hypercholesterolemia and additional coronary risk factors. Clin Pharmacol Ther. Apr1999;65(4):439-47.

Torres O, et al. Treatment of hypercholesterolemia in NIDDM with policosanol. Diabetes Care. Mar1995;18(3):393-7.

Fraga V, et al. Effect of policosanol on in vitro and in vivo rat liver microsomal lipid peroxidation. Arch Med Res. 1997;28(3):355-60.

Arruzazabala ML, et al. Protective effect of policosanol on atherosclerotic lesions in rabbits with exogenous hypercholesterolemia. Braz J Med Biol Res. Jul2000;33(7):835-840.

[554] Satyavati GV. Gum Guggul (Commiphora Mukul)—The Success Story of an Ancient Insight Leading to a Modern Discovery. Indian J Med Res. 1988;87:327-35.

Satyavati GV, Dwarakanath C, Tripathi SN. Experimental Studies on Hypocholesterolemic Effect of Commiphora Mukul. Indian J Med Res. Oct1969;57(10):1950-62.

Satyavati GV, et al. Guggulipid: A Promising Hypolipidemic Agent from Gum Guggul (Commiphora Wightii). Econ Med Plant Res. 1991;5:48-82.

To find out more or to speak to a nutritional counselor for free, just visit us at:
www.CuresForTheBody.com

Verma SK, et al. Effect of Commiphora Mukul (Gum Guggulu) in Patients of Hyperlipidemia with Special Reference to HDL-Cholesterol. Indian J Med Res. Apr1988;87:356-60.

Tripathi YB, et al. Thyroid Stimulatory Action of (Z)-Guggulsterone: Mechanism of Action. Planta Med. 1988;54(4):271-77.

Baldwa VS, et al. Effects of Commiphora Mukul (Guggul) in Experimentally Induced Hyperlipidemia and Atherosclerosis. J Assoc Physicians India. 1981;29(1):13-17.

[555] Ernst E. Cardioprotection and Garlic. Lancet. 1997;349(9045):131.

Steiner M, et al. A Double-blind Crossover Study in Moderately Hypercholesterolemic Men that Compared the Effect of Aged Garlic Extract and Placebo Administration on Blood Lipids. Am J Clin Nutr. 1996;64(6):866-70.

Agarwal KC. Therapeutic Actions of Garlic Constituents. Med Res Rev. 1996;16(1):111-24.

Fogarty M. Garlic's Potential Role in Reducing Heart Disease. Br J Clin Pract. 1993;47(2):64-65.

Orekhov AN, et al. Direct Anti-atherosclerosis-related Effects of Garlic. Ann Med. 1995;27(1):63-65.

Kiesewetter H, et al. Effect of Garlic on Platelet Aggregation in Patients with Increased Risk of Juvenile Ischaemic Attack. Eur J Clin Pharmacol. 1993;45(4):333-36.

Bordia A. Effect of Garlic on Blood Lipids in Patients with Coronary Heart Disease. Am J Clin Nutr. 1981;34(10):2100-03.

Bordia A, et al. Protective Effect of Garlic Oil on the Changes Produced by 3 Weeks of Fatty Diet on Serum Cholesterol, Serum Triglycerides, Fibrinolytic Activity and Platelet Adhesiveness in Man. Indian Heart J. 1982;34(2):86-88.

Kendler BS. Garlic (Allium sativum) and Onion (Allium cepa): A Review of Their Relationship to Cardiovascular Disease. Prev Med. 1987;16(5):670-85.

Arora RC, et al. The Long-term Use of Garlic in Ischemic Heart Disease—An Appraisal. Atherosclerosis. 1981;40(2):175-79.

Koscielny J, et al. The Antiatherosclerotic Effect of Allium sativum. Atherosclerosis. May1999;144(1):237-49.

Ide N, et al. Aged Garlic Extract Attenuates Intracellular Oxidative Stress. Phytomedicine. May1999;6(2):125-31.

Garlic Oil: No Impact on Lipids. Harv Heart Lett. Sep1998;9(1):6.

Weber ND, et al. In Vitro Virucidal Effects of Allium sativum (garlic) Extract and Compounds. Planta Med. Oct1992;58(5):417-23.

Freeman F, et al. Garlic Chemistry: Stability of s-2-propenyl)-2-propene-1-sulfinothioate (allicin) in Blood, Solvents, and Simulated Physiological Fluids. J Agric Food Chem. 1995;43:2332-2338.

Egen-Schwind C, et al. Metabolism of Garlic Constituents in the Isolated Perfused Rat Liver. Planta Med. Aug1992;58(4):301-5.

Egen-Schwind C, et al. Pharmacokinetics of Vinyldithiins, Transformation Products of Allicin. Planta Med. Feb1992;58(1):8-13.

[557] Endo A, Kuroda M, Tusija Y. ML-336, ML-236B and ML-236C, New Inhibitors of Cholesterogenesis Produced by Penicillium citrinum. J of Antibiotics. 1976;(29):1346-48.

Grundy SM. HMG-CoA Reductase Inhibitors for Treatment of Hypercholesterolemia. New England J of Medicine. 1988;(319):24-33.

To find out more or to speak to a nutritional counselor for free, just visit us at:
www.CuresForTheBody.com

Wang J, Lu Z, Chi J, et al. Multicenter Clinical Trial of the Serum Lipid-lowering Effects of a Monascus purpureus (red yeast) Rice Preparation from Traditional Chinese Medicine. Current Therapeutic Research. 1997;(58):964-78.

Shen Z, Yu P, Sun M, et al. A Prospective Study on Zhitai Capsule in the Treatment of Primary Hyperlipidemia. National Medical J of China. 1996;(76):156-57.

Heber D, Yip I, Ashley J, et al. A Chinese Red Yeast Rice Dietary Supplement Significantly Reduces Cholesterol Levels. FASEB J. 1998;12(A206):abstract 1201.

Bonovitch K, Colfer H, Davidson M, et al. A Multi-center Center Study of Cholestin in Subjects with Elevated Cholesterol. Abstracts of the National Medical Ass Scientific Assembly. Aug1998:1-6.

Wei J, Yang H, Zhang C, et al. A Comparative Study of Xuezhikang and Mevalotin in Treatment of Essential Hyperlipidemia. Chinese J of New Drugs. 1997;(6):265-68.

[558] Terpstra AH, Lapre JA, de Vries HT, et al. Hypocholesterolemic Effect of Dietary Psyllium in Female Rats. Ann Nutr Metab. Dec2000;44(5-6):223-228.

Davidson MH, et al. Long-term effects of consuming foods containing psyllium seed husk on serum lipids in subjects with hypercholesterolemia. Am J Clin Nutr. Mar1998;67(3):367-76.

Jenkins DJ, Kendall CW, Vuksan V, Vidgen E, Parker T, Faulkner D, et al. Soluble fiber intake at a dose approved by the US Food and Drug Administration for a claim of health benefits: serum lipid risk factors for cardiovascular disease assessed in a randomized controlled crossover trial. Am J Clin Nutr. May2002;75(5):834-839.

Brown L, et al. Cholesterol-lowering effects of dietary fiber: a meta-analysis. Am J Clin Nutr. Jan1999;69(1):30-42.

Anderson JW, et al. Long-term cholesterol-lowering effects of psyllium as an adjunct to diet therapy in the treatment of hypercholesterolemia. Am J Clin Nutr. Jun2000;71(6):1433-1438.

Haskell WL, et al. Role of water-soluble dietary fiber in the management of elevated plasma cholesterol in healthy subjects. Am J Cardiol. Feb1992;69(5):433-9.

Trautwein EA, et al. Psyllium, not pectin or guar gum, alters lipoprotein and biliary bile acid composition and fecal sterol excretion in the hamster. Lipids. Jun1998;33(6):573-82.

Seamon KB, et al. Forskolin: Its Biological and Chemical Properties. Advances in Cyclic Nucleotide and Protein Phosphorylation Research. Vol 20. New York: Raven Press; 1986:1-150.

Doi K, et al. The Effect of Adenylate Cyclase Stimulation on Endocochlear Potential in the Guinea Pig. Eur Arch Otorhinolaryngol. 1990;247(1):16-19.

Kreutner RW. Bronchodilator and Antiallergy Activity of Forskolin. European Journal of Pharmacology. 1985;111:1-8.

Christenson JT, et al. The Effect of Forskolin on Blood Flow, Platelet Metabolism, Aggregation and ATP Release. Vasa. 1995;24(1):56-61.

Agarwal KC, et al. Significance of Plasma Adenosine in the Antiplatelet Activity of Forskolin: Potentiation by Dipyridamole and Dilazep. Thromb Haemost. 1989;61(1):106-10.

Marone G, et al. Inhibition of IgE-mediated Release of Histamine and Peptide Leukotriene from Human Basophils and Mast Cells by Forskolin. Biochem Pharmacol. 1987;36(1):13-20.

[559] "Acid resistant lipase as replacement in chonic pancreatic exocrine insuffieiency: a study in dogs." Gut 30: 1012-15 (1989)

[560] "Abstracts of efficacy studies using acid stable lipase (Aspergillus niger). British Socity of Gastroenterology.

[561] "Enyzme therapy in experimentally produced atherosclerosis." L.E. Mawdesley-Thomas. Enzymologia 31: 65-82 (1966).

[562] "Effect of lipase ingestion on blood lipid levels" James C. McPherson, et al. Proceedings of the Society of Experimental Biology and Medicine 115: 514-17 (1964)

[563] Zacconi, C., V. Bottazzi, A. Rebecchi, E. Bosi, P.G. Sarra, and L. Tagliaferri, 1992, Serum cholesterol levels I axenic mice colonized with Enterococcus faecium and lactobacillus acidophilus, Microbiologica, 15:413-417

[564] Pauling L. How to Live Longer and Feel Better. New York: WH Freeman and Company; 1987:118-21.

Hemila H. Does vitamin C alleviate the symptoms of the common cold? – A review of current evidence. Scan J Infec Dis. 1994;26(1):1-6.

Van Straten M, Josling P. Preventing the common cold with a vitamin C supplement: a double-blind, placebo-controlled survey. Adv Ther. May2002;19(3):151-9.

[565] Meydani SN, et al. Antioxidant modulation of cytokines and their biologic function in the aged. Z Ernahrungswiss. 1998;37(1):35-42.

[566] Garland ML, et al. The role of zinc lozenges in the treatment of the common cold. Ann Pharmacother1998;32:63-69.

Marshall S. Zinc gluconate and the common cold. Review of randomized controlled trials. Can Fam Physician. 1998;44:1037-42.

Novick SG, et al. Zinc-induced suppression of inflammation in the respiratory tract, caused by infection with HRV and other irritants. Med Hypotheses. 1997;49(4):347-57.

[567] Bouic PJD. Immunomodulation in HIV/AIDS: The Tygerberg/Stellenbosch university experience. AIDS Bulletin. Sept1997;6(3):18-20.

Clerici M, Bevilacqua M, Vago T, et al. An Immunoendocrinological Hypothesis of HIV Infection. Lancet. Jun1994;343:1552-1553.

Donald PR, Lamprecht JH, Freestone M, et al. A Randomized Placebo-controlled Trial of the Efficacy of Beta-sitosterol and Its Glucoside as Adjuvants in the Treatment of Pulmonary Tuberculosis. International Journal of Tuberculosis and Lung Disease. Jul 1997;1(5):518-522.

erges RR, Windele J, Trampisch HJ, et al. Randomized, Placebo-controlled, Double-blind Clinical Trial of B-sitosterol in Patients with Benign Prostatic Hyperplasia. Lancet. Jun1995;345(8964):1529-32.

Plat J, Kerckhoffs DA, Mensink RP. Therapeutic Potential of Plant Sterols and Stanols. Curr Opin Lipidol. Dec2000;11(6):571-6.

Turner RB, et al. Ineffectiveness of echinacea for prevention of experimental rhinovirus colds. Antimicrob Agents Chemother. Jun2000;44(6):1708-9.

[568] Snow JM. Echinacea (Moench) spp. Asteraceae. Protocol Journal of Botanical Medicine. 1996;2(2):18-23.

Vomel VT. The effect of a nonspecific immunostimulant on the phagocytosis of erythrocytes and ink by the reticulohistiocyte system in the isolated, perfused liver of rats of various ages. Arzneim Forsch/Drug Res. 1984;34:691-95.

DM, et al. In vitro effects of echinacea and ginseng on natural killer and antibody-dependent cell cytotoxicity in healthy subjects and chronic fatigue syndrome or acquired immunodeficiency syndrome patients. Immunopharmacology. 1997;35(3):229-35.

Wichtl M, in N. A. Bisset, ed. Herbal Drugs and Phytopharmaceuticals. Stuttgart: Scientific Press; 1994:182-84.

Schoneberger D. The influence of immune-stimulating effects of pressed juice from Echinacea purpurea on the course and severity of colds. Forum Immunologie. 1992;8:2-12.

Braunig B, et al. Echinacea purpurea root for strengthening the immune response in flu-like infections. Zeitschrift Phytother. 1992;13:7-13.

Braunig B, et al. Therapeutical experiences with Echinacea pallida for influenza-like infections. Naturheilpraxis. 1993;1:72-75.

Grimm W, et al. A Randomized Controlled Trial of the Effect of Fluid Extract of Echinacea purpurea on the Incidence and Severity of Colds and Respiratory Infections. Am J Med. Feb1999;106(2):138-43.

Brinkeborn RM, et al. Echinaforce and Other Echinacea Fresh Plant Preparations in the Treatment of the Common Cold. A Randomized, Placebo Controlled, Double-blind Clinical Trial. Phytomedicine. Mar1999;6(1):1-6.

Bauer R, et al. Analysis of alkamides and caffeic acid derivatives from Echinacea simulata and E. paradoxa roots. Planta Medica. 1991;57:447-449.

Wagner H, et al. Immunstimulerend wirkende polysaccharide (heteroglykane) aus hoheren Pflanzen. Arneim-Forsch. 1985;35:1069-1075.

Grimm W, et al. A Randomized Controlled Trial of the Effect of Fluid Extract of Echinacea purpurea on the Incidence and Severity of the Colds and Respiratory Infections. Am J of Medicine. 1999;109:139-143.

[569]Newall CA, et al. Herbal Medicines: A Guide for Health Care Professionals. London, England: The Pharmaceutical Press; 1996:151-52.

Berberine. Altern Med Rev. Apr 2000;5(2):175-7. Zhang MF, et al. Antidiarrheal and anti-inflammatory effects of berberine. Chung Kuo Yao Li Hsueh Pao. 1989;10(2):174-76.

Sun D, et al. Berberine sulfate blocks adherence of Streptococcus pyogenes to epithelial cells, fibronectin, and hexadecane. Antimicrobial Agent and Chemotherapy. 1988;32(9):1370-1374.

Sabir M, et al. Study of Some Pharmacological Actions of Berberine. Indian J Physiol Pharmacol. 1971;15(3):111-32.

[570] Chang CY, et al. Effects of Astragalus membranaceus on enhancement of mouse natural killer cell activity. Chung Kuo I Hsueh Ko Hsueh Yuan Hsueh Pao. 1983;5(4):231-34.

Zhao KS, et al. Positive modulating action of shengmaisan with Astragalus membranaceus on anti-tumor activity of LAK cells. Immunopharmacology. 1990;20(3):471.

Chang H, et al. Pharmacology and Application of Chinese Materia Medica. Singapore; Chinese University of Hong Kong. World Scientific. 1987:4.

Chu DT, et al. Immune restoration of local xenogeneic graft-versus-host reaction in cancer patients in in-vitro and reversal of cyclophosphamide-induced immune suppression in the rat in vivo by fractionated Astragalus membranaceus. Chung Hsi I Chieh Ho Tsa Chih. Jun1989;9:351-54.

Chu DT, et al. Immune Restoration of Local Xenogeneic Graft-versus-host Reaction in Cancer Patients in In-Vitro and Reversal of Cyclophosphamide-induced Immune

Suppression in the Rat in vivo by Fractionated Astragalus membranaceus. Chung Hsi I Chieh Ho Tsa Chih. Jun1989;9:351-54.Geng CS, et al. Advances in immuno-pharmacological studies on Astragalus membranaceus. Chung Hsi I Chieh Ho Tsa Chih. 1986;6(1):62-64.

Kelly GS. Larch Arabinogalactan: Clinical Relevance of a Novel Immune-enhancing Polysaccharide. Altern Med Rev. Apr1999;4(2):96-103.

[571] Hauer J, et al. Mechanism of Stimulation of Human Natural Killer Cytotoxicity by Arabinogalactan from Larix occidentalis. Cancer Immunol Immunother. 1993;36(4):237-44.

[572] Elmer GW, et al. Biotherapeutic agents. A neglected modality for the treatment and prevention of selected intestinal and vaginal infections. JAMA. Mar1996;275(11):870-6.

Hilton E, et al. Ingestion of yogurt containing Lactobacillus acidophilus as prophylaxis for candidal vaginitis. Ann Intern Med. Mar1992;116(5):353-7.

Fitzsimmons N, Berry DR. Inhibition of Candida albicans by Lactobacillus acidophilus: evidence for the involvement of a peroxidase system. Microbios. 1994;80(323):125-33.

Jack M, et al. Evidence for the involvement of thiocyanate in the inhibition of Candida albicans by Lactobacillus acidophilus. Microbios. 1990;62(250):37-46.

[573] Aquino R, et al. Plant Metabolites. Structure and in Vitro Antiviral Activity of Quinovic Acid Glycosides from Uncaria tomentosa and Guettarda platypoda. J Nat Prod. 1989;52(4):679-85.

Aquino R, et al. Plant Metabolites. New Compounds and Anti-inflammatoy Activity of Uncaria tomentosa. J Nat Prod. 1991;54(2):453-59.

Wagner H, et al. The Alkaloids of Uncaria tomentosa and Their Phagocytosis-stimulating Action. Planta Med. 1995;5:419-23.

Jones K. Cat's Claw: Healing Vine of Peru. Seattle. Sylvan Press. 1995;48-49.

Aquino R, et al. New Polyhydroxylated Triterpenes from Uncaria tomentosa. J Nat Prod. 1990;53(3):559-64.

Sandoval-Chacon M. Antiinflammatory actions of cat's claw: the role of NF-kappaB. Aliment Pharmacol Ther. Dec1998;12(12):1279-89.

Visioli F. Antiatherogenic components of olive oil. Curr Atheroscler Rep. Jan2001;3(1):64-7.

Visioli F, et al. Oleuropein, the bitter principle of olives, enhances nitric oxide production by mouse macrophages. Life Sci. 1998;62(6):541-6.

Renis HE. In vitro antiviral activity of calcium elenolate. Antimicrob. Agents Chemother. 1970;167-72.

Heinze JE, et al. Specificity of the antiviral agent calcium elenolate. Antimicrob Agents Chemother. Oct1975;8(4):421-5.

Bennani-Kabchi N, et al. Effects of Olea europea var. oleaster leaves in hypercholesterolemic insulin-resistant sand rats. Therapie. Nov1999;54(6):717-23.

Gonzalez M, et al. Hypoglycemic activity of olive leaf. Planta Medica. 1992;58:513-515.

Freeman F, et al. Garlic Chemistry: Stability of s-2-propenyl)-2-propene-1-sulfinothioate (allicin) in Blood, Solvents, and Simulated Physiological Fluids. J Agric Food Chem. 1995;43:2332-2338.

Egen-Schwind C, et al. Metabolism of Garlic Constituents in the Isolated Perfused Rat Liver. Planta Med. Aug1992;58(4):301-5.

To find out more or to speak to a nutritional counselor for free, just visit us at:
www.CuresForTheBody.com

Egen-Schwind C, et al. Pharmacokinetics of Vinyldithiins, Transformation Products of Allicin. Planta Med. Feb1992;58(1):8-13.

Hammer KA, et al. In-vitro activity of essential oils, in particular Melaleuca alternifolia (tea tree) oil and tea tree oil products, against Candida spp. J Antimicrob Chemother. Nov1998;42(5):591-5.

Long MM, et al. Tea tree oil in the treatment of tinea pedis. Australas J Dermatol. 1992;33(3):145-9.

[574] Bisignano G, et al. On the in-vitro antimicrobial activity of oleuropein and hydroxytyrosol. J Pharm Pharmacol. Aug1999;51(8):971-4.

Bisignano G, et al. On the in-vitro antimicrobial activity of oleuropein and hydroxytyrosol. J Pharm Pharmacol. Aug1999;51(8):971-4.

[575] Ernst E. Cardioprotection and Garlic. Lancet. 1997;349(9045):131.

Steiner M, et al. A Double-blind Crossover Study in Moderately Hypercholesterolemic Men that Compared the Effect of Aged Garlic Extract and Placebo Administration on Blood Lipids. Am J Clin Nutr. 1996;64(6):866-70.

Adetumbi M, et al. Allium sativum (Garlic)—A Natural Antibiotic. Med Hypoth. 1983;12:227-37.

Pai ST, et al. Antifungal Effects of Allium sativum (Garlic) Extract Against the Aspergillus Species Involved in Otomycosis. Lett Appl Microbiol. 1995;20(1):14-18.

Weber ND, et al. In Vitro Virucidal Effects of Allium sativum (garlic) Extract and Compounds. Planta Med. Oct1992;58(5):417-23.

[576] Altman PM. Australian tea tree oil. Australian J Pharmacy. 1988;69:276-78.

Penfold AR, et al. Some notes on the Essential oil of M. alternifolia. Aust J Dent. 417-4181930.

Mann CM, et al. The outer membrane of pseudomonas aeruginosa NCTC 6749 contributes to its tolerance to the essential oil of melaleuca alternifolia. Lett Appl Microbiol. Apr2000;30(4):294-7.

Carson CF, et al. Efficacy and safety of tea tree oil as a topical antimicrobial agent. J Hosp Infect. Nov1998;40(3):175-8.

Cox SD, et al. The mode of antimicrobial action of the essential oil of Melaleuca alternifolia (tea tree oil). J Appl Microbiol. Jan2000;88(1):170-5.

Carson CF, et al. Susceptibility of methicillin-resistant Staphylococcus aureus to the essential oil of Melaleuca alternifolia. J Antimicrob Chemother. Mar1995;35(3):421-4.

May J, et al. Time-kill studies of tea tree oils on clinical isolates. J Antimicrob Chemother. May2000;45(5):639-643.

Nenoff P, et al. Antifungal activity of the essential oil of Melaleuca alternifolia (tea tree oil) against pathogenic fungi in vitro. Skin Pharmacol. 1996;9(6):388-94.

[577] Ionescu G, et al. Oral Citrus seed extract. J Orthomolecula Med. 1990;5(3):72-74.

Arimi SM. Campylobacter infection in humans. East Afr Med J. Dec1989;66(12):851-5.

Fitzgerald JF. Colonization of the gastrointestinal tract. Mead Johnson Symp Perinat Dev Med. 1977;(11):35-8.

[578] Girodon F, Galan P, Monget AL. Impact of Trace Elements and Vitamin Supplementation on Immunity and Infections in Institutionalized Elderly Patients. Arch Intern Med. 1999;159:748-754.

[579] Udo Erasmus, Fats that Heal Fats that Kill, Flax, new research, Lignans. Pg. 284.

[580] Lee, I-Min. Harvard Medical School, "Physical Activity and Cancer," PCPFS Research Digest 2:2.

[581] A. Sanchez et al. "Role of Sugars in Human Neutrophilic Phagocytosis," Am J Clin Nutr 26 (1973):1180-4.

W. Ringsdorf, E. Cherakin, and R. Ramsay, "Sucrose, Neutrophil Phagocytosis, and Resistance to Disease,Dent Surv 52 (1976):46-8.

J. Bernstein et al., "Depression of Lymphocyte Transformation Following Oral Glucose Ingestion," Am J Clin Nutr 30 (1977):613.

[582] Mitsuoka, T. The effect of nutrition on intestinal flora. Nahrung. 28: 619-625. 1984.

[583] Manning AP, et al. Towards positive diagnosis of the irritable bowel. BMJ. 1978;2:653.

[584] Gaynes BN, Drossman DA. The role of psychosocial factors in irritable bowel syndrome. Baillieres Best Pract Res Clin Gastroenterol. 1999;13(3):437-52.

[585] Borok G. Irritable Bowel Syndrome and Diet. Gastroenterology Forum. Apr1994;29.

Bennett WG, Cerda JJ. Benefits of Dietary Fiber Myth or Medicine? Postgraduate Medicine. Feb1996;99(2):153-172.

Mac Mahon M, et al. Ispaghula husk in the treatment of hypercholesterolaemia: a double-blind controlled study. J Cardiovasc Risk. Jun1998;5(3):167-72.

Hotz J, et al. Effectiveness of plantago seed husks in comparison with wheat brain on stool frequency and manifestations of irritable colon syndrome with constipation. Med Klin. Dec1994;89(12):645-51.

Chapman ND, et al. A comparison of mebeverine with high-fibre dietary advice and mebeverine plus ispaghula in the treatment of irritable bowel syndrome: an open, prospectively randomised, parallel group study.
Br J Clin Pract. Nov1990;44(11):461-6.

Fernandez-Banares F, et al. Randomized clinical trial of Plantago ovata seeds (dietary fiber) as compared with mesalamine in maintaining remission in ulcerative colitis. Spanish Group for the Study of Crohn's Disease and Ulcerative Colitis (GETECCU). Am J Gastroenterol. Feb1999;94(2):427-33.

Hallert C, et al. Ispaghula husk may relieve gastrointestinal symptoms in ulcerative colitis in remission. Scand J Gastroenterol. Jul1991;26(7):747-50.

[586] Freeman GL. Psyllium hypersensitivity. Ann Allergy. Dec1994;73(6):490-2.

Wong PW, et al. How to deal with chronic constipation. A stepwise method of establishing and treating the source of the problem. Postgrad Med. Nov1999;106(6):199-200, 203-4, 207-10.

Tomas-Ridocci M, et al. The efficacy of Plantago ovata as a regulator of intestinal transit. A double-blind study compared to placebo. Rev Esp Enferm Dig. Jul1992;82(1):17-22.

[587] Kaya E, Gur ES, Ozguc H, et al. L-glutamine enemas attenuate mucosal injury in experimental colitis. Dis Colon Rectum. Sep1999;42(9):1209-15.

Fujita T, Sakurai K. Efficacy of glutamine-enriched enteral nutrition in an experimental model of mucosal ulcerative colitis. Br J Surg. 1995;82:749-751.

[588] Cavallo G, et al. Changes in the blood zinc in the irritable bowel syndrome: a preliminary study. Minerva Dietol Gastroenterol. Apr1990;36(2):77-81.

Valberg LS, et al. Zinc absorption in inflammatory bowel disease. Dig Dis Sci. Jul1986;31(7):724-31.

[589] Chapkin RS, et al. Dietary Influences of Evening Primrose and Fish Oil on the Skin of Essential Fatty Acid-deficient Guinea Pigs. J Nutr. 1987;117(8):1360-70.

Dutta-Roy AK, et al. Effects of Linoleic and Gamma-linolenic Acids (Efamol Evening Primrose Oil) on Fatty Acid-binding Proteins of Rat Liver. Mol Cell Biochem. 1990;98(1-2):177-82.

Dib A, et al. Effects of Gamma-linolenic Acid Supplementation on Pregnant Rats Fed a Zinc-deficient Diet. Ann Nutr Meta. 1987;31(5):312-19.

[590] Resorption of Enzymes in Enzyme therapy. Max Wolf and Karl Ransberger. (New York: Vantage Press, 1972). Pp26-33

[591] Nobaek S, et al. Alteration of intestinal microflora is associated with reduction in abdominal bloating and pain in patients with irritable bowel syndrome. Am J Gastroenterol. May2000;95(5):1231-8.

Rees WD. Treating Irritable Bowel Syndrome With Peppermint Oil. Br Med J. Oct1979;2(6194):835-836.

Pittler MH. Peppermint Oil for Irritable Bowel Syndrome: A Critical Review and Metaanalysis. Am J Gastroenterol. Jul1998;93(7):1131-1135.

Liu JH, et al. Enteric-coated Peppermint-oil Capsules in the Treatment of Irritable Bowel Syndrome: A Prospective, Randomized Trial. J Gastroenterol. Dec1997;32(6):765-768.

Nash P, et al. Peppermint Oil Does Not Relieve the Pain of Irritable Bowel Syndrome. Br J Clin Pract. Jul1986;40(7):292-293.

[592] Shulz V, et al. Rational Phythotherapy: A Physician's Guide to Herbal Medicine. New York: Springer-Verlag; 1996:187-190.

Beesley A, et al. Influence of Peppermint Oil on Absorptive and Secretory Processes in Rat Small Intestine. Gut. Aug1996;39(2):214-219.

[593] Aquino R, et al. Plant Metabolites. Structure and in Vitro Antiviral Activity of Quinovic Acid Glycosides from Uncaria tomentosa and Guettarda platypoda. J Nat Prod. 1989;52(4):679-85.

Aquino R, et al. Plant Metabolites. New Compounds and Anti-inflammatory Activity of Uncaria tomentosa. J Nat Prod. 1981;54(2):453-59.

Wagner H, et al. The Alkaloids of Uncaria tomentosa and Their Phagocytosis-stimulating Action. Planta Med. 1995;5:419-23.

Jones K. Cat's Claw: Healing Vine of Peru. Seattle: Sylvan Press; 1995:48-49.

Aquino R, et al. New Polyhydroxylated Triterpenes from Uncaria tomentosa. J Nat Prod. 1990;53(3):559-64.(9)

Sandoval-Chacon M. Antiinflammatory actions of cat's claw: the role of NF-kappaB. Aliment Pharmacol Ther. Dec1998;12(12):1279-89.

Aziz NH. Comparative antibacterial and antifungal effects of some phenolic compounds. Microbios. Jan1998;93(374):43-54.

Visioli F, et al. Oleuropein, the bitter principle of olives, enhances nitric oxide production by mouse macrophages. Life Sci. 1998;62(6):541-6.

Renis HE. In vitro antiviral activity of calcium elenolate. Antimicrob. Agents Chemother. 1969;167-72.

To find out more or to speak to a nutritional counselor for free, just visit us at:
www.CuresForTheBody.com

Heinze JE, et al. Specificity of the antiviral agent calcium elenolate. Antimicrob Agents Chemother. Oct1975;8(4):421-5.

Bennani-Kabchi N, et al. Effects of Olea europea var. oleaster leaves in hypercholesterolemic insulin-resistant sand rats. Therapie. Nov1999;54(6):717-23.

Gonzalez M, et al. Hypoglycemic activity of olive leaf. Planta Medica. 1992;58:513-515.

[594] Bisignano G, et al. On the in-vitro antimicrobial activity of oleuropein and hydroxytyrosol. J Pharm Pharmacol. Aug1999;51(8):971-4.

Tassou CC. Effect of phenolic compounds and oleuropein on the germination of Bacillus cereus T spores. Biotechnol Appl Biochem. Apr1991;13(2):231-7.

[595] Ionescu G, et al. Oral Citrus seed extract. J Orthomolecula Med. 1990;5(3):72-74.

Arimi SM. Campylobacter infection in humans. East Afr Med J. Dec1989;66(12):851-5.

Fitzgerald JF. Colonization of the gastrointestinal tract. Mead Johnson Symp Perinat Dev Med. 1977;(11):35-8.

[596] Walker AF, Middleton RW, Petrowicz O. Artichoke leaf extract reduces symptoms of irritable bowel syndrome in a post-marketing surveillance study. Phytother Res. Feb2001;15(1):58-61.

[597] Cecil's Textbook of Information - 21st edition (2000). pp 687-691

[598] Lewis MJ, Whorwell PJ. Bran: may irritate irritable bowel. Nutrition. May1998;14(5):470-1.

[599] Borok G. Irritable Bowel Syndrome and Diet. Gastroenterology Forum. Apr1994;29.

[600] Gremse DA, et al. Irritable bowel syndrome and lactose maldigestion in recurrent abdominal pain in childhood. South Med J. Aug1999;92(8):778-81.

Enck P, et al. Prevalence of lactose malabsorption among patients with functional bowel disorders. Z Gastroenterol. May1990;28(5):239-41.

[601] Fernandes, C.F., K.M. Shahani, and M.A. Amer. 1987 Therapeurtic role of dietary lactobacilli and lactobacilic fermented dairy products. FEMS Microbiol. Rev., 46:343-356

[602] Nobaek S, et al. Alteration of intestinal microflora is associated with reduction in abdominal bloating and pain in patients with irritable bowel syndrome. Am J Gastroenterol. May2000;95(5):1231-8.

[603] King TS, et al. Abnormal colonic fermentation in irritable bowel syndrome. Lancet. Oct1998;352 (9135):1187-9.

[604] Drs. Emanuel Cheraskin, Marshall Ringsdorf, Jr. and Emily Sisley explain in The Vitamin C Connection (1983) (page 213)

[605] ibid.

[606] "Intestinal digestion and maldigestion of dietary carbohydrates" Gary M. Grey Annual review of Medicine 22; 391-404 (1971).

[607] Shahani, K.M. and A.D. Ayebo, 1980, Role of dietary lactobacilli in gastrointestinal microecology, Proc. VI International Symposium on Intestinal Microecology, Amercian Journal of Clinical Nutrition, 33 (11), 2448-2457

[608] "The absorption of protolytic enzymes from the gastrointestinal tract" Joseph M. Miller Clinical Medicine 75: 35-40 (1968)

[609] Proteolytic enzymes A therapeutic evaluation: Sol Sherry and Anthony P. Fletcher. Clinical Pharmacology and Therapeurtics 1: 202-6 (1961)

[610] ibid

To find out more or to speak to a nutritional counselor for free, just visit us at:
www.CuresForTheBody.com

[611] "Effect of lipase ingestion on blood lipid levels" James C. McPherson, et al. Proceediongs of the Society of Experimental Biology and Medicine 115: 514-17 (1964)

[612] ibid

[613] "Application of Enzymes Supplements" by A.V. Modyanov and V.R. Zel'ner in Handbook of Nutritional Supplements: Volume II, Agricultural Use edited by Miloslav Rechcigl, Jr. (Boca Raton, Fl: CRC Press, 1983).

[614] "Substrate specificity in pinocytosis and intalysosomal protein digestion." J.B. Lloyd in Proteolysis and Physiological Regulation edited by D.W. Ribbons and K. Brew. (New York: Academic Press, 1976)

[615] Specific Enymes that easily digest Protein completely down to there most usable form. Protease, Peptidase, Bromelains – "Influence of an enzyme from Aspergillus oryzae, Protease I on some components of the fibrinolytic system." Hans Kiessling and Roland Svensson. Acta Chemie Scandinavia 24: 569-79 (1970)

[616] Mongey AB, Hess EV. The role of environment in systemic Lupus erythematosus and associated disorders. In: Wallace DJ, Hahn BH, eds. Dubois' Lupus Erythematosus, 5th ed. Baltimore: Williams & Wilkins; 1997:31-47.

[617] Sanchez-Guerrero J, et al. Postmenopausal Estrogen Therapy and The Risk for Developing Systematic Lupus Erthematosus. Annals of Internal Medicine. Mar 1995;122(6):430433.

[618] Udo Erasmus, Fats That Heal Fats That Kill, pg. 272, 277

[619] Lees, R. & Karel, M. *Omega 3 Fatty Acids in Health and Disease.* Basel, Switzerland. Dekker. 1990.

[620] Molad Y, et al, FERUM cobalamin and transcobalamin levels in systemic lupus erythematosus. Am J Med. Feb1990;88(2): 141-4.

[621] Ayers S, Mihan R. Lupus erythematosus and vitamin E: an effective and nontoxic therapy. Cutis. Jan 1979;23(1):49-52, 54.

[622] Zhao KS, et al. Positive Modulating Action of Shengmaisan with Astragalus membranaceus on Anti-tumor of LAK Cells. Immunopharmacology. Dec 1990; 20.

[623] Dorman HJ, et al. Antimicrobacterial agents from plants: antibacterial activity of plant volatile oils. J Appl Microbiol. Feb 2000;88(2): 308-16.

[624] Ionescu G, et al. Hypoglycemic activity of olive leaf. Planta Medica. 1992;58: 513-515.

[625] G, Gaspardy, et al. Pheumatology and Physical Medicine. 11: 14-9. 1971.

[626] Plat J, Kerckhoffs DA, Menskink RP. Therapeutic Potential of Plant Sterols and Stanols. Curr Opin Lipidol. Dec 2000;11(6):571-6.

[627] Jones, G. Hypercholestermic and hypoglyceridemic effect of acidophilus yogurt, MS thesis, University of Nebraska-Lincoln.

[628] National Institute of Arthritis and Musculoskeletal and Skin Diseases, National Institutes of Health, Bethesda, MD 20892, January 1999

[629] Molad Y, et al, FERUM cobalamin and transcobalamin levels in systemic lupus erythematosus. Am J Med. Feb1990;88(2): 141-4.

[630] Facchinetti F, et al. Magnesium prophylaxis of menstrual migraine: effects on intracellular magnesium. Headache. May 1991;31(5):298-301.

[631] Schoenen J, et al. Effectiveness of high-dose riboflavin in migraine prophylaxis. A randomized controlled trail. Neurology. Feb1998;50(2):466-70.

To find out more or to speak to a nutritional counselor for free, just visit us at:
www.CuresForTheBody.com

[632] Thys-Jacobs S. Vitamin D and calcium in menstrual migraine. Headache. Oct1994;34(9):544-6.

[633] Tolerability of Iron; A comparison of Bis-glycino Iron and Ferrous Sulfate. Clinical Theraputics/Vl. 13, No. 5, 1991.

[634] National Institute of Arthritis and Musculoskeletal and Skin Diseases, National Institutes of Health, Bethesda, MD 20892, January 1999

[635] Zhu ZJ, et al. Studies on the active constituents of Momordica charantia L. Yao Hsueh Hsueh Pao. 1990;25(12):898-903.

[636] Amann W. Amenorrhea. Favorable Effect of Agnus castus (Agnolyt) on Amenorrhea. ZFA. Stuttgart. 1982;58(4):228-31.

Sliutz G, et al. Agnus castus Extracts Inhibit Prolactin Secretion of Rat Pituitary Cells. Hormone and Metabolic Research. 1993;25:253-55.

[637] Lieberman S. A Review of the Effectiveness of Cimicifuga racemosa (black cohosh) for the Symptoms of Menopause. J Womens Health. Jun1998;7(5):525-29.

[638] Volz HP, et al. Kava-kava Extract WS 1490 Versus Placebo in Anxiety Disorders - A Randomized Placebo-controlled 25-week Outpatient Trial. Pharmacopsychiatry. Jan1997;30(1):1-5.

[639] Dutta-Roy AK, et al. Effects of Linoleic and Gamma-linolenic Acids (Efamol Evening Primrose Oil) on Fatty Acid-binding Proteins of Rat Liver. Mol Cell Biochem. 1990;98(1-2):177-82.

[640] Udo Erasmus, Fats that Heal Fats that Kill, Arthritis, pg. 354

[641] Lieberman S. A Review of the Effectiveness of Cimicifuga racemosa (black cohosh) for the Symptoms fo Menopause. J Womens Health. Jun1998;7(5):525-29.

[642] Koeda M, et al. Studies on the Chinese Crude Drug "Shoma." IX. Three Novel Cyclolanostanol Xylosides, Cimicifugosides H-1, H-2 and H-5, from Cimicifuga Rhizome. Chem Pharm Bull. Tokyo. May1995;43(5):771-76.

[643] Snow JM. Curcuma longa L. (Zingiberaceae). Protocol Journal of Botanical Medicine. 1995;1(2):43-46.

[644] Johnson ES, et al. Efficacy of Feverfew as Prophylactic Treatment of Migraine. British Medical Journal. 1985;291:569-73.

[645] Chapkin RS, et al. Dietary Influences of Evening Primrose and Fish Oil on the Skin of Essential Fatty Acid-deficient Guinea Pigs. J Nutr. 1987;117(8):1360-70.

[646] Altura Bm and Altura BT. Magnesium and vascular tone and reactivity. Blood Vessels. 1978: 15: 5-16.

[647] Weaver K. Magnesium and Its Role in Vascular Reactivity and Coagulation. Contemp Nutr. 1987;12(3):1.

[648] Heaney, RP: Calcif Tisa int (1990) 46, 300-4.

[649] Lucchinetti CF, Rodriguez M. The controversy surrounding the pathogenesis of the multiple sclerosis lesion. Mayo Clin Proc. 1997;72:665-678.

[650] Compston A. The epidemiology of multiple sclerosis: Principles, achievements, and recommendations. Ann Neurol. 1994;36:S211-S217.

[651] Nieper H. THE NIEPER REGIMEN FOR THE TREATMENT OF MULTIPLE SCLEROSIS. The Brewer Science Library. 1994.

To find out more or to speak to a nutritional counselor for free, just visit us at:
www.CuresForTheBody.com

[652] Yasui M, Ota K. Experimental and clinical studies on dysregulation of magnesium metabolism and the aetiopathogenesis of multiple sclerosis. Magnes Res. Dec1992;5(4):295-302.

[653] Reynolds EH. Multiple sclerosis and vitamin B12 metabolism. J Neuroimmunol. Oct1992;40(2-3):225-30.

[654] Yasui M, et al. Zinc concentration in the central nervous system in a case of multiple sclerosis—comparison with other neurological diseases. No To Shinkei. Oct1991;43(10):951-5.

[655] Jong SC, et al. Medicinal Benefits of the Mushroom Ganoderma. Adv Appl Microbiol. 1992;37:101-34.

[656] Swank R. Multiple sclerosis: fat-oil relationship. Nutrition. Sep1991;7(5):368-76.

[657] Yan GQ, Wnag SZ, Ahou RH and Sun SZ: Endemic selenium intoxication of humans in China. Am J Clin Nutr 37: 872-81, 1983.

[658] "Application of Enzyme Supplements" by A.V. Modyanov and V.R. Zel'ner in Handbook of Nutritional Siupplements; Volume II, Agricultural Use edite by Miloslav Rechcigl, Jr. (Boca Raton, Fl: CRC Press, 1983).

[659] Ayebo A.D., I.A. Angelo and K.M. Shanhani, 1981, Effect of ingesting Lactobacillus acidophilus mild upon fecal flora and enzyme activity in humans. Milchwissenschaft, 35: 730-733.

[660] Mulcare, J. "Multiple Sclerosis." in *Exercise Management for Persons with Chronic Diseases and Disabilities*. Champaign, IL: Human Kinetics, 1997: 189-193.

[661] General Variable Immunologic Deficiency with MS. Clin. Med. 1990 May; 68 (5:90-4).

[662] Dib A, et al. Effects of Gamma-linolenic Acid Supplementation on Pregnant Rats Fed a Zinc-deficient Diet. Ann Nutr Meta. 1987;31(5):312-19.

[663] Reynolds EH. Multiple sclerosis and vitamin B12 metabolism. J Neuroimmunol. Oct1992;40(2-3):225-30

[664] Johnson S. The possible role of gradual accumulation of copper, cadmium, lead and iron and gradual depletion of zinc, magnesium, selenium, vitamins B2, B6, D, and E and essential fatty acids in multiple sclerosis. Med Hypotheses. Sep2000;55(3):239-241.

[665] Johnson S. The possible role of gradual accumulation of copper, cadmium, lead and iron and gradual depletion of zinc, magnesium, selenium, vitamins B2, B6, D, and E and essential fatty acids in multiple sclerosis. Med Hypotheses. Sep2000;55(3):239-241.

[666] Swank R. Multiple sclerosis: fat-oil relationship. Nutrition. Sep1991;7(5):368-76.

[667] Plat J, Kerckhoffs DA, Mensink RP. Therapeutic Potential of Plant Sterols and Stanols. Curr Opin Lipidol. Dec2000;11(6):571-6.

[668] Jong SC, et al. Medicinal Benefits of the Mushroom Ganoderma. Adv Appl Microbiol. 1992;37:101-34.

[669] Dutta-Roy AK, et al. Effects of Linoleic and Gamma-linolenic Acids (Efamol Evening Primrose Oil) on Fatty Acid-binding Proteins of Rat Liver. Mol Cell Biochem. 1990;98(1-2):177-82.

[670] Dworkin RH, et al. Linoleic Acid and Multiple Sclerosis: A Reanalysis of Three Double-blind Trials. Neurology. Nov1984;34(11):1441-45.

[671] Suprunov NI, et al. Determination and Study of Lignan Distribution in the Fruits of Schisandra chinensis (Turcz.) Baill. Farmatsiia. May1972;21(3):34-37.

To find out more or to speak to a nutritional counselor for free, just visit us at:
www.CuresForTheBody.com

[672] Nishiyama N, et al. An Herbal Prescription, S-113m, Consisting of Biota, Ginseng and Schizandra, Improves Learning Performance in Senescence Accelerated Mouse. Biol Pharm Bull. Mar1996;19(3):388-93.

[673] Sorensen TI. The genetics of obesity. Metabolism. Sep1995;44(9 Suppl 3):4-6.

[674] Field AE, Coakley EH, Must A, Spadano JL, Laird N, Dietz WH, et al. Impact of overweight on the risk of developing common chronic diseases during a 10-year period. Arch Intern Med. 9 Jul 2001; 161 (13): 1581-6.

[675] Wilson PW, D'Agostino RB, Sullivan L, Parise H, Kannel WB. Overweight and obesity as determinants of cardiovascular risk: the Framingham experience. Arch Intern Med. Sep2002;162(16):1867-72.

[676] Effect of lipase ingestion on blood lipid levels: James C. McPherson, et al. Proceedings of the Society of Experimental Biology and Medicine 115: 514-17 (1964)

[677] Tisdale MJ and Dhesi JK. Inhibition of weight loss by omega-3 fatty acids in an experimental cachexia model. Cancer Res; 50(16): 5022-6. Aug 15 1990.

[678] Anderson RA. Effects of chromium on body composition and weight loss. Nutr Rev. Sep1998;56(9):266-70.

[679] Sergio W. A Natural Food, the Malabar Tamarind, May be Effective in the Treatment of Obesity. Med Hypotheses. 1998;27(1):39-40.

[680] Peuhkuri, K.,M Hukkanen, R. Beale, j.M. Polak, H. Vapaatalo and R. Korpela, 1997, Age and continues lactose challenge modify lactase protein expression and enzyme activity in gut epithelium in the rat, J. Physiol. Pharmacol., 48:719720

[681] JMed. 2002:33 "1-4": 247-64 Curtus Arntium as a thermogenic, Weight-dedction replacement for ephedra: An overview. Preuss HG. Georgetown Universtiy medcenter, Washington DC 20057 USA

[682] Yamasaki M, et al. Dietary effect of conjugated linoleic acid on lipid levels in white adipose tissue of Sprague-Dawley rats. Biosci Biotechnol Biochem. Jun1999;63(6):1104-6.

[683] West DB, et al. Effects of conjugated linoleic acid on body fat and energy metabolism in the mouse. Am J Physiol. Sep1998;275(3 Pt 2):R667-72.

[684] Gaullier JM, Halse J, Hoye K, et al. Conjugated linoleic acid supplementation for 1 y reduces body fat mass in healthy overweight humans. Am J Clin Nutr. Jun2004;79(6):1118-25.

[685] Morris BW, et al. Glucose-dependent uptake of chromium in human and rat insulin-sensitive tissues. Clin Sci. Apr1993;84(4):477-82.

[686] Anderson RA. Effects of chromium on body composition and weight loss. Nutr Rev. Sep1998;56(9):266-70.

[687] Sergio W. A Natural Food, the Malabar Tamarind, May Be Effective in the Treatment of Obesity. Med Hypotheses. 1988;27(1):39-40.

[688] Sullivan AC, et al. Effect of (-)-Hydroxycitrate upon the Accumulation of Lipid in the Rat. II. Appetite. Lipids. 1974;9:129-34.

[689] Sullivan AC, et al. Metabolic Regulation as a Control for Lipid Disorders. I. Influence of (—)-hydroxycitrate on Experimentally Induced Obesity in the Rodent. American J of Clinical Nutrition. 1977;30:767-76.

To find out more or to speak to a nutritional counselor for free, just visit us at:
www.CuresForTheBody.com

[690] McGarry JD, et al. In Support of the Roles of Malonyl-CoA and Carnitine Acyltransferase I in the Regulation of Hepatic Fatty Acid Oxidation and Ketogenesis. J Biol Chem. 1979;254:8163-68.

[691] McCarty MF, et al. Inhibition of Citrate Lyase May Aid Aerobic Endurance. Med Hypotheses. 1995;45(3):247-54.

[692] Heymsfield SB, et al. Garcinia cambogia (hydroxycitric acid) as a Potential Anti-obesity Agent: A Randomized Controlled Trial. JAMA. Nov1998;280(18):1596-600.

[693] US Department of Health and Human Services: Physical Activity and Health: A Report of the Surgeon General, Atlanta, DHHS, Centers for Disease Control and Prevention, National Center for Chronic Disease Prevention and Health Promotion, 1996

Benefits and Recommendations for Physical Activity Programs for All Americans. *Circulation* 1996;94:857-862.

[694] Jenkins, David, et al. "Glycemic Index of Food: A Physiological Basis for Carbohydrate Exchange. American Journal of Clinical Nutrition. 34: 360-66.

[695] Jenkins, David, et al. "Glycemic Index of Food: A Physiological Basis for Carbohydrate Exchange. American Journal of Clinical Nutrition. 34: 360-66.

[696] Rudin, D.O. & Felix, C. The Omega-3 Phenomenon, New York, NY. Rawson Associates. 1987.

[697] McPherson, James C., et al. Effect of lipase ingestion on blood lipid levels. *Proceedings of the Society of Experimental Biology and Medicine.* 115: 514-17. 1964.

[698] Curro F, et al. Fucus vesiculosis L. nel Trattamento Medico Dell'Obesita e delle Alterazioni Metaboliche Connesse. Arch Med Interna. 1976;28:19-32.

[699] Tripathi YB, et al. Thyroid Stimulatory Action of (Z)-Guggulsterone: Mechanism of Action. Planta Med. 1998;54(4):271-77.

[700] Basal secretion f digestive enzymes. Jacob Meyer, et al: Archives of Internal Medicine 65: 171-7 (1940)

[701] Wyshak G, Frisch RE. Carbonated Beverages, Dietary Calcium: The Dietary Calcium/Phosphorus Ratio, and Bone Fractures in Girls and Boys. J Adolescent Health. 1994;15:210-15.

[702] Kiel DP, et al. Caffeine and the Risk of Hip Fracture: The Framingham Study. Am J Epidemiol. Oct1990;132(4):675-84.

[703] Orwoll ES, Klein RF. Osteoporosis in men. Endocr Rev. 1995; 16:87-116.

[704] Riggs BL, Melton LJ III. Involutional osteoporosis. N Engl J Med. 1986;314:1676-1686.

[705] Eriksen EF, Kudsk H, Emmertsen K, et al. Bone remodeling during calcitonin excess: reconstruction of the remodeling sequence in medullary thyroid carcinoma. Bone. 1993;14:399-401.

[706] Hurley DL, Tiegs RD, Wahner HW, et al. Axial and appendicular bone mineral density in patients with long-term deficiency or excess of calcitonin. N Engl J Med. 1987;317:537-541.

[707] Feskanich D, et al. A prospective study of thiazide use and fractures in women. Osteoporos Int. 1997;7(1):79-84.

[708] Albanese AA, et al. Effects of Calcium and Micronutrients on Bone Loss of Pre- and Postmenopausal Women. Scientific Exhibit Presented to the American Medical Association. Atlanta GA. Jan1981;24-26.

To find out more or to speak to a nutritional counselor for free, just visit us at:
www.CuresForTheBody.com

[709] Kritz-Silverstein D, Goodman-Gruen DL. Usual dietary isoflavone intake, bone mineral density, and bone metabolism in postmenopausal women. J Womens Health Gend Based Med. Jan2002;11(1):69-78.

[710] Cohen L, Kitzes R. Infrared Spectroscopy and Magnesium Content of Bone Mineral in Osteoporotic Women. Isr J Med Sci. 1981;17:1123-25.

[711] Hart JP, et al. Electrochemical Detection of Depressed Circulating Levels of Vitamin K1 in Osteoporosis. J Clin Endocrinol Metab. 1985;60:1268-69.

[712] Gaby A. Preventing and Reversing Osteoporosis. Rocklin, CA: Prima Publishing; 1994:33.

[713] Volpe SL, et al. The relationship between boron and magnesium status and bone mineral density in the human: a review. Magnes Res. 1993;6(3):291-6.

[714] Barnes S. Evolution of the health benefits of soy isoflavones. Proc Soc Exp Biol Med. 1998;217:386-398.

[715] Leung A, et al. Encyclopedia of Common Natural Ingredients Used in Foods, Drugs, and Cosmetics. New York: Wiley-Interscience Publication; 1996:306-308.

[716] Chiechi LM. Dietary Phytoestrogens in the Prevention of Long-term Postmenopausal Diseases. Int J Gynaecol Obstet. Oct1999;67(1):39-40.

[717] The Physician and Sports Medicine. Vol. 26 – No. 2. February, 1998.

[718] Antonios TF, MacGregor GA. Salt intake: potential deleterious effects excluding blood pressure. J Hum Hypertens. Jun1995;9(6):511-5.

[719] Laitinen K, Valimaki M. Bone and the 'comforts of life.' Ann Med. Aug1993;25(4):413-25.

[720] Metz JA, et al. Intakes of Calcium, Phosphorus, and Protein, and Physical Activity are Related to Radial Bone Mass in Young Adult Women. Am J Clin Nutr. 1993;58(4):537-42.

[721] Halpner AD, Kellermann G, Ahlgrimm MJ, Arndt CL, Shaikh NA, Hargrave JJ, Tallas PG. The effect of an ipriflavone-containing supplement on urinary N-linked telopeptide levels in postmenopausal women. J Womens Health Gend Based Med. Nov2000;9(9):995-8.

[722] Ohta H, Komukai S, Makita K, Masuzawa T, Nozawa S. Effects of 1-year ipriflavone treatment on lumbar bone mineral density and bone metabolic markers in postmenopausal women with low bone mass. Horm Res. 1999;51(4):178-83.

[723] Agnusdei D, Bufalino L. Efficacy of ipriflavone in established osteoporosis and long-term safety. Calcif Tissue Int. 1997;61(Suppl 1):S23-7.

[724] Gennari C, Adami S, Agnusdei D, Bufalino L, Cervetti R, Crepaldi G, et al. Effect of chronic treatment with ipriflavone in postmenopausal women with low bone mass. Calcif Tissue Int. 1997;61(Suppl 1):S19-22.

[725] Baumann TJ. In: DiPiro JT, Talbert RL, Yee GC, Matzke GR, Wells BG, Posey LM, eds. Pharmacotherapy, A Pathophysiologic Approach, 4th ed. Stamford, Conn: Appleton & Lange; 1999:1014-26.

[726] Oral anti-inflammatory enzyme therapy in injuries I professional footballers. P.S. Boyne and H. Medhurst. The practitioner 1948: 543-6 (1967)

[727] Jacob SW, et al. The Miracle of MSM: The Natural Solution for Pain. New York: GP Putnam's Sons; 1999:57-58.

[728] Leeb BF, et al. A metaanalysis of chondroitin sulfate in the treatment of osteoarthritis. J Rheumatol. Jan2000;27(1):205-11.

To find out more or to speak to a nutritional counselor for free, just visit us at:
www.CuresForTheBody.com

[729] Bucsi L, Poor G. Efficacy and tolerability of oral chondroitin sulfate as a symptomatic slow-acting drug for osteoarthritis (SYSADOA) in the treatment of knee osteoarthritis. Osteoarthritis Cartilage. May1998;6(Suppl A):31-6.

[730] McAlindon TE, et al. Glucosamine and chondroitin for treatment of osteoarthritis: a systematic quality

assessment and meta-analysis. JAMA. Mar2000;283(11):1469.

[731] Lopes Vas A. Double-blind clinical evaluation of the relative efficacy of ibuprofen and glucosamine sulphate in the management of osteoarthrosis of the knee in out-patients. Curr Med Res Opin. 1982;8(3):145-9.

[732] Lindahl O, Lindwall L. Double Blind Study of Valerian Preparations. Pharmacol. Biochem. Behav. 1989;32(4):1065-66.

[733] Benefits and Recommendations for Physical Activity Programs for All Americans. *Circulation*996;94:857-862

[734] Rovetta G, Monteforte P, Molfetta G, Balestra V. A two-year study of chondroitin sulfate in erosive osteoarthritis of the hands: behavior of erosions, osteophytes, pain and hand dysfunction. Drugs Exp Clin Res. 2004;30(1):11-6.

[735] Ammon HP, et al. Pharmacology of Curcuma longa. Planta Med. Feb1991;57(1):1-7.

[736] Mascolo N, Jain R, Jain SC, et al. Ethnopharmacologic Investigation of Ginger (Zingiber officinale). J Ethnopharmacol. Nov1989;27(1-2):129-40.

[737] Langner E, Greifenberg S, Gruenwald J. Ginger: History and Use. Adv Ther. Jan1998;15(1):25-44.

[738] Srivastava KC, Mustafa T. Ginger (Zingiber officinale) and Rheumatic Disorders. Med Hypotheses. May1989;29(1):25-8.

[739] Makheja AM, et al. The Active Principle in Feverfew. Lancet. 1981;2(8254):1054.

[740] Mills SY, et al. Effect of a proprietary herbal medicine on the relief of chronic arthritic pain: a double-blind study. Br J Rheumatol. Sep1996;35(9):874-8.

[741] Simpson LO. The etiopathologies of premenstrual syndrome as a consequence of altered blood rheology: A new hypothesis. Med Hypothesis. 1988;25(4).

[742] Shapiro SS. Treatment of dysmenorrhea and premenstrual syndrome with non-steroidal anti-inflammatory drugs. Drugs. Oct1988;36(4):475-90.

[743] Eriksson E. Serotonin reuptake inhibitors for the treatment of premenstrual dysphoria. Int Clin Psychopharmacol. May1999;14(2S):27-33s.

[744] Abraham GE. Nutritional factors in the etiology of the premenstrual tension syndrome. Reprod Med. 1983;28(7):446-64.

[745] Facchinetti F, et al. Oral magnesium successfully relieves premenstrual mood changing Obstet Gynecol. 1991;78(2(:177-81. Aldercreutz H. Phytoestrogens: Epidemiology and anpossible role in cancer prevention. Environ Health Perspect. 1995:104S(7):103-12. Barnes S. Evolution of the health benefits of soy isoflavones. Proc Soc Exp Biol Med. 1998;217(3):386-98.

[746] Steinberg PN. Isoflavones and the New Concentrated Soy Supplements. New York: Healing Wisdom Publiscations; 1996:4-7

[747] Collins, E.B. and P. Hardt, 1980, Inhibition of Candida albicans by Lactabacillus acidophilus. J. Dairy Sci. 63, 830-832.

[748] Brush MG, et al. Pyridoxine in the treatment of premenstrual syndrome: a retrospective survey in 630 patients. Br J Clin Pract. 1988;42(110:448-52.

To find out more or to speak to a nutritional counselor for free, just visit us at:
www.CuresForTheBody.com

[749] London RS, et al. Efficacy of alpha-tocopherol in the treatment of the prementstrual syndrome. J Reprod Med 1987;32(6):400-4. Ferslew KE, et al. Pharmacokinetics and bioavailability of the RRR and all racemic stereoisomers of alpha-tocopherol in humans after single oral administration. JClin Pharmacol. 1993;33(1):84-8

[750] Jarry H, et al. the Endocrine Effects of Constituents of Cimicifuga racemosa. 2. In vitro Binding of Constituents to Estrogen Receptors. Planta Med. Aug.1985;4:316-19.

[751] Amann W. Amenorrhea. Favoravle Effect of Agnus castus (Agnolyt) on Amenorrhea ZFA. Stuttgart. 1982;58(4):228-31. Milewicz. A, et al. Vitex Agnus castus Extact in the Treatment of Luteal Phase Defects Due to Latent Hyperporlactinemia. Results of a Randomixed Placebo-controlled Double-blind Study. Arzneim Forsch?Drug Res. 1993;43(7):752-56. Hillebrand H. The Treatment of Premenstrual Aphthous Ulcerative Stomatitis with Agnolyt.

Z Allgemeinmend. 1964;40(36):1577. McGibbon D. Premenstrual Syndrome. CMAJ. 1989;141(11):1124-25.

[752] Zhu DPQ. Dong Quai. Am J Chin Med. 1987;15(3-4):117-25. Hirata JD, et al. Does Dong quai Have Estrogenic Effects in Postmenopausal Women Double-blind, Placebo-controlled Trial. Fertil Steril. 1997;68(6):981-86.

[753] Newall CA, et al. Herbal Medicines: A Guide for Health Care Professionals. London: The Pharmaceutical Press; 1996:96-97.

[754] Volz HP, et al. Kav-kave Extarct WS 1490 Versus Placebo in Anxiety Disorder Randomized Placebo-controlled 25-week Outpatient Trial. Pharmacopsychiatry. An1997;30(1):1-5.

[755] Nordfors M, Hatvig P. Hypericum Perforatum in the Treatment of Mild Depression. Larkritidningen. 1997;94:2365-67. Bloomfield H, et al. Can Depression Be Successfully Treated with a Safe, Inexpensive Medically Proven Herb Available Without a Prescription? Hypericum an Depression. California: Prelude Press; 1996;7:S57-S59. Murray M. Natural Aternative to Prozac. New Your: William Morrow and Company, Inc. 1996:137.

[756] What your doctor may not tell you about menopause. John R Lee, M.D. Warner Books. 0-44667144-4. Pg 263-76.

[757] N.A.P.S (National Association for Premenstrual Syndrome) Exercise & PMS

[758] John R. Lee, M.D., Jesse Hanley, M.D., Virginia Hopkins and David Zava, PH.D. "What Your Doctor May Not Tell You About Premenopause (1999), Menopause (1996) and Breast Cancer (2002)" Warner Books.

[759] Smeltzer SC, Bare BG. Medical Surgical Nursing. 7th Ed.Philadelphia: JB Lippincott Co. 1992.

[760] Journal of the American Medical Association 276: 1957-1996

[761] Di Silverio F, et al. Evidence that Serenoa repens Extract Displays an Antiestrogenic Activity in Prostatic Tissue of Benign Prostatic Hypertrophy Patients. European Urologv. 1992;21(4):309-14.

[762] Pavon Maganto E. Zinc in prostatic physiopathology. I. Role of zinc in the physiology and biochemistry of the prostatic gland. Arch Esp Urol. Mar1979;32(2):143-52.

[763] Clinton SK, et al. Cis-trans lycopene isomers, carotenoids, and retinol in the human prostate. Cancer Epidemiol Biomarkers Prev 1996 Oct;5(10):823-833.

[764] Clark LC, et al. Decreased incidence of prostate cancer with selenium supplementation: results of a double-blind cancer prevention trial. Br J Urol. May1998;81(5):730-4.

To find out more or to speak to a nutritional counselor for free, just visit us at:
www.CuresForTheBody.com

[765] Heinonen, OP. Prostate cancer and supplementation with alpha tocopherol and beta-carotene: Incidence and mortality in a controlled trial. J Natl Cancer Inst. Mar1998;90(6):440-446.

[766] Barlet A, et al. Efficacy of Pygeum africanum Extract in the Medical Therapy of Urination Disorders Due to Benign Prostatic Hyperplasia: Evaluation of Objective and Subjective Parameters. A Placebo-controlled Double-blind multicenter Study. Wien Klin Wochenschr. Nov1990;102(22):667-73.

[767] Krzeski T, et al. Combined Extracts of Urtica dioica and Pygeum africanum in the Treatment of Benign Prostatic Hyperplasia: Double-blind Comparison of Two Doses. Clin Ther. 1993;15(6):1011-20.

[768] Rose DP and Connolly JM. Effects of fatty acids and eicosanoid synthesis inhibitors on the growth of two human prostate cancer cell lines. Prostate; 18(3): 243-54. 1991.

[769] Resolution of an artificially induced hematoma in the influence of a proteolytic enzyme." Robert M. Woolf, et al. The Journal of Trauma 5: 491-4 (1965)

[770] Anderson, A.J.C. Refining of Oils and Fats. Williams (ed). Elmsford, MY. Paergamon Press. 1962.

[771] Progress in the Chemistry of Fats and other Lipids. Holman, T. (ed) Elmsford. NY. Pergamon Press. 1951-1977.

[772] Edward Howell. Enzyme Nutrition. Enzymes to the Rescue. Pg 139.

[773] Fahim MS, et al. Zinc arginine, a 5 alpha-reductase inhibitor, reduces rat ventral prostate weight and DNA without affecting testicular function. Andrologia. Nov1993;25(6):369-375.

[775] Clinton SK, et al. Cis-trans lycopene isomers, carotenoids, and retinol in the human prostate. Cancer Epidemiol Biomarkers Prev 1996 Oct;5(10):823-833.

[775] Gerster H. The potential role of lycopene for human health. J Am Coll Nutr. Apr1997;16(2):109-126.

[776] Clark LC, et al. Decreased incidence of prostate cancer with selenium supplementation: results of a double-blind cancer prevention trial. Br J Urol. May1998;81(5):730-4.

[777] Heinonen, OP. Prostate cancer and supplementation with alpha tocopherol and beta-carotene: Incidence and mortality in a controlled trial. J Natl Cancer Inst. Mar1998;90(6):440-446.

[778] Briley M, et al. Permixon, a New Treatment for Prostatic Benign Hyperplasia, Acts Directly at the Cytosolic Androgen Receptor in Rat Prostate. J Steroid Biochem. 1979;10:483-86.

[779] Di Silverio F, et al.Evidence that Serenoa repens Extract Displays an Antiestrogenic Activity in Prostatic Tissue of Benign Prostatic Hypertrophy Patients. European Urologv. 1992;21(4):309-14.

[780] Plosker GL, et al. Serenoa repens (Permixon). A Review of Its Pharmacology and Therapeutic Efficacy in Benign Prostatic Hyperplasia. Drugs Aging. 1996;9(5):379-95.

[781] Di Silverio F, et al. Plant Extracts in BPH. Minerva Urol Nefrol. 1993;45(4):143-49.

[782] Krzeski T, et al.Combined Extracts of Urtica dioica and Pygeum africanum in the Treatment of Benign Prostatic Hyperplasia: Double-blind Comparison of Two Doses. Clin Ther. 1993;15(6):1011-20.

[783] Wagner H, et al. Biologically Active Compounds from the Aqueous Extract of Urtica dioica. Planta Med. 1989;55(5):452-54.

To find out more or to speak to a nutritional counselor for free, just visit us at:
www.CuresForTheBody.com

[784] Boone K. Withania – The Indian Ginseng and Anti-aging Adaptogen. Nutrition and Healing. Jun1998;5(6):5-7.

[785] Chang CY, et al. Effects of Astragalus membranaceus on Enhancement of Mouse Natural Killer Cell Activity. Chung Kuo I Hsueh Ko Hsueh Yuan Hsueh Pao. Aug1983;5(4):231-34.

[786] Rege NN, et al. Adaptogenic Properties of Six Rasayana Herbs Used in Ayurvedic Medicine. Phytother Res. Jun1999;13(4):275-91.

[787] Lobo A, et al. Reduction of homocysteine levels in coronary artery disease by low-dose folic acid combined with vitamins B6 and B12. Am J Cardiol. Mar1999;83(6):821-5.

[788] ibid.

[789] ibid.

[790] Urberg M, et al. Hypocholesterolemic effects of nicotinic acid and chromium supplementation. J Fam Pract. Dec1988;27(6):603-6.

[791] Urberg M, et al. Hypocholesterolemic effects of nicotinic acid and chromium supplementation. J Fam Pract. Dec1988;27(6):603-6.

[792] Bertolini S, et al. Lipoprotein changes induced by pantethine in hyperlipoproteinemic patients: adults and children. Int J Clin Pharmacol Ther Toxicol. 1986;24(11):630-7.

[793] Moody JA, et al. Effects of long-term oral administration of L-arginine on the rat erectile response. J Urol. Sep1997;158(3 Pt 1):942-7.

[794] Elsakka M, et al. New Data Referring to Chemistry of Withania Somnifera Species. Rev Med Chir Soc Med Nat Lasi. Apr1990;94(2):385-87.

[795] Boone K. Withania – The Indian Ginseng and Anti-aging Adaptogen. Nutrition and Healing. Jun1998; 5(6): 5-7.

[796] Zhu J, et al. CordyMax Cs-4: A Scientific Product Revie. Pharmanex Phytoscience Review Series. 1997.

[797] Deng X, et al. Clinical Study of Fermentation Product of Cordyceps sinensis on Treatment of Hyposexuality. J Administration Traditional Chinese Med. 1995;5(supp):23-24.

[798] Lynch SM, et al. Ascorbic acid and atherosclerotic cardiovascular disease. Subcell Biochem. 1996;25:331-67.

[799] Chan AC. Vitamin E and atherosclerosis. J Nutr. 1998;128(10):1593-6.

[800] Mortensen SA, et al. Dose-related decrease of serum coenzyme Q10 during treatment with HMG-CoA reductase inhibitors. Mol Aspects Med. 1997;18 Suppl:S137-44.

[801] Bisignano G, et al. On the in-vitro antimicrobial activity of oleuropein and hydroxytyrosol. J Pharm Pharmacol. Aug1999;51(8):971-4.

[802] Majamaa H, Isolauri E. Probiotics: a novel approach in the management of food allergy. J Allergy Clin Immunol. Feb1997;99(2):179-85.

[803] Cardui mariae fructus (Milk Thistle fruit). Commission E Monograph. Bundesanzeiger, no 50. Mar1986.

[804] Horrobin DF. Essential fatty acid metabolism and its modification in atopic eczema. Am J Clin Nutr. Jan2000;71(1 Suppl):367S-72S.

[805] Horrobin DF. Essential fatty acid metabolism and its modification in atopic eczema. Am J Clin Nutr. Jan2000;71(1 Suppl):367S-72S.

To find out more or to speak to a nutritional counselor for free, just visit us at:
www.CuresForTheBody.com

[806] David TJ, et al. Low serum zinc in children with atopic eczema. Br J Dermatol. Nov1984;111(5):597-601.

[807] Campos R, et al. Silybin Dihemisuccinate Protects Against Glutathione Depletion and Lipid Peroxidation Induced by Acetaminophen on Rat Liver. Planta Medica. 1989;55:417-19.

[808] Ionescu G, et al. Oral Citrus seed extract. J Orthomolecula Med. 1990;5(3):72-74.

[809] Newall CA, et al. Herbal Medicine: A Guide for Health-Care Professionals. Cambridge: Pharmaceutical Press; 1996:36-37.

[810] Wahn U, et al. Atopic eczema: how to tackle the most common atopic symptom. Pediatr Allergy Immunol. 1999;10(12 Suppl):19-23.

[811] Petkov V, Manolov P. Pharmacological analysis of the iridoid oleuropein. Drug Res. 1972;22(9):1476-86.

[812] Visioli F, et al. Oleuropein, the bitter principle of olives, enhances nitric oxide production by mouse macrophages. Life Sci. 1998;62(6):541-6.

[813] Ewing CI, et al. Failure of oral zinc supplementation in atopic eczema. Eur J Clin Nutr. Oct1991;45(10):507-10.

[814] Valenzuela A, et al. Selectivity of Silymarin on the Increase of the Glutathione Content in Different Tissues of the Rat. Planta Medica. 1989;55:1550-52.

[815] Fitzgerald JF. Colonization of the gastrointestinal tract. Mead Johnson Symp Perinat Dev Med. 1977;(11):35-8.

[816] Skene, DJ., et al. Use of melatonin in the treatment of phase shift and sleep disorders Adv Exp Med Biol. 1999;467:79-84.

Dagan Y., et al. Evaluating the role of melatonin in the long-term treatment of delayed sleep phase Syndrome (DSPS). Chronobiol Int. Nov 1998;15(6):655-66

[817] Bruni O., Ferri R., Miano S., Verrillo E., I- 5-hydroxytryptophan treatment of sleep terrors in children.Eur J Pediatr. Jul 2004; 163(7):402-7

[818] Volz HP, et al kava-kava extract WS 1490 Versus Placebo in Anxiety Disorders- A Randomized PlaceboControlled 25-week Outpatient Trial. Pharmacopsychiatry . Jan 1997:30(1) 1:5

[819] Newall CA, Et al. Herbal Medicines: A Guide for Health Care Professionals. London. The pharmaceutical Press; 1996:206-207.

[820] Lindahl O., Lindwall L., Double Blind Study of Valerian Preparations. Pharmacol Biochem Behav.1989;32(4):1065-66.

Leathwood PD, et al. Aqueous Extract of Valerian Root (Valeriana officinalisL.) Improves Sleep Quality In Man. Pharmacol Biochem Behav. 1982;17:65-71.

Balderer G, et al. Effect of Valerian on Human Sleep. Psvchopharmacology 1985;87:406-09.

[821] Wichti M., in Bisset NA, ed. Herbal Drugs and phytopharmaceuticals. Stuttgart Press Scientific 1994:140-42.

[822] Newall CA, et al Herbal Medicines: A Guide for Health Care Professionals. London: The Pharmaceutical Press; 1996:162-163.

Bradley PR, ed. British Herbal Compendium, vol 1. Bournemouth: British Herbal Medicine Association; 1992:128-129.

To find out more or to speak to a nutritional counselor for free, just visit us at:
www.CuresForTheBody.com

[823] Hornyak M, et al. Magnesium therapy for periodic leg movements-related insomnia and restless legs syndrome: an open pilot study. Sleep. Aug1998;21(5):501-5.

[824] O'Keeffe ST, Gavin K, Lavan JN. Iron status and restless legs syndrome in the elderly. Age Ageing. May1994;23(3):200-3.

[825] Kolb E. Some new biochemical knowledge on the effect of nutritional factors on brain function. Z Gesamte Inn Med. Dec1987;42(24):689-95.

[826] Beyer CE, Steketee JD, Saphier D. Antioxidant properties of melatonin - an emerging mystery. Biochem Pharmacol. Nov1998;56(10):1265-72.

[827] Beyer CE, Steketee JD, Saphier D. Antioxidant properties of melatonin - an emerging mystery. Biochem Pharmacol. Nov1998;56(10):1265-72.

[828] Volz HP, et al. Kava-kava Extract WS 1490 Versus Placebo in Anxiety Disorders - A Randomized Placebo-controlled 25-week Outpatient Trial. Pharmacopsychiatry. Jan1997;30(1):1-5.

[829] Newall CA, et al. Herbal Medicines: A Guide for Health Care Professionals. London: The Pharmaceutical Press; 1996:206-207.

[830] Lindahl O, Lindwall L. Double Blind Study of Valerian Preparations. Pharmacol Biochem Behav. 1989;32(4):1065-66.

[831] Gutierrez S, Ang-Lee MK, Walker DJ, Zacny JP. Assessing subjective and psychomotor effects of the herbal medication valerian in healthy volunteers. Pharmacol Biochem Behav. May2004;78(1):57-64.

[832] Wichtl M, in Bisset NA, ed. Herbal Drugs and Phytopharmaceuticals. Stuttgart: Scientific Press; 1994:140-42.

[833] U. Ulthaus. J.J. Staub, A. Ryff-DeLeche, et al.

"LDL/HDL-changes in Subclinical Hypothyroidism: Possible Risk Factors for Coronary Heart Disease." Clinical Endocrinology 28 (1998):158-63.

J.W. Dean and P.B.S. Fowler. "Ezaggerated Responsiveness to Thyrotrophin Realeaing Hormone: A Risk Factor in Women with Artery Disease," Brit Med J 290 (1985):1555-61.

[834] Azizi F, et al. Treatment of goitrous hypothyroidism with iodized oil supplementation in an area of iodine deficiency. Exp Clin Endocrinol Diabetes. 1996;104(5):387-91.

Vono J, et al. The effect of oral administration of iodine to patients with goiter and hypothyroidism due to defective synthesis of thyroglobulin. Thyroid. Feb1996;6(1):11-5.

[835] Olivieri O, et al. Low selenium status in the elderly influences thyroid hormones. Clin Sci (Colch). Dec1995;89(6):637-42.

Wu HY, et al. Selenium deficiency and thyroid hormone metabolism and function. Sheng Li Ko Hsueh Chin Chan. Jan1995;26(1):12-6.

Vanderpas JB, et al. Selenium deficiency mitigates hypothyroxinemia in iodine-deficient subjects. Am J Clin Nutr. Feb1993;57(2 Suppl):271S-275S.

[836] Curro F, et al. Fucus vesiculosis L. nel Trattamento Medico Dell'Obesita e delle Alterazioni Metaboliche Connesse. Arch Med Interna. 1976;28:19-32.

Newall CA, et al. Herbal Medicines: A Guide for Health Care Professionals. London: The Pharmaceutical Press; 1996:124-126.

Burkholder PR. Drugs from the Sea. Armed Forces Chem J. 1963;17(6):12-16.

To find out more or to speak to a nutritional counselor for free, just visit us at:
www.CuresForTheBody.com

Duke, James A. Handbook of phytochemical constituents of GRAS herbs and other economic plants. Boca Raton, FL: CRC Press; 1992.

Shilo S, et al. Iodine-induced hyperthyroidism in a patient with a normal thyroid gland. Postgrad Med J. Jul1986;62(729):661-2.

Dimitriadou, et al. Iodine goiter. Proc Royal Soc Med. 1961;54:345-346.

[837] Misra GC, et al. Malabsorption in thyroid dysfunctions. J Indian Med Assoc. Jul1991;89(7):195-7.

[838] Dirican M, Tas S. Effects of vitamin E and vitamin C supplementation on plasma lipid peroxidation and on oxidation of apolipoprotein B-containing lipoproteins in experimental hyperthyroidism. J Med Invest. Feb1999;46(1-2):29-33.

[839] Seven A, et al. Biochemical evaluation of oxidative stress in propylthiouracil treated hyperthyroid patients. Effects of vitamin C supplementation. Clin Chem Lab Med. Oct1998;36(10):767-70.

[840] Bianchi G, et al. Oxidative stress and anti-oxidant metabolites in patients with hyperthyroidism: effect of treatment. Horm Metab Res. Nov1999;31(11):620-4.

[841] Benvenga S, Ruggeri RM, Russo A, Lapa D, Campenni A, Trimarchi F. Usefulness of L-carnitine, a naturally occurring peripheral antagonist of thyroid hormone action, in iatrogenic hyperthyroidism: a randomized, double-blind, placebo-controlled clinical trial. J Clin Endocrinol Metab. Aug2001;86(8):3579-94.

[842] Jarosz M, et al. Effects of high dose vitamin C treatment on Helicobacter pylori infection and total vitamin C concentration in gastric juice. Eur J Cancer Prev. 1998;7:449-454.

Dubey SS, et al. Ascorbic acid, dehydroascorbic acid, glutathione and histamine in peptic ulcer. Indian J Med Res. Dec1982;76:859-62.

Novoderzhkina IuG, Cherentsov AM. Effect of diet therapy on the changes of vitamin C content in the blood and urine of patients with chronic gastritis and peptic ulcer. Vopr Pitan. May1993;(3):13-6.

[843] Mahmood T, et al. Prevention of duodenal ulcer formation in the rat by dietary vitamin A supplementation. JPEN J Parenter Enteral Nutr. Jan1986;10(1):74-7.

Patty I, et al. A comparative dynamic study of the effectiveness of gastric cytoprotection by vitamin A, De-Nol, sucralfate and ulcer healing by pirenzepine in patients with chronic gastric ulcer (a multiclinical and randomized study). Acta Physiol Hung. 1984;64(3-4):379-84.

Horwitt MK. Plasma tocopherol, hemolysis and dietary unsaturated lipid relationships in man. Fed Proc. 1958;17:245.

al-Moutairy AR, Tariq M. Effect of vitamin E and selenium on hypothermic restraint stress and chemically-induced ulcers. Dig Dis Sci. Jun1996;41(6):1165-71.

Arutiunian VM, et al. Use of alpha-tocopherol acetate (vitamin E) and sodium nucleinate in the treatment of patients with stomach and duodenal ulcer. Klin Med (Mosk). Apr1983;61(4):52-4.

Toteva ET, et al. Use of alpha-tocopherol in the complex treatment of patients with peptic ulcer. Vrach Delo. Feb1988;(2):79-81.

Watanabe T, et al. Zinc deficiency delays gastric ulcer healing in rats. Dig Dis Sci. Jun1995;40(6):1340-4.

To find out more or to speak to a nutritional counselor for free, just visit us at:
www.CuresForTheBody.com

Escolar G, Bulbena O. Zinc compounds, a new treatment in peptic ulcer. Drugs Exp Clin Res. 1989;15(2):83-9.

Jimenez E, et al. Meta-analysis of efficacy of zinc acexamate in peptic ulcer. Digestion. 1992;51(1):18-26.

Bandyopadhyay B, Bandyopadhyay SK. Protective effect of zinc gluconate on chemically induced gastric ulcer. Indian J Med Res. Jul1997;106:27-32.

Banos JE, Bulbena O. Zinc compounds as therapeutic agents in peptic ulcer. Methods Find Exp Clin Pharmacol. 1989;11(Suppl 1):117-22.

Jimenez E, et al. Meta-analysis of efficacy of zinc acexamate in peptic ulcer. Digestion. 1992;51(1):18-26.

Bandyopadhyay B, Bandyopadhyay SK. Protective effect of zinc gluconate on chemically induced gastric ulcer. Indian J Med Res. Jul1997;106:27-32.

Banos JE, Bulbena O. Zinc compounds as therapeutic agents in peptic ulcer. Methods Find Exp Clin Pharmacol. 1989;11(Suppl 1):117-22.

Cho CH, Ogle CW. Does increased gastric mucus play a role in the ulcer-protecting effects of zinc sulphate? Experientia. Jan1978;34(1):90-1.

Abou-Mohamed G, et al. Effect of Zinc on Antiinflammatory and Ulcerogenic Activities of Indomethacin and Diclofenac. Pharmacology. 1995;50:266-272.

[844] Nair S, et al. Micronutrient antioxidants in gastric mucosa and serum in patients with gastritis and gastric ulcer: does Helicobacter pylori infection affect the mucosal levels? J Clin Gastroenterol. Jun2000;30(4):381-5.

Horwitt MK. Tocopherol requirements in man. Fed Proc. 1959;18:530.

[845] Watanabe T, et al. Zinc deficiency delays gastric ulcer healing in rats. Dig Dis Sci. Jun1995;40(6):1340-4.

Escolar G, Bulbena O. Zinc compounds, a new treatment in peptic ulcer. Drugs Exp Clin Res. 1989;15(2):83-9.

[846] Okabe S, et al. Effects of acetylsalicylic acid (ASA), ASA plus L-glutamine and L-glutamine on healing of chronic gastric ulcer in the rat. Digestion. 1976;14(1):85-8.

Shive W, et al. Glutamine in treatment of peptic ulcer. Texas State J Med. 1957;53:840-843.

Yan R, et al. Early enteral feeding and supplement of glutamine prevent occurrence of stress ulcer following severe thermal injury. Chung Hua Cheng Hsing Shao Shang Wai Ko Tsa Chih. May1995;11(3):189-92.

Akamatsu H, et al. Mechanism of Anti-inflammatory Action of Glycyrrhizin: Effect on Neutrophil Functions Including Reactive Oxygen Species Generation. Planta Medica. 1991;57:119-21.

Kimura Y, et al. Effects of Chalcones Isolated from Licorice Roots on Leukotriene Biosynthesis in Human Polymorphonuclear Neutrophils. Phytotherapy Res. 1988;2:140-45.

Shinada M, et al. Enhancement of Interferon-gamma Production in Glycyrrhizin-Treated Human Peripheral Lymphocytes in Response to Concanavalin A and to Surface Antigen of Hepatitis B Virus. Proc Soc Exp Biol Med. 1986;181(2):205-10.

Abe N, et al. Interferon Induction by Glycyrrhizin and Glycyrrhetinic Acid in Mice. Microbiol Immunol.

1982;26:535-39.

Van Marle J, et al. Deglycyrrhizinated Liquorice (DGL) and the Renewal of Rat Stomach Epithelium. European Journal of Pharmacology. 1981;72:219-25.

Wilson JA. A Comparison of Carbenoxolone Sodium and Deglycyrrhizinated Liquorice in the Treatment of Gastric Ulcer in the Ambulant Patient. British Journal of Clinical Practice. 1972;26:563-66.

D'Imperio N, et al. Double-blind Trial in Duodenal and Gastric Ulcers. Acta Gastro-Enterologica Belgica. 1978;41:427-34.

Rees WD, et al. Effect of Deglycyrrhizinated Liquorice on Gastric Mucosal Damage by Aspirin. Scandinavian J of Gastroenterology. 1979;14:605-07.

Visioli F, et al. Oleuropein, the bitter principle of olives, enhances nitric oxide production by mouse macrophages. Life Sci. 1998;62(6):541-6.

Renis HE. In vitro antiviral activity of calcium elenolate. Antimicrob Agents Chemother. 1969:167-72.

Heinze JE, et al. Specificity of the antiviral agent calcium elenolate. Antimicrob Agents Chemother. Oct1975;8(4):421-5.

Bennani-Kabchi N, et al. Effects of Olea europea var. oleaster leaves in hypercholesterolemic insulin-resistant sand rats. Therapie. Nov1999;54(6):717-23.

Gonzalez M, et al. Hypoglycemic activity of olive leaf. Planta Medica. 1992;58:513-515.

[847] Wilson JA. A Comparison of Carbenoxolone Sodium and Deglycyrrhizinated Liquorice in the Treatment of Gastric Ulcer in the Ambulant Patient. British Journal of Clinical Practice. 1972;26:563-66.

Van Marle J, et al. Deglycyrrhizinated Liquorice (DGL) and the Renewal of Rat Stomach Epithelium. European Journal of Pharmacology. 1981;72:219-25.

Morgan AG, et al. Comparison between Cimetidin and Caved-S in the Treatment of Gastric Laceration, and Subsequent Maintenance Therapy. Gut. 1982;23:545-51.

Tangri KK, et al. Biochemical Study of Anti-inflammatory and Anti-arthritic Properties of Glycyrrhetic Acid. Biochemical Pharmacology. 1965;14:1277-81.

[848] Bisignano G, et al. On the in-vitro antimicrobial activity of oleuropein and hydroxytyrosol. J Pharm Pharmacol. Aug1999;51(8):971-4.

Petkov V, Manolov P. Pharmacological analysis of the iridoid oleuropein. Drug Res. 1972;22(9):1476-86.

Juven B, et al. Studies on the mechanism of the antimicrobial action of oleuropein. J Appl Bact. 1972;35:559.

[849] Huwez FU, et al. Mastic gum kills Helicobacter pylori. N Engl J Med. Dec1998;339(26):1946.

Huwez FU, Al-Habbal MJ. Mastic in treatment of benign gastric ulcers. Gastroenterol Japon. 1986;21:273–74.

Al-Said MS, Ageel AM, Parmar NS, Tariq M. Evaluation of mastic, a crude drug obtained from Pistacia lentiscus for gastric and duodenal anti-ulcer activity. J Ethnopharmacol. 1986;15:271–78.

Al-Habbal MJ, Al-Habbal Z, Huwez FU. A double-blind controlled clinical trial of mastic and placebo in the Treatment of duodenal ulcer. J Clin Exp Pharm Physiol. 1984;11:541-4.

Ali-Shtaveh MS, et al. Antifungal activity of plant extracts against dermatophytes. Mycoses. 1999;42(11-12):665-72.

Iauk L, et al. In vitro antimicrobial activity of Pistacia lentiscus L. extracts: preliminary report. J Chemother. Jun1996;8(3):207-9.

Saito H, et al. [Effects of aloe extracts, aloctin A, on gastric secretion and on experimental gastric lesions in rats]. Yakugaku Zasshi. May1989;109(5):335-9.

Wang HH, et al. Aloe-emodin effects on arylamine N-acetyltransferase activity in the bacterium Helicobacter pylori. Planta Med. Mar1998;64(2):176-8.

[850] Sotnikova EP. [Therapeutic use of aloe in experimental stomach ulcers]. Vrach Delo. Jun1984;(6):71-4.

[851] Salminen, S., E. Isolauri and T. Onnela, 1995, Gut flora in normal and disordered states. Chemotherapy, 41: 5-15

[852] J.M. Beazell. "The effect of supplemental amylase on digestion." *The Journal of Laboratory and Clinical Medicine* 27: 308-19 (1941)

[853] Western Journal of Medicine August 2000

[854] De Roos, Nicole M, et al. "Consumption of a Solid Fat Rich in Lauric Acid Results in a More Favorable Serum Lipid Profile in Healthy Men and Women than Consumption of a Solid Fat Rich in trans-fatty Acids," Journal of Nutrition (2001): 131:242-245.

Prior, I. A., et al. "Cholesterol, coconuts, and diet on Polynesian atolls: a natural experiment: the Pukapuka and Tokelau Island studies," American Journal of Clinical Nutrition (1981): 34: 1552-1561.

St-Onge, Marie-Pierre, P.J.H. Jones, "Physiological Effects of Medium-Chain Triglycerides: Potential Agents in the Prevention of Obesity," Journal of Nutrition (2002): 132:329-332.

[855] Petschow, Byron W., et al. "Susceptiblity of Helicobacter pylori to Bactericidal Properties of Medium-Chain Monoglycerides and Free Fatty Acids ," Antimicrobial Agents and Chemotherapy (February 1996): 302-306.

[856] M. Boero et al., "Candida Overgrowth in Gastric Juice of Peptic Ulcer Subjects on Short-and long-Term Treatment with H2-Receptor Antagonists." Digestion 28 1983):158-63.

[857] Fernandes, C.F. and K.M. Shahani, 1989, Modulation of antibiosis by lactobacilli and yogurt and tits healthful and beneficial significance, in proceedings of National Yogurt Association, New York, NY pp. 145-59.

[858] "Effect of lipase ingestion on blood lipid levels" James C. McPherson, et al. Proceedings of the Society of Experimental Biology and medicine 115: 514-17 (1964)

[859] Bennett JE. Pathogenic fungi. In: Sherris JC, ed. Medical Microbiology. 2nd ed. New York. Elsevier. 1991:440.

[860] M. Woodhead, "Antibbiotic Resistance," Brit J Hosp Med 56 (1996):314-15.

M. Cohen, "Epidemiology of Drug Resistance: Implications for a Post-Antibiotic Era,' Science 257 (1992):1050-5.

World Health Organization, Fighting Disease, Fostering Development: Report of the Director General (London:HMSO, 1996).

[861] Udo Erasmus, Fats that Heal Fats that Kill, Flax, new research, Lignans. Pg. 284.

[862] Elmer GW, et al. Biotherapeutic agents. A neglected modality for the treatment and prevention of selected intestinal and vaginal infections. JAMA. Mar1996;275(11):870-6.

Hilton E, et al. Ingestion of yogurt containing Lactobacillus acidophilus as prophylaxis for candidal vaginitis. Ann Intern Med. Mar1992;116(5):353-7.

Fitzsimmons N, Berry DR. Inhibition of Candida albicans by Lactobacillus acidophilus: evidence for the involvement of a peroxidase system. Microbios. 1994;80(323):125-33.

Jack M, et al. Evidence for the involvement of thiocyanate in the inhibition of Candida albicans by Lactobacillus acidophilus. Microbios. 1990;62(250):37-46.

[863] R.D. Smyth, et al. "Systemic biochemical changes following the oral administration of a proteolytic enzyme, bromelain." Archives of International Pharmacodynamics 136: 230-6 (1962)

[864] Aquino R, et al. Plant Metabolites. Structure and in Vitro Antiviral Activity of Quinovic Acid Glycosides from Uncaria tomentosa and Guettarda platypoda. J Nat Prod. 1989;52(4):679-85.

Aquino R, et al. Plant Metabolites. New Compounds and Anti-inflammatoy Activity of Uncaria tomentosa. J Nat Prod. 1991;54(2):453-59.

Wagner H, et al. The Alkaloids of Uncaria tomentosa and Their Phagocytosis-stimulating Action. Planta Med. 1995;5:419-23.

Jones K. Cat's Claw: Healing Vine of Peru. Seattle. Sylvan Press. 1995;48-49.

Aquino R, et al. New Polyhydroxylated Triterpenes from Uncaria tomentosa. J Nat Prod. 1990;53(3):559-64.

Sandoval-Chacon M. Antiinflammatory actions of cat's claw: the role of NF-kappaB. Aliment Pharmacol Ther. Dec1998;12(12):1279-89.

Visioli F. Antiatherogenic components of olive oil. Curr Atheroscler Rep. Jan2001;3(1):64-7.

Visioli F, et al. Oleuropein, the bitter principle of olives, enhances nitric oxide production by mouse macrophages. Life Sci. 1998;62(6):541-6.

Renis HE. In vitro antiviral activity of calcium elenolate. Antimicrob. Agents Chemother. 1970;167-72.

Heinze JE, et al. Specificity of the antiviral agent calcium elenolate. Antimicrob Agents Chemother. Oct1975;8(4):421-5.

Bennani-Kabchi N, et al. Effects of Olea europea var. oleaster leaves in hypercholesterolemic insulin-resistant sand rats. Therapie. Nov1999;54(6):717-23.

Gonzalez M, et al. Hypoglycemic activity of olive leaf. Planta Medica. 1992;58:513-515.

Freeman F, et al. Garlic Chemistry: Stability of s-2-propenyl)-2-propene-1-sulfinothioate (allicin) in Blood, Solvents, and Simulated Physiological Fluids. J Agric Food Chem. 1995;43:2332-2338.

Egen-Schwind C, et al. Metabolism of Garlic Constituents in the Isolated Perfused Rat Liver. Planta Med. Aug1992;58(4):301-5.

Egen-Schwind C, et al. Pharmacokinetics of Vinyldithiins, Transformation Products of Allicin. Planta Med. Feb1992;58(1):8-13.

Hammer KA, et al. In-vitro activity of essential oils, in particular Melaleuca alternifolia (tea tree) oil and tea tree oil products, against Candida spp. J Antimicrob Chemother. Nov1998;42(5):591-5.

Long MM, et al. Tea tree oil in the treatment of tinea pedis. Australas J Dermatol. 1992;33(3):145-9.

[865] Bisignano G, et al. On the in-vitro antimicrobial activity of oleuropein and hydroxytyrosol. J Pharm Pharmacol. Aug1999;51(8):971-4.

To find out more or to speak to a nutritional counselor for free, just visit us at:
www.CuresForTheBody.com

Bisignano G, et al. On the in-vitro antimicrobial activity of oleuropein and hydroxytyrosol. J Pharm Pharmacol. Aug1999;51(8):971-4.

[866] Ernst E. Cardioprotection and Garlic. Lancet. 1997;349(9045):131.

Steiner M, et al. A Double-blind Crossover Study in Moderately Hypercholesterolemic Men that Compared the Effect of Aged Garlic Extract and Placebo Administration on Blood Lipids. Am J Clin Nutr. 1996;64(6):866-70.

Adetumbi M, et al. Allium sativum (Garlic)—A Natural Antibiotic. Med Hypoth. 1983;12:227-37.

Pai ST, et al. Antifungal Effects of Allium sativum (Garlic) Extract Against the Aspergillus Species Involved in Otomycosis. Lett Appl Microbiol. 1995;20(1):14-18.

Weber ND, et al. In Vitro Virucidal Effects of Allium sativum (garlic) Extract and Compounds. Planta Med. Oct1992;58(5):417-23.

[867] Altman PM. Australian tea tree oil. Australian J Pharmacy. 1988;69:276-78.

Penfold AR, et al. Some notes on the Essential oil of M. alternifolia. Aust J Dent. 417-4181930.

Mann CM, et al. The outer membrane of pseudomonas aeruginosa NCTC 6749 contributes to its tolerance to the essential oil of melaleuca alternifolia. Lett Appl Microbiol. Apr2000;30(4):294-7.

Carson CF, et al. Efficacy and safety of tea tree oil as a topical antimicrobial agent. J Hosp Infect. Nov1998;

40(3):175-8.

Cox SD, et al. The mode of antimicrobial action of the essential oil of Melaleuca alternifolia (tea tree oil). J Appl Microbiol. Jan2000;88(1):170-5.

Carson CF, et al. Susceptibility of methicillin-resistant Staphylococcus aureus to the essential oil of Melaleuca alternifolia. J Antimicrob Chemother. Mar1995;35(3):421-4.

May J, et al. Time-kill studies of tea tree oils on clinical isolates. J Antimicrob Chemother. May2000;45(5):639-643.

Nenoff P, et al. Antifungal activity of the essential oil of Melaleuca alternifolia (tea tree oil) against pathogenic fungi in vitro. Skin Pharmacol. 1996;9(6):388-94.

[868] Ionescu G, et al. Oral Citrus seed extract. J Orthomolecula Med. 1990;5(3):72-74.

Arimi SM. Campylobacter infection in humans. East Afr Med J. Dec1989;66(12):851-5.

Fitzgerald JF. Colonization of the gastrointestinal tract. Mead Johnson Symp Perinat Dev Med. 1977;(11):35-8.

[869] Hauer J, et al. Mechanism of Stimulation of Human Natural Killer Cytotoxicity by Arabinogalactan from Larix occidentalis. Cancer Immunol Immunother. 1993;36(4):237-44

[870] Lee, I-Min. Harvard Medical School, "Physical Activity and Cancer," PCPFS Research Digest 2:2.

[871] M. Boero et al., "Candida Overgrowth in Gastric Juice of Peptic Ulcer Subjects on Short- and long-term treatment with H2-Receptor antagonists." Digestion 28 (1983):158-63

[872] Guillot, N., 1959, Elaboration par Lactobacillus adicdophilus d'un produit actif contre Candida albicans, Ann. Ist. Pasteur 95, 194-207.

Chapter 5

Optimal Nutrition Plan

The need for nutrition

Proper nutrition is an extremely important element for optimal health. When it comes to generating permanent change, there is no exercise program, supplement, powder, or pill that will work by itself. For optimal health, the cells must have the constant nourishment that comes from balanced nutrition. Athough nutrition has received a lot of attention in the past few years, even the most concerned consumers may find it difficult to decipher the truth. Hype permeates the media, leaving misinformation and confusion in its wake. We are left to choose between several options, all about as unhealthy, and perplexing, as the next. We wonder which is better: grapefruit diets, protein diets, or juice fasts; low-fat, no-fat or fat blockers; diet candy or diet pills; this food or that fad.

Though nutrition information seems readily available, the statistics show that something is sorely amiss. We live in an age of advanced technology and affluence, yet thousands of North Americans are malnourished. Poor nutrition is so prevalent that it is seriously affecting the overall health of the American people. In fact, eight out of the top ten causes of death today are directly related to our diet. We are overweight and undernourished. Individuals continue to die sooner than they should and to live less productive lives – simply because of poor nutritional habits. According to Dr. Herman Tarnower, "You can be malnourished in affluent suburbia as well as in the Third World. In most cases, it takes the form of eating too much of the wrong things."

To find out more or to speak to a nutritional counselor for free, just visit us at: www.CuresForTheBody.com

Advances in understanding nutrition have helped to virtually eliminate deficiency diseases such as pellagra, rickets, goiter, anemia, beriberi and scurvy. However, in place of these diseases, largely because of the prevalence of quick-fix, highly processed convenience foods, we now experience a host of other disorders.

For the most part, we get enough food to satisfy our hunger, but because the foods we eat are full of empty calories, we are often seriously deficient in nutrients. "Large sectors of the U.S. population are chronically deficient in nutrients; that is, malnourished, even though they look normal or even overweight," stated Joseph D. Beasley, M.D. and Jerry Swift, M.A. in *The Kellogg Report: The Impact of Nutrition, Environment and Lifestyle on the Health of Americans.*

Source of the Problem

Jean Mayer pointed out some of the reasons for this widespread problem in her report of the findings of the White House Conference on Food, Nutrition and Health. She stated, "The nutritive value of snack foods, a more and more important component of our daily intake of food, was extremely low, and there was essentially no leadership in encouraging or requiring its improvement.

Each year, the advertising industry concentrated a major portion of its efforts on the promotion of our least nutritious foods; namely candy, soft drinks, beer, and a host of crisp-fried snack items that are consumed in great quantities, particularly by our young people."

I suppose advertisers who market cigarettes, coffee, white flour, sugar and other highly processed foods should be commended. Many of them have fulfilled their assignments and have done an outstanding job of disclaiming the health hazards and hiding the dangers associated with their products. Similarly, shouldn't researchers receive some sort of recognition for spending millions of dollars and thousands of hours trying to discredit the obvious, and searching, instead, for ways to say that their unsafe products are actually good?

Sound studies clearly, consistently and overwhelmingly show that rich foods such as white flour, sugars, processed foods and meats and dairy products are a major cause of premature death and disability. However, the money interests behind these industries continue to win out. A great deal of money is spent every year to convince us that black is white and white is truly black. Think about the term "junk food." The term itself should be a warning, yet brightly colored packages and clever slogans entice us to nonchalantly (and smilingly) consume our daily dose of garbage. Dr. George Biggs, professor of nutrition at the University of California, Berkeley speaks about these "worthless" foods: "About 17 percent of our calories come from isolated fats – fats that are added back to foods, as in the frying of doughnuts and the making of candies and pastries. Another 17 percent of our calories are in the form of sugar, so we're actually getting some 34 percent of our calories from foods with virtually no vitamins or minerals. Then, we get another 16 percent from heavily milled refined white flour."

So, we have to ask the question: **How can we get all the necessary vitamins and minerals if 50 percent of the calories we consume are derived from fat, sugar and processed foods from which the vitamins and minerals are removed?**

Sweet Sabotage

It seems as if marketers have done a great job of luring us into the center of the pond and then have left us there like sitting ducks waiting for the deadly consequences of poor dietary habits to set in. Sugar consumption continues to skyrocket, soaring to over 170 pounds per person per year. Americans drink an average of over 53 gallons of carbonated soft drinks per person per year total, which far surpasses the total of milk, real fruit juice and bottled water combined. We consume only 2/3 as much flour and grains as our grandparents ate in 1910; and even though our grain consumption is higher than it was in 1970, we aren't eating more whole grains and oatmeal but more doughnuts, cookies and brownies.

As our diets continue to go downhill, volumes of research continue to prove what the Assistant Secretary of Health, Robert E. Windom stressed several years ago, saying, "Diseases such as heart disease, stroke, cancer and diabetes remain leading causes of death and disability in the United States. Substantial scientific research over the past decades indicates that diet can play an important role in prevention of such conditions."

Additional evidence that how we eat in North America is affecting our health is to watch what happens in developing countries as they adopt our way of eating. In May of 1997, *U.S. News and World Report* noted that **as our fries-and-shake habits have spread to other countries, the rates of cancer, heart disease and stroke have risen sharply.** Anthelme Brillat-Savarin's statement from 1825 is all-too true, and should have been heeded. He said, "The destiny of countries depends on the way they feed themselves." An echoing warning came from Senator George McGovern when, as a member of the Senate Select Committee on Nutrition, he said, "The simple fact is that our diets have changed radically within the last 50 years...These dietary changes represent as great a threat to public health as smoking."

Unfortunately, those warnings have been waylaid by the claims made by individuals and companies whose interest is not in your health but in their own profitability. Though studies and statistics prove otherwise, various companies and trade associations have the audacity to make utterly ridiculous statements. For example, the National Cattlemen's Association would like us to believe that: "Beef is highly digestible – more digestible, in fact, than vegetables." The American Medical Association also showed their ignorance regarding nutrition when they said, "White flour is a wholesome food and has a proper place in the well balanced, adequate diet." And, the National Association of Margarine Manufacturers tried to pull the wool over consumers' eyes in publications they funded, which stated, "There is no clear evidence...that trans-fatty acids at levels consumed by Americans have important adverse effects on blood cholesterol fractions..."

What kind of credible information do you think you are receiving when you realize that The Dairymen's Association or the Beef Industry Council pay for dietary brochures distributed by the American Heart Association? What do you think the American Dietetic Association is inclined to promote when a great deal of their funding comes from companies like M & M Mars, Sarah Lee and Coca-Cola and from trade groups such as the Sugar Association and the National Livestock and Meat Board? Sounds almost like the old poison apple trick from Snow White and the Seven Dwarfs, doesn't it? We simply must take a different look at how we eat and which messages we heed.

"Re-examine all you have been told at school or church or in any book, dismiss what insults your soul, and your flesh shall be a great poem," said Walt Whitman in the preface to *Leaves of Grass* in 1855. I encourage you now to re-examine what you have been told in terms of health, dismiss what insults your well-being and listen instead to sound reason that will allow your flesh (and all the other parts of the body) to function at optimal levels.

Eating our Way to an Early Grave

A balanced, nutritious diet can prevent the most treacherous health conditions of our day; yet, many people continue to eat their way to disease, disabilities and an early grave. How can you reverse the trend for you and your family? What foods should you eat? What needs to be eliminated from your diet? To eat for health doesn't mean that you have to eat costly, pre-packaged meals. Nor does it mean that you'll have to stop eating at your favorite restaurants or fast-food establishments. Instead, by simply re-examining how you look at food, you can learn to make healthier choices whether preparing meals at home or eating out.

As nature planned it, food is meant to fuel and nourish the body... and also to provide additional oxygen to the cells. In the midst of our busy, hectic lives we eat for all the wrong reasons. We eat to satisfy hunger pangs, rather than with the intent to provide the body with the nutrients it needs to function at optimal levels for the rest of the day. In addition, we often eat for emotional reasons; i.e., because we're bored, nervous, angry or stressed. At times we eat to quench a sugar craving or an urge for salt. Often we are simply trying to gratify a sense of taste that has become over-active because of the rich foods we indulge in regularly. Ads on television, social gatherings with friends, and the smell of fresh baked goods all prompt us to eat succulent sweets and assorted goodies.

Don't Simply Feed Your Face!

Interestingly, many of us have used an old cliché when we are heading for lunch or dinner, saying something like, "I'm going to go feed my face;" and in many cases, that's all we are doing. Often, when we grab food on the run, eat whatever sounds good at the moment, and don't take care to select healthy foods, we end up merely "feeding our faces," rather than balancing our nutrition and supplying the entire body with the fuel it needs to perform at optimal levels. We would be much better off if we would approach mealtimes with the attitude of, "I'm going to feed my cells." The individual cells of the body are living units that breathe, eat, reproduce and even die. It is within the cells that nutrients are converted to energy. It is there that proper metabolism is maintained. It is within the cells that optimal health is generated. Every person in the world is made up of trillions of these cells, and every person's cells need the exact same things to carry on the processes of life.

Contrary to the many fad diets that try to convince consumers that one person needs more protein, while another needs more fat, while yet another should concentrate on carbohydrates, every person's cells need the same balance of nutrients, and the same rich sources of oxygen to remain in a healthy, regenerative state. The cell's main source of fuel is from carbohydrates (glucose). Proteins (amino acids) are the next most important element for energy production in the cells. Then, fats – known as essential fatty acids – are also needed in limited amounts. Micronutrients (vitamins, minerals and enzymes), water and oxygen must also be available to the cells.

Whether a person is a professional athlete, a sick patient or a person who is just trying to be healthier, his or her cells require the same ratio of carbohydrates, protein and fat as anyone else's. The ratio should be the same, even though the total amount of food intake might be much greater for one person than another. Rather than altering that ratio in order to lose body fat or to build muscle, or to otherwise encourage the body to be at its genetic best, the important thing is to look at lifestyle practices and medical conditions that may be interfering with the body's ability to break nutrients down and deliver them to the cells where they are needed.

Give the Cells What They Need

We will further explore the importance of this ratio later in this chapter. For now, it is important to remember that the underlying goal, for every individual, should be to give the cells what they need, and that what the cells need is the same for every individual. Understanding that the purpose of eating is to feed and oxygenate the cells helps us select foods that are beneficial to that process, rather than opting for foods that interfere with that and actually starve our cells.

By considering this important underlying principle, I have created seven recommendations that I call the "Seven Rules of Cellular Nutrition." These seven principles should be at the core of your nutrition plan and should serve as guidelines whenever you make a food selection. If you want to achieve optimal health, consider these seven core concepts to be immutable and start right now to make them your standard in terms of nutrition.

The Rules of Cellular Nutrition

The seven rules of cellular nutrition are:
1. Eat more raw food.
2. Replace bad fat with good.
3. Avoid white flour and highly processed foods.
4. Avoid white sugar and other high glycemic foods.
5. Eliminate carbonated beverages.
6. Drink more water.

7.   Balance your diet using a 60-20-20 ratio.

1. Eat More Raw Food.

The benefits of natural foods have been well documented and new findings are constantly being published. For example, in recent years, scientists have identified nutrients known as phytochemicals in raw foods and have found them to be extremely beneficial. Though no one fully understands all the benefits of raw food, we do know that they supply life-giving enzymes and that they contain more oxygen than foods that are cooked and processed. Simply put, raw foods are more alive, so naturally, they are more life-giving and health-enhancing. Oxygen and enzymes are not available in foods that have been cooked or processed. Oxygen and the minute, highly complex protein molecules known as enzymes work together to help digest food and make it useable in the body. When food is cooked or processed, enzymes are destroyed and oxygen is no longer present in that food. The full burden of digestion then falls on the body. Although the body can supply some digestive enzymes to help with this process, those stores are limited. Once digestive enzymes are depleted, the body next draws from its supply of metabolic enzymes. This means that enzymes that are intended for other important processes in the body – including immune function, energy production, and the functioning of every organ system, including the workings of the brain – are being used for digestion instead. At the same time, because the body is being overworked, it has less time and energy to take in oxygen, creating a greater deficiency in this area as well.

Over-taxing the body by eating foods that are enzyme and oxygen deficient can lead to numerous diseases and lowered immune function. In other words, eating cooked and processed foods causes sickness, premature aging and even early death! The key is to constantly replenish the body's enzyme supply and to increase the body's oxygen intake by eating foods as close to their natural state as possible. The closer to nature, the more enzyme and oxygen-rich the foods are. The more processed and refined, the more nutrient deficient and laced with additives and toxins foods are. Consider the contrast in terms of health value between the following two dinners:

– A salad of various dark greens and homegrown tomatoes. Chicken with the skin removed and baked. Fresh (raw) sweet potato slices. Fresh broccoli, steamed, with a dab of butter. Dessert of honeydew melon with a slice of raw cheese.

To find out more or to speak to a nutritional counselor for free, just visit us at:
www.CuresForTheBody.com

– A gelatin salad with canned fruit and whipped cream. Hot dogs on a bun with canned chili and canned cheese spread, prepared mustard. Potato chips or french fries. Canned baked beans with brown sugar and catsup. Dessert of cream-filled doughnuts and ice cream bars.

We are so used to eating foods that are so highly processed that they are virtually "man-made." We definitely need to return to foods that are natural and raw. Look for foods that come from nature. Remember that there is no spring that flows with carbonated water, there are no Twinkie plants, no french fry vines. (No matter how hard my children try to convince me, I have yet to see a licorice tree!)

When selecting snacks, opt for raw carrots, raw almonds, or some other raw enzyme and oxygen-rich food. As a snack, try peeling a sweet potato and cutting it in slices or "carrot sticks." This is one of the most nutritious snacks you could eat.

Along with healthy snacking, do whatever you can to make sure that you include at least some raw food, such as a raw salad or side dish, with each meal. While fixing dinner at home, you may want to put out raw vegetables or raw nuts for you and your family to eat as an appetizer. You'll soon find that you will develop a taste for raw, naturally sweet fruits and vegetables. You will also find that raw foods will help you feel satisfied much quicker and won't leave you feeling tired and lethargic after a meal.

2. Replace Bad Fat with Good.

In recent years, fat has been looked at as the "bad guy," an enemy to be eliminated at all cost. Unfortunately, the cost of completely eliminating fat from the diet has not been considered. Trimming fat to less than 20 percent of the total food intake can cause numerous health concerns. Fat is actually required for health. It is essential for energy and for healthy skin and hair. Fat is also necessary for absorption of some vitamins and for proper functioning of all the body's systems. We badly need fats for cell membranes, body structure, healthy skin, reproduction, hormones and bile, warmth and protection. Certain fats even help to curb the appetite; and without fat, calorie burning significantly shuts down. (Contrary to what most people have been led to believe, trimming fat can make you fat! Could this be why the general population is 54% fatter, even though we have significantly reduced our overall caloric intake?)

Now, this doesn't mean you should run out and order the greasiest french fries you can find. While fat is good for you, all fat is not the same. Udo Erasmus, author of *Fats that Heal, Fats that Kill*, put it this way,

"The fats that heal have different molecular structures than those that kill. Their healing or killing potential rests in these molecular differences-differences that make them behave differently in our body." Raw fats, cold-processed fats and "extra virgin" fats – such as the fats in avocados and nuts, cold-pressed canola oil or extra virgin olive oil – supply the body with energy-producing, health-generating essentials. That's because these fats, like other foods that are "close to nature," are richer in enzymes and oxygen! (Still, it is important to remember that all fats and oils have more carbon and hydrogen-and less oxygen-than carbohydrates.)

Fats that are highly processed (and are, therefore, enzyme deficient and oxygen depleted) – such as the fats you take in when you eat french fries, fried eggs rolls or any other fried or greasy foods – cannot be easily digested and used by the body. Because these fats cannot be readily broken down and used for energy, they are, instead, stored as body fat. Trying to use such fats puts such tremendous strain on the body that processed fats are a primary cause of premature aging. Also, fat that cannot be broken down in the body actually sticks together in clumps and clogs the blood vessels. This slows the blood flow, decreasing the nutrients and oxygen that can be delivered to the tissues and organs. Saturated fats form aggregates (clots) that block and cause spasms in the blood vessels. Thus, undigested fats can lead to strokes, chest pain, heart attack, fatigue, decreased endurance, loss of hearing, reduced lung function and elevated blood pressure. In addition, such fats can actually go "rancid" in the system, producing harmful free radicals and increasing the risk of cancer and diabetes. In *Nutrition*, authors Hamilton and Whitney defined free radicals as "molecular fragments that can damage the body's cells and can accelerate the aging process, cause cancer and initiate the process...that causes plaque to form in the arteries."

Dr. J. Silverman reported a study of 47 countries comparing fat intake and cancer incidence and found the higher the processed fat in the diet, the higher the rate of breast cancer. John A. McDougall, M.D. reported in his book, *The McDougall Plan*, that countless other research studies support those findings and prove that cancers of the colon, kidneys, ovaries, testicles and prostate are more common in populations which consume diets that are high in processed fat.

Again, it is not the consumption of fat per se, but the eating of cooked and processed fat that leads to the deadliest diseases we know today – heart disease, stroke, cancer, obesity and other fat-related conditions. Yet, even with the surge of information regarding the hazards of high-fat diets and the many low-fat and no-fat foods on the market today, we are still eating 25 percent more added fats and oils than we did in 1970. By "added" fats, I mean fats that aren't found naturally in foods, but are added during cooking and processing. In almost every case, these added fats are the highly processed, harmful varieties that we've been discussing here.

Fats Are Killing Us

With this rise in enzyme and oxygen-deficient fats, degenerative diseases have also risen correspondingly. Statistics show that over two-thirds of the people living in affluent nations die from three conditions – heart disease, cancer and diabetes – that are linked directly to fats. According to the National Center for Health Statistics and The Surgeon General's Report on Nutrition and Health, excess fat is the prime culprit that contributes to 85 percent of the total healthcare costs in the United States – accounting for more deaths than cigarettes, alcohol and HIV infections combined.

Obviously, an entire book could be written on this important subject; but for our current discussion, a rudimentary understanding will suffice. However, before I leave this topic and tell you more about how to select good fats, I need to extend a warning about hydrogenation and trans-fats.

Hydrogenation has been called "the worst stage of oil processing" because it drastically changes natural oils by "saturating" them with hydrogen atoms. Though proven to render these fats extremely harmful, the food industry continues to use this process because it allows manufacturers to create cheap, spreadable (and marketable!) products like margarine, vegetable spreads and shortening. Though this may be a benefit for manufacturers, it is certainly not for the consumers. Hydrogenation creates fats that are not commonly found in nature and which are known to be exceptionally hazardous to health. "In fact, the molecular structure of hydrogenated oils has been so radically disorganized that it is largely unrecognizable and unusable by the body," states The Kellogg Report.

Complete hydrogenation results in extremely hard fats that don't spoil. (Could the fact that they don't spoil be a clue that they no longer have any "life" left in them?) Since hydrogenation is accomplished by using a metal catalyst, some hydrogenated oils may be contaminated with metal. Also, the completely hydrogenated fats may contain unnatural fatty acid fragments and other altered molecules that cannot be used by the body and may be toxic.   As bad as complete hydrogenation is, partial hydrogenation can be even worse, creating what are known as trans-fatty acids. Products such as shortening, margarine, shortening oils and partially hydrogenated vegetable oils contain large quantities of trans-fatty acids. Ross Hume Hall in *Food for Naught: The Decline in Nutrition* states that trans-fats are "disastrous biochemically." Trans-fatty acids increase total cholesterol levels and triglycerides, while decreasing the beneficial HDL cholesterol. Trans-fats have also been shown to interfere with the detoxification processes of the liver. These unnatural, chemically altered fats also block the function of the good fats (essential fatty acids) that the body needs. Studies show that people who eat this type of fat have a much higher risk of dying from heart disease and cancer. So, when it comes to fat, the first step is to eliminate harmful fats from your diet. Next, I recommend that you limit your intake of good fats to 20 percent of your total daily intake. Some healthy fat is absolutely essential for health. However, most Americans consume way too much, with 37 percent of their total food intake coming from fat. The World Health Organization recommends that total fat intake should be only 15 to 30 percent.

To derive the benefits of fats without over-taxing the body, I recommend that 20 percent of your calories be from fat. Read labels carefully, and use the following calculation to determine the fat content of the food you buy:

EXAMPLE: 97% Fat Free Frozen Dinner

Nutrition Information

1 serving = 200 calories

Carbohydrates... 10 grams

Protein..............13 grams

Fat..................10 grams

Multiply the total fat grams by 10 to get the total fat calories in one serving. In the case of this example, the total fat grams is 10, so the total fat calories is 100. Divide the result by the total number of calories in one serving. One hundred fat calories divided by 200 total calories, equals .5. Multiply the result by 100 to get the percent of fat. In this example, .5 x 100 = 50, meaning this food is 50% fat (even though it is labeled as 97% fat free!). It's obvious from the above example that labels claiming that a food is "97% fat free" or has "50% less fat" are misleading. Advertisers can get away with such things because they can make claims based on volume only. To understand how this works, think about a bottle of water. If you were to add one drop of oil to that water, you may have one drop of oil to 99 drops of water. In that case, you could say your water was 99 percent fat free-by volume. However, in reality, if you were to look at the caloric content, 100 percent of the calories in that water – every one of the calories – are from fat. Shouldn't it then be labeled "100% fat?" Even if you are able to find prepared foods with a low fat-calorie content, remember that much of the fat in those pre-cooked, highly processed foods is unhealthy. I recommend that you avoid pre-packaged, "warm-them-up-at-home" meals, even if they claim to be "healthy" and low in fat. The good news is that there are "good" and healthy options for the high-fat potato chips, crackers, pork rinds, corn nuts, meat sticks, and other greasy, grimy snacks. You can find baked whole wheat crackers, baked tortilla chips, baked potato chips, raw trail mix, and other "acceptable" and very "snackable" options. The trick is to sort the "good" from the "bad and ugly" fats.

Obviously, you should also stay away from french fries and other deep fat fried foods, and you will want to eliminate the hydrogenated or partially-hydrogenated fats and oils that you currently use for cooking or dressings. You should also know that the new "fat substitutes" (such as Olestra) are not healthy alternatives. Initial studies show that these "fake fats" are definitely not an improvement on what Mother Nature provides, and my prediction is that time will reveal even more problems stemming from these fat substitutes.

Get to Know the Good Fats

Yes, trim the fat, but don't eliminate fat altogether. People who have chosen to do away with fat in their diets are often at great health risk. When it comes to fat, your goal should be to become "Fat-wise," rather than "Fat-free."The following information about good fats will help you accomplish that goal.

There are two fatty acids, linoleic acid (LA) and linolenic acid (LNA), that our bodies cannot produce, and that we must, therefore, obtain from our foods. They are called "essential fatty acids" because our bodies must have them. These fatty acids are crucial in the process of deriving energy from our food. They are mandatory for proper growth, mental state, skin condition, learning ability, liver and hormone function, vitality, and even behavioral patterns.

LA and LNA contain nine calories per gram but rather than using those calories solely for energy, our bodies use them for hormonal, electrical, and structural functions (as long as they have not been formed into trans-fatty acids by heating them at too high a temperature). When your intake of these EFAs is high, your metabolic rate and fat burn-off is increased. This means an increase in vitality and a decrease in body fat.

I strongly recommend that you take this information to heart. Carefully read the next section to discover just how to obtain the maximum benefit by incorporating healthy fats into your cooking and eating habits.

The "Good-Guy" Fats

Some of the richest sources of LA are cold-pressed safflower oil, sunflower oil and grape seed oils. The best readily available sources of LNA are raw flaxseeds, raw walnuts and raw wheat germ. (I strongly encourage you to eat a teaspoon of ground flaxseeds daily. They are by far the richest source of LNA.) Most oils on the market today are processed with heat and chemicals. Often the oils are bleached and deodorized. These processes remove and destroy not only the natural taste of these oils, but also the natural antioxidants, oil-soluble vitamins and enzymes.

Cold-processed and Expeller-pressed oils

The healthiest oils – ones with their antioxidants, vitamins and enzyme properties still intact – are "cold-pressed" and then stored in dark bottles and refrigerated. No heat or chemicals are used in the processing of these oils. Because processing does not diminish the taste, these are "full-flavored" oils; so, it may take time to adjust to their flavor, but once you do, you'll never want the tasteless, highly processed oils you're accustomed to eating now. Cold-processed oils are very unstable and should not be used for cooking. Cooking with these oils will easily form trans-fatty acids. The only exception to this rule is "extra virgin olive oil," which is still "cold-pressed" but is much more stable. This is the reason that I recommend using extra virgin olive oil in cooking. See the recipes provided later in this chapter.

The next best oils are those that are often termed "expeller-pressed" on the label. These oils are heat-processed, but by lower temperatures to ensure that trans-fatty acids are not produced. These oils have a milder taste. Therefore, you may want to mix expeller-pressed oils with "cold-pressed" varieties until a taste for the cold-pressed oils is acquired. Cold-pressed and expeller-pressed oils are found, almost exclusively, in health food stores.

Healthy Sources of Fat

The following is a list of some healthy fat sources. This list can help you in designing your daily intake to include the recommended 20 percent of your total caloric intake from healthy fats. Each of the listed items provides approximately 20 calories from fat (2 g.):

- 2 Tbsp. grated raw cheese (not packed)
- 2 Tbsp. mashed avocado
- 1/2 tsp. oil from the following list: expeller-pressed safflower oil, extra virgin olive oil or (particularly for salads) cold-pressed oils i.e., walnut, soybean, safflower, sesame-untoasted
- 1/2 tsp. butter (raw, if available)
- 1/2 tsp. mayonnaise (made from expeller-pressed oil)
- 1 tsp. peanut butter (non-hydrogenated only)
- 11/2 tsp. raw nuts (i.e., walnuts, pecans, almonds)

Foods high in fat such as nuts, seeds, avocados, etc. should always be eaten raw. In many areas you can even get raw dairy products that are available from reputable dairies and have undergone strict testing procedures. If raw, commercially produced dairy products are available, I recommend that you opt for those over the highly processed dairy products.

3. Avoid white flour and highly processed foods.

The recommendation, "Stay away from white flour," may be the single most important nutrition tip in this book. White flour should be avoided like poison because, in many ways, it is poison. During refining, wheat goes through up to two dozen processes. Nutrient-poor, starchy material is extracted from the wheat and the nutritious seed at the center – the wheat germ – is discarded. The mineral-rich wheat bran that makes up the high-fiber shell is also trashed. At least twenty-five different nutrients are lost during refining. The resulting high-calorie, low-nutrient white flour is sold in the form of hamburger buns, tortillas, pastries, pasta, breads and cakes-often with claims as to how healthy certain of those products are. In many cases, bread sacks are adorned with a picture of the Eating Right Pyramid in an effort to convince consumers that they are getting the "grains" that should make up the bulk of the diet. However, what marketers call grains hardly warrant that title. One authority calls refining a "nutrient-devastating

To find out more or to speak to a nutritional counselor for free, just visit us at:
www.CuresForTheBody.com

series of industrial procedures." Almost all of the flour and grain products that we use today have gone through dozens of processes, including high-pressure steel rolling, scouring, grinding and magnetic separation.

When white flour was first introduced in the marketplace, it caused a great deal of sickness and even some deaths. At the outset of World War II, army physicals showed that the nation's fighting men were gravely deficient in nutrients. The government took a closer look at white flour and other refined grains and began requiring that they be "enriched" or "fortified," meaning nutrients had to be added back before they could be sold to the public. One problem: The government required that only B1, B2, B3 and iron be replaced, despite the fact that milling also destroys many other nutrients of equal importance to health. Many scientists and investigators – including Dr. Weston A. Price in the 1930s, Surgeon Captain Thomas Cleave in the 1950s, and Nobel laureate Linus Pauling in the 1970s – have found that "nutrient restoration as practiced today is woefully inadequate and misleads the public into relying on nutrient-deficient foods." They seem to agree with Dr. Harvey Wiley, the original FDA commissioner, who said, "Those who impose white bread upon the nation have worked an evil... Woe to this nation unless it reestablishes the fundamentals of nutrition which white flour and other denatured foods have broken down."

White flour and refined grains are extremely detrimental as far as health is concerned. These stripped down versions of grains contain less fiber, fewer nutrients and more absorbable calories than whole grains. The weevil beetle, which normally thrives on wheat, cannot survive on white flour.

Roger Williams, author of Physicians Handbook of Nutritional Science, set out to show the difference between a "complete" product and the standard "enriched" grocery store varieties. He found that after 90 days on the commercial bread diet, about 2/3 of the study animals had died of malnutrition and those still living were severely stunted. On the other hand, practically all of the rats that had eaten bread with all the nutrients intact were alive and growing.

In a study conducted by a famous breakfast food company in 1942, the results were similar. Four sets of rats were given special diets. One group received plain whole wheat, water, vitamins and minerals and lived over a year on the diet. The second group received only water and vitamins, and they lived for about eight weeks. The third group lived only a month on their diet of sugar and water. However, the fourth group, which received refined, puffed wheat cereal, vitamins and water died in two weeks! The study concluded that there was something actually toxic about eating the highly processed puffed wheat. Yet, while the company has known about this for over 40 years, they continue to market their products. Studies show that white flour products "ball up" in the system, much like a piece of white bread forms a gummy ball when you roll it between the palms. Highly refined grain products actually draw minerals out of the body, depleting important nutrients the body needs. Recent studies also show that white flour (along with sugar) "caramelizes" in the system, leading to premature aging, clogging of the arteries and other health concerns.

White flour and the many products made from white flour and processed grains are seriously devoid of nutrients-even if the packages claim they are fortified and enriched. As you select foods, remember that those closest to their natural state are much more nutrient-rich and more health promoting than foods that are altered by refining and processing. Avoid refined grains like poison. Rather than white flour, select whole grain bread, rolls, pancakes, tortillas and other baked goods. Don't let another slice of that airy, mineral-robbing, nutrient-void white bread touch your lips! Eat whole grain cereals, not the puffy, "fortified" pre-sweetened types. Try whole wheat, spinach or other vegetable-based pastas; and choose brown rice over white rice. Bottom line is this: If it says "enriched" or "fortified" on the label, stay away!

4. Avoid white sugar and other high glycemic foods.

"Just a spoonful of sugar..." seems to be the theme song for many Americans. Unfortunately, sugar intake has skyrocketed, and most Americans consume far more than "just a spoonful of sugar" each day. Statistics show that sugar consumption has hit an all-time high of 170 pounds of sugar a year for each person in the United States. We continue to eat more and more of a substance that is not even a food! (Why do you suppose sugar is one of the substances on a list of food additives requiring prior approval by the FDA?) Refined sugar, in its various forms, is so stripped of nutrients that it ceases to have any nutritive value at all. "Refining of raw cane sugar into white sugar removes most (93%) of the ash, and with it go the trace elements necessary for metabolism of the sugar: 93 percent of the chromium, 89 percent of the manganese, 98 percent of the cobalt, 83 percent of the copper, 98 percent of the zinc and 98 percent of the magnesium," says Henry Schroeder in *The Trace Elements and Man*. He goes on to explain what happens to all the nutrition that is taken out of the sugar, saying, "These essential elements are in the residue molasses, which is fed to cattle." Jean Mayer in *A Diet for Living* says, "Let me point out that sugar is a new food. It didn't exist in the diet in the West until the seventeenth century. And the argument that sugar is an essential food is a lot of nonsense." Not only is sugar not essential, since even the trace elements that are necessary for metabolism of the sugar are gone, it is actually a "negative nutrient." In order for the body to metabolize refined sugar, it must confiscate nutrients from the body. Thus, the more sugar you eat, the less nourished you become.

Eating syrups, candies, soft drinks, and other foods that are high in refined sugars produces a surge of energy. This is because the body is working hard and fast to metabolize these non-foods. When you eat refined sugars that are devoid of the nutrients needed for metabolism, carbon dioxide is produced in the system and the acid balance is upset. In other words, sugar upsets the system's homeostasis without providing the necessary nutrients (and oxygen!) to bring the body back into balance. By contrast, when we eat foods that naturally contain sugar (like carrots, for example), acid is produced inside the cell in the same way it is when we consume refined sugar. However, minerals and other nutrients in the carrot (such as sodium, potassium, calcium and magnesium) are available to the body and provide the neutralizing effect that maintains balance within the body.

A Nation of Suga-holics

Sugar-rich, nutrient-poor foods make up a disproportionate share of many Americans' diets. One study shows that sugars (both refined and natural) make up over one fourth of the average American's daily caloric intake. Such nutrient-impoverished foods crowd out the foods that are high in nutrients, leaving individuals with excess calories, but still malnourished. We have become a nation of suga-holics. Many of us are literally addicted to sugar and high-sugar foods. Much of this comes not from common table sugar use, but sugar that is added to foods during processing. The food industry routinely adds sugar to virtually every processed food. Ketchup has long been recognized as a food high in sugar. (But, did you know that on a per-calorie basis, ketchup has almost twice as much sugar as ice cream?) Other foods like mayonnaise and sauerkraut, once made without sugar, now contain added sugars. In a way, the food industry has tricked the general public with the introduction of the many foods labeled low fat or non-fat. Consumers think they are buying a better, healthier product, when in actuality most of these foods are extremely high in sugar content.

The impact of this over-consumption of sugar is enormous. Sugar has been linked to diabetes, high blood pressure, athero-sclerosis, behavioral

To find out more or to speak to a nutritional counselor for free, just visit us at:
www.CuresForTheBody.com

disorders, and even cancer. William B. Grant, Ph.D. says that sugar should be given more heed when it comes to heart health. It is his belief that "eating too much sugar is the most important risk factor for coronary heart disease in women 35 and over, and that dietary fat, followed by too much sugar, are the primary culprits for developing coronary heart disease in men 35 and over."Researchers also believe that sugar can be responsible for learning disabilities, aggressive behavior and depression. In this matter, as in others discussed previously, marketers have gone to great lengths to have us believe that sugar is not that bad, especially for our children. Materials promoted by the American Dietetic Association, which were written and produced by the Sugar Association, try to make us believe, "Sugar has a mildly quieting effect on some children." Obviously they have never been around children the day after they have eaten an entire bag of Halloween treats!

Actually, sugar increases stress and tension, which in turn increases cravings for sweets. Stress and sugar work hand-in-hand to contribute to the wave of ill-health. Stress stimulates the breakdown of serotonin; it also triggers the release of the hormone cortisol, which stimulates the production of a chemical in the brain called neuropeptide Y. As levels of NPY go up and serotonin levels go down, sugar cravings increase. Marketers seem to know this and know they can keep us in a downward spiral that keeps us buying candy bars and cupcakes. They tell us, "Grab a certain candy bar when you're on the run and in the middle of a high-stress day," "Drink pre-sweetened fruit drinks to feel better fast," and other such ads that tempt us to turn to sweets in times of stress. Marketers have also made ridiculous statements when it comes to obesity and sugar, such as "Sugar doesn't make you fat." Contrary to what these heralders of hype try to make us believe, the consumption of sugars and high-sugar foods play a major role in the epidemic of obesity that plagues our country.

The appetite control center in the brain knows when you are nutrient deficient.

When your diet is high in sugary, nutrient-negative foods, that control center continues to signal that more food is needed to supply the nutrients you need. "Given the low nutrient density of the American diet and the nutrient-depleting action of certain foods, individuals...may become so deficient in certain nutrients that they eat compulsively in an insatiable metabolic drive to obtain them." The National Academy of Sciences has called obesity "the commonest form of malnutrition in the Western nations."

To find out more or to speak to a nutritional counselor for free, just visit us at:
www.CuresForTheBody.com

© Copyright 2004 Erica, Inc.

Not only does refined sugar rob you of nutrients, foods that are high in sugar content cause insulin surges and sudden, unstable swings in blood sugar. These sugary foods are called "high glycemic." Eating high glycemic foods increases irritability. The body's tendency to convert food calories into body fat is also increased. The over-stimulation of insulin from eating high glycemic foods can cause people to eat 60 to 70 percent more at the next meal. Low glycemic foods, on the other hand, promote a slow, moderate rise in blood sugar. This keeps hunger in check and diminishes mood swings and cravings. Low glycemic foods also encourage the body to convert stored body fat to energy.

I once went to a seminar that was promoted as a "weight loss" seminar. The gentleman presenting it told his audience that it made absolutely no difference where their calories came from. He even brought out a slice of angel food cake smothered in strawberries and topped with non-fat whipped cream to show that you could find "low-fat" (and, therefore, "legal?") desserts. As noted above, sugar creates an artificial appetite. In addition, "the minerals in the body become unbalanced, enzymes don't function correctly, food does not digest properly, and allergies occur. Allergies cause addiction, addiction causes cravings, and overeating is the result," says Nancy Appleton, PhD in her book, *Lick the Sugar Habit*. Studies with rats, such as those conducted by F. Lucas and A. Scalfani and reported in *Physiological Behavior*, suggest that sugar alone may be as disasterous as fat alone in promoting obesity.

Don't think you are safe by using artificial sweeteners either. Aspartame, saccharin and other sweeteners have been shown to cause the same, or even greater, insulin surges as sugar. In many ways they are even more damaging to health. For example, aspartame is made up of phenylalanine, aspartic acid and methanol (wood alcohol), which are released into the bloodstream when aspartame is digested. High levels of these substances can affect the synthesis of neurotransmitters in the brain and can increase blood pressure. Aspartame can also affect sleep and hunger. Over a thousand complaints regarding aspartame have been registered by the FDA, by Woodrow C. Monte, who is the director of the Food Science and Nutrition Laboratory at Arizona State University, and by Dr. Richard Wurtman of the Massachusetts Institute of Technology. These complaints include dizziness, visual impairment, ear buzzing, severe muscle aches, high blood pressure and others. Remember, aspartame and other sweeteners are "artificial," and, therefore, are even more foreign to the body than natural sugars.

To find out more or to speak to a nutritional counselor for free, just visit us at:
www.CuresForTheBody.com

Glycemic Guidelines

The following general guidelines can help you determine which foods are most desirable in terms of sugar content and which foods should be avoided because they will significantly raise blood sugar. Notice that these guidelines do not consider nutrient value. Some foods that are nutrient-rich may be high glycemic. These foods need to be balanced with low-glycemic foods rather than being avoided all together.

Breads: Coarse, whole grain breads, including cracked or sprouted whole wheat bread or any whole grain bread are the best. Select breads that feel "heavy" and avoid the light, airy white or commercial whole wheat breads. Most English muffins, bagels and Matzoh are high glycemic, and, so, are less desirable.

Cereal/Grains: Again, select coarse, compact varieties of cereal, such as high-bran types (All-Bran) or other whole grain cereals. Coarse, rolled oatmeal is best, the finer "5-minute" variety is medium glycemic, and the instant "Quick" type is high glycemic. Similarly, brown rice or regular white rice is low while instant rice has a high glycemic content.

Pasta: Almost all pasta is low glycemic. However, beware of the added sauces and cheeses.

Legumes and Starchy Vegetables: Most beans and peas fall into the low glycemic category. Sweet potatoes and yams are also low glycemic. However, baked potatoes, lima beans and winter squash are in the less desirable category.

Vegetables: Almost all vegetables are low glycemic. Note the exceptions in the Starchy Vegetable category (above). Carrots are also an exception. They are high in sugar content and should always be balanced with a low-glycemic food.

Fruits: Like vegetables, almost all fruits and natural fruit juices are in the low-glycemic range. Bananas and canned fruits are in the mid-range. Fruits to avoid or use in combination with another food are pineapple, raisins, watermelon and sugar-sweetened fruit juices.

Dairy: Low-fat milk and milk products are the most desirable in terms of their glycemic rating. (That's why low-fat frozen yogurt sweetened with fructose makes a great treat.) Whole milk, ice milk, ice cream, sugar-sweetened yogurt are on the high-glycemic end.

Soups: Low fat, low sugar versions are available, e.g., Health Valley, Nile Spice, Pritikin, certain Progresso varieties, and Campbell's Healthy Request. Most other commercial soups have high-starch content, making them less desirable; and the powdered, "Cup of Soup" instant soups often contain corn syrup, making them high glycemic.

Sugars: The best sugars are fructose and lactose. Fructose is found mainly in fruits, or may also be added to foods as a sweetener. Lactose is found in milk products, including yogurt. These two sugars, fructose and lactose, are metabolized slowly and through a different process than is glucose, so they are much lower on the glycemic index. However, even these "safer" sugars should be taken in limited amounts. (Many people lack the enzyme to break down lactose.) Also avoid foods that are high in sugar-particularly hidden sugars-and, therefore, "spike" insulin levels. Note, for example, that white bread is higher on the glycemic index than is sucrose (table sugar). Don't think that this means I recommend table sugar; I don't! I'm merely saying to be aware of other things that are just as bad.

Bottom line, as far as sugary foods are concerned, do whatever you can to eat low or medium glycemic foods and to eliminate refined sugars from your diet. Such sugars are often listed on the label using other terms, including corn syrup, sucrose, glucose or dextrose. Don't be fooled by the term, "high fructose corn syrup." This, too, is a highly processed and unhealthy form of sugar. These various types of sugar should be eliminated. If you need to use some kind of sweetener, replace the harmful, highly refined sugars with fructose or with Stevia. As noted above, fructose can be more readily metabolized and enters the cells more slowly, without causing insulin swings. Fructose looks and smells like the table sugar you are familiar with. It can be found at health food stores and some grocery stores. An even better option is called Stevia. Stevia, a natural sweetener from a plant, is much sweeter than refined sugar and is available at health food stores.

5. Eliminate carbonated beverages.

Soda pop sales soared from 192 servings per person in 1960 to 493 in 1976. Since then, with the new soft drink brand names, new flavors and creative packaging, not to mention the "super size" containers available at every convenience store, the vertical rise has continued. The U.S. Department of Agriculture reports that between 1960 and 1980, soft drink consumption increased 300%. By 1982, Americans were consuming more soft drinks than milk. Today, one company, the Coca-Cola Company, brags that over 8000 of their drinks are consumed every second!

Via soft drinks, we are taking in tons (literally!) of sugar, as well as truckloads of caffeine, artificial dyes, flavors and preservatives. However, even more harmful than sugar and caffeine is the acid in carbonated drinks.

To find out more or to speak to a nutritional counselor for free, just visit us at:
www.CuresForTheBody.com

Soft drinks contain carbonic, malic, erythorbic and phosphoric acids. These acids change the pH in the digestive system, thus, significantly interfering with digestion. Recall from earlier in this chapter that the purpose of food is to fuel the body with nutrients and oxygen. Carbonated drinks actually do the opposite. Since they interfere with the very process that allows food to be broken down and delivered where it is needed within the body, carbonated drinks drain the body of potential energy. By drinking a soda with a meal, even the most balanced, healthy menu can be sabotaged because nutrients in the food are not digested and absorbed. You simply won't get the nutrition you need if you wash your healthy foods down with a carbonated drink.

Understanding that carbonated beverages interfere with digestion may shed some light on another issue. Often people who drink "diet" sodas find that they still seem to have trouble losing weight. Could this be because they are not properly digesting their food due to the acid they are getting from these drinks? And, what about the sharp rise in osteoporosis in recent years? Could that rise be tied primarily to the rise in soft drink consumption? Studies show that the acids in carbonated drinks increase calcium loss.

For strong bones, improved digestion and increased health, get off the soda. Individuals who drink a lot of soda pop or other carbonated beverages can see dramatic health improvements almost *overnight* if they will change this habit. Carbonated beverages have no place in the diet. Also, please note that while some people think they are safe drinking "Perrier" water, this is a false assumption. Perrier or "sparkling" water is carbonated, just like soda pop. Eliminate carbonated beverages from your diet. Replace them with water, fresh fruit juices or fresh vegetable juices.

6. Drink more water.

Some experts say that water is the most important nutrient. Ninety percent of the body is water, and for optimal health, the body needs to be constantly rehydrated. The performance of the individual cells and the tissues of the body depend on the quality and quantity of the water you drink. Studies show that hydration is particularly important in warding off autoimmune disease and that aging, in many cases, is actually a process of dehydration. Water is lost in urine, sweat and even when we breathe. Athletes and others who train heavily can use over two gallons of water a day. Even light exercise requires half a gallon of water. Proper hydration helps the body to eliminate toxins and shed unwanted body fat. While body water can be replenished with any beverage, water is best. This is because anything that is added to water actually slows absorption. Water passes easily through the semi-permeable membranes of the intestine, but other particles may not. So, I suggest you drink water, and plenty of it. However, I'm not suggesting that you drink tap water. Tap water, depending on where you live, may be contaminated with parasites, pesticides and other environmental toxins. There is no such thing as clean water out of a tap. Avoid it. Also, as mentioned earlier, stay away from Perrier or sparkling water. Neither tap water nor sparkling water is a healthy way to rehydrate. Beyond those two don't's, there really aren't many restrictions when it comes to water. The key is simply to drink more water. Some people recommend spring water, others insist that you have to drink distilled water. Countless reverse osmosis and home distillers are on the market. While the controversy over which kind of water is cleanest and safest rages on, until further research is available, I recommend using any purified or distilled water.

7. Balance your diet using the 60-20-20 ratio.

Harvard Proposes New Food Pyramid

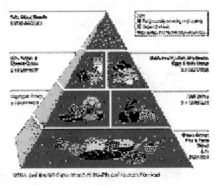

Every five years, the United States Department of Agriculture (USDA) and Department of Health and Human Services (DHHS) release dietary guidelines that provide nutritional advice to Americans. These guidelines are meant to serve as the basis of the well-recognized "Food Guide Pyramid" *(see figure at right)* that categorizes foods and suggests the number of servings people should eat from each food group. The pyramid shape shows the proportion of the total diet that certain food groups are to compose. Food groups at the wide base of the pyramid, for example, are to be eaten in greater quantity than food groups that appear toward the narrower top.

When new recommendations are due, a committee of invited experts offer changes to the guidelines based on the findings from new research studies. The USDA and DHHS then review these recommendations and release the new, revised guidelines. The latest set of Dietary Guidelines for Americans was released in May 2000.

To find out more or to speak to a nutritional counselor for free, just visit us at:
www.CuresForTheBody.com

These newest guidelines emphasize, for example, the importance of eating grains (especially whole grains), vegetables and fruits, and for the first time describe ways in which to keep food safe to eat. The guidelines also urge Americans to be physically active and achieve and maintain a healthy weight.

While some of the recommendations in the new guidelines sit well with Harvard researchers, several cause disagreement.

Dr. Meir Stampfer, Professor in the Departments of Epidemiology and Nutrition and Chair of the Department of Epidemiology at the Harvard School of Public Health, served on the committee for the 2000 guidelines. He feels that additional changes should have been made to the recommendations. Dr Stampfer is a world-renowned investigator whose research has shown strong associations between dietary and other lifestyle modifications and disease prevention, such as heart disease and cancer. An authority in this area, he believes that the current recommendations have not incorporated the latest research findings for fear of confusing the public with dietary advice that may appear to contradict long ingrained recommendations. He hopes that future revisions of the guidelines and food pyramid will reflect this accumulating evidence.

A New Healthy Eating Pyramid

In response to the federal government's Food Guide Pyramid, Dr. Stampfer and his colleagues, including Dr. Walter Willet, Chair of the Department of Nutrition, have developed a new healthy eating pyramid that reflects the latest research on the optimal diet (*see figure at left*). Some highlights of this version:

- Whole grain foods, vegetable oils, and fruits and vegetables are emphasized.

- Physical activity and weight control are emphasized.

- Red meat and refined grains (like white bread and white rice) are de-emphasized and listed as items that should only be eaten sparingly.

- Nuts and legumes receive their own category.

- Dairy products are de-emphasized and placed in a category with calcium supplements.

- A daily multivitamin tablet is recommended for most people, and moderate daily alcohol intake is a healthy option unless this does not make sense for the individual.

Some authors, including Barry Sears and Dr. Barry Atkins, perpetuate the unfounded claim that high protein diets are the way to go. Diet plans like "The Zone" have captured the interest of many individuals who have been led to believe that high-protein diets raise testosterone and sex-hormone-binding globulin levels and reduce the levels of cortisol, the hormone that breaks muscle down. In other words, many people have been convinced that a high-protein diet will help them gain lean muscle and lose body fat. This couldn't be further from the truth. In fact, studies show the exact opposite. It is high-carbohydrate diets that actually raise testosterone and sex-hormone-binding globulin as studies by Columbia University and Rockefellar Hospital prove. In addition, high-carbohydrate diets were proven to reduce cortisol levels. Who knows where Mr. Sears, Mr. Atkins and the other high-protein advocates got their facts? Apparently they didn't look into the research.

You may have heard anecdotal evidence that seems to support the widely publicized high-protein diets. However, you need to understand the primary reason that some people see results. Protein is a diuretic, which means a person on a high-protein diet may experience some initial weight loss, but the loss is mostly from water weight and doesn't represent a drop in body fat. Also, individuals on high protein diets are most likely using their own organs and tissues for fuel, since high-protein doesn't supply the ready energy that comes from carbohydrates. While some people may experience initial results from a high-protein diet, they are most likely being encouraged by the false hopes that come from water-weight loss, while doing a great deal of harm to their overall health.

When our diet contains more proteins than we need, the excess must be broken down in the liver, and undue stress is placed on this important organ and on the kidneys as well. Also, as the protein is broken down and excreted, it takes with it vital minerals. One of the most important minerals lost when excess protein is eaten is calcium. Painful calcium kidney stones can result, and calcium can be pulled from the bones, resulting in osteoporosis. High protein diets are a leading cause of gouty arthritis and can increase the chances of developing allergies. Some studies show that diets high in protein can even cause brain damage.

Like the high-protein diet hoaxes, high-fat diets have occasionally been touted as the way to achieve maximum weight loss. These diets claim to

To find out more or to speak to a nutritional counselor for free, just visit us at:
www.CuresForTheBody.com

work because fats supposedly digest slower and suppress appetite longer. While fat is necessary for proper metabolism, large amounts of just any kind of fat is not the answer. Processed fats (any fat that has been heated) can't be thoroughly digested. As discussed earlier, this kind of fat puts a great deal of stress on the body and is often left undigested in the system. This undigested fat is stored in the tissues, blocks the arteries and circulates in the blood stream, leading to such diseases as heart disease, diabetes and obesity. In addition, diets that are high in fat can lead to ketone-induced kidney damage. Fatty diets have also been linked to increased cancer risk.

High fat diets are definitely not health-promoting. Rather than dealing with the health risks of taking in extra fat, the key is to supply the body with proper amounts of the kind of fat that can be broken down for use in the body.

Balancing Act

Absolutely, the best way to balance your nutrition is to eat 60 percent of your foods from high-quality, complex carbohydrates (including whole grains, fresh fruits and vegetables); 20 percent from good protein sources; and 20 percent from readily digestible fats. At this point you may be thinking, "Okay, fine, you've given me all this great nutrition information, but how do I get started?" I'm glad you asked! I want you to have the freedom to design your own menus and meals. Our goal is not to have you tied to someone's apron strings for the rest of your life. Instead, we want you to have enough education in the basics of sound nutrition that you can be self-sufficient when it comes to selecting what you want to eat (and when you want to eat it!). We do know, however, that the best way to learn how to make proper selections is to have a step-by-step plan that provides exact guidelines at first, and then gradually helps you transition into making all those decisions on your own.

My experience of watching hundreds of others over the past decade plus, suggests that you will be much more likely to see quick results and also to have the necessary motivation to continue a lifestyle of sound nutrition if you will do the following: For six weeks, follow the F.I.T.N.E.S.S. System Nutritional Plan as closely as you can. Note that during the first two weeks, the foods that you are "allowed" to eat are outlined exactly. Then, beginning with week three, the plan explains additional foods you can eat and modifications you can make as the program progresses.

Once you have completed the six-week program, you may choose to repeat the F.I.T.N.E.S.S. System Nutritional Plan for a second six weeks. Or, you may feel you have had a good enough "jump start" and your results have been such that you can start to fashion your own food plan. Don't worry. We don't want you to slide right back into your unhealthy habits, so we're not going to kick you out of the nest and send you on your way without giving you some "flying instructions." This manual provides nutrition information that will help you select foods whether you are at home or on the road. It includes a comprehensive list of the healthiest fast food and restaurant options; and, following that list, you'll find hints for preparing foods in your own kitchen in the healthiest way. Use what you have learned from following the six-week Nutritional Plan along with the Guidelines for Eating Out and the Recipes and Hints. Within a short time, selecting healthy items from any menu or any aisle in the grocery store will be almost "second nature." Best of all, by following sound nutritional principles as outlined in this book, you will soon see definite improvements in your overall health and well being. Improvements are inevitable; they come as the natural result of taking in foods that provide additional nutrients and oxygen to the cells.

Six Weeks to Success

As explained above, you will experience the greatest success and most immediate results if you follow the F.I.T.N.E.S.S. System Nutritional Plan for six weeks. At the end of the six weeks, if you choose to do so, you may repeat the plan for another six weeks.

The F.I.T.N.E.S.S. System Nutrition Plan

Weeks One and Two

Breakfast
> One piece of fruit
> 1/2 cup Raw Cereal Blend (recipe below) with 1/2 cup skim milk, soy milk, fresh juice or water

Raw Cereal Blend   Yield: 1 serving
> 1/4 c. prepared cereal (Grape Nuts, Shredded Wheat and Bran, Fiber One or Fiber Wise)

To find out more or to speak to a nutritional counselor for free, just visit us at:
www.CuresForTheBody.com

1 tsp. raw nuts or seeds (slivered almonds, pumpkin or sunflower seeds)

1/4 c. old fashioned rolled oats

1 tsp. raw wheat germ

Pinch of flax seeds

Raw, organic honey or fructose to taste (optional)

Mix all ingredients together, and serve with skim milk, soy milk, fresh juice or water.

Note: Pre-mixed Raw Cereal Blend is available for purchase from Optimal Health Systems.

Morning Snack

1 serving of whole food powder in 8 oz. skim milk, soy milk, fresh juice or water OR one piece of fresh fruit OR one serving fresh vegetables.

Lunch

Large salad with white meat (chicken, turkey or fish). Use any vegetables in your salad. Remember that the denser, darker vegetables provide the highest amount of nutrients. For example, use green or red leaf lettuce rather than iceberg.

Dressing: vinegar or lemon juice with 1 tsp. of "healthy" oil, such as grape seed oil, cold pressed canola oil or extra virgin olive oil. Add Mrs. Dash seasoning, if desired.

Afternoon Snack

1 serving of whole food powder in 8 oz. skim milk, soy milk, fresh juice or water OR one piece of fruit OR one serving of fresh vegetables

Dinner

For dinner, eat a whole grain, a lean meat and vegetables (and remember to include at least some raw!). Here are five different examples of "acceptable" dinners:

• Turkey Sandwich on whole grain bread, with vegetables (lettuce, tomato, sprouts, etc.)

To find out more or to speak to a nutritional counselor for free, just visit us at:
www.CuresForTheBody.com

- Fish, brown rice, green salad
- Mexican Dinner: Chicken fajita (chicken, onions, peppers) on steamed corn tortilla
- Italian Dinner: Marinara sauce on whole wheat or spinach pasta, fish, green salad
- Oriental Dinner: Brown rice, chicken, steamed vegetables

Water

Drink six to eight 8-oz. glasses of water daily.

Nutrition Guidelines — Weekly Instructions

Weeks One and Two

For the first two weeks, follow the Nutrition Plan as closely as possible. While this plan may seem unfamiliar and perhaps a little strict at first, following it to a "t" will ensure that you achieve the greatest possible results from the program.

By including raw foods and certain supplements, the Nutrition Plan is designed to add to the "oxygen" benefits of this complete program.

If you feel hungry at first, you may add second servings, but only of the foods listed. If you do choose to eat more food, be sure to keep the percentages the same. For example, if you eat additional chicken or fish at dinnertime, add additional carbohydrates (salad, etc.) as well. Some people find that an extra serving of the Raw Cereal Blend is all they need in order to feel full and satisfied throughout the day.

Weeks Three and Four

During the next two weeks, you may choose to make the following modifications:

Breakfast

For breakfast, rather than Raw Cereal Blend, you may eat Oat Bran Cereal OR Optimal Whole Grain Pancakes (see recipe on pages 487 & 488).

Lunch

During the third and fourth week, rather than the salad, you may have:

- Turkey, Chicken or Tuna Sandwich on whole wheat or whole grain bread
- Mix tuna with 1 tsp. mustard, if desired, or with 1 tsp. "healthy" oil (grape seed oil, cold-pressed canola or extra virgin olive oil)
- Add tomatoes, lettuce, sprouts, cucumber slices or other vegetables

Dinner

For dinner, follow recommendations for Weeks One and Two.

Water

Continue to drink six to eight 8-oz. glasses of water and take the supplements as recommended.

Weeks Five and Six

Breakfast

Along with any of the breakfast options for the first four weeks, during Weeks Five and Six, you may add: Scrambled Egg Beaters or scrambled egg whites.

Lunch and Dinner

You may eat out according to the Eating Out Guidelines that follow on page 482-485.

Water

Continue to drink six to eight 8-oz. glasses of water and to take the recommended supplements.

Guidelines for Eating Out

General Recommendations

Remember that you want to eat foods as close to their natural state as possible and that you want to eat half of your daily intake raw, if possible. At most restaurants and fast food establishments, you can order some kind of raw fruits or vegetables as part of your meal or as a side

To find out more or to speak to a nutritional counselor for free, just visit us at:
www.CuresForTheBody.com

dish.

Drink water, lemon water or herb tea. Stay away from carbonated drinks, coffee, tea or alcohol.

Order foods the way YOU want them. You will find that most restaurants are accommodating.

Mexican

Have:

Chicken soft tacos

Chicken, fish, shrimp or vegetable fajitas

Chicken or bean burritos (with whole pinto or black beans)

Whole black beans

Salsa

How to order:

Request corn or wheat tortillas, grilled or steamed with no oil.

Ask them to hold the cheese.

Add your choice of whole beans, lettuce, tomato, guacamole, avocados.

Avoid:

Refried beans (order black beans or whole pinto beans instead)

Chips (order a grilled corn tortilla instead.)

White flour tortillas (many restaurants offer wheat, tomato or spinach tortillas)

Nachos

Beef and pork

Fried entrees

Sour cream and cheese (replace with extra guacamole)

Oriental

Have:

Stir-fried dishes with lean meats and vegetables.

How to order:

Choose steamed rice, not fried. Ask for brown rice, if available. Order soup if you want, but if you can see oil on the top, skim it off with the back of your spoon.

Avoid:

Won tons, egg rolls and other fried dishes, including fried rice

Sweet and sour dishes

Tofu (generally very high in fat)

Italian

Have:

Pasta dishes with lean meats—such as clams, shrimp, lobster, oysters and chicken—and with marinara or tomato sauce (and vegetables, if available)

How to Order:

Ask for whole wheat or spinach pasta.

Order clear white sauce, marinara or tomato sauces with vegetables.

Select sauces with lean meat or ask them to eliminate the meat.

Avoid:

Cheese-filled pastas

Dishes with sausage or other high-fat meats

Sauces made with cream, butter or cheese (choose clear white sauce or tomato sauces instead)

Veal Parmesan

Ravioli (cheese or beef)

Beef lasagna

American

Have:

Salads

Lean meats (chicken, fish, lobster, crab legs, shrimp) that are grilled, steamed or baked. You can also have shish kabobs made with vegetables and any of the meats listed.

Whole grain breads

Vegetables, raw or steamed

To find out more or to speak to a nutritional counselor for free, just visit us at:
www.CuresForTheBody.com

Baked potatoes

Non-creamy or whole bean soups (If fat is on the top of the soup, skim it off with the back of your spoon. If soup has meat, eat the vegetables and leave the meat behind to avoid extra fat.)

How to order:

Select all-vegetable salads or salads with lean meats. Ask them to hold the bacon-flavored bits, croutons and cheese. Egg whites are okay, but avoid egg yolks. For dressing, use lemon juice, vinegar and/or salt and pepper.

You can ask for low-fat salad dressing or other sauces to be served on the side. Then, use approximately one teaspoon of dressing and dilute it with lemon juice or vinegar. Rather than pouring the diluted dressing over the top of your food, dip the food into the sauce.

Ask to have vegetables steamed without butter and with no sauces.

Order a slice of avocado or lemon wedges to flavor your baked potato, but don't add butter or sour cream.

Ask to have meats grilled, steamed or baked without added butter or oil.

Ask for cocktail sauce, lemon wedges or vinegar (according to your taste).

Avoid:

French fries or fried potato skins

Fried chicken or buffalo wings and other fried meats

All fatty toppings, gravies or dressings for salads or potatoes

Breakfast

Have:

Omelets made with egg whites and vegetables

Whole grain toast, pancakes or waffles

Low-fat yogurt with fresh fruit

Oatmeal or a healthy dry cereal with non-fat (skim) milk

Fresh fruit

Steamed hash browns

How to order:

To find out more or to speak to a nutritional counselor for free, just visit us at:
www.CuresForTheBody.com

Ask for scrambled egg whites or omelets made with egg whites only.

Request that no butter or oil be used to cook eggs.

Order dry toast, pancakes or waffles.

Ask for "100% fruit" spread or order fresh fruit to eat over pancakes or waffles.

Ask that the hash browns be steamed, not cooked with oil.

Avoid:

White bread, pancakes or waffles (Many restaurants offer whole grain pancakes and waffles.)

High-sugar cereals

Sausage, bacon or ham

Fried hash browns

Recipes and Menu Suggestions:

The following section suggests foods that can be eaten for breakfast, lunch and dinner as well as some snack ideas and recommendations for ways to add raw foods to your daily diet. In many cases, you will find that recipes and/or preparation suggestions are provided for the recommended foods.

Some of the ingredients referred to in this section (i.e., raw apple cider vinegar, fructose, etc.) are found primarily in health food stores. Also, it may be helpful for you to know that most health food stores will order items for you if they do not currently carry them.

To cook the low-fat, health-promoting dishes in this book, you don't need a lot of fancy equipment or special pans. However, I do recommend one item. If you don't already have a large, deep skillet with a non-stick surface, I suggest you get one since you will be using it often for cooking healthy foods.

BREAKFAST Recipes and Menu Suggestions

Pancakes made with whole wheat pancake mixes or using a recipe with whole wheat flour (see recipe for Optimal Whole Grain Pancakes on page 488). Use egg whites and no oil. Adding flaxseeds (approximately 1 tsp. per cup of batter) will add some healthy, essential fatty acids and a "nutty" flavor to your pancakes. Other add-in options:

To find out more or to speak to a nutritional counselor for free, just visit us at:
www.CuresForTheBody.com

Blueberries, bananas, raw wheat germ.

French toast using whole grain bread dipped in egg whites thinned with a little water or with skim milk (Add cinnamon to egg, if desired.)

Scrambled egg whites cooked in Cooking Spray (see page 486 for recipe) Leave in part of the yolk, if desired.

Omelets with egg whites (leave part of the yolk). After cooking, add raw cheese, if desired, and cover until melted. Cereal, low fat, low sugar varieties. Add raw, "old-fashioned" oats, flaxseeds, or raw wheat germ to store-bought cereals. Even better, the Optimal Cereal Blend (the same cereal included in the Six-week Program) is a great health-supporting choice. You can mix a batch of this cereal according to the recipe provided below, or order Optimal Cereal Blend by calling Optimal Health Systems at (800) 890-4547.

Oatmeal, cracked wheat, or pre-packaged whole grain cereals sweetened with fructose instead of sugar.

Fresh (raw) juices or juices "not from concentrate."

Raw Milk if available commercially in your area. Otherwise, use skim or 1% milk.

Whole grain toast with "100%-fruit" jam or jellies.

Cinnamon toast made with whole grain bread. Spread toast with Better Spread, then sprinkle with cinnamon mix (one part cinnamon to three parts fructose).

Hash Browns or country-style potatoes made from left-over baked potatoes and cooked with a little Cooking Spray (page 496).

Raw Cereal Blend   Yield: 1 serving

1/4 c. prepared cereal (Grape Nuts, Shredded Wheat and
  Bran, Fiber One or Fiber Wise)

1 tsp. raw nuts or seeds (slivered almonds, pumpkin or
  sunflower seeds)

1/4 c. old fashioned rolled oats

1 tsp. raw wheat germ

To find out more or to speak to a nutritional counselor for free, just visit us at:
www.CuresForTheBody.com

Pinch of flax seeds

Raw, organic honey or fructose to taste (optional)

Mix all ingredients together, and serve with skim milk, soy milk, fresh juice or water.

Optimal Whole Grain Pancakes

1 c. whole-wheat or multi-grain pancake mix (Arrowhead
   Mills Multi-Grain is a good, mild-tasting choice.)

1/4 c. old-fashioned rolled oats

1 tsp. crystalline fructose (optional)

1/2 tsp. baking powder

1/2 tsp. crushed raw flaxseeds

1/2 tsp. raw wheat germ

1/4 tsp. ground cinnamon or allspice (optional)

2 dashes salt (optional)

1 c. skim milk or water

1/4 c. fresh or thawed frozen blueberries, sliced fresh
   bananas or diced fresh apples

 In a medium bowl, mix all dry ingredients. Add the milk or water to the dry ingredients. Blend. Add additional milk or water, if necessary, until batter is proper consistency. Fold in fruit.

Lightly spray nonstick griddle with Cooking Spray (page 496) and pre-heat griddle over medium heat. Ladle 1/4 cup of the batter onto the griddle for each pancake. When the tops of the pancakes are covered with bubbles, flip them over and cook until golden brown. Serve with 100-percent fruit spread or Fructose Syrup.

Fructose Syrup

1 c. water

2 c. crystalline fructose

1 1/4 tsp. natural maple flavoring

 In a small saucepan over medium heat, bring water to a boil. Add fructose and stir until dissolved. Simmer approximately 10 minutes. Add maple flavoring and stir to blend. Remove from heat. Syrup will thicken as it cools.

To find out more or to speak to a nutritional counselor for free, just visit us at:
www.CuresForTheBody.com

LUNCH AND DINNER Recipes and Menu Suggestions

Quick pan-steamed vegetables, can be prepared by spraying a non-stick skillet with Cooking Spray, heating over high heat, adding your choice of vegetables (i.e., broccoli, cauliflower, carrots, etc.), and stirring continuously for approximately three minutes. While cooking, add hot water as needed, one tablespoon at a time, to keep moisture in the pan. Cover pan with a lid and remove from heat. Sprinkle with small amount of raw cheese (if available) or a small amount of Better Spread (page 495).

Whole wheat or corn tortillas can be served as a side dish or used as the foundation for a healthy meal. To soften tortillas, spray a non-stick skillet with Cooking Spray (page 496) and place over medium-high heat. Place tortilla in the pan. After about 30 seconds, spray the top side of the tortilla and turn it over. Heat for about 30 seconds more.

For **Soft Chicken Tacos**, warm corn tortillas as explained above. (You may also want to put two tortillas together, one on top of the other, with 1 Tbsp. raw cheese in the middle). Add Versatile Chicken with seasoning option 1, 2 or 3 (page 492).

Serve Mexican foods (i.e., burros, tacos, etc.) with shredded lettuce or cabbage, sliced radishes, chopped onions, tomatoes, or avocados, etc. for a variety of raw veggies as fillings, toppings or side choices. Also offer Fresh Salsa (page 495), Yogurt Cheese (page 495), sliced olives (only in small amounts because of their high fat content). If commercially produced raw cheese is available, grate a small amount over your Mexican dish.

Easy Spanish Rice: Measure ingredients for brown rice as directed on the package. Then, before cooking, for every 1 cup of rice, add to the water: 1 additional Tbsp. water; 1/2 tomato, diced; 1/4 yellow onion, diced; one small clove garlic, minced or pressed; 1/4 tsp. salt; 1/4 tsp. Lawry's Seasoned Salt (with no MSG); and 1/8 tsp. cayenne or 1 tsp. very finely minced jalapeno (optional).

For **Chicken Burros**, use whole-wheat tortillas (Alvarado St. Bakery is a good brand). Use fat-free refried beans. Add Versatile Chicken (made with any of the seasoning options [page 492]); a scoop of whole fat-free black beans; and/or Spanish Rice (see above) for filling, if desired. Also, any of the items listed in the Mexican foods tip above may be used as fillings or side items.

Build your own **Nachos**. Place baked tortilla chips on a cookie sheet covered with foil. Sprinkle with raw grated cheese (if available) and place in oven on broil for approximately one minute or until cheese is just melted (watch very closely). Serve with your choice of Versatile Chicken options (page 4902) and fat free refried beans.

Short-grain brown rice is very tasty. When making brown rice, try adding a little extra water or using fat-free chicken broth in place of the water to make rice more tender.

Salad bar: Use dark green lettuces, spinach and shredded cabbage. Add boiled egg whites; cooked beans; grilled, stir-fried, or Versatile Chicken (page 492), or tuna for protein. Add your choice of diced/ sliced vegetables (i.e., tomatoes, green peppers, broccoli, cauliflower, celery, mushrooms), frozen corn or peas, grated carrots, thinly sliced red onions, sprouts, diced avocado, and a small amount of raw, grated cheese (if available). Top with vinegar, a healthy oil, or dressing made with good oils and salt and pepper. Use dressing sparingly and rather than pouring it over the salad, dip your fork into dressing before each bite.

For **Taco Salad**, top lettuce with choice of Chili Beans (page 495), diced tomatoes, avocado, yellow or green onions, small amount of sliced black or green olives and raw grated cheese, salsa, and Yogurt Cheese (page 495) instead of sour cream.

Salad Dressings: Look for varieties at the health food store that are made with expeller-pressed oils or extra virgin olive oil. Also use fresh lemon or lime juice, raw apple cider vinegar, balsamic vinegar, raw red wine vinegar, extra virgin olive oil, and salt and pepper. Small amounts of avocado, raw cheese, soy "bacon bits," pine nuts, walnuts or pumpkin seeds add great flavor.

Build your own **Healthy-Stacked Potato**. Use baked or boiled potatoes as your base. If desired, season with salt and pepper. For more moisture, you may add a little hot water. Top with your choice of Chili Beans (page 494) or Versatile Chicken (page 492), pan-steamed vegetables (see the Lunch/Dinner tip, above) salsa, avocado, sliced mushrooms, Yogurt Cheese (page 495) and a small amount of raw, grated cheese (if available) or sliced black olives.

Make **Oh-So-Healthy Spaghetti** using whole-wheat noodles. Try cooking them 1 to 3 minutes longer than the package recommends. Since this cooks out some of the strong wheat flavor, it is a good way to help children get used to whole-wheat noodles. For the sauce, use your favorite low-fat spaghetti sauce (check the ingredients and select a sauce with no added sugars). Add Versatile Chicken (page 492) prepared with seasoning option 1. If you serve the sauce and noodles separately, extra noodles keep well in a storage bag. To reheat, place noodles in a saucepan with 1 Tbsp. water. Cover with lid and heat on low. For garlic/mushroom spaghetti, preheat a non-stick skillet sprayed with Cooking Spray (page 496) for one minute over medium heat. Sauté sliced mushrooms with minced or pressed garlic. Cover and remove from heat. Serve with spaghetti.

For **Garlic Bread**, line a cookie sheet with foil and place pieces of whole grain bread on top. Spread each piece with 1/4 tsp. Better Spread (page 495) and sprinkle with garlic salt. Place in oven on broil for approximately one minute to warm.

For **Honey Bread**, follow instructions for Garlic Bread above, but omit garlic salt. Spread with raw organic honey after bread is removed from the oven. For only one or two pieces of bread, toast lightly in toaster (about 30 sec.) then apply topping.

For **Quick Pizzas**, start with a whole grain bagel or a slice of whole grain bread. Top with pizza or spaghetti sauce and your choice of chopped vegetables (i.e., green peppers, yellow onions, mushrooms, broccoli, green or black olives, pineapple tidbits). You may want to add Versatile Chicken (page 492) prepared with seasoning option 1. Next, top with 1 to 2 Tbsp. raw, grated cheese. Bake at 400 degrees for 5 minutes.

Make **"Healthy Hamburgers"** using ground chicken or turkey breast instead of beef. Season with garlic salt, Lawry's Seasoned Salt (with no MSG), and pepper. Barbecue sauce is very good on these burgers.

To find out more or to speak to a nutritional counselor for free, just visit us at:
www.CuresForTheBody.com

You may want to top with 1 Tbsp. raw, grated cheese. Assemble on whole wheat bun with your choice of thinly sliced onions, tomatoes, and pickles. Add relish, catsup, and stone-ground mustard to taste.

Scrumptious Sandwiches start with whole grain bread. Use stone-ground mustard, vinegar, a small amount of mayonnaise made with expeller pressed safflower oil, avocado, or raw grated cheese. Use a lot of fresh vegetables (i.e., cucumbers, mushrooms, bell peppers, red or yellow onions, and watercress). Choose 3 oz. of lean meat (i.e., shrimp, turkey, or turkey breast). You may use Versatile Chicken (below) prepared with seasoning option 1, and using thin strips of chicken in place of ground chicken).

For a tuna sandwich, mix water-packed tuna with the following ingredients: 1/2 tsp. mayonnaise with 1/4 tsp. mild-tasting extra virgin olive oil (Santini is good) per sandwich. Add diced celery, onions, apples, bell peppers, dill pickles and water chestnuts. For added flavor, include a few slivered almonds.

Versatile Chicken

1 lb. ground chicken or turkey breast

Seasoning Option 1

1 large clove garlic, minced or pressed

1 tsp. salt

1 tsp. Italian Seasoning

1/4 tsp. pepper

1/4 tsp. Lawry's Seasoned Salt with no MSG

Seasoning Option 2

1 small clove garlic, minced or pressed

1 pkg. Taco or Chili Mix with no MSG (Hain brand meets this criterion)

Seasoning Option 3

1 large clove garlic, minced or pressed

1 Tbsp. fresh lemon or lime juice

1 Tbsp. fresh cilantro or parsley, chopped

1 tsp. salt

To find out more or to speak to a nutritional counselor for free, just visit us at:
www.CuresForTheBody.com

1/4 tsp. Lawry's Seasoned Salt with no MSG

1/8 tsp. pepper

1/8 tsp. cayenne

Place chicken in medium-sized non-stick skillet over medium-high heat.

With a spoon or spatula, break up chicken into marble-sized pieces and continue to move the pieces around in the pan until fully cooked and brown on all sides.

Remove pan from heat and add your choice of seasoning options. Stir for one minute to mix well.

Note: One pound of chicken breast, thinly sliced or cubed before cooking may be used in place of the ground chicken or turkey breast.

Browned Chicken (approx. five 3-oz. servings)

1 lb. chicken tenders or 1 lb. boneless, skinless split chicken
   breasts

1 large clove garlic, minced or pressed

Spray a large non-stick skillet with Cooking Spray (page 498) and place over medium-high heat to preheat.

Heat until water sizzles when a few drops are sprinkled on pan, place chicken and garlic into pan.

Let cook until chicken is brown on one side (about 7 minutes). Turn, and continue to cook until brown on the other side (about 5 minutes).

Choose one of the sauces listed below, and add it to the chicken in the pan. Continue cooking until chicken is no longer pink in the middle. To check, slit chicken with a knife in its thickest part.

This chicken, with any of the sauce options, is very good served with cooked brown rice.

Mock 7-Up Sauce

3/4 cup fructose

1/2 cup fresh lemon juice

1/4 cup soy sauce (with no MSG, sugars or colorings)

I cup water

To find out more or to speak to a nutritional counselor for free, just visit us at:
www.CuresForTheBody.com

Luau Sauce

1 small onion, thinly sliced (optional)

1 bell pepper, thinly sliced (optional)

1/4 cup fructose

1/4 cup soy sauce

1 Tbsp. lemon juice

1 cup water

1 can pineapple chunks in their own juice OR

1 can apricots in their own juice

If using apricots, use only the juice for the sauce, and add in the apricots after the chicken is done cooking.

Honey Barbecue Sauce

1 cup barbecue sauce

1/4 cup water

1 Tbsp. raw, organic honey

1 Tbsp. fresh lemon juice

Pacific Sauce

1 medium green pepper, cut in strips

1 medium onion, cut in thin strips

2 Tbsp. soy sauce

1 12-oz. jar Heinz Fat-Free Chicken Gravy

1 12-oz. can mandarin orange segments, drained (optional)

1 can pineapple tidbits, drained (optional)

*If fruit is used, put it in at the end of cooking time.

*May also serve over cooked whole wheat noodles.

Chili Beans

1 lb. ground chicken or turkey

1 pkg. Hain brand chili mix (or other MSG-free chili mix)

1 can (15 oz.) kidney beans

1 can stewed tomatoes

To find out more or to speak to a nutritional counselor for free, just visit us at:
www.CuresForTheBody.com

1/4 tsp. fructose (optional)

Brown ground meat. Add chili mix, beans, tomatoes and
fructose. Stir and heat.

Yogurt Cheese

Plain or flavored nonfat yogurt

Place a strainer in a bowl. Empty one container of yogurt into the
strainer. Cover and refrigerate for 24 hours. The liquid will drain out,
and what remains is yogurt cheese.

Fresh Salsa

1 lb. fresh tomatoes, finely diced

2 medium tomatoes, pureed in blender

1 medium onion, finely diced

1 to 2 jalapenos, minced (optional)

3 green onions with some chives, chopped

2 medium cloves garlic, minced or pressed

1 tsp. raw apple cider vinegar

1 tsp. raw lemon or lime juice

Mix all ingredients together. Add diced avocado if desired.

Better Spread

1/2 c. raw butter or butter, softened

3/8 tsp. salt

1/2 c. your choice of cold pressed, unrefined oils

Mix all ingredients together until smooth. This recipe makes a spread
that is much softer, right from the fridge, than butter. It also makes
whole grain breads more palatable because it penetrates into the
breads, softening them. (This is also true of the peanut butter version
listed below.)

Peanut butter version: Use approx. 1 jar non-hydrogenated peanut
butter in place of butter. May also add 1/2 cup raw almond butter to
this mixture.

To find out more or to speak to a nutritional counselor for free, just visit us at:
www.CuresForTheBody.com

Cooking Spray

1 c. extra virgin olive oil
1/2 cup water
Dark plastic or glass spray bottle

Mix oil and water together in spray bottle. Keep spray in a dark cupboard away from light and heat. (When using the spray, always use it and then return it immediately to the cupboard.) After several uses, you may need to add more water so the Cooking Spray will continue to spray evenly.

RAW FOOD SUGGESTIONS

Following are some ways to add more raw food to your diet. These are also great ideas for helping children eat more raw foods.

• Select a fruit that is in season but would normally not be eaten with a meal (i.e., grapefruit), and serve it as the first course. (Often children will eat something with the family that they wouldn't eat on their own!)

• Serve a dinner salad as a first course instead of with the rest of the meal. (Most people will eat much more salad, if served this way.)

• Serve fresh fruits of the season for dessert.

• Have raw vegetables washed and stored in plastic storage bags ready to take out of the refrigerator and into the car with you. This is a great snack for you, and when children see you eating vegetables, it's amazing how they start asking for some too. Vegetables like carrots, zucchini, cucumber slices and celery are very clean snacks!

• Experiment by mixing raw dry-blended flaxseeds with the foods you eat. You'll find that in many foods you won't even taste them, and you'll be getting the benefits.

• Remember that fruits and vegetables are high in water and fiber. While neither the water or the fiber have any calories, they add to the sense of fullness you feel when you eat. They require more chewing than cooked foods and, therefore, slow eating down.

To find out more or to speak to a nutritional counselor for free, just visit us at:
www.CuresForTheBody.com

• Garlic is called for in many of the recipes in this manual. Raw garlic can be minced or pressed and is not only a good flavoring, but it has also been shown to enhance immune function. A product called "Breath Assure" can help if you are worried about bad breath from garlic, onions, etc.

HEALTHY SNACKS AND DESSERTS

Recipes and Suggestions

Frozen fruits, i.e., banana slices, strawberries, mangos, pineapple chunks, peaches, etc. (Freezing foods does not destroy their enzymes)

"100% Fruit" fruit rolls

Fresh, raw fruits

Raw vegetables. Dilute vegetable dip with lemon juice or raw apple cider vinegar to reduce calories per tablespoon. NOTE: To clean fruits and vegetables, wash them in water with a capful of white vinegar and a few drops of Oxy-Pure (available from OHS). Lay them out on a bath towel covered with paper towel to dry. This will wash away any pesticides or chemicals that may be on your produce.

Raw nuts are an excellent snack as they supply a good fat source. Eat nuts very sparingly if you are trying to lose weight. To make salt that will stick to raw nuts, place one cup sea salt in a blender and blend on highest speed until salt is very fine powder. Use 1 tsp. of this salt for every 1 lb. nuts. Stir salt around with nuts for about three minutes to coat evenly.

Low-fat yogurt sweetened with fruit juices or fructose. Add raw wheat germ (store in refrigerator only), flaxseeds, pre-soaked wheat berries (soak in water overnight) or raw rolled oats.

Raw trail mix made from raw nuts, raw sunflower and pumpkin seeds, date pieces, sun-dried raisins, etc. (Trader Joe's has a good selection of these items.)

Baked tortilla chips with Fresh Salsa (page 497) or baked potato chips. (Avoid chips made with Olestra.)

Make **banana splits or sundaes** with vanilla frozen yogurt (fructose sweetened). Top with fresh or frozen fruits blended with a little fructose, if desired. Also look for chocolate toppings made without refined sugars. Sprinkle sparingly with a few raw pecans or slivered almonds.

For **Cookies**, use whole wheat pastry flour or "white wheat" flour (available at Trader Joe's) in place of white flour. Use fructose in place of sugar and reduce amount by 1/4 to 1/3. For every 1/2 cup of brown sugar called for in the recipe, substitute 1/2 cup fructose plus 3/4 tsp. unsulphured molasses and 1 tsp. vanilla. For each 1/2 cup butter, margarine or shortening called for in a recipe, substitute 2 tsp. water mixed with 1 Tbsp. light tasting extra virgin olive oil .

Snacks such as baked potato crisps and turkey jerky are okay for picnics or road trips but should be used in moderation.

Make a **milk shake** by blending vanilla frozen yogurt (fructose sweetened), a small amount of milk and fresh or frozen fruits of your choice (i.e., strawberries, bananas, pineapple).

Musieli

16 oz. fructose or juice-sweetened strawberry yogurt

2 large apples, peeled and chopped

2 large bananas, sliced

1 cup sliced strawberries or fresh or frozen thawed blueberries

1/2 cup chopped raw pecans

Mix all ingredients together in a medium bowl. (Does not keep well.)

DRINK SUGGESTIONS
Purified water

To find out more or to speak to a nutritional counselor for free, just visit us at:
www.CuresForTheBody.com

Fresh vegetable juices

Fresh fruit juices

Herb teas (may sweeten with raw organic honey (preferred) or fructose and add flavor with fresh lemon)

For a "Virgin Strawberry Daiquiri," place ingredients in a blender in this order: 16 oz. fresh or frozen strawberries, 4 ounces lime juice, 1/2 cup fructose, and 4 cups ice. Blend on medium-high until smooth.

Fresh Lemonade

5 cups water

3/4 cups fructose

11/2 cups freshly squeezed lemon juice

Mix all ingredients well and add ice or refrigerate before serving.

HEALTHIER COOKING INGREDIENTS AND PRODUCTS

When selecting ingredients, remember to choose items that are as close to nature as possible. The following list represents a "hierarchy" that you should use when selecting foods. The list is in descending order, with the healthiest listed first.

Raw organic

Raw

Frozen (freezing foods does not destroy their enzymes) or dried without preservatives and at low temperatures (sun-dried if possible)

Bottled raw (i.e., Clausin's pickles are not cooked)

Baked

Canned

Microwaved (never recommended!)

Ingredient Replacement Suggestions

Many of these ingredients listed below as replacement suggestions are found in health food stores. If the health food store nearest you does not carry them make sure to request that they carry them in the future. Stores are usually very willing or will at least order them for you.

INGREDIENT	REPLACE WITH
Mayonnaise	Mayonnaise made with expeller pressed safflower or Canola oil
Hydrogenated oils to be used in baking(Shortening, margarine, etc.)	Real butter
Cooking oil to be used in foods that will be heated. (i.e. pancakes, cornbread, etc.)	A very mild tasting extra virgin olive oil ("Santini"brand is one) or any expeller-pressed oil
Margarine used to spread on bread	Better Spread (page 495)
Commercial cooking sprays (Pam)	Cooking Spray (page 496) (Use for sautéing, stir-frying, preparing cookie sheets and baking dishes, etc.)
Hydrogenated peanut butter	Non-hydrogenated peanut butter

If you will keep your intestinal "playing field" full of friendly flora, the disease-causing bacteria will have to go elsewhere to find a field!

WHAT ABOUT SUPPLEMENTS? ARE THEY NEEDED? IS THERE SCIENTIFIC PROOF? IF SO, HOW MUCH AND WHAT KIND?

The Game of LIFE

View on Supplementation

In search of health, thousands of people seem to be unaware of their potential for LIFE. Particularly when it comes to supplementation, most individuals seem to be confused. Is there an answer? Is there scientific proof that shows we need to add back certain nutrients on a daily basis? This paper will prove, using peer reviewed research, the unequivocal need for restoring on a daily basis five kinds of nutrients that are lost due to current lifestyle and environmental factors. It will also explain a simple, cost effective way to accomplish that.

To find out more or to speak to a nutritional counselor for free, just visit us at:
www.CuresForTheBody.com

First, we need to explain that, though crucial, supplementation is just one aspect of health. It is important to provide yourself with a complete game plan that will allow you to be successful with LIFE.

This plan includes everything you need to have F.I.T.N.E.S.S.—Focused, Intense Thought; Nutrition; Exercise and Specific Supplementation. With this plan, you can quit hoping or wishing for health. This plan is clear, concise and strategic making it easy to win in LIFE. It will virtually guarantee success, allowing you to fully expect to reach the goal of optimal health.

As noted above, one of the most important strategies for the winning game is specific supplementation. Here we will point out some of the most misleading options available, and provide you with the rules to sort them out and thus, play the game of LIFE successfully to reach and maintain optimal health.

Note: Nutritional supplements have become a multi-billion dollar industry, and it seems as if some people are trying to support that industry all by themselves—judging by the number of products they take!

This section will help you see how you can restore all of the nutrients you need for health, without having to invest in a ton of supplements. **In fact, our goal is to help you take fewer supplements** as you improve your lifestyle and apply the F.I.T.N.E.S.S. principles. Read on!

Scoping out the playing field

In the playing field we call "Supplementation," there are thousands of distractions that beckon with flashy wording and promising phrases:

> Pop this product to sleep better!
> Double your dose of this vitamin for whatever ails you!
> Swallow this supplement for a stronger immune system!
> Take two tablets for tummy aches!
> Drink this down to feel younger and more energetic!

How do you stay focused? If you were to stop and involve yourself with all the distractions along the way, you would never reach your ultimate goal of winning the game for optimal health. Rather than sitting on the sidelines or disregarding the rules as you play the game, wouldn't you rather be winning with every opportunity and enjoying the quality of life that you won?

To find out more or to speak to a nutritional counselor for free, just visit us at:
www.CuresForTheBody.com

When it comes to health, most people are playing the wrong game. In the United States alone, 1.5 million people die every year from diseases that are largely *preventable*![1] We are literally killing ourselves through the lifestyle choices we make on a daily basis. Though one of the richest nations in the world, *malnutrition* is rampant in the United States.[2]

The answer isn't to make still another wrong play by taking supplements that you don't need or would actually do you more harm. Instead, the game plan for optimal health is pretty straightforward. All you need to make are five strategic plays and you are well on your way to win a life of health and wellness. In fact, when it comes to supplementation, you may want to think of the Game to Optimal Health as having 5 plays!

#1 – Enzyme Advantage

Cooked and processed foods are perhaps the single most detrimental deterrent to optimal health. That's a pretty bold statement when you consider the many health hazards that we deal with on a daily basis, but it's not an exaggeration. You sit out on the bench every time you eat cooked and processed foods—which, for most people, is every time they eat a meal or a snack!

Here's why: Enzymes are minute protein molecules that are found naturally in foods we eat.[3] These protein molecules serve a vital purpose. They are catalysts that make possible the chemical reactions that digest our food and break it down to useable, absorbable nutrients. Enzymes are the life force that is found in foods and then transferred to our bodies to keep every system functioning optimally.

Problems arise because most of the foods we eat are enzyme-deficient. Enzymes are destroyed at temperatures of 118°F. or above.[4] That means that almost any kind of food preparation method destroys enzymes. Anytime you cook, microwave, fry, bake, grill or otherwise process your foods, you subject yourself to the dangerous consequences of eating enzyme-deficient foods. How bad is that really, and just what happens when you eat foods that are devoid of enzymes?

Mother Nature must have known we wouldn't eat all of our foods raw, so our bodies do have a backup supply of digestive enzymes to draw from. However, that supply is limited and depleting this supply places undue stress on the body. In other words, whenever we eat cooked or processed foods (which for most people is every meal!), we cause our bodies to work harder than necessary.[5]

To find out more or to speak to a nutritional counselor for free, just visit us at:
www.CuresForTheBody.com

When the body's resources are being commandeered to accomplish digestion, they aren't readily available to do other things—such as warding off disease or delaying the aging process or burning stored body fat. That's right. Eating cooked and processed foods can lead to frequent sickness, premature aging and increased storage of body fat and countless other problems.[6]

Cooked and processed foods are so hard on the body that they actually bring on a condition called *digestive leucocytosis.* The body considers cooked food to be a foreign substance, an unwanted invader and eating cooked food causes the white blood cell count to rise just as it does when the body is sick or has ingested poison![7]

Further, if enzymes are not present in the food you eat, not only is the body overtaxed, but also food is often only partially digested. This causes additional problems, including allergies, lethargy and deadly plaque build-up in the blood vessels.

Eventually, as your body's stores of digestive enzymes are depleted, you become unable to digest certain foods at all. For example, if you were to use up your supply of lactase enzymes (from eating enzyme-deficient milk products) you would become lactose intolerant.

All the while that we are inordinately using up our digestive enzymes by eating enzyme-deficient foods, the body is trying to compensate in yet another way—by next pulling from its supply of metabolic enzymes. These enzymes *can* be called upon to facilitate digestion, but their primary purpose is to run other processes of the body.

Plainly, it is not a good thing to be using enzymes to accomplish digestion when those enzymes are supposed to regulate the heart, lungs, or kidneys instead. However, that is exactly what happens. The body places a priority on digestion and goes to great lengths to do whatever is necessary to make sure foods are properly broken down and assimilated.

Some experts recognize the extreme toll this places on the body. They believe that enzyme deficiency is a factor in *all* disease and even determines lifespan. Dr. Edward Howell, who studied enzyme nutrition for over 50 years, wrote:

> *Humans eating an enzymeless diet use up a tremendous amount of their enzyme potential in lavish secretions of the pancreas and other digestive organs. The result is a shortened lifespan (65 years or less as compared with 100 or more), illness, and lowered resistance to stresses of all types, physiological and environmental.*[8]

To find out more or to speak to a nutritional counselor for free, just visit us at:
www.CuresForTheBody.com

Effects of Enzyme-Deficient Foods

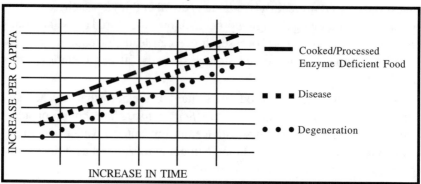

Over time, as more and more people consume cooked and processed (and, therefore enzyme-deficient) foods, the rate of disease and degeneration increases proportionately.

Initially, the body may react to enzyme deficiency with what we call "indigestion." Minor discomforts — burping, heartburn, abdominal pain and bad breath as well as excess gas, skin problems, diarrhea, constipation and more — can be linked to consuming foods that are devoid of enzymes. Headaches, mental fatigue, nervousness, lack of concentration, memory loss, insomnia and nightmares can all result when the body doesn't have enzymes readily available in the foods we eat. A lack of enzymes also interferes with hormone production, inhibits cellular repair and causes chronic digestive problems. (These types of problems are common! One in thirteen hospitalizations is a result of chronic digestive disorders.[9])

There is an ironic twist in this whole scenario. Most people, when they experience the first signs of indigestion, have no idea that those signs are tied to enzyme deficiency and are a signal that digestion is compromised. Rather than looking for a way to promote digestion and make sure the burden is taken off the body, most people who experience indigestion further interfere with the process by taking antacids or acid blockers, which stop the digestive process in its tracks.[10] While this may dissuade the symptoms, it doesn't solve the problem, and is detrimental to overall health and well being.

The need for restoring the body's enzyme supply is unquestionable. Taking supplemental enzymes preserves the body's own vital enzyme stores. Many people who take an enzyme supplement notice that they aren't lethargic or sleepy after a meal, the discomfort of indigestion is gone and—for many— food allergies disappear. Enzyme supplementation has been shown to

To find out more or to speak to a nutritional counselor for free, just visit us at:
www.CuresForTheBody.com

alleviate mild, and even severe or chronic, digestive disorders. Many people—who may not have noticeable digestive problems but who understand the benefits of enzymes—say they take enzyme supplements as a way to ward off the aging process, bolster the immune system and protect themselves from the incredible toll cooked and processed foods can place on the body.

Obviously, in today's world, it is virtually impossible to eat a diet of only raw foods. And, if you—or any other individual who has lived on the typical North American diet—were even to start doing that today, you still need a way to restore the enzymes that have been depleted to this point if you are to experience optimal health.

Along with changing your diet and adding more raw foods, the way to preserve the body's vital enzyme supply is by taking an enzyme supplement each time you eat foods that are cooked or processed. In recent years, as more and more people become aware of the need for enzymes, many products have cropped up on the market. While some have value, many others are incomplete, and thus, ineffective.

In order to promote complete digestion, an enzyme supplement must contain the full complex of enzymes. Pineapple enzymes or papaya enzymes are single plant enzyme products and are devoid of the enzymes needed to completely digest food. Likewise, products that contain protease only initiate the process of protein digestion. Protease breaks protein down to a peptide. In the peptide form, protein can't be used by the body and can actually cause more harm than good. To break peptides down to useable amino acids requires peptidase as well.

Amylase will break carbohydrates down into disaccharides. Since disaccharides are still not in a form the body can use—and, like peptides, can cause havoc in the system—cellulase, lactase, maltase and invertase must also be included to finish the job and break the carbohydrates all the way down to useable simple sugars.[11]

Similarly, lipase, the enzyme that digests fat, must have certain minerals present in order to accomplish its job.[12]

Many products on the market contain animal enzymes, such as pepsin. While animal enzymes may indeed promote digestion, they have a limited pH range. This limited range means that they work in only one stage of the three-stage process of digestion. In addition, animal enzymes don't work in conjunction with the natural processes of the body. Rather than restoring the body's enzyme supply and allowing it to function at optimal levels, animal enzymes supplant (or take the place of) this supply and cause the body to stop producing enzymes of its own.

To find out more or to speak to a nutritional counselor for free, just visit us at:
www.CuresForTheBody.com

Taking an enzyme supplement helps the body in yet another way. Not only does a complete, pure plant enzyme supplement help break foods down, enzymes also assist with the absorption and delivery of vitamins and minerals, making these nutrients readily available for use in the body.

You now understand the dangers of enzyme depletion and how to avoid the side effects of eating cooked and processed foods. It's now up to you to choose to stay off the bench and successfully win the first inning with the enzyme advantage—The Game of LIFE benefits with enzyme supplementation.

Choose to be free of indigestion and chronic digestive problems, to preserve your enzyme stores for important metabolic function, to promote optimum nutrient absorption and fat metabolism by doing what I call "eating responsibly." When you eat foods that are cooked and processed and, therefore, devoid of enzymes, make sure you don't let enzyme deficiencies overtax your system and deprive you of the optimal health you want and deserve. Avoid the many health hazards on the enzyme deficiency disadvantage—distractions such as lactose intolerance and inability to digest milk products; fat intolerance and the resulting dangers of heart disease; sugar intolerance and the precursory steps to diabetes; and the ravages of lethargy, food allergies and toxicity that can result from undigested food particles.

Stay in the game for optimal health by taking an enzyme supplement each time you eat a snack or a meal that contains foods that are cooked or processed.

#2 Probiotic Defense

The next nutrient necessity is probiotics. Again, this is an inning of the game of health that many people have never traversed. Most of us are unfamiliar with the benefits of probiotics and the danger we put ourselves in when we fail to take advantage of those benefits.

What are probiotics, and why the need? Antibiotics have been used for a number of years to fight infections and ward off harmful bacteria. Antibiotics means "against or opposed to life."[13]

Probiotics, on the other hand, means "promoting or favoring life." Probiotics are living organisms—also known as bacteria or flora—that colonize and flourish in the healthy intestine. These friendly bacteria are vital to health and to the proper functioning of the intestinal tract. In fact, the healthy intestine contains approximately three pounds of friendly flora.[14]

These bacteria strains function as a backup to our body's immune system. They promote health by secreting antibiotic-like substances, such as lactic acid, acetic acid, hydrogen peroxide and others. Though these substances are produced in tiny amounts, they have a wide-range of activity against salmonella, pseudomonas, E. coli and other harmful food-borne bacteria.[15]

When the intestine is flourishing with friendly bacteria, there is no room for the harmful, disease-causing strains to implant and grow.

Not only do probiotics help to detoxify and suppress pathogens, they also promote proper digestion. Certain strains are particularly beneficial as they produce abundant amounts of the enzyme lactase; thus, are effective in helping many individuals tolerate dairy foods.[16]

Unfortunately, this is another area that has been generally dealt with in a way that has further exaggerated the problem, rather than addressing it.

Consider the problem: As stated above, the healthy intestine requires the presence of friendly bacteria. However, common dietary and lifestyle factors destroy those bacteria.

Stress—with daily pressures of family life, work and finances that seem to be a fact of life for most of us—is to blame for much of the probiotic depletion each of us experiences today. Probiotics are also depleted by strong antibacterial herbs, cortisone, carbonated drinks, lack of sleep, laxatives and birth control pills.[17] Poor diet, toxins in the blood stream and emotional upset further rob the body of the flora it needs. Natural aging also takes a toll on our probiotic stores.

Studies show that most North Americans have less than half the amount of flora needed for optimal health.[18] As bowel flora is depleted, the body is subject to numerous diseases, including colitis, diabetes, meningitis, rheumatoid arthritis, thyroid disease and even bowel cancer. A deficiency in friendly bacteria can bring on a host of additional problems associated with bowel toxicity.

Following the route that depletes probiotics has taken thousands of people further and further from optimal health. The results have been staggering. Infectious diseases that once were considered to be under control have reemerged with more ferocity than ever. Flus and colds are more frequent, more debilitating than ever.[19]

To find out more or to speak to a nutritional counselor for free, just visit us at:
www.CuresForTheBody.com

Whenever an individual experiences the results of a depleted probiotic supply, their doctor's first inclination is often to treat the resulting infection or virus with an *anti*biotic. Ironically, the strategy used to protect us from disease further complicates the situation and actually puts us at greater risk. Antibiotics not only kill the bad bacteria, they also wipe out the good strains (those same strains that have already been depleted by the lifestyle and environmental factors noted above).

Females may be all too familiar with this vicious cycle. How many women have gone to the doctor because they had a cold or ear infection, were given an antibiotic, and within a few weeks have had to go back to see the doctor, this time with a yeast infection? The antibiotic may have done its job of killing the bacteria that caused the cold or infection, but at the same time, it depleted the stores of friendly flora that keep the yeast overgrowth in check.

Yet, antibiotics are still often prescribed indiscriminately, even for minor ailments, without any thought as to whether they are really necessary for that situation. Don't think that because you haven't taken an antibiotic lately that your probiotic supply is fine.

Even though you haven't had a written prescription for an antibiotic, chances are you have still taken significant amounts of antibiotics during the past few months. You see, animals (including cows, pigs and chickens) are fed antibiotics in order to keep them well and to promote growth. In fact, in North America, half of the antibiotics produced—over 20 million pounds each year—are fed to animals. Dairy products as well contain high levels of antibiotics.[20]

What is the answer then, if our lifestyles and environmental factors are taking away from our supply of friendly flora? How can an individual continue to win without a constant supply?

The Game of LIFE, then, requires probiotic supplementation. Many products of the market (acidophilus or salivarius supplements) are single-strain products, so don't provide the combination of benefits that can come from a blend of several different strains.

When selecting a probiotic supplement, look for stabilized strains of bacteria. Stabilized strains of bacteria are hearty and resilient, able to survive the many changes in pH and temperature encountered before reaching the lower intestine where the bacteria can grow.

As the friendly flora grows and fills in the spaces in your intestine, there will be no "vacancies" where bad bacteria can implant. Choose to protect yourself from toxins and harmful bacteria and the resulting infectious

To find out more or to speak to a nutritional counselor for free, just visit us at:
www.CuresForTheBody.com

diseases by restoring your friendly bacteria. Nutritionally, flora can be restored by eating yogurt and other fermented foods. However, unless you are eating such foods on a daily basis, you are most likely not getting enough flora to make up for what is lost due to dietary and environmental factors.

With the factors of constant stress, overuse of prescription antibiotics, and antibiotics in our foods, flora supplementation is really the only way to ensure optimum bacteria balance. Remember, flora supplementation is particularly important if you are under stress. Your flora supply should also be restored through supplementation if you have recently taken antibiotics or are planning for or recovering from surgery. Flora supplementation can be particular beneficial for individuals who are lactose intolerant. Also, anyone who is frequently sick, has recently been exposed to an infectious disease, or is experiencing symptoms of bowel toxicity may find flora to be extremely helpful.[21]

Don't mess around this inning in the Game of LIFE. Make a choice to improve and protect your immune system from the ravages of stress and lifestyle, rather than leaving yourself open for any bacterial invader that comes your way every time you eat, drink or breathe. It will serve you well and take you closer to your success of health if you will make flora supplementation part of your game winning strategy.

#3 – Vitamin Offense

By taking enzymes and flora, you will have a significant advantage in the Game of LIFE. But, what about the more traditional nutrients that you have always heard about? What about vitamins and minerals? Was your mother right when she told you to eat your vegetables to get these nutrients?

A U.S. Department of Agriculture study substantiates what your mother may have advocated. It found that most Americans are getting well below the Recommended Daily Allowances for most vitamins. Another survey showed that 97% of Americans have some sort of nutritional deficiency.[22] Where has all the nutrition gone?

First, take a look at the modern diet. Many people seem to be getting by on junk food diets of high-fat fast foods, salty snacks and sugar-loaded desserts. One research study found that on any given day almost half of the American population doesn't eat even one piece of fruit. Eighteen percent have neglected to eat even one vegetable.[23] To make matters worse, even the fruits and vegetables that we do eat are often canned, frozen or otherwise processed.

The same processing methods that destroy the enzymes in foods also take a toll on the other nutrients. Add to that the poor crop rotation, depletion of the soil, the use of pesticides, the presence of environmental toxins, the practice of harvesting foods before they are ripe and many other commonplace farming practices, and you end up with foods that are seriously lacking in the nutrients.[24]

While it was once easy to come by vitamins and minerals from our foods, in today's environment, even selecting food properly may not ensure that you are getting all the nutrients you may think.

Whole Food Vitamin C

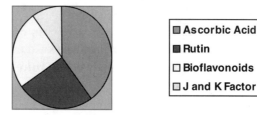

Cabbage once contained high amounts of vitamin C. Now, with current growing and processing methods, it has none. The protein content of wheat has dropped from 17 percent to only about 9 percent.[25] Even the same foods can vary in nutrient content simply because of growing conditions. One study showed that the vitamin A content in tomatoes can vary from 640 CIU to over 3,000 CIU depending upon where they are grown.[26]

Somehow, we need to find a way to take up the slack and restore the vitamins and minerals that our bodies **must** have if we are to enjoy optimal health.

Now you may think that you can get along just fine with a minor nutrient deficiency. Think again! Minor deficiencies manifest themselves first as something seemingly insignificant. Your hair may lose its sheen. Your fingernails may have ridges or your lips may crack. You may bruise easily or you may feel unusually sluggish in the afternoon. Soon, however, those minor deficiencies can develop into major problems.

Vitamins have been described as "missing keys," and like a key, "they fit into tiny chemical locks that free the body's…regulatory networks, each vitamin is a complex organic molecule that fills in specific missing links throughout the body's chemistry."[27]

What happens when certain "chemical locks" are left locked, simply because you haven't supplied the body with the necessary vitamins? What may begin as a minor deficiency symptom can quickly elevate into a significant problem and health concern. Knowing that vitamins are key, it becomes obvious that they are, indeed, crucial. Their role is significant as they supply the keys necessary to balance and nourish the body, support it in its hundreds of processes and promote its healing and regeneration. In the body, vitamins work in tandem with enzymes and with minerals, assisting these other nutrients to perform their roles.

As noted previously, the general public is often misled by marketing mires to bend the rules. In terms of vitamin supplementation, this is again the case. First, many people have been led to believe that vitamin supplementation is simply not necessary. This is definitely a dangerously mismarked byway. The Food and Nutrition Encyclopedia puts the matter to rest, saying, "There is no question that nutrient supplements, used properly, are critical to restoring and sometimes to maintaining human health."[28]

Even those who understand the need for vitamin supplementation fail to comprehend the subtle—but significant—difference between whole food vitamins and synthetics. In order for the vitamin (the key) to be of any use in the body, it must be absorbed into the cells. The fitting of the missing keys into their tiny slots in your biochemistry takes place within the trillions of cells that make up the body. Unfortunately, if you were to take any one of many commercially produced vitamins on the market you could still be malnourished, simply because the vitamins in these supplements are only fractions of the complete key, and, thus, are not useable on the cellular level.

In actuality, synthetic or chemically purified substances that are labeled and sold as vitamins are not really vitamins at all. They are only fragments of the key the body needs. In this fractionated, incomplete form, the so-called vitamin becomes a non-food and, rather than a nourishing, sustaining effect in the body, it acts like a drug. Synthetic vitamins are unrecognizable in the body. In their fractionated form, they don't fit into the keyhole.[29]

Whole food vitamins, on the other hand, are alive. They are moving, functioning composites that contain all the co-factors necessary to perform their role within the body.

Synthetic vitamins have the exact opposite effect than you would want from a vitamin supplement. For example, alpha tocopherol is sold as "vitamin

To find out more or to speak to a nutritional counselor for free, just visit us at:
www.CuresForTheBody.com

E." Actually, this is only a portion of the complete vitamin E complex and in this form it loses up to 99 percent of its potency or function. In essence, it is no longer vitamin E. This is obvious when you realize that, in its whole food form, vitamin E supports bone health and strength. However, large doses of alpha tocopherol actually cause the bone to release minerals to compensate for this incomplete, synthetic source of vitamin E.

The way the body handles these nutritional fractions is to use up its own reserves to create the entire complex (the key that will fit the lock).

For example, taking ascorbic acid instead of whole vitamin C would force the body to use its own reserves of J Factor, K factor, rutin, and the other portions of the complete vitamin C. The result could actually deplete the body's supply. This means that taking synthetic vitamins may not replenish nutrients, but could very easily *cause* a deficiency.[30]

In addition to improper function and inability to perform a role in the body, fractionated vitamins stimulate nerve activity and increase blood sugar pickup (a drug-like reaction). These vitamin forms are rushed through the body for elimination (which may cause a temporary euphoric feeling, but doesn't encourage repair or regeneration).[31]

Though synthetic vitamins are the most prevalent kind on the market today, consumers beware! These vitamins are the most inexpensive form to produce and market. The companies who put them on the shelf are much more interested in your wallet than in your wellbeing.

An interesting event just happened in Denmark. The government of has pulled all of the Kellogg cereals from the shelves and will not permit them back on until all the "synthetic" vitamins are taken out. Finally, a country that understands whole food vitamins and has researched the evidence!!

Hold out for whole food vitamins. You can now make an informed decision that will allow you to have the benefits and balance of bounteous whole food vitamin stores. **Supplement your diet with a whole food vitamin source to steer clear of the minor vitamin deficiencies that can result in major problems.** By restoring your critical vitamin balance, you'll notice that your skin, hair and nails are healthier. You won't have constant mood swings and you will no longer crumble under the daily stresses you have to face. Vitamin balance can help you experience the advantages of increased energy, greater mental clarity and fewer aches and pains. Since whole food vitamins support the body's natural healing processes, every illness or disease responds more favorably if the right kind of vitamins are available to the body.

To find out more or to speak to a nutritional counselor for free, just visit us at:
www.CuresForTheBody.com

This is an area where too many people try to bend the rules of the game. They reach for a one-each-day type of vitamin, thinking they are doing themselves a favor, and don't realize that they are reducing their potential to win. Still sick and tired, they wonder what's wrong, thinking to themselves, "But, I take my vitamins!"

Don't fall by the wayside with this way of thinking. **Add back what is missing due to current lifestyle and environmental factors by taking whole food vitamins and experience the added benefits for health!**

#4 – Mineral Pass

Minerals have drawn a great deal of attention during recent months. Minerals have made a showing in the gym scene, where individuals are trying to find ways to add muscle mass and increase strength. They are also receiving added attention from women over the age of 35 who are beginning to understand the risks associated with osteoporosis. Still others look to minerals as a way to alleviate symptoms of arthritis, enhance immunity and improve mental function.

Once almost an afterthought, just a nice addition to a daily dose of vitamins, mineral supplementation has now come into its own. Mineral experts and proponents of mineral supplementation remind us, "Lacking vitamins, the system can make some use of the minerals, but lacking minerals, the vitamins are often useless. While our bodies can manufacture some of the vitamins we need, they must rely completely upon outside sources for an adequate supply of minerals."[32]

Minerals are essentially tiny rocks. Found in the soil, minerals are taken up into plants and delivered to our bodies in the foods that we eat. Though they make up only about 4% of our total body weight, minerals are involved in more body processes than perhaps any other basic nutrient.[33]

As we discussed earlier, enzymes play a crucial role as catalysts, as the life force behind every bodily process. Let's now take that concept a step further. Understand that minerals are the catalysts behind these catalysts. Minerals are necessary in order to activate enzymes so they can perform their important duties in the body.[34]

As enzyme catalysts, minerals help our bodies grow and maintain themselves, they regulate body processes and they supply us with energy. If there are only slight changes in the normal mineral composition inside the cell, "the alteration may result in profound physiological consequences."[35]

To find out more or to speak to a nutritional counselor for free, just visit us at:
www.CuresForTheBody.com

It is minerals that provide the medium for cellular activity, determine the osmotic properties of body fluids, and regulate electrolyte balance. That's

CALCIUM ABSORPTION

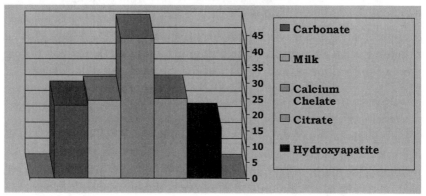

As this graph indicates, the form of calcium that is amino acid bound is absorbed and used by the body much more effectively than the calcium found in milk or in any other supplemental form of calcium.

a lot of big words that simply mean that bone formation, blood formation, nerve function and proper composition of the body's fluids all depend on the minute particles known as minerals. Deficiencies in these minute particles can be manifest in a number of ways, from aching joints, brittle fingernails, and prematurely gray hair. For women, menstrual cycles can become irregular. Long-term mineral deficiencies can contribute to atherosclerosis and heart problems, prostate problems, and ulcers and can even increase the risk of cancer.[36]

Obviously, minerals are important. However, the question comes to mind, "When minerals are needed in such tiny amounts and are available in the foods we eat, why do we need to take a mineral supplement?"

Ah, welcome to what may very well be the most controversial section in the game book for LIFE. In fact, many people think this section for LIFE is still "under investigation" because there seem to be so many twists and turns and divergent plays to make. Here you will have to watch the game carefully to stay in the lead and sort fact from fiction.

To begin, let's take a look at just why the body's mineral reserves need to be restored. As noted above, minerals are found naturally in the foods we eat. However—just as is the case with the vitamins that are available from our foods—many minerals are in short supply. Soil depletion means foods simply don't absorb as many minerals to begin with. Then, the refining and processing of foods further diminishes the available minerals.

Chromium is deficient in the American diet largely because of refining of sugar, flour and fats.[37] The refining of raw cane sugar also removes "89% of the manganese, 98% of the cobalt, 83% of the copper, 98% of the zinc and 98% of the magnesium."[38]

Similar mineral loses can be seen when wheat is refined into white flour. This process removes "40% of the chromium, 86% of the manganese, 76% of the iron, 89% of the cobalt, 68% of the copper, 78% of the zinc and 48% of the molybdenum, all trace elements essential for life or health."[39] Also lost during the refining process are large amounts of calcium, phosphorus, magnesium, potassium and sodium.

Along with poor growing and processing procedures, other factors can diminish our mineral stores. Imbalances of vitamins, amino acids and other nutrients can decrease the body's ability to absorb minerals. Stress, white flour products and other processed foods, lack of sleep and prescription drugs all pull minerals from the body, leaving a lack that must be filled.

However, in recent years, the misconceptions have multiplied. Audiocassette tapes, billboards and magazine ads perpetuate bogus claims about the benefits of colloidal minerals or some other "hot" mineral of the moment. Each successive ad seems to become bolder, some saying they contain "over 40 minerals," others claiming "72 essential minerals," and one ad indicated they had 90 minerals in their product.

Many people have altered the rules; even though "everything but the kitchen sink" and "the more minerals we can supplement the better" approach is erroneous and dangerous.

To stay in the lead, The Game of LIFE requires evading the misconceptions about mineral supplementation and focusing on the plays ahead. We have established the need to restore our mineral supplies. So, just how do you go about that in a way that doesn't create even greater distractions for your health?

For many years, scientists have known that minerals were present in animal and human tissue, but these minerals were believed to be contaminants. As methods of scientific analysis have improved, many of these minerals have now been shown to be essential to life and health. Others, however, have been tagged as the toxins that they are.[40]

How do you know which minerals are essential and which are purely poison to the system? Basically, minerals are considered essential if a

To find out more or to speak to a nutritional counselor for free, just visit us at:
www.CuresForTheBody.com

deficiency in that mineral results in impaired biological function and if that impairment is preventable or reversible by taking that particular mineral. Scientists deem a mineral as "essential" if it meets the following criteria:

a) It is present in all healthy tissue.

b) Its concentration from one animal to the next is generally constant.

c) Its withdrawal from the body results in reproducible physiological and structural abnormalities.

d) Its addition prevents or reverses those abnormalities.

e) The deficiency-induced abnormalities are accompanied by specific biochemical changes.

f) Those biochemical changes can be prevented or cured when the deficiency is prevented or cured.[41]

Essential minerals are essential in that they directly or indirectly function in supplying energy, they aid in growth and maintenance of the body tissue, and they assist in the regulation of body processes. Yes, minerals *are* essential, but this isn't to say that 40 or 50 or 90 minerals are needed for health. According to the National Research Council, "there are only 17 minerals or elements of substantiated nutritional value."[42] Eight others may have some relevance, but "evidence for requirements and essentialness is weak…essentialness to the human diet has never been demonstrated."[43]

As clear as the research is on the benefits of these particular minerals, it also plainly proves the dangers of taking minerals that are *not* essential. For example, some marketing magicians have conjured up clever campaigns touting the benefits of taking supplemental silver. Yet, why would anyone recommend taking silver when the toxic effects are well documented? Furthermore, why would anyone who is concerned about his or her health think of taking in a mineral that is most often written about in toxicology books as if it were a poison?

Similarly, gold, which is also touted as a beneficial mineral, has been shown to be extremely detrimental to the kidneys, the immune system, the skin and the bone marrow, even causing bone marrow failure.[44]

Rather than supplementing minerals based on hearsay and twisted rationale, why not take a look at what research and logic clearly prove. As noted above, research shows that there are only 17 minerals that are essential for health. Of that 17, there are three that are prevalent enough in the typical American diet. The others, however, must be supplemented, and they must be supplemented in a form that the body can assimilate.

To find out more or to speak to a nutritional counselor for free, just visit us at:
www.CuresForTheBody.com

When we drink or eat fruits or vegetables, we take in minerals that were once in the soil. In this natural form, minerals are bound to amino

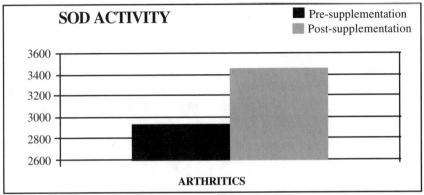

When arthritic patients were given the building blocks of SOD, blood levels of SOD (the body's own antioxidant) increased significantly.

acids. In this form they are referred to as "chelated" minerals, from the Greek work, "chele," meaning "claw." The amino acids "claw" onto the minerals, facilitating their transport into the cells of the body. It is key to remember that these minerals are rocks, and, as such, they must have the assistance of amino acids in order to travel to the sites where they are needed and penetrate the cell walls where they will do their work.

Minerals that are not chelated (oyster shells and other forms on the market) are not absorbed and used by the body. Because these mineral forms are not assimilated and used by the body, they can build up in the system and create toxic effects. Could this be why you have heard reports of iron toxicity or other toxic reactions to minerals? Most likely, the reports stem from a person having taken minerals that are not being absorbed.

Taking non-chelated minerals puts additional strain on the body, since the body attempts to supply the necessary amino acids required for the chelation process. In other words, the body *will* attempt to chelate minerals itself, but this overtaxes the system and robs amino acids that should be used for other processes.

Seeing the importance of chelation, some companies have responded with claims that their products contain "chelated" minerals. (Again, this stretch of the highway gets a little treacherous. Don't be fooled.) Indeed, some have bound their minerals to picolinatic acid (chromium picolinate) or some other inferior binding agent. Studies show that increased intake of a mineral picolinate caused **more** of the same mineral to be excreted in the

To find out more or to speak to a nutritional counselor for free, just visit us at:
www.CuresForTheBody.com

urine. In other words, the minerals were not metabolized and incorporated into the tissues.[45]

Stay in the game by choosing to ignore the many false claims. Rely only on minerals that are bound to amino acids. As noted above, this kind of minerals can be found in foods. In addition, one company called Albion Laboratories has studied and perfected this process and holds over 50 international patents into the chelation process. Extensive studies by independent researchers prove that amino acid chelated minerals from Albion are far superior to any other supplemental form of mineral. Though this form of mineral is available for purchase from Albion by any supplement manufacturer, most opt to include minerals that are far less effective, simply because they are cheaper.

The amino acid chelated minerals from Albion work exactly like the chelated minerals found in foods. Because of this fact, they are absorbed much better (up to 400 times better), more of the mineral is retained in the tissues, and they are safer than any other form on the market.

Executing the Mineral Pass without being distracted on the field may seem tricky at first. The opposing fans and experienced opponents have been known to make you lose focus. Take heart, the answer to restoring your mineral supplies and putting points on the scoreboard is quite straightforward.

All you need to do is remember the simple facts of nature: First, remember that we each desperately need those "rocks" that make up such a minute amount of our total makeup. Without tiny amounts of a few minerals that have been labeled "essential," health is impossible. Also, remember that because of current lifestyle and environmental factors, these minerals are in short supply, necessitating supplementation. Last, in selecting a mineral supplement, don't forget that the most natural, and therefore, the most readily absorbable and most effective minerals are those that are chelated with an amino acid.

You can choose to complete the Mineral Pass, simply by ignoring the false—albeit flashy—marketing ploys and sticking to the type of minerals that nature and research prove to be the best.

#5 – Antioxidant Attitudes

The last stretch of the game is the most recent addition to the strategies for a winning game. While the other areas that we have discussed thus far—enzymes, probiotics, vitamins and minerals—have been studied for decades, the group of nutrients known as antioxidants are relatively new kids on the block.

Why the sudden interest and the strong recommendations for antioxidant?

To understand their importance requires understanding another term: free radicals. Sounds almost like a bunch of rowdy teenagers, doesn't it? And, there may very well be some similarities, when you consider the havoc free radicals cause!

Free radicals are highly reactive molecules. Created by environmental toxins, electronic devices, sunlight, pesticides and chemicals, free radicals are oxygen molecules that are missing an electron. Since billions of tons of toxins are dumped into our soil, air and water every year, you can see how we can say that these unstable molecules enter the body every time we drink water, eat food or breathe. Additional free radicals are created within the body, as a result of stress, over-exercise, aging, and the natural functioning of the immune system.

These free radicals "attack" the stable, healthy cells of the body, looking for the electron they are missing. The healthy cells of our bodies are subjected to over 10,000 hits from free radicals every day, according to some experts. As the cells are bombarded, the cell lining becomes weak, allowing disease to set in and leading to premature degeneration.

This constant weakening process, known as "oxidation," has been linked to a number of diseases, including cancer, stroke, atherosclerosis and cataracts. Free radical damage has also been linked to joint pain, shortness of breath, eye strain, excess bruising and age spots.

The body does have the capability to deal with a limited number of free radicals and to keep the oxidative process in check. However, the prevalence of environmental toxins has created an ever-increasing number of free radicals that the body has to deal with. Most people's natural free radical fighting abilities are overtaxed. Even people who live in rural areas are at risk. Those who work around paint, chemicals and computers should especially heed this warning.

To find out more or to speak to a nutritional counselor for free, just visit us at:
www.CuresForTheBody.com

In order to stop the process of damaging oxidation and defuse these unstable free radical molecules, our bodies need nutrients called antioxidants. Antioxidants can actually stop the harmful chain reaction and can even repair damage that has already been caused by free radicals.

Jumping on the antioxidant bandwagon, many companies have proclaimed the benefits of one nutrient or another. This section of the Highway is complex. It requires a many-pronged approach, taking care to rely on the most effective antioxidant nutrients available.

For example—"ACES"—Vitamins A, C, E and the mineral, selenium— are widely recognized for their antioxidant benefits. While some advertisers laud vitamin E over the others, or some try to capitalize on the antioxidant benefits of selenium, why wouldn't you rather have the combined benefits of all of these powerful antioxidant nutrients? As discussed earlier, to get maximum antioxidant benefit from your vitamin A, C and E supplementation, you should be taking these in their whole food form. In fact, recent studies echo the importance of whole food vitamins in this regard. Vitamin E has been shown to be a powerful antioxidant. However, if the synthetic form of vitamin E is taken, it has the opposite effect, actually contributing to the problems that should be alleviated by an antioxidant.

Along with whole food vitamins A, C, E and selenium, there are other important sources of antioxidant nutrients that shouldn't be ignored if you want to adequately protect yourself from the ravages of free radicals. Extensive research into certain of these compounds was conducted in France by Dr. Jacques Masquelier. He found that the positive benefits of longevity and good health, which many people who drank wine experienced, could be attributed to proanthocyanidins found in the grapes used to make the wine. The same class of nutrients found in grape seed and grape seed extract is also found in pine bark extract. They have been proven to be twenty times more effective than vitamin C and fifty times more effective than vitamin E in terms of antioxidant protection.

There is one other consideration that must be addressed at this inning of the game. While many companies supply antioxidant nutrients, few take advantage of the most powerful antioxidant of all. The most potent free radical fighter is already present in the body. Known as Super Oxide Dismutase (SOD), this natural defense against free radicals is the most effective force that the body has. As mentioned earlier, however, this defense is in such great demand that it is difficult for the body to keep pace with the onslaught. Unfortunately, despite what some companies may say, SOD can not be supplemented. Supplemental SOD is destroyed in the digestive system before it is ever absorbed and made available for use in the body. There is a way, however, to restore the body's own free radical fighting forces, and that is to supply it with the building blocks needed to create more SOD. These SOD building blocks are specific, highly absorbable minerals, which supply what the body needs to make its own antioxidant.

Effect of SOD Precursors:

Don't give free radicals free reign, allowing them to leave their wake of damaged cells, degeneration and disease. By choosing to have the Antioxidant Attitude you can have one more of the many advantages available to the successful outcome of the game. You can fight back against free radicals and the 80 different diseases that have been linked to their ravages.

Take a multi-faceted approach of supplying your body with the finest antioxidant ingredients available, including vitamin A, C, E and selenium and proanthocyanidins from grape seed, grape seed extract and pine bark extract. Even more importantly, become a better free radical fighter on your own. Ward off free radical damage by supplying the body with the precursors necessary to create more SOD, the body's own ultra-powerful antioxidant. Don't allow your health to fall victim to the prevalence of environmental toxins and the natural stresses of life. Give your health a hand by boosting its free radical fighting forces.

Plus, Here's the Game Plan

This plan and explanation of the rules for the Game of LIFE makes the playing time towards optimal health easier and more enjoyable. The plan—and the wealth of research behind it—makes it obvious that there are certain nutrients that are depleted because of current lifestyle and environmental factors.

1. **Enzymes** are unavailable in our over-cooked, over-processed diets.

2. **Probiotics**, depleted by stress, poor diets and the prevalence of antibiotic use, are in such short supply that our immune systems and digestive processes are compromised.

3. With our food sources sadly devoid of **vitamins**, many of us are malnourished and dangerously deficient in the nutrients we need for health.

To find out more or to speak to a nutritional counselor for free, just visit us at:
www.CuresForTheBody.com

4. Even the minute amounts of **minerals** needed for healthy functioning of every bodily process are no longer readily available and are further depleted by dietary and lifestyle habits.

5. Plus, our body's **antioxidant** forces are unable to keep pace with the constant bombardment from free radical molecules.

To reach optimal health, there is simply no choice but to play the game in order to provide the body with what it needs by restoring each of these nutrient areas.

From this book, you can see that there are many intricacies along the way. Deception and obstacles abound and disregard for the rules could easily lead you astray. Your game plan is a good tool to keep you from losing the game.

Knowing that the best plan is useless unless it is implemented, we simply haven't handed you a rule book and walked away. **We have created a step by step strategy that will allow you to swiftly and easily play your position.** The strategy itself seems almost too good to be true.

There are companies in the market that have recognized this need and have created some great products to help you with this. The lead author's company has combined these nutrients into two products to make it easy to supplement. GNC and other companies have these five nutrients on their shelves. Just make sure you pick the right form of the nutrient as we have discussed in this chapter. At the end of the book we have listed some other great people and companies that sell reputable products. By being responsible, you will find that you can take very little of these nutrients as you improve your eating habits as discussed previously.

The results are staggering...

Housewives, professional athletes, students, business executives, teenagers, rehab patients and thousands of others have experienced the benefits of improved immunity, greater energy, increased ability to lose excess body fat, enhanced digestion, fewer mood swings and cravings and an overall sense of well-being and optimal health!

You can have the same amazing benefits. Stake your claim and start up your new vehicle that will take you—without fail—down the road to greater health. **Get started on the five essentials today.** The lead author has trained thousands of individuals over the years. The quickest and greatest improvement in health and performance has always occurred when

To find out more or to speak to a nutritional counselor for free, just visit us at:
www.CuresForTheBody.com

the clients have improved their basic nutrition along with taking the basic nutrients needed for health.

CHAPTER 5 FOOTNOTES

[1]U.S. Surgeon General Report, 1988.

[2]Beasley, Joseph D., M.D. and Jeffrey Swift, M.A. *The Kellogg Report: The Impact of Nutrition, Environment and Lifestyle on the Health of Americans.* New York: The Institute of Health Policy and Practice, 1989, pg. 108-9.

[3]Howell, Dr. Edward. *Enzyme Nutrition.* New Jersey: Avery Publishing Group, 1985, p. 2.

[4]*Ibid.,* p. 4.

[5] *Ibid.,* p. 6-7.

[6] *Ibid.,* p. 15-6.

[7] Kautchakoff, Paul, M.D. "The Influence of Food Cooking on the Blood Formula of Man," Lausanne, Switzerland, 1930.

[8]Howell, *op. cit.*

[9]National Digestive Disease Information Clearinghouse http://www.niddk.nih.gov/DD-statistics/DD-statistics.html

[10]Garrett, Laurie. *The Coming Plague: Newly Emerging Diseases in a World out of Balance.* New York: Penguin Books, 1994.

[11] Gray, Gary M. "Intestinal Digestion and Maldigestion of Dietary Carbohydrates." *Annual Review of Medicine* 22:391-404, 1971.

[12] McPherson, James C., *et al.* "Effect of lipase ingestion on blood lipid levels." *Proceedings of the Society of Experimental Biology and Medicine* 115: 5124-17 (1964).

[13]Chaitow, Leon, N.D., D.O. and Natasha Trenew. *Probiotics.* London: Harper Collins, 1990.

[14]Shahani, Khem M., Ph.D. and Nagendra Rangavajhyala, Ph.D. "Role of Probiotics in Clinical Nutrition and Immunity" Paper presented at the Annual Conference of the International American Associations of Clinical Nutritionists, Orlando, FL, August 28-31, 1997.

[15]Fernandes CF, Shahani, KM, Amer MA. Therapeutic role of dietary lactobacilli and lactobacillic fermented dairy foods. FEMS *Microbiol Rev* 1987;46:343-356.

[16]Fernandes, CF Ph.D. and Khem Shahani, Ph.D. "Lactose intolerance and its modulation with lactobacilli and other microbial supplements." *Journal of Applied Nutrition* Vol. 41, Number 2, 1989.

[17]Shahani, *op. cit.*

[18]Huenel, H. "Human Normal and Abnormal Gastrointestinal Flora" American Journal of Clinical Nutrition, 1970; 23: 1433-9.

[19]Garrett, *op. cit.*

[20]*Ibid.*

[21]Fernandes and Shahani, KM. Amer MA, *op. cit.*

[22]USDA Report

[23]*Ibid.*

To find out more or to speak to a nutritional counselor for free, just visit us at:
www.CuresForTheBody.com

[24]"Composition of Foods." Agriculture Handbook, Nov. 8, U.S. Dept. of Agriculture.

[25]*Ibid.*

[26]Kellogg, *op.cit.,* pg 74.

[27]Beasley, Joseph D., M.D. and Jeffy Swift, M.A. *The Kellogg Report: The Impact of Nutrition, Environment and Lifestyle on the Health of Americans.* New York: The Institute of Health Policy and Practice, 1989, pg. 70.

[29]Proceedings of the National Academy of Sciences, 1997.

[30]New England Journal of Medicine, Vol. 333, No. 21.

[31]Robbins, Joel, M.D., D.C. Nutrition in the Practice: A Practical Guide on Incorporating Nutrition into any Health Care Practice. Oklahoma: Health Dynamics Corporation, 1997.

[32]Ashmead, H. DeWayne, Ph.D., F.A.C.N. *Conversations on Chelation and Mineral Nutrition.* Connecticut: Keats Publishing, Inc. 1989, pg. 11.[28]Ensminger, *et al. The Food and Nutrition Encyclopedia.* 1983: 2203.

[33]*Advanced Nutrition in Human Metabolism.* West Publishing.

[34]Ashmead, H. DeWayne. Intestinal Absorption of Metal Ions.

[35]Ashmead, H. DeWayne, Ph.D., F.A.C.N., *Conversations on Chelation and Mineral Nutrition.* Connecticut: Keats Publishing, Inc. 1989, .p. 18

[36]H. DeWayne Ashmead, Ph.D. Mineral Nutrition in Your Life and Health.Connecticut: Keats Publishing, Inc., 1989.

[37]Kellogg, *op. cit.* pg. 115.

[38]Schroeder, Henry A. "Frontiers in Trace Element Research," Keynote address at a sumposium, "Trace Elements and Brain Functions," held at Princeton, NJ, Oct. 24-26, 1973.

[39]Kellogg, *op. cit.* pg. 116.

[40]Herrick, John B. "Minerals in Animal Nutrition." *The Roles of Amino Acid Chelates in Animal Nutrition.* New Jersey: Noyes Publications, 1993.

[41]Mertz, W. "Some aspects of nutritional trace element research," Federation Proceeding, Federation of American Societies for Experimental Biology, Soc. Exp. Biol. 29:1482-1488, 1970.

[42]"Minerals…Trace Minerals…Ultra Trace Minerals: Is Supplementation Safe?" Albion Research Notes: A Compilation of Vital Research Updates on Human Nutrition. May, 1996 Vol. 5, No. 2.

[43]*Ibid.*

[44]*Ibid,* pg. 3

[45]Seal, C. "Influence of dietary picolinic acid on mineral metabolism in the rat," Am Nutr Met 32:186 (4) 1988.

Chapter 6
Where Do We Go From Here?

By now your head is spinning and a lot of new education and information is soaking in. Hopefully you have determined to take responsibility for your health care and start applying some of the basic proven benefits of nutrition that we just discussed.

Our desire with this book to this point was to educate and motivate you to take charge of your health choices. Now it is time for you to create a goal and the plan to accomplish it. The first step in doing this is to create a viable "Focused Intense Thought." In other words, create a goal that drives you daily into making the right choices and sticking with your plan. Here is a process that the lead author teaches based on motivational research.

Optimal Health and Fitness Begin with Focused, Intense Thought.

Before changing any of your eating habits, before changing the way you exercise, before changing the supplements you use, you must first change your mind.

Your current state of health is a result of how you think about health. A few years ago it may have seemed an eccentric idea, a supposition that was truly "out there" to imagine that what you think affects your physical being.

Today, it is known that this is more than a far-fetched notion. It is a scientifically proven fact that thoughts play themselves out in the form of physical reactions within the body.

Well-known author and philosopher, Deepak Chopra M.D., teaches "Your health is the sum total of all the impulses, positive and negative, emanating from your consciousness. For every state of consciousness, there is a corresponding state of physiology, for example, You are what you think."

Every thought, no matter how fleeting, has an effect on your physical being.

This is not to suggest that you can merely think happy thoughts and become well. While light-hearted musing may help somewhat, it requires a much more structured and well-planned process to create the kind of thought that will impact your health for good. The thought must become a driving force,it must be focused and intense.

Focused, Intense Thought is the foundation to reach optimal health. Thus, the process explained in this chapter is one of the most valuable things that you can learn from this book.

Thoughts Produce Results

"Experts agree on one thing. People will never make serious changes in their bodies without first making a change in their thinking," says Constance Cardozo.

So, how do you change your thinking? For years, the lead author ran a one-on-one health and strength-training clinic where a "whole" program – including specific principles of exercise, nutrition and supplementation – was proven to be extremely effective. There were a few individuals, however, who didn't see the same dramatic results that most people did or who weren't able to reach their goals as quickly as they'd like. Working with the trainers, he closely examined the way these people approached fitness and health. He discovered that there was a direct correlation between what these people thought and how well they progressed.

The people who had a distinct, clear vision of what they wanted to achieve progressed towards their goals much more quickly . Those who were wishy-washy and hadn't created a distinct mental image of what they wanted to accomplish often struggled to achieve results. Based on this discovery, the lead author began incorporating the added aspect of having each client describe and verbalize his or her goal and of making that goal a focused, intense thought using the process described below.

Almost across the board they saw positive effects. Those people who were already seeing improvement felt even more satisfied and rewarded when they identified the exact end result they desired, and then could see themselves accomplishing what they had envisioned. Others, who had

To find out more or to speak to a nutritional counselor for free, just visit us at:
www.CuresForTheBody.com

decided that improvement was hard to come by found that, by focusing on the specific results they wanted, success came fairly easily.

From rudimentary beginnings in this area we have carefully researched this process and honed it in clinical settings. The step-by-step process outlined below has proven to be successful over and over in helping individuals improve their health and reach fitness goals. By following this process, you will derive the benefits that come from adding the necessary component of Focused, Intense Thought to an overall program.

How to Create a Focused, Intense Thought

1. Establish a "baseline" as a starting point.

Our thoughts can be tricky and many of us rationalize, often without even knowing it. All of us seem to do it to one degree or another. Sandy can fit in the same pants she did last year, so she ignores the fact that they are tighter than ever. Even though Lee's cholesterol levels have risen steadily over the past three years, he attributes it to the natural process of aging, and figures, "It's still lower than Bob's!" Tonya's energy is at rock bottom, but she blames it on her busy work schedule and believes her lethargy will end as soon as she can take a vacation.

Before we can create a new mental image of health, we need to take a realistic view of where we are. Several assessment methods can help give you a clear picture of your current state of health and fitness and can show you areas in which you may need to improve. Along with body weight, circumference measurements, and body fat percentage, you may also want to have your cholesterol and blood pressure checked. In addition, it is recommended that you write down a brief description of how you currently feel and any symptoms of ill-health you may now experience on a regular basis. It will be extremely rewarding to look back in a few weeks and see the many ways in which your health has improved. Then, continue with this process of creating a mental image which will help you improve the baseline numbers you come up with.

2. Create a mental image of health and find a picture that illustrates that image.

To find out more or to speak to a nutritional counselor for free, just visit us at:
www.CuresForTheBody.com

Now that you have completed the Assessment and have a clear idea of exactly where you are, take a few moments to think about where you would like to be. Relax and let your imagination wander as you think about health and what it means to you. Picture times in your life when you felt the most energetic or when you were able to accomplish the most. Imagine how it would be to have the strength and vitality you desire. From the myriad of pictures you envision, focus on one that particularly represents health to you and motivates you at this time. This is the vision that will drive your accomplishments and will continue to supply the motivation you need in order to succeed.

Next, find a photograph or a picture out of a magazine that illustrates the vision of what you want in terms of health. Any picture that shows the vitality you envision or the activities you want to be able to participate in will work. Put this picture on your mirror or some other place where you will see it often. With the many things you have to think about each day, this picture is practically a necessity. Such a picture will keep your goal at the forefront of your mind and will help strengthen your image of health and make that image a governing factor, thus supplying the impetus to initiate change.

3. Use spaced repetition.

To make sure that the vision you have created becomes a driving force, use a process known as spaced repetition. Set aside a few minutes each day to relax and focus on the image that represents health to you. You only need to take a few seconds to pause, close your eyes, and focus on that healthy mental image. Selecting a specific time for this will help you be more consistent. You may want to conduct a "vision session" when you take your supplements or just before your workout.

Here's what you need to do: As you focus on your image of optimal health, inhale sharply and completely. Hold that breath for seven seconds, continuing to savor the image in your mind. Then exhale forcefully. Repeat one more time.

To find out more or to speak to a nutritional counselor for free, just visit us at:
www.CuresForTheBody.com

4. Strengthen the vision.

Another way to make the image in your mind more intense, and thus increase the benefits of this method, is to create a written statement describing the kind of health you want for yourself. Rather than simply saying, "I want to feel good," or "I want to have more lean muscle," pick a particular event or a date-specific activity. In writing, describe that event in detail as if you are participating in it, include vivid descriptions of how you feel and even what the surroundings look like.

For example, you could imagine and describe the opening seconds of a sporting event that you are fit and healthy enough to participate in. You could describe yourself, trim and energetic, boarding the plane to take off on an exotic vacation. Even something as simple as a description of slipping into a new outfit or receiving a compliment can help motivate you and reinforce your mental image.

When you have created a written statement, use it in conjunction with your daily "vision session." To do so, read your statement two or three times, then proceed with the vision session as described above.

The technique of Focused, Intense Thought is so simple that some may consider it inconsequential. That is far from the truth. Focused, Intense Thought can make the difference between success and failure. Because it is vital is exactly why it is at the foundation of a successful health goal. Begin today. Add this important element to your total program of health, and start changing your wellness by changing the way you think!

Assembling your team:

In order to achieve your health goals, you need to have a team of experts surrounding you and assisting you in choosing what directions to take with medical crisis care, nutrition, motivation, exercise and supplementation.

Here is a suggested layout for the type of people you want on your team:

Medical Crisis Care - Interview and choose a doctor that will listen to and answer your questions. If the doctor follows great lifestyle practices of proper nutrition and exercise for themselves, then they will be more likely to support yours. Make sure your doctor will do specific tests and prescribe specific drugs while showing why the benefits of the drug he or she is prescribing outweigh the side effects.

Nutrition - Find a good company or person who teaches nutrition. Make sure they teach the basics and they don't ever recommend diets that take out a major food group. If they believe and follow the nutritional research laid out in this book, then you are on the right track. Make sure the nutritionist or company works with a lot of people that can provide referrals.

Motivation - Having two people for this part of your team is beneficial. First, find someone in your life that can motivate and encourage you to stick to your goals. Second, find a person or company that specializes in personal development and motivation. The lead author uses different books and seminars from different people but there must be one used each month.

Exercise - Hire a personal trainer that will listen to your plan and train you properly. Or find an expert in the field that you can rely on either through books or videos and follow their programs.

Supplementation – Choose a company where you can learn who formulates their products. Make sure they believe in whole food supplements and not natural or synthetic. Ask for the fact sheets and research on the formulas and make sure you will get the technical help needed.

Your team doesn't have to be people you have met. You can have a member of your team be someone that has written many books that you have studied.

Example "Health Team"

Jill

Medical - Jill chose Dr. George who listened to her goals of wanting to have more energy and to lower her risk for diseases that might shorten her quality of life. Dr. George communitcated to Jill that he would explain any recommendations he had and why it would help her achieve her goals faster.

Nutrition - Jill picked a company that laid out healthy basic nutrition plans and taught her how to shop and cook healthy meals.

Motivation - Jill reads a book a month from an author in the "Nightingale Conant" group which is a self help motivation group with many speakers and authors.

Exercise - Jill works with a personal trainer twice a week. In addition, he helps monitor her exercise when she is on the road.

Supplementation - Jill filled out a nutritional questionniare form and, with the help of a counselor, determined what nutrients she should be taking. She receives updates once a month on any new changes or research that will benefit her from her supplement company of choice.

Once you assemble your team, consult with each one at least once a month. As you do this you will naturally start making choices that will benefit your health and longevity. Having a team will inspire you to be outgoing and excited to reach your goals. Do this and you will achieve great success in not just your health, but other areas of your life.

To find out more or to speak to a nutritional counselor for free, just visit us at:
www.CuresForTheBody.com

Chapter 7
Putting It All Together

It is very important for you to assess your current health, and to make a committed step toward taking responsibility for improved health. Let's review what you have learned from this book so far:

You have discovered the detrimental effects of relying totally on our crisis care medical system for your health care.

You have been educated on the medical and nutritional approaches to conditions and diseases.

You have received a complete layout of nutritional guidelines from basic education and research to specific eating plans.

You have learned the basics of supplementation to help you cut through the hype presented in the market.

You have been taught to assemble a team of experts to surround you, so you can make the best decisions for your own health care.

After training thousands of people over the last decade the author has seen different things work for different people. Here are a few suggestions to see what might fit the best with your goals and priorities:

1. Pick two or three things from the book that will help you improve your health and work on them. Slowly add additional principles to your life as you master the first ones. Maybe you will start by eliminating the use of white flour and sodas and then eventually red meat. Maybe you will decide to actively work with your primary care physician to reduce and possibly eliminate the intake of prescription drugs by improving your diet and lifestyle.

2. Assemble your team and write down a complete program. Then aggressively pursue your goals. This choice takes some discipline.

To find out more or to speak to a nutritional counselor for free, just visit us at:
www.CuresForTheBody.com

3.   The most popular approach is to have a counselor that is part of your team as you start a 4-6 week program. This counselor can help you create small attainable goals and provide support to help you reach your goals.

No matter which suggestion you choose to follow, we have assembled many resources for you as you start to travel down your road to optimal health. Feel free to call the following people and/or companies to see if they might fit into your team. They are respected within the industry and can help you obtain the answers you need.

The lead author's company, **Optimal Health Systems,** trains thousands of doctors and professional athletes around the world on nutritional testing programs, nutritional plans, and whole food supplements. Their products are not available in chain health food stores but are available through health professionals. Optimal Health Systems also offers products and free nutritional counseling over the phone. You can take a web based questionnaire to help understand your specific needs. By completing the questionnaire a Nutritional Counselor at Optimal Health System will work to educate and motivate you to reach your goals. You can reach Optimal Health Systems by calling **1-866-341-2622.**

Author of *Look Hot, Live Long* and *The Hot Buns Diet,* **Chris Lydon, M.D.** is available for fitness seminars, nutritional counsulting, and personal appearances. For more information, or to contact Chris, please visit her website at: **www.chrislydon.com.**

Becky Greer, Nationally Certified Nutritional Microscopist, Nutritional Consultant, and a former Coronary and Intensive Care Nurse, changed her focus of interest from disease care to preventive disease education and care after 15 years of working as a nurse. Instead of taking care of people during and after suffering the ill effects of their lifestyle choices, she wanted to help people change the direction they were heading. As she studied nutrition and disease prevention, her passion for nutrition grew as she gained the realization that proper "nutrition and exercise" were the keys to prevention. She operates a nutritional counseling business and can be reached on her website at **www.leanandhealthybydesign.com**.

Richard A. Passwater, PhD has been a research biochemist since 1959. His first areas of research interest were in the development of pharmaceuticals, spectrophotoluminescence, and analytical chemistry. His laboratory research led to his discovery of biological antioxidant synergism in 1962 that has been the focus of his research and patents ever since. In 1970, Dr. Passwater shifted the emphasis of his research from pharmaceuticals to nutrients. In 1975 his bestselling book *Supernutrition: Megavitamin Revolution* was credited with legitimizing megavitamin therapy. Dr. Passwater has continued to research nutritional supplements and has now published over 40 books and pamphlets, as well as over 450 articles on nutrition and nutritional supplements.

There are more than 200 nutritional articles that may be of interest to you on Dr. Passwater's website. Please feel free to browse around and come back often. He will continue to add to this wide-ranging spectrum of information on nutritional issues that are important to us all. Also available is information regarding his 40 books. His website address is **www.drpasswater.com**.